ANNIE

Mortgage Lending Fundamentals and Practices

Mortgage Lending Fundamentals and Practices

Second Edition

Marshall W. Dennis

Reston Publishing Company, Inc.
A Prentice-Hall Company
Reston, Virginia

Library of Congress Cataloging in Publication Data

Dennis, Marshall W.
   Mortgage lending fundamentals and practices.

   Includes bibliographies and index.
   1. Mortgage loans—United States.   I. Title.
HG2040.5.U5D44   1983   332.7′22′0973   82-25013
ISBN 0-8359-4653-3

© 1983 by
Reston Publishing Company, Inc.
A Prentice-Hall Company
Reston, Virginia

10 9 8 7 6 5 4 3 2

Printed in the United States of America

Contents

List of Figures

Preface

The second edition of *Mortgage Lending Fundamentals and Practices* represents the substantial changes in mortgage lending in the last decade. Although the changes are incorporated in the text, the basic purpose remains the same: to communicate and explain the fundamentals of mortgage lending in as simple and concise a manner as possible. It is designed for either a new employee of a mortgage lender or a college student studying real estate finance and wanting to supplement that study with practical mortgage lending fundamentals.

A new employee of any mortgage lender will probably need at least the first six months to understand both the specific job requirements and some of the fundamentals of mortgage lending. This book is for that individual, whether the employing mortgage lender be a commercial bank, a savings and loan association, a mutual savings bank, or a mortgage company.

The academic backgrounds of those entering the mortgage lending field today ranges from solid real estate finance training to no formal academic training. Whatever the background, all of these students can and will succeed if they have the ability to learn and apply what they have learned. No prior knowledge of any part of mortgage lending is assumed in this book. The reader is assumed to possess only the ability and willingness to learn.

This book will discuss each topic beginning with the fundamentals and will develop them to the point where the reader will have a basic understanding of that topic. Not all topics will be applicable to every mortgage lender, nor even be of interest to all readers, but to understand the basics of modern mortgage lending each subject included needs to be comprehensively understood. Changes occur so rapidly in this segment of the economy, that an area in which a particular mortgage lender is not involved today may be where the growth and profit scene is tomorrow. All mortgage lenders should prepare for this growth and change by either employing suitably educated personnel or providing that education.

While explaining the fundamentals of mortgage lending, this book also examines the similarities and differences which exist among mortgage lenders. Basically, therefore, this text is designed to fulfill the need all mortgage lenders have for a basic text to prepare new employees for the important job of helping finance the growing real estate needs of this country.

Marshall W. Dennis

ACKNOWLEDGMENTS

I am deeply indebted to a number of people for valuable assistance in preparing this book. These recognized experts in their field have either read portions of the book and suggested appropriate improvements or prepared case studies.

John Fitzmaurice, Vice President, General Electric Mortgage Insurance Corp., Cincinnati, Ohio

Edwin R. Godwin, Senior Vice President, Mortgage and Trust, Inc., Houston, Texas

Gary Hammond, Vice President, First Federal Savings and Loan of Arizona, Phoenix, Arizona

Robert F. MacSwain, Assistant Vice President, Hartford Life Insurance Co., Hartford, Connecticut

Kevin A. North, Mortgage Loan Department, Hartford Life Insurance Co., Hartford, Connecticut

Donna J. Pillard, Vice President, Carruth Mortgage Co., New Orleans, Louisiana

Dr. James Porterfield, Professor of Finance, Graduate School of Business, Stanford University, Stanford, California

Thomas A. Ronzetti, Vice President, Federal National Mortgage Association, Washington, D.C.

Donald D. Wipf, Assistant Vice President, Perpetual American Federal Savings and Loan, Washington, D.C.

I would also like to thank Carol Suttmiller of the Institute of Financial Education who assisted in the 1983 revision of the text.

For those possible errors, omissions, or faulty analyses, the author assumes full and sole responsibility.

Marshall W. Dennis

Mortgage Lending
Fundamentals
and Practices

Introduction

SCOPE OF BOOK

Any attempt to analyze or answer all of the many questions inherent to mortgage lending would result in a series of treatises too complex to be of value or benefit to the student or the new practitioner. Instead, this book is designed to provide the theoretical and practical framework necessary to begin understanding the increasingly complex field of mortgage lending.

Throughout this book additional readings are listed which the more advanced student may want to review. Reference will be made to other publications for review and study regarding subjects not related directly to the design of this book or which are too complex to be included.

REAL ESTATE INVESTMENT DECISIONS

Many important real estate finance analyses and decisions must be made by a potential mortgage borrower *before* seeking a mortgage loan. Practically all of these are beyond the scope of this book, although they will be mentioned here. Although these issues can be quite complex, they are basic to each transaction and a potential borrower should carefully analyze each one. The issues are (generally) as applicable whether the loan is for a residential or income property.

These real estate finance issues include:

- The return of capital (equity)
- The return on investment
- The income tax shelter

- The degree of liquidity (ability to sell)
- The effectiveness of leverage (use of borrowed funds to increase yield)
- The cost of money (interest rate)
- The risk factor

After analyzing each issue, a potential borrower should relate each conclusion to the other issues and then make a decision on whether to proceed toward seeking a mortgage loan.

Although a mortgage loan officer may want to review these decisions with a borrower, the analyses and the necessary decisions usually have been made by the borrower. Of course a mortgage loan officer must analyze all relevant decisions when determining whether a mortgage loan should be made. However, since these decisions should occur before seeking a mortgage loan, they will not be discussed in this book. The subject of this book concerns those questions or issues that occur after the decision to borrow has been made and a mortgage loan sought.

LENDING CUSTOMS AND PRACTICES

Major differences exist among mortgage lenders regarding the actual mortgage lending process. For example, the origination of mortgage loans, whether residential or income property, is possibly the most important function in the mortgage lending process. But the manner in which a commercial bank originates mortgages is often radically different from that of a mortgage company or a savings and loan institution. In fact, even within an industry group, the origination function is most often performed according to company policy or philosophy rather than industry custom. Therefore, the origination function will not be discussed in this book.

The marketing of mortgage loans is another difficult area to discuss adequately in a book of this nature. Many mortgage lenders, such as small savings and loan associations, still originate mortgages only for their own portfolio and consequently engage in no mortgage marketing. Others, such as mortgage companies, originate all mortgage loans for sale to others. Among mortgage lenders active in marketing loans, each establishes its own individual methods and policies. Although marketing of mortgage loans will not be discussed specifically, the important secondary mortgage market and its institutions will be examined.

MORTGAGE LENDERS

Some of the basic philosophies or strategies of mortgage lenders (e.g. whether to participate in government subsidized lending programs) are at opposite extremes of the real estate financing spectrum from their competitors. In general, all mortgage lenders have worked diligently to provide for the real estate financing needs of this nation and their success has made this the best housed nation in the world. Yet, more could be done and greater cooperation among mortgage lenders could prepare the way for greater accomplishments.

All mortgage lenders are dealing with the same product and rendering the same service—financing real estate. Although they may obtain funds for lending in different ways and have varying degrees of regulation, their basic purpose is the same. Some commentators on the mortgage industry claim that the inability of mortgage lenders to work more closely together is the result of competition and, therefore, it cannot be expected that one lender would assist another when the result could be lost business. If the industry is going to solve the major real estate finance problems of today (such as the inability of the average family to afford the average priced home), all lenders will have to combine their financial expertise and political influence.

Major mortgage lenders include:

- Savings and loan associations
- Commercial banks
- Mortgage companies
- Mutual savings banks
- Real estate investment trusts

The total number of such lenders and their branches is about 60,000. And at some point in 1983, one of these lenders will originate a mortgage loan which will push the nation's outstanding mortgage debt beyond the mind-boggling $1.7 trillion mark. Regardless of which mortgage lender originates that or any other mortgage, all perform basically the same function for a borrower.

MORTGAGE LENDING FUNCTIONS

All mortgage lenders perform some or all of the following functions:

1. The origination of mortgage loans
   a. residential
   b. income property
   c. construction
2. The processing of mortgage loans
   a. conventional
   b. government insured or guaranteed
3. The appraisal of real estate
4. The underwriting of mortgage loans
   a. residential
   b. income property

5. The administration of mortgage loans
   a. loan approval
   b. loan closing
   c. loan servicing
   d. collections
   e. tax and insurance account processing
6. The marketing of mortgage loans
   a. packaging
   b. fulfilling commitments
   c. secondary mortgage market operations

SPECIAL AREAS OF EMPHASIS

The first chapter in this book concerns the history and evolution of mortgage lending. It provides essential material for a serious student of mortgage lending. Unless past problems and failures of mortgage lending are understood and resolved, they will occur again. Further, it would be difficult to comprehend the present position of mortgage lending without examining its history.

The chapter on Government Regulations and Consumer Protection should be read as a part of the history chapter but not necessarily at the same time. The recommendation is for this chapter to be read last since it provides a good review of the developments in mortgage lending which have produced the current position.

A chapter on Real Estate Law is included to provide the reader with both a basic review of law as it relates to real estate and mortgage lending, and as a reference for material covered in other chapters.

The last two chapters are supplements for training purposes. The first chapter contains three residential case studies which are as actually submitted, although some facts have been changed. Many people in mortgage lending do not have the opportunity to see the complete product of the mortgage lending process. The packaging of these loans should be studied in order to determine what should be included for the protection of both the borrower and lender.

The last section is an extensive glossary of the language of the industry. An important first step toward becoming a competent practitioner is understanding the vocabulary used.

SUGGESTED READINGS

Bagby, Joseph R. *Real Estate Financing Desk Book,* Englewood Cliffs, New Jersey: Institute for Business Planning, Inc., 1975.

Beaton, William R. *Real Estate Finance.* Englewood Cliffs, New Jersey: Prentice Hall, Inc., 1975.

———. *Real Estate Investment.* Englewood Cliffs, New Jersey: Prentice Hall, Inc., 1971.

Boykin, James H. *Financing Real Estate,* Lexington, Massachusetts: Lexington Books, D. C. Heath & Co., 1979.

Clark, William Dennison. "Leverage: Magnificent Mover of Real Estate," *Real Estate Review* (Winter 1972), pp. 8–13.

Cooper, James R. *Real Estate Investment Analysis.* Lexington, Massachusetts: Lexington Books, D. C. Heath & Co., 1974.

Graaskamp, J.A. *A Guide to Feasibility Analysis.* Chicago: Society of Real Estate Appraisers, 1970.

Maisel, Sherman J., and Roulac, Stephen E. *Real Estate Investment and Finance.* New York: McGraw-Hill Book Co., Inc., 1976.

Martin, Wendall H. "Tax Shelter and the Real Estate Analyst," *The Appraisal Journal* (January 1975), pp. 17–28.

Robinson, Gerald J. *Federal Income Taxation of Real Estate.* Boston: Warren, Gorham & Lamont, Inc., 1974.

Roulac, Stephen E. "Life Cycle of a Real Estate Investment," *Real Estate Review* (Fall 1974), pp. 113–17.

Wendt, Paul F. and Cerf, Alan R. *Real Estate Investment Analysis and Taxation.* New York: McGraw-Hill Book Co., Inc., 1969.

Chapter 1

The History of Mortgage Lending

Mortgage lending, as presently utilized in the United States, is a relatively recent development, although many of the basic concepts date back to the beginning of recorded history. To fully understand how mortgage lending works today, an appreciation of the historical development of mortgage lending will provide many of the answers to why lending is where it is today.

The underlying product in all real estate activities is land. Some sociologists claim that the use of, the desire to acquire, and the need to regulate the transfer of land were the fundamental reasons for the development of government and laws. As government units developed, laws were formulated to govern the ownership and use of land. Because of the importance of land, it was soon being used as security for the performance of an obligation, such as repaying debts or the fulfillment of military service.

ANCIENT CONCEPTS OF MORTGAGE LENDING

Evidence of transactions involving land as security has been uncovered in such ancient civilizations as Babylonia and Egypt. Many of the basic principles of mortgage lending, including the essential elements of naming the borrower and the lender and describing the property, were developed in these early civilizations. For example, there is evidence that the Egyptians were the first to use surveys to describe mortgaged land. This was undoubtedly necessitated by the annual flooding of the Nile River, which often obliterated property markers.

During the period when Greek civilization was at its peak, the temple leaders loaned money with real estate as security. In fact, throughout history organized religion has taken a strong interest in real estate.

The Roman Empire developed mortgage lending to a high level of sophistication, beginning with the *fiducia*. This transaction was an actual transfer of possession and title to land. It was subject to an additional agreement stating that if the borrower fulfilled the obligation, a reconveyance would occur. As Roman government became stronger and the law more clearly defined, a new concept of security, called the *pignus,* was developed. No title transfer occurred. Instead the land was "pawned." According to this concept, title and possession remained with the borrower, but the lender could take possession of the property at any time if it was deemed a possibility of default existed.

However, the most important Roman development regarding mortgages was the *hypotheca,* which was a pledge. The hypotheca was similar to the lien theory (described later) that exists in most states in this country today. The title remained with the borrower, who was also allowed to retain possession of the property. Only if an actual default occurred, i.e., a failure on the part of the borrower to perform, was the lender entitled to take possession of and title to the land.

As the Roman Empire receded throughout Europe during the Dark Ages, a Germanic law introduced a new concept. A borrower was given a choice whether to fulfill an obligation or lose the security. If the mortgagor defaulted, the mortgagee had to look exclusively to the property itself. This security system was called a *gage* in Germanic law; something was deposited for the performance of an agreement. As the Dark Ages continued and the governmental authority of Rome weakened to the point where lenders were not sure they would have support from the central authorities in securing their debts, the *hypotheca* system decayed and died, and the more primitive concept of the *fiducia* returned.

ENGLISH DEVELOPMENTS

Later, in Europe, a new system of government and social structure, the feudal system, became widespread. The feudal system was an all-encompassing form of government that affected the economy, the military and the administration of government. The essential element of the feudal system was the totality of the king's control. He was the owner of all lands. He would grant the *use* of this land to certain lords in return for military fealty. Lords given the use of the land were permitted to continue on the land as long as they fulfilled a military obligation to the king. If this obligation was not fulfilled, or if the lord died, the use of the land was revoked and given to others. In this situation, land served as a security for the performance of an obligation— military service.

Along with the feudal system of land tenure, the Germanic system of the *gage* was introduced into early English law by William of Normandy in 1066 following the successful invasion of England. The word *mortgage* was not found in English literature until after the Norman invasion. It derives from the French words *mort,* which means "dead" or "frozen" (the land is "dead," since the mortgagor could not use or derive income from it), and *gage,* which means "pledge".

During the early years after the Norman invasion, it was the Catholic Church that primarily established the civil law in England. The Church stated that the charging of any interest for money loaned was *usury;* therefore, mortgage lending (along with other business transactions) was not an important feature in the economic system of that time.

Throughout the development of the common law in England, there occurred a gradual shift from a concept of favoritism or protection of the mortgagee, to favoritism or protection of the mortgagor. Finally, the common law reached a more balanced position. The initial concept (mortgagee favoritism) was dictated by the realities of the economic and legal systems that existed at this early stage of mortgage development. Mortgage lending was not a common occurrence during this period for two reasons: 1) there was very little need for it, and 2) no incentive to lend existed without the ability to collect interest. The mortgage lending that did occur was not for the purpose of providing funds to purchase real estate, but usually to finance large purchases, for example, of a new mill, or livestock, or perhaps to prepare a dowry for a daughter. Since lenders could not collect interest on these loans, they would take both title *and* possession of a designated portion of the borrower's land and thus be entitled to all rents and profits. When the obligation was fulfilled, title was reconveyed to the mortgagor. If the mortgagor defaulted, the mortgagee would permanently retain title and possession of the mortgaged land. The mortgagee was also still entitled to expect performance of the underlying obligation.

During the 15th century, courts of equity allowed the mortgagor to perform the obligation, even after the required date, and redeem the property. This concept was expanded and by 1625 nearly all existing mortgage lending practices had ended because a mortgagee never knew when a mortgagor might perform and thus redeem the property. To alleviate this problem, mortgagees would petition the court for a decree requiring the mortgagor to redeem the property within six months or lose the right to do so.

A more balanced position resulted which required the mortgagor to still relinquish title to the land, but to retain possession. If a default occurred, the mortgagor had a specified period of time in which to redeem the property.

This concept, called *title theory,* was brought to America and formed the basis of American mortgage law. After the Revolutionary War, however, the concept was changed by some states to the more modern *lien theory.* Under this theory, title remains with the mortgagor, and the mortgagee has only a lien against the property which can be exercised if the underlying obligation is not fulfilled.

AMERICAN DEVELOPMENTS

The American Revolutionary War was followed by a westward expansion which was financed by land development banks borrowing primarily in Europe to finance their land purchases in the developing West. Much of this land acquisition was speculative and eventually culminated in the bankruptcy of nearly all these early land development banks. Little, if any, real estate financing was done on an organized basis from the early 1800s until after the Civil War.

During the first 75 years of this country's history, the population was located primarily on small farms passed down through families. Little need existed for mortgage lending except for an occasional purchase of new land or for seed money. The small amount of mortgage lending that did occur during this period was provided primarily by family and friends. It is important to realize that until the 1920s, the largest category of mortgage lenders in the United States was individuals, not financial institutions.

Thrift Institutions

The birth of various thrift institutions provided a change in mortgage lending. The first mutual savings bank, the Philadelphia Savings Fund Society, was started Dec. 2, 1816. Of greater long-term importance to mortgage lending was the organization of the first building society in the U.S. Modeled after societies that had existed in England and Scotland for 50 years, the Oxford Provident Building Association was organized Jan. 3, 1831 in Frankford, Penn. This association, like the ones that soon followed, was intended to exist only long enough for all the organizers to obtain funds to purchase homes. Ironically, the first loan made by this association became delinquent and another member of the association assumed the debt and took possession of the house.

Later, other associations were formed, providing a popular means for the expansion of building associations across the United States.

Even with these new financial institutions, mortgage lending was still not an important part of the economy in the first half of the 19th century. Most families still lived on farms, which met basically all their requirements. No urgent need for savings existed. Away from the farm there were few employment opportunities where excess cash could be accumulated for savings. The concept of saving was still new, and the number of active savers was very small. Then, as now, the impetus for mortgage lending was the inflow of savings to the institutions that would lend funds.

Mortgage Companies

After the Civil War, expansion continued and change resumed. Starting with a new westward expansion which opened virgin lands for farming, a regular farm mortgage business developed in the predominantly rural Midwest. The Midwest is an area where many mortgage companies began, and it still has one of the heaviest concentrations of mortgage companies.

Most of these companies did not originate mortgage loans for their own portfolios, as did the thrift institutions. Rather, such loans were for direct sale to wealthy individuals or to institutional investors such as life insurance companies. Most of these individual and institutional investors were located on the East coast and needed local mortgage companies to originate loans for them. This need resulted in the mortgage loan correspondent system.

The bulk of the mortgage business consisted of financing farms, usually with a prevailing loan-to-value ratio of 40 percent. An occasional 50 percent loan might be made on a farm in a well-developed area. The term of the loan was short (less than five years), with interest payable semi-annually and the principal paid at the end of the term. By 1900, outstanding farm mortgages originated by these mortgage companies totalled more than $4 billion.

During this period of time, the move to urban areas began to increase, swelled by ever-mounting numbers of immigrants. In 1892, the United States League of Savings Associations was founded in response to the expanding savings and loan industry. These institutions provided urban residents a place to save money and a source of funds to use in purchasing homes. These mortgages made by savings and loans associations usually were repaid on an installment basis, not at the expiration of the term as were mortgages from other types of lenders.

Commercial Banks

Commercial banks made few real estate loans until after the Civil War when a sudden demand for loans to finance new farmsteads encouraged state-chartered commercial banks to make low-ratio farm mortgages. Except for a brief period of time, federally-chartered commercial banks could not make real estate loans. This competition from state-chartered banks eventually forced a change in federal banking law. In 1913 the *Federal Reserve Act* authorized federally-chartered banks to lend money on real estate. This initial authorization limited mortgage loans to improved farms for a five-year term with the loan-to-value ratio of 50 percent. This authorization was extended in 1916 to include one-year loans on urban real estate.

Many changes have occurred in both state and federal laws relating to the types and terms of mortgage loans made by commercial banks. These changes tended to lag behind advances made by other mortgage lenders, but the contribution made by commercial banks has been meaningful, especially in those areas of the country where they function as the principal mortgage lender.

Turn of the Century

During the period from 1870 to the early 1900s, a few mortgage companies in or near urban areas began to make loans on single-family houses. This initially constituted a very small percentage of their business but gradually grew to account for more and more total origination volume. The Farm Mortgage Bankers Association, which was formed in 1914, was changed to the Mortgage Bankers Association in 1923 to reflect the increasing accent on residential lending.

In the first two decades of this century the typical loan made by a mortgage company on a single-family dwelling called for no more than a 50 percent loan-to-value ratio, with a three-to-five-year mortgage term. There were no provisions for *amortization* of the loan and interest was generally payable semi-annually. The majority of these mortgages were renewed upon maturity, since few families had the money to retire the debt. The mortgage companies originating these mortgages charged from one to three percent of the amount of the loan as a fee. Upon renewal, an additional one percent fee would be charged.

As the 20th century progressed, thrift institutions, especially savings and loan associations, continued to expand. The mutual savings banks, which had their greatest growth after the Civil War, remained principally in the New England states, but the savings and loans continued to grow and spread across the country. During this time, thrift institutions originated short-term mortgage loans for their own portfolios, with some installment-type mortgages.

All mortgage lenders participated in the real estate boom years of the 1920s. This was a period of unrestrained optimism. Most Americans believed growth and prosperity would continue forever. Real estate prices appreciated as much as 25 to 50 percent per year during the first half of the decade. Many lenders forgot their underwriting standards, believing that inflating prices would bail out any bad loan. As with any speculative period, the end came and, along with it, many personal fortunes were dissipated.

Depression Era

The real estate boom of the 1920s began to show signs of weakening long before the stock market crash. By 1927, real estate values that had appreciated in the early 1920s began to decline dramatically. Following the disastrous dive of the stock market in 1929 the entire economy of the United States was in danger of collapse. Real estate values plunged to less than half the level of the year before. The ability of both the individual borrower and the income property mortgagor to meet quarterly or semi-annual interest payments was reduced by the large-scale unemployment that followed the collapse of the stock market and by the loss of economic vitality throughout the nation.

Because periodic amortization of mortgages was not common, a six-month lag often occurred before an institutional investor realized a mortgage was in trouble. In addition, the various financial institutions were faced with a severe liquidity problem which sometimes required them to sell vast real estate and mortgage holdings under very unfavorable conditions. This need to sell real estate holdings to obtain cash, coupled with a rise in foreclosures and tax sales, severely depressed an already-crumbling real estate market. Many individual homeowners were threatened with property loss even if they retained their jobs, because when their five-year mortgages expired, many were unable to refinance their mortgages because lenders were caught in a liquidity crisis and did not have the funds to lend.

Thrift institutions also experienced problems during this period even though some of their mortgagors had installment type mortgages. As many workers lost their jobs and unemployment reached 25 percent, the savings inflow diminished drastically. All types of financial institutions began to fail, savers withdrew funds and the liquidity crisis worsened for all lenders. In the early 1930s, many savings and loan associations failed due to financial problems associated with heavy withdrawals by savers and a high foreclosure rate. This foreclosure rate reached such a high level that by 1935, 20 percent of all savings and loan mortgage assets were in the "real estate owned" category.

The vast majority of all foreclosures during the 1930s were made by second and third mortgagees, who needed to foreclose immediately on a defaulted property to protect what little security they may have had. The highest number of foreclosures occurred from 1931–1935, averaging 250,000 each year. The increasing number of foreclosures, especially on family farms in the Midwest, forced the beginning of compulsory moratoria. In the Midwest, where economic deterioration was aggravated by the dust bowl storms, the cry for moratoria reached the stage of near rebellion, and some violence occurred. Reacting to the hysteria sweeping the farm belt and some of the larger cities, many mortgagees voluntarily instituted forbearance, some for as long as two years. The first law requiring a mortgage moratorium became effective in Iowa on Feb. 8, 1933. In the next 18 months, 27 states enacted legislation suspending nearly all foreclosures. Most of the moratorium laws enacted during this period were to last for two years or less, although many were re-enacted and allowed to continue as law until the early 1940s.

It is important to note that during the period when these laws were in effect, there still were some foreclosures. The determining factor on whether to grant relief was the soundness of a debtor's fundamental economic position. If it were determined that a debtor would eventually lose the land anyway, it was considered a waste of time and an injustice to the creditor to postpone the foreclosure or grant a moratorium. The moratoria of the early 1930s did not provide an actual solution to the underlying economic problems, but they did provide time in which public unrest could be soothed and the federal government could introduce some economic remedies.

GOVERNMENT INTERVENTION

The federal government realized that the drop in real estate values would continue to add to the depression of the entire economy, preventing its revitalization. Therefore, the government instituted a series of programs designed to help stabilize real estate values and, hopefully, the entire economy. This marked the beginning of a drastic reversal in previous governmental-political philosophy, which had more or less been laissez-faire.

Beginning in the last year of the Hoover Administration, federal legislation usurped, to a large measure, control over real estate and mortgage lending activities which previously had been left to the states. (For a complete discussion of these programs and others, see Chapter *13,* Government Regulations and Consumer Protection.)

The first legislation designed to meet the threat of the Depression was the Reconstruction Finance Corporation (RFC) in 1932, which, among other things, provided liquidity to commercial banks. Shortly thereafter, the Federal Home Loan Bank (FHLB) was created to provide central credit facility to home finance institutions, primarily savings and loan associations. The next major legislation was the Home Owners' Loan Act (HOLA) in 1933, which provided for federal charters for savings and loan associations and created the Home Owners Loan Corporation (HOLC) to provide emergency relief to home owners by refinancing or purchasing defaulted mortgages. This program kept many tens of thousands of families from losing their homes in the 1930s.

One of the most far reaching enactments of this period was the National Housing Act of 1934 which created the Federal Housing Administration (FHA) and, in addition, the Federal Savings and Loan Insurance Corporation (FSLIC). FSLIC and the Federal Deposit Insurance Corporation (FDIC) were instrumental in encouraging depositors to return desperately needed deposits to financial institutions. FHA has provided the framework and the impetus necessary for the development of a true national mortgage market. FHA has also been credited with either initiating or making popular many innovations in mortgage lending, such as the long-term, self-amortizing mortgage loan.

THE GROWTH ERA

A minimal amount of single-family construction occurred from 1926 to 1946 as a result of the Depression and World War II. At the end of the war, however, five million servicemen returned home, and a tremendous demand for housing was created. The government, as part of its responsibility to returning veterans, passed the Servicemen's Readjustment Act of 1944. One of the major products of this act was a program which provided a desirable means of financing homes for veterans, the most distinguishing feature of which is the lack of a downpayment requirement for eligible veterans. Rates have been set at or slightly below the FHA rate. No mortgage insurance premiums are collected from the participants, since the program is not meant to be self-supporting, as is the FHA.

The highly liquid position of financial institutions was the second great impetus to the rapid expansion of single-family dwelling construction following World War II. In 1945, more than half of their assets were tied up in the no-risk but low-yielding securities they were obligated to purchase during World War II. At the end of the war, these bonds could be sold and the cash converted into securities with a higher return through the use of mortgage loans.

The greatest boom in housing construction in the history of this country and possibly the world became a reality with these two government programs (FHA and VA), the build-up demand for housing and the liquid position of lenders. Since that time, the mortgage market has been the largest user of long-term credit in the entire American economy.

During the period of 1946 to 1955, almost all new dollars invested in real estate mortgages were used to finance single-family housing. However, as the demand for housing peaked and began to diminish, some lenders realized that the new suburban communities would need shopping centers, office buildings and even apartment houses. A new investment philosophy began to emerge with the developing income property mortgage market.

This change in investment philosophy among lenders, especially life insurance companies, resulted from the need for these new properties and a realization that higher yields could be obtained with less expense. For example, it was less expensive for an institutional lender to make a $1 million apartment loan than to make 50 $20,000 single-family loans. The change in some lenders' investment philosophy is further illustrated by the fact that in 1955, three out of every four dollars being invested by life insurance companies in long-term mortgages were in single-family loans. By 1960, the ratio had changed to two out of every four dollars, and during the first half of the 1970s almost all new dollars invested were for income property mortgages. As life insurance companies shifted their lending philosophy, thrift institutions absorbed a larger percentage of single-family mortgage loans.

RECENT MORTGAGE LENDING

The most productive boom in real estate construction and financing in the United States has occurred during the past 35 years. More housing units and other types of buildings have been constructed during this period than in all the years since this country was founded. Much of the credit for this boom can be attached to the availability of capital at a reasonable rate and the corresponding creation of the secondary mortgage market. For example, FNMA was given expanded purchasing authority in 1970, and was joined by the Federal Home Loan Mortgage Corporation (FHLMC) in that year to provide secondary market facilities for conventional mortgages originated by savings and loan associations. While the housing boom changed the landscape of the American countryside, the new office buildings, apartment complexes and shopping centers provided the amenities and services needed by the new families in these homes.

The federal government was not the only government in the 1970s involved in either providing or stimulating housing for low and moderate income families. Before 1960, the state of New York had the only state housing agency, but by 1975 nearly all states had some type of housing agency. Although some have used tax-exempt bonds to raise revenue to lend to home buyers at below-market interest rates, many have fulfilled their social responsibility by providing financing for multi-family units.

During the 1970s, the rapid growth and equally rapid decline of a new mortgage lender—the real estate investment trust, or REIT—occurred. Authorized by a 1960 amendment to the tax laws, REITs were originally designed to provide a type of "mutual fund" interest or equity ownership in real estate for the investing public. By purchasing a share of stock, a shareholder had an interest in a trust that owned and managed real estate. A combination of inexperienced management, poor underwriting of loans, the oil embargo, a recession, and the unforeseeable dramatic increase in the prime interest rate brought disaster to the REITs. Most short-term trusts charged an interest rate that floated from three to five percent above the prime rate. The increase in the prime rate to 12 percent in 1974 forced many builder/developers into default, since few projects could carry an interest rate of 17 percent. The result was massive foreclosures and losses to the REITs. Although only a few trusts became bankrupt, most had substantial portions of their assets in an "interest non-accrual" category for a period of time. Most REITs will probably survive past reversals, but the public's confidence in them may have been shattered by the spectacular drop in REIT share prices.

THE DECADE OF CHANGE

The 1970s will be remembered as the decade when mortgage lending changed in a variety of ways. The 1970s witnessed positive developments such as mortgage-backed securities, alternative mortgage instruments and, in general, more sources of needed capital. Regrettably, the 1970s and 1980s will also be remembered as the period when recession and double-digit inflation combined to produce drastic changes for the nation's economy in general and mortgage lending in particular. The events which produced such a traumatic and mutable decade included, among others, a 1000 percent increase in the cost of imported oil, wage-price controls, the Vietnam War and environmental safeguards which produced little real growth but consumed much capital. The results were a stagnant stock market, a prime interest rate near 20 percent, gold at over $800 an ounce, and mortgage rates over 17 percent. One of the most unfortunate results was that by the end of the decade, only 15 percent of the American families could afford the average priced home.

Throughout the 1970s, the chronic inflation rate, high interest rate and periodic capital shortages were the major problems for mortgage lending. These problems and the mentioned positive aspects of this decade led to some basic changes in mortgage lending and mortgage lenders. These changes will be discussed in the chapters that follow.

SUGGESTED READINGS

Bryant, Willis R. *Mortgage Lending Fundamentals and Practices.* New York: McGraw-Hill Book Co., Inc., 1962.

Colean, Miles L. *Mortgage Companies: Their Place in the Financial Structure.* Englewood Cliffs, New Jersey: Prentice-Hall, Inc., 1962.

Dennis, Marshall W. "Mortgage Banking: Steeped in History and Bright with Promise," *The Mortgage Banker* (October 1973), pp. 88–105.

Downs, Anthony. *Federal Housing Subsidies: How Are They Working?* Lexington, Massachusetts: Lexington Books, D. C. Heath & Co., 1973.

Halperin, Jerome Y., and Brenner, Michael J. "Opportunities Under the New Section 8 Housing Program," *Real Estate Review* (Spring 1976), pp. 67–75.

Harriss, C. Lowell. *History and Policies of the Home Owners' Loan Corporation.* New York: National Bureau of Economic Research, Inc., 1951.

Hoffmann, G. J., Jr. *The Mortgage Banker of Yesterday and Today.* Jacksonville, Florida: Stockton, Whatley, Davin & Company, 1956.

Klaman, Saul B. *The Postwar Rise of Mortgage Companies.* New York: National Bureau of Economic Research, Inc., 1959.

Lodge, Edgar A. *A Mortgage Analysis 1906–1934.* Home Title Guaranty Company, 1935.

Pease, Robert H. and Kerwood, Lewis O., eds., *Mortgage Banking.* New York: McGraw-Hill Book Co., Inc., 1965.

Ring, Alfred A. *Real Estate Principles and Practices.* Englewood Cliffs, New Jersey: Prentice-Hall, Inc., 1972.

Skilton, Robert H. *Government and the Mortgage Debtor* (1929 to 1939). Philadelphia: University of Pennsylvania, 1944.

Unger, Maurice A. *Real Estate.* Cincinnati, Ohio: South-Western Publishing Co., 1974.

Weimer, Arthur M., Hoyt, Homer, and Bloom, George F. *Real Estate.* New York: The Ronald Press Co., 1972.

Chapter 2

The Role of Mortgage Lending in the Economy

Mortgage lending, in addition to fulfilling certain sociological demands, is a principal and essential ingredient of our nation's economy. Viewed in another perspective, mortgage lending allows for the fruition of one of the "American Dreams," that is, owning a home. It also provides a process through which an attractive return on savings can be realized and needed funds can be borrowed.

Mortgage lending could not fulfill these functions without many and varied types of mortgage lenders. The common requisite for all mortgage lenders is the accumulation of sufficient savings to produce the capital needed for mortgage loans. Unless financial intermediaries have access to sufficient savings, capital shortages result and credit restraints occur, affecting all mortgage lenders, often with disastrous results. This was the situation during 1973-74 and 1979-82. Secondary mortgage markets can assist during these periods of credit restraint but cannot solve the basic problem of a lack of savings flow to the mortgage lenders. (See Chapter 7, Secondary Mortgage Markets and Institutions.)

CAPITAL FORMATION

The funds required by the financial market are derived primarily from the savings of individuals and businesses. Savings of individuals, in the form of either deposits at financial institutions or reserves that accumulate in whole life insurance policies, account for approximately 90 percent of total savings. Savings inflows are not constant and the savings function must compete with food, shelter, clothing, transportation, recreation and other real or perceived demands for the after-tax income of an individual. Those individuals who do save are motivated by such needs and desires as accumulating funds for retirement, future security, major purchases, college, and others.

In recent years, the percentage of disposable income the American public has put into savings has decreased alarmingly. The reasons for this decline include the relatively low interest paid on passbook savings, which inhibits savings. This decrease in savings forces mortgage lenders to develop alternate sources of funds, such as money market certificates, which necessarily force up the interest rate for new mortgage loans.

Changes in the economy directly affect savings in some manner. For example, if the business cycle is down and unemployment increases, individuals may increase savings because of uncertainty over their employment. The result could be a savings inflow which theoretically should cause interest rates to decline as more dollars chase less demand. On the other hand, with a downturn in the business cycle and an increase in unemployment, those unemployed may have to withdraw savings for living expenses.

If the economy is expanding, savings may also accumulate since the demand for funds could reach a point where high interest rates attract more savings. On the other hand, if the economy is expanding, the demand for funds and interest rates may reach the legal limit on interest financial intermediaries can pay on savings. This could influence savers to reinvest elsewhere at a higher yield. The effect, known as *disintermediation*, is a massive savings outflow, which is devastating to mortgage lending. This occurred most recently in 1979-81. Although future economic cycles may change the result, the past seems to indicate that when the economy overheats, disintermediation will occur as savers seek the highest return on their funds.

Money market funds have become a new and strong competitor to financial institutions as savers seek the highest return on their funds. Savers can deposit as little as $1,000 and earn yields considerably higher than traditional types of savings accounts. The money market funds also provide easy access to the savers' money through checks and credit cards. However, they do not provide either insurance or any protection against declining rates as other types of accounts do. Money market funds grew to over $181 billion in 1981 from $3 billion in 1975.

During periods of high demand for credit (normally, the apex of a business cycle) the capital markets are usually unable to satisfy the combined demands for credit of individuals, government and business. Mortgage lending usually suffers during such periods since the price of money, as indicated by the interest rate, is either too high for most mortgage loans to be economically feasible or forced up against a state usury ceiling. Because real estate in general and mortgage lending in particular are the losers in a credit crunch, they have often been classified as countercyclical. This means that real estate activity, and consequently mortgage lending, usually expands when the general business cycle is down and credit demands are low. Conversely, as the economy begins to improve and demand for credit from other users increases, real estate activity begins to slow down as interest rates increase. This somewhat simplified explanation demonstrates the direct relationship between the availability of credit and real estate activity.

MORTGAGE MARKETS

Two general markets, capital and money, comprise the total financial market.[1] The mortgage market is only a part of the complete capital market. Within the capital market, a specific demand for funds, e.g. mortgages, must compete with other instruments, such as corporate bonds. Yet, mortgage lending has used more credit in the past 30 years than any other segment of the American economy, exceeding even the staggering credit demands of the federal government. (See Figure 2–1.)

GROWTH IN SELECTED TYPES OF CREDIT
(BILLIONS OF DOLLARS)

Type of Credit	1960	1981*	Increase
Total Credit Outstanding	$779.9	$5,127.7	$4,347.8
Residential Mortgage Loans:			
One- to Four-family Homes	141.9	1,018.5	876.6
Apartments	20.8	144.3	123.5
Total	162.7	1,162.7	1,000.1
Corporate and Foreign Bonds	90.2	533.2	443.0
State and Local Government Obligations.	70.8	361.4	290.6
Consumer Credit	65.1	411.4	346.3
Mortgages on Commercial Properties ...	33.4	279.1	245.7
Federal Debt	243.1	1,146.7	903.6

Note: Components may not add to totals due to rounding.
*Preliminary.
Sources: Federal Reserve Board; United States League of Savings Associations.

Figure 2–1.

If the composite demand for available funds is high, the price for these funds (the interest rate) will probably be high as well. Therefore, the price of money is subject to supply and demand like any other commodity. For example, if those who are demanding funds for mortgages are willing to pay the price for the funds, credit will be made available. But if corporate demand is also high and corporations are willing to pay a price equal to that offered by mortgages, funds will generally flow to bonds to the detriment of mortgage lending. The explanation for this relative attractiveness of corporate capital instruments lies in the unique characteristics of mortgage debt which requires a higher yield because of the lack of uniformity in mortgages, lower liquidity and the problems and delays of foreclosure. Although inflation and demand and supply of funds are the most important factors in the rise and fall of interest rates, the degree of risk inherent in any mortgage loan or bond offering also is influential.

PUBLIC DEBT VS. PRIVATE DEBT

When any federal, state, or local government spends more money than it collects, it must borrow in the same markets in which the issuers of bonds and mortgages borrow. In this manner they provide greater competition for the available capital. The federal government in particular has been in a severe deficit position recently, a condition which many economists believe was the basic cause of the persistent inflation in the 1970s and 1980s. The inflation and resulting high interest rates have played havoc both in the money markets and capital markets, and all users of credit have suffered.

Many times the fiscal policy of the federal government forces the Federal Reserve to act in an attempt to moderate the inflationary impact of federal borrowing.

FEDERAL RESERVE

In addition to its banking functions, the Federal Reserve has credit control responsibility over the nation's economy through financial institutions. The Federal Reserve has several methods of implementing this control.

Reserve requirements. By increasing the amount of money a member institution must have in its reserve account, less money is available to be loaned. Conversely, if the Federal Reserve policy is to increase the amount of money in order to make credit easier to obtain, it can lower the reserve requirement.

Open Market Operations. This commonly used method allows the Federal Reserve to decrease the supply of money by selling treasury securities on the open market. The securities are paid by checks drawn on commercial banks. This decreases their reserves, therefore reducing the amount of funds which can be loaned. If the Federal Reserve intends to increase the supply of money, it will buy the securities by issuing a check drawn upon itself.

Discount Rate. The Federal Reserve operates a service of discounting (paying less than par) commercial paper from member institutions. By discounting, the Federal Reserve provides funds which can be loaned. If the discount rate is increased, (considered as the interest rate that a member institution pays the Federal Reserve), it becomes more difficult for an institution to borrow to obtain necessary reserves. Consequently, the interest rate a member institution must then charge a borrower increases. If the discount rate is lowered, borrowing is easier for a financial institution and the interest rate charged to a borrower could be lowered.

FINANCIAL INTERMEDIARIES

Although the savings of individuals are the most important part of capital formation and mortgage lending, these individual savers are not investing or lending their money directly. Most individuals have neither the time nor the expertise to make sound investment decisions regardless of whether their investment vehicle is mortgages or stocks and bonds. Instead of direct investments, most savers use financial experts who can accumulate the funds of many savers and then invest them at a higher net yield to the saver. These experts are called *financial intermediaries* and include, among others:

- Commercial banks
- Credit unions
- Life insurance companies
- Mutual savings banks
- Savings and loan associations
- Pension funds

TOTAL ASSETS OF FINANCIAL INTERMEDIARIES AT YEAR-END
(BILLIONS OF DOLLARS)

Financial Intermediary	1960	1965	1970	1975	1980	1981*
Commercial Banks	$257.6	$377.3	$ 576.2	$ 964.9	$1,703.7	$1,808.7
Savings Associations	71.5	129.6	176.2	338.2	630.7	663.8
Life Insurance Companies.....	119.6	158.9	207.3	289.3	479.2	521.4
Mutual Savings Banks	40.6	58.2	79.0	121.1	171.6	175.6
Finance Companies	27.6	44.7	64.0	99.1	198.6	224.6
Investment Companies	17.0	35.2	47.6	42.2	58.4	55.2
Credit Unions	5.7	10.6	18.0	38.0	71.7	77.7
Private Pension Funds	38.1	73.6	110.4	146.8	286.8	310.9
State and Local Pension Funds.	19.7	34.1	60.3	104.8	198.1	226.2
Money Market Funds	—	—	—	3.7	74.4	181.9
Total	$597.4	$922.2	$1,339.0	$2,148.1	$3,873.2	$4,246.0

*Preliminary.
Sources: CUNA International, Inc.; Federal Home Loan Bank Board; Federal Reserve Board; Institute of Life Insurance; Investment Company Institute; National Association of Mutual Savings Banks; U.S. League of Savings Associations.

Figure 2–2.

These financial intermediaries have various alternatives for investing the accumulated funds of individuals and others, depending upon laws, regulations and custom. One of the attractive alternatives in addition to stocks and bonds is mortgages, and these intermediaries and others, such as mortgage companies, are the principal mortgage lenders.

MORTGAGE LENDERS

The primary economic function of a mortgage lender is to facilitate the flow of money into and through the mortgage market. A mortgage lender obtains funds accumulated by itself or other institutions such as savings and loan associations, commercial banks and life insurance companies and makes these funds available to borrowers in the form of mortgage loans. By bringing together borrowers and lenders from different economic sectors and geographic locations, a mortgage lender contributes to a more efficient allocation of the economy's resources.

The classification *mortgage lender* is used to describe those institutions or organizations at least partially engaged in the primary mortgage market; that is, the extending of funds directly to a borrower. Mortgage lenders may also purchase mortgages originated by other mortgage lenders either directly through fulfilled commitments or the secondary markets. This classification includes:

- Savings and loan associations
- Commercial banks
- Mortgage companies
- Mutual savings banks
- Life insurance companies
- Real estate investment trusts
- Credit Unions[2]

These mortgage lenders originate nearly all mortgage loans, including all types of residential and income-producing property loans, and hold about 70 percent of the total outstanding mortgage debt. (See Figure 2–3.)

A complete discussion on the development of these mortgage lenders, how they are organized and their mortgage lending activity is included in Chapters 3 and 4, the Mortgage Lenders.

**MORTGAGE LOANS OUTSTANDING, BY TYPE OF PROPERTY
AND LENDER, YEAR-END 1981***
(BILLIONS OF DOLLARS)

	Residential Properties					
Lender	One- to Four-family	Multi-family	Total	Commercial Properties	Farm Properties	Total Mortgage Loans
Savings Associations.......	$ 432.7	$ 38.3	$ 470.9	$ 47.3	†	$ 518.3
Commercial Banks.........	172.5	14.9	187.5	90.7	$ 8.5	286.6
Mutual Savings Banks	65.4	17.4	82.8	17.1	0.1	100.0
Life Insurance Companies ..	18.0	20.1	38.1	89.0	13.2	140.2
All Others................	329.9	53.6	383.5	35.0	80.2	498.7
Total.....................	$1,018.5	$144.3	$1,162.7	$279.1	$101.9	$1,543.8

Note: Components may not add to totals due to rounding.
*Preliminary.
†Less than $50 million.
Sources: Federal Home Loan Bank Board; Federal Reserve Board.

Figure 2–3.

MORTGAGE INVESTORS

The classification *mortgage investor* is used to describe those institutions that usually do not originate mortgage loans but are important holders of mortgage debt. This classification includes:

- Federal National Mortgage Association (FNMA)
- Government National Mortgage Association (GNMA)
- Retirement and pension funds
- Federal agencies
- State housing agencies
- Life insurance companies

These mortgage investors acquire the mortgages they hold either directly from the mortgage lenders or through the operations of the secondary market. Historically, the most important of these mortgage investors, FHLMC, FNMA and GNMA, will be discussed in detail in Chapter 7, Secondary Mortgage Markets and Institutions. The others will be discussed briefly at the end of Chapter 4, The Mortgage Lenders.

TRENDS IN MORTGAGE LENDING

More changes currently are influencing mortgage lending than at any other time since the 1930s. These changes affect how needed funds for mortgage financing are raised and loaned. After the turmoil in real estate finance of the 1970s, many borrowers and lenders questioned both the traditional manner of obtaining funds for mortgage lending and the mortgage instruments. The recent history of high inflation and unsettled monetary conditions has increased the need for modernization of the basic mortgage lending industry.

Mortgage lenders have difficulty with the traditional fixed interest rate mortgage when interest rates fluctuate rapidly because of excessive demands for credit, the advent of abnormal inflation, or a combination of both. If interest rates throughout the economy increase, thrift institutions must increase the rate of interest paid on deposits to hold those deposits. If the rate of interest on deposits does not keep pace with general interest rate increases, disintermediation occurs and depositors withdraw their funds and reinvest elsewhere. Disintermediation for mortgage lenders and particularly thrift institutions results in no available funds for mortgage loans. And a credit crunch occurs as it did in 1973-74 and again 1979-81.

On the other hand, if a thrift institution attempts to keep deposits by increasing the rate of interest paid to depositors, its cost of capital and lending increases. The problem is that while a thrift institution must pay the increased rate to all depositors, it is limited on its return to previously-negotiated interest rates on mortgages in its portfolio. Since the return on the mortgage portfolio remains constant or only slightly increases as the rate paid for deposits increases dramatically, the net return becomes tenuous.

MONEY MARKET CERTIFICATES

After thrift institutions had experienced yet another bout of disintermediation during the high interest period of 1974 with the expected result of scarcity of mortgage funds, regulatory authorities authorized a new type of savings instrument to help prevent future outflows—the Money Market Certificate (MMC). This certificate was first issued in June, 1978 and was indexed to the six-month Treasury bill rate. A saver could use this MMC to invest a minimum $10,000 in a six-month certificate that would yield .25 percent higher than Treasury bills, the traditional haven for savers during periods of high interest. By being able to offer the traditional .25 percent differential (commercial banks also offered this $10,000 MMC) and having authority to exceed the Regulation Q ceiling on interest rates, thrift institutions were able to stem disintermediation to a meaningful degree.

Regulatory changes later prohibited compounding of interest and the differential when the index exceeded 9 percent. The result of these regulatory changes was that the market share of MMC increased at commercial banks and decreased at thrifts. Later regulatory changes put a minimum ceiling of 7.75 percent on this MMC. From the very beginning of MMC, they have been the major factor in the continuation of savings inflow to all deposit-type mortgage lenders which has prevented disintermediation to a large degree and allowed for a continuation of mortgage lending activities.

However, the mortgage lenders that relied on MMC extensively for mortgage funds soon learned that these certificates were adding to the already rising cost of borrowing. Then, in late 1979, another certificate with a 30-month maturity was authorized. This certificate is indexed to the market yield of outstanding treasury securities of comparable maturity plus the differential. In addition to the earnings problem resulting from the high interest rates paid on MMCs, depository institutions faced continuing disintermediation as the short-term certificates matured. The net effect of both of these new money market certificates is that not only has the cost of borrowing drastically increased, but the length of time these high costs are locked in has increased. These higher costs will keep mortgage rates higher for a longer period than otherwise would occur as the economy cooled.

When the market rates drop, a mortgage lender still may suffer, since a borrower many times simply refinances at a lower rate after paying any prepayment penalty. If lenders are to remain in the mortgage market during periods of extended inflation or rapid interest rate fluctuation, alternate forms of finance must be used.

ALTERNATIVE MORTGAGE INSTRUMENTS

An equitable solution to mortgage lenders' need to maintain a sufficient spread between cost of borrowing and cost of lending may be found in one of the following alternative mortgage instruments. The most common is the *variable rate mortgage* (VRM). Variable rate mortgages are the direct result of inflation and are designed to increase a lender's return on mortgages already made with the variable rate feature to a level sufficient to maintain a profitable spread and to keep that lender in the mortgage market. This type of loan has existed in other countries for many years and has proven satisfactory to both borrower and lender.

This alternative first gained wide acceptance in this country among state-chartered savings and loan associations and commercial banks in California in the high inflation years of the late 1970s. Many financial institutions after being authorized to make variable rate loans made over 50% of their loans using this alternative. Federally chartered savings and loan associations were given authority to make this type of loan in 1979. Many other states have followed California's lead and authorized this type of loan.

The basic concept is that the interest rate on the underlying mortgage will change according to the *prevailing market interest rate* as fixed by an acceptable standard. An example of this could be a cost of money index at a Federal Home Loan Bank. Changes in the underlying rate, after being communicated to a borrower, could be changed by at least 0.10 percent but not more than

0.25 percent at each adjustment. Adjustment periods would probably be quarterly or semi-annually. If an index calls for a downward adjustment, a lender is obligated to make it—adjustments are optional on the up side. Usually the interest rate can only be increased a maximum amount (2½ percentage points under federal regulations) over the life of the mortgage. If a borrower is not satisfied with the rate change, prepayment is allowed with no penalty.

The adjustable mortgage loan (AML) is one of the more recent alternative mortgage instruments. It was authorized in 1981 and allows lenders to adjust interest rates without regulatory caps. Like the VRM and RRM, it allows for adjustments to the interest rate on the mortgage. The interest rate corresponds directly to the movement of an interest rate index. A lender can use any index that is verifiable by the borrower and is beyond the control of the lender.

Another alternative which is receiving much attention recently is the *renegotiable rate mortgage*—similar to the *Canadian roll-over mortgage*. This type of mortgage, which federally chartered savings and loans were authorized to make in 1980, is based on the type used in Canada since the late 1960s. Similar to a degree to the regular 25- or 30-year self-amortizing mortgage, a borrower repays the loan as if it was a long-term loan, except that at the end of a period (usually 3 to 5 years) the loan in effect comes due. A borrower can automatically have it renewed with the same lender (a lender is obligated to renew) but the interest rate will be at the current market rate. The new rate could be higher (maximum increase of 5% over life of loan) or lower than the old rate. If a borrower does not want to accept the new rate, a new lender is sought, (if desired or needed) and repayment is made with no penalty.

A third alternative to the fixed rate mortgage is the *graduated payment mortgage* (GPM). Although this program is not designed to encourage mortgage lenders to remain in the long-term mortgage market, it does provide a means for young couples to purchase homes at an initially lower-than-normal monthly debt service. This program recognizes that incomes do increase, and that a larger payment could be made later to offset the initial lower debt service and fully amortize the mortgage loan within the normal 25- to 30-year term.

Somewhat similar to the GPM is the *Flexible Loan Insurance Program* (FLIP) which became popular in the late 1970s. This privately administered program basically allows for partial monthly payment of the mortgage to come from a pledged savings account. By putting a part of what normally would be a required downpayment into a savings account and then using a part of it each month to supplement the mortgage payment for a short period (3 to 5 years), a borrower can afford to obtain a larger mortgage and thus more house. At the end of the period of supplemental payment from the savings account (which is now depleted), the monthly mortgage payment will increase to the total monthly amount the lender was receiving. By this time, a borrower's income should have increased to allow for the increased payment.

Date_____, 19_____

ADJUSTABLE MORTGAGE LOAN ADJUSTMENT NOTICE

Your loan with_____

secured by a _____ on property located at _____

_____ is scheduled to be adjusted on _____, 19_____.

The outstanding balance of your loan on that date based on the remaining monthly payments due by that date will be

$_____. Unless you elect to pay the loan in full by that date you will be charged _____ % on

your loan for the next _____ months. This rate is based on_____

index which currently is _____ and will be in effect until the next payment adjustment date which is

_____, 19_____. Rate adjustments will occur on _____

between this payment adjustment and the next payment adjustment date.

Your monthly payment, based on that rate will be $_____, beginning with the payment due on _____,

19 _____.

You should be aware of the following information concerning your loan since the last payment adjustment:

1. Rate adjustment(s) took place on _____.
2. Rates on the rate adjustment date(s) were _____.
3. Index values on the rate adjustment date(s) were _____.
4. Date(s) which the principal loan balance was adjusted were _____.
5. The net change in the principal loan balance since the last payment adjustment is $_____.

Rate adjustment date(s) which fall between your current payment adjustment date and your next payment adjustment date are
_____.

You may pay off the entire loan or a part of it without penalty at any time.

If you have any questions about this notice, please contact:

_____
NAME

_____
TITLE

_____
PHONE NUMBER

43077-7 (7/81)
AML Adjustment Notice

SAF Systems and Forms
American Savings & Accounting Supply, Inc.

BORROWER

Figure 2-4. *Adjustable Mortgage Loan Adjustment Notice.*

MORTGAGE-BACKED BONDS

As real estate in general, and single-family units in particular, rebounded from the lows of 1975–76, the need for new sources of mortgage money produced new vehicles for generating the needed capital. The most important innovation was the private mortgage-backed bond, which had no governmental guarantee. This allows both thrift institutions and commercial banks to raise new funds by pooling existing mortgages and selling a bond backed by these mortgages. The mortgages in these pools are either FHA-insured, VA-guaranteed, or have private mortgage insurance. Standard and Poor's has given many of these bonds its AA rating because of the existence of private or governmental insurance and because the bonds are over-collateralized from 125 to 160 percent of face value. (One issuer pledged $340 million of mortgages to collateralize the $200 million worth of bonds.) Other issues insured by private mortgage insurance were not over-collateralized.

TAX-EXEMPT HOUSING BONDS

Prior to 1978, state housing finance agencies were the only governmental entities using tax-exempt bonds to provide financing for mortgage borrowers. Their normal method of financing was to borrow money and then provide below market rate loans to low- and moderate-income groups. In mid 1979, the city of Chicago also began using tax-exempt bonds, but this program was designed for middle-income buyers and, as a result, created a storm of controversy.

The concept behind using tax-exempt bonds for financing is quite simple. An issuer, whether state or city, is able to sell its tax-exempt bonds in the captial market with an interest rate substantially below taxable bonds because of the tax savings to investors. This money is then channeled through various mortgage lenders to the mortgage borrower. As a result of this low cost borrowing, mortgagors often get a loan 2 or 3 percentage points below the conventional market rate.

The various state programs in past years caused little reaction as they attempted to help the low- and moderate-income groups, but when some new programs developed which intended to assist middle-income groups, the concern of many segments of society became vocal.

The Mortgage Subsidy Bond Act of 1981 resulted from this rising concern. The Act severely restricts the use of tax-exempt mortgage bonds issued by state and local housing authorities. It limits eligibility of buyers and imposes purchase price ceilings and limitations on states' annual volumes. The rates to the mortgagors cannot exceed the tax-exempt bond rate by more than 1 percent. Finally, the law calls for the tax-exempt privilege on single-family housing bonds to be terminated on December 31, 1983.

SUGGESTED READINGS

Aaron, Henry J. *Shelter and Subsidies: Who Benefits from Federal Housing Policies?* Washington, D.C.: The Brookings Institution, 1972.

Brueggeman, William B., and Baesel, Jerome B. "The Mechanics of Variable Rate Mortgages and Implications for Home Ownership as an Inflation Hedge," *The Appraisal Journal* (April 1976), pp. 236–46.

Candilis, Wray O. *Variable Rate Mortgage Plans.* Washington, D.C.: The American Bankers Association, 1971.

Cassidy, Henry I. "Price-Level Adjusted Mortgages versus Other Mortgage Instruments," *Federal Home Loan Bank Board Journal* (January 1981), pp. 3–7.

Grebler, Leo. "The New System of Residential Mortgage Finance," *The Appraisal Journal* (April 1976), pp. 434–48.

Hoagland, Henry E., Stone, Leo D., and Brueggeman, William B. *Real Estate Finance,* 6th Ed. Homewood, Illinois: Richard D. Irwin, Inc., 1977.

Jacobs, D. P., Farwell, and Neave, E. H. *Financial Institutions.* Homewood, Illinois: Richard D. Irwin, Inc., 1972.

McFarland, Stuart R. "Alternative Mortgage Instruments Offer Key to Expanded Lending Market," *The Mortgage Banker* (September 1978), pp. 7–16.

Seldin, Maury, and Swesnik, Richard H. *Real Estate Investment Strategy.* New York: Wiley-Interscience, 1970.

Stansell, Stanley R., and Miller, James A. "How Variable Rate Mortgages Would Affect Lenders," *Real Estate Review* (Winter 1976), pp. 116–18.

Tucker, Donald P. "The Variable-Rate Graduated-Payment Mortgage," *Real Estate Review* (Spring 1975), pp. 71–80.

Vitt, Lois A., and Bernstein, Joel H. "Convertible Mortgages: New Financing Tool?" *Real Estate Review* (Spring 1976), pp. 33–37.

Wiedemer, John P. *Real Estate Finance*, 2nd Ed. Reston, Virginia: Reston Publishing Company, 1977.

Yardeni, Dr. Edward. "Is the Housing Industry Still Cyclical?" *Federal Home Loan Bank Board Journal* (February 1980), pp. 16–23.

NOTES

1. The basic difference between the two markets is the maturity of the financial instruments. Money market instruments (U.S. Treasury Bills, corporate commercial paper, etc.) mature in less than one year. Capital market instruments (bonds and mortgages) mature in more than one year.

2. Although state-chartered credit unions have had the authority to make long-term mortgage loans for a number of years, they have not been a significant factor in mortgage lending. Federally chartered credit unions were given the authority in 1977 to make long-term mortgage loans but only to their own members.

Chapter 3

The Mortgage Lenders—
Part One

Commercial Banks,
Mortgage Companies,
and REITS

This first of two chapters on mortgage lenders will discuss commercial banks, mortgage companies and real estate investment trusts. The second chapter on mortgage lenders will discuss savings and loan associations, mutual savings banks and all other lenders. Mortgage lenders are described as those financial intermediaries that actually originate mortgage loans as contrasted with mortgage investors that hold mortgage debt but do not originate any loans.

About 67 percent of the nation's outstanding mortgage debt is held by four major mortgage lenders. (See Figure 2-3.) Only one of those, commercial banks, will be discussed in this chapter. It is important to note that holding mortgage debt does not mean that the institution or intermediary necessarily originated the mortgage. For example, mortgage companies have originated more than 75 percent of all FHA-VA mortgages made, yet mortgage companies are not listed as holders of any mortgage since they sell all mortgages originated. On the other hand, life insurance companies are listed as holding a substantial amount of mortgage debt although most of this debt was originated by mortgage companies and then sold to life insurance companies.

COMMERCIAL BANKS (CBs)

Commercial banks have both the largest collective membership at about 15,000 (with about 30,000 branches) and greatest total assets with just under 50 percent of the total assets of all financial institutions. CBs are second only to savings and loan associations in their holdings of the total outstanding mortgage debt. They are first in origination of income-property loans and construction mortgages, and are second to savings and loan associations in origination of residential mortgages.

A commercial bank is a private financial institution organized to accumulate funds primarily through time and demand deposits and to make these funds available to finance the nation's commerce and industry. In recent years, commercial banks have expanded their real estate finance operations from mostly short-term mortgage loans to include long-term loans.

Development

Except for a one-year period following the enactment of the *National Bank Act of 1863,* federally-chartered commercial banks were not allowed to make real estate loans until relatively recently. During the period from 1863 to 1913 state-chartered banks thrived since they were able to make real estate loans. Then in 1913, the *Federal Reserve Act* provided the authorization for federally-chartered commercial banks to make mortgage loans. The typical CB mortgage loan during this early period was a 50 percent loan-to-value ratio for a five-year term with the principal payable at the end of the term and with interest payable semiannually.

Commercial banks in the 1930s were in a position similar to that of other financial institutions—distressed by being illiquid—and consequently many failed. (In fact, the number of commercial banks decreased from more than 30,000 to about 16,000.) During the early months of President Franklin D. Roosevelt's first term, many new federal laws affecting the economy were enacted. The Federal Deposit Insurance Corporation (FDIC), authorized by the *Banking Act of 1933,* helped restore confidence in commercial banks and encouraged badly needed funds to flow back into bank vaults to provide liquidity for new loans. Currently, the FDIC insures deposits in all commercial banks up to $100,000.

Organization and Regulation

Commercial banks are chartered by either the federal government through the comptroller of the currency, or a state banking agency. State-chartered banks outnumber federally chartered banks by about two to one, although more assets are in the federally chartered CBs. State-chartered CBs may be members of the Federal Reserve System, but only 1,000 (or 10 percent) are members. All federally chartered must be members, however. This central banking system, comprising 12 Federal Reserve Districts,[1] provides many services to its members such as issuing currency, holding bank reserves, discounting loans, and serving as a check clearinghouse. (For a discussion of how the Federal Reserve operates to control economic developments, see page 20.)

Mortgage Lending Activity

Commercial banks are quite different from other major mortgage lenders. They are neither organized for nor economically inclined toward mortgage lending. CB funds are short-term and derived mainly from passbook savings and deposits in checking accounts. Long-term lending is generally not attractive. CBs are interested in commercial loans which are normally short-term and provide a better match between the maturity of assets (loans) and liabilitites (deposits). When commercial loan demand is high, practically all CB funds flow to meet that demand and mortgage loans are neglected. During those periods in the business cycle when commercial loan demand is light, CBs have recently placed excess funds in real estate. This excess credit of CBs can be damaging to real estate in general as some unsound mortgage loans result. The CB problem loans in the 1970s, primarily to real estate investment trusts, can be traced directly to 1972–73 when CBs held funds with little commercial loan demand. Much of the current real estate assets of CBs resulted from these poor loan judgments made during that time.

Some CBs holding companies have recently become more active in mortgage lending either by purchasing a mortgage company or establishing their own, while others have formed REITs.

The mortgage lending activity of commercial banks is more diverse than other lenders. Banks not only engage in both government and conventional residential mortgage lending, but also are the largest income-property lender. They are the largest mortgage lender for construction loans and help finance other lenders, especially mortgage companies, by issuing lines of credit which allow for the "warehousing" of loans until needed for delivery to an investor.

Currently, construction loans on residential and income-properties comprise a large percentage of mortgage financing activity by banks. These loans are normally classified as ordinary commercial loans, not real estate loans on the bank's books. The interest rate on these loans is generally two to five points about the prime rate depending on the borrower. These loans are attractive to CBs because of the yield and because the loan is short term (6 to 36 months) making it similar to the bank's source of funds.

The board of governors of the Federal Reserve System issues regulations affecting real estate lending activity by member banks. State-chartered banks are governed by the regulations of the responsible state agency. These regulations usually are similar to those of the Federal Reserve. The current regulations of the Federal Reserve allow loans up to 90 percent of value to be amortized up to 30 years with no limit on the loan amount, although they are subject to the $93,750 limit in the secondary market. A bank can lend up to 70 percent of its deposits or 100 percent of capital and surplus, whichever is greater. CBs may have up to 10 percent of real estate loan units in a "basket," or nonconforming classification. Leasehold loans are allowed if the lease extends at least 10 years past the date of full amortization.

MORTGAGE COMPANIES

A mortgage company usually is identified as a mortgage banker, but that term is somewhat misleading since it implies that the lender is a depository for funds like other banks. Mortgage companies are not depositories but can be classified as intermediaries since they serve as financial bridges between borrowers and lenders.

Less than 1,000 mortgage companies exist throughout the United States although the majority are located in traditional capital-deficit areas such as the South and West. They render a valuable service to both the borrower and the ultimate investor by moving funds by means of mortgage originations and sales from capital-surplus areas to areas where insufficient capital exists for needed growth.

Unlike previously discussed mortgage lenders, a mortgage company does not intentionally hold mortgages for its own benefit. All mortgages originated are sold to mortgage investors either directly or through the secondary market. Mortgage companies originate about as many residential mortgages as commercial banks although both originate far less than savings and loan associations. Mortgage companies originate about 75 percent of all FHA-VA mortgages, most of which are currently being pooled in mortgage-backed securities guaranteed by GNMA. Only commercial banks originate more income-property loans than mortgage companies.

Development

Mortgage companies developed to fulfill a need for farm financing in the second half of the 19th century. Following the Civil War, new farm lands were opened in the Ohio Valley and further west which required an infusion of credit from the capital-surplus areas in New England. Originally, a few real estate agents, attorneys and some commercial bankers made the needed mortgage loans and then sold the mortgages either to wealthy individuals or institutions in the east. This practice grew until farm mortgage lending specialists developed and formed the first mortgage companies. At the turn of the century approximately 200 mortgage companies were originating 50 percent loan-to-value ratio farm mortgages with five-year maturities and principal paid at maturity.

Following World War I, the migration from the farms to the developing urban areas accelerated, and a few of the more aggressive mortgage companies began to make single-family mortgage loans. Regarding loan ratio and term, this type of loan was similar to the farm mortgage loans made by mortgage companies for the previous 50 years. The non-amortized mortgage, which normally required refinancing at the expiration of the term, was one of the principle reasons for the large number of families who lost their homes in the depression of the 1930s. The liquidity crisis which prevented other financial institutions from refinancing mortgage loans as they became due had a multiplied effect for mortgage companies.

In the early 1930s, officials of the federal government realized that to prevent more basic political changes from occurring some basic economic changes were needed. The first step taken toward stabilizing the economy was to put a floor under depreciating real estate values. Not only was demand at a low point, but values were being forced down by an ever-increasing foreclosure rate. The Federal Home Loan Bank System was begun in 1932 to help the savings and loan associations, but the Home Owners Loan Corporation (HOLC) in 1933 allowed all lenders to exchange defaulted mortgages for government bonds. This program helped save many family homes as HOLC restructured the mortgage and put it on an amortized basis. It also helped stabilize real estate values since foreclosed mortgages were not forced on the market.

The Federal Housing Administration (FHA), created by the National Housing Act of 1934, provided the main stimulus to the formation of modern mortgage companies. Approximately 80 percent of current mortgage companies were formed after 1934. FHA established minimum standards for both the borrower and the real estate before it would insure a mortgage loan. FHA insurance protected mortgage lenders. FHA minimum standards prompted life insurance companies to seek permission from state insurance commissioners to make out-of-state loans with higher loan-to-value ratios and longer terms. State regulatory authorities eventually agreed to the request and mortgage companies soon began originating FHA-insured mortgages for sale to life insurance companies.

FHA adopted the HOLC practice of amortizing mortgage loans, thus creating a need to service loans sold to investors. Servicing meant that a mortgage company would collect the monthly principal and interest and then forward it to an investor, in addition to ascertaining that taxes and insurance were paid and the property generally maintained. If a default occurred, the mortgage company had the responsibility of curing it, if possible. If not, the mortgage company would handle the foreclosure. The servicing function is what clearly separates the mortgage company from the mortgage broker, who simply handles the sale of a mortgage loan and is then finished with the transaction.

Mortgage companies grew slowly during the slow-growth period of the Depression and World War II. But at the end of the war three factors led to one of the greatest real estate booms this country has ever seen:

1. Pent-up demand for housing because of minimal housing construction for nearly 20 years.
2. The Veterans Administration's mortgage guarantee for eligible veterans.
3. The bountiful financial capacity created by the sale of previously-obligatory government bonds.

This single-family housing boom lasted well into the 1950s, and mortgage companies originated the vast majority of the FHA-VA mortgages made. By the 1960s, the interest of permanent investors (particularly life insurance companies) turned toward income-property loans. So the mortgage companies developed the expertise that also enabled them to originate these multi-million dollar loans.

The evolution of mortgage companies has produced a modern financial institution that is capable of adapting to changes in financial conditions and government activity. Today, most mortgage companies have dual capabilities —single-family housing and income-property production—while some companies specialize in one or the other.

Some or all of the following functions are performed by the modern mortgage company:

1. Originates mortgages on single-family and/or income-property for sale to investors
2. Arranges construction financing, gap financing and interim financing
3. Warehouses single-family loans
4. Services loans sold to investors

Organization and Regulation

The mortgage banking function is performed primarily by mortgage companies, but some commercial banks and savings and loans serve basically the same function. Some of these latter institutions have purchased mortgage companies in order to compete with other mortgage companies.

Unlike the other mortgage lenders, mortgage companies are not chartered by either state or federal government but simply follow either the partnership or incorporation laws and requirements of the state in which the respective company is located. The mortgage company is also unique by not being subject to direct regulation and supervision. If a mortgage company is an approved FHA lender or an FNMA-approved seller/servicer, it is subject to periodic audits. HUD has recently attempted to exercise more control by issuing regulations governing several areas of concern, among them how a mortgagee handles delinquency problems with a mortgagor. During the early 1970s when activity in mergers and acquisitions between commercial banks and mortgage companies were common, the Federal Reserve attempted to exercise some control by requiring approval prior to ownership changes.

Mortgage Lending Activity

The manner in which a mortgage company conducts its residential lending business differs considerably from other lenders. The principal reason for this difference is that mortgage companies usually do not have their own funds to close residential loans. Life insurance companies and other depository institutions can attract their funds needed for mortgage lending directly, but mortgage companies must borrow before they can lend.

Financing the Mortgage Company

Mortgage companies finance lending activity either by the sale of *commercial paper* or by drawing on a line of credit with a commercial bank. Historically, the latter was the primary way of obtaining funds, but commercial paper has recently become equally important. Commercial paper is a short-term debt instrument for which the maximum term is usually 180 or 270 days and that carries a fixed rate for a fixed term. Mortgage companies use this alternative during those periods in the economic cycle when the rate for commercial paper is lower than the prime rate. In addition to the lower cost of borrowing, the need for *compensating balances*—funds left on deposit with a commercial bank to provide increased incentive to lend funds—is either diminished or non-existent. If a commercial bank lends its support to the commercial paper by backing it with an irrevocable letter of credit, the bank will require a fee and some compensating balances. On the other hand, if commercial paper is sold under the name of a holding company of the mortgage company, no compensating balances are required, but the parent company must have a recognizable credit rating before it can render this valuable service to a subsidiary mortgage company. The problem with selling commercial paper is that the market is quite volatile, and during periods of tight money only high-cost funds can be obtained and then only by those companies with the highest credit ratings.

The second alternative for obtaining funds needed by a mortgage company is by drawing on a line of credit with a commercial bank. The loan from the commercial bank will be fully collateralized by closed mortgage loans and repaid from the proceeds of a periodic sale of a group of mortgages to either a permanent investor or in the secondary mortgage market. This process is called *warehousing*. It aptly describes the constant flow of closed mortgages which secure the bank loan into the commercial bank. There the closed mortgages remain until a group, or pool of mortgages, typically $1 million worth, is sold to an investor.

Commercial banks are attracted to this type of loan because it is short-term, involves little risk and because the mortgages that serve as collateral are usually obligated by a commitment to an investor. Commercial banks require this line of credit to be supported by compensating balances usually of 20 percent of the maximum line of credit. These required compensating balances sometimes are tax and insurance escrows collected by a mortgage company and deposited with the lending bank until needed.

A mortgage company pays the prime rate or higher for the borrowed funds, depending on its credit rating and the money market. This often allows for a small marketing profit between the cost of borrowing and the interest rate on the underlying mortgage.

Because of its unique financial characteristics, a mortgage company usually obtains a *commitment* from either a permanent investor, such as a mutual savings bank, or government agency, such as GNMA. That investor agrees to purchase the originated mortgages. A commitment is a contractual agreement between an investor, who agrees to purchase a certain amount of mortgages at a stated interest rate with certain maturities and type of property, and a mortgage company, which agrees to supply them. The commitment agreement may also stipulate whether servicing is to be granted, how it is to be handled, and the fee involved. A commitment, depending on the terms, can require delivery, which is a *take-out commitment,* either immediately or in the future, usually within four months. It may not require delivery at all. This is called a *stand-by commitment.* The commitment may be supported by a fee payable by the mortgage company to the investor and which may be refunded if the commitment is fulfilled. If it is a stand-by commitment, the fee is not refunded.

Mortgage companies earn revenue from four sources:

1. An origination fee charged to each borrower
2. A servicing fee charged to the investor
3. Any marketing difference between the interest rate of the underlying mortgage and the rate required by the commitment
4. Any warehousing difference between interest rate of funds borrowed and loaned

Both residential (FHA-VA and conventional) and income-property loans are originated by mortgage companies for sale to the following investors:

1. Life insurance companies—primarily income-property
2. Mutual savings banks—primarily residential
3. Savings and loan associations—all types of loans
4. Federal National Mortgage Association—primarily residential
5. Government National Mortgage Association—primarily residential
6. Commercial banks—primarily income-property
7. Pension funds—all types of loans

Since mortgage companies are not directly regulated on mortgage limits, ratios, lending areas or types of loans, their only limitations are those imposed by purchasers of mortgages or insuring or guaranteeing agencies or companies.

REAL ESTATE INVESTMENT TRUSTS (REITs)

The real estate investment trust is of recent origin and the smallest in the percentage of total outstanding mortgage debt held (about one percent) of the major mortgage lenders. At the beginning of 1980, 218 REITs held more than $12 billion in total assets. This asset total has dropped from the historical peak of over $21 billion in 1974.

Development

The forerunner of the modern REIT existed in Massachusetts for many years before changes in federal tax law in 1960 allowed for the development of shareholder-owned trusts that could be treated as conduits for tax purposes in which trusts would not be taxed on those earnings passed to shareholders. The key provisions to the Internal Revenue Code were:

1. A trust, in order to qualify for conduit status, must distribute 90 percent of annual net income to shareholders
2. 75 percent of assets must consist of either mortgages or real estate equities and
3. 75 percent of the trust's earnings must come from those assets.

REITs grew slowly until 1968 when total assets reached $1 billion. This amount doubled in 1969 and by the end of 1970 assets were nearly $5 billion. Growth in the number of REITs and their total assets exploded after 1970, peaking in 1974 when more than 200 REITs had total assets in excess of $21 billion. The success story changed after 1974 because of a combination of overbuilding, poor and improper underwriting, construction material shortages and record-high interest rates. The outlook in general for REITs has been blurred ever since.

During the early 1960s, the REIT industry was dominated by equity trusts which purchased and operated existing income properties. These early trusts provided professionally selected and managed real estate investment opportunities for the small investor, similar to the way mutual funds operated in stocks and bonds. During this same period of time, a few mortgage trusts existed which invested in long-term mortgages. Following the credit crunch of 1966, these trusts became more active in the short-term construction and development (C&D) market, which, until that time, had been dominated by commercial banks. The earnings of these short-term trusts allowed for an increase in their book value which facilitated the sale of additional shares of stock at a premium, the proceeds of which could be used for future leverage.

These short-term trusts produced such phenomenal results that many mortgage companies, commercial banks and life insurance companies followed the trend and formed their own REITs to share in the attractive earnings. From 1970 to 1973 the total assets of all REITs increased from $4.7 billion to more than $20 billion and the number of REITs increased from less than 100 to more than 200.

Much of the real estate construction boom of the early 1970s was funded by these REITs and consequently, when the boom ended in 1974, the result was devastating for most REITs. Without a doubt, a lot of real estate construction occurred in the early 1970s because some REITs were forced to put all available funds to work immediately to produce the earnings necessary to pay high dividends to expectant shareholders. To accomplish this task, many REITs turned to short-term, variable-cost bank loans on which interest rates floated at or above the prime, and to the sale of commercial paper to finance lending operations and increase leverage. The burden of satisfying the debt service requirements of these bank loans forced many trusts into more aggressive lending. This resulted both in a lowering of underwriting standards and massive overbuilding of certain types of properties in some areas, such as condominiums in Florida.

In 1974, several events combined to produce a general economic recession which was actually a depression for the real estate industry:

1. The oil embargo which made recreational properties located far from population centers unattractive
2. A shortage of construction materials which resulted in costly construction delays
3. Record-high interest rates which made construction mortgages floating three to five percent over prime uneconomical.

Massive losses to REITs resulted with corresponding losses to their shareholders. Many of the larger short-term trusts had more than 70 percent of assets in a nonaccruing interest status, which resulted in no dividends being paid to shareholders. As a result, stock prices plummeted and many investors became disillusioned with REITs. Some economic commentators expected many REITs to become bankrupt during these difficult years, but only a few did. The reason many survived was that creditor banks did not want to transfer real estate losses from REITs' balance sheets to their own by demanding payment on past due loans. Some REITs recently relinquished their tax-free status to become publicly-owned companies. This allows them to carry forward losses to balance future earnings.

The future for REITs is blurred, but it appears many will probably survive past problems, possibly in a merged form, and again make an important contribution to the real estate finance needs of this nation. In 1977, some of the stronger trusts began making new loans and paying dividends to their shareholders. Many of the pure equity trusts experienced little difficulty during the dark days of 1974 and 1975 and have continued to pay dividends on a regular basis.

Organization and Regulation

The trustees of a REIT, elected by the shareholders, have a function similar to the board of directors of a corporation. Trustees have a responsibility to formulate the trust's general investment philosophy, although the implementation usually is entrusted to an independent advisor. This advisor, which may also lend its name to the trust, is normally a mortgage company, a commercial bank or a life insurance company. In return for its professional services involving originating, underwriting and servicing of loans, the advisor receives a fee, usually ranging from 0.5 to 1.25 percent of the dollar value of the assets managed.

REITs are not directly regulated by either the federal government or state governments. However, they must satisfy the securities law. Since REITs have no restrictions on types of loans, loan amounts, loan-to-value ratios or locations, they can fill a void in real estate finance that other mortgage lenders cannot.

Mortgage Lending Activity

A unique source of funds for mortgage lending exists with REITs. Unlike most other mortgage lenders, which, except for mortgage companies, are depository-type institutions, REITs raise funds through the sale of shares and debt securities or bank borrowing. As a result, the cost of funds to REITs is considerably higher than the cost to other mortgage lenders. Consequently, REITs have tended to focus their lending in those areas of real estate finance that offer higher returns even though higher risks may be involved. An example would be construction and development loans. A few REITs make C&D loans for tract homes, but because of their yield requirements, REITs usually do not make long-term, single-family mortgages. In addition to C&D loans, REITs make sale-leaseback loans, long-term income-property loans and short-term gap or interim loans.

NOTES

1. Federal District Banks are located in Boston, New York, Philadelphia, Richmond, Atlanta, Cleveland, St. Louis, Chicago, Minneapolis, Kansas City, Dallas, and San Francisco.

Chapter 4

The Mortgage Lenders—
Part Two
Savings and Loan Associations,
Mutual Savings Banks,
Life Insurance Companies, and
All Others

This second chapter on mortgage lenders includes a discussion of the thrift institutions—savings and loan associations and mutual savings banks, both of which are of paramount importance to home financing. Life insurance companies are examined as an evolving financial intermediary; i.e., one that was an important home lender but which now is almost completely an income property lender. Finally, all other entities that operate in and affect the mortgage market are discussed. The chapter begins with savings and loan associations, which are the largest holders of residential mortgage debt.

SAVINGS AND LOAN ASSOCIATIONS (S&Ls)

The unique role of savings and loan associations in the nation's economy is the pooling of savings of individuals for investment in residential mortgages. Although the name may be different in some states (e.g. homestead associations, building and loan, etc.), their role remains the same. S&Ls operate in all 50 states and number about 4,300 (with about 17,788 branches) and are the largest of all mortgage lenders in total mortgage debt held and in annual origination volume. Although the percentage held may vary from year to year depending on savings inflow, S&Ls originate about 40 percent of all residential mortgages and 17 percent of all income-property mortgages each year. The mortgage portfolio of S&Ls at the end of 1979 consists of approximately 85 percent in one-to-four family and apartment loans and the remaining 15 percent in income-property loans and other loans.

Development

From the founding of the first association in 1831 (Oxford Provident Building Association in Frankfort, PA), S&Ls have spread across the U.S. as they have provided funds for the housing growth of the nation. Although the greatest number of associations was reached in 1927 when more than 12,000 were in existence, the contribution they have made toward providing housing finance has continued to increase since then. S&Ls provided much of the institutional financing of urban homes for middle-income Americans before the 1930s.

The 1930s were years of dramatic change for S&Ls. More than half of those in existence failed during this time and more than 25 percent of S&L mortgage assets were in default. In addition to the general economic depression, the major problem for S&Ls during the early '30s was a lack of liquidity. This liquidity crisis was caused by the financial panic of the American public following the stock market crash which precipitated a rush on all financial institutions to withdraw savings. As non-amortized, short-term mortgages came due, many creditworthy mortgagors were unable to refinance their mortgages because the associations had no funds. Many homes were lost as a result. To help alleviate this liquidity problem, the Federal Home Loan Bank System (FHLB) was created by Congress on July 22, 1932. The FHLB has provided liquidity during periods of credit restraint for member associations and has served the industry in the way that the Federal Reserve System has served the needs of commercial banks. The law provided for the creation of 12 regional banks to serve each geographical area.[1]

Another important step toward the development of the modern S&L occurred with the creation of the Federal Savings and Loan Insurance Corporation (FSLIC) as authorized by Title IV of the *National Housing Act of 1934*. This step was vital for the restoration of faith in the safety of deposits in S&Ls and paved the way for new deposits which were needed before any new mortgage loans could be made. The maximum insurance protection for each account in member S&Ls is currently $100,000.

Organization and Regulation

Savings and loan associations may be chartered by either a state or the federal government and can be either mutual or stock associations. State charters account for about 60 percent of existing associations, with 40 percent operating under federal charter. In a mutual association all depositors automatically become shareholders of the association, whereas a stock association is owned by private stockholders. Until recently, all federally chartered associations had to be mutual. Since 1975, upon application to the

FHLB, some federally-chartered associations have been allowed to convert to stock associations.

Federal associations are required to belong to both the FHLB and the FSLIC. Although state-chartered associations are not so required, most belong to one or both. If a state-chartered association does not belong to the FSLIC, state insurance is available. Those state-chartered associations that join the FHLB are subject to the regulations of the FHLB, but they also have access to funds for lending during periods of tight credit. During those periods when savings inflows are not sufficient to meet the demand for mortgage credit or savings withdrawal, member S&Ls can turn to the FHLB for help. In addition to lending funds, another way the FHLB assists S&Ls in tight credit periods is by changing the liquidity requirement. The liquidity, or cash on hand requirement, set by law to range from four to ten percent of total assets, assures that sufficient assets are available if a depositor wants to make a withdrawal. These liquidity reserves are usually held in United States government securities. By lowering the liquidity requirement, more money becomes available for lending. The ability to borrow directly from a regional bank has allowed member associations to continue to make mortgage loans even during periods of severe savings outflow. For example, in 1973 member associations borrowed in excess of $7 billion to offset deposit withdrawals. The FHLB acquires the funds through the sale of bonds and notes in the open market.

Those state-chartered associations which do not belong to the FHLB are regulated by their respective state on lending area, types of loans, loan-to-value ratio and maximum loan amount. These regulations normally are similar to federal regulations although state regulations often are more liberal.

S&L's ability to compete for deposits in recent years was increased by their authority to offer a differential—a .25 percent higher interest rate than commercial banks. However, the differential is being gradually phased out. Passage of the Depository Institutions Deregulation and Monetary Control Act of 1980 authorized the orderly deregulation of all depository financial institutions and the phase out of interest rate maximums and the differential by 1986.

Mortgage Lending Characteristics

Unlike other private financial institutions, savings and loan associations basically exist to accumulate savings from individuals which are then used to finance home ownership. Originally, S&Ls were concerned only with local housing needs, and this is still their primary interest. Many S&Ls have become active in the secondary mortgage market both as buyers and sellers. Beginning in 1978, S&Ls for the first time became net sellers of mortgages in the secondary mortgage market. This development is significant in that it demonstrates

CONDENSED STATEMENT OF CONDITION OF ALL SAVINGS ASSOCIATIONS AS OF DECEMBER 31, 1981*

Item	Amount (Millions)	Percentage of Total
ASSETS:		
Mortgage Loans Outstanding	$518,350	78.1%
Insured Mortgages and Mortgage-backed Securities	33,451	5.0
Mobile Home Loans	4,003	0.6
Home Improvement Loans	5,882	0.9
Loans on Savings Accounts	5,244	0.8
Education Loans	1,646	0.2
Other Consumer Loans	2,483	0.4
Cash and Investments Eligible for Liquidity	48,534	7.3
Other Investments	14,222	2.1
Federal Home Loan Bank Stock	5,300	0.8
Investment in Service Corporations	3,810	0.6
Building and Equipment	9,327	1.4
Real Estate Owned	2,800	0.4
All Other Assets	8,792	1.3
Total Assets	$663,844	100.0%
LIABILITIES AND NET WORTH:		
Savings Deposits:		
Earning Regular Rate or Below	$101,823	15.3%
Earning in Excess of Regular Rate	422,551	63.7
Federal Home Loan Bank Advances	62,794	9.5
Other Borrowed Money	26,303	4.0
Loans in Process	6,369	1.0
All Other Liabilities	15,612	2.4
Net Worth	28,392	4.3
Total Liabilities and Net Worth	$663,844	100.0%

Note: Components may not add to totals due to rounding.
*Preliminary.
Sources: Federal Home Loan Bank Board; United States League of Savings Associations.

Figure 4–1.

a change in lending philosophy from one dominated by local concerns to one affected and shaped by the nation's economy.

Because of acquired local expertise and previous legal limitations on their lending area, most S&Ls seldom become involved in either FHA-insured or VA-guaranteed mortgages. Instead, S&L funds are invested in local conventional mortgages originated primarily for association portfolios. This type of residential mortgage comprises 90 percent of the total number of mortgages held by S&Ls.

With respect to mortgage activity, S&Ls have historically given primary emphasis to residential lending and secondary emphasis to income-property lending, although they are becoming important income-property lenders in some areas. All thrift institutions are encouraged by federal tax benefits to invest at least 80 percent of assets in residential mortgages.

MUTUAL SAVINGS BANKS (MSBs)

Mutual savings banks often have been categorized as commercial banks and at other times as S&Ls. Although an MSB has some of the characteristics of both, it actually is a thrift institution. MSBs are unique, private financial institutions where many individuals keep their savings. Approximately 459 exist in 17 states and Puerto Rico, although more than 60 percent of the total are located in New York and Massachusetts. MSBs, which had total assets of $175 billion at the end of 1981, hold just under 10 percent of the total outstanding mortgage debt and originate about six to eight percent of all residential and commercial mortgages each year. Since MSBs are thrift institutions, this percentage is quite cyclical, depending on savings inflows.

Development

The first mutual savings bank was founded in the same state as the first savings and loan association—Pennsylvania. The Philadelphia Saving Fund Society, the nation's largest mutual savings bank, began in 1816 and was followed in 1817 by the Provident Institute for Savings in Boston. The Boston facility was the first savings bank in New England.

Unlike the early building societies, these institutions were organized to provide facilities to encourage saving by the small wage earner who was being thoroughly ignored by the other financial institutions. They were well received and began to spread throughout the New England states. By 1875 the number of MSBs had reached a peak of 674. The MSB concept never spread far from its origins, probably due to the change in building societies that encouraged savings, and to the development of savings deposits at commercial banks.

Organization and Regulation

Since these institutions are mutual organizations, no stockholders exist. Instead, all depositors share ownership. An MSB is managed by a self-perpetuating board of trustees, usually comprised of prominent local and business leaders.

In 1979 changes in federal law allowed for MSBs to be federally chartered, but at present, very few are. Practically all MSBs are chartered by states, therefore the regulations that govern their operations vary from state to state. The only exception to state regulations is the Federal regulation (Reg Q) on interest rates. State regulations establish guidelines for deposits, reserves, the extent of mortgage lending allowed, as well as maximum loan amounts, loan terms and loan-to-value ratios. These limits are usually similar to those of S&Ls and are governed, if sales are expected, by the secondary mortgage market limits.

An MSB may be a member of the FHLB (and therefore subject to FHLB regulation) but only a few hold membership. All except those in Massachusetts provide federal insurance (FDIC) to depositors, the amount of insurance being $100,000. Massachusetts provides full insurance coverage for all deposits.

Mortgage Lending Activity

MSBs differ from other thrift institutions in that they are not obligated to invest a set amount of money in mortgages. Some may make personal loans and consumer loans, and all MSBs buy government and private securities in addition to making mortgage loans on residential and income properties. MSBs have always considered mortgage lending to be important and currently about 65 percent of their assets are in mortgages. Other assets include corporate bonds, U.S. Treasury and federal agency obligations, corporate stock, and state and local government debt. The percentage in mortgages has varied throughout the years as the risk and yield in mortgage lending changed and alternate investments became available. The percentage of assets invested in mortgages dropped after the Depression but began to climb again with the rapid growth of the low-risk FHA and VA mortgage loan programs after World War II.

In the current mortgage market, MSBs originate both conventional and FHA-VA mortgages for their own portfolios. Since the majority of MSBs are located in capital-surplus areas and therefore have more funds than are demanded locally, they normally purchase low-risk FHA-VA and conventional mortgages from other mortgage lenders, particularly mortgage companies, in capital-short areas of the country.

LIFE INSURANCE COMPANIES (LICs)

There are about 1,825 life insurance companies in the United States. LICs have a long history of mortgage lending and currently hold about 9 percent of the outstanding mortgage debt. Their total assets at the end of 1981 exceeded $520 billion of which about 30 percent is in the form of mortgages. The mix of mortgages between residential (1-4 family) and income-property has changed drastically in the past 30 years. During the residential boom years of the late 1940s and early 1950s, more than 60 percent of the mortgages held were residential, but this mixture is now reversed and more than 60 percent of mortgages held are income-property. LICs differ significantly from other mortgage lenders in the way mortgage loans are acquired. Practically all residential mortgages and many income-property mortgages are originated by other mortgage lenders, primarily mortgage companies, who then sell to an LIC. However, LICs are considered to be mortgage lenders rather than investors because some income-property mortgages loans are made directly to borrowers such as builders and developers without the aid of an intermediary. In addition, some LICs will make mortgage loans only if they are originated by their own regional offices.

Development

The first 25 years of the 20th century witnessed the development and public acceptance of life insurance as a major repository for savings. As more and more American families sought the protection of life insurance, the assets of LICs increased dramatically—ten-fold since 1940. Most life insurance contracts written today, as in the past, are ordinary life insurance policies in which cash value accrues in addition to the death protection. The death protection is the sole feature of term insurance.

Life insurance premium payments provide a steady and substantial cash inflow which life insurance companies can project into the future to balance long-term liabilities, such as death benefits, with safe long-term assets such as mortgages. Mortgages, of course, must compete with other investment alternatives—stocks, bonds and, in some situations, real estate ownership. In any given year, for example, bonds may provide a greater yield to LICs with less risk and greater liquidity than other investment alternatives. Therefore, funds will flow to bonds. Mortgage holdings of LICs as a percentage of total assets have been relatively constant over the past 20 years, although currently only about 27 percent of total assets are in mortgages, down about eight percent since 1970.

An LIC's cash inflow comes from premiums on policies, earnings on investments, and repayments of investment principal. This inflow is usually well-regulated and anticipated, but it occasionally puts pressures on a company to put these funds to work immediately.

Until the Depression of the 1930s, the farm mortgage was the primary interest of LICs. Some of these loans were originated directly, but most were originated by mortgage companies which then sold the mortgages to LICs located primarily in the Northeast. This was the beginning of one of the most successfully, mutually beneficial business relationships in the U.S. economy. This relationship still continues and is referred to as the *correspondent system.*

The correspondent system became an important way of transacting the mortgage lending business for LICs after the creation of the FHA in 1934. Following the changes in state regulation of LICs, due in a major part to the FHA, they relied heavily on correspondents in various parts of the country to originate loans. The rationale for this system was that the lender could rely on the local expert to originate financially sound loans and in this way the lender would not have the expense of attempting to duplicate that local expertise. In return for this assistance, an LIC would commit to buy a certain dollar amount of mortgages on a periodic schedule, providing a ready market for all loans originated. The LIC would also agree to buy only from one mortgage company and in return expect its commitments to be satisfied. A mortgage company, depending on its size, may have a correspondent relationship with only one investor or with several at the same time.

"The understanding between the loan correspondent who originates and sells loans and the investor who buys such loans is usually covered by a servicing contract. This contract may be one covering all loans which are sold by a correspondent, or each loan may be covered by an individual short form of servicing contract. Such a contract is usually made with the expectation that it will be a continuing arrangement over a long period of time and that it will result in a steady submission of new loans. Its purpose is to avoid misunderstandings about the rights and duties of those who are bound by it."[2]

Regulations

Life insurance companies are regulated by state laws which control either the activities of those LICs located within the state, those doing business within the state, or both. As a general rule, LICs located elsewhere but doing business in a state are limited to the same extent as those within the state.

LICs are considered national lenders because they are not limited to a certain geographical area, as are S&Ls. As a general rule, LICs may make a loan-to-value ratio loan up to 75 percent as established by an appraisal. Most states do not limit the term of the loans, although a term in excess of 30 years is uncommon.

The loan amount as established by state regulation is usually a factor based on total assets. For example, in New York, an insurance company is limited on any one loan to two percent of total assets.

Mortgage Lending Activity

LICs have an advantage over other mortgage lenders—the predictable inflow of funds. This advantage may be partially off-set by policy loans during periods of disintermediation, but it allows for more orderly planning of mortgage investments by LICs.

Many insurance companies, especially the larger ones, are not currently purchasing residential mortgages. Normally, most new dollars invested in mortgages are for income-property mortgages. This investment philosophy can be expected to change periodically as the yields to be realized in residential mortgages exceeds that for income-property mortgages. When LICs do purchase residential mortgages, they normally purchase them in either GNMA or other structured pools. (For additional information on this subject, see Chapter 9, Fundamentals of Income-Property Mortgage Lending).

Some LICs only invest in mortgage loans originated by their regional offices while other LICs rely completely on the correspondent system. Many LICs will consider a *direct placement* in which a builder or developer sends the loan application directly to a life insurance company. But many others expect most loans to come from intermediaries such as mortgage companies.

OTHER MORTGAGE INVESTORS

Although the previously discussed mortgage lenders originate practically all mortgage loans and hold a large percentage of the nation's outstanding mortgage debt, they are not the only mortgage investors. Others will be discussed in their order of importance.

Federal National Mortgage Association (FNMA)

This one-time governmental agency, which is now a privately-owned corporation, is the largest single holder of residential mortgage debt, owning in excess of $61 billion at the end of 1981. FNMA does not originate any mortgages directly and is normally associated with the secondary mortgage market. A complete discussion of FNMA appears in Chapter 7, Secondary Mortgage Markets and Institutions.

Governmental National Mortgage Association (GNMA)

GNMA is a governmental agency created in 1968 when FNMA became privately owned. It is another important mortgage investor that does not originate mortgages. In addition to engaging in the secondary market, GNMA is the principal means by which the federal government subsidizes home ownership or stimulates the housing industry. The GNMA mortgage-backed security has brought traditionally non-mortgage investors into the mortgage market. A complete discussion of GNMA appears in Chapter 7, Secondary Mortgage Markets and Institutions.

Federal Home Loan Mortgage Corporation (FHLMC)

This is a relatively new (1970) secondary mortgage market participant and does not hold as much mortgage debt in its own name as others in the secondary mortgage market, such as FNMA. A complete examination of FHLMC and its role in supporting the conventional mortgage market appears in Chapter 7, Secondary Mortgage Markets and Institutions.

Retirement and Pension Funds

The funds accumulated in these retirement programs are for the future security of the participants; therefore, the primary investment objective is security for the funds invested. The number of funds and assets of retirement and pension funds are growing. At the end of 1981, their total assets were $536 billion.

Until recently, mortgages have not been a significant investment alternative to stocks and bonds for these funds. The reasons are:

1. These funds have not had the technical expertise necessary to invest in mortgages.
2. The need to reinvest the monthly payment of principal and interest did not appeal to them.
3. The lack of market quotations on mortgages was contrary to their daily needs.

The *Employee Retirement Income Security Act* of 1974 (ERISA) placed an increased duty on trustees of these funds to exercise greater care in selecting investments to achieve greater diversification and reduce the chances of substantial losses. The lack of performance in the stock and bond markets in recent years has forced fund trustees to consider mortgages as investment alternatives. The GNMA mortgage-backed security provided a bond-type investment that eliminated most of the previous objections to mortgage investments while still providing a yield comparable to high-rated stocks and bonds. Many retirement and pension funds are currently acquiring the expertise to consider long-term mortgages originated by various mortgage lenders as investments.

Credit Unions

A credit union is a specialized thrift institution and one of the fastest growing financial organizations in the American economy. A recent change in federal regulations may stimulate this growth. Since April, 1977 federal credit unions have been authorized to make residential mortgage loans to their members. State-regulated credit unions have had this authority for many years. This activity is expected to begin slowly, but at some future point credit unions could become a significant factor in residential mortgage finance. The problems credit unions will have to overcome are basically the same ones retirement and pension funds are facing.

Federal Agencies

In addition to GNMA and FHLMC, other federal agencies hold about three percent of the total outstanding mortgage debt.[3] The Federal Land Bank held more than $25 billion in farm mortgages and the Farmers Home Administration held in excess of $1 billion in 1981. The Federal Housing Administration and the Veterans Administration held more than $7 billion of mortgages they either insured or guaranteed.

State Housing Agencies

Most states now have a state housing agency of one type or another that has the responsibility of providing shelter for low- and moderate-income families. The funds used in the various programs are often raised from the sale of tax-exempt bonds. The resulting cost of funds for these agencies is relatively low. Many of the state programs subsidize only the mortgage interest rates without the state purchasing the mortgage. Other programs authorize the state to purchase the mortgage and then resell it in the secondary market. These state housing agencies could become more important in the future depending on the position taken by the federal government on providing shelter for low- and moderate-income families.

SUGGESTED READINGS

Bryant, Willis R. *Mortgage Lending Fundamentals and Practices.* New York: McGraw-Hill Book Co., Inc., 1962.

Campbell, Kenneth D. *Mortgage Trusts: Lenders with a Plus.* New York: Audit Publications, Inc., 1969.

Davidson, Harold A. "The Pension Funds Increasing Real Estate Commitment," *Real Estate Review* (Spring 1981), pp. 115–119.

Edwards, Raoul D. "The Thrift Industry: Is Housing Enough?" *United States Banker* (February 1980), pp. 24–35.

Hines, Mary Alice. "The REIT Shakeout in 1974," *Real Estate Review* (Winter 1975), pp. 56–59.

Hoagland, Henry E., Stone, Leo D., and Brueggeman, William B. *Real Estate Finance,* 6th Ed. Homewood, Illinois: Richard D. Irwin, Inc., 1977.

Jacobs, D.P., and Neave, E.H. *Financial Institutions*. Homewood, Illinois: Richard D. Irwin, Inc., 1972.

Klaman, Saul B. *The Postwar Rise of Mortgage Companies*. New York: National Bureau of Economic Research, Inc., 1959.

McMichael, Stanley L., and O'Keefe, Paul T. *How to Finance Real Estate*. Englewood Cliffs, New Jersey: Prentice-Hall, Inc., 1967.

Wrocklage, France E. "Pension Fund Investment for Income Property Mortgages," *The Mortgage Banker* (October 1980), pp. 55-61.

NOTES

1. These regional banks are located in Boston, New York, Pittsburgh, Indianapolis, Chicago, Cincinnati, Greensboro (N.C.), Little Rock, Topeka, Des Moines, San Francisco, and Seattle.

2. Pease and Kerwood, Editors, Mortgage Banking, McGraw-Hill, New York, 2nd Ed., 1963, page 315.

3. Federal Reserve Bulletin, September 1979, page A41.

Chapter 5

Security Instruments

PART ONE
MORTGAGES AND DEEDS OF TRUST

A mortgage and a deed of trust (sometimes called a trust deed or trust indenture) are alternate forms of real estate finance instruments used in many states. The purpose of each is to provide an instrument for the lender of money to obtain a security interest in that real estate which is securing the debt.

An excellent definition of a mortgage, which could be expanded to include a deed of trust, is found in Black's Law Dictionary, 4th Edition:

> ". . . a pledge or security of particular property for the payment of a debt or the performance of some other obligation, whatever form the transaction may take, but is not now regarded as a conveyance in effect, though it may be cast in the form of a conveyance."

As it exists today in the United States, the mortgage is unique in many features, but its fundamentals are based on the common law as it developed in England over the past 900 years.

HISTORICAL DEVELOPMENT

The classic common law mortgage, which developed in England after the Norman invasion in 1066, was well developed and established by 1400. Basically it was an actual conveyance, and title transfer, of the real estate serving as security for the debt. For a conveyance to be effective under the common law, possession of that real estate actually had to pass, putting the mortgagee in possession of the real estate.

The instrument conveying the real estate title to the mortgagee contained a *defeasance clause* whereby the mortgagee's title was defeated if payment was made on the due date, called the *law day*. Originally, when title and possession were in the hands of the mortgagee, all rents and profits generated by the land could be retained by the mortgagee. This practice was established because a mortgagee could not charge interest on a loan; any interest was usury, which was illegal. After this law changed and interest could be charged, the mortgagee was forced to credit all rents and profits to the credit of the mortgagor.

Early common law mortgages did not require any action on behalf of mortgagees to protect their rights if a mortgagor failed to perform. Since a conveyance had already been made, the mortgagee had title and possession, and thus the only effect of the mortgagor's nonperformance was the termination of the possibility of *reversion* through the defeasance clause.

The harsh result of a mortgagor not performing after the due date, even when not personally at fault, led mortgagors to petition the king for redress from an inequitable practice. Eventually, the courts of equity gave relief to mortgagors by allowing them to redeem their real estate through payment with interest of the past due debts. This was called the *equity of redemption*. By 1625, this practice had become so widespread that mortgagees were reluctant to lend money with real estate as security since they never knew when a mortgagor might elect to redeem the real estate. Mortgagees attempted to change this by inserting a clause in mortgages whereby the mortgagor agreed not to seek this redress. But courts of equity refused to allow the practice and would not enforce the clause. In order to restore an equitable balance, the courts began to decree that a mortgagor had a certain amount of time after default, usually six months, in which to redeem the real estate. If this were not done, the mortgagor's equity of redemption would be cancelled or foreclosed. This action soon became known as a foreclosure suit and is still used in some states today. (See Part 2 of this chapter, Foreclosure and Redemption.)

AMERICAN MORTGAGE LAW

The most important change in the common law that has occurred in American law relates to the concept of who actually owns the real estate that is serving as security for the performance of an obligation. The common law held that the mortgagee was the legal owner of the real estate while it served as security. This was called the *title theory;* the mortgagee had the title. Shortly after the Revolutionary War, a New Jersey court held that a mortgagor did not lose title to real estate serving as security. The court's reasoning was since the law already recognized the right of a mortgagor to redeem the real estate after default, the law had to accept a continuing ownership interest in the mortgagor. The court held that a mortgage created only a security interest in the mortgagee and that title should therefore remain with the mortgagor. This is the law in 28 states today and is called the *lien theory*. Although 23 states still classify themselves as either intermediate or title theory states, actually all states recognize the mortgagor as the legal owner of the real estate. The principal difference between these two theories is in the manner of foreclosure. Currently, mortgagors are able to do as they please with mortgaged real estate as long as the activity does not interfere with the security interest of a mortgagee.

According to current law, any interest in real estate that can be sold can be mortgaged, including a fee simple, a life estate or a lease. The determining factor is whether a mortgagee can be found willing to lend money with that particular interest as security.

THE SECURITY INTEREST

The Mortgage Debt

The debt secured by a mortgage is evidenced by either a promissory note or a bond (Figure 5–1). Normally, the mortgage and the note are separate documents, but in some jurisdictions they are combined. The note should be negotiable so that the originating mortgagee can assign it. This is normal practice for some mortgage lenders such as a mortgage company. The mortgage must, in one way or another, acknowledge and identify the debt it secures. When the entire debt has been paid, the mortgage that secured it loses its effectiveness and no longer creates a lien. A *notice of satisfaction,* or notice of full payment of a mortgage, should be recorded when a debt is paid to clear the *cloud on the title* created by the mortgage.

The Mortgage Instrument

The mortgage instrument, like a deed, does not have to appear in any particular form. There are no set requirements except that it must be in writing. Any wording that clearly indicates the purpose of the instrument, which is to create a security interest in described real estate for the benefit of a mortgagee, is sufficient.

If a conveyance is made to a mortgagee that appears to be a *deed absolute* but is actually intended to be a *conveyance* as security for a debt, all state courts have uniformly held that transaction to be a mortgage even if a defeasance clause is missing. If the parties agree in writing that money will be advanced with the debt for those funds secured by a later mortgage and a mortgage is not executed, the law holds that a creditor has a security interest in the real estate. This interest is called an *equitable mortgage*.

A valid mortgage instrument should include (Figure 5–3):

NOTE

US $ ....

.........................., Illinois
City

........................., 19....

FOR VALUE RECEIVED, the undersigned ("Borrower") promise(s) to pay.........................
...., or order, the principal sum of
....Dollars, with
interest on the unpaid principal balance from the date of this Note, until paid, at the rate of.....................
......................percent per annum. Principal and interest shall be payable at.....................
...., or such other place as the Note holder may
designate, in consecutive monthly installments of...
..........................Dollars (US $.........................), on the.................
............day of each month beginning........................., 19..... Such monthly installments
shall continue until the entire indebtedness evidenced by this Note is fully paid, except that any remaining indebtedness, if not sooner paid, shall be due and payable on...

If any monthly installment under this Note is not paid when due and remains unpaid after a date specified by a notice to Borrower, the entire principal amount outstanding and accrued interest thereon shall at once become due and payable at the option of the Note holder. The date specified shall not be less than thirty days from the date such notice is mailed. The Note holder may exercise this option to accelerate during any default by Borrower regardless of any prior forbearance. If suit is brought to collect this Note, the Note holder shall be entitled to collect all reasonable costs and expenses of suit, including, but not limited to, reasonable attorney's fees.

Borrower shall pay to the Note holder a late charge of.........................percent of any monthly installment not received by the Note holder within.........................days after the installment is due.

Borrower may prepay the principal amount outstanding in whole or in part. The Note holder may require that any partial prepayments (i) be made on the date monthly installments are due and (ii) be in the amount of that part of one or more monthly installments which would be applicable to principal. Any partial prepayment shall be applied against the principal amount outstanding and shall not postpone the due date of any subsequent monthly installments or change the amount of such installments, unless the Note holder shall otherwise agree in writing.

Presentment, notice of dishonor, and protest are hereby waived by all makers, sureties, guarantors and endorsers hereof. This Note shall be the joint and several obligation of all makers, sureties, guarantors and endorsers, and shall be binding upon them and their successors and assigns.

Any notice to Borrower provided for in this Note shall be given by mailing such notice by certified mail addressed to Borrower at the Property Address stated below, or to such other address as Borrower may designate by notice to the Note holder. Any notice to the Note holder shall be given by mailing such notice by certified mail, return receipt requested, to the Note holder at the address stated in the first paragraph of this Note, or at such other address as may have been designated by notice to Borrower.

The indebtedness evidenced by this Note is secured by a Mortgage, dated.............................
........................, and reference is made to the Mortgage for rights as to acceleration of the indebtedness evidenced by this Note.

....

....

....
Property Address   *(Execute Original Only)*

ILLINOIS —1 to 4 Family—6/75—FNMA/FHLMC UNIFORM INSTRUMENT

Figure 5-1.

ADJUSTABLE RATE NOTE

NOTICE TO BORROWER: THIS NOTE CONTAINS A PROVISION ALLOWING FOR CHANGES IN THE INTEREST RATE. INCREASES IN THE INTEREST RATE WILL RESULT IN HIGHER PAYMENTS. DECREASES IN THE INTEREST RATE WILL RESULT IN LOWER PAYMENTS.

. . . . , 19 . . . . , ...

City   *State*

. . . .

Property Address   *City*   *State*   *Zip Code*

1. BORROWER'S PROMISE TO PAY

In return for a loan that I have received, I promise to pay U.S. $ . . . . (this amount will be called "principal"), plus interest, to the order of the Lender. The Lender is . . . .
NAME OF FINANCIAL INSTITUTION

I understand that the Lender may transfer this Note. The Lender or anyone who takes this Note by transfer and who is entitled to receive payments under this Note will be called the "Note Holder".

2. INTEREST

Interest will be charged on that part of outstanding principal which has not been paid. Interest will be charged beginning on the date I receive principal and continuing until the full amount of principal I receive has been paid.

Beginning on the date of this Note, I will pay interest at a yearly rate of . . . . % (the "Initial Interest Rate"). The interest rate that I will pay will change in accordance with Section 4 of this Note until my loan is paid. Interest rate changes may occur on the . . . . day of the month beginning on . . . . , 19 . . . . and on that day of the month every . . . . months thereafter. Each date on which the rate of interest may change will be called a "Change Date".

3. PAYMENTS

(A) Time and Place of Payments

I will pay principal and interest by making payments every month. I will make my monthly payments on the . . . . . day of each month beginning on . . . . , 19 . . . . . I will make these payments until I have paid all of the principal and interest and any other charges, described below, that I may owe under this Note. I will pay all sums that I owe under this Note no later than . . . . , ... (the "final payment date").

I will make my monthly payments at . . . **1234 Main Street – Anytown, U.S.A. 12345** . . . . or at a different place if required by the Note Holder.

(B) Borrower's Payments Before They Are Due

I have the right to make payments of principal at any time before they are due. A payment of principal only is known as a "prepayment". When I make a prepayment, I will tell the Note Holder in writing that I am doing so. I may make a full prepayment or a partial prepayment without paying any penalty. The Note Holder will use all of my prepayments to reduce the amount of principal that I owe under this Note. If I make a partial prepayment, there will be no delays in the due dates of my monthly payments unless the Note Holder agrees in writing to those delays. My partial prepayment will reduce the amount of my monthly payments after the first Change Date following my partial prepayment. However, any reduction due to my partial prepayment may be offset by an interest rate increase.

(C) Amount of Monthly Payments

My initial monthly payments will be in the amount of U.S. $ . . . . If the interest rate that I pay changes, the amount of my monthly payments will change. Increases in the interest rate will result in higher payments (unless my prepayments since the last Change Date offset the increases in my monthly payments). Decreases in the interest rate will result in lower payments. The amount of my monthly payments will always be sufficient to repay my loan in full in substantially equal payments by the final payment date. In setting the monthly payment amount on each Change Date, the Note Holder will assume that the Note interest rate will not change again prior to the final payment date.

COLORADO—ADJUSTABLE RATE LOAN NOTE—6/81—FHLMC UNIFORM INSTRUMENT   44106-3 **SAF Systems and Forms**

Figure 5-2.

4. INTEREST RATE CHANGES

(A) The Index

Any changes in the interest rate will be based on changes in an interest rate index which will be called the "Index". The Index is the: [*Check one box to indicate Index.*]

(1) ☐* "Contract Interest Rate, Purchase of Previously Occupied Homes, National Average for all Major Types of Lenders" published by the Federal Home Loan Bank Board.

(2) ☐* . . . .
. . . .

If the Index ceases to be made available by the publisher, or by any successor to the publisher, the Note Holder will set the Note interest rate by using a comparable index.

(B) Setting the New Interest Rate

To set the new interest rate, the Note Holder will determine the change between the Base Index figure and the Current Index figure. The Base Index figure is . . . . The Current Index figure is the most recent Index figure available . . . . days prior to each Change Date. If the amount of the change is less than one-eighth of one percentage point, the change will be rounded to zero. If the amount of the change is one-eighth of one percentage point or more, the Note Holder will round the amount of the change to the nearest one-eighth of one percentage point.

If the Current Index figure is larger than the Base Index figure, the Note Holder will add the rounded amount of the change to the Initial Interest Rate. If the Current Index figure is smaller than the Base Index figure, the Note Holder will subtract the rounded amount of the change from the Initial Interest Rate. The result of this addition or subtraction will be the preliminary rate. If there is no change between the Base Index figure and the Current Index figure after rounding, the Initial Interest Rate will be the preliminary rate.

[*Check one box to indicate whether there is any maximum limit on interest rate changes; if no box is checked, there will be no maximum limit on changes.*]

(1) ☐ If this box is checked, there will be no maximum limit on changes in the interest rate up or down. The preliminary rate will be the new interest rate.

(2) ☐ If this box is checked, the interest rate will not be changed by more than . . . . percentage points ⁄ n any Change Date. The Note Holder will adjust the preliminary rate so that the change in the interest rate will not be more than that limit. The new interest rate will equal the figure that results from this adjustment of the preliminary rate.

(C) Effective Date of Changes

Each new interest rate will become effective on the next Change Date. If my monthly payment changes as a result of a change in the interest rate, my monthly payment will change as of the first monthly payment date after the Change Date.

(D) Notice to Borrower

The Note Holder will mail me a notice by first class mail at least thirty and no more than forty-five days before each Change Date if the interest rate is to change. The notice will advise me of:

(i)   the new interest rate on my loan;

(ii) the amount of my new monthly payment; and

(iii) any additional matters which the Note Holder is required to disclose.

5. BORROWER'S FAILURE TO PAY AS REQUIRED

(A) Late Charge for Overdue Payments

If the Note Holder has not received the full amount of any of my monthly payments by the end of . . . . calendar days after the date it is due, I will pay a late charge to the Note Holder. The amount of the charge will be . . . . % of my overdue payment of principal and interest. I will pay this late charge only once on any late payment.

(B) Notice from Note Holder

If I do not pay the full amount of each monthly payment on time, the Note Holder may send me a written notice telling me that if I do not pay the overdue amount by a certain date I will be in default. That date must be at least 30 days after the date on which the notice is mailed to me.

(C) Default

If I do not pay the overdue amount by the date stated in the notice described in (B) above, I will be in default. If I am in default, the Note Holder may require me to pay immediately the full amount of principal which has not been paid and all the interest that I owe on that amount.

Even if, at a time when I am in default, the Note Holder does not require me to pay immediately in full as described above, the Note Holder will still have the right to do so if I am in default at a later time.

---

* *If more than one box is checked or if no box is checked, and Lender and Borrower do not otherwise agree in writing, the first Index named will apply.*

Figure 5–2. *Continued.*

(D) Payment of Note Holder's Costs and Expenses

If the Note Holder has required me to pay immediately in full as described above, the Note Holder will have the right to be paid back by me for all its reasonable costs and expenses to the extent not prohibited by applicable law. Those expenses may include, for example, reasonable attorneys' fees.

6. WAIVERS

Anyone who signs this Note to transfer it to someone else (known as an "endorser") waives certain rights. Those rights are (A) the right to require the Note Holder to demand payment of amounts due (known as "presentment") and (B) the right to require the Note Holder to give notice that amounts due have not been paid (known as "notice of dishonor").

7. GIVING OF NOTICES

Except for the notice provided in Section 4(D), any notice that must be given to me under this Note will be given by mailing it by certified mail. All notices will be addressed to me at the Property Address above. Notices will be mailed to me at a different address if I give the Note Holder a notice of my different address.

Any notice that must be given to the Note Holder under this Note will be given by mailing it by certified mail to the Note Holder at the address stated in Section 3(A) above. Notices will be mailed to the Note Holder at a different address if I am given a notice of that different address.

8. RESPONSIBILITY OF PERSONS UNDER THIS NOTE

If more than one person signs this Note, each of us is fully and personally obligated to pay the full amount owed and to keep all of the promises made in this Note. Any guarantor, surety, or endorser of this Note is also obligated to do these things. The Note Holder may enforce its rights under this Note against each of us individually or against all of us together. This means that any one of us may be required to pay all of the amounts owed under this Note.

Any person who takes over my rights or obligations under this Note will have all of my rights and must keep all of my promises made in this Note. Any person who takes over the rights or obligations of a guarantor, surety, or endorser of this Note is also obligated to keep all of the promises made in this Note.

9. LOAN CHARGES

It could be that this loan is subject to a law which sets maximum loan charges and that law is interpreted so that the interest or other loan charges collected or to be collected in connection with this loan would exceed permitted limits. If this is the case, then: (A) any such loan charge shall be reduced by the amount necessary to reduce the charge to the permitted limit; and (B) any sums already collected from me which exceeded permitted limits will be refunded to me. The Note Holder may choose to make this refund by reducing the principal I owe under this Note or by making a direct payment to me. If a refund reduces principal, the reduction will be treated as a partial prepayment.

10. THIS NOTE SECURED BY A MORTGAGE

In addition to the protections given to the Note Holder under this Note, a Mortgage, dated . . . ., 19. . . . . protects the Note Holder from possible losses which might result if I do not keep the promises which I make in this Note. That Mortgage describes how and under what conditions I may be required to make immediate payment in full of all amounts that I owe under this Note. One of those conditions relates to any transfer of the property covered by the Mortgage. In that regard, the Mortgage provides in paragraph 17:

17. Transfer of the Property; Assumption. If all or any part of the Property or an interest therein is sold or transferred by Borrower without Lender's prior written consent, excluding (a) the creation of a lien or encumbrance subordinate to this Mortgage, (b) the creation of a purchase money security interest for household appliances, (c) a transfer by devise, descent or by operation of law upon the death of a joint tenant or (d) the grant of any leasehold interest of three years or less not containing an option to purchase, Lender may, at Lender's option, declare all the sums secured by this Mortgage to be immediately due and payable. Lender shall have waived such option to accelerate if, prior to the sale or transfer, Lender and the person to whom the Property is to be sold or transferred reach agreement in writing that the credit of such person is satisfactory to Lender and that the interest payable on the sums secured by this Mortgage shall be at such rate as Lender shall request. If Lender has waived the option to accelerate provided in this paragraph 17, and if Borrower's successor in interest has executed a written assumption agreement accepted in writing by Lender, Lender shall release Borrower from all obligations under this Mortgage and the Note.

If Lender exercises such option to accelerate, Lender shall mail Borrower notice of acceleration in accordance with paragraph 14 hereof. Such notice shall provide a period of not less than 30 days from the date the notice is mailed within which Borrower may pay the sums declared due. If Borrower fails to pay such sums prior to the expiration of such period, Lender may, without further notice or demand on Borrower, invoke any remedies permitted by paragraph 18 hereof.

Figure 5-2. *Continued.*

MORTGAGE

THIS MORTGAGE is made this.............................day of..........................,
19...., between the Mortgagor,...
.................................(herein "Borrower"), and the Mortgagee,....................
..NAME OF FINANCIAL INSTITUTION............................., a corporation organized and existing
under the laws of......................................, whose address is.......................
..1234 Your Street....Your City, Your State................................(herein "Lender").

WHEREAS, Borrower is indebted to Lender in the principal sum of...............................
......................................Dollars, which indebtedness is evidenced by Borrower's note
dated........................(herein "Note"), providing for monthly installments of principal and interest,
with the balance of the indebtedness, if not sooner paid, due and payable on..............................
...................;

To SECURE to Lender (a) the repayment of the indebtedness evidenced by the Note, with interest thereon, the payment of all other sums, with interest thereon, advanced in accordance herewith to protect the security of this Mortgage, and the performance of the covenants and agreements of Borrower herein contained, and (b) the repayment of any future advances, with interest thereon, made to Borrower by Lender pursuant to paragraph 21 hereof (herein "Future Advances"), Borrower does hereby mortgage, grant and convey to Lender, with power of sale, the following described property located in the County of...................................., State of Massachusetts: which has the address of...................................., ...,

[Street]   [City]

..........................(herein "Property Address");

[State and Zip Code]

TOGETHER with all the improvements now or hereafter erected on the property, and all easements, rights, appurtenances, rents, royalties, mineral, oil and gas rights and profits, water, water rights, and water stock, and all fixtures now or hereafter attached to the property, all of which, including replacements and additions thereto, shall be deemed to be and remain a part of the property covered by this Mortgage; and all of the foregoing, together with said property (or the leasehold estate if this Mortgage is on a leasehold) are herein referred to as the "Property".

Borrower covenants that Borrower is lawfully seised of the estate hereby conveyed and has the right to mortgage, grant and convey the Property, that the Property is unencumbered, and that Borrower will warrant and defend generally the title to the Property against all claims and demands, subject to any declarations, easements or restrictions listed in a schedule of exceptions to coverage in any title insurance policy insuring Lender's interest in the Property.

MASSACHUSETTS—1 to 4 Family—7/78—**FNMA/FHLMC UNIFORM INSTRUMENT**   43721-0 SAF

IN WITNESS WHEREOF, Borrower has executed this Mortgage under seal.

....
—Borrower

....
—Borrower

COMMONWEALTH OF MASSACHUSETTS,......................................County ss:

On this..............day of.............., 19...., before me personally appeared.................
...., and
acknowledged the foregoing to be...............free act and deed.

My Commission expires:

....
Notary Public

Figure 5–3.

ADJUSTABLE RATE LOAN RIDER

**NOTICE: THE SECURITY INSTRUMENT SECURES A NOTE WHICH CONTAINS
A PROVISION ALLOWING FOR CHANGES IN THE INTEREST RATE. IN-
CREASES IN THE INTEREST RATE WILL RESULT IN HIGHER PAYMENTS.
DECREASES IN THE INTEREST RATE WILL RESULT IN LOWER PAYMENTS.**

This Rider is made this . . . . . . day of . . . ., 19. . . . , and is incorporated into and shall
be deemed to amend and supplement the Mortgage, Deed of Trust, or Deed to Secure Debt (the "Security Instrument") of the same date given by the undersigned (the "Borrower") to secure Borrower's Note to . . . .
NAME OF FINANCIAL INSTITUTION . . . .
(the "Lender") of the same date (the "Note") and covering the property described in the Security Instrument and
located at . . . .

Property Address

Modifications. In addition to the covenants and agreements made in the Security Instrument, Borrower and
Lender further covenant and agree as follows:

A. INTEREST RATE AND MONTHLY PAYMENT CHANGES

The Note has an "Initial Interest Rate" of . . . . . %. The Note interest rate may be increased or decreased on the
. . . . . day of the month beginning on . . . ., 19 . . . and on that day of the month every
. . . . . months thereafter.

Changes in the interest rate are governed by changes in an interest rate index called the "Index". The Index is the:
[Check one box to indicate Index.]

(1) ☐* "Contract Interest Rate, Purchase of Previously Occupied Homes, National Average for all Major
Types of Lenders" published by the Federal Home Loan Bank Board

(2) ☐* . . . .

. . . .
*[Check one box to indicate whether there is any maximum limit on changes in the interest rate on each Change Date; if no box is checked there will
be no maximum limit on changes.]*

(1) ☐ There is no maximum limit on changes in the interest rate at any Change Date.

(2) ☐ The interest rate cannot be changed by more than . . . . . percentage points at any Change Date.

If the interest rate changes, the amount of Borrower's monthly payments will change as provided in the Note. Increases in the interest rate will result in higher payments. Decreases in the interest rate will result in lower payments.

B. LOAN CHARGES

It could be that the loan secured by the Security Instrument is subject to a law which sets maximum loan charges
and that law is interpreted so that the interest or other loan charges collected or to be collected in connection with the
loan would exceed permitted limits. If this is the case, then: (A) any such loan charge shall be reduced by the amount
necessary to reduce the charge to the permitted limit; and (B) any sums already collected from Borrower which exceeded permitted limits will be refunded to Borrower. Lender may choose to make this refund by reducing the principal
owed under the Note or by making a direct payment to Borrower.

C. PRIOR LIENS

If Lender determines that all or any part of the sums secured by this Security Instrument are subject to a lien
which has priority over this Security Instrument, Lender may send Borrower a notice identifying that lien. Borrower
shall promptly act with regard to that lien as provided in paragraph 4 of the Security Instrument or shall promptly
secure an agreement in a form satisfactory to Lender subordinating that lien to this Security Instrument.

D. TRANSFER OF THE PROPERTY

If there is a transfer of the Property subject to paragraph 17 of the Security Instrument, Lender may require (1)
an increase in the current Note interest rate, or (2) an increase in (or removal of) the limit on the amount of any one interest rate change (if there is a limit), or (3) a change in the Base Index figure, or all of these, as a condition of Lender's
waiving the option to accelerate provided in paragraph 17.

By signing this, Borrower agrees to all of the above.

. . . . (Seal)
—Borrower

. . . . (Seal)
—Borrower

---

* *If more than one box is checked or if no box is checked, and Lender and Borrower do not otherwise agree in writing, the first Index named will apply.*

ADJUSTABLE RATE LOAN RIDER—6/81—FHLMC UNIFORM INSTRUMENT   44295-4 **SAF Systems and Forms**

Figure 5–4.

1. Names of the mortgagor and mortgagee
2. Words of conveyance or a mortgaging clause
3. Amount of the mortgage, interest rate, terms of payment and, in some jurisdictions, a repeat of the provisions of the promissory note or bond
4. Description of the real estate securing the debt
5. Clauses to protect the rights of the parties
6. Date
7. Signature of the mortgagor
8. Any additional requirements particular to the jurisdiction, such as acknowledgment.

Clauses to Protect the Rights of the Parties

The above-mentioned elements are the framework upon which a complete mortgage instrument is built. A mortgage instrument should contain clauses to solve all foreseeable problems, and they should be sufficient to protect both parties (Figure 5–3). Of course there are many types of clauses; but the most typical and important ones are the acceleration clause, the prepayment clause and the payment clause. Other clauses, such as those relating to *eminent domain* or *assignment of rent,* for example, are recommended if either party considers it necessary.

Acceleration clause. The acceleration clause is the most important clause in the entire mortgage for the protection of the mortgagee. This clause is generally found in both the mortgage and the instrument that evidences the debt. It states that the entire amount of the debt can be accelerated at the mortgagee's election if the mortgagor defaults or breaches any stated covenant (paragraph 18, Figure 5–5).

(In some states, automatic acceleration clauses are allowed, but these should be avoided if possible, because other options for curing defaults or breaches are available to the mortgagee and may be more beneficial.)

The most common defaults or breaches of covenants by a mortgagor that could trigger acceleration are:

- Failure to pay principal and interest when due
- Failure to pay taxes or insurance when due
- Failure to maintain the property
- Committing waste (destructive use of property)

For the past 15 years, some mortgagees have inserted clauses providing for acceleration if a mortgagor either further mortgages the secured real estate or sells the real estate with the mortgage still attached (paragraph 17, Figure 5–5). This clause ostensibly protects the mortgagee from a change in risk.

Prepayment clause. A mortgagee, especially an institutional investor, lends money with the expectation that it will be repaid over a period of time at a certain, usually fixed rate as stipulated in the mortgage. The mortgagee relies on this schedule of repayment to determine future financial strategy, and

UNIFORM COVENANTS. Borrower and Lender covenant and agree as follows:

1. Payment of Principal and Interest. Borrower shall promptly pay when due the principal of and interest on the indebtedness evidenced by the Note, prepayment and late charges as provided in the Note, and the principal of and interest on any Future Advances secured by this Mortgage.

2. Funds for Taxes and Insurance. Subject to applicable law or to a written waiver by Lender, Borrower shall pay to Lender on the day monthly installments of principal and interest are payable under the Note, until the Note is paid in full, a sum (herein "Funds") equal to one-twelfth of the yearly taxes and assessments which may attain priority over this Mortgage, and ground rents on the Property, if any, plus one-twelfth of yearly premium installments for hazard insurance, plus one-twelfth of yearly premium installments for mortgage insurance, if any, all as reasonably estimated initially and from time to time by Lender on the basis of assessments and bills and reasonable estimates thereof.

The Funds shall be held in an institution the deposits or accounts of which are insured or guaranteed by a Federal or state agency (including Lender if Lender is such an institution). Lender shall apply the Funds to pay said taxes, assessments, insurance premiums and ground rents. Lender may not charge for so holding and applying the Funds, analyzing said account, or verifying and compiling said assessments and bills, unless Lender pays Borrower interest on the Funds and applicable law permits Lender to make such a charge. Borrower and Lender may agree in writing at the time of execution of this Mortgage that interest on the Funds shall be paid to Borrower, and unless such agreement is made or applicable law requires such interest to be paid, Lender shall not be required to pay Borrower any interest or earnings on the Funds. Lender shall give to Borrower, without charge, an annual accounting of the Funds showing credits and debits to the Funds and the purpose for which each debit to the Funds was made. The Funds are pledged as additional security for the sums secured by this Mortgage.

If the amount of the Funds held by Lender, together with the future monthly installments of Funds payable prior to the due dates of taxes, assessments, insurance premiums and ground rents, shall exceed the amount required to pay said taxes, assessments, insurance premiums and ground rents as they fall due, such excess shall be, at Borrower's option, either promptly repaid to Borrower or credited to Borrower on monthly installments of Funds. If the amount of the Funds held by Lender shall not be sufficient to pay taxes, assessments, insurance premiums and ground rents as they fall due, Borrower shall pay to Lender any amount necessary to make up the deficiency within 30 days from the date notice is mailed by Lender to Borrower requesting payment thereof.

Upon payment in full of all sums secured by this Mortgage, Lender shall promptly refund to Borrower any Funds held by Lender. If under paragraph 18 hereof the Property is sold or the Property is otherwise acquired by Lender, Lender shall apply, no later than immediately prior to the sale of the Property or its acquisition by Lender, any Funds held by Lender at the time of application as a credit against the sums secured by this Mortgage.

3. Application of Payments. Unless applicable law provides otherwise, all payments received by Lender under the Note and paragraphs 1 and 2 hereof shall be applied by Lender first in payment of amounts payable to Lender by Borrower under paragraph 2 hereof, then to interest payable on the Note, then to the principal of the Note, and then to interest and principal on any Future Advances.

4. Charges; Liens. Borrower shall pay all taxes, assessments and other charges, fines and impositions attributable to the Property which may attain a priority over this Mortgage, and leasehold payments or ground rents, if any, in the manner provided under paragraph 2 hereof or, if not paid in such manner, by Borrower making payment, when due, directly to the payee thereof. Borrower shall promptly furnish to Lender all notices of amounts due under this paragraph, and in the event Borrower shall make payment directly, Borrower shall promptly furnish to Lender receipts evidencing such payments. Borrower shall promptly discharge any lien which has priority over this Mortgage; provided, that Borrower shall not be required to discharge any such lien so long as Borrower shall agree in writing to the payment of the obligation secured by such lien in a manner acceptable to Lender, or shall in good faith contest such lien by, or defend enforcement of such lien in, legal proceedings which operate to prevent the enforcement of the lien or forfeiture of the Property or any part thereof.

5. Hazard Insurance. Borrower shall keep the improvements now existing or hereafter erected on the Property insured against loss by fire, hazards included within the term "extended coverage", and such other hazards as Lender may require and in such amounts and for such periods as Lender may require; provided, that Lender shall not require that the amount of such coverage exceed that amount of coverage required to pay the sums secured by this Mortgage.

The insurance carrier providing the insurance shall be chosen by Borrower subject to approval by Lender; provided, that such approval shall not be unreasonably withheld. All premiums on insurance policies shall be paid in the manner provided under paragraph 2 hereof or, if not paid in such manner, by Borrower making payment, when due, directly to the insurance carrier.

All insurance policies and renewals thereof shall be in form acceptable to Lender and shall include a standard mortgage clause in favor of and in form acceptable to Lender. Lender shall have the right to hold the policies and renewals thereof, and Borrower shall promptly furnish to Lender all renewal notices and all receipts of paid premiums. In the event of loss, Borrower shall give prompt notice to the insurance carrier and Lender. Lender may make proof of loss if not made promptly by Borrower.

Unless Lender and Borrower otherwise agree in writing, insurance proceeds shall be applied to restoration or repair of the Property damaged, provided such restoration or repair is economically feasible and the security of this Mortgage is not thereby impaired. If such restoration or repair is not economically feasible or if the security of this Mortgage would be impaired, the insurance proceeds shall be applied to the sums secured by this Mortgage, with the excess, if any, paid to Borrower. If the Property is abandoned by Borrower, or if Borrower fails to respond to Lender within 30 days from the date notice is mailed by Lender to Borrower that the insurance carrier offers to settle a claim for insurance benefits, Lender

Figure 5-5. *FNMA/FHLMC uniform covenants.*

is authorized to collect and apply the insurance proceeds at Lender's option either to restoration or repair of the Property or to the sums secured by this Mortgage.

Unless Lender and Borrower otherwise agree in writing, any such application of proceeds to principal shall not extend or postpone the due date of the monthly installments referred to in paragraphs 1 and 2 hereof or change the amount of such installments. If under paragraph 18 hereof the Property is acquired by Lender, all right, title and interest of Borrower in and to any insurance policies and in and to the proceeds thereof resulting from damage to the Property prior to the sale or acquisition shall pass to Lender to the extent of the sums secured by this Mortgage immediately prior to such sale or acquisition.

6. Preservation and Maintenance of Property; Leaseholds; Condominiums; Pianned Unit Developments. Borrower shall keep the Property in good repair and shall not commit waste or permit impairment or deterioration of the Property and shall comply with the provisions of any lease if this Mortgage is on a leasehold. If this Mortgage is on a unit in a condominium or a planned unit development, Borrower shall perform all of Borrower's obligations under the declaration or covenants creating or governing the condominium or planned unit development, the by-laws and regulations of the condominium or planned unit development, and constituent documents. If a condominium or planned unit development rider is executed by Borrower and recorded together with this Mortgage, the covenants and agreements of such rider shall be incorporated into and shall amend and supplement the covenants and agreements of this Mortgage as if the rider were a part hereof.

7. Protection of Lender's Security. If Borrower fails to perform the covenants and agreements contained in this Mortgage, or if any action or proceeding is commenced which materially affects Lender's interest in the Property, including, but not limited to, eminent domain, insolvency, code enforcement, or arrangements or proceedings involving a bankrupt or decedent, then Lender at Lender's option, upon notice to Borrower, may make such appearances, disburse such sums and take such action as is necessary to protect Lender's interest, including, but not limited to, disbursement of reasonable attorney's fees and entry upon the Property to make repairs. If Lender required mortgage insurance as a condition of making the loan secured by this Mortgage, Borrower shall pay the premiums required to maintain such insurance in effect until such time as the requirement for such insurance terminates in accordance with Borrower's and Lender's written agreement or applicable law. Borrower shall pay the amount of all mortgage insurance premiums in the manner provided under paragraph 2 hereof.

Any amounts disbursed by Lender pursuant to this paragraph 7, with interest thereon, shall become additional indebtedness of Borrower secured by this Mortgage. Unless Borrower and Lender agree to other terms of payment, such amounts shall be payable upon notice from Lender to Borrower requesting payment thereof, and shall bear interest from the date of disbursement at the rate payable from time to time on outstanding principal under the Note unless payment of interest at such rate would be contrary to applicable law, in which event such amounts shall bear interest at the highest rate permissible under applicable law. Nothing contained in this paragraph 7 shall require Lender to incur any expense or take any action hereunder.

8. Inspection. Lender may make or cause to be made reasonable entries upon and inspections of the Property, provided that Lender shall give Borrower notice prior to any such inspection specifying reasonable cause therefor related to Lender's interest in the Property.

9. Condemnation. The proceeds of any award or claim for damages, direct or consequential, in connection with any condemnation or other taking of the Property, or part thereof, or for conveyance in lieu of condemnation, are hereby assigned and shall be paid to Lender.

In the event of a total taking of the Property, the proceeds shall be applied to the sums secured by this Mortgage, with the excess, if any, paid to Borrower. In the event of a partial taking of the Property, unless Borrower and Lender otherwise agree in writing, there shall be applied to the sums secured by this Mortgage such proportion of the proceeds as is equal to that proportion which the amount of the sums secured by this Mortgage immediately prior to the date of taking bears to the fair market value of the Property immediately prior to the date of taking, with the balance of the proceeds paid to Borrower.

If the Property is abandoned by Borrower, or if, after notice by Lender to Borrower that the condemnor offers to make an award or settle a claim for damages, Borrower fails to respond to Lender within 30 days after the date such notice is mailed, Lender is authorized to collect and apply the proceeds, at Lender's option, either to restoration or repair of the Property or to the sums secured by this Mortgage.

Unless Lender and Borrower otherwise agree in writing, any such application of proceeds to principal shall not extend or postpone the due date of the monthly installments referred to in paragraphs 1 and 2 hereof or change the amount of such installments.

10. Borrower Not Released. Extension of the time for payment or modification of amortization of the sums secured by this Mortgage granted by Lender to any successor in interest of Borrower shall not operate to release, in any manner, the liability of the original Borrower and Borrower's successors in interest. Lender shall not be required to commence proceedings against such successor or refuse to extend time for payment or otherwise modify amortization of the sums secured by this Mortgage by reason of any demand made by the original Borrower and Borrower's successors in interest.

11. Forbearance by Lender Not a Waiver. Any forbearance by Lender in exercising any right or remedy hereunder, or otherwise afforded by applicable law, shall not be a waiver of or preclude the exercise of any such right or remedy. The procurement of insurance or the payment of taxes or other liens or charges by Lender shall not be a waiver of Lender's right to accelerate the maturity of the indebtedness secured by this Mortgage.

12. Remedies Cumulative. All remedies provided in this Mortgage are distinct and cumulative to any other right or remedy under this Mortgage or afforded by law or equity, and may be exercised concurrently, independently or successively.

13. Successors and Assigns Bound; Joint and Several Liability; Captions. The covenants and agreements herein contained shall bind, and the rights hereunder shall inure to, the respective successors and assigns of Lender and Borrower, subject to the provisions of paragraph 17 hereof. All covenants and agreements of Borrower shall be joint and several. The captions and headings of the paragraphs of this Mortgage are for convenience only and are not to be used to interpret or define the provisions hereof.

14. Notice. Except for any notice required under applicable law to be given in another manner, (a) any notice to Borrower provided for in this Mortgage shall be given by mailing such notice by certified mail addressed to Borrower at the Property Address or at such other address as Borrower may designate by notice to Lender as provided herein, and (b) any notice to Lender shall be given by certified mail, return receipt requested, to Lender's address stated herein or to such other address as Lender may designate by notice to Borrower as provided herein. Any notice provided for in this Mortgage shall be deemed to have been given to Borrower or Lender when given in the manner designated herein.

15. Uniform Mortgage; Governing Law; Severability. This form of mortgage combines uniform covenants for national use and non-uniform covenants with limited variations by jurisdiction to constitute a uniform security instrument covering real property. This Mortgage shall be governed by the law of the jurisdiction in which the Property is located. In the event that any provision or clause of this Mortgage or the Note conflicts with applicable law, such conflict shall not affect other provisions of this Mortgage or the Note which can be given effect without the conflicting provision, and to this end the provisions of the Mortgage and the Note are declared to be severable.

16. Borrower's Copy. Borrower shall be furnished a conformed copy of the Note and of this Mortgage at the time of execution or after recordation hereof.

17. Transfer of the Property; Assumption. If all or any part of the Property or an interest therein is sold or transferred by Borrower without Lender's prior written consent, excluding (a) the creation of a lien or encumbrance subordinate to this Mortgage, (b) the creation of a purchase money security interest for household appliances, (c) a transfer by devise, descent or by operation of law upon the death of a joint tenant or (d) the grant of any leasehold interest of three years or less not containing an option to purchase, Lender may, at Lender's option, declare all the sums secured by this Mortgage to be immediately due and payable. Lender shall have waived such option to accelerate if, prior to the sale or transfer, Lender and the person to whom the Property is to be sold or transferred reach agreement in writing that the credit of such person is satisfactory to Lender and that the interest payable on the sums secured by this Mortgage shall be at such rate as Lender shall request. If Lender has waived the option to accelerate provided in this paragraph 17, and if Borrower's successor in interest has executed a written assumption agreement accepted in writing by Lender, Lender shall release Borrower from all obligations under this Mortgage and the Note.

If Lender exercises such option to accelerate, Lender shall mail Borrower notice of acceleration in accordance with paragraph 14 hereof. Such notice shall provide a period of not less than 30 days from the date the notice is mailed within which Borrower may pay the sums declared due. If Borrower fails to pay such sums prior to the expiration of such period, Lender may, without further notice or demand on Borrower, invoke any remedies permitted by paragraph 18 hereof.

NON-UNIFORM COVENANTS. Borrower and Lender further covenant and agree as follows:

18. Acceleration; Remedies. Except as provided in paragraph 17 hereof, upon Borrower's breach of any covenant or agreement of Borrower in this Mortgage, including the covenants to pay when due any sums secured by this Mortgage, Lender prior to acceleration shall mail notice to Borrower as provided in paragraph 14 hereof specifying: (1) the breach; (2) the action required to cure such breach; (3) a date, not less than 30 days from the date the notice is mailed to Borrower, by which such breach must be cured; and (4) that failure to cure such breach on or before the date specified in the notice may result in acceleration of the sums secured by this Mortgage and sale of the Property. The notice shall further inform Borrower of the right to reinstate after acceleration and the right to bring a court action to assert the non-existence of a default or any other defense of Borrower to acceleration and sale. If the breach is not cured on or before the date specified in the notice, Lender at Lender's option may declare all of the sums secured by this Mortgage to be immediately due and payable without further demand and Lender may invoke the STATUTORY POWER OF SALE and any other remedies permitted by applicable law. Lender shall be entitled to collect all reasonable costs and expenses incurred in pursuing the remedies provided in this paragraph 18, including, but not limited to, reasonable attorney's fees.

If Lender invokes the STATUTORY POWER OF SALE, Lender shall mail a copy of a notice of sale to Borrower, and to any other person required by applicable law, in the manner provided by applicable law. Lender shall publish the notice of sale and the Property shall be sold in the manner prescribed by applicable law. Lender or Lender's designee may purchase the Property at any sale. The proceeds of the sale shall be applied in the following order: (a) to all reasonable costs and expenses of the sale, including reasonable attorney's fees and costs of title evidence; (b) to all sums secured by this Mortgage; and (c) the excess, if any, to the person or persons legally entitled thereto.

19. Borrower's Right to Reinstate. Notwithstanding Lender's acceleration of the sums secured by this Mortgage, Borrower shall have the right to have any proceedings begun by Lender to enforce this Mortgage discontinued at any time prior to the earlier to occur of (i) the fifth day before sale of the Property pursuant to the power of sale contained in this Mortgage or (ii) entry of a judgment enforcing this Mortgage if: (a) Borrower pays Lender all sums which would be then due under this Mortgage, the Note and notes securing Future Advances, if any, had no acceleration occurred; (b) Borrower cures all breaches of any other covenants or agreements of Borrower contained in this Mortgage; (c) Borrower pays all reasonable expenses incurred by Lender in enforcing the covenants and agreements of Borrower contained in this Mortgage and in enforcing Lender's remedies as provided in paragraph 18 hereof, including, but not limited to, reasonable attorney's fees; and (d) Borrower takes such action as Lender may reasonably require to assure that the lien of this Mortgage, Lender's interest in the Property and Borrower's obligation to pay the sums secured by this Mortgage shall continue unimpaired.

Figure 5-5. *Continued.*

Upon such payment and cure by Borrower, this Mortgage and the obligations secured hereby shall remain in full force and effect as if no acceleration had occurred.

20. Assignment of Rents; Lender in Possession. As additional security hereunder, Borrower hereby assigns to Lender the rents of the Property, provided that Borrower shall, prior to acceleration under paragraph 18 hereof or abandonment of the Property, have the right to collect and retain such rents as they become due and payable.

Upon acceleration under paragraph 18 hereof or abandonment of the Property, Lender shall be entitled to enter upon, take possession of and manage the Property and to collect the rents of the Property including those past due. All rents collected by Lender shall be applied first to payment of the costs of management of the Property and collection of rents, including, but not limited to, reasonable attorney's fees, and then to the sums secured by this Mortgage. Lender shall be liable to account only for those rents actually received.

21. Future Advances. For the purposes permitted by applicable law and upon request of Borrower, Lender, at Lender's option prior to release of this Mortgage, may make Future Advances to Borrower. Such Future Advances, with interest thereon, shall be secured by this Mortgage when evidenced by promissory notes stating that said notes are secured hereby. At no time shall the principal amount of the indebtedness secured by this Mortgage, not including sums advanced in accordance herewith to protect the security of this Mortgage, exceed the original amount of the Note plus US$. . . . .

22. · Release. Upon payment of all sums secured by this Mortgage, Lender shall discharge this Mortgage without cost to Borrower. Borrower shall pay all costs of recordation, if any.

Figure 5-5. *Continued*

could be at an economic disadvantage if forced to accept early payments. This disadvantage would be the result of either having to give up a high interest rate or having to reinvest the funds immediately.

The law is clear; a mortgagee does not have to accept early payment unless so obligated in the mortgage itself. If a mortgagor desires the option of early payment, the provision should be negotiated before the mortgage is executed and be included in the mortgage. Many mortgagees will stipulate in the mortgage that prepayment can be made if a penalty is paid—usually a certain percentage of the outstanding debt. Mortgagees may waive this penalty if they want to remove low-yielding mortgages from their portfolios, but a mortgagor would normally have no desire in prepaying a mortgage with a low interest rate. Since 1979, mortgages sold to FNMA or FHLMC may not include a prepayment penalty.

Payment clause. The most obvious clause in a mortgage is the one by which a mortgagor agrees to pay the obligation in an agreed-upon manner. Reference usually is made to the note or bond whereby a mortgagor was obligated to pay a certain amount of money. A separate clause may stipulate a covenant to pay taxes and hazard insurance (with a mortgagee payable clause) as they became due on the encumbered real estate. However, this often is a part of the payment clause. A mortgagee may require taxes and insurance to be placed in escrow and collected monthly as part of the mortgage payment.

Deeds of Trust

Before deeds of trust can be used in any state, special enabling legislation must be enacted, since the deed of trust was not known in the common law. One of the basic legal differences between a mortgage and a deed of trust is that a mortgage is a two-party instrument between a mortgagor and a mortgagee, while a deed of trust is a three-party instrument between a borrower, a lender and a third party, called a *trustee* (Figure 5-6). If a deed of

DEED OF TRUST

(TRUST INDENTURE UNDER THE SMALL TRACT FINANCING ACT)

THIS DEED OF TRUST is made this . . . . day of . . . . ,
19 . . . ., among the Grantor, ...
. . . . (herein "Borrower"), ...
. . . . (herein "Trustee"), and the Beneficiary,
. . . . , a corporation organized and
existing under the laws of . . . ., whose address is . . . .
. . . . (herein "Lender").

BORROWER, in consideration of the indebtedness herein recited and the trust herein created, irrevocably grants
and conveys to Trustee, in trust, with power of sale, the following described property located in the County of
. . . . , State of Montana:

which has the address of . . . . , ... ,

                                     [Street]   [City]
. . . . (herein "Property Address");

    [State and Zip Code]

TOGETHER with all the improvements now or hereafter erected on the property, and all easements, rights,
appurtenances, rents (subject however to the rights and authorities given herein to Lender to collect and apply such
rents), royalties, mineral, oil and gas rights and profits, water, water rights, and water stock, and all fixtures now or
hereafter attached to the property, all of which, including replacements and additions thereto, shall be deemed to be
and remain a part of the property covered by this Deed of Trust; and all of the foregoing, together with said property
(or the leasehold estate if this Deed of Trust is on a leasehold) are herein referred to as the "Property";

To SECURE to Lender (a) the repayment of the indebtedness evidenced by Borrower's note dated . . . .
. . . . (herein "Note"), in the principal sum of . . . .
. . . . Dollars, with interest thereon, providing for monthly installments
of principal and interest, with the balance of the indebtedness, if not sooner paid, due and payable on . . . .
. . . . ; the payment of all other sums, with interest thereon, advanced
in accordance herewith to protect the security of this Deed of Trust; and the performance of the covenants and
agreements of Borrower herein contained; and (b) the repayment of any future advances, with interest thereon, made
to Borrower by Lender pursuant to paragraph 21 hereof (herein "Future Advances").

Borrower covenants that Borrower is lawfully seised of the estate hereby conveyed and has the right to grant and
convey the Property, that the Property is unencumbered, and that Borrower will warrant and defend generally the
title to the Property against all claims and demands, subject to any declarations, easements or restrictions listed in a
schedule of exceptions to coverage in any title insurance policy insuring Lender's interest in the Property.

MONTANA—1 to 4 Family—6/75—FNMA/FHLMC UNIFORM INSTRUMENT   30 FHLMC MONTANA—AS & AS (2651)

Figure 5-6.

IN WITNESS WHEREOF, Borrower has executed this Deed of Trust.

....
—Borrower

....
—Borrower

STATE OF MONTANA, ...County ss:

On this....................day of....................., 19...., before me, a Notary Public for the State of Montana, personally appeared.. ....known to me to be the person(s) whose name(s)................ subscribed to the foregoing instrument, and acknowledged to me that...............executed the same.

My Commission expires:

....
Notary Public for Montana
Residing at..................................., Montana

REQUEST FOR RECONVEYANCE

TO TRUSTEE:

The undersigned is the holder of the note or notes secured by this Deed of Trust. Said note or notes, together with all other indebtedness secured by this Deed of Trust, have been paid in full. You are hereby directed to cancel said note or notes and this Deed of Trust, which are delivered hereby, and to reconvey, without warranty, all the estate now held by you under this Deed of Trust to the person or persons legally entitled thereto.

Date:.........................   ....

———————————— (Space Below This Line Reserved For Lender and Recorder) ————————————

Figure 5-6. *Continued.*

UNIFORM COVENANTS. Borrower and Lender covenant and agree as follows:

1. Payment of Principal and Interest. Borrower shall promptly pay when due the principal of and interest on the indebtedness evidenced by the Note, prepayment and late charges as provided in the Note, and the principal of and interest on any Future Advances secured by this Deed of Trust.

2. Funds for Taxes and Insurance. Subject to applicable law or to a written waiver by Lender, Borrower shall pay to Lender on the day monthly installments of principal and interest are payable under the Note, until the Note is paid in full, a sum (herein "Funds") equal to one-twelfth of the yearly taxes and assessments which may attain priority over this Deed of Trust, and ground rents on the Property, if any, plus one-twelfth of yearly premium installments for hazard insurance, plus one-twelfth of yearly premium installments for mortgage insurance, if any, all as reasonably estimated initially and from time to time by Lender on the basis of assessments and bills and reasonable estimates thereof.

The Funds shall be held in an institution the deposits or accounts of which are insured or guaranteed by a Federal or state agency (including Lender if Lender is such an institution). Lender shall apply the Funds to pay said taxes, assessments, insurance premiums and ground rents. Lender may not charge for so holding and applying the Funds, analyzing said account or verifying and compiling said assessments and bills, unless Lender pays Borrower interest on the Funds and applicable law permits Lender to make such a charge. Borrower and Lender may agree in writing at the time of execution of this Deed of Trust that interest on the Funds shall be paid to Borrower, and unless such agreement is made or applicable law requires such interest to be paid, Lender shall not be required to pay Borrower any interest or earnings on the Funds. Lender shall give to Borrower, without charge, an annual accounting of the Funds showing credits and debits to the Funds and the purpose for which each debit to the Funds was made. The Funds are pledged as additional security for the sums secured by this Deed of Trust.

If the amount of the Funds held by Lender, together with the future monthly installments of Funds payable prior to the due dates of taxes, assessments, insurance premiums and ground rents, shall exceed the amount required to pay said taxes, assessments, insurance premiums and ground rents as they fall due, such excess shall be, at Borrower's option, either promptly repaid to Borrower or credited to Borrower on monthly installments of Funds. If the amount of the Funds held by Lender shall not be sufficient to pay taxes, assessments, insurance premiums and ground rents as they fall due, Borrower shall pay to Lender any amount necessary to make up the deficiency within 30 days from the date notice is mailed by Lender to Borrower requesting payment thereof.

Upon payment in full of all sums secured by this Deed of Trust, Lender shall promptly refund to Borrower any Funds held by Lender. If under paragraph 18 hereof the Property is sold or the Property is otherwise acquired by Lender, Lender shall apply, no later than immediately prior to the sale of the Property or its acquisition by Lender, any Funds held by Lender at the time of application as a credit against the sums secured by this Deed of Trust.

3. Application of Payments. Unless applicable law provides otherwise, all payments received by Lender under the Note and paragraphs 1 and 2 hereof shall be applied by Lender first in payment of amounts payable to Lender by Borrower under paragraph 2 hereof, then to interest payable on the Note, then to the principal of the Note, and then to interest and principal on any Future Advances.

4. Charges; Liens. Borrower shall pay all taxes, assessments and other charges, fines and impositions attributable to the Property which may attain a priority over this Deed of Trust, and leasehold payments or ground rents, if any, in the manner provided under paragraph 2 hereof or, if not paid in such manner, by Borrower making payment, when due, directly to the payee thereof. Borrower shall promptly furnish to Lender all notices of amounts due under this paragraph, and in the event Borrower shall make payment directly, Borrower shall promptly furnish to Lender receipts evidencing such payments. Borrower shall promptly discharge any lien which has priority over this Deed of Trust; provided, that Borrower shall not be required to discharge any such lien so long as Borrower shall agree in writing to the payment of the obligation secured by such lien in a manner acceptable to Lender, or shall in good faith contest such lien by, or defend enforcement of such lien in, legal proceedings which operate to prevent the enforcement of the lien or forfeiture of the Property or any part thereof.

5. Hazard Insurance. Borrower shall keep the improvements now existing or hereafter erected on the Property insured against loss by fire, hazards included within the term "extended coverage", and such other hazards as Lender may require and in such amounts and for such periods as Lender may require; provided, that Lender shall not require that the amount of such coverage exceed that amount of coverage required to pay the sums secured by this Deed of Trust.

The insurance carrier providing the insurance shall be chosen by Borrower subject to approval by Lender; provided, that such approval shall not be unreasonably withheld. All premiums on insurance policies shall be paid in the manner provided under paragraph 2 hereof or, if not paid in such manner, by Borrower making payment, when due, directly to the insurance carrier.

All insurance policies and renewals thereof shall be in form acceptable to Lender and shall include a standard mortgage clause in favor of and in form acceptable to Lender. Lender shall have the right to hold the policies and renewals thereof, and Borrower shall promptly furnish to Lender all renewal notices and all receipts of paid premiums. In the event of loss, Borrower shall give prompt notice to the insurance carrier and Lender. Lender may make proof of loss if not made promptly by Borrower.

Unless Lender and Borrower otherwise agree in writing, insurance proceeds shall be applied to restoration or repair of the Property damaged, provided such restoration or repair is economically feasible and the security of this Deed of Trust is not thereby impaired. If such restoration or repair is not economically feasible or if the security of this Deed of Trust would be impaired, the insurance proceeds shall be applied to the sums secured by this Deed of Trust, with the excess, if any, paid to Borrower. If the Property is abandoned by Borrower, or if Borrower fails to respond to Lender within 30 days from the date notice is mailed by Lender to Borrower that the insurance carrier offers to settle a claim for insurance benefits, Lender is authorized to collect and apply the insurance proceeds at Lender's option either to restoration or repair of the Property or to the sums secured by this Deed of Trust.

Unless Lender and Borrower otherwise agree in writing, any such application of proceeds to principal shall not extend or postpone the due date of the monthly installments referred to in paragraphs 1 and 2 hereof or change the amount of such installments. If under paragraph 18 hereof the Property is acquired by Lender, all right, title and interest of Borrower in and to any insurance policies and in and to the proceeds thereof resulting from damage to the Property prior to the sale or acquisition shall pass to Lender to the extent of the sums secured by this Deed of Trust immediately prior to such sale or acquisition.

Figure 5-6. *Continued.*

6. Preservation and Maintenance of Property; Leaseholds; Condominiums; Planned Unit Developments. Borrower shall keep the Property in good repair and shall not commit waste or permit impairment or deterioration of the Property and shall comply with the provisions of any lease if this Deed of Trust is on a leasehold. If this Deed of Trust is on a unit in a condominium or a planned unit development, Borrower shall perform all of Borrower's obligations under the declaration or covenants creating or governing the condominium or planned unit development, the by-laws and regulations of the condominium or planned unit development, and constituent documents. If a condominium or planned unit development rider is executed by Borrower and recorded together with this Deed of Trust, the covenants and agreements of such rider shall be incorporated into and shall amend and supplement the covenants and agreements of this Deed of Trust as if the rider were a part hereof.

7. Protection of Lender's Security. If Borrower fails to perform the covenants and agreements contained in this Deed of Trust, or if any action or proceeding is commenced which materially affects Lender's interest in the Property, including, but not limited to, eminent domain, insolvency, code enforcement, or arrangements or proceedings involving a bankrupt or decedent, then Lender at Lender's option, upon notice to Borrower, may make such appearances, disburse such sums and take such action as is necessary to protect Lender's interest, including, but not limited to, disbursement of reasonable attorney's fees and entry upon the Property to make repairs. If Lender required mortgage insurance as a condition of making the loan secured by this Deed of Trust, Borrower shall pay the premiums required to maintain such insurance in effect until such time as the requirement for such insurance terminates in accordance with Borrower's and Lender's written agreement or applicable law. Borrower shall pay the amount of all mortgage insurance premiums in the manner provided under paragraph 2 hereof.

Any amounts disbursed by Lender pursuant to this paragraph 7, with interest thereon, shall become additional indebtedness of Borrower secured by this Deed of Trust. Unless Borrower and Lender agree to other terms of payment, such amounts shall be payable upon notice from Lender to Borrower requesting payment thereof, and shall bear interest from the date of disbursement at the rate payable from time to time on outstanding principal under the Note unless payment of interest at such rate would be contrary to applicable law, in which event such amounts shall bear interest at the highest rate permissible under applicable law. Nothing contained in this paragraph 7 shall require Lender to incur any expense or take any action hereunder.

8. Inspection. Lender may make or cause to be made reasonable entries upon and inspections of the Property, provided that Lender shall give Borrower notice prior to any such inspection specifying reasonable cause therefor related to Lender's interest in the Property.

9. Condemnation. The proceeds of any award or claim for damages, direct or consequential, in connection with any condemnation or other taking of the Property, or part thereof, or for conveyance in lieu of condemnation, are hereby assigned and shall be paid to Lender.

In the event of a total taking of the Property, the proceeds shall be applied to the sums secured by this Deed of Trust, with the excess, if any, paid to Borrower. In the event of a partial taking of the Property, unless Borrower and Lender otherwise agree in writing, there shall be applied to the sums secured by this Deed of Trust such proportion of the proceeds as is equal to that proportion which the amount of the sums secured by this Deed of Trust immediately prior to the date of taking bears to the fair market value of the Property immediately prior to the date of taking, with the balance of the proceeds paid to Borrower.

If the Property is abandoned by Borrower, or if, after notice by Lender to Borrower that the condemnor offers to make an award or settle a claim for damages, Borrower fails to respond to Lender within 30 days after the date such notice is mailed, Lender is authorized to collect and apply the proceeds, at Lender's option, either to restoration or repair of the Property or to the sums secured by this Deed of Trust.

Unless Lender and Borrower otherwise agree in writing, any such application of proceeds to principal shall not extend or postpone the due date of the monthly installments referred to in paragraphs 1 and 2 hereof or change the amount of such installments.

10. Borrower Not Released. Extension of the time for payment or modification of amortization of the sums secured by this Deed of Trust granted by Lender to any successor in interest of Borrower shall not operate to release, in any manner, the liability of the original Borrower and Borrower's successors in interest. Lender shall not be required to commence proceedings against such successor or refuse to extend time for payment or otherwise modify amortization of the sums secured by this Deed of Trust by reason of any demand made by the original Borrower and Borrower's successors in interest.

11. Forbearance by Lender Not a Waiver. Any forbearance by Lender in exercising any right or remedy hereunder, or otherwise afforded by applicable law, shall not be a waiver of or preclude the exercise of any such right or remedy. The procurement of insurance or the payment of taxes or other liens or charges by Lender shall not be a waiver of Lender's right to accelerate the maturity of the indebtedness secured by this Deed of Trust.

12. Remedies Cumulative. All remedies provided in this Deed of Trust are distinct and cumulative to any other right or remedy under this Deed of Trust or afforded by law or equity, and may be exercised concurrently, independently or successively.

13. Successors and Assigns Bound; Joint and Several Liability; Captions. The covenants and agreements herein contained shall bind, and the rights hereunder shall inure to, the respective successors and assigns of Lender and Borrower, subject to the provisions of paragraph 17 hereof. All covenants and agreements of Borrower shall be joint and several. The captions and headings of the paragraphs of this Deed of Trust are for convenience only and are not to be used to interpret or define the provisions hereof.

14. Notice. Except for any notice required under applicable law to be given in another manner, (a) any notice to Borrower provided for in this Deed of Trust shall be given by mailing such notice by certified mail addressed to Borrower at the Property Address or at such other address as Borrower may designate by notice to Lender as provided herein, and (b) any notice to Lender shall be given by certified mail, return receipt requested, to Lender's address stated herein or to such other address as Lender may designate by notice to Borrower as provided herein. Any notice provided for in this Deed of Trust shall be deemed to have been given to Borrower or Lender when given in the manner designated herein.

15. Uniform Deed of Trust; Governing Law; Severability. This form of deed of trust combines uniform covenants for national use and non-uniform covenants with limited variations by jurisdiction to constitute a uniform security instrument covering real property. This Deed of Trust shall be governed by the law of the jurisdiction in which the Property is located.

Figure 5–6. *Continued.*

In the event that any provision or clause of this Deed of Trust or the Note conflicts with applicable law, such conflict shall not affect other provisions of this Deed of Trust or the Note which can be given effect without the conflicting provision, and to this end the provisions of the Deed of Trust and the Note are declared to be severable.

16. Borrower's Copy. Borrower shall be furnished a conformed copy of the Note and of this Deed of Trust at the time of execution or after recordation hereof.

17. Transfer of the Property; Assumption. If all or any part of the Property or an interest therein is sold or transferred by Borrower without Lender's prior written consent, excluding (a) the creation of a lien or encumbrance subordinate to this Deed of Trust, (b) the creation of a purchase money security interest for household appliances, (c) a transfer by devise, descent or by operation of law upon the death of a joint tenant or (d) the grant of any leasehold interest of three years or less not containing an option to purchase, Lender may, at Lender's option, declare all the sums secured by this Deed of Trust to be immediately due and payable. Lender shall have waived such option to accelerate if, prior to the sale or transfer, Lender and the person to whom the Property is to be sold or transferred reach agreement in writing that the credit of such person is satisfactory to Lender and that the interest payable on the sums secured by this Deed of Trust shall be at such rate as Lender shall request. If Lender has waived the option to accelerate provided in this paragraph 17, and if Borrower's successor in interest has executed a written assumption agreement accepted in writing by Lender, Lender shall release Borrower from all obligations under this Deed of Trust and the Note.

If Lender exercises such option to accelerate, Lender shall mail Borrower notice of acceleration in accordance with paragraph 14 hereof. Such notice shall provide a period of not less than 30 days from the date the notice is mailed within which Borrower may pay the sums declared due. If Borrower fails to pay such sums prior to the expiration of such period, Lender may, without further notice or demand on Borrower, invoke any remedies permitted by paragraph 18 hereof.

NON-UNIFORM COVENANTS. Borrower and Lender further covenant and agree as follows:

18. Acceleration; Remedies. Except as provided in paragraph 17 hereof, upon Borrower's breach of any covenant or agreement of Borrower in this Deed of Trust, including the covenants to pay when due any sums secured by this Deed of Trust, Lender prior to acceleration shall mail notice to Borrower as provided in paragraph 14 hereof specifying: (1) the breach; (2) the action required to cure such breach; (3) a date, not less than 30 days from the date the notice is mailed to Borrower, by which such breach must be cured; and (4) that failure to cure such breach on or before the date specified in the notice may result in acceleration of the sums secured by this Deed of Trust and sale of the Property. The notice shall further inform Borrower of the right to reinstate after acceleration and the right to bring a court action to assert the non-existence of a default or any other defense of Borrower to acceleration and sale. If the breach is not cured on or before the date specified in the notice, Lender at Lender's option may declare all of the sums secured by this Deed of Trust to be immediately due and payable without further demand and may invoke the power of sale and any other remedies permitted by applicable law. Lender shall be entitled to collect all reasonable costs and expenses incurred in pursuing the remedies provided in this paragraph 18, including, but not limited to, reasonable attorney's fees.

If Lender invokes the power of sale, Lender shall give Trustee notice of the occurrence of an event of default and of Lender's election to cause the Property to be sold. Lender or Trustee shall record a notice of sale in each county in which the Property or some part thereof is located, and Trustee shall mail copies of such notice in the manner prescribed by applicable law to Borrower and to the other persons prescribed by applicable law. After the lapse of such time as may be required by applicable law and after posting on the Property and publication of the notice of sale, Trustee, without demand on Borrower, shall sell the Property at public auction to the highest bidder at the time and place and under the terms designated in the notice of sale in one or more parcels and in such order as Trustee may determine. Trustee may postpone sale of all or any parcel of the Property by public announcement at the time and place of any previously scheduled sale. Lender or Lender's designee may purchase the Property at any sale.

Trustee shall deliver to the purchaser Trustee's deed conveying the Property so sold without any covenant or warranty, expressed or implied. The recitals in the Trustee's deed shall be prima facie evidence of the truth of the statements made therein. Trustee shall apply the proceeds of the sale in the following order: (a) to all reasonable costs and expenses of the sale, including, but not limited to, reasonable Trustee's and attorney's fees and costs of title evidence; (b) to all sums secured by this Deed of Trust; and (c) the excess, if any, to the person or persons legally entitled thereto or to the clerk or recorder of the county in which the sale took place.

19. Borrower's Right to Reinstate. Notwithstanding Lender's acceleration of the sums secured by this Deed of Trust, Borrower shall have the right to have any proceedings begun by Lender to enforce this Deed of Trust discontinued at any time prior to the earlier to occur of (i) sale of the Property pursuant to the power of sale contained in this Deed of Trust or (ii) entry of a judgment enforcing this Deed of Trust if: (a) Borrower pays Lender all sums which would be then due under this Deed of Trust, the Note and notes securing Future Advances, if any, had no acceleration occurred; (b) Borrower cures all breaches of any other covenants or agreements of Borrower contained in this Deed of Trust; (c) Borrower pays all reasonable expenses incurred by Lender and Trustee in enforcing the covenants and agreements of Borrower contained in this Deed of Trust and in enforcing Lender's and Trustee's remedies as provided in paragraph 18 hereof, including, but not limited to, reasonable attorney's fees; and (d) Borrower takes such action as Lender may reasonably require to assure that the lien of this Deed of Trust, Lender's interest in the Property and Borrower's obligation to pay the sums secured by this Deed of Trust shall continue unimpaired. Upon such payment and cure by Borrower, this Deed of Trust and the obligations secured hereby shall remain in full force and effect as if no acceleration had occurred.

20. Assignment of Rents; Appointment of Receiver; Lender in Possession. As additional security hereunder, Borrower hereby assigns to Lender the rents of the Property, provided that Borrower shall, prior to acceleration under paragraph 18 hereof or abandonment of the Property, have the right to collect and retain such rents as they become due and payable.

Upon acceleration under paragraph 18 hereof or abandonment of the Property, Lender, in person, by agent or by judicially appointed receiver, shall be entitled to enter upon, take possession of and manage the Property and to collect the rents of the Property including those past due. All rents collected by Lender or the receiver shall be applied first to payment of the costs of management of the Property and collection of rents, including, but not limited to, receiver's fees, premiums on receiver's bonds and reasonable attorney's fees, and then to the sums secured by this Deed of Trust. Lender and the receiver shall be liable to account only for those rents actually received.

Figure 5-6. *Continued.*

21. Future Advances. Upon request of Borrower, Lender, at Lender's option prior to full reconveyance of the Property by Trustee to Borrower, may make Future Advances to Borrower. Such Future Advances, with interest thereon, shall be secured by this Deed of Trust when evidenced by promissory notes stating that said notes are secured hereby. At no time shall the principal amount of the indebtedness secured by this Deed of Trust, not including sums advanced in accordance herewith to protect the security of this Deed of Trust, exceed the original amount of the Note plus US$..................

22. Reconveyance. Upon payment of all sums secured by this Deed of Trust, Lender shall request Trustee to reconvey the Property and shall surrender this Deed of Trust and all notes evidencing indebtedness secured by this Deed of Trust to Trustee. Trustee shall reconvey the Property without warranty and without charge to the person or persons legally entitled thereto. Such person or persons shall pay all costs of recordation, if any.

23. Substitute Trustee. Lender, at Lender's option, may from time to time remove Trustee and appoint a successor trustee to any Trustee appointed hereunder. Without conveyance of the Property, the successor trustee shall succeed to all the title, power and duties conferred upon the Trustee herein and by applicable law.

24. Area of Property. The area of the Property is not more than fifteen acres.

Figure 5-6. Continued

trust is used, a borrower conveys title for the real estate securing a debt to a trustee who holds it until the obligation is satisfied, at which time title is conveyed back to the borrower. This is for the benefit of the lender.

Another theoretical difference is the necessity of a mortgagee foreclosing on a mortgage if there has been a default. On the other hand, in most states there is no requirement for a foreclosure with its time-consuming court proceedings if a deed of trust is used. Instead, the trustee has the power of sale to satisfy the debt. Some states, however, require a foreclosure even if the financing vehicle is a deed of trust. Regardless of the situation, there is always a requirement for a public sale. (See Part 2 of this chapter, Foreclosure and Redemption.)

In using a deed of trust there is generally no statutory right of redemption as there is with a mortgage. This is one of the most important reasons for a mortgagee to use a deed of trust rather than a mortgage. In many jurisdictions, a mortgagor has a period of time to redeem the property after default and foreclosure. If the right to redeem exists, this period varies from six months to two years, depending on the state. To a mortgagor, the advantage of a deed of trust is that a mortgagee does not have the right to a deficiency judgment. A deficiency judgment is the result of a lawsuit to make up the difference between the amount obtained at a foreclosure sale and the mortgage obligation.

TRANSFERS OF MORTGAGED REAL ESTATE

In all jurisdictions, whether the title or lien theory is followed, the mortgagor has the ability to transfer real estate that is serving as security for a debt and has options on the method of transfer.

Free and clear. The grantor (the one transferring) could transfer the land free and clear. This would occur if a mortgagor satisfied the obligation secured by the real estate and presumes the mortgage could be prepaid. In such an event, a prepayment penalty might be required. Much mortgaged real estate sold today is transferred in this manner, with a new owner obtaining new financing, since inflation has produced greater equity in real estate than a purchaser would want to buy for cash. Therefore, a new purchaser normally would rather finance the purchase price than assume the mortgage and pay cash for the equity. During periods of exceedingly high interest rates as occurred in 1979–81, purchasers may desire to assume an existing lower interest rate mortgage and pay cash or use another financing technique for the equity.

Subject to the mortgage. The grantor could transfer the real estate subject to the mortgage, with the grantee (the one to whom the property is transferred) paying the grantor for any equity. If this occurs, the original mortgage remains effective and the personal liability of the original mortgagor to pay the mortgage continues, although the mortgage payment will probably be made by the grantee from that point on. The grantee becomes the legal owner of the real estate after the sale, although it continues to serve as security for the original mortgage. The grantee assumes no personal liability for the original mortgage payment and could decide to abandon the real estate with no danger of contingent liability. If the grantee stops the mortgage payment and the mortgagee forecloses, the grantee loses only equity in the real estate while the original mortgagor is liable for any amount of the obligation not satisfied by the sale of the mortgaged real estate.

Assumption of the mortgage. The real estate could be transferred to the grantee who would buy the grantor's equity and assume the mortgage. This is the most common manner in which real estate is transferred in those cases where the existing mortgage remains intact. In this situation, the grantee assumes personal liability for satisfying the mortgage debt, while the original mortgagor retains only secondary liability. (See Figure 5–7.)

Recently some mortgagees have inserted clauses into conventional mortgages to either prohibit the transfer of the mortgage or make the transfer conditional on the approval of the mortgagee. Other mortgagees, especially savings and loan associations, have inserted *due-on-sale clauses* in conventional mortgages, accelerating the entire debt if the real estate is sold with the mortgage still intact. The stated rationale for such a clause is to protect the mortgagee's security interest by forcing the new mortgagor to meet the mortgagee's underwriting requirements. Often, however, the real reason is to force the grantee to assume an increase in the interest rate from the rate on the assumed mortgage to the higher current rate. The validity of these clauses has evolved to the point that most but not all courts currently enforce the mortgagee's right to accelerate. Most states have enacted legislation specifically prohibiting due-on-sale clauses. This trend could accelerate as alternative mortgage instruments become common, providing mortgagees some protection on their yields.

Many mortgagors, after selling the real estate to the grantee who assumes the mortgage, have requested that the mortgagee sign a *novation contract* which would end any secondary liability on the part of the original mortgagor. Many mortgagees have agreed to sign, but normally the assuming grantee must agree to an increase in the interest rate to the prevailing rate.

ASSUMPTION AGREEMENT

WITHOUT RELEASE   *Loan No.* _____

WHEREAS   NAME OF FINANCIAL INSTITUTION

loaned _____

_____

the sum of _____Dollars

($_____), evidenced by note and mortgage dated _____and recorded

as Document No._____in_____County, _____;

WHEREAS, said Borrowers have sold said property to the undersigned Purchasers and said Purchasers desire to assume and agree to pay said indebtedness and perform all the obligations under said Loan Contract, and said Association is willing to consent to said transfer of title, and assumption of said indebtedness, but is not willing to release said Borrowers from their present liability on said note and mortgage.

THEREFORE, in consideration of the mutual covenants and agreements herein contained, IT IS HEREBY AGREED as follows:

1. The Association does hereby consent to the sale and conveyance of said premises by the aforesaid Borrowers to said Purchasers.

2. The Purchasers do hereby assume and agree to pay said mortgage indebtedness, evidenced by said note and mortgage, and to perform all of the obligations provided therein, it being agreed and understood that as of this date said indebtedness is

_____Dollars ($_____),

and that the interest rate shall be _____% per annum, and that monthly payments shall be made beginning the

_____day of_____, 19_____, in the sum of

_____Dollars ($_____) per month, to be applied first to interest and the balance to principal until said indebtedness is paid in full, and that, in addition, said Purchasers will pay the sum of

_____Dollars ($_____), estimated to be sufficient to pay taxes and insurance on said property, which estimate may be revised, making a total

current payment of_____Dollars ($_____) per month.

3. The Borrowers agree that their present liability under said mortgage loan shall not be impaired, prejudiced or affected in any way whatsoever by this Agreement, or by sale or conveyance of said premises, or by the assumption by the Purchasers of said mortgage loan, or by any subsequent change in the terms, time, manner or method of payment of said indebtedness, or any part thereof, contracted by the Association and the Purchasers or the transferees of the Purchasers, whether or not such changes or such transfers have been consented to by the Borrowers.

This assumption by said Purchasers is joint and several and shall bind them, their heirs, personal representatives, successors and assigns.

IN WITNESS WHEREOF, the parties have hereunto executed this instrument this_____day of

_____, 19_____.

_____   _____

_____   _____

Borrowers   Purchasers

          NAME OF FINANCIAL INSTITUTION

          By _____
          Authorized Signature

THIS INSTRUMENT WAS PREPARED BY: ATTEST:

          _____
          Secretary

44047-9 (1/74)
35 AAG—Assumption Agreement, Without Release

SAF Systems and Forms
(American Savings & Accounting Supply, Inc.)

Figure 5–7.

Assignments of Mortgages

Many originators of mortgage loans, such as mortgage companies, originate loans for sale to other investors. Any mortgage lender has the right to assign a mortgage even if the mortgagor is unaware of the assignment.

The instrument by which mortgages are assigned should be in writing and the assignment should be recorded immediately to protect the assignee from another possible assignment.

At the time of assignment, the mortgagor may be required to sign an *estoppel certificate*. This is a statement by the mortgagor that there is a binding obligation not yet satisfied, and that the mortgagor has no defenses against the mortgagee. An assigned mortgage has full effect and the mortgage payments may be made directly to the assignee or through the original mortgagee.

PART TWO
FORECLOSURE AND REDEMPTION

DEFAULT

A mortgagor who breaches any of the covenants in a mortgage is considered to be in default. A default is normally caused by a nonpayment of principal and interest, but could also result from a failure to pay taxes, provide hazard insurance or maintain the premises. A mortgage instrument is usually worded in such a manner that the mortgagee has certain options in the event of a default. Even if automatic acceleration is required in a mortgage it may not be the best choice for a mortgagee and is certainly not the best alternative for a mortgagor.

There are many reasons why a mortgagor defaults on mortgage obligations. The more common reasons for residential mortgage defaults read like a list of personal tragedies, and usually are:

- Loss of employment
- Strike
- Death of a wage-earner
- Credit over-extension or bankruptcy
- Illness of a wage-earner or mounting family medical expenses
- Marital problems

Income-property mortgage defaults could occur from the reasons listed above, plus:

- Economic slowdown
- Inflation
- Loss of top management
- Loss of a key industry

In practically all situations, a mortgagee does not want to foreclose if it can be prevented. Although the average American may not believe it, mortgagees not only dislike foreclosure, but generally lose money if they must foreclose.[1] After all, most mortgagees are in the business of lending money, not owning or managing real property.

Typically, a loan is delinquent 30 days before a mortgagee or its agent (e.g., a mortgage company) takes any action. This is primarily because of the awareness that people may occasionally miss a payment because of vacation, forgetfulness or some other logical reason. Although most mortgages provide for acceleration 30 days after the due date for a payment, few are immediately accelerated.

After 30 days, a mortgagee or the agent will attempt to contact the mortgagor to determine why a required payment has not been received. This initial inquiry may enable a mortgagee to resolve the problem and, after charging a late fee to partially offset additional expenses, allow the mortgage to continue. If the mortgage is FHA-insured, however, the mortgagee may not be able to accelerate if the mortgagor has submitted at least 50 percent of past due amounts.

If a mortgagee does not require a late fee or accelerates and reinstates the mortgage, it still retains all options, including the right to accelerate for future defaults. Together, a mortgagee and mortgagor are normally able to handle any personal problems that may have led to the delinquency. For example, in a case where a borrower is sick and cannot work for six months, a mortgagee may choose:

- To collect just a portion of the past due amount immediately
- To make a second mortgage to bring the loan current
- To extend the term
- To look to other solutions tailored to the needs of both parties that will rectify the problem.

The percentage of single-family loans that are delinquent 30 days or more changes with swings in the economy and unemployment. But the percentage in foreclosure is near an historic low. (Figure 5–8.) This is due in part to the fact that the inflationary period of the early 1970s has given most homeowners enough equity in their homes to sell (thus keeping their equity) if they have problems making the mortgage payment rather than let it be sold at foreclosure.

FORECLOSURE

After all attempts to cure a default fail, a mortgagee must move to foreclose and protect its investment. It is important for all to realize that when a mortgagee or its agent forecloses a defaulted mortgage, it is only fulfilling its fiduciary responsibility to protect the funds loaned which are actually the savings public's money, whether in the form of passbook savings or life insurance.

There are various forms of foreclosure, depending on state law. Any time before a foreclosure sale or other disposition, a mortgagor or anyone claiming through the mortgagor, such as a spouse or junior lienholders, may exercise the equitable right of redemption. This right is exercised by paying the mortgagee the outstanding balance plus interest and costs and applies to all foreclosures.

MORTGAGE FORECLOSURES BY INSURED ASSOCIATIONS

Year	All Mortgage Loans		Conventional Loans		FHA and VA Loans	
	Number	Rate[1]	Number	Rate[1]	Number	Rate[1]
1965	53,788	.570%	41,817	.512%	11,971	.947%
1970	19,493	.186	12,777	.141	6,176	.461
1971	20,464	.189	11,278	.121	9,186	.549
1972	22,958	.199	10,045	.104	12,913	.687
1973[2]	25,275	.208	10,639	.103	14,636	.770
1974	24,230	.192	11,945	.112	12,285	.623
1975	24,979	.195	15,538	.142	9,441	.491
1976	22,542	.168	15,800	.138	6,742	.353
1977	19,900	.141	13,468	.110	6,432	.351
1978	17,502	.117	12,214	.092	5,288	.303
1979	16,767	.108	12,764	.092	4,003	.246
1980	20,211	.129	17,050	.120	3,161	.202
1981[3]	13,083	.166	11,215	.156	1,868	.246

[1]Percentage of loans held.
[2]New series.
[3]January through June; foreclosure rates are annualized.
Source: Federal Home Loan Bank Board.

Figure 5–8. *(Reprinted from* Savings and Loan Fact Book '82, © *1982 by the United States League of Savings Associations.)*

As mentioned previously, the first judicial method of cutting off a mortgagor's equity of redemption was known as *strict foreclosure.* If not redeemed within a set time, a court decree transferred the mortgagor's interest to the mortgagee irrespective of any equity of the mortgagor in the property. This result was grossly unfair to the mortgagor. Therefore, a more balanced approach followed which provided for selling the property to secure the debt. The proceeds of the sale went first to satisfy the mortgagee, then other lienholders, and then to the mortgagor.

The four modern methods of foreclosure, depending on the law of a state, are: (See Figure 5–9.)

1. Judicial proceeding
2. Power of sale
3. Strict foreclosure
4. Entry and possession

Judicial Proceeding

Most states provide for mortgage foreclosure through a court proceeding. This method best protects the interests of the various parties. The action is much like any other civil suit in that the case must be brought in the court with jurisdiction, either a circuit or district court of the state where the real estate is located. The procedure involved requires a complaint naming the borrower, who now is the defendant, alleging that a mortgage was executed by the defendant using specifically described real estate as security for a loan and that a default has occurred whereby the mortgagee has had to accelerate. The complaint will request foreclosure.

The defendant always has an opportunity to answer the allegations with any defenses available. For example, the defendant may attempt to prove that:

- no mortgage existed
- the mortgage was satisfied
- no default occurred
- the interest rate was usurious

If the decision of a court is in favor of a mortgagee, the decree of foreclosure terminates the equitable right of redemption at the time of sale, and a mortgagor loses all rights to the real property except the right to any excess proceeds from sale after secured parties are paid. The exception is if a state has a statutory right of redemption. The court decree will order a sale and the manner for its execution. Many courts will include an *upset price* in the decree which is the acceptable minimum bid at the sale. The court usually specifies the officer, such as a sheriff or referee, who will conduct the sale after giving the statutory notice of the sale. To encourage purchasers, a successful bidder acquires title to the property unencumbered by any interest, except that of the mortgagor's statutory right of redemption, if allowed.

With one possible exception, anyone who can contract can purchase property at a foreclosure sale. Some states prevent a defaulting mortgagor from purchasing since the unencumbered title would cut off the rights of junior lienholders. Probably the best laws are those that allow a mortgagor to repurchase at a foreclosure sale where all liens on the real estate prior to foreclosure reattach.

The key element in this form of foreclosure is that the sale must be accepted or confirmed by the court retaining jurisdiction. This requirement is for the protection of both the mortgagor and junior lienholders since a court will not approve a price which is unconscionably low.

State	Nature of Mortgage	Customary Security Instrument	Predominant Method of Foreclosure	Redemption Period (Months) (If customary security instrument used)	Possession During Redemption (If customary security instrument used)	Deficiency Judgment Allowed?
Alabama	Title	Mortgage	Power of Sale	12	Purchaser	Yes
Alaska	Lien	Trust Deed	Power of Sale	None	—	No
Arizona	Lien	Trust Deed	Judicial	None	—	Yes
Arkansas	Intermediate	Mortgage	Power of Sale	12	Purchaser	Yes
California	Lien	Trust Deed	Power of Sale	None	—	No
Colorado	Lien	Trust Deed	Power of Sale	2½	Mortgagor	Yes
Connecticut	Intermediate	Mortgage	Strict Foreclosure	None	—	No
Delaware	Intermediate	Mortgage	Judicial	None	—	No
Dist. of Columbia	Intermediate	Trust Deed	Power of Sale	None	—	Yes
Florida	Lien	Mortgage	Judicial	None	—	Yes
Georgia	Title	Security Deed	Power of Sale	None	—	Yes
Hawaii	Title	Trust Deed	Power of Sale	None	—	Yes
Idaho	Lien	Trust Deed	Power of Sale	None	—	Yes
Illinois	Intermediate	Mortgage	Judicial	12	Mortgagor	No
Indiana	Lien	Mortgage	Judicial	3	Mortgagor	Yes
Iowa	Lien	Mortgage	Judicial	6	Mortgagor	No
Kansas	Lien	Mortgage	Judicial	12	Mortgagor	Yes
Kentucky	Lien	Mortgage	Judicial	None	—	Yes
Louisiana	Lien	Mortgage	Judicial	None	—	Yes
Maine	Title	Mortgage	Entry and Possession	12	Mortgagor	Yes
Maryland	Title	Trust Deed	Power of Sale	None	—	Yes
Massachusetts	Intermediate	Mortgage	Power of Sale	None	—	Yes
Michigan	Lien	Mortgage	Power of Sale	6	Mortgagor	Yes
Minnesota	Lien	Mortgage	Power of Sale	12	Mortgagor	Yes
Mississippi	Intermediate	Trust Deed	Power of Sale	None	—	Yes
Missouri	Intermediate	Trust Deed	Power of Sale	12	Mortgagor	Yes
Montana	Lien	Mortgage	Judicial	12	Mortgagor	Yes
Nebraska	Lien	Mortgage	Judicial	None	—	No
Nevada	Lien	Mortgage	Power of Sale	None	—	Yes
New Hampshire	Title	Mortgage	Power of Sale	None	—	Yes
New Jersey	Intermediate	Mortgage	Judicial	None	—	No
New Mexico	Lien	Mortgage	Judicial	1	Purchaser	Yes
New York	Lien	Mortgage	Judicial	None	—	Yes
North Carolina	Intermediate	Trust Deed	Power of Sale	None	—	No
North Dakota	Lien	Mortgage	Judicial	12	Mortgagor	Yes
Ohio	Intermediate	Mortgage	Judicial	None	—	Yes
Oklahoma	Lien	Mortgage	Judicial	None	—	Yes
Oregon	Lien	Trust Deed	Power of Sale	None	—	Yes
Pennsylvania	Title	Mortgage	Judicial	None	—	Yes
Rhode Island	Title	Mortgage	Power of Sale	None	—	No
South Carolina	Lien	Mortgage	Judicial	None	—	Yes
South Dakota	Lien	Mortgage	Power of Sale	12	Mortgagor	Yes
Tennessee	Title	Trust Deed	Power of Sale	None	—	No
Texas	Lien	Trust Deed	Power of Sale	None	—	Yes
Utah	Lien	Mortgage	Judicial	6	Mortgagor	Yes
Vermont	Intermediate	Mortgage	Strict Foreclosure	6	Mortgagor	Yes
Virginia	Intermediate	Trust Deed	Power of Sale	None	—	Yes
Washington	Lien	Mortgage	Judicial	12	Purchaser	Yes
West Virginia	Intermediate	Trust Deed	Power of Sale	None	—	Yes
Wisconsin	Lien	Mortgage	Power of Sale	None	—	Yes
Wyoming	Lien	Mortgage	Power of Sale	6	Mortgagor	Yes

CAVEAT This chart only lists the customary form of security instrument used in each state and not all the forms that could be used. Therefore, the method of foreclosure and period of redemption (if allowed) will be listed only for the customary form and not for all possible security instruments. The reader is further cautioned that many states have extensive qualifications and limitations on the period of redemption and for obtaining a delinquency judgment.

Consult a local attorney for details.

Figure 5-9. *State by state comparison of selected aspects of fore-closure.*

Power of Sale

This method is sometimes called *foreclosure by advertisement* since the clause creating a power of sale calls for an advertisement to give notice of the sale. This method is used primarily with deeds of trust, but it can be used with mortgages.

The power to use this method rather than the more cumbersome judicial proceeding comes from a clause that is part of the securing instrument. The clause specifically explains how the sale will be carried out. This method does not preclude a mortgagor's statutory right of redemption if it exists, although many states do not allow such a right if the instrument is a deed of trust.

Foreclosure by advertisement requires procedures which vary among the states. Therefore, extreme care should be taken to insure that proper notice is given and that other requirements are fulfilled. The proceeds from the sale are distributed in the same way as those in a judicial proceeding.

Strict Foreclosure

As mentioned earlier, this was the original method of foreclosure. It is still used in some states which classify themselves as title theory states. The action involves a court of equity and requests a decree giving a mortgagor a period of time to exercise the equitable right of redemption or lose all rights to the property with title vesting irrevocably in the mortgagee. When requesting this type of relief, a mortgagee must be able to prove all allegations just as it must in judicial proceedings.

Entry and Possession

Entry and possession is used only in Maine, Massachusetts, New Hampshire and Rhode Island. After default, a mortgagee gives the mortgagor notice that possession will be taken. If the mortgagor does not agree peacefully to relinquish possession, the mortgagee will have to use a judicial method. This "peaceful possession" needs to be witnessed and recorded. If the mortgagor does not redeem in the statutory period, title vests with the mortgagee.

Deed in Lieu

An alternative to foreclosure which may be of benefit to both the mortgagor and mortgagee would be the execution of a deed transferring the secured real estate to the mortgagee in lieu of foreclosure. The benefits to a mortgagor would include not being subject to the embarrassment of a foreclosure suit or possibly being liable for a deficiency judgment. A mortgagee would benefit by immediately acquiring title to the real estate for a quick sale.

For a deed in lieu to be effective in transferring title, the existing mortgage liability of the mortgagor must be extinguished. If not, the transaction and deed will be considered as nothing more than a new security agreement.

The mortgagee must carefully consider the consequences of this alternative before it is used. If a mortgagee decides to take a deed in lieu of foreclosure, the rights of junior lienholders will not be extinguished. On the other hand, if a mortgagee forecloses, junior lienholders' rights are extinguished if not satisfied by the proceeds of the sale, but the mortgagor has the right of redemption which can be of serious consequence to a mortgagee.

Redemption

In addition to the equity of redemption already discussed, 26 states provide another form of redemption right which begins to accrue to a mortgagor or those claiming through the mortgagor after foreclosure and sale depending on the type of security instrument. This is called the statutory right of redemption because it only exists if created by statute. This redemption period ranges from six months to two years depending on the state.

There are two reasons for a statutory right of redemption: 1) to provide a mortgagor with a chance to keep the real estate, and 2) to encourage bidders at foreclosure sales to bid the market value. The first is more important in agricultural states where a bad growing season can be followed by bumper crops. This right would provide a method for a mortgagor to keep the farm. This same reasoning applies in some income-property situations, but rarely in a residential case. The second reason is equally important for all types of real estate since a bidder at a forced sale would more likely bid the true market value rather than chance later divesture by the mortgagor.

The right of redemption currently has a limited impact on single-family transactions since most of these transactions use a trust deed rather than a mortgage. This makes a difference because many states do not allow the statutory right of redemption with a trust deed based on the concept that a grantor had conveyed all interest to the trustee at the creation of the transaction and consequently had nothing on which to base the redemption.[2] Other states allow it, regardless of what the transaction is called, because if real estate secures a debt, then the transaction is a mortgage and all rights attach. Even if the redemption right exists for a mortgagor, it is seldom exercised by single-family mortgagors who are more likely to sell their property before foreclosure if there is equity to protect.

The right, as previously mentioned, is important to agricultural or income-property mortgagors. If a mortgagor wants to redeem, it must be done within the statutory period by paying the purchaser the price paid at the foreclosure sale, not the outstanding balance on the mortgage, plus interest and costs.

One of the problems inherent with this right usually emerges in a jurisdiction that allows a mortgagor to retain possession during the redemption period. This is necessary if a farmer is to have the advantage of a good year, but it can be catastrophic with income-property if a mortgagor with financial difficulties cannot or will not properly maintain the property. Mortgagees so deeply dread this possibility that many will "trade" their right to a deficiency judgment for immediate possession, possibly by taking a *deed in lieu* of foreclosure.

Other Considerations

In some states, a mortgagee could elect to sue rather than foreclose, based on the promissory note the mortgagor signed. If allowed, the decision might be based on the fact a mortgagee does not believe a forced sale would yield sufficient compensation, but a judgment based on the note could attach to all the debtor's property, and yield full compensation.

Some states allow a mortgagee to sue on the mortgage and force a sale and if not fully compensated, also sue on the note and get a deficiency judgment.

SUGGESTED READINGS

Hebard, Edna L., and Meisel, Gerald S. *Principles of Real Estate Law.* Cambridge, Massachusetts: Schenkman Publishing Co., 1967.

Kratovil, Robert. *Modern Mortgage Law and Practice.* Englewood Cliffs, New Jersey: Prentice-Hall, Inc., 1972.

———. *Real Estate Law.* Englewood Cliffs, New Jersey: Prentice-Hall, Inc., 1974.

Lusk, Harold F. *The Law of the Real Estate Business.* Homewood, Illinois: Richard D. Irwin, Inc., 1975.

NOTES

1. "It is perhaps the normal situation to find any project in foreclosure to be in need of substantial repair. Many mortgagors, during a period of diminishing income, utilize the net income to keep the mortgage current as long as possible, keeping maintenance expenses to a bare minimum. When the evil day arrives that the income will no longer cover the mortgage payments, he falls into default and the subject of the foreclosure action is a property which requires substantial expenditures to place it in properly inhabitable condition, and to make it attractive to the rental market." Court quoting FHA comments in *U.S. vs. Stadium Apartments, Inc., 425F. 2d 358, 365 (1970).*

2. Comment, Comparison of California Mortgages, Trust Deeds, and Land Sales Contracts, *7 U.C.L.A. Law Review* 83 (1959).

Chapter 6

Underwriting the Residential Loan

The term *underwriting* is used in many segments of the American economy to describe the process of analyzing information relating to risk and making a decision whether or not to accept that risk. In real estate, underwriting is an integral part of the mortgage lending process, regardless of the type of loan or the type of property securing the mortgage. Although similarities exist in the underwriting of all types of real estate loans, the differences are fundamental and of great importance. This chapter examines the steps in underwriting a residential loan. The underwriting of an income producing property loan will be covered in Chapter 9, Fundamentals of Income Property Mortgage Lending.

INTRODUCTION

All mortgage loans involve the risk of possible loss to a mortgage lender or investor. The underwriting involved to determine this risk on a residential mortgage loan requires the gathering and analysis of much information about both the applicant and the real estate which will secure the loan.

This underwriting could involve more than just that accomplished by a mortgage lender. On any one residential loan, three separate underwriting reviews could occur at various stages on the mortgage lending cycle:

1. A *mortgage lender* should analyze the risk and determine whether to lend funds to a borrower for a period of time secured by a certain piece of real estate.
2. A *mortgage insuror* or *guarantor* will determine if mortgage insurance is to be written, or a guarantee made based on the loan as submitted.
3. A *permanent investor* will determine if the mortgage or mortgages as submitted will be purchased.

Each of these underwriters will analyze the submission and estimate the risk to the institution being represented and determine if the benefits are sufficient to balance the risk. Mortgage lending is a risk business and a lender must be willing to take a business risk to earn a fee or make a profit and satisfy the real estate financing needs of the nation. All mortgage lenders have a responsibility to attempt to satisfy a request for a mortgage loan as long as the risk is fully analyzed and acceptable. The duty to make a loan if at all possible must be balanced by a mortgage lender's duty to protect funds loaned, which are the savings of depositors or life insurance policy holders.

Of the three mentioned underwriting stages, mortgage lenders have the most difficult underwriting task because they face the delinquency problems that can result from improperly underwritten mortgages. A mortgage company also has a unique problem. Unlike other mortgage lenders, a mortgage company underwrites a loan knowing that loan must be sold to a permanent investor either directly or through the secondary market. If a loan in not attractive as made, a substantial discount may be needed to make it marketable. This can involve considerable loss to a mortgage company. Since most other mortgage lenders have the option of placing mortgages they originate in their own portfolios, their marketing loss potential for a poorly underwritten mortgage is less than that of a mortgage company. All lenders, of course, share the danger that a poorly underwritten mortgage may become delinquent.

If a default occurs, the cost of either curing the default or foreclosing could eliminate present or future profit made from either marketing or servicing. For example, loss could result from a poorly underwritten mortgage if the defaulted loan is in a pool of mortgages securing a GNMA mortgage-backed security. In this situation, the originating mortgage lender must pay the monthly accrued principal and interest to the security holder from its own funds. As is evident, the underwriting phase in the mortgage lending cycle can have a lasting effect, obligating the originating mortgage lender to exercise professional expertise in underwriting.

Unfortunately, no uniform underwriting guidelines exist for all residential mortgage loans. Mortgage lenders have had to adopt and follow different underwriting rules, regulations and formulas depending on whether a residential mortgage loan was conventional (i.e., no government insurance or guarantee), FHA-insured or VA-guaranteed.[1] Many of these differences are not of major significance in underwriting but instead affect loan processing. If a specific difference exists on an important point, it will be explained; otherwise a composite of these underwriting guidelines will be used in this chapter. It is important to realize only guidelines exist, not specific, precise formulas that can be applied to every applicant. Underwriting is an art, not a science, and the successful underwriter is one who can analyze all relevant material and make a mortgage loan if justified while protecting the assets of others.

Government and Underwriting Guidelines

The 1970s witnessed the Federal Government becoming the final arbitrator of underwriting guidelines in its attempt to end all discriminatory practices and reach equalitarian goals in mortgage lending. The burden shifted from an applicant having to demonstrate they were qualified for a mortgage loan to a lender having to establish an applicant was not so qualified. This shift in the burden of proof makes a mortgage lender liable for civil and/or criminal penalties if the letter and spirit of the law are not followed exactly. For a more complete discussion of these developments, see Chapter 13, Government Regulations and Consumer Protection.

INITIAL INTERVIEW

The underwriting process for a residential loan begins with the initial interview between a lender and a potential borrower. The importance of this face-to-face interview cannot be emphasized enough since it allows for counseling if a borrower is attempting to borrow more than he or she can handle. It also allows a mortgage lender to save future time and paperwork if the borrower is obviously not qualified. But, and this must be emphasized, a mortgage lender must allow an application to be made if a borrower desires to make one unless, in the normal course of business, the lender does not extend that type of credit. If application is made, certain disclosures are triggered (ECOA, Truth-in-Lending, RESPA) and an applicant must be notified within 30 days of the outcome of a complete application. These disclosures will be discussed in detail later in this chapter and Chapter 13, Government Regulations and Consumer Protection.

During the interview, a lender should apply the various general guidelines to establish whether the underwriting process should continue. For a lender, these guidelines are not absolute formulas but are used only to assist in establishing whether a borrower is qualified. Typical underwriting guidelines or requirements include:

I. Acceptable ratios for housing expenses and long-term debt.
    A. Housing expenses
        1. Conventional. For a conventional mortgage, the monthly principal, interest, taxes, insurance and others (such as condominium or home-owners' association fees) should *not* exceed 25–28 percent of *gross monthly income.*
        2. FHA. For an FHA mortgage (and similar to a VA guaranteed) the ratio is 35 percent of *net effective income* (gross income minus federal income tax).
    B. Long-term debt
        1. Conventional. For a conventional mortgage, the monthly debt

service, taxes, insurance and other monthly obligations extending beyond 10 months into the future should not exceed 33–36 percent of gross monthly income.

2. FHA. For an FHA mortgage, the monthly debt service, taxes, insurance and other monthly obligations extending beyond 10 months into the future should not exceed 50 percent of net effective income (for this ratio add FICA and state and local income tax to federal income tax when establishing net effective income).

II. Stable employment history

III. Adequate liquid assets for closing and moving expenses

IV. Strong mortgagor motivation

V. Acceptable credit history

VI. Acceptable real estate

These guidelines are derived from the requirements of mortgage insurors, secondary mortgage market institutions or government regulations. The acceptable ratios for conventional mortgages have a slight spread because at the date of publication, FNMA and FHLMC had different published ratios. It is expected a uniform approach will soon reappear.

It should be emphasized again, if an applicant desires to apply for a mortgage loan, the lending officer should not discourage the application. A lending institution should also have a published underwriting and loan policy statement which can be provided to any interested party.

After an application has been made, the underwriting begins in earnest and a mortgage lender will request supporting documentation and necessary verifications. (See Chapter 15, Residential Mortgage Loan Case Studies.)

An underwriter will be particularly interested in:

- Financial capability of a borrower
- Credit characteristics of a borrower
- Real estate securing the mortgage

FINANCIAL CAPABILITY OF THE BORROWER

A borrower's income provides the means for the repayment of the mortgage debt and other household and long-term debts. Not only is current income important, but the prospect for continuation of that income must be determined. The *Request for Verification of Employment* form (Figure 6–2) request from an employer the amount of current income, type of income, tenure of employment and probability of continued employment.

The amount of income usually is not an item of controversy, but the type of income can be. If all income is derived from commissions or bonuses, an obvious problem exists regarding the possibility of lower sales income in a

NAME OF FINANCIAL INSTITUTION
1234 Street
Your City, State 00000

RESIDENTIAL LOAN APPLICATION

MORTGAGE APPLIED FOR	Amount	Interest Rate	No. of Months	Monthly Payment Principal & Interest	Escrow/Impounds (to be collected monthly)
☐ Conventional ☐ FHA ☐ VA	$	%		$	☐ Taxes ☐ Hazard Ins. ☐ Mtg. Ins. ☐

Prepayment Option

SUBJECT PROPERTY

Property Street Address	City	County	State	Zip	No. Units

Legal Description (Attach description if necessary)   Year Built

Purpose of Loan: ☐ Purchase ☐ Construction-Permanent ☐ Construction ☐ Refinance ☐ Other (Explain)

Complete this line if Construction-Permanent or Construction Loan

Lot Value Data	Original Cost	Present Value (a)	Cost of Imps. (b)	Total (a + b)	ENTER TOTAL AS PURCHASE PRICE IN DETAILS OF PURCHASE.
Year Acquired $	$	$	$		

Complete this line if a Refinance Loan

Year Acquired	Original Cost	Amt. Existing Liens	Purpose of Refinance	Describe Improvements [ ] made [ ] to be made
$	$			Cost $

Title Will Be Held In What Name(s)	Manner In Which Title Will Be Held

Source of Down Payment and Settlement Charges

This application is designed to be completed by the borrower(s) with the lender's assistance. The Co-Borrower Section and all other Co-Borrower questions must be completed and the appropriate box(es) checked if ☐ another person will be jointly obligated with the Borrower on the loan, or ☐ the Borrower is relying on income from alimony, child support or separate maintenance or on the income or assets of another person as a basis for repayment of the loan, or ☐ the Borrower is married and resides, or the property is located, in a community property state.

BORROWER				CO-BORROWER		
Name		Age	School Yrs	Name	Age	School Yrs
Present Address No. Years ☐ Own ☐ Rent				Present Address No. Years ☐ Own ☐ Rent		
Street				Street		
City/State/Zip				City/State/Zip		
Former address if less than 2 years at present address				Former address if less than 2 years at present address		
Street				Street		
City/State/Zip				City/State/Zip		
Years at former address ☐ Own ☐ Rent				Years at former address ☐ Own ☐ Rent		

Marital Status	☐ Married ☐ Separated ☐ Unmarried (incl. single, divorced, widowed)	DEPENDENTS OTHER THAN LISTED BY CO BORROWER NO. AGES	Marital Status	☐ Married ☐ Separated ☐ Unmarried (incl. single, divorced, widowed)	DEPENDENTS OTHER THAN LISTED BY BORROWER NO. AGES

Name and Address of Employer	Years employed in this line of work or profession? ___ years Years on this job ___ ☐ Self Employed*	Name and Address of Employer	Years employed in this line of work or profession? ___ years Years on this job ___ ☐ Self Employed*

Position/Title	Type of Business	Position/Title	Type of Business

Social Security Number***	Home Phone	Business Phone	Social Security Number***	Home Phone	Business Phone

GROSS MONTHLY INCOME				MONTHLY HOUSING EXPENSE **			DETAILS OF PURCHASE	
Item	Borrower	Co-Borrower	Total		PRESENT	PROPOSED	Do Not Complete If Refinance	
Base Empl. Income	$	$	$	Rent	$		a. Purchase Price	$
Overtime				First Mortgage (P&I)		$	b. Total Closing Costs (Est.)	
Bonuses				Other Financing (P&I)			c. Prepaid Escrows (Est.)	
Commissions				Hazard Insurance			d. Total (a + b + c)	$
Dividends/Interest				Real Estate Taxes			e. Amount This Mortgage	
Net Rental Income				Mortgage Insurance			f. Other Financing	( )
Other† (Before completing, see notice under Describe Other Income below.)				Homeowner Assn. Dues			g. Other Equity	( )
				Other:			h. Amount of Cash Deposit	( )
				Total Monthly Pmt.	$	$	i. Closing Costs Paid by Seller	( )
				Utilities			j. Cash Reqd. For Closing (Est.)	$
Total	$	$	$	Total	$	$		

DESCRIBE OTHER INCOME

◁ B—Borrower C—Co-Borrower

NOTICE:† Alimony, child support, or separate maintenance income need not be revealed if the Borrower or Co-Borrower does not choose to have it considered as a basis for repaying this loan.

	Monthly Amount
	$

IF EMPLOYED IN CURRENT POSITION FOR LESS THAN TWO YEARS COMPLETE THE FOLLOWING

B/C	Previous Employer/School	City/State	Type of Business	Position/Title	Dates From/To	Monthly Income
						$

THESE QUESTIONS APPLY TO BOTH BORROWER AND CO-BORROWER

If a "yes" answer is given to a question in this column, explain on an attached sheet.	Borrower Yes or No	Co-Borrower Yes or No	If applicable, explain Other Financing or Other Equity (provide addendum if more space is needed).
Have you any outstanding judgments? In the last 7 years, have you been declared bankrupt?			
Have you had property foreclosed upon or given title or deed in lieu thereof?			
Are you a co-maker or endorser on a note?			
Are you a party in a law suit?			
Are you obligated to pay alimony, child support, or separate maintenance?			
Is any part of the down payment borrowed?			

*FHLMC/FNMA require business credit report, signed Federal Income Tax returns for last two years, and, if available, audited Profit and Loss Statements plus balance sheet for same period.

**All Present Monthly Housing Expenses of Borrower and Co-Borrower should be listed on a combined basis.

***Neither FHLMC nor FNMA requires this information.

FHLMC 65 Rev. 8/78   FNMA 1003 Rev. 8/78

Figure 6-1.   *FNMA/FHLMC residential loan application.*

This Statement and any applicable supporting schedules may be completed jointly by both married and unmarried co-borrowers if their assets and liabilities are sufficiently joined so that the Statement can be meaningfully and fairly presented on a combined basis; otherwise separate Statements and Schedules are required (FHLMC 65A/FNMA 1003A). If the co-borrower section was completed about a spouse, this statement and supporting schedules must be completed about that spouse also. ☐ Completed Jointly ☐ Not Completed Jointly

ASSETS		LIABILITIES AND PLEDGED ASSETS			
Indicate by (*) those liabilities or pledged assets which will be satisfied upon sale of real estate owned or upon refinancing of subject property					
Description	Cash or Market Value	Creditors' Name, Address and Account Number	Acct. Name if Not Borrower's	Mo. Pmt. and Mos. left to pay	Unpaid Balance
Cash Deposit Toward Purchase Held By	$	Installment Debts (include "revolving" charge accts)		$ Pmt./Mos.	$
Checking and Savings Accounts (Show Names of Institutions/Acct. Nos.)				/	
Stocks and Bonds (No./Description)				/	
Life Insurance Net Cash Value Face Amount ($)		Other Debts Including Stock Pledges		/	
SUBTOTAL LIQUID ASSETS	$				
Real Estate Owned (Enter Market Value from Schedule of Real Estate Owned)		Real Estate Loans		/	
Vested Interest in Retirement Fund					
Net Worth of Business Owned (ATTACH FINANCIAL STATEMENT)					
Automobiles (Make and Year)		Automobile Loans		/	
Furniture and Personal Property		Alimony, Child Support and Separate Maintenance Payments Owed To		/	
Other Assets (Itemize)					
		TOTAL MONTHLY PAYMENTS		$	
TOTAL ASSETS	A $	NET WORTH (A minus B) $		TOTAL LIABILITIES	B $

SCHEDULE OF REAL ESTATE OWNED (If Additional Properties Owned Attach Separate Schedule)							
Address of Property (Indicate S if Sold, PS if Pending Sale or R if Rental being held for income)	Type of Property	Present Market Value	Amount of Mortgages & Liens	Gross Rental Income	Mortgage Payments	Taxes, Ins. Maintenance and Misc.	Net Rental Income
		$	$	$	$	$	$
TOTALS →		$	$	$	$	$	$

LIST PREVIOUS CREDIT REFERENCES

B–Borrower C–Co-Borrower	Creditor's Name and Address	Account Number	Purpose	Highest Balance	Date Paid
				$	

List any additional names under which credit has previously been received _____

AGREEMENT   The undersigned applies for the loan indicated in this application to be secured by a first mortgage or deed of trust on the property described herein, and represents that the property will not be used for any illegal or restricted purpose, and that all statements made in this application are true and are made for the purpose of obtaining the loan. Verification may be obtained from any source named in this application. The original or a copy of this application will be retained by the lender, even if the loan is not granted   The undersigned ☐ intend or ☐ do not intend to occupy the property as their primary residence

I/we fully understand that it is a federal crime punishable by fine or imprisonment, or both, to knowingly make any false statements concerning any of the above facts as applicable under the provisions of Title 18, United States Code, Section 1014.

_____ Date _____   _____ Date _____
Borrower's Signature   Co-Borrower's Signature

INFORMATION FOR GOVERNMENT MONITORING PURPOSES

The following information is requested by the Federal Government if this loan is related to a dwelling, in order to monitor the lender's compliance with equal credit opportunity and fair housing laws. You are not required to furnish this information, but are encouraged to do so. The law provides that a lender may neither discriminate on the basis of this information, nor on whether you choose to furnish it. However, if you choose not to furnish it, under Federal regulations this lender is required to note race and sex on the basis of visual observation or surname. If you do not wish to furnish the above information, please initial below

BORROWER: I do not wish to furnish this information (initials) _____   **CO-BORROWER:** I do not wish to furnish this information (initials) _____

RACE/ ☐ American Indian, Alaskan Native ☐ Asian, Pacific Islander   RACE/ ☐ American Indian, Alaskan Native ☐ Asian, Pacific Islander
NATIONAL ☐ Black ☐ Hispanic ☐ White SEX: ☐ Female   NATIONAL ☐ Black ☐ Hispanic ☐ White SEX: ☐ Female
ORIGIN ☐ Other (specify) _____ ☐ Male   ORIGIN ☐ Other (specify) _____ ☐ Male

FOR LENDER'S USE ONLY

(FNMA REQUIREMENT ONLY) This application was taken by ☐ face to face interview ☐ by mail ☐ by telephone

_____   _____
(Interviewer)   Name of Employer of Interviewer

FHLMC 65 Rev. 8/78   REVERSE   FNMA 1003 Rev. 8/78

Figure 6-1.   *Continued.*

Federal National Mortgage Association

REQUEST FOR VERIFICATION OF EMPLOYMENT

FNMA

INSTRUCTIONS: LENDER- Complete items 1 thru 7. Have applicant complete item 8. Forward directly to employer named in item 1.
EMPLOYER-Please complete either Part II or Part III as applicable. Sign and return directly to lender named in item 2.

PART I - REQUEST

1. TO *(Name and address of employer)*	2. FROM *(Name and address of lender)*		
3. SIGNATURE OF LENDER	4. TITLE	5. DATE	6. LENDER'S NUMBER *(optional)*

I have applied for a mortgage loan and stated that I am now or was formerly employed by you. My signature below authorizes verification of this information.

7. NAME AND ADDRESS OF APPLICANT *(Include employee or badge number)*	8. SIGNATURE OF APPLICANT

PART II - VERIFICATION OF PRESENT EMPLOYMENT

EMPLOYMENT DATA	PAY DATA		

| 9. APPLICANT'S DATE OF EMPLOYMENT | 12A. CURRENT BASE PAY (Enter Amount and Check Period) ☐ ANNUAL ☐ HOURLY ☐ MONTHLY ☐ OTHER $ _____ ☐ WEEKLY *(Specify)* | 12C. FOR MILITARY PERSONNEL ONLY | |

PAY GRADE

10. PRESENT POSITION		TYPE	MONTHLY AMOUNT
	12B. EARNINGS	BASE PAY	$
11. PROBABILITY OF CONTINUED EMPLOYMENT	TYPE / YEAR TO DATE / PAST YEAR	RATIONS	$
13. IF OVERTIME OR BONUS IS APPLICABLE, IS ITS CONTINUANCE LIKELY?	BASE PAY $ / $	FLIGHT OR HAZARD	$
	OVERTIME $ / $	CLOTHING	$
	COMMISSIONS $ / $	QUARTERS	$
OVERTIME ☐ YES ☐ NO		PRO PAY	$
BONUS ☐ YES ☐ NO	BONUS $ / $	OVER SEAS OR COMBAT	$

14. REMARKS *(if paid hourly, please indicate average hours worked each week during current and past year)*

PART III - VERIFICATION OF PREVIOUS EMPLOYMENT

15. DATES OF EMPLOYMENT	16. SALARY/WAGE AT TERMINATION PER (Year) (Month) (Week) BASE _____ OVERTIME _____ COMMISSIONS _____ BONUS _____
17. REASON FOR LEAVING	18. POSITION HELD

19. SIGNATURE OF EMPLOYER	20. TITLE	21. DATE

The confidentiality of the information you have furnished will be preserved except where disclosure of this information is required by applicable law. The form is to be transmitted directly to the lender and is not to be transmitted through the applicant or any other party.

PREVIOUS EDITION WILL BE USED UNTIL STOCK IS EXHAUSTED

FNMA Form 1005
Rev. June 78

Figure 6-2. *Request for verification of employment.*

subsequent year which would not support the continuation of the commission income at the present level. As a rule, if the past two or three years establish the current level as "normal," the income should be given full consideration. If income derived from overtime or part-time work is necessary to qualify the loan, a lender should establish whether the additional income is expected to continue and whether the amount of that income is reasonable for the additional employment.

Self-employed applicants should be required to furnish a balance sheet and profit and loss statements in addition to a copy of federal income tax returns for the last two or three years to support the claim of income received. Tax returns also may be requested in other situations to verify income claims, such as if income from securities is the main support for mortgage payments.

Following the 1976 amendments to the *Equal Credit Opportunity Act* (ECOA), a mortgage lender must consider all types of income, including public assistances, when determining the sufficiency of income. This will be discussed in detail later.

FHA-insured Mortgage

HUD-FHA uses *net effective income,* or monthly income minus estimated federal income tax, in analyzing a mortgagor's financial capacity for an FHA-insured loan. HUD-FHA applies a guideline of 35 percent of net effective income as the maximum amount that should be applied to housing expense. (VA guidelines are approximately the same as HUD-FHA).

Housing expenses, according to HUD-FHA regulations, include:

- Principal and interest
- Mortgage insurance
- Hazard insurance
- Taxes and special assessments
- Maintenance
- Utilities
- Homeowner association fees

Conventional Mortgage

A conventional mortgage is one with no government insurance or guarantee. A conventional mortgage utilizes *gross monthly income,* which is income before any deductions, in analyzing a mortgagor's financial capacity to carry the mortgage debt. The suggested guideline is that principal, interest, taxes and insurance, and homeowner's association fees if applicable, should not exceed 25–28 percent of gross monthly income.

Long-term Debts

It is recognized that different mortgagors with the same income and the same housing expenses may have other financial obligations which will affect their future financial capacity. The permissible ratio of these other liabilities against income varies according to the type of mortgage sought. For an FHA-insured mortgage, the guideline suggests prospective housing expenses and other recurring expenses should not exceed 50 percent of net effective income. (To establish net effective income for this ratio, subtract FICA, state and local income tax in addition to federal income tax from gross income.) FHA defines recurring expenses as those extending a year or more into the future. For a conventional mortgage, the relationship of total monthly obligations (obligations extending beyond 10 months into the future) should not exceed 33–36 percent of gross monthly income.

CREDIT CHARACTERISTICS OF THE BORROWER

Of great concern to any mortgage lender is the answer to the question of the status of the applicant's credit record. If an applicant has demonstrated an inability to handle financial obligations, the amount of current income and its relationship to outstanding obligations is more crucial. In some situations, a mortgage lender may not be able to justify a loan to an applicant regardless of current income because of past credit problems. In all situations, an applicant should be given the opportunity to explain and possibly justify credit problems.

A mortgage lender must be aware of two important limitations on credit information gathering. The first is the *Fair Credit Reporting Act*[2] which is designed to insure fair and accurate reporting of information regarding consumer credit. A mortgage lender seeking credit information from a consumer reporting agency must certify the purpose for which the information is sought and use it for no other purpose. The act prohibits investigative reports which are based on interviews with neighbors and others relating to character, general reputation, mode of living and other subjective areas. Certain previous credit information (such as a bankruptcy more than seven years before) is also prohibited unless the principal is $50,000 or more. If credit is denied, the consumer must be notified if the denial is based on information contained in a credit report.

A more recent federal law of far reaching effect is the *Equal Credit Opportunity Act* (ECOA)[3] which became law on October 28, 1975 and was substantially changed by amendments effective March 23, 1977. ECOA prohibits a creditor from discriminating in the extending of credit based on:

- Race
- Color
- National origin

- Sex
- Marital Status
- Age (provided borrower can legally contract)
- The fact that all or part of income is derived from a public assistance program

A loan application form may ask if the applicant is unmarried, married or separated, but not whether the applicant is divorced. Questions concerning an applicant's spouse are prohibited unless:

- Spouse will be contractually liable
- Spouse's income will be used to qualify
- Applicants live in a community property state
- Applicant will use child support, alimony or separate maintenance payments from a spouse or former spouse to qualify

Questions concerning fertility, birth control practices or the possibility of children in the future may not be asked, although the age and current number of children may be asked.

The act further states that no classification of income such as part-time or retirement may be rejected automatically, but must be analyzed in view of its probable continuation. In addition, if a woman's income is being relied upon, it cannot be assumed she will become pregnant or, that it will prevent further employment if she does.

Finally, a mortgage lender must notify an applicant within 30 days of receipt of a completed application whether the loan has been approved substantially as submitted or rejected. If the loan is rejected, the applicant must be informed of the specific reasons. (See Figure 6–3.)

Within the legal framework of the credit information limitations, a mortgage lender should gather as much information as possible on an applicant's credit record. The analysis of the information supplied in a credit report by a reputable reporting agency (Figure 6–4) should be directed at four key areas:

1. History of past credit: how much credit has the applicant had and what have been the repayment terms?
2. Type of credit: has the applicant had a past real estate loan, an auto loan or other installment type loans?
3. Attitude toward credit: are the active accounts current, and is there any recent bankruptcy or judgment?
4. Lapses in employment or debt repayment history: how many unexplained lapses, and for how long?

DATE _____

Applicant's Name: _____

Applicant's Address: _____

Description of Account, Transaction, or Requested Credit: _____

_____

Description of Adverse Action Taken: _____

_____

_____

PRINCIPAL REASON(S) FOR ADVERSE ACTION CONCERNING CREDIT

☐ Credit application incomplete
☐ Insufficient credit references
☐ Unable to verify credit references
☐ Temporary or irregular employment
☐ Unable to verify employment
☐ Length of employment
☐ Insufficient income
☐ Excessive obligations
☐ Unable to verify income
☐ Inadequate collateral
☐ We do not grant credit to any applicant on the terms and conditions you request.
☐ Other, specify: _____

_____

☐ Too short a period of residence
☐ Temporary residence
☐ Unable to verify residence
☐ No credit file
☐ Insufficient credit file
☐ Delinquent credit obligations
☐ Garnishment, attachment, foreclosure, repossession, or suit
☐ Bankruptcy

DISCLOSURE OF USE OF INFORMATION OBTAINED FROM AN OUTSIDE SOURCE

☐ Disclosure inapplicable
☐ Information obtained in a report from a consumer reporting agency

Name: _____

Street Address: _____

_____

Phone: _____

☐ Information obtained from an outside source other than a consumer reporting agency. Under the Fair Credit Reporting Act, you have the right to make a written request, within 60 days of receipt of this notice, for disclosure of the nature of the adverse information.

Creditor's name: _____

Creditor's address: _____

_____

Creditor's telephone number: _____

Figure 6–3. *Statement of credit denial, termination, or change.*

EQUIFAX / RETAILERS COMMERCIAL AGENCY   CONFIDENTIAL

MORTGAGE LOAN REPORT   SPECIMEN - ALL ENTITIES FICTITIOUS

Acct. No. 00000	Report Made By Equifax ☐ Retailers ☒ Atlanta OFFICE
Date 00-0-00	REPORT FROM_____
NAME (& Spouse) JONES, RICHARD C. (JULIA)	*(If not city in heading)* *(State whether former addr., etc.)*
Address Atlanta, Ga., 234 Lark Street	Case or File Number___ M-276589
Emp-Occ. XYZ Corporation - Manager	
Bus. Add. Atlanta, Ga., 456 Peachtree St.	Property Address 18 Meadow Lane, Atlanta, Ga.

1. Time known by each source?   1. 3yrs., 5yrs., Intv. Wife
2. Are name & addresses correct as given?   2. Yes
3. About what is age? (If around 21, verify if possible.)   3. 34
4. Is applicant married? How long married? No. dependents (including spouse)?   4. Yes   How long? 7yrs.   No. of deps.? 3
5. Name of Employer.   5. XYZ Corporation
6. What is nature of business? (State kind of trade or industry.)   6. Building Material Mfg.
7. Position held—how long with present employer?   7. Manager   How long? 5yrs.
8. Is present employment reasonably secure?   8. Yes
9. Work full time steadily? (If not, how many days per week?)   9. Yes
10. Employment *status* changed within the past two years?   10. No
11. Annual earned income from employment or business?   11. $ 17,000 Exact ☒   Estimated ☐
12. Approximate annual income, if any, from other sources. (Investments, rentals, pensions.)   12. $ 250   Source: Invest.
13. What would you estimate net worth?   13. $ 35,000
14. Does applicant own home or rent?   14. Own Home
15. If rents home, what is amount of monthly rental?   15. $ -
16. If spouse employed, give name of employer.   16. Housewife
17. Position held—approximate ANNUAL INCOME.   17. -   Income $___-___
18. Approximate number of years employed.   18. -
19. Do you learn of any failures, bankruptcies, mortgage foreclosures, suits, judgments or garnishments? (If so, state which. Give details.)   19. None

SPECIMEN All entities fictitious (watermark)

REMARKS: (Please write a separate paragraph on each)

20. CREDIT RECORD: Set out CREDIT RECORD in tabular form below.

21. BUSINESS—FINANCES: Cover business history for minimum of two years. If any change in employment within 2 years, list names and locations of former connection. Cover financial position, giving breakdown on worth. Cover income from investments, rentals, pensions, etc., showing source and regularity.

22. RESIDENCE: Show how long subject has lived at this address and former addresses if developed. Comment when information developed on credit responsibility or financial difficulties may affect earnings or paying ability. (DO NOT REPORT INVESTIGATIVE CONSUMER INFORMATION.)

Trade Line	How Long Selling	Date Last Sale	Highest Credit	Terms of Sale	Amount Owing	Amount Past Due	Paying Record
Bank-Mtge.	6-73	–	$26,102	$96.45/Mo.	$21,472	None	Satis.-J
Dept. Store	4-75	5-78	550	Revolving	None	None	30 Day Slow-I
Bank-Auto	3-77	–	4,000	100/Mo.	2,200	$100	30 Day Slow-J
Oil Card	7-75	4-78	76	Revolving	None	None	Prompt-I

BUSINESS-FINANCES: Richard C. Jones is employed as a manager for the XYZ Corporation at the above captioned address and has been so employed for the past 5 years, earning $17,000 per year as verified by employer. Subject has $250 annual additional income from stock dividends. The subject's net worth consists of equity in home, savings, automobile and household effects.

RESIDENCE: The subject is married to Julia for the past 7 years and has two children, ages 5 years and 3 years. They have resided at 234 Lark Street, Atlanta, Ga. for the past 5 years where they are buying.

WFG/st
2cc

Equifax Inc.
Form 1667—2-76 U.S.A.

Figure 6–4. *Sample credit report for mortgage loan purposes. (Use of this form a courtesy of Retailers Commercial Agency, Inc., Atlanta, Georgia.)*

AVAILABLE ASSETS

The size of the equity or down payment is of great importance to an underwriter. The experience of many investors has shown that less risk is present in loans with a higher equity or down payment. The applicant must have sufficient assets not only to make the required down payment, but to close the transaction as well. Sufficient assets for both can be ascertained by a *Request for Verification of Deposit* (Figure 6-5). In some situations, a down payment may be made from funds supplied by parents or relatives of the applicants. This is acceptable as long as funds are legally a gift not to be repaid and the donors sign an affidavit to that effect (Figure 6-6).

REAL ESTATE SECURING THE MORTGAGE

The third stage in underwriting a residential mortgage loan involves an analysis of the real estate which will secure the mortgage debt. Although it is expected that the income of a borrower will be available to fulfill the mortgage obligation, a mortgage lender must protect both its own position and that of any investor, if applicable, by having adequate security for the debt. The adequacy of the security will be established by an appraisal. (See Figure 11-2.)

An appraisal is an opinion or estimate of value made by an appraiser who is either an independent fee appraiser or employed by a mortgage lender. The appraisal not only helps establish the adequacy of the security but also establishes the value of the security upon which the loan-to-value ratio will be applied.[4] (See Chapter 11, Appraising Real Estate for Mortgage Loan Purposes.)

An underwriter will use the appraisal and other information—such as city growth plan—to evaluate the following:

1. *Physical security.* The age, equipment, architectural design, quality of construction, floor plan and site features are considered in establishing the adequacy and future value of the physical security.

2. *Location.* The type of neighborhood in which the subject property is located, its condition and its proximity to amenities is of paramount importance. The availability of public transportation and public utilities will add to the attractiveness of the location. A mortgage lender must be careful that the appraisal report does not produce a discriminatory result by a general negative stance being taken in regard to a particular neighborhood.

3. *Local government.* The amount of property tax can have a great effect on future marketability. Building codes, deed restrictions and zoning ordinances help to maintain housing standards and promote a high degree of homogeneity.

FNMA

Federal National Mortgage Association
REQUEST FOR VERIFICATION OF DEPOSIT

INSTRUCTIONS: LENDER - Complete Items 1 thru 8. Have applicant(s) complete Item 9. Forward directly to depository named in Item 1.
DEPOSITORY - Please complete Items 10 thru 15 and return DIRECTLY to lender named in Item 2.

PART I - REQUEST

1. TO (Name and address of depository)	2. FROM (Name and address of lender)

3. SIGNATURE OF LENDER	4. TITLE	5. DATE	6. LENDER'S NUMBER (Optional)

7. INFORMATION TO BE VERIFIED

TYPE OF ACCOUNT	ACCOUNT IN NAME OF	ACCOUNT NUMBER	BALANCE
			$
			$
			$
			$

TO DEPOSITORY: I have applied for a mortgage loan and stated in my financial statement that the balance on deposit with you is as shown above. You are authorized to verify this information and to supply the lender identified above with the information requested in Items 10 thru 12. Your response is solely a matter of courtesy for which no responsibility is attached to your institution or any of your officers.

8. NAME AND ADDRESS OF APPLICANT(s)	9. SIGNATURE OF APPLICANT(s)

TO BE COMPLETED BY DEPOSITORY

PART II - VERIFICATION OF DEPOSITORY

10. DEPOSIT ACCOUNTS OF APPLICANT(s)

TYPE OF ACCOUNT	ACCOUNT NUMBER	CURRENT BALANCE	AVERAGE BALANCE FOR PREVIOUS TWO MONTHS	DATE OPENED
		$	$	
		$	$	
		$	$	
		$	$	

11. LOANS OUTSTANDING TO APPLICANT(s)

LOAN NUMBER	DATE OF LOAN	ORIGINAL AMOUNT	CURRENT BALANCE	INSTALLMENTS (Monthly/Quarterly)	SECURED BY	NUMBER OF LATE PAYMENTS
		$	$	$ per		
		$	$	$ per		
		$	$	$ per		

12. ADDITIONAL INFORMATION WHICH MAY BE OF ASSISTANCE IN DETERMINATION OF CREDIT WORTHINESS:
(Please include information on loans paid-in-full as in Item 11 above)

13. SIGNATURE OF DEPOSITORY	14. TITLE	15. DATE

The confidentiality of the information you have furnished will be preserved except where disclosure of this information is required by applicable law. The form is to be transmitted directly to the lender and is not to be transmitted through the applicant or any other party.

PREVIOUS EDITION WILL BE USED UNTIL STOCK IS EXHAUSTED

FNMA Form 1006
Rev. June 78

Figure 6–5. *Request for verification of deposit.*

GIFT LETTER

TO WHOM IT MAY CONCERN:

I, _____ , do hereby certify that I have
        donor

made a gift of $_____ to my _____
                                relationship

to be applied toward the purchase of the property located at

_____

I further certify that there is no repayment expected or implied
on this gift either in the form of cash or future services from

_____ and/or _____
       recipient   co-recipient

_____
               donor

Date _____

ACKNOWLEDGMENT

I, _____ , and I, _____

hereby certify to the receipt of the gift made by_____

in the amount of $_____to be applied toward the purchase of

the referenced property.

_____
Purchaser

_____
Purchaser

Date_____

Figure 6-6. *Typical gift letter.*

UNDERWRITING WORKSHEET

	Verified	Acceptable
I. Financial Capability		
A. Of the applicant		_____
1. Primary employment	_____	_____
2. Self-employed	_____	_____
3. Secondary employment	_____	_____
4. Other income	_____	_____
B. Of the co-applicant (if any)		_____
1. Primary employment	_____	_____
2. Self-employed	_____	_____
3. Secondary employment	_____	_____
4. Other income	_____	_____
II. Credit Characteristics		_____
A. Past real estate loans	_____	_____
B. Installment loans	_____	_____
C. Bankruptcy, judgments	_____	_____
D. Lapses	_____	_____
III. Real Estate (Security)		_____
A. Structure		_____
1. Age ____ years		_____
2. Amenities		_____
3. Condition		_____
B. Neighborhood		_____
C. Local Government		_____

Figure 6–7. *Underwriting worksheet.*

LOAN ANALYSIS

LOAN NUMBER

SECTION A – LOAN DATA

1. NAME OF BORROWER	2. AMOUNT OF LOAN $	3. CASH DOWN PAYMENT ON PURCHASE PRICE $

SECTION B – BORROWER'S PERSONAL AND FINANCIAL STATUS

4. APPLICANT'S AGE	5. OCCUPATION OF APPLICANT	6. NUMBER OF YEARS AT PRESENT EMPLOYMENT	7. LIQUID ASSETS (Cash savings, bonds, etc.) $	8. CURRENT MONTHLY RENTAL OR OTHER HOUSING EXPENSE $
9. IS SPOUSE EMPLOYED? ☐ YES ☐ NO	10. SPOUSE'S AGE	11. OCCUPATION OF SPOUSE	12. NUMBER OF YEARS AT PRESENT EMPLOYMENT	13. AGE OF OTHER DEPENDENTS

SECTION C – ESTIMATED MONTHLY SHELTER EXPENSES (This Property)

SECTION D – DEBTS AND OBLIGATIONS (Itemize and indicate by (√) which debts considered in Section E, Line 42)

	ITEMS	AMOUNT		ITEMS	(√)	MO. PAYMENT	UNPAID BAL.
14.	TERM OF LOAN: YEARS		23.			$	$
15.	MORTGAGE PAYMENT (P&I)(@____%)	$	24.				
16.	REALTY TAXES		25.				
17.	HAZARD INSURANCE		26.				
18.	SPECIAL ASSESSMENTS		27.				
19.	MAINTENANCE		28.				
20.	UTILITIES (Including heat)		29.				
21.	OTHER		30.	JOB RELATED EXPENSE (Child care, etc.)			
22.	TOTAL	$	31.	TOTAL	$		$

SECTION E – MONTHLY INCOME AND DEDUCTIONS

	ITEMS		SPOUSE	BORROWER	TOTAL
32.	GROSS SALARY OR EARNINGS FROM EMPLOYMENT		$	$	$
33.	DEDUCTIONS	FEDERAL INCOME TAX			
34.		STATE INCOME TAX			
35.		RETIREMENT OR SOCIAL SECURITY			
36.		OTHER (Specify)			
37.		TOTAL DEDUCTIONS	$	$	$
38.	NET TAKE-HOME PAY				$
39.	PENSION COMPENSATION OR OTHER NET INCOME (Specify)				
40.	TOTAL (Sum of lines 38 and 39)		$	$	$
41.	LESS THOSE OBLIGATIONS LISTED IN SECTION D WHICH SHOULD BE DEDUCTED FROM INCOME				
42.	TOTAL NET EFFECTIVE INCOME				$
43.	LESS ESTIMATED MONTHLY SHELTER EXPENSE (Line 22)				
44.	BALANCE AVAILABLE FOR FAMILY SUPPORT				$

45. PAST CREDIT RECORD ☐ SATISFACTORY ☐ UNSATISFACTORY	46. DOES LOAN MEET VA CREDIT STANDARDS? (Give reasons for decision under "Remarks," if necessary, e.g., borderline cases) ☐ YES ☐ NO

47. REMARKS (Use reverse, if necessary)

SECTION F – DISPOSITION OF APPLICATION

☐ Recommend that the application be approved since it meets all requirements of Chapter 37, Title 38, U.S. Code and applicable VA Regulations and directives.

☐ Recommend that the application be disapproved for the reasons stated under "Remarks" above.

48. DATE	49. SIGNATURE OF EXAMINER
50. FINAL ACTION ☐ APPROVE APPLICATION ☐ REJECT APPLICATION	51. DATE	52. SIGNATURE AND TITLE OF APPROVING OFFICIAL

VA FORM **26-6393**
SEP 1974

EXISTING STOCK OF VA FORM 26-6393, JUL 1973, WILL BE USED.

Figure 6-8. *VA loan analysis form.*

THE UNDERWRITING DECISION

When all information relating to a borrower's financial capabilities, credit characteristics and the physical security are present a decision must be made to accept, reject or modify the mortgage loan application.

All of the items must be reviewed individually and in conjunction with other items being considered. For example, a number of credit characteristics may have deficiencies that are not serious when considered alone, but when combined with other characteristics could affect a mortgagor's ability or willingness to pay, possibly leading to a future default. Although all underwriters should attempt to approve a loan application if at all prudently possible, the approval of a loan that will become delinquent is a disservice to the borrower, the mortgage lender and those it represents.

SUGGESTED READINGS

Pease, Robert H., and Kerwood, Lewis O., eds. *Mortgage Banking.* New York: McGraw-Hill Book Co., Inc., 1965.

Shenkel, William M. *Modern Real Estate Principles.* Dallas, Texas: Business Publications, Inc., 1977.

————. *Real Estate Finance.* Washington, D.C.: American Bankers Association, 1976.

Unger, Maurice A. *Real Estate.* Cincinnati, Ohio: South-Western Publishing Co., 1974.

Weimer, Arthur M., Hoyt, Homer, and Bloom, George F. *Real Estate* (7th ed.). New York: John Wiley & Sons, 1978.

NOTES

1. For FHA-insured single-family mortgage, see HUD Handbook, *Mortgage Credit Analysis Handbook* (4155.1), July 1972 as amended pages 1–29. For VA-guaranteed mortgage, see VA *Lenders Handbook,* December 1969.

2. Effective April 25, 1971, Title VI of the *Consumer Credit Protection Act,* as amended, 15 USC 1601 et. seq.

3. Also known as *Regulation B,* effective March 23, 1977, Title VII of the *Consumer Credit Protection Act,* as amended, 15 USC 1601 et. seq. Please note: This brief review is *not* intended in any way to be a complete discussion of ECOA. Competent counsel should be consulted concerning all laws governing the granting of credit in your jurisdiction.

4. All financial institutions are limited by federal or state laws to certain loan-to-value ratios for loans in their portfolios.

Chapter 7

Secondary Mortgage Markets and Institutions

INTRODUCTION

One of the most important reasons for the sharp increase in real estate lending activity since the end of World War II has been the demand for and the general availability of mortgage money at reasonable rates. The demand resulted from both the pent-up housing market of the Depression and war years, and the movement to and population growth in the sunbelt states. These areas did not have sufficient capital to meet the demand; therefore, availability of capital was essential to continued growth. This availability, although sporadic at times, has been largely the result of the development of a secondary market for mortgages. During periods of tight money or credit restraints such as existed in 1969–70, 1974, and 1979–81, the activity of the secondary market accounted for a large portion of the residential lending that did occur. Today, the activity of the secondary market provides the foundation for all mortgage lending with yearly transactions approximating $22 billion.

Primary vs. Secondary

The distinction between what is known as the *primary* and *secondary* mortgage markets is not always clear, and one is often used to describe activity in the other. The term *secondary market* is not used often in regard to income-property loan mortgage transactions, although the possibility exists for a true income-property loan secondary market in the future.

Most authorities agree that a primary market exists when a lender extends funds directly to a borrower. This would occur whether the lender is originating the mortgages for its own portfolio (e.g., most thrift institutions) or for sale to another investor (e.g., a mortgage company). (See Chapters 3 and 4, The Mortgage Lenders).

The secondary market exists when primary lenders and permanent investors buy and sell existing mortgages from each other. This activity could occur as part of the normal course of business for the mortgage lender, or be utilized only during periods of credit restraints.

> "The secondary market for residential mortgages is that part of the mortgage market in which existing mortgages are bought and sold. The primary market, on the other hand, is that part of the market in which mortgages are originated. Thus, the primary market involves an extension of credit and the secondary market a sale of the credit instrument."[1]

The authors of this statement further limit this definition by excluding mortgages originated with a prior commitment from an investor.

> "This definition excludes transactions from the secondary market that were preceded by the buyer's promise to purchase the loans prior to their acquisition by the seller. In such "sales" the transaction is no more than a transfer from agent to principal and is, therefore, assigned to the primary market. Thus, the definition of the secondary market is limited to sales of mortgages without prior commitment from the buyer."[2]

When these quotes were published the type of commitment used was a firm commitment which established contractually the obligation the originator had to deliver and the investor had to buy. The current practice of many institutions active in the secondary market is to use a *standby commitment* which provides an originator with the opportunity to deliver if no better price is available elsewhere. A fee is charged to the originator for this commitment.

ECONOMIC FUNCTIONS OF THE SECONDARY MORTGAGE MARKET

In order to provide the needed economic assistances to mortgage lending, a secondary mortgage market should perform these four important economic functions:

1. *Provide liquidity.* Many investors who have traditionally not invested in mortgages, such as pension funds, trust accounts and credit unions, are now beginning to invest in mortgages because the required liquidity is present. These investors are interested in the relatively higher yields available with mortgages, and realize that a ready market exists if they are forced to liquidate their holdings.

2. *Moderate the cyclical flow of mortgage capital.* During periods of general capital shortage, the funds available for mortgages are usually very scarce (e.g., 1969–70, 1974 and 1979–81) and real estate activity slows down. The financial institutions operating in the secondary market during these periods can purchase existing mortgages from the primary mortgage lenders, and in this way provide funds for additional mortgages to be originated.

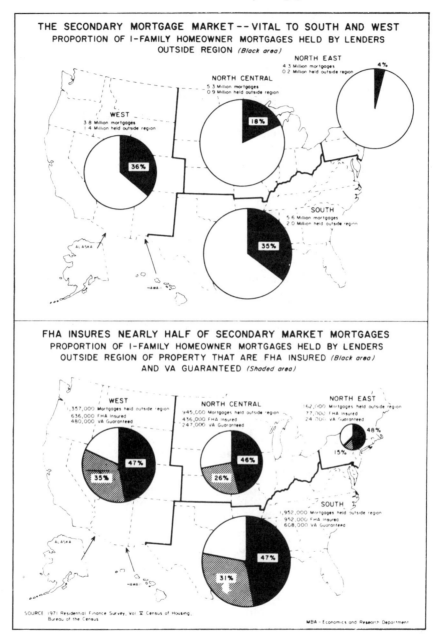

Figure 7-1. *Sectionalized maps from the Mortgage Bankers Association of America, Economics and Research Department.*

3. *Assist the flow of capital from surplus areas to deficit areas.* The operations of the secondary market allow an investor in a capital-surplus area, such as New England, to invest in mortgages originated in a capital deficit area such as the South and West, thus providing capital for needed growth. (Figure 7–1)

4. *Lessen the geographical spread in interest rates and allow for portfolio diversification.* The mobility of capital allows for a moderation of the geographical differences in mortgage interest rates to the borrower since capital will flow to areas of high interest, pressuring the rate downward. In addition, regional risk, e.g., a large industry closing, is spread to more investors, lessening its effect.

FINANCIAL INSTITUTIONS ACTIVE IN THE SECONDARY MARKET

Federal National Mortgage Association (FNMA)

Any discussion of secondary markets must start with the Federal National Mortgage Association, also known as "Fannie Mae." FNMA is the most active participant historically and currently is also the largest purchaser of residential mortgages.

The importance of an effective secondary market has been recognized since 1924, when a bill was introduced in Congress to establish a system of national home loan banks which could purchase first mortgages. The legislation failed to become law. The first federal attempt to establish and assist a national mortgage market was the Reconstruction Finance Corporation (RFC), created in 1935, followed in 1938 by a wholly-owned subsidiary, the National Mortgage Association of Washington, soon renamed the Federal National Mortgage Association

In 1950, FNMA was transferred to the Department of Housing and Urban Development (HUD)[3], and was later partitioned into two separate corporations by amendments to the Housing and Urban Development Act of 1968. This was done to permit the new FNMA to support more actively the mortgage market outside the federal budget.

One of these corporations, named the Government National Mortgage Association (GNMA, or "Ginnie Mae") remained in HUD and retained the special assistance and loan liquidation functions of the old FNMA. GNMA will be discussed in greater detail in a later section.

The second corporation was to be basically private, though some regulatory control remained with HUD. It retained the Federal National Mortgage Association's name, as well as the assets and responsibility for secondary market operations.

Today, the corporation is run by a 15-member board of directors, consisting of 10 selected by the stockholders and five appointed by the President of the United States. Approximately 60 million shares are currently outstanding and traded regularly on the New York Stock Exchange.

FNMA finances its secondary market operations by tapping the private capital markets using both short and long-term obligations. The short-term obligations are discount notes, which, as the term implies, are sold to investors at a price less than the face amount at maturity. At the end of 1981, FNMA had $17 billion outstanding in such discount notes. The long-term obligations are called *debentures* and are generally issued with maturities ranging from two to 25 years. At the end of 1981, $37 billion was outstanding.[4]

FNMA must produce its earning from the spread between its borrowing cost and the yield on its mortgage investment. Since it is a stockholder-owned corporation, it must keep the cost of borrowing below its portfolio yield, although for a brief period the rates for short-term funds may be higher than mortgage rates. This last occurred in 1974.

Secondary Market Operations

Mortgages are purchased by FNMA only from approved seller/servicers that number approximately 3,500 and who have outstanding commitments to deliver mortgages.

An approved seller/servicer can obtain a commitment from FNMA by participating in the *Free Market System* (FMS) auction usually held every two weeks. Participants are charged one basis point (or .02 percent) of the offer as an offering fee to bid competitively by phone against other seller/servicers. Each bid is to deliver up to $3 million in mortgages at a stated yield to FNMA. A seller/servicer may make up to 5 bids each in the government-backed and conventional auction. After analyzing the bids, the trends in the capital markets, and the cost of borrowing, FNMA accepts bids representing a range of yields and issues contracts obligating itself for a four-month period to buy mortgages at the yield specified in the accepted bid.

The commitment the successful bidder obtained from FNMA does not obligate the seller/servicer to deliver to FNMA. Instead, it gives the seller/servicer the right to deliver if no better price can be obtained elsewhere, and this is known as an optional delivery commitment or a "put" option. A fee of .2 percent of the commitment amount is charged to the seller/servicer.

In addition to the competitive bid, a seller/servicer may submit a noncompetitive bid limited to $400,000 by which the yield to FNMA will be the weighted average of all accepted competitive bids at that particular auction.

Another program allows a seller/servicer to obtain a forward 9- or 12-month convertible standby commitment at a yield established by FNMA. These commitments are available for fixed rate and adjustable rate mortgages and are usually used to protect builders of new construction against sharp interest rate changes. This commitment can be converted after the first four-month period to match the weighted average yield of the most recent FMS auction. Processing commitment and delivery of conversion fees are also charged for this commitment.

Types of Mortgages

FHA/VA

Prior to 1970, the only mortgages FNMA was authorized to purchase were FHA-insured and VA-guaranteed loans. This requirement was based on FNMA being a federally-chartered corporation charged with the responsibility of supporting the nation's goal of providing adequate housing for low and moderate income families through a program of supplementing liquidity to the residential mortgage market. This responsibility was fulfilled initially by dealing only with FHA-insured and VA-guaranteed mortgages since these programs provided the financing for most families in these income levels. In 1980, a new program was added (with a separate auction) whereby FNMA would purchase FHA graduated payment mortgages.

Conventional

The law was changed by the *Emergency Home Finance Act of 1970,* and FNMA was authorized to purchase conventional mortgages (i.e., those not guaranteed or insured by the federal government). Its prime responsibility though, was still to support the government programs. The first purchases under the new conventional program began in early 1972 after a lengthy study to determine the correct underwriting procedure for these non-government insured loans.

The dollar amount of conventional mortgages in the FNMA portfolio has increased dramatically since the program began in 1972. (See Figure 7–2.) Recently, more conventional mortgages are purchased than FHA/VA, and commitments issued are about equal. (See Figure 7–4.)

Adjustable Rate Mortgage

FNMA began a program in the purchase of adjustable rate mortgages in mid-1981. FNMA purchases eight different types of ARMs tied to five different indices. Some of the plans have payment caps, while others do not.

Condominiums and PUDs

FNMA added another program in 1974 to purchase mortgages on condominiums and planned unit developments (PUDs).

Project mortgages (those with government mortgage insurance commitments) are purchased under either an immediate purchase contract or a 24-month standby commitment depending on the current status of the project. The yield to FNMA for project mortgages is a fixed published yield which may be adjusted if market conditions warrant.

Dollars in millions, except per share amounts *For The Year*	1981	1980	1979	1978	1977	1976
Summary Statements of Operations:						
Mortgage portfolio income (loss), net of costs..........	$ (485)	$ (42)	$ 241	$ 294	$ 251	$ 203
Commitment and other fees..	125	68	60	106	73	44
Loss on sales of mortgages	—	—	(2)	—	(6)	(3)
Income (loss) before Federal income taxes	(360)	26	299	400	318	244
Provision for Federal income taxes.............	(170)	12	137	191	153	117
Net income (loss)	$ (190)	$ 14	$ 162	$ 209	$ 165	$ 127
Per share:						
Earnings (loss):						
Primary	$ (3.22)	$ .24	$ 2.81	$ 3.81	$ 3.15	$ 2.62
Fully diluted	(3.22)	.23	2.68	3.47	2.77	2.18
Cash dividends	.40	1.12	1.28	1.15	1.00	.88
Commitments Issued:						
Portfolio:						
FNMA:						
Home: Government insured or guaranteed	$ 2,971	$ 5,570	$ 5,698	$ 9,119	$ 6,240	$3,827
Conventional	6,360	2,511	4,441	9,829	4,605	2,168
Total home mortgages	9,331	8,081	10,139	18,948	10,845	5,995
Project	—	2	40	11	6	1
Total FNMA	9,331	8,083	10,179	18,959	10,851	5,996
FNMA/GNMA tandem plans	—	—	—	—	43	241
Total portfolio	$ 9,331	$ 8,083	$10,179	$18,959	$10,894	$6,237
Conventional mortgage- backed securities	$ 3,259	$ —	$ —	$ —	$ —	$ —
Mortgages Purchased:						
Home: Government insured or guaranteed	$ 2,284	$ 5,272	$ 5,388	$ 6,620	$ 2,284	$ 824
Conventional	3,827	2,802	5,410	5,682	2,366	2,513
Total home mortgages.....	6,111	8,074	10,798	12,302	4,650	3,337
Project	2	27	7	1	130	269
Participation in project construction loans	—	—	2	2	4	26
Total mortgages	$ 6,113	$ 8,101	$10,807	$12,305	$ 4,784	$3,632
Average gross yield on mortgages purchased	15.75%	12.64%	10.48%	9.46%	8.80%	9.10%

Figure 7–2. *FNMA financial and statistical summary. (Source: 1981 Annual Report, Federal National Mortgage Association.)*

Dollars in millions, except per share amounts						
For The Year	*1981*	*1980*	*1979*	*1978*	*1977*	*1976*
Debt Issued:						
Short-term notes	**$30,185**	$17,654	$10,567	$ 9,621	$ 3,090	$3,650
Debentures	**10,221**	11,000	9,900	10,400	5,550	5,600
Subordinated capital						
debentures	—	500	—	—	200	300
Mortgage-backed bonds	—	—	156	—	—	—
Total...................	**$40,406**	$29,154	$20,623	$20,021	$ 8,840	$9,550
Average Cost	**16.22%**	13.37%	10.72%	8.49%	6.89%	6.86%

Figure 7–2. *Continued.*

FNMA ACTIVITY
(MILLIONS OF DOLLARS)

Year	Loan Purchases	Loan Sales	Total Portfolio (Year-end)
1960	$ 980	$ 42	$ 2,903
1965	757	46	2,520
1970	5,078	. . .	15,502
1971	3,574	336	17,791
1972	3,699	211	19,791
1973	6,127	71	24,175
1974	6,953	4	29,578
1975	4,263	2	31,824
1976	3,606	86	32,904
1977	4,780	67	34,370
1978	12,303	5	43,311
1979	10,812	. . .	51,091
1980	8,099	. . .	57,327
1981	6,112	. . .	61,412

Note: Data adjusted to exclude functions transferred to GNMA in 1968.
Source: Federal National Mortgage Association.

Figure 7–3.

In 1978, FNMA added a participation loan purchase and sale program designed to make funds available in older urban areas. This program currently is limited to single-family conventional mortgages submitted by an approved seller/servicer that executes a participation loan agreement. FNMA will purchase a majority interest of 60 to 90 percent from an originating lender that retains servicing. The remaining interest may be retained by the originating lender or sold to another investor.

Government National Mortgage Association (GNMA)

The Government National Mortgage Association, known as Ginnie Mae, was organized within HUD under the authority of the Housing and Urban Development Act of 1968 which split the old FNMA into two separate entities—FNMA and GNMA.

GNMA was given authority to operate in the following three areas, the first two of which were inherited from the old FNMA:

1. *The special assistance function* (SAF). Under this function, GNMA was authorized to make available below-market interest rate loans to low-income families who normally could not obtain loans through private means. An example would be one of the Tandem Plans through which GNMA purchases below-market interest rate mortgages for sale to FNMA at market yield with GNMA absorbing any loss.

2. The *management and liquidation of previously originated (old FNMA) mortgages.*

3. *The mortgage-backed security program.* Under this new program, GNMA will guarantee the timely payment of principal and interest on mortgage-backed securities composed of FHA-insured, VA-guaranteed or Farmers Home Administration mortgages and issued by an FHA-approved mortgagee and sold to an investor.

It is in this last area that GNMA has had its greatest effect on mortgage lending and the secondary markets.

The primary purpose behind the rebirth of a mortgage-backed security was to attract more funds into the housing markets by providing a liquid instrument with a governmental guarantee to traditional non-mortgage investors.

The mortgage lender usually is a mortgage company since most FHA/VA mortgages are originated by this type of lender. This lender seeks a commitment from GNMA to guarantee a pool of acceptable mortgages.[5] A mortgage lender/issuer of a GNMA mortgage-backed security must be an FHA-approved mortgagee with a net worth of at least $100,000, depending on the amount of the pool. In addition, GNMA requires an issuer to establish guidelines to insure prudent business practices are followed by security dealers. When the commitment is received (with an annual guaranty fee of .06 percent), a mortgage lender can rely on GNMA's guarantee of the certificate when the underlying mortgages are either originated or purchased and then packaged. These certificates are sold to investors with the full faith and credit of the United States behind the monthly payment of principal and interest.

In addition to the better-known, single-family mortgage-backed security, GNMA is authorized to guarantee pools of FHA/VA mobile home mortgages, FHA-insured hospital mortgages and securities backed by a single FHA-insured multi-family mortgage.

The mortgage-backed security has been well received by both traditional and non-traditional mortgage investors. Many credit unions, pension funds, trusts and individuals who never had invested in mortgages before now have a vehicle to do so. These security instruments, usually purchased from a securities dealer that will also make a market in the security, provide the holder with:

- High yielding government security
- Liquidity
- Safety
- Monthly cash flow

To date, over $100 billion of GNMA securities have been issued and the total is currently increasing at the rate of two billion a month.

The mortgages in a single-family mortgage pool must be homogeneous in the interest rate and term of the loan. The coupon rate on the security will be 50 basis points (½ percent) less than the internal rate of the underlying mortgages. Of this, 44 basis points are to compensate the issuer for servicing the loan and six to GNMA as a guarantee fee.

Although others exist, the most popular form of mortgage-backed security is the *modified pass-through security*. Under this program, the issuer must pay the scheduled monthly payment of principal and interest to the holder whether or not the mortgagors pay the issuer. If the issuer defaults on the obligation to the holder, GNMA will take over the pool and make the payment.

During periods of extreme credit restraint GNMA has been authorized to purchase mortgages as a means of stimulating the housing industry. The Emergency Home Purchase Assistance Act of 1974 is an example of this authorization. It authorized GNMA to purchase conventional mortgages at a below market interest rate. Initially $3 billion worth was purchased. This was the first time GNMA was authorized to purchase mortgages not insured or guaranteed by the government.

A futures market in GNMA pass-through exists on the Chicago Board of Trade where investors competitively trade contracts to buy or sell securities at a negotiated price at a specified date in the future. The market enables lenders to pass along the interest rate risk of dealing in these securities to speculators who are more willing to gamble on interest rate trends.

GNMA MORTGAGE-BACKED
SECURITY PROGRAM
(MILLIONS OF DOLLARS)

Year	*Pass-through Securities*		*Bonds Sold*
	Applications	*Issues*	
1970	$ 1,126	$ 452	$1,315
1971	4,374	2,702	300
1972	3,854	2,662	. . .
1973	5,529	3,249	. . .
1974	6,203	4,784	. . .
1975	10,449	7,366	. . .
1976	25,394	13,765	. . .
1977	31,076	16,230	. . .
1978	35,014	15,359	. . .
1979	53,820	24,592	. . .
1980	58,701	20,648	. . .
1981	36,915	14,253	. . .

Source: Government National Mortgage Association.

Figure 7–4.

Federal Home Loan Mortgage Corporation (FHLMC)

The Emergency Home Finance Act of 1970, in addition to giving FNMA the power to purchase conventional mortgages, authorized the establishment of the Federal Home Loan Mortgage Corporation, also known as "Freddie Mac" or The Mortgage Corporation. It was originally intended to provide secondary market facilities for members of the Federal Home Loan Bank System but has been slightly modified to include others.

FHLMC's particular function is to provide secondary market support for conventional mortgages originated primarily by savings and loans, although commercial banks and mortgage companies (since 1978) may also participate. Sellers who are nonmembers of the FHLB system are charged .5 percent of amounts purchased in addition to any applicable fees.

FHLMC has three home purchase programs:

1. Conventional fixed-rate home mortgages
2. Multifamily home mortgages
3. Adjustable-rate mortgages (ARM)

FHLMC will purchase whole loans or participation in all three programs. The fixed-rate mortgage program has both immediate delivery and an eight-

FEDERAL HOME LOAN MORTGAGE CORPORATION ACTIVITY
(MILLIONS OF DOLLARS)

| Year | Mortgage Transactions | | Loan Portfolio (Year-end) | | |
	Purchases	Sales	Total	FHA-VA	Conventional
1970	$ 325	. . .	$ 325	$ 325	. . .
1971	778	$ 113	968	821	$ 147
1972	1,297	407	1,788	1,502	286
1973	1,334	409	2,604	1,800	804
1974	2,190	53	4,586	1,961	2,625
1975	1,713	1,521	4,987	1,881	3,106
1976	1,127	1,797	4,269	1,675	2,594
1977	4,124	4,640	3,267	1,450	1,817
1978	6,526	6,426	3,091	1,299	1,792
1979	5,721	4,544	4,052	1,159	2,893
1980	3,722	2,526	5,056	1,090	3,966
1981	3,800	3,532	5,237	1,047	4,190

Source: Federal Home Loan Mortgage Corporation.

Figure 7–5.

month forward plan. The multifamily and ARM programs have immediate deliveries which are mandatory within 60 days of contract date.

Most commitments from FHLMC call for mandatory delivery within 60 days of contract date. Failure to deliver could bring a two-year suspension of the right to sell to FHLMC.

Until May 1977, the yield to FHLMC was administratively set by FHLMC, but now a bid price system similar to FNMA's auction is used to set a net yield[6] to FHLMC.

In 1981, FHLMC added a mortgage swap program. The program enables eligible sellers to exchange home mortgages or participation interests in conventional home mortgages for FHLMC Mortgage Participation Certificates (PCs). These PCs represent undivided interests in those mortgages.

Financing Mortgage Purchases

FHLMC finances its secondary market operations somewhat differently than FNMA. Rather than finance its purchases entirely with debt securities in the capital market, as does FNMA, FHLMC finances its mortgage purchases with capital generated from the sale of either whole mortgages or participations in groups of mortgages, in addition to debt securities. It effectively buys and sells mortgages.

The total FHLMC mortgage commitments issued in 1981 were $6.6 billion. (See Figure 7–6.) This increase was the result of the dramatic shortage of

	1981	*1980*
For the Year Ending December 31		
Commitment Activity		
Mortgages		
Commitments (including Guarantor)....	$ 6,632,330	$ 3,856,050
Purchases	$ 3,744,018	$ 3,689,766
Number of Loans Purchased...........	83,428	73,276
PCs and GMCs		
Commitments (including Guarantor)....	$ 6,300,728	$ 2,425,300
Settlements.........................	$ 3,529,157	$ 2,526,568
Long-Term Debt		
Issued	$ 400,000	$ 1,050,000
Retired	(388,894)	(215,083)
Net................................	$ 11,106	$ 834,917
Income Statement Highlights		
Revenue from Total Portfolio...........	$ 626,453	$ 493,052
Interest Expense.....................	556,939	416,526
Net Interest Spread	69,514	76,526
Other Expenses, Net	38,610	42,940
Net Income	$ 30,904	$ 33,586

Figure 7-6. *FHLMC purchase and sales activity, 1980 and 1981. (Source: 1981 Federal Home Loan Mortgage Corporation Annual Report.)*

capital needed to finance the lending activity of savings and loans ($3.7 billion was actually purchased).

By way of offsetting the purchase program Mortgage Participation Certificates (PCs) are sold to thrift institutions which gives them an undivided interest in the pooled mortgages. The monthly payment of principal and interest is guaranteed by FHLMC.

In addition to the PC program, FHLMC periodically issues Guaranteed Mortgage Certificates (GMC) for sale to traditional non-mortgage investors such as bank trusts and pension funds. Interest is payable semi-annually with the GMCs and principal annually. In the PC program, interest and principal are payable monthly.

Uniform Documentation

In order for mortgages to be readily saleable in a secondary market, a degree of uniformity must exist. Before FHLMC joined FNMA in the secondary market the required uniformity existed because all mortgages sold in the secondary market were either FHA-insured or VA-guaranteed. After 1970, conventional mortgages could also be bought and sold in the secondary market and a need developed for uniform documentation.

Both FNMA and FHLMC have worked diligently to produce the state-by-state uniform documents that all mortgage lenders needed. GNMA has also adopted these forms which include among others:

- Mortgage note
- Deeds of trust
- Mortgage
- Loan application
- Appraisal form
- Verification Documents

These forms can also be used for VA-guaranteed mortgages if a VA-guaranteed loan rider is added to the mortgage or deed of trust to make the mortgage instrument conform to special VA requirements. These forms regrettably cannot be used for FHA-insured loans; FHA-approved forms must be used. This may change in the future.

These uniform forms may contain some minor variations to comply with different state laws.

SUGGESTED READINGS

Bennewitz, Dall. *Introduction to the Secondary Mortgage Market: A Primer.* Chicago, Illinois: U.S. League of Savings Associations, 1980.

Connolly, James J. "The GNMA Market: A Retrospective," *The Mortgage Banker* (September 1980), pp. 16–19.

Karl, Max. "Don't Overlook Secondary Mortgage Markets," *Bankers Magazine* (September–October 1979), pp. 68–71.

NOTES

1. Jones, Oliver H., and Grebler, Leo. *The Secondary Mortgage Market: Its Purpose, Its Performance and Its Potential,* Los Angeles: Real Estate Research Program, UCLA, 1961, p. 4.

2. Ibid.

3. It was originally called the Housing and Home Finance Agency until 1965 when the present cabinet-level department was created.

4. 1979 Annual Report of the Federal National Mortgage Association.

5.   An acceptable pool of mortgages (in an aggregate amount of at least $1 million) would contain only the same type of mortgage (such as all single-family with the same interest rate and maturity). The government-insured or guaranteed mortgage cannot be older than one year at the time of the GNMA commitment.

6.   A net yield means the originating lender must add on any servicing fee. However, FNMA purchases on a gross yield basis and pays for servicing at ⅜ percent of the principal balance. FHLMC, on the other hand, purchases on a net servicing basis and, consequently, is not concerned with specific servicing fees.

7.   1981 Annual Report of the Federal Home Loan Mortgage Corporation.

Chapter 8

Mortgage Insurance—
Government and Private

The function of mortgage insurance, whether government or private, is to make mortgage investments more attractive by lessening risk and providing liquidity. With mortgage insurance, a permanent mortgage investor has an alternative to foreclosed real estate; an alternative which will release the investor from an asset that might decline in value.

Mortgage insurance offers lenders the opportunity to make higher percentage loans with lower downpayments to more people because of less risk. The variations on this basic concept can be traced to whether the insurance is government or private, and whether it is for a single-family loan or an income-property loan.

Before examining government and private insurance programs, a brief review of the historical development of this concept will be helpful to an understanding of present mortgage insurance practices.

HISTORICAL DEVELOPMENT

Although some of the early title insurance companies insured the mortgage in addition to the title, the first law providing statutory authority for this type of insurance was not enacted until 1904 in New York.

The social and demographic changes that emerged after 1900 (particularly following World War I) led mortgage lending into a more important position in the American economy. As mortgage lending became more prevalent and important, mortgage insurance became more accepted and desired and mortgage companies began taking an interest in the concept.

It was customary during this period for a mortgage company either to exchange a new mortgage for a defaulted one or to buy back a troubled loan sold to an investor. As the real estate boom of the 1920s continued, this custom gave way to the actual guaranteeing of principal and interest by a new entity—a mortgage guaranty company. During their peak years (1925–1932), as many as 50 of these companies were in operation, located primarily in the state of New York.

These companies prospered by originating and selling mortgages with a guaranty either as whole loans to institutional investors or as mortgage participation bonds to individual investors. The units sold to individual investors were usually in $500 or $1,000 denominations. Yield and apparent safety made the units very attractive. A trustee would hold the mortgage and be responsible for foreclosure if any default in payment occurred. The prevailing viewpoint during this period of time was that real estate values would continue to appreciate, and if any lax underwriting or appraising occurred, the resulting questionable mortgage would be saved by inflation. This optimism affected the investing public. Large portions of accumulated savings were invested in mortgage bonds issued by apparently successful mortgage guaranty companies.

Due to the general optimism about the economy and the *laissez-faire* attitude of the government, these mortgage guaranty companies were virtually unregulated. This lack of regulation often led to poor underwriting, self-dealing, fraud, and ultimately to a lack of adequate reserves to meet any meaningful emergency.

Before the stock market crash of 1929, the real estate industry was in serious trouble. As real estate values started to drop, the emergency the mortgage guaranty companies could not survive had arrived, and it was inevitable that these companies would not survive the bank holiday declared by President F. D. Roosevelt in March 1933. Many billions of dollars were lost by institutional investors with similarly tragic results to private investors because of the failure of these companies. The collapse left such an ugly mark on the real estate finance industry that private mortgage insurance did not reappear for almost 25 years.

Government (FHA) Insurance

The years immediately following the stock market crash witnessed much debate on the advisability and proper role of the government in the nation's economy. One segment of the economy that many agreed could benefit from government action was real estate. Those in favor of stimulation reasoned that expanding waves from a healthy real estate industry would have a multiplied effect on the remainder of a depressed economy. The National Housing Act of 1934 contained provisions to help stimulate the construction industry and created the Federal Housing Administration (FHA) to encourage lenders to make real estate mortgages again by providing government-backed mortgage insurance as protection. Title I of this law provided initially free insurance to lenders who loaned money for home improvements and repairs.

Title II provided for the establishment of a Mutual Mortgage Insurance Fund to be funded by premiums paid by mortgagors out of which any claims by the protected lenders could be satisfied. Initially, the mortgagor paid an annual insurance premium of .5 percent based on the original amount. (The premium is now computed on the unpaid balance.)

The basic program under this Act was Section 203(b), designed to provide government insurance to lenders who made loans on 1-4 family houses. (Most have been single-family.) This program is still successfully meeting national housing needs after helping to provide housing for more than 10 million families.

Now a part of the Department of Housing and Urban Development (HUD), the FHA has other insurance programs (Figure 8-1), each designed to meet a specific problem. But the Mutual Mortgage Insurance Fund remains the largest and most important.

It should be understood that the legislation to establish FHA was faced with opposition from some thrift institutions that believed the federal government should not get involved in housing. Even after enactment, FHA did not meet with great acceptance among the financial centers, since many felt mortgage insurance as a concept was discredited, and even if not discredited, the government should not get involved in what was basically a private enterprise.

History, however, has proven this to be a shortsighted belief, especially in view of the many changes for which FHA has paved the way in real estate finance. As an example, FHA insurance has allowed for the development of a national mortgage market by providing for the transferability, and thus the liquidity, of mortgage instruments. The FHA-insured mortgage was attractive to many investors because it established property and borrower standards with a corresponding reduction in risk.

The FHA mortgage insurance program allowed life insurance companies to justify a successful request to offer loans with higher loan-to-value ratios with lower downpayments to state insurance commissioners. The program also gave them the opportunity to lend across the nation. With this new authorization, life insurance companies could lend in those areas of the country that desperately needed capital. Subsequently they could receive a higher yield than what was previously available in the capital-surplus area of New England, where most of the major life insurance companies were located. Mortgage companies were the principal intermediaries for moving this capital from capital-surplus areas to capital-poor areas by originating mortgages with FHA insurance and selling them to life insurance companies.

One of the primary reasons for the increase in home ownership from about 40 percent of all homes occupied in 1930 to about 65 percent today is the leadership provided by FHA that led to:

- Established property and borrower standards
- Mortgage insurance

- Amortized mortgage payments
- Higher loan-to-value ratios
- Longer terms

These factors have contributed to the higher percentage of home ownership and to a financial environment conducive to a rebirth of private mortgage insurance.

Mortgage loans to be insured by FHA could be originated by any of the various mortgage intermediaries, although as a practical matter about 75 percent have been originated by mortgage companies. Initially, this high percentage of origination was due to the local lending philosophy of the other mortgage lenders and the correspondent system that developed between mortgage lenders and life insurance companies. Most FHA-insured mortgages are still originated by mortgage companies.

203 Mutual Mortgage Insurance and Insured Improvement Loans.

(b) One-to-four Family Housing.

(h) One-Family Housing for Disaster Victims.

(i) Outlying Properties; One-Family Non-farm or Farm Housing.

(m) Vacation Homes.

207 Multifamily Housing Mortgage Insurance.
Rental Housing of eight or more Units.
Mobile Home Parks.

213 Cooperative Housing Mortgage Insurance.
Dwelling Unit Released from a Cooperative Project-Sales Mortgage.
Management-type Cooperative Projects of five or more Units.
Sales-type Cooperative Projects of five or more Units.
Investor-sponsored Cooperative Projects of five or more Units.

220 Urban Renewal Mortgage Insurance and Insured Improvement Loans.
One-to-eleven Family Housing in Urban Renewal Areas.
Construction of two or more Units in Approved Urban Renewal Area.

221 Low Cost and Moderate Income Mortgage Insurance.

(d)(2) One-to-four Family Housing for Low and Moderate Income Families and Displaced Families.

(h) Individual Units Released from 222(h) Project Mortgage.

Figure 8–1. *HUD-FHA mortgage insurance programs.*

(i) Conversion of 221(d)(3) Below Market Interest Rate Rental Project into Condominium Plan.

(d)(3) Housing Projects (Below Market Interest Rate) for Housing Moderate Income Families, Individuals 62 or Older, or Handicapped.

(d)(3) Same as above, but with Market Interest Rate Program and Rent Supplement Program.

(d)(4) Housing Projects for Moderate Income Families. Market Interest Rate Program for Profit-motivated Sponsors.

(h) Substandard Housing for Subsequent Resale after Rehabilitation.

(j) Conversion of 221(d)(3) Rental Project into a Cooperative Project.

222 Servicemen's Mortgage Insurance
One-Family Housing for Servicemen.

223 Miscellaneous Housing Insurance.
Housing and Mortgage Insurance for Housing in Declining Neighborhoods.
Insurance for Government-Acquired Properties.

231 Housing Mortgage Insurance for the Elderly.
Housing Project of eight or more Units for Occupancy by Elderly or Handicapped.

232 Nursing Homes and/or Intermediate Care Facilities Mortgage Insurance.
Housing for 20 or more Patients.

233 Experimental Housing Mortgage Insurance.
Proposed or Rehabilitated Housing Using Advanced Technology.
Rental Housing Using Advanced Technology.

234 Condominium Housing Mortgage Insurance.

(c) Individual Units in Condominium Projects.

(d) Condominium Projects with four or more Units.

235 Mortgage Insurance and Assistance Payments.

(i) One-Family Unit in Single- or Two-Family Dwelling. Open-end advances permitted in connection with previously insured mortgage.

(j) Individual Units Released from 235(j) Rehabilitation Sales Project Mortgage.

(k) Housing for Lower Income Families.

Figure 8-1. *Continued.*

236 Mortgage Insurance and Interest Reduction Payments.
Rental and Cooperative Housing for Lower Income Families, Individuals 62 or over, or Handicapped.

237 Special Mortgage Insurance for Low and Moderate Income.
Special Credit Risks; Single-Family Units.

240 Mortgage Insurance on Loans for Title Purchase.
Purchase of Fee Simple Title.

241 Supplementary Financing for FHA Project Mortgages.

242 Mortgage Insurance for Hospitals.
Construction or Rehabilitation of Non-profit and Proprietary Hospitals.

244 Mortgagee Coinsurance

245 Graduated Payment Mortgage

803/809/810 Armed Services Housing.

809 One-to-Four Family Housing for Civilian Employees at or near R & D Installations.

810(h) Individual Units Released from 810 (g)Multifamily Mortgage.

810(f) Rental Housing with eight or more Units for Military or Civilian Personnel.

810(g) Same as above, but for Later Resale as Single-Family Housing.

1000 Mortgage Insurance for Land Development.
Purchase of Land for Development of Building Sites for Subdivisions or New Communities.

1100 Mortgage Insurance for Group Practice Facilities.
Construction of Rehabilitation of Facilities for Dentistry, Medicine or Optometry Practice.

Note: This chart is intended for quick reference to HUD-FHA insurance programs. Check for specific details in the appropriate FHA issuances.
Source: Department of Housing and Urban Development, *Housing in the Seventies,* A report of the National Housing Policy Review, Washington, D.C., 1974.

Figure 8-1. *Continued.*

FHA INSURANCE TODAY

Although the various FHA programs have performed admirably and have allowed for changes in real estate finance that have affected all mortgage lenders whether FHA insurance was used or not, and although the total is still high, the percentage of homes insured by FHA declined in the 1970s.

The reasons for this decline are many, but would have to include:

1. The unjustified length of time it takes to get a commitment from FHA.
2. The periodically low FHA maximum insured loan amount for Section 203(b), which precluded large areas of the country (because of the high cost of real estate) from the program.
3. The maximum interest rate limit for FHA-insured loans set by HUD, which is usually far below the market rate, thus requiring discount points.

The Housing and Community Development Act of 1980 provided for an increase in FHA-insured mortgage amounts to a level which allowed for some increase in activity. The limit was again increased in 1982. The new limit for single-family dwellings is $82,000 and for two- to four-family units it is from $92,000 and $129,500. Therefore, under the basic Section 203(b) program, for a fee of .5 percent which is paid by the borrower, FHA will insure a lender for 97 percent of the first $25,000 of acquisition cost, and 95 percent of the remainder, up to a maximum insured amount of $82,000 for single-family dwellings.

FHA-INSURED MORTGAGE AND OTHER LOANS MADE
(MILLIONS OF DOLLARS)

Year	Total	Home Mortgages	Project Mortgages	Property Im- provement Loans
1960	$ 6,293	$ 4,601	$ 711	$ 982
1965	8,689	7,465	591	634
1970	11,982	8,114	3,251	617
1971	14,689	10,375	3,641	674
1972	12,320	8,067	3,448	805
1973	7,591	4,473	2,286	832
1974	5,915	3,934	1,225	756
1975	7,863	6,166	976	721
1976	9,619	6,362	2,315	942
1977	12,808	8,841	2,818	1,149
1978	15,534	11,140	3,014	1,380
1979	22,393	18,167	2,678	1,548
1980	22,092	16,459	3,987	1,646
1981	14,323	10,278	2,779	1,266

Note: Components may not add to totals due to rounding.
Source: Federal Housing Administration.

Figure 8-2.

As an example, if Mr. and Mrs. Jones want to purchase a home which had total acquisition costs (including closing costs) of $67,000, their downpayment would be as follows:

$$3\% \text{ (non-insured) of } \$25,000 = \$\ \ 750$$
$$5\% \text{ (non-insured) of } \$42,000 = \underline{\$2,100}$$

Total Downpayment $2,850

With FHA insurance on a $64,150 loan ($67,000 − $2,850), the monthly payment of principal and interest including .5 percent FHA insurance at 11 percent for 30 years would be $635.72.

Chapter 6, Underwriting the Residential Loan, discusses the requirements the property must meet and the income the family must have to obtain this mortgage insurance.

VETERANS ADMINISTRATION

As a gesture to returning World War II veterans, Congress enacted the *Servicemen's Readjustment Act of 1944*, which authorized the Veterans Administration (VA) to guarantee loans (among other benefits) made to eligible veterans.[1] The original guarantee was for the first 50 percent of the loan amount of $2,000, whichever was less. This has been increased through the years to the current guarantee of $27,500, or 60 percent of the loan whichever is less. The VA issues a *Certificate of Reasonable Value* (CRV) that establishes the amount on which these figures are based. A veteran borrower does not pay a premium for the mortgagee's protection as with an FHA-insured loan. Instead, any loss is paid by the government without benefit of a premium-supported fund. The maximum interest rate for a VA-guaranteed mortgage, like the FHA rate, is an artificially set rate which often requires that discount points be charged to a seller.

Originally, this program was designed to allow a veteran to buy a home with no money down, and it still operates on that concept. Consequently, a veteran now can buy a home costing up to $100,000 with no downpayment, assuming income is sufficient to support the payment. The current $27,500 guarantee is the reason no downpayment is required. It means that although the lender is lending $100,000, only $72,500, or 72 percent of value, is made with any risk. If foreclosure is necessary, the real estate typically should bring at least the $72,500 the lender had as a risk, which, combined with the $27,500 guarantee, will make the lender whole.

If a veteran wanted to buy a home appraised at more than $100,000, a lender would probably either require a downpayment equal to the amount in excess

VA-GUARANTEED HOME
MORTGAGE LOANS MADE
(DOLLAR AMOUNTS IN MILLIONS)

Year	Number	Amount
1960	145,000	$ 1,985
1965	164,000	2,652
1970	168,000	3,440
1971	282,000	5,961
1972	370,000	8,293
1973	316,000	7,467
1974	310,000	8,206
1975	299,000	8,884
1976	329,000	10,419
1977	389,000	13,901
1978	365,000	14,447
1979	357,000	16,674
1980	266,000	14,500
1981	143,000	7,903

Source: Veterans Administration.

Figure 8–3.

of $100,000 to keep the loan within the 72 percent loan-to-value ratio or obtain private mortgage insurance for the coverage.

Veterans who believe they are eligible for a VA-guaranteed loan must apply to the VA for a certificate of eligibility which establishes eligibility and the amount of the guarantee available. The 1974 law which increased the guarantee also provided for re-entitlement of benefits if all prior VA-guaranteed mortgages had been repaid or, if assumed, released.

PRIVATE MORTGAGE INSURANCE

After a lapse of a quarter of a century, private mortgage insurance companies (MICs) returned as FHA insurance programs proved successful. The first of the reborn MICs was Mortgage Guaranty Insurance Corporation (MGIC), organized in 1957 under a Wisconsin state law passed in 1956. As the first, MGIC remains the largest of the current MICs and receives the most premium dollars.

The reasons for the rebirth of the MICs and their impressive growth since then ranges from the slow red-tape procedures of government programs with their low mortgage amounts to the desire of mortgage lenders to have a program which allowed home-buyers to purchase higher-priced homes with low downpayments. These high ratio conventional mortgages became increas-

GROWTH IN MORTGAGE INSURANCE
(DOLLAR AMOUNTS IN BILLIONS)

Year-end	Private Mortgage Insurance	One- to Four-family FHA/VA Insurance	Insurance as a % of Home Mortgage Debt
1960	$ 0.3	$ 56.4	40.0%
1965	3.3	73.1	34.6
1970	7.3	97.3	35.1
1971	9.6	105.2	35.0
1972	17.5	113.0	35.1
1973	27.4	116.2	34.5
1974	33.6	121.3	34.5
1975	40.0	127.7	34.2
1976	49.3	133.5	32.8
1977	62.8	141.6	31.2
1978	80.5	153.4	30.6
1979	95.2	172.9	30.5
1980	105.3	195.2	31.3
1981*	114.3	205.9†	31.5†

*Preliminary.
†September 30.
Sources: Federal Housing Administration; Federal Reserve Board; Mortgage Insurance Companies of America; Veterans Administration.

Figure 8–4.

ingly popular in the 1970s, and once these mortgages could be traded in the secondary market, most mortgage lenders, in particular savings associations, began to offer them.

Protection for insured mortgage lenders and the general public that was missing with the old mortgage insurance companies is present now because all MICs are carefully regulated by the laws of the state in which they are organized as well as the states where they do business. The regulating entity is normally the state insurance commission or department.

The specific regulations vary among the states but generally provide that an MIC can insure only a fully amortized first lien on a 1–4 family residence that does not exceed 95 percent of fair market value. This originally was 90 percent but was changed by the *Emergency Home Loan Financing Act of 1970*, which allowed FNMA and FHLMC to purchase 95 percent conventional mortgages. Before an MIC can begin insuring loans, it must meet minimum limits for paid-in capital and surplus. Then its insurance exposure is limited to 25 times the value of the capital.

Three types of reserves must be maintained by MICs:

Unearned Premium Reserve. Premiums received but unearned for the term of a policy are placed in this reserve.

Loss Reserve. This reserve is established for losses or potential losses on a case-by-case basis as the company learns of defaults and foreclosures. It also includes a reserve for losses incurred, but not reported.

Contingency Reserve. This is a special reserve required by law to protect mortgage lenders against the type of catastrophic loss that can occur in severe economic periods. Half of each premium dollar received goes into this reserve and cannot be used by an MIC for 10 years, unless losses in a calendar year exceed 35 percent of earned premiums and the insurance commissioner of the state where the insurer is domiciled concurs in the withdrawal.

Before a mortgage lender can do business with an MIC, the lender must be approved in regard to its capacity to underwrite, appraise and service (if required) the high-ratio loans to be insured. An approved lender can get a commitment to insure within a day or two of submitting the application. The contents of the application and underwriting standards for MICs is discussed in Chapter 6, Underwriting the Residential Loan.

COMPARISON OF GOVERNMENT AND PRIVATE MORTGAGE INSURANCE

The differences between FHA mortgage insurance, a VA guarantee and private mortgage insurance are many and, in some cases, debatable as to which is preferable. These would include:

Insurance. The VA-guaranteed mortgage requires no premium from the borrower. An FHA-insured mortgage requires the borrower to pay an insurance premium of .5 percent of the outstanding balance for the life of the loan. MICs will provide insurance for .25 percent of the principal balance after the first year. At the lender's option, the premium can be dropped any time, although probably not until the loan-to-value ratio reaches 80 percent. This is in keeping with the requirements of FNMA and FHLMC which stipulates that the exposure on loans in excess of 80 percent be reduced to 75 percent through private mortgage insurance; however, the insurance may be dropped at the lender's option when the loan to value reaches 80 percent. MICs charge a premium in the first year that ranges from .25 to 1.0 percent, depending on the loan-to-value ratio.

Downpayment required. If the mortgage is VA-guaranteed, veterans normally do not need to make a downpayment unless the mortgage exceeds $100,000. For an FHA-insured mortgage, the borrower must put up equity of three percent of the first $25,000 of appraised value and five percent of the remainder up to a maximum insured amount of $67,500. If the insurance comes from an MIC, the downpayment could be as little as five percent with no loan limit (except for the secondary mortgage market limits) as long as the borrower has the capacity to repay.

Coverage. The VA guarantee protects the lender to the extent of 60 percent of the mortgage or $27,500, whichever is less. A mortgage insured by FHA under the basic 203(b) program protects the lender on the whole loan up to the insured amount to a maximum of $67,500. A mortgage insured by an MIC protects the top 20 or 25 percent of the lender's exposure.

Processing time. With VA allowing approved mortgagees to make commitments, the time for processing is now quite reasonable. The FHA processing time is supposed to be five working days, but can be as much as several weeks. An approved MIC lender is normally able to get a commitment within a day or two.

Interest rate. Both the VA and FHA programs have a maximum interest rate which is set administratively. This interest rate is often below the market rate requiring discount points to increase the investor's yield to the market.[2] Since an MIC-insured loan is normally made on a conventional mortgage, the market rate is used and points generally are not required.

Assumption. Neither VA nor FHA mortgages have a due-on-sale clause. Because of this the mortgage can be transferred to a new buyer and the mortgage lender can charge only a reasonable fee for transferring the records. Practically all conventional mortgages, whether insured by an MIC or not, contain due-on-sale clauses which could prevent the transfer of the mortgage upon sale.

Prepayment penalty. Neither FHA nor VA mortgages contain a prepayment penalty. Many conventional mortgages do.

INCOME-PROPERTY MORTGAGE INSURANCE

Following the success of the home mortgage insurance programs by the various MICs, the predictable expansion into income-property mortgage insurance occurred in 1967 when MGIC offered both income-property mortgage insurance and lease guarantees.

This original income-property mortgage insurance to protect mortgage lenders provided for coverage on the top 20 percent of an income-property loan. If a default occurred, a protected lender had to foreclose and then tender title to the insurer. The insurer, at its election, could decide on whether to pay 100 percent of the amount due under the loan and take title or pay 20 percent of the loan and leave title with the lender. The five-year premium for this insurance ranged from 1.75 to 2.90 percent of the loan, depending on the type of property.

As originally offered, the lease guarantee program guaranteed the total amount of fixed rent over a period ranging from a minimum of five years to a maximum of 20 years. Although percentage rents were excluded, additional rent from tax increases were allowed if a proper tax escalation clause existed.

The guarantee extends to the landlord after an eviction and protects until a new tenant is found. If the new tenant pays less rent than the guaranteed amount, the insurer pays the difference. In reality, this program was designed for the benefit of a mortgage lender who decided to make a mortgage loan based on a loan guarantee which would allow for an uninterrupted flow of income to amortize the mortgage.

Depending on the lease term, the premium for this guarantee ranged from 2.80 to 5.40 percent of the amount of rent guaranteed.

Both of these programs were profitable for insurance until the recession of 1974. This national recession was actually a depression for the real estate industry and resulted in tremendous underwriting losses for those MICs engaged in income-property mortgage insurance and lease guarantee. In 1975 the losses were so massive that most existing programs were scrapped, forcing a complete re-examination of the basic concepts and underwriting criteria.

The involved MICs realized that insuring an income property mortgage was far riskier and involved more variables than were present in home mortgage insurances. In addition, many mortgage lenders, especially those only interested in credit transactions, took the position that if a particular mortgage or lease needed to be insured or guaranteed to be attractive, it was better not to become involved at all.

Faced with mounting underwriting losses and the poor acceptance by lenders, most MICs reconsidered their approach to income-property mortgage insurance and instituted new programs which provided for less exposure to the insurer. As an example, CLIC,[3] with about 85 percent of the market, abolished the lease guarantee program and decreased its exposure on income-property mortgage insurance to either the top 10 or 15 percent, depending on which program was selected, and dropped its set premium schedule.

The current program offers a 10-year policy followed by annual renewals. The premium is established by CLIC after reviewing the risk. If a default occurs, the insured lender must foreclose and offer a merchantable title to CLIC which, at its option, can either pay 10 percent (or 15 percent depending on program) of the claim[4] or the original amount of the loan, whichever is less, or pay 100 percent of the claim and take title.

Income-property mortgage insurance's future is clouded by the severe recession of 1974–75 and the losses suffered by both mortgage lenders and insurers. The acceptability of income-property mortgage insurance by most lenders has not occurred yet, but a period of relatively stable economic progress should provide the opportunity.

SUGGESTED READINGS

Browne, Diana G. "The Private Mortgage Insurance Industry, The Thrift Industry and The Secondary Mortgage Market: Their Interrelationships." *Akron Law Review*, Vol. 12, Spring, 1979.

Brownstein, Philip N. "Federal Housing Administration: An Ever-Growing Force, An Ever-Growing Necessity," *The Mortgage Banker* (April 1979), pp. 46–52.

Doehler, Steven P. "Private Mortgage Insurance—Its Expanding Role," *The Mortgage Banker* (March 1980), pp. 44–46.

Rapkin, Chester. *The Private Insurance of Home Mortgages*. New York: Columbia University, 1973.

Wood, Burton C. "The 1980 Housing Bill," *The Mortgage Banker* (December 1980), pp. 22–23.

NOTES

1. A VA guarantee is not technically mortgage insurance, although the effect is the same, because a mortgage lender is protected and thus encouraged to make loans.

2. Discount points (or "points") are used to increase the effective yield of an FHA or VA mortgage (with administratively set interest rates) to a current level. For example, assume the FHA interest rate is 9 percent while the current market yield required is 9.5 percent. In order to induce an investor to purchase the 9 percent FHA mortgage rather than one at 9.5 percent, the 9 percent FHA mortgage would have to be discounted to increase the investor's yield. If the FHA mortgage is for $10,000 at 9 percent for 30 years, the investor would discount the mortgage by 3.41 (341 basis points) and purchase it at 96.59; that is $9,659. (The discount amount can be obtained from typically available tables.) The investor will pay $9,659 for the mortgage (while the mortgagor repays the entire $10,000), thereby increasing the yield from the 9 percent coupon rate to 9.5 percent (assuming the average 12 years before prepayment). The $341 difference will be paid by the seller of the home the mortgage is being used to finance because the law prohibits an FHA or VA buyer from paying discount points.

3. Commercial Loan Insurance Corporation, a subsidiary of MGIC Investment Corporation.

4. A claim includes the unpaid principal balance, accumulated interest, real estate taxes and hazard insurance premiums advanced, cash for repairs and foreclosure costs.

Chapter 9

Fundamentals of Income-Property Mortgage Lending

INTRODUCTION

The classification of real estate known as income property (or commercial) can be defined as that real estate conceived, built and operated for the purpose of producing income. This income is realized either as actual cash or on the income-property owner's balance sheet as a tax shelter. This income can be *actual,* (e.g., if an owner has leased the property) or *imputed* (e.g., if an owner occupies the property). This is contrasted with residential real estate which is an *amenity* property.

Another major difference between residential and income property is how the income of a borrower is treated. In financing residential real estate, the income of a borrower, and the stability of that income, are of primary importance in determining whether the loan is made. The income-producing capability of commercial real estate itself establishes the value and thus the amount of financing available.

The income property classification can be divided further into *general use* and *special use* property. A general use property could be a retail space in a shopping center since that space could be used by many different types of retail outlets. Churches, factories, bowling alleys and grain elevators are examples of special use properties because their special architectural requirements are useable only for a specific purpose. As a general rule, permanent mortgage investors would rather lend on a general use property than on a special use property since the alternate use potential provides greater security if an occupying tenant does not renew the lease or if a lender has to foreclose.

Since permanent mortgage investors take a greater risk with a special use property, they insist on greater protection through such items as a higher interest rate, personal or corporate guarantees or pre-leasing requirements.

General use properties include:

- Apartment buildings
- Office buildings
- Retail outlets
- Shopping centers
- Industrial (multi-purpose)
- Some warehouses

Special use properties include:

- Hotels and motels
- Mobile home parks
- Churches
- Banks
- Nursing homes and hospitals
- Theaters
- Restaurants

Another classification of income property is based on whether the lender is looking primarily to the real estate as the security for the mortgage loan, as in a real estate loan, or is looking to the credit of either the mortgagor or the tenant who has signed a long-term *net lease*.[1] This would be a credit loan. A credit loan is of increasing importance to many long-term investors who have learned through experience that real estate values can depreciate as well as appreciate.

The ideal credit loan for a permanent investor would be one that fully amortizes over a period of time during which the property is completely leased by an AAA tenant (national credit) with a net lease obligating the tenant for that period and with the rent equal to or exceeding the debt service. In this situation, the lender's risk exposure is limited to the extreme improbability of the tenant declaring bankruptcy. (Leases and their important clauses are discussed in Chapter 10, The Lease and Leasehold Financing.)

Unlike a credit loan where a lender has the security of a valuable tenant and the real estate, a pure real estate mortgage loan offers only the real property as security. Normally this is sufficient security but the risk to a lender is greater. This increased risk is derived from the possibility that the real estate may not be aesthetically or economically attractive to tenants in the future. If that occurs, existing tenants may not renew their leases and new tenants may be difficult to attract. The result of such a situation is usually that a mortgagor defaults on the mortgage because insufficient funds are generated by the property, thereby forcing the lender to foreclose.

ANALYZING THE INCOME PROPERTY LOAN

Typically, there are three parties to this type of loan:

1. Borrower
2. Mortgage intermediary
3. Permanent lender

The analysis of this type of loan must be extensive to protect and provide information for all parties involved. A borrower must be satisfied that the property to be bought or built will provide a reasonable return on the investment. This of course will vary according to each borrower's unique financial position after consideration of taxes, leverage, cash flow and depreciation. No single income property arrangement will satisfy all needs or all borrowers.

The mortgage intermediary (e.g., mortgage company or savings and loan) between the borrower and the permanent mortgage investor, must be convinced that the concept is sound and possible to place before time and effort is invested in underwriting and packaging the deal. A permanent mortgage investor is not involved at this stage unless the loan is being made directly.

Of particular importance to all parties are two questions: will this arrangement create more value than it will cost to produce and will the projected income be of sufficient magnitude and duration to pay operating expenses, service the debt and provide an acceptable return to the borrower. In regard to the first question, disregarding tax considerations for the moment, a project costing $10 million to build but which is worth only $10 million or less at completion is one that should never have been started. Of course, a borrower may intend to get only tax benefits from a particular transaction.

Every income property loan should be analyzed according to:

- Feasibility
- Location
- Timing
- Borrower
- Real estate

Feasibility

Although a permanent investor will regard location as the paramount issue because of concern for the safety of its investment, both the borrower and the mortgage intermediary are initially concerned with the concept. Questions must be answered, such as: Will this project work at any cost? Does a need exist that this project can satisfy on a practical basis? If the answer is yes then it must be determined if the transaction can create value and give the borrower the requested loan while protecting the interest of the permanent investor.

Figure 9–1 is an example of an analysis made after the acceptance (positive feasibility) of a concept.

Location

Although a few deals will work almost anywhere, good location usually is required. The garden apartment proposal in Figure 9–1 is a good example of a type of loan that requires a good location.

Assume Joe Developer has plans for a 150-unit garden apartment. He provides the following information:

COST

Hard cost (land and construction)	
$17,000 per unit x 150	$2,550,000
Soft cost (architectural and engineering)	
10% of hard cost	255,000
Financing cost (construction interest and points)	127,000
Total Cost	$2,932,000

INCOME

Average rent for 1 & 2 bedroom units	
(tenant pays utilities)	
$300 per month x 12 x 150	$ 540,000
Vacancy factor—5 percent	–27,000
Effective Gross Income	$ 513,000

EXPENSES

Real estate taxes (est.)	15%	
Insurance	4%	
Maintenance	10%	
Management	6%	
Reserve & Misc.	5%	
	40% of Effective Gross Income	$ –205,000
NET INCOME		$ 307,800

Figure 9–1. *Step-by-step income property analysis.*

FINANCING

Capitalization rate[1] 10¼%

$\dfrac{307,800}{.1025}$ = **$3,002,926 value**[2] established by **Income Capitalization Method**[3], say $3,000,000.

75% Loan-to-value ratio[4]

$3,000,000 x .75 = $2,250,000 loan

Rate[5] 9½ for 28 years

Monthly principal and interest, $19,163 x 12 = $229,950 **debt service**[6]

Constant[7] $\dfrac{229,950}{2,250,000}$ = 10.22

Debt coverage[8] $\dfrac{307,800}{229,950}$ = 1.34

Break-even point[9] $\dfrac{435,150}{540,000}$ = .80

Cash flow[10] $513,000 - 205,200 - 229,950 = $77,850

Figure 9-1. *Continued.*

[1]Capitalization rate—a rate used to convert into present value a series of future installments of net income. Used to establish value. (See Chapter 11, **Appraising Real Estate for Mortgage Loan Purposes,** for an explanation of how this rate is established.

[2]Value—an estimate arrived at by dividing the net income by the capitalization rate. Required in order to apply maximum legally allowed loan-to-value ratio.

[3]Income Capitalization Method—the most important appraisal technique used to establish an estimate of value based on a capitalization of net income.

[4]Loan-to-value ratio—in most cases, permanent investors are limited by law to lending only 75 percent of the value of an interest in real estate.

[5]Rate—the interest rate upon which the loan is to be repaid over a specific term, normally established by money market conditions.

[6]Debt service—the annual amount of principal and interest necessary to amortize the loan over its term.

[7]Constant—the percentage of the original loan paid in equal, annual payments (monthly principal and interest x 12) that provides for repayment of the loan over the term. In other words, the percentage that the annual debt service is to the original loan amount.

[8]Debt coverage—the amount of times (stated as a ratio) the net income covers (is over) the debt service.

[9]Break-even point—a percentage of occupancy required to produce sufficient income to meet operating expenses and debt service.

[10]Cash flow—the amount of cash derived from the real estate after debt service and expenses but *before* depreciation and income taxes.

As the location for the proposed construction is analyzed, particular emphasis should be placed on competing properties, population growth, income level, stability of employment, accessibility by automobile and public transportation, and any other factor which will affect the project at this location. This is often called a *market analysis.*

Timing

Assuming that the concept is financially sound, the figures work and a good location exists, the timing of the project is of crucial importance. If three months before the project is completed a similar one is opened elsewhere, in all probability this so-called good deal will fail, or at best have trouble renting. A rent cut may be necessary to attract tenants. The mortgage intermediary *must* investigate to determine whether or not other, similar projects are being planned.

Borrower

An entrepreneur is the most important link in the whole income-property financing chain. Without an entrepreneur's skill and a desire to create value where none existed or to increase existing value, the entire field of income property financing would be entirely different.

It is imperative that this entrepreneur have a successful track record. This record should be indicative of the entrepreneur's ability as a manager, because many developers want to manage the completed project to save management fees which normally are five percent of gross income.

The permanent mortgage investor is interested only in the borrower's ability to build the project according to plans and specifications and, most importantly, within budget. After the project is completed and funding by the permanent mortgagee has occurred, the borrower takes on secondary importance behind the tenants and the real estate.

Some permanent investors will attempt to get personal endorsements which obligate a borrower to repay the mortgage debt if a default occurs. Although these have questionable value in some jurisdictions, the entire financial condition of the borrower must be open to examination. An audited financial statement of the borrower's personal and professional status should be obtained.

Real Estate

For many years the value of the real estate served as the matrix for establishing the mortgage loan. It was assumed that a lender should be able to appraise the value of the real estate against which it was lending and by lending 75 percent of value have sufficient protection against any possible loss through the 25 percent equity if problems developed. Normally this is a valid assumption, but lenders have learned that most of the value created has a direct correlation to the general economic climate. A change in the economy could affect spending, which in turn could affect the mortgaged premises. Because of these problems, many lenders started to consider not only the real estate as security, but also the credit of both the borrower and long-term tenants.

THE INCOME-PROPERTY LENDING PROCESS

The stages through which an income property loan progresses are not always in the same order. But for the purpose of this text, the stages will be organized in a typical sequence.

The origination of this type of loan by a mortgage lender is generally quite different from the origination of a typical residential mortgage loan. The tract business, which is important to residential mortgage lending, is normally not available. Instead, origination resembles the residential spot business as satisfied builder-developers return for additional or new financing. Income property borrowers tend not to remember who helped finance their last deal. If your competitor is quoting rates an eighth or a quarter point lower, they will probably get the business.

If a mortgage lender such as a mortgage company has a correspondent relationship with an institutional investor (e.g., life insurance company) that investor may refer business directly received to the mortgage company.

The feasibility stage usually follows in which the mortgage lender analyzes the data to determine if a proposed transaction is possible. The format is much like the method previously suggested.

Assume a transaction looks like a deal that can be structured and placed. At this stage a mortgage lender will take an application from the borrower and may also require a good faith deposit of one or two percent of the amount sought. In addition to showing that a borrower has some cash to begin the project, this deposit prevents a borrower from shopping a commitment—that is, trying to get one at a lower interest rate or for a longer term. A mortgage intermediary will earn its fee when a commitment is obtained from a permanent lender according to the application, irrespective of whether the borrower accepts it. (See page 170 for a further discussion of commitment and standby fees.)

An application gives an originator a period of time in which to place the loan—usually 30 to 90 days. Since an application insures a fee if the loan is placed, time can be spent to underwrite the loan completely. This stage requires a complete analysis of the projected numbers and the estimation of value by an appraiser using the income approach primarily and the cost and market data approaches as a check. (See Chapter 11, Appraising Real Estate for Mortgage Loan Purposes.)

The *capitalization rate* and the *constant* are figures that can be used as pawns in negotiations with a permanent mortgage investor. A permanent lender may require a high capitalization rate and be willing to trade a longer mortgage term for it, or the borrower may want a lower constant and be willing to accept a higher interest rate in return. All factors should be negotiable, as long as both parties feel protected. An investor who insists on getting as much out of a loan as possible may end up being the owner—something it does not want.

All supporting data and documentation should be submitted to the investor in a carefully prepared loan submission. In some cases, this is all the investor will see, although all income property real estate should be inspected before a loan is funded.

Assuming a loan as submitted, or modified, is acceptable to the permanent mortgage investor, a *firm commitment* will be offered. At this point the mortgage intermediary's fee is earned. The closing of a loan, or *preclosing* if construction must still occur, normally terminates the production phase.

The last stage is the important one of servicing the mortgage loan. Many times, a permanent investor will require a few loans from a mortgage intermediary before granting servicing—others never grant it. (See Chapter 12, Closing and Administering the Mortgage Loan.)

PERMANENT MORTGAGE INVESTORS

Four main groups of permanent investors hold more than 80 percent of all long-term mortgages on income-producing real estate. These same four groups (See Figure 2-3) have been active for many years in all types of long-term mortgage lending, although their emphasis has shifted periodically from one type of loan to another.

All mortgage investors are concerned and motivated by *return on* and *return of* investment. Return on investment is the interest that is charged for the use of the money for the term of the loan. This interest rate is determined by the marketplace and the risk involved. Return of the investment is the repayment of the principal and is of primary concern to a mortgage investor.

As an investor reviews a potential loan, it is concerned with the degree of risk involved, because the risk element will affect the interest rate. If the risk is high, probably no interest rate will balance it, but if the risk is only moderate, a higher than normal interest rate may make the investment attractive. At this point, an investor would have to decide if the higher interest rate might jeopardize the basic deal and force foreclosure in the future.

An additional item to be considered by a mortgage investor, especially an insurance company, is the alternative investments which are competing for available investable dollars. These alternative investments would include bonds and real estate equities.

SUGGESTED READINGS

Archer, Wayne R. "Income Property Loans and Related Problems," *Federal Home Loan Bank Board Journal* (October 1980), pp. 13–15.

Britton, James A. and Kerwood, Lewis O., eds. *Financing Income-Producing Real Estate*. New York: McGraw-Hill Book Co., Inc., 1977.

Chesborough, Lowell D. "Do Participation Loans Pay Off?" *Real Estate Review* (Summer 1974), pp. 94–100.

Halper, Emanuel M. "What is a New Net Net Net Lease?" *Real Estate Review* (Winter 1974), pp. 9–14.

Handorf, William C. and Finley, Jane B. "Interest Capitalization and Project Profitability," *Real Estate Review* (Spring 1978), pp. 54–58.

Hoyt, Richard W. and Raffa, Basil J. "A Formula for Estimating Project Feasibility," *The Mortgage Banker* (October 1980), pp. 80–85.

Kempner, Paul S. "Investments in Single-Tenant Net Leased Properties," *Real Estate Review* (Summer 1974), pp. 131–34.

Robinson, Gerald J. *Federal Income Taxation of Real Estate*. Boston: Warren, Gorham & Lamont, Inc., 1974.

Sillcocks, H. Jackson. "Financing Sense in Real Estate Sales and Leasebacks," *Real Estate Review* (Spring 1975), pp. 89–95.

Unger, Maurice A. *Real Estate*. Cincinnati, Ohio: South-Western Publishing Co., 1974.

NOTES

1. A net lease is one where the tenant is responsible for all taxes, insurance, maintenance and operating expenses.

Chapter 10

The Lease and Leasehold Financing

INTRODUCTION

The business side of real estate is normally concerned with the building, sale, financing or leasing of real estate. The leasing aspect of real estate is extensive considering all the various and often complicated types of leases and leasing arrangements. Consumers and members of the real estate fraternity alike are exposed to leasing in one form or another. As a result everyone needs to be aware of the legal and financial aspects of leasing. The legal term for the interest or estate created by a lease is *leasehold estate*. (See Chapter 14, Fundamentals of Real Estate Law.)

The Importance of Leases

A lease fulfills various economic functions. To the tenant,[1] a lease establishes the contractual right to use and possess the real property of another. To the landlord, it creates the contractual right to collect rent. To a landlord, rent represents either a return on the investment, income to pay the mortgage on the leased real property, or both. The second alternative takes on greater importance when discussing income-producing real property, because a primary reason for the construction of income-producing real estate is to lease to a tenant whose rent will retire the mortgage and produce a reasonable net profit.

The law historically has considered a lease to be both a *conveyance* of real estate and a *contract*. It is considered a conveyance because the landlord is parting with a possessory right to the real estate for a period of time. Under a lease, a landlord gives up the right to use the real estate and, until the expiration of the lease, has only limited rights of a reversionary nature unless further rights have been reserved. For example, under common law, nonpayment of rent did not give a landlord the right to dispossess a tenant because the lease conveyed possession of the land to a tenant for the period of the lease. This rule, of course, has been modified by statute in all states. Another common law rule was that a tenant could not use lack of repairs to justify nonpayment of rent. But this has also been changed by statute in many states to alleviate the problems of slum landlords who continue to collect rent without making repairs.

A lease is considered a contract because it includes clauses containing certain covenants which are guarantees or promises. Since a lease is a contract as well as a conveyance, suit can be brought for breach of contract without terminating the lease. For example, if a tenant has a lease with a covenant requiring the landlord to make repairs to the leased premises but no repairs are made, the tenant can sue for breach of contract to repair, without destroying the lease. In another example, if a shopping center landlord has a valuable tenant who breaches a covenant, the landlord can retain that valuable tenant and still enforce the lease by suing for breach of contract on the appropriate covenant.

All leases, whether for a simple apartment or a complex industrial park, are basically the same. One lease may contain more clauses than another to resolve particular problems, but all will have the same basic elements. A review of the various clauses follows with an explanation of their function and importance. The clauses discussed will be examined from the viewpoint of understanding the different needs of both the landlord and tenant. It is important to emphasize that real estate laws differ among the states, and a local attorney should be consulted about any specific questions regarding leases.

The key to working with leases is to understand the lease itself. Any landlord or tenant should be able to find an answer to any question that could conceivably arise in the wording. The primary reason for a lease is to establish the *rights and duties* of both the landlord and tenant. The Statute of Frauds (each state has a statute named after the original English statute) requires that all leases for a period of more than one year be in writing. But as a practical matter all leases should be in writing for the protection of the parties involved.

Credit Loans

Due to recent and rapid fluctuations in the cost (interest rate) and value of money (inflation), long-term mortgage investors have been extremely hesitant to make loans based only on the real estate securing the debt. They have turned to making credit loans and in some cases, exclusively.

As mentioned previously, a permanent investor may look primarily at the credit of a tenant in determining whether to make the loan and how much to

EQUIFAX / RETAILERS COMMERCIAL AGENCY
CREDIT FIRM REPORT

SPECIMEN - ALL ENTITIES FICTITIOUS

CONFIDENTIAL

Acct. No. 00000   File No. Y-2567548   Report Made By Equifax ☐ Retailers ☒   Atlanta ____OFFICE

00-0-00
ACME CARD SHOP, INC.
Atlanta, Ga., 1675 Grady Street

Transaction: Lease of Space
Amount: $ 18,000/3 years

BUSINESS RECORD:
Check type business organization:
☒ Corporation—List names of officers.
☐ Partnership—List names of partners.
☐ Individual Proprietorship—List owner's name.

FULL NAME	TITLE	AGE	HOW LONG IN FIRM?	IF LESS THAN 2 YEARS WHAT WAS FORMER JOB?
Marvin Brown	President	43	5yrs.	
Louis Carter	Vice-Pres.	46	5yrs.	
Jane Lewis	Treasurer	41	5yrs.	

1. No. Years Known. 5yrs., 3yrs., 5yrs.
2. Date Business Started. 5-1-73
3. Line of business (Mfg., Wholesale, Retail) Retail Sales
4. Type products or Services rendered. Greeting cards, magazines, novelty items
5. Any suits, judgments, foreclosures, repossessions, bankruptcy against firm or members learned? None

6. Is Character of firm and members as to honesty and fair dealing good? If No, explain. Yes
7. Estimated Net Worth. $ 25,000
8. Estimated Gross Annual Sales. $ 175,000
9. Is Firm regarded as operating profitably at present? If not, explain. Yes
   Any factors which will adversely affect future success? If yes, explain. No

REMARKS: Amplify any irregular features above. Write separately paragraphs on the following:
CREDIT RECORD: Sources—Banks, Commercial Houses. Set out separately and specifically the experience and how regarded as a credit risk. Quote any legal records in file. Comment on any suits, judgments or bankruptcies developed through sources.
BUSINESS HISTORY: Describe size and nature of business, produce manufactured or sold or services rendered and scope of operations (local, state, national). Comment on present success and standing and future prospects for success. Cover experience and previous connection of each member of firm if in business less than 2 years. Show number of employees, if developed. Comment on location of business—whether inside city, uptown, suburban or out on highway. Cover any unusual competition which might affect this business.
FINANCES: Show kind of property that makes up worth of business. Try to develop assets and liabilities. Do they own or lease the building? Secure and attach or quote up-to-date financial statement if available. (If individually owned business, cover total net worth of owner in addition to net worth of business.)
FARM: If farm operating as firm, also cover information on farm.

CREDIT RECORD:
Bank of Atlanta: Bank officer reports paid unsecured loan in 4 figures, paid as agreed.
Bank of Athens: Bank officer reports open unsecured loan in 4 figures since 6-76, paying as agreed.
ABC Card Co.:   Dealing with this firm for 5 years, high credit $3500, pays 30 days, good account.
Business Landlord: Rental of business space paid promptly, $700 per month, satisfactory tenant.

BUSINESS HISTORY: The Acme Card Shop, Inc. is a moderate size retail greeting card store which was incorporated in the State of Georgia in 1973 and the above named officers have been with this firm since its inception. The firm engages in the sale of greeting cards, magazines and novelty items and employs 10 people. The firm has operated from the above location for the past 5 years and is a closed corporation. The firm has operated on a local level only and has been successful at this location.

FINANCES: The firm's net worth is estimated at $25,000 based upon bank account, inventory and equipment. Gross annual sales are estimated at $175,000 and these figures were obtained from the firm's accountant. This firm appears to be financially sound and prospects for the future appear favorable.

WFG/st
2cc

Equifax Inc.
Form 411—2-76 U.S.A.

Figure 10-1. *Sample credit report on a business for leasing purposes.*

lend when analyzing an income property loan application. Accordingly, the real estate takes on a secondary role as security. This lender is interested in determining whether the tenant is a recognizable credit—with either a national or regional reputation. In this way the lender can reasonably determine whether or not the tenant's net lease[2] will be sufficient to meet the debt service, which includes mortgage interest and principal. For example, if a major auto manufacturer executes a 30-year net lease at X dollars a year, a lender probably will make a mortgage loan to be amortized within 30 years if the debt service is also X dollars or, ideally, less. The ability to analyze a lease in a credit transaction is very important for both a mortgage originator and permanent investor.

THE LEASE

An effective lease should include the following:

- The parties to the lease
- An agreement to lease
- A description of the leased premises
- The term of the lease
- A rental agreement
- The rights and duties of all parties
- Signatures

Parties to the lease. It is necessary to identify the parties to the lease. When dealing with a corporation, reference should be made to the articles of incorporation which give the corporation the power to be either a landlord or a tenant. It is important that neither landlord nor tenant be a minor because a minor has the legal right to disaffirm a contract.

Agreement to lease. This is a contract between the parties whereby a landlord agrees to give possession of the premises to the tenant in return for certain promises by the tenant, including payment of rent, for a period of time.

Description of the premises. It is advisable to examine a landlord's title to the premises to prevent a tenant being evicted because of a title defect. The leased premises must be clearly identifiable. A description of the premises is usually sufficient, such as, the building at 727 South 3rd Street, or a legal description which identifies and locates the property being leased. If a part of a building is leased, the tenant has the right to use other parts of the building, including stairs, halls, toilets and other areas, even if not so stated within the lease.

Term of the lease. Although the vast majority of leases, especially residential leases, are for periods of less than 10 years, many commerical leases are for longer periods and may last for generations. Many states require that a lease last no longer than 99 years, making it important to determine at the time the lease is drawn how long it will last.

Lease Check List

I. Parties
A. Landlord
B. Tenant

II. Premises
A. Location
B. If less than all, what part

III. Term
A. Lease signed
B. Commences
C. Expires

IV. Rent
A. Base rent
B. Percentage
 i. Of gross income
 ii. Any offsets
C. Covenant to pay
D. Assignments of rent
 i. To investor
 ii. After foreclosure

V. Expenses
A. Escalation
B. Base year

C. Who is responsible for:

	Lessor	Lessee
Real estate taxes	___	___
Hazard insurance	___	___
Public liability insurance	___	___
Janitorial	___	___
Electricity	___	___
Elevators	___	___
Water	___	___
Fuel	___	___
Trash removal	___	___
Landscaping	___	___
Parking area	___	___
Air cond.	___	___
Repairs and maintenance	___	___
Other	___	___

VI. Assignment and subletting
A. Allowed?
B. Novation, or keep tenant liable
C. Increase rental to whom

VII. Mortgages
A. Leasehold mortgages allowed
B. Subordination
C. Limit of fee mortgage to lease income
D. Future mortgages subordinated

VIII. Condemnation
A. Tenants' share
B. Landlord share

Figure 10-2. *Lease checklist.*

Although a landlord is not obligated to renew a lease unless contracted to do so, it is typical to include in the lease the option to renew if the tenant is in good standing. If the option to renew exists, it will not benefit a sub-tenant. If the mortgage is based on the credit of a tenant, the option to renew would be critical if the lease term was less than the term of the mortgage. However, this would be an unusual situation since the mortgagee would normally require the protection of the lease.

If the option is exercised, the rental amount due under a renewed lease must be determined or the option to renew at a rent to be fixed in the future will be unenforceable because of uncertainty. Some courts have held *contra* if the rent can be established by a reasonable method such as an appraisal, formula, or equation. Under all circumstances, a lease should stipulate how the tenant is to give notice to renew and how much notice is to be given.

Rental agreement. As far as a landlord is concerned, the reason a lease exists is to produce income. Under the common law, rent was payable at the end of a rental period. Today, most landlords require that rent be paid at the beginning of the rental period. A tenant should realize rent paid in advance is not refundable if the premise is not occupied, unless the contract is contra. A lease should not only state the amount of the rent and when it is due, but also include a covenant to pay the rent. Then, if nonpayment occurs, the landlord can sue on the breach of the covenant to pay, instead of having to terminate the lease. Of course, nonpayment can justify termination of the lease if the landlord determines that it is the best alternative. If a tenant with the right to sublet does so, then the landlord has the right to sue the original tenant for any unpaid rent by the subtenant.

Rights and duties of the parties. As mentioned earlier, if a lease is prepared correctly, it should answer as many potential questions as possible regarding the rights and duties of the landlord and tenant. A discussion of some of the more common clauses designed to solve lease problems follows.

1. *Assignment of rent clause.* When dealing with commercial leases, one of the clauses that often creates conflicts involves rent assignments to the landlord's mortgagee. A permanent mortgage investor may require a direct assignment of rent clause because it is not confident of the financial stability of the landlord and, in effect, has made the mortgage on the credit of the tenant. In this case, the investor may insist on a direct assignment of the rents, although this would be unusual, whereby the tenant pays the investor who then takes out principal and interest. Some money may be placed in escrow for taxes and insurance and the difference rebated to the landlord. A more common type of direct assignment occurs when an investor requires a landlord to include a clause that obligates the tenant to forward all rent to the investor rather than to the landlord if there is a default on the mortgage.

2. *Tax clause.* Real estate taxes are a landlord's responsibility, but the lease can require a tenant to pay these taxes and often does. For example, if the lease is a net lease, the tenant is obligated to pay the real estate taxes, among other expenses. (See the section of the escalation clause for an additional explanation.)

3. *Insurance clause.* The landlord and tenant should clearly state in the lease who is responsible for obtaining and paying insurance. In a commercial lease, this could include public liability insurance, rental insurance, fire insurance, boiler insurance, glass insurance, elevator insurance, and any other type of insurance needed. For the protection of the landlord, the lease should require that insurance policies cannot be cancelled for nonpayment of premiums or materially amended unless the landlord has been given sufficient notice.

If a tenant has the obligation to pay taxes, insurance, etc., the lease should contain a requiring covenant. These obligations could be included as additional rent allowing a landlord to sue for nonpayment of rent if a tenant pays the contract rent but not the additional rent.

4. *Assignment clause.* In an assignment of a lease, a tenant is transferring all interests in the lease and, in effect, creating a new lease. This creates a new tenant who pays rent directly to the same landlord. With an assignment, the original tenant retains the obligation to the landlord. Therefore, a tenant cannot disregard an obligation to pay rent simply by assigning the lease to another party. If a tenant sublets, then the tenant in effect becomes a landlord since the entire interest under the lease is not being transferred. In this situation, as with an assignment, the prior tenant retains the obligation to the landlord.

Any tenant has the right to assign a lease unless the landlord has restricted the right. Most sophisticated landlords hold back the right to assign or sublet, except with their approval. Normally, this approval will be given because many landlords realize that without the right to transfer a particular lease, a tenant might not be able to sell a business (such as a restaurant) located on or in the leased premises. If a lease allows a transfer with approval, the approval cannot be capriciously withheld. Any increase in rent should go to the landlord if a landlord does allow a tenant to assign or sublet.

5. *Escalation clauses.* The basic reason for escalation clauses is to protect a landlord from inflation and in this way protect the investment. Although most residential leases do not include escalation clauses, many commercial leases now contain them. A few apartment leases also have such clauses. A tenant should insist that an escalation clause affect all tenants on an equal basis.

The escalation clause based on the escalation of taxes is most common. At the time a lease is drawn, it is impossible to predict the level of future taxes. Taxes will probably rise at least at the rate of inflation, which also is indeterminable. If taxes are to be paid completely by the tenant, no need exists for an escalation clause. The clause is required only if increases are to be paid by the tenant. Any increase should be calculated on a base year, and the lease should clearly define the base year. The first three years after the building is completed and 80 percent occupied could be the base year for determining the amount of taxes to be passed on to the tenant. A tenant may want a landlord to agree that the tenant can contest tax increases in the landlord's name.

Escalation clauses for operating expense exist for the same reason as those for taxes. Escalation clauses should include the increases in wages, supplies, repairs or similar expenses. A base year again is advisable if the increases are to be paid by the tenant. Some experts have suggested an operating expenses escalation clause based on the government cost-of-living index, but this index does not always reflect the items included under operation expenses. It seems better to have actual increases passed through to the tenant, especially in an inflationary economy.

6. *Percentage clause.* Another way to protect a landlord against inflation is through the use of percentage leases. These can also exist for the benefit of a tenant. In a percentage lease, any additional rent generally is computed over a base rent or a base amount. This base rent is usually lower than what both parties expect a business to normally pay for a similar premise (economic rent) that has no percentage lease. After a certain gross income level has been reached, a percentage of the excess amount becomes additional rent to the landlord.

A percentage lease allows a tenant to stay in business during adverse economic times, since the rent being paid for the premises is actually less than the rent paid if it were based purely on current economics or the rent of competing businesses. On the other hand, a percentage lease allows a landlord to participate in good times through the increased income a tenant is generating by the use of the real property owned by the landlord.

It is important for all parties to understand that a percentage lease is not a partnership, even though profits are shared. A partner is liable for losses. Consequently, courts have been clear in stating that a percentage lease does not make a landlord a partner with a tenant. Suppose the base rent is $5,000 per year and, if the business grosses more than $100,000 for the year, the landlord will receive five percent of the amount over $100,000 as additional rent. If the business grosses $500,000, the additional rent to the landlord would be $20,000 (.05 × $400,000 = $20,000), or a total rent of $25,000.

Percentage leases should be based on the gross income of a business. Gross income rather than net income is suggested because a tenant might include improper expense items to arrive at net income. Another reason for using gross income is that there may be additional income generated from the premises but still related to the lease, such as repairs. Therefore, a lease should explicitly define gross income.

The percentage a landlord would receive over the base amount varies from area to area and from business to business. The range may be anywhere from half of one percent for a chain supermarket to 60 percent for a parking lot. The base rent is usually payable monthly, while the percentage rent based on gross income will probably be calculated and made payable at the end of the calendar or fiscal year.

7. *Other clauses.* A covenant to do business is necessary with a percentage lease, and it should clearly state that a tenant has an obligation to continue in business. The reason for this clause is clear. Business might be too good and a tenant will realize that the percentage rent is higher than expected. Business may be bad and the tenant will not want to continue in business. Either way, the landlord is affected. Therefore, a continuous operation clause should be made part of the covenant to do business requiring that the tenant remain in business the entire year to insure that a peak period is not missed. It also should prevent a tenant from operating only when business is good, then closing shop for the remainder of the year and prorating income over the entire year.

In addition to the clauses that make a percentage lease operative, a radius clause should be used. Under a radius clause, a tenant cannot operate a second business within a certain area if that business would compete with the one under lease. The radius might be determined in miles if a small community is involved, or by blocks in a large urban area. This clause prevents a tenant from competing with its own business. Such competition would keep income and the percentage rent down. A problem with radius clauses and competition is the questionable legality of preventing a tenant from advertising its other stores.

Mortgages and Leases

Whenever these two topics are discussed, the paramount issue is one of priorities. The simplest rule is the first to be recorded will have a superior position, meaning that if a lease exists on real estate in question before a mortgage encumbers that real estate, the lease is protected and will continue even if a mortgage forecloses.

If the lease is subsequent to the mortgage, then the lease is in jeopardy. If the need to foreclose occurs, in most states the lease would be terminated by a foreclosure proceeding. The legal reason for this is that a tenant is in possession of the premises based on a landlord's (mortgagor's) right to possession. But upon foreclosure the landlord is no longer entitled to possession. This is not the case if the lease predates the mortgage since the mortgagee is bound by the mortgagor's contract with the tenant.

Termination of a lease as a result of foreclosure is not always the desired result for a mortgagee. As mentioned, some mortgages are made based either on the fact that tenants are available or on the credit rating of a tenant. To lose such a tenant could make the property less valuable. A solution to this problem is to make the mortgage subordinate to the important subsequent lease so if the need to foreclose should arise, the valuable tenant will not be lost.

LEASEHOLD FINANCING

As leasehold interests have become more common and important in commercial real estate, various techniques have developed which enable sophisticated landlords, developers and tenants to realize the maximum value from their real estate interest. These techniques include the use of the sale-leaseback and the use of the leasehold interest as security for a mortgage.

A leasehold interest has sufficient determinable value to be one of these financing techniques if the term of the lease is long enough, the rent reasonable, and the real estate desirable. However, many of the decisions on financing the lease and which technique to use are based on tax considerations. A complete explanation of these tax considerations is beyond the scope of this text, but the more obvious ones will be discussed.

Sale-Leaseback

This technique has been used for many years but in the past 25 years or so has become a common financing technique. It gained acceptance when various state laws were amended to allow insurance companies to purchase real estate for investment rather than be limited solely to legally-prescribed loan-to-value mortgages.

A sale-leaseback simply is a sale of real estate to a buyer who simultaneously leases it back to the seller. For example, assume Ajax Steel owns a smelter and the land on which the smelter is located and wants to sell the land, then immediately lease it back. The reasons for this apparently simple transaction are many, but could include any or all of the following:

1. The seller, who did not want its capital tied up in real estate, would rather use the capital to expand its business or acquire additional inventory.
2. The transaction allows a seller to obtain 100 percent of the value of the land sold. If the seller had decided to mortgage, it could have received only up to a maximum of 75 percent of value.
3. The rent the seller has to pay for the leased premises is deductible for income tax purposes and usually less, ideally, than the debt service on a mortgage.

For the buyer, the several advantages of this transaction would include:

1. Greater security for an investment since title is held by the buyer.
2. Normally higher yield than could be obtained from making a mortgage loan because of no usury limitations. Also the buyer often becomes a participant in gross income.
3. An appreciating asset.

This technique also can be used in many situations that require additional financing. For example, assume a developer owns land upon which an office building has been constructed and a permanent mortgage obtained for 75 percent of value. The developer could sell the land under the building and lease it back using the proceeds from the sale to obtain what amounts to 100 percent financing of the office building.

During the prosperous days of 1971–1973 of the Real Estate Investment Trusts, the purchase of land under income-producing real estate, with a net lease back to the seller/tenant, provided an investment without any management problems associated with the land itself. This desirable investment also produced the yield REITs needed on their investments.

If a sale-leaseback is successfully negotiated, a question may arise later concerning whether the transaction was really a sale or a disguised 100 percent mortgage. All aspects of the transaction must be carefully analyzed including sale price, rent, and the amount of the repurchase price. The required documents also must be carefully drafted to prevent one of the parties or, more probably, the Internal Revenue Service, from alleging the transaction was a mortgage. If a court holds the transaction was a disguised mortgage, then the tenant/mortgagor is the legal owner and the landlord/mortgagee has merely a security interest. In addition to the tax consequences of the transaction being a mortgage, the existence of a usurious interest rate is probable. Courts have held that the test for determining whether a sale-leaseback transaction is a sale or a mortgage is the intent of the parties.[3]

Financing the Leasehold Interest

A lease can be mortgaged just as any other interest in real estate that can be sold. The danger of lending money on a lease is that there may be no tangible security. The mortgagee of a fee can always foreclose and obtain the real property, if necessary, but the mortgagee of a lease may only have the lease as security. If the leasehold mortgagor also owns the building on the leased land, then the leasehold mortgagee will have a much stronger security position.[4]

A leasehold mortgagee faces two dangers: 1) the lease could be cancelled by the landlord for some nonperformance by the tenant; or 2) the lease could be cancelled by foreclosure by a feehold mortgagee if the lease is subsequent to a mortgage on the fee.[5] Usually, the mortgagee of a leasehold interest will require an estoppel certificate from the landlord which states that there is no back rent due, no set-offs, no liens, no prior default, nor any other reason why the lease would be vulnerable. The best protection for a leasehold mortgagee would be an agreement that any nonperformance by the tenant would allow the lease to continue until the mortgagee is given a chance to cure the default.

If a lease is prior to a mortgage on the fee, the tenant, and thus its mortgagee, need not be concerned about a foreclosure of the fee mortgage, but if the fee mortgage is prior to the lease, foreclosure could terminate the lease. Even if the lease is subsequent to the fee mortgage, a leasehold interest could be protected by a nondisturbance agreement which states that the fee mortgagee will not destroy the lease if a foreclosure of the fee mortgage occurs. A nondisturbance agreement is useless in some states, since their laws require that if a foreclosure occurs, all subsequent leases are terminated. In those states, a subordination agreement is needed by which the fee mortgagee subordinates its mortgage to the lease.

Normally, a mortgagee of a fee would be willing to subordinate since the lease makes the security more valuable. In some situations a mortgagee may not want to subordinate, because it may feel a property unencumbered by leases would be easier to sell.

This concept is not always easy to understand especially in those situations where mortgages exist on both the fee interest and the leasehold interest. For example, assume ABC is the owner of a shopping center, upon which the PDQ Insurance Company has a mortgage. ABC leases a quarter acre on the edge of the parking lot to XYZ to build a coffee shop. XYZ's coffee shop is constructed and XYZ obtains a permanent mortgage on its leasehold interest from the LUV Insurance Company. At the request of LUV, PDQ Insurance Company subordinated its mortgage on the fee to XYZ's lease in order that XYZ could get the leasehold mortgage. This subordination was acceptable to PDQ because it then had greater security for its mortgage in the lease payment from XYZ.

An example which combines a sale-leaseback and a mortgage of a leasehold interest and also portrays the conflicting claims and motivations of the parties involved follows:

Mr. A owns a parcel of valuable real estate which has been in the family for a number of years and upon which he plans to build an office building. Mr. A does not have the cash to begin construction although a local commercial bank will provide a construction mortgage if Mr. A can obtain sufficient cash.

In order to obtain this cash, Mr. A decides to sell the land to B Investment Company which will simultaneously lease the land back to him under a long-term net lease at a rental amount which provides B with an attractive yield on its investment and a participation in future rental income. Mr. A receives 100 percent of the value of the land in cash—as contrasted with a typical 50 percent of value loan on an unimproved real estate—and is therefore able to get a construction loan for the construction of the office building. The office building is then constructed on his leasehold estate (interest).

Mr. A now wants to obtain a permanent mortgage from C Insurance Company to pay off the construction mortgage and get his cash out. C is willing to make the leasehold mortgage with the building and leasehold interest as security but only if B will subordinate its fee interest to the mortgage. The reason for this demand is that C, the leasehold mortgagee, is concerned about its security which in reality is the leasehold interest of Mr. A. This interest could disappear if the lease is terminated by a default by the tenant, Mr. A.

This security interest of C could be protected by requiring B to notify C of any default and allowing C a chance to cure the default, but this is not acceptable to C. C's primary fear is the possibility that the office building will be difficult to rent and consequently Mr. A would probably default on his lease payment. B would then notify C to cure the default or lose the lease and, for all practical purposes, the building. C does not want to be in a situation where it would have to foreclose the mortgage and become the owner of a leasehold interest, which is uneconomical. C will therefore insist that B's fee be subordinated in order that a foreclosure of the leasehold interest will wipe out the fee interest of B allowing for the sale of the land and building. The B Investment Company will probably agree to subordinate its interest because it realizes its fee will be more valuable with an improvement and its participation in rent can only occur if an improvement exists.

SUGGESTED READINGS

Bohon, Davis T. *Complete Guide to Profitable Real Estate Leasing.* Englewood Cliffs, New Jersey: Prentice-Hall, Inc., 1969.

Dennis, Marshall W. "Close Scrutiny Helps Avoid Legal Troubles in Commerical Leases," *The Mortgage Banker* (December 1974), pp. 27–34.

Friedman, M. R. *Friedman on Leases.* New York: Practicing Law Institute, 1974.

Levy, Daniel S. "ABC's of Shopping Center Leases," *Real Estate Review* (Spring 1971), pp. 12–16.

McMichael, Stanley L., and O'Keefe, Paul T. *Leases: Percentage, Short and Long Term.* Englewood Cliffs, New Jersey: Prentice-Hall, Inc., 1974.

Orendorf, James M. "Origination and Servicing: The Income Property Loan from Cradle to Grave," *The Mortgage Banker* (October 1978), pp. 144–146.

NOTES

1.   The term landlord (lessor) and tenant (lessee) will be used in place of the less understood legal terms.

2.   The term net lease will be used to define the situation where the tenant is obligated to pay all taxes, insurance, operating, and maintenance expenses.

3.   See, In Re San Francisco Industrial Park, Inc., 307 F. Supp. 271, 274 (N.D. Calif. 1969).

4.   Normally, the only time a leasehold mortgage is made with only the lease as security is when the purpose of the loan is to finance inventory, or other short-term capital needs.

5.   A mortgagee will only make a leasehold mortgage if the loan is fully amortized before the expiration of the lease. Some require that the loan be fully amortized before 75 percent of the term of the ground lease expires.

Chapter 11

Appraising Real Estate for Mortgage Loan Purposes

INTRODUCTION

The purpose of this chapter is to provide an overview of the fundamentals of real estate appraisal, define the standard terminology used, and explain the common methods of estimating value. An appraisal of real estate is a supportable estimate of value made by a technically trained specialist as of a specific date.[1] The value being sought could be insurable value or assessed value, but is most often market value.

An appraisal may be required to provide an estimate of value in almost any stage of a real estate transaction or activity. For example, at any given moment an appraisal of real estate may be needed to estimate:

- Assessed value for taxation purposes
- Insurance value
- Market value for sale or exchange purposes
- Market value for mortgage loan purposes
- Compensation in condemnation proceedings
- Rental value

The value determined for the same piece of real estate can vary according to the purpose of the appraisal; the estimated value for insurance purposes could be much different from the value estimated for condemnation purposes. In this chapter the value to be estimated will be market value since most mortgage lenders are required by law or regulation to lend only a certain percentage of market value.

VALUE

A clear, concise definition of value is difficult if not impossible to obtain because the concept of value means many different things. One of the classical definitions holds that value is the capacity of an economic good to command other goods in exchange. In other words, the value of an object is established by what it can get in exchange, or value represents that point stated as a price where supply and demand coincide or intersect.

Market value of real estate is that price a property would bring on the open market if offered for sale during a reasonable period of time by a seller not forced to sell and if sought by a purchaser not forced to buy. The *market price* is that price for which the real estate actually sells. In theory, market value and price should be the same, but they rarely are. For example, a seller may decide to accept less (market price) than asked (market value) in order to facilitate the sale if the seller believes time is more valuable than the difference in money.

PRINCIPLES OF REAL ESTATE VALUE

Value of a given piece of real estate does not remain the same. The value can be changed by:

1. Shifts in social standards and ideals such as population growth or decline
2. Economic developments such as the opening or closing of a large industrial plant
3. Modifications of governmental regulations affecting zoning or building codes
4. Shifts in traffic patterns or road networks

If these factors remain constant, the market value of a given piece of real estate may still change as a result of the following more basic value determinants:

1. *Supply and demand.* Real estate is similar to all other marketable commodities in that its value is increased or decreased by supply and demand.

2. *Highest and best use.* Market value of real estate is influenced most by whether the real estate is being put to its highest and best use. This use is defined as that providing the greatest net return over a period of time. This return could be in terms of money or amenities (living in a house as opposed to renting it).

3. *Diminishing returns.* This principle recognizes that continuing additions to the whole will not continue to increase the value of the whole by the value of the addition after a certain point.

4. *Substitution.* This basic principle perceives that the upper limit of the value of the real estate tends to be established by the cost of acquiring an equally-desirable substitute property.

THE APPRAISAL PROCESS

Since an appraisal is intended to solve a problem; that is, to estimate value, the problem must be clearly stated as to what type of value is sought. The process required to provide this estimate of value necessitates identification of the following:

- The real estate to be appraised
- Property rights involved
- Type of value to be estimated
- Function or use of the appraisal

To accomplish the assigned task, an appraiser must review and analyze all data relating to the economic background of the region, city and neighborhood of the subject property, the demographic profile, amenities and, finally, of the subject property itself (Figure 11–1). The next step in the process is the application of one or more of the three approaches to value.

Market Data Approach

This approach to value, often referred to as the *direct sales comparison approach,* uses market data on sale prices of similar properties to estimate value. This is the most common approach used for single-family residential properties. The principle of substitution is evident since the value of a property similar to the subject property should closely approximate the value of the subject property. The market value for the comparables is best substantiated by the actual recent sales prices.

An appraiser will use as many recent sales of similar or comparable properties as possible and the more used, the better will be the estimate. The market price will be adjusted for whatever physical differences exist between the comparables and the subject property. Any features of a comparable that are not found in the subject property are subtracted from the value of the comparable to suggest the value of the subject property. On the other hand, features in the subject property not present in the comparable are added to the value of the comparable to adjust the value. The basis formula is as follows:

Value of comparable property ± adjustments = Value of subject property

For example, if house A with a finished basement worth $6,000 currently sells for $61,000 and is otherwise comparable to house B, then the estimate of value for house B would be $55,000: The house A value of $61,000–$6,000 for finished basement = House B value of $55,000.

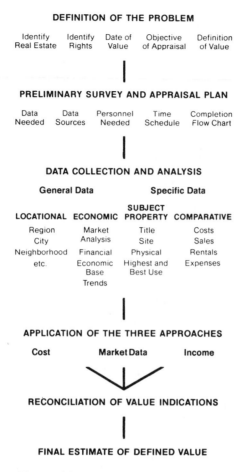

Figure 11–1. *The appraisal process.*

Cost Approach

This approach to estimating value often is referred to as the *summation approach.* It combines the cost of replacing or reproducing the improvements with the value of the land and is often considered most important when dealing with non-residential, non-income-producing, special purpose real estate, such as a public library, or when used as a check against other approaches. The concept behind this approach is that an investor would not pay more for an improvement on the open market than it would cost to build a new one.

The cost that is estimated in order to arrive at a value of a subject property by the cost approach is either reproduction cost or replacement cost.

1. *Reproduction cost.* The current amount of money needed to construct a new duplicate structure.

2. *Replacement cost.* Some structures cannot be duplicated at any reasonable cost. Therefore, the cost sought is the cost to construct a structure with the same utility.

When figuring cost for either reproduction or replacement, both direct costs such as supplies, labor and profits, and indirect costs including fees, taxes and financing costs, are listed.

The appraiser considers the fact that the subject property will not be the same as a reproduced structure because of depreciation or loss in value to the subject property. Therefore, adjustments must be made to either the reproduction or replacement cost reflecting existing depreciation. Depreciation includes:

1. *Physical deterioration.* A loss in value from the cost of a new structure is made equal to the loss of economic life in the subject property caused by wear and tear. This physical deterioration may or may not be curable.

2. *Functional obsolescence.* A loss in value resulting from structural components, such as bathrooms, kitchens or in the overall layout, that are outmoded or inefficient as judged by current desires or standards.

3. *Economic obsolescence.* A loss in value resulting from changes external to the property such as changes in zoning classifications, sharp increases in property taxes or other negative influences.

The cost approach can be explained simply:

Cost of reproduction or replacement – depreciation + land value =
Value of subject property

For example, assume the problem is to estimate the value of an old public library which has depreciated 50 percent. The cost to build a new public library (reproduction cost) is $1.5 million and the land is valued at $100,000. The estimate of value is made in this way:

Cost $1,500,000 – depreciation of $750,000 + land, $100,000 =
$850,000 value of subject property

Income Approach

This approach to estimating value uses the net operating income of the property. Although the other two approaches can be used for residences and other types of property, this approach is normally used to arrive at the value for income-producing real estate such as office buildings, apartments and other commercial establishments. The concept is that an ascertainable

RESIDENTIAL APPRAISAL REPORT

File No.

To be completed by Lender

| Borrower Martin, John R. & Pamela S. | Census Tract | Map Reference |

Property Address 2800 Linden Lane

City Springfield   County Fairfax   State Virginia   Zip Code 22132

Legal Description Lot 42, Section 2, Olde Forge Subdivision

Sale Price $ 35,000   Date of Sale current   Loan Term 30 yrs   Property Rights Appraised ☒Fee ☐Leasehold ☐DeMinimis PUD

Actual Real Estate Taxes $ 700   (yr) Loan charges to be paid by seller $ Other sales concessions

Lender/Client Blake Mortgage Company   Address Lendertown, Virginia

Occupant R.J. Miller   Appraiser Jones & Co.   Instructions to Appraiser

NEIGHBORHOOD

				Good	Avg.	Fair	Poor
Location	☒Urban	☐Suburban	☐Rural				
Built Up	☒Over 75%	☐25% to 75%	☐Under 25%	Employment Stability	☒	☐	☐	☐
Growth Rate ☐Fully Dev.	☐Rapid	☒Steady	☐Slow	Convenience to Employment	☐	☒	☐	☐
Property Values	☐Increasing	☒Stable	☐Declining	Convenience to Shopping	☐	☒	☐	☐
Demand/Supply	☐Shortage	☒In Balance	☐Over Supply	Convenience to Schools	☒	☐	☐	☐
Marketing Time	☒Under 3 Mos.	☐4–6 Mos.	☐Over 6 Mos.	Adequacy of Public Transportation	☒	☐	☐	☐

Present Land Use 75% 1 Family ___% 2–4 Family ___% Apts. 25% Condo ___% Commercial

___% Industrial ___% Vacant ___%

Change in Present Land Use ☒Not Likely   ☐Likely (*)   ☐Taking Place (*)

(*) From ___ To ___

Predominant Occupancy ☒Owner   ☐Tenant   ___% Vacant

Single Family Price Range $ 31,000 to $ 40,000   Predominant Value $ 36,000

Single Family Age 17 yrs to 20 yrs   Predominant Age 18 yrs

	Good	Avg.	Fair	Poor
Recreational Facilities	☐	☐	☒	☐
Adequacy of Utilities	☒	☐	☐	☐
Property Compatibility	☐	☒	☐	☐
Protection from Detrimental Conditions	☒	☐	☐	☐
Police and Fire Protection	☒	☐	☐	☐
General Appearance of Properties	☐	☒	☐	☐
Appeal to Market	☐	☒	☐	☐

Note: FHLMC/FNMA do not consider race or the racial composition of the neighborhood to be reliable appraisal factors.

Comments including those factors, favorable or unfavorable, affecting marketability (e.g. public parks, schools, view, noise) None

SITE

Dimensions 70' X 150' = 10,500 Sq. Ft. or Acres   ☐Corner Lot

Zoning classification A-1

Highest and best use: ☒Present use   ☐Other (specify)

Present improvements ☒do ☐do not conform to zoning regulations

	Public	Other (Describe)	OFF SITE IMPROVEMENTS	Topo	level
Elec.	☒		Street Access: ☒Public ☐Private	Size	average
Gas	☒		Surface asphalt	Shape	rectangular
Water	☒		Maintenance: ☒Public ☐Private	View	satisfactory
San.Sewer	☒		☒Storm Sewer ☒Curb/Gutter	Drainage	good

☐Underground Elect. & Tel. ☒Sidewalk ☒Street Lights   Is the property located in a HUD Identified Special Flood Hazard Area? ☒No ☐Yes

Comments (favorable or unfavorable including any apparent adverse easements, encroachments or other adverse conditions) None

IMPROVEMENTS

☒Existing ☐Proposed ☐Under Constr.   No. Units 1   Type (det, duplex, semi/det, etc.) detached   Design (rambler, split level, etc.) rambler   Exterior Walls brick

Yrs. Age: Actual ___ Effective ___ to ___   No. Stories 1

Roof Material comp. shingle   Gutters & Downspouts ☒None aluminum   Window (Type): wood sash   Insulation ☐None ☐Floor

☐Storm Sash ☐Screens ☒Combination   ☒Ceiling ☐Roof ☒Walls

☐Manufactured Housing   50% Basement   ☒Floor Drain   Finished Ceiling full

Foundation Walls cinder block   ☒Outside Entrance   ☐Sump Pump   Finished Walls full

☐Concrete Floor   ___% Finished   Finished Floor full

☐Slab on Grade ☐Crawl Space   Evidence of: ☐Dampness ☐Termites ☐Settlement

Comments

ROOM LIST

Room List	Foyer	Living	Dining	Kitchen	Den	Family Rm.	Rec. Rm.	Bedrooms	No. Baths	Laundry	Other
Basement							X			X	
1st Level	X	X	X	X				3	2		
2nd Level											

Finished area above grade contains a total of 6 rooms, 3 bedrooms, 2 baths. Gross Living Area ___ sq. ft. Bsmt Area ___ sq. ft.

Kitchen Equipment: ☒Refrigerator ☒Range/Oven ☒Disposal ☒Dishwasher ☒Fan/Hood ☐Compactor ☐Washer ☐Dryer

HEAT: Type for air Fuel gas Cond. good   AIR COND: ☒Central ☐Other   ☒Adequate ☐Inadequate

INTERIOR FINISH & EQUIPMENT

Floors	☒Hardwood ☒Carpet Over 75% ___	
Walls	☒Drywall ☐Plaster ☐ ___	
Trim/Finish	☐Good ☒Average ☐Fair ☐Poor	
Bath Floor	☒Ceramic ☐ ___	
Bath Wainscot	☒Ceramic ☐ ___	

Special Features (including energy efficient items) fireplace

ATTIC: ☒Yes ☐No ☐Stairway ☐Drop-stair ☒Scuttle ☐Floored

Finished (Describe) ___ ☐Heated

CAR STORAGE: ☐Garage ☐Built-in ☐Attached ☐Detached ☒Car Port

No. Cars 1 ☒Adequate ☐Inadequate Condition good

FIREPLACES, PATIOS, POOL, FENCES, etc. (describe) None

PROPERTY RATING

	Good	Avg.	Fair	Poor
Quality of Construction (Materials & Finish)	☒	☐	☐	☐
Condition of Improvements	☒	☐	☐	☐
Room sizes and layout	☐	☒	☐	☐
Closets and Storage	☐	☒	☐	☐
Insulation—adequacy	☐	☒	☐	☐
Plumbing—adequacy and condition	☐	☒	☐	☐
Electrical—adequacy and condition	☐	☒	☐	☐
Kitchen Cabinets—adequacy and condition	☐	☒	☐	☐
Compatibility to Neighborhood	☐	☒	☐	☐
Overall Livability	☐	☒	☐	☐
Appeal and Marketability	☐	☒	☐	☐

Yrs. Est. Remaining Economic Life 40 to ___   Explain if less than Loan Term.

COMMENTS (including functional or physical inadequacies, repairs needed, modernization, etc.) None

FHLMC Form 70 Rev. 7/79   ATTACH DESCRIPTIVE PHOTOGRAPHS OF SUBJECT PROPERTY AND STREET SCENE   FNMA Form 1004 Rev. 7/79

Figure 11–2. *FNMA/FHLMC residential appraisal report.*

VALUATION SECTION

Purpose of Appraisal is to estimate Market Value as defined in Certification & Statement of Limiting Conditions (FHLMC Form 439/FNMA Form 1004B). If submitted for FNMA, the appraiser must attach (1) sketch or map showing location of subject, street names, distance from nearest intersection, and any detrimental conditions and (2) exterior building sketch of improvements showing dimensions.

COST APPROACH

Measurements	No. Stories			Sq. Ft.
55' x 25'	x 1	=		1,375
19' x 12	x 1	=		228
x	x	=		
x	x	=		
x	x	=		
x	x	=		

Total Gross Living Area (List in Market Data Analysis below) _____

Comment on functional and economic obsolescence: _____

ESTIMATED REPRODUCTION COST – NEW – OF IMPROVEMENTS:

Dwelling 1,600 Sq. Ft. @ $ 19.00	=	$	30,400
Sq. Ft. @ $	=		
Extras bsmt. rec. room	=		600
Special Energy Efficient Items _____	=		
Porches, Patios, etc.	=		
Garage/Car Port 140 Sq. Ft. @ $ 5.00	=		700
Site Improvements (driveway, landscaping, etc.)	=		800
Total Estimated Cost New	=	$	32,500

Physical | Functional | Economic

Less Depreciation $ 4,000 | $ | $ = $ (4,000)

Depreciated value of improvements . . . . . . = $ 28,500

ESTIMATED LAND VALUE . . . . = $ 7,000
(If leasehold, show only leasehold value)

INDICATED VALUE BY COST APPROACH . . = $ 35,500

The undersigned has recited three recent sales of properties most similar and proximate to subject and has considered these in the market analysis. The description includes a dollar adjustment, reflecting market reaction to those items of significant variation between the subject and comparable properties. If a significant item in the comparable property is superior to, or more favorable than, the subject property, a minus (-) adjustment is made, thus reducing the indicated value of subject; if a significant item in the comparable is inferior to, or less favorable than, the subject property, a plus (+) adjustment is made, thus increasing the indicated value of the subject.

MARKET DATA ANALYSIS

ITEM	Subject Property	COMPARABLE NO. 1		COMPARABLE NO. 2		COMPARABLE NO. 3	
Address	2800 Linden	2463 Brinkley		2765 Lemen		3215 Essex	
Proximity to Subj.		2 blocks		1 block		2 blocks	
Sales Price	$ 35,000		$ 33,900		$ 36,000		$ 34,990
Price/Living area	$		$		$		$
Data Source	MLS	MLS		MLS		MLS	
Date of Sale and Time Adjustment	DESCRIPTION	DESCRIPTION	+(−)$ Adjustment 500	DESCRIPTION	+(−)$ Adjustment 500	DESCRIPTION	+(−)$ Adjustment 500
Location	good	good		good		exc	−200
Site/View	good	good		good		good	
Design and Appeal	good	good		exc	−250	good	
Quality of Const.	good	good		good		good	
Age	19 yrs	19 yrs		17 yrs		18 yrs	
Condition	good	good		good		good	
Living Area Room Count and Total	Total 6 B-rms 3 Baths 2	Total 6 B-rms 3 Baths 2		Total 6 B-rms 3 Baths 2		Total 6 B-rms 3 Baths 2	
Gross Living Area	1600 Sq.Ft.	1600 Sq.Ft.		1700 Sq.Ft.	−1000	1650 Sq.Ft.	−500
Basement & Bsmt. Finished Rooms	1	1/2	600	1/2 - 2	−350	1/2	600
Functional Utility	good	good		good		good	
Air Conditioning	cent.	cent		cent		cent	
Garage/Car Port	c/p	c/p		none	600	c/p	
Porches, Patio, Pools, etc.	none	none		patio	−400	none	
Special Energy Efficient Items	none	none		none		none	
Other (e.g. fireplaces, kitchen equip., remodeling)	firepl	firepl		firepl		firepl	
Sales or Financing Concessions	13% down	10% down		15% down		10% down	
Net Adj. (Total)		☒ Plus; ☐ Minus $ 1,100		☐ Plus;☒ Minus $ 900		☐ Plus; ☒Minus $ 100	
Indicated Value of Subject		$ 35,000		$35,100		$34,890	

Comments on Market Data ___ These sales are the three most recent rambler transactions.

INDICATED VALUE BY MARKET DATA APPROACH . . . . $ 35,000

INDICATED VALUE BY INCOME APPROACH (If applicable) Economic Market Rent $ 235 /Mo. x Gross Rent Multiplier 150 = $ 35,250

This appraisal is made ☐ "as is" ☐ subject to the repairs, alterations, or conditions listed below ☐ completion per plans and specifications.

Comments and Conditions of Appraisal: _____

Final Reconciliation: ___ Market approach is most indicative of suject's current market value and was given the most weight.

Construction Warranty ☐ Yes ☒ No Name of Warranty Program _____ Warranty Coverage Expires _____

This appraisal is based upon the above requirements, the certification, contingent and limiting conditions, and Market Value definition that are stated in
☐ FHLMC Form 439 (Rev. 10/78)/FNMA Form 1004B (Rev. 10/78) filed with client_____ 19____ ☐ attached.

I ESTIMATE THE MARKET VALUE, AS DEFINED, OF SUBJECT PROPERTY AS OF _____ 19____ to be $ 35,000

Appraiser(s) _R D Smith_ Jones & Co. Review Appraiser (If applicable) _____

☐ Did ☒ Did Not Physically Inspect Property

FHLMC Form 70 Rev. 7/79

REVERSE
43570-1 SAF Systems and Forms

FNMA Form 1004 Rev. 7/79

Figure 11-2. *Continued.*

relationship exists between the income a property earns and the price, or value, someone would be willing to pay for that property.

Obviously, this approach can be used only for those properties that have or will have income, but a special technique called the *gross rent multiplier* (GRM) can be used either to estimate value for a single-family residence or to serve as a check against the other approaches. The theory behind GRM is that the same market will influence both the sales price and the rental price and, therefore, both tend to move up or down in tandem. This relationship can be expressed as a ratio:

$$\frac{\text{Sale price}}{\text{Gross income}} = \text{GRM}$$

Thus, if a house recently sold for $72,000 and rented for $500 a month, the GRM would be:

$$\frac{\$72,000}{\$500} = 144$$

Thus, if the appraisal assignment is to estimate the value of a house comparable to another property being rented at $450 a month, the result would be:

$450 \times 144 = \$64,800$—value of subject house by the income approach.

However, before considering the final estimate of value, the other approaches must be considered.

With respect to income-producing properties, the first step in the income approach is to ascertain the *net operating income* of the property being appraised. This requires establishing *gross income* from which an allowance for vacancy is deducted to arrive at *effective gross income.* Net operating income is derived by deducting *operating expenses* from effective gross income. Operating expenses include all expenses necessary to produce the income, such as utilities, repairs, insurance, real estate taxes and wages, but does not include indirect expenses such as financing costs, income taxes and depreciation.

When net operating income is known, an appraiser can use various techniques to convert this income into a present value. This process is called *capitalization,* and the desired result is to discount the future income to a present value. In other words, the discounting of the future income determines the *present value* of that stream of income (Figure 9-1).

Analyzing the concept from a basic position, this process is used to establish how much money a person would pay for, or value, the right to receive a certain amount of income for a period of time. For example, if a person could receive $100 per year on an investment for 10 years and wanted a 10 percent return on the investment, the worth, or present value, of that future stream of income would be calculated:

$$\text{Value} = \frac{\text{income}}{\text{rate of return}} \quad \text{or} \quad V = \frac{I}{R} \quad \text{or} \quad \$1,000 = \frac{\$100}{.10}$$

The 10 percent return the investor sought in this example is called the *capitalization rate* and the process of converting the income stream to present value is called *capitalization.*

The capitalization rate, or cap rate, to be applied to the income stream is at times a difficult figure to establish, since it is a reflection of market conditions. A small change in the expected rate of return can have an appreciable effect on value as the following example demonstrates:

$$\frac{\$1,000 \text{ annual income}}{.10 \text{ return}} = \$10,000 \text{ value}$$

$$\frac{\$1,000 \text{ annual income}}{.09 \text{ return}} = \$11,111 \text{ value}$$

$$\frac{\$1,000 \text{ annual income}}{.11 \text{ return}} = \$9,090 \text{ value}$$

Many students of real estate have been confused by academic explanations of how a capitalization rate is established and given false hope by practitioners who explain it simply as "whatever the market will bear." An analysis of capital investment motivation reveals that an investor wants two returns:

1. Return on investment—the interest an investor wants to earn on an investment
2. Return of investment—the return of capital or the recapture of invested capital

Since in theory land does not depreciate in value, it should return the capital invested at some time in the future when it is sold. Therefore, no present need exists to provide for recapture of the capital in land. In land only situations, the capitalization rate would consist solely of the interest, or discount rate, an investor wanted as a return on the investment. Requirements by investors for rates of return vary according to their needs and many outside influences, but the most important influence is the competition for investment dollars from other sources, in addition to real estate. One method by which an individual interest rate can be constructed is the *summation method* which reflects the various risks inherent in an investment that are summed up or added together. For example, the return on land only that is necessary to attract capital is computed by assigning to each element of risk an interest rate that is indicative of its relative weight. For example:

safe rate of interest (as established
by a "safe" investment, e.g.,
U.S. Treasury bills)   .06

risk rate (a need for a greater return
as risk increases)   .02

non-liquidity rate (an interest penalty
because of lack of liquidity)   .01

management burden (an interest
penalty because of a need
to manage the investment)   .01
                                                       ————
                                                        .10

This 10 percent interest rate would be the capitalization rate for the stream of income from land only.

If the land is improved with a structure, the capitalization rate will include the interest rate as the return on capital and a *recapture rate* as the return of capital. The capital must be partially recaptured each year to provide for a complete return of the capital investment over the life of the improvement. There are three methods of computing recapture—straight-line, sinking-fund, and annuity. If a property had an economic life of 25 years, the recapture, figured on the straight-line method, would require a four percent (100 percent ÷ 25 years = 4 percent) recapture per year. The sinking-fund and annuity methods add back to the amount recaptured the value of the interest the recaptured capital can earn.

Therefore, if the net operating income is produced by both the improvements and the land, the capitalization rate to capitalize that income will include the interest rate or discount rate and the recapture rate. For example:

Interest rate (return on)	.10
Recapture rate (return of)	.04
Capitalization rate	.14

There are other techniques for applying a capitalization rate to various segments of income, but those techniques are beyond the scope of this text.

CORRELATION OF VALUE

An appraiser should always strive to use the three approaches—market data, cost and income—in estimating value to provide as valid an estimate as possible. In most situations, the estimates of value after using all three approaches should be fairly similar. (See Figure 11-2, Valuation Section, for an example of a residential appraisal that embraces all three approaches.) If the estimates are widely divergent, the data-gathering method and analysis for each approach must be carefully reviewed. If the estimates remain far apart, the appraiser must consider the purpose of the appraisal. If the appraisal is to estimate value for a condemnation suit, the market data is most important. For insurance purposes, the replacement cost is most important. If the appraisal is for mortgage loan purposes on an income-producing property, then the income approach should be emphasized. It is in the correlation of value that an appraiser's skill is recognized and the problem of estimating value answered.

SUGGESTED READINGS

Graaskamp, J. A. *A Guide to Feasibility Analysis*. Chicago: Society of Real Estate Appraisers, 1970.

Kahn, Sanders A., and Case, Frederick E. *Real Estate Appraisal and Investment*. New York: The Ronald Press Co., 1976.

Kinnard, William N., Jr. *Income Property Valuation*. Lexington, Massachusetts: Lexington Books, D. C. Heath & Co., 1971.

Ratcliff, Richard U. *Real Estate Analysis*. New York: McGraw-Hill Book Co., Inc., 1961.

Ring, Alfred A. *The Valuation of Real Estate*. Englewood Cliffs, New Jersey: Prentice-Hall, Inc., 1970.

Thorne, Oakleigh J. "Real Estate Financial Analysis—The State of the Art," *The Appraisal Journal* (January 1974), pp. 7–37.

Troisi, Frank X. "Is It One, Two or Three Approaches to Value?" *Real Estate Review* (Fall 1978), pp. 94–98.

Troxel, Jay C. "Rates: Capitalization and Interest," *The Appraisal Journal* (January 1975), pp. 71–80.

Wendt, Paul F. *Real Estate Appraisal: Review and Outlook*. Athens, Georgia: University of Georgia Press, 1974.

_____, and Cerf, Alan R. *Real Estate Investment Analysis and Taxation*. New York: McGraw-Hill Book Co., Inc., 1969.

NOTES

1. A trained specialist is one certified by either The Society of Real Estate Appraisers or The American Institute of Real Estate Appraisers.

Chapter 12

Closing and Administering the Mortgage Loan

PART ONE
CLOSING THE MORTGAGE LOAN

INTRODUCTION

After a decision (probably by a loan committee) to make a mortgage loan has been made, the loan proceeds to loan closing. The term *loan closing* as used in mortgage lending refers to the process of formulating, executing and delivering all documents required by a permanent investor, the disbursement of the mortgage funds, and the protection of the investor's security. A clear distinction should be drawn between this type of closing and a real estate sales closing in which a different set of documents would be required, such as a purchase agreement, sales contract, and a closing statement, among others. Of course, as is a usual situation, if the sale also includes financing, both sets of documents or a combination of the two would be required. The process of loan closing begins with the taking of the mortgage application and the issuance of a commitment letter, and concludes in the exchanging of documents and funds and the recording of all pertinent instruments. It is important to realize that a loan closing is not the end of the mortgage lending cycle, which continues through servicing until the loan is finally repaid or refinanced.

Essential documents that should be contained in a complete mortgage file vary by state and also by property type; that is, residential or commercial. A lender's peculiar requirements can also add or delete from this. As in any discussion involving legal documents, state law requires caution. When establishing a loan closing process, competent counsel should be consulted on state law concerning any of the documents discussed.

Loan closing, depending on the custom in the jurisdiction, can be handled by either an outside attorney, an escrow agent, a title insurance company, or the closing staff of the mortgage lender. Whatever method is used, the purpose of loan closing is the same; that is, to assure the loan is closed according to all laws of the state; therefore, providing the mortgage lender with a first lien on the property. At one time, most closings were handled by an outside attorney, but now more and more mortgage lenders have staff members who are qualified loan closers to prepare and analyze all necessary closing documents. This is probably true only for residential property. An income property investor may want to close the loan in-house. Care should be exercised to determine whether state law requires a licensed attorney to close a loan. There are many types of loan closings, including the closing of construction loans, loans to be warehoused and loans with the permanent investor. This chapter is concerned primarily with the closing of permanent loans.

CLOSING A RESIDENTIAL LOAN

The following documents are discussed relative to the closing of a residential mortgage loan. The process of gathering, producing and preparing the necessary documents and the careful checking of all forms is often referred to as a *preclosing procedure*. The documents needed for a commercial mortgage loan will be discussed in a separate section to follow. The documents usually need not appear in any particular order in a loan file (some secondary mortgage market transactions may require the documents in a specified order). Therefore, they are listed here in alphabetical order with a discussion of the reason for the required document. A few examples of these documents can be found as exhibits in this chapter; others can be found in the case studies of Chapter 15.

Appraisal. The appraisal is necessary for all real estate loans. It is usually made by a designated appraiser who may be either a fee appraiser or an in-house appraiser. The amount of the loan is established by the appraised value of the property and loan-to-value ratio requirement of the investor. The appraisal is also needed to prove that the permanent investor has satisfied the legal loan-to-value ratio established in the particular state.

If the loan is guaranteed by the Veterans Administration, a Certificate of Reasonable Value (CRV) establishes the maximum loan amount. If the loan is insured by the Federal Housing Administration, FHA Form 2800, Mortgagee's Application for Property Appraisal, is required. Page 5 informs the mortgagee of the final FHA approval. If the mortgage loan is not guaranteed by VA or insured by FHA, the appraisal will probably be on FNMA/FHLMC, Form 1004.

Assignment of Mortgage. If the mortgage is being purchased from a mortgage lender who originated it for later sale, an instrument assigning the mortgage to a permanent investor and an estoppel certificate should be included in the loan file.

Building restrictions. Any local building restrictions that affect the mortgaged premise should be contained in the loan file with a statement as to whether this property meets local building restrictions. This may be contained in a lawyer's opinion.

Cancelled mortgage. If the loan being closed is for the purpose of refinancing a previous loan, the original mortgage and note should appear in the file and be cancelled, with the satisfaction of that mortgage recorded.

Certificate of occupancy. In all new construction and refurbishing that requires it, a certificate issued by the local authorities should appear declaring that the building is habitable.

Closing statement. The closing statement for a mortgage closing (like a closing statement for the sale) will determine how the proceeds are to be apportioned to the parties. A receipt signed by the mortgagor is required, indicating that loan proceeds have been disbursed according to instructions.

Commitment letter. A commitment letter should be examined closely since it establishes the contractual rights and obligations between the lender and the borrower. Comparison should be made between this commitment letter and the application for the loan to determine if the applicant is receiving everything required. If the mortgage is to be insured, guaranteed, or sold to FHA, VA, FNMA, GNMA, FHLMC or one of the MICs, their commitment letter should also appear.

Contract of sale. If a loan is requested for the purchase of an existing property, the contract of sale should be in the loan file to verify an actual sale and to assist later in verifying the appraisal of the property.

Credit report. A credit report on the borrower is normally required in all loans. This report is usually accomplished by a local company if the loan is for a residential borrower.

Chattel lien. If personal property is serving as security in addition to the real estate, a financing statement or other document creating the lien is required.

Deed. If a loan is to purchase property, a copy of the deed should be included in the loan file, along with instructions to record.

Disbursement papers. Instructions are required on how funds are to be delivered to the mortgagor or to other involved parties.

Escrow. If the transaction involved has been closed in escrow, a copy of the escrow agreement should be in the loan file; and when the term escrow, or impoundment, is used to describe the way mortgage payments are to be made, this agreement should also be in the loan file.

FHA/VA. All documents required by an FHA-insured or VA-guaranteed loan—e.g., credit report, verification of employment, building certificate, certificate of occupancy, flood insurance, etc.—should be in the loan file for both residential and multifamily properties.

Good Faith Estimate. Lender must provide at loan application a written estimate of charges payable at settlement. (See Figure 12-1.) See Chapter 13, Government Regulations and Consumer Protection.

Insurance policies. In a residential file, the required insurance policy (probably a home-owners) covering losses for fire, liability, and any other hazard should exist with a mortgagee loss payable clause.

Loan application. At the time of closing, both the mortgagor and the mortgagee should review the loan application to determine that the loan is delivered as requested. The application is important to a mortgage lender because it establishes various fees and who is to pay them.

Mortgage or deed of trust. A mortgage or a deed of trust creating the security interest must appear in the loan file. Any chattel liens on personal property, or any financing statements should also appear. Recording instructions are required to protect all parties.

Mortgagor's affidavit. A mortgagor should be required to sign certain affidavits attesting to any current position regarding divorce proceedings, judgments or liens, or any recent improvement on the real estate or other pertinent facts that would affect the mortgage loan.

Note. It is essential to include a properly-executed promissory note. The note creates the obligation to repay the debt which is secured by the mortgage and it should state the amount of the loan, the term, the interest rate, and any other pertinent conditions. This note may also be recorded.

Photographs. Photographs of good, clear quality are required to adequately show the mortgaged real estate.

Private mortgage insurance documents. All documents required by a mortgage insurance company to issue their insurance as well as a copy of their commitment should appear in the loan file.

Survey. Since the real estate is the loan security, it is in the mortgagee's interest that a survey be made to identify correctly the property and determine if any encroachments exist.

Title insurance or examination. In all loans, it is essential that title be examined, or that an approved ALTA title insurance policy or binder be included. (See Figure 12–2.) This requirement establishes who has right to the real estate and therefore, who must execute the mortgage to encumber it. The title examination should also disclose any prior encumbrances, tax liens or other interests.

Truth-in-Lending. The requirements of the Consumer Credit Protection Act of 1968 and the 1980 Truth-in-Lending Simplification Act are covered extensively in Chapter 13, Government Regulation and Consumer Protection. Basically, the loan file must contain a Loan Cost Disclosure Statement which will disclose both the Annual Percentage Rate and the total finance charge.

Verification reports. The mortgage lender should verify all relevant statements made on the loan application by obtaining verifying documentation. The most commonly used verification forms are those for employment and deposits.

GOOD FAITH ESTIMATE
OF SETTLEMENT CHARGES

**NAME OF
FINANCIAL INSTITUTION**
Anytown, U.S.A. 12345

Listed below is the Good Faith Estimate of Settlement Charges made pursuant to the requirements of the Real Estate Settlement Procedures Act (RESPA). These figures are only estimates and the actual charges due at settlement, may be different. This is not a commitment.

		Estimated Charge	or	Range	of	Charges
801	Loan Origination Fee	$			to	
	(Includes Item No.)					
802	Loan Discount	$			to	
803	Appraisal Fee	$			to	
804	Credit Report				to	
805	Lender's Inspection Fee				to	
806	Mortgage Insurance Application Fee				to	
807	Assumption Fee				to	
901	Interest				to	
902	Mortgage Insurance Premium				to	
1101	Settlement or Closing Fee	$			to	
1102	Abstract or Title Search	$			to	
1105	Document Preparation	$			to	
1106	Notary Fees	$			to	
1107	Attorney Fees	$			to	
	(Includes Item No.)					
1108	Title Insurance	$			to	
	(Includes Item No.)					
1201	Recording Fees	$			to	
1301	Survey	$			to	
1302	Pest Inspection	$			to	
		$			to	
		$			to	

In lieu of individual settlement charges, the lender at its option may elect to absorb all settlement charges and charge a fixed amount. If so, instead of amounts, all of the services and items checked above are included in the following fixed amount, in accordance with Section 3500.7(f) and 3500.8(d)(2), of the Real Estate Settlement Procedures Act. $ —————

This form does not cover all items you will be required to pay in cash at settlement, for example, deposits in escrow for real estate taxes and insurance. You may wish to inquire as to the amounts of such other items, as you may be required to pay other additional amounts at settlement.

THIS SECTION TO BE COMPLETED BY LENDER ONLY IF A PARTICULAR PROVIDER OF SERVICE IS REQUIRED

Listed below are providers of service which we require you use. The charges or range indicated in the Good Faith Estimate above are based upon the corresponding charge of the below designated providers.

Designated Charge Item No. Phone No.	Item No. Phone No.
Service Provided	
Providers Name	
Address	
We (☐ do), (☐ do not), have a business relationship with the above named provider.	We (☐ do), (☐ do not), have a business relationship with the above named provider.

Delivery of the above Good Faith Estimate and the booklet entitled "Settlement Costs and You" is hereby acknowledged.

Applicant's Signature,
or Mailed By:
Date

Address of Subject Property

44510-6 (*3/77)
GFE-1 Good Faith Estimate

SAF Systems and Forms
(American Savings & Accounting Supply, Inc.)

Figure 12–1. *Good faith estimate of settlement charges.*

COMMONWEALTH LAND
TITLE INSURANCE COMPANY
(a stock company)   PHILADELPHIA, PENNSYLVANIA

COMMITMENT FOR TITLE INSURANCE

Commitment No.

801 − 365457

File No. ___3062 MV___

SCHEDULE A

1. Effective Date: 20th   day of   August, 1977   , at   4:30   .M.

2. Policy or Policies to be issued: Amount

   (a)   ALTA Owner − 1970   ☐ Form B   ☐ Form A $ _____
           (Amended 10-17-70)

   Proposed Insured:

           Victoria E. Fowler

   (b) ☐   ALTA Loan Policy − 1970 (Amended 10-17-70) $35,900.00_____

   Proposed Insured: ☒ Conv ☐ FHA ☐ VA

           Perpetual Federal Savings and Loan Association

3. The estate or interest in the land described or referred to in the Commitment and covered herein is
   and is at the effective date hereof vested in   Kettler Brothers, Inc. (a Maryland Corporation)

4. The land referred to in this Commitment is situated in the County of   Montgomery
   State of   Maryland   , and described as follows:

   Lot numbered 3, in the subdivision known as, "Plat 277, Lots 3   through   49,
   Being a resubdivision of Lots 182 to 195, CLUBSIDE, Part of Section 2-A,
   MONTGOMERY VILLAGE", as per Plat thereof duly recorded among the Land Records
   of Montgomery County, Maryland in Plat Book 100 at Plat 11262.

   Property Address: #3 Ridgeline Drive
                       Gaithersburg, Maryland   20760

   SETTLEMENT DATE: September 9, 1977

   Betts, Clogg & Murdock
   PO Box 2186
   Gaithersburg, Maryland   20760

Countersigned: _____

James G. Hollis   Authorized Officer or Agent
American Land Title Association Commitment − 1966
Schedule A   Valid Only If Schedule B and Cover Are Attached
Form 1004-2 (6-77)

ORIGINAL

Figure 12−2. *Commitment for title insurance.*

168

Commitment No. 801-365257

File No. 3062 MV

Schedule B — Section 1

The following are the requirements to be complied with:

1. Instrument creating the estate or interest to be insured must be executed and filed for record, to-wit:

    a. Proper deed vesting fee simple title to Victoria E. Fowler.

    b. Deed of Trust from above named party securing Perpetual Federal Savings and Loan Association in the amount of $35,900.00.

2. Pay the full consideration to, or for the account of, the grantors or mortgagors.

3. Pay all taxes, charges, assessments, levied and assessed against subject premises, which are due and payable.

4. Satisfactory evidence should be had that improvements and/or repairs or alterations thereto are completed; that contractor, sub-contractors, labor and materialmen are all paid; and have released of record all liens or notice of intent to perfect a lien for labor or material.

5. FREE & CLEAR

Schedule B — Section 2

Schedule B of the policy or policies to be issued will contain exceptions to the following matters unless the same are disposed of to the satisfaction of the Company:

1. Defects, liens, encumbrances, adverse claims or other matters, if any, created, first appearing in the public records or attaching subsequent to the effective date hereof but prior to the date the proposed Insured acquires for value of record the estate or interest or mortgage thereon covered by this Commitment.

CONTINUED

NOTE: AN OWNER'S POLICY ISSUED IN CONNECTION WITH THIS COMMITMENT WILL CONTAIN THE FOLLOWING PRE-PRINTED EXCEPTIONS:

1. Rights or claims of parties other than Insured in actual possession of any or all of the property.
2. Unrecorded easements, discrepancies or conflicts in boundary lines, shortage in area and encroachments which an accurate and complete survey would disclose.
3. Unfiled mechanics' or materialmen's liens.

American Land Title Association Commitment 1966
Schedule B
Form 1004-7 (10-74)

ORIGINAL

Figure 12-2. *Continued.*

Uniform Settlement Statement (HUD-1). This statement (see Figure 12–3) is required at loan closings by the Real Estate Settlement Procedures Act of 1974 (RESPA). The statement offers the borrower and seller a full disclosure of known or estimated settlement costs.

CLOSING AN INCOME PROPERTY LOAN

Many of the documents required to close a residential loan are the same as those required to close an income property loan. A few, such as the various RESPA documents, are not needed, but other documents are required. These will be discussed in the following section, along with the different functions that some documents perform in a commercial loan closing.

The commitment is one of the documents that has a much more sophisticated function to perform in an income property loan closing than in a residential loan. In today's market, where interest rates experience wide fluctuations and institutional investors need to protect their future income stream, new concepts have been developed to prevent a builder or other mortgagor from "walking" a commitment.

When an investor, including a life insurance company or other investor such as a REIT, issues a commitment to fund a loan, it normally asks for either a _standby deposit_ or a _commitment fee._ A standby deposit is for a commitment issued by an investor to a builder who needs a hedge against being able to locate either a permanent investor, or one at an attractive interest rate. The investor will probably not have to fund this commitment since the interest rate is substantially higher than the market.

The builder may expect interest rates to decline before the permanent financing is needed, but in order to secure a construction loan, the builder will need some type of takeout. The standby commitment can be used for this purpose, in addition to being an escape if the interest rates move up dramatically. An investor will charge one or two nonrefundable points for such a commitment.

On a regular commitment, with a fee of one or two points, an investor fully expects to fund the commitment. This commitment fee may or may not be refundable. In the past, with a commitment fee of one or two percent of the loan amount, an investor was normally assured that the loan would be delivered; but in the past few years, with the interest rate changing abruptly, a one- or two-point fee has not meant necessarily that the investor who made the commitment would get the loan. In such a market, the forfeiture of two points can be recovered easily by a borrower who has walked away from a loan commitment to take advantage of a rapid drop in interest rates. For example, this could occur if the builder subsequently obtained another commitment from another investor that was one percent lower. The builder would be able to make up the forfeited two-point commitment fee within a couple of years because of the lower interest rate. Everything after that would be profit.

A.	B. TYPE OF LOAN
U. S. DEPARTMENT OF HOUSING AND URBAN DEVELOPMENT	1. ☐ FHA 2. ☐ FmHA 3. ☐ CONV. UNINS. 4. ☐ VA 5. ☐ CONV. INS.
	6. File Number: 　　　　　　7. Loan Number:
SETTLEMENT STATEMENT	8. Mortgage Insurance Case Number:

C. **NOTE:** *This form is furnished to give you a statement of actual settlement costs. Amounts paid to and by the settlement agent are shown. Items marked "(p.o.c.)" were paid outside the closing; they are shown here for informational purposes and are not included in the totals.*

D. NAME OF BORROWER:	E. NAME OF SELLER:	F. NAME OF LENDER:

G. PROPERTY LOCATION;	H. SETTLEMENT AGENT:	I. SETTLEMENT DATE:
	PLACE OF SETTLEMENT:	

J. SUMMARY OF BORROWER'S TRANSACTION		K. SUMMARY OF SELLER'S TRANSACTION	
100. GROSS AMOUNT DUE FROM BORROWER:		**400. GROSS AMOUNT DUE TO SELLER:**	
101. Contract sales price		401. Contract sales price	
102. Personal property		402. Personal property	
103. Settlement charges to borrower *(line 1400)*		403.	
104.		404.	
105.		405.	
Adjustments for items paid by seller in advance		*Adjustments for items paid by seller in advance*	
106. City/town taxes　　　to		406. City/town taxes　　　to	
107. County taxes　　　to		407. County taxes　　　to	
108. Assessments　　　to		408. Assessments　　　to	
109.		409.	
110.		410.	
111.		411.	
112.		412.	
120. GROSS AMOUNT DUE FROM BORROWER		**420. GROSS AMOUNT DUE TO SELLER**	
200. AMOUNTS PAID BY OR IN BEHALF OF BORROWER:		**500. REDUCTIONS IN AMOUNT DUE TO SELLER:**	
201. Deposit or earnest money		501. Excess deposit *(see instructions)*	
202. Principal amount of new loan(s)		502. Settlement charges to seller *(line 1400)*	
203. Existing loan(s) taken subject to		503. Existing loan(s) taken subject to	
204.		504. Payoff of first mortgage loan	
205.		505. Payoff of second mortgage loan	
206.		506.	
207.		507.	
208.		508.	
209.		509.	
Adjustments for items unpaid by seller		*Adjustments for items unpaid by seller*	
210. City/town taxes　　　to		510. City/town taxes　　　to	
211. County taxes　　　to		511. County taxes　　　to	
212. Assessments　　　to		512. Assessments　　　to	
213.		513.	
214.		514.	
215.		515.	
216.		516.	
217.		517.	
218.		518.	
219.		519.	
220. TOTAL PAID BY/FOR BORROWER		**520. TOTAL REDUCTION AMOUNT DUE SELLER**	
300. CASH AT SETTLEMENT FROM/TO BORROWER		**600. CASH AT SETTLEMENT TO/FROM SELLER**	
301. Gross amount due from borrower *(line 120)*		601. Gross amount due to seller *(line 420)*	
302. Less amounts paid by/for borrower *(line 220)*	(　　)	602. Less reductions in amount due seller *(line 520)*	(　　)
303. CASH (☐ FROM) (☐ TO) BORROWER		**603. CASH (☐ TO) (☐ FROM) SELLER**	

Figure 12-3.   *HUD settlement statement.*

L. SETTLEMENT CHARGES

	PAID FROM BORROWER'S FUNDS AT SETTLEMENT	PAID FROM SELLER'S FUNDS AT SETTLEMENT
700. TOTAL SALES/BROKER'S COMMISSION based on price $ @ % =		
Division of Commission (line 700) as follows:		
701. $ to		
702. $ to		
703. Commission paid at Settlement		
704.		
800. ITEMS PAYABLE IN CONNECTION WITH LOAN		
801. Loan Origination Fee %		
802. Loan Discount %		
803. Appraisal Fee to		
804. Credit Report to		
805. Lender's Inspection Fee		
806. Mortgage Insurance Application Fee to		
807. Assumption Fee		
808.		
809.		
810.		
811.		
900. ITEMS REQUIRED BY LENDER TO BE PAID IN ADVANCE		
901. Interest from to @ $ /day		
902. Mortgage Insurance Premium for months to		
903. Hazard Insurance Premium for years to		
904. years to		
905.		
1000. RESERVES DEPOSITED WITH LENDER		
1001. Hazard insurance months @ $ per month		
1002. Mortgage insurance months @ $ per month		
1003. City property taxes months @ $ per month		
1004. County property taxes months @ $ per month		
1005. Annual assessments months @ $ per month		
1006. months @ $ per month		
1007. months @ $ per month		
1008. months @ $ per month		
1100. TITLE CHARGES		
1101. Settlement or closing fee to		
1102. Abstract or title search to		
1103. Title examination to		
1104. Title insurance binder to		
1105. Document preparation to		
1106. Notary fees to		
1107. Attorney's fees to		
(includes above items numbers;)		
1108. Title insurance to		
(includes above items numbers;)		
1109. Lender's coverage $		
1110. Owner's coverage $		
1111.		
1112.		
1113.		
1200. GOVERNMENT RECORDING AND TRANSFER CHARGES		
1201. Recording fees: Deed $; Mortgage $; Releases $		
1202. City/county tax/stamps: Deed $; Mortgage $		
1203. State tax/stamps: Deed $; Mortgage $		
1204.		
1205.		
1300. ADDITIONAL SETTLEMENT CHARGES		
1301. Survey to		
1302. Pest inspection to		
1303.		
1304.		
1305.		
1400. TOTAL SETTLEMENT CHARGES (enter on lines 103, Section J and 502, Section K)		

HUD-1 Rev. 5/76

Figure 12–3. *Continued.*

Today, due to the extreme difficulty in assuring the deliverability of a loan for which a commitment has been issued, lenders have developed other methods to protect their interest. These would be in addition to the agreement in the commitment itself not to place the loan with another investor.

One such method investors have developed to protect their interests and assure delivery of the loan is the tripartite agreement, or buy/sell. There are three essential parties to this agreement:

1. The construction lender who agrees and contracts to sell the loan to the permanent investor upon completion
2. The permanent investor who agrees to buy the loan from the construction lender upon completion
3. The borrower or developer who promises to do nothing to interfere with the transaction.

Many investors now require a loan to be preclosed to assure that a builder takes down the permanent loan. This, in effect, closes the loan even though the building has not been constructed. As a result, the builder is precluded from going to another investor for financing since the new investor could not get a first lien—and the builder would also be in default to the first investor.

Other documents needed in an income property loan file, in addition to those already mentioned in the residential file, include:

Articles of incorporation. If the mortgagor is a corporation, the articles of incorporation should be included in the loan file to establish corporate powers, in addition to a copy of the by-laws or minutes empowering the officer to sign a mortgage.

Financial statement. Audited or certified financial statements of the borrower's financial position for the past fiscal year should be in the file, and in some instances, W-2 Forms.

Insurance policies. In an income property loan, the required insurance policies covering losses for fire, theft, personal injury, rent and any other hazard should exist with a mortgagee loss payable clause.

Lawyer's opinion letter. A local attorney's opinion letter concerning usury, zoning, and any other issues determined by local law is required by most investors in income-property loans.

Leases. A list of key tenants, lease arrangements and tenants' ability to sublet or assign, plus any subordination agreement, is essential in a commercial loan file. Any assignment of a rent clause applicable to the particular lease should also be documented. If the mortgage loan is based on the credit of the tenants, the leases may require prior approval of the investor and this approval should be in the loan file.

Partnership agreement. If the mortgagor is a partnership, a copy of the partnership agreement creating the partnership and its authority to act should be in the loan file.

Personal endorsement. If a permanent lender requires a mortgagor to become personally liable on the note, the personal endorsement must be in the loan file.

Plans and specifications. The permanent loan is based on the improvements being constructed according to agreed plans and specifications. Therefore, the agreement to any changes should be in the loan file.

Subordination agreement. In an income property loan, agreements should appear in the loan file if there is a requirement for a subordination of a previous mortgage to the current mortgage or the subordination of a current lease to a subsequent mortgage.

Tax bills. A permanent lender will want to make certain that all taxes are current on the security. This can be established by the stamped tax bills.

Tripartite or buy/sell agreement. If there is an interceding construction loan, this agreement involving a borrower, a construction lender, and a permanent investor should be present to establish the rights and duties of the parties.

PART TWO
MORTGAGE LOAN ADMINISTRATION

INTRODUCTION

After the closing of the mortgage loan, the next step in the mortgage lending process involves the loan administration or servicing department. This function can be both the most difficult and the most profitable of any of the steps in the lending process for any mortgage lender. The difficulty stems from the myriad of problems that can develop when dealing with people and their problems. If handled correctly and in sufficient volume, servicing has the potential to produce a profit to the mortgage lender which may be needed to offset other lending related losses.

"The modern concept of mortgage loan administration includes all activities which complement mortgage loan production and enhance its profitability."[1]

The purpose of this section is to discuss briefly the basic principles of mortgage loan administration. Mortgage loan administration involves all of the essential mortgage loan activities necessary to do the following things:

- Render the required service to the mortgagor
- Protect the security of the mortgagee
- Produce a profit for the servicer

Therefore, mortgage loan administration can be defined as the total effort required to perform both the day-to-day management or administrative function, and the servicing of mortgage loans.

Mortgage loan administration is required of all mortgage lenders (except possibly mortgage brokers), whether they originate residential or income property loans and whether some or all of the loans are sold to other investors. Mortgage companies have been closely associated with the servicing part of mortgage loan administration because of the volume of mortgage loans they have originated and sold to other mortgage investors (either directly or through GNMA mortgage-backed securities) while continuing to service the same loans. Mortgage companies were servicing in excess of $250 billion of mortgage loans sold to other mortgage investors at the end of 1981. Other mortgage lenders were also servicing for other mortgage investors, but not as extensively as mortgage companies. As an example, many savings and loan associations sell originated loans into the secondary market, but many of them and other mortgage lenders retain most of the mortgages they originate for their own portfolio.

SERVICING RESPONSIBILITY

The first task is to establish a servicing file, and then to mail notification of first payment to the borrower. This should be the last time correspondence is required unless notice of increased monthly payment is necessary because of increased taxes or insurance, or the borrower is late in a payment.

If mortgages to be serviced have been sold to another mortgage lender or mortgage investor such as FHLMC, the servicing relationship is established by either a *commitment letter* or a *servicing contract.* This contractual relationship should continue for the life of the mortgage loans, but it can be terminated. Termination can be either for cause—some failure to perform on the part of the servicer—or, in some cases, without cause. If servicing is withdrawn without cause, then it is common for an investor to pay a fee, typically one percent of amount serviced, as compensation.

The responsibilities of a servicer are usually described in detail in a servicing contract or in a servicing manual supplied by an investor. These responsibilities typically include:

1. Monthly collection of principal and interest from the mortgagor and disbursement to the investor
2. Collection and periodic payment of real estate taxes
3. Collection and periodic payment of required insurance
4. Any other activity necessary to protect the investor's security interest

To successfully fulfill these responsibilities, a servicer of a mortgage loan will need either trained people or separate departments to perform five functions:

1. *Cashier.* The cashier is responsible for a) receiving payments, b) de-

positing these payments and, c) transmitting this information to loan accounting.

2. *Loan Accounting.* This function is responsible for notifying investors that a deposit has been made to their account, or drawing a check (payable to an investor) to distribute principal and interest less any servicing fee.

3. *Collection.* The purpose of this function is to collect those payments past due. In many ways, this is the most difficult function, but it is also the most essential for a successful servicing operation. If collection is impossible, then this function is also responsible for initiating foreclosure proceedings. See Chapter 5, Security Instruments.

4. *Insurance.* The mortgage lender is responsible for protecting an investor's security interest by determining that adequate insurance exists and is current with a mortgagee payable clause. Some mortgage lenders sell this insurance as a service to their borrowers.

5. *Taxes.* To protect an investor's first lien, a mortgage lender must collect and pay all real estate taxes and assessments due on the security.

SERVICING INCOME

In addition to origination fees and possible marketing profits, the fee a mortgage lender receives from an investor for servicing a mortgage provides practically all income (in addition to interest on the mortgage, of course) of a mortgage lender. During those periods of the business cycle when mortgage loan demand is low, the servicing income often provides a mortgage lender with the means to stay in business. In the current mortgage market, many mortgage lenders are unable to generate a profit from the origination process, especially if a large percentage of total originations are either FHA or VA. This is because the origination fee for those mortgages by law is only one percent of the loan amount. These mortgage lenders must look to servicing income to offset origination losses, and sometimes marketing losses, to produce a net profit from mortgage lending. The 1970s experienced a period of such high inflation that the tradition of servicing profitability came into serious question. The question centered around the fact that servicing income for each mortgage loan will continue to decrease each year while expenses to service each loan will continue to increase.

This servicing income is generated by a servicer retaining a previously agreed upon fraction of one percent of the outstanding principal balance collected monthly. The fraction is applied only if the payment is collected. After receiving the monthly payment of principal and interest, a servicer forwards that amount less the servicing fee to the investor. For example, assume the outstanding mortgage balance of a 10 percent loan is $30,000 as of January 1st and the interest payment is $250 with a servicing fee of 3/8 of 1 percent per month. The February 1st remittance to the investor will be

$240.63 ($250 interest payment – $9.37 servicing fee of 1/12 of 3/8 of 1 percent of $30,000 = $240.63).

The servicing fee is typically 3/8 of one percent per month for residential mortgages and ranges from 1/10 to 1/8 of one percent for income property loans. Some investors put a maximum on annual servicing income from one mortgage loan at $4,000 to $5,000.

Other fees that a mortgage lender can generate from servicing include late payment fees when a mortgage payment is 15 days past due and transfer fees if the mortgage is being assumed.

SUGGESTED READINGS

Britton, James A., and Kerwood, Lewis O., eds. *Financing Income-Producing Real Estate*. New York: McGraw-Hill Book Co., Inc., 1977.

DeHuszar, William I. *Mortgage Loan Administration*. New York: McGraw-Hill Book Co., Inc., 1972.

Duffy, Robert E., Jr. "The Real Estate Settlement Procedures Act of 1974," *Real Estate Review* (Winter 1976), pp. 86–93.

Klein, Walter C., Jr. and Watson, Beverly A. "The Whys and Hows of Record Retention," *The Mortgage Banker* (April 1979), pp. 63–67.

NOTES

1.   William I. DeHuszar. *Mortgage Loan Administration*. New York: McGraw-Hill Book Co., Inc., p. 3.

Chapter 13

Government Regulation and Consumer Protection

ROLE OF GOVERNMENT

The government's role in the management or shaping of the nation's economy in general, and mortgage lending in particular, is one that has been analyzed and debated many times—and undoubtedly will continue in the future. There seems to be little argument that government, regardless of whether it is federal, state or local, has an obligation to its citizens to provide adequate shelter for all—even if they cannot afford it themselves. There are many arguments, though, regarding how to provide this basic necessity. Over the past decade, the federal government tried helping people in need of shelter in a variety of ways. First, they tried providing rent assistance, then tried mortgage assistances so people could purchase rather than rent, and finally returned to subsidizing rent payments. Assuming that government does have an obligation to provide in one way or another, this basic necessity of shelter, what other real estate or mortgage lending obligations does it have?

Recently, some commentators have suggested that excessive governmental interference into what should be a private enterprise (housing) has resulted in increased housing costs to the extent that fewer families now can afford the average-priced home than at any time in recent history. Obviously, some governmental laws and regulations have had a commendable impact on real estate and mortgage lending. The *Interstate Land Sales Full Disclosure Act* (1968) which helped to prevent fraudulent land sales is an obvious example. Many of these new laws and regulations were necessitated by excesses and failures on the part of the lending community; nevertheless, the contribution of some of these laws cannot be overstated. In fact, one governmental creation, the Federal Housing Administration, has provided the framework for a modern, vibrant mortgage lending system that has made this the best housed nation in the world.

But, lately some mortgage lenders have argued that the government has interjected itself so deeply into mortgage lending that it has hindered mortgage lending. For example, more laws and regulations affecting mortgage lending have been enacted since 1968 than in all preceding years. Following is a list of major federal laws and regulations affecting mortgage lending.

1913—Federal Reserve Act. Established the Federal Reserve System and authorized federally chartered commercial banks to make real estate loans.

1916—Federal Farm Loan Act. Provided for the formation of Federal Land Bank Associations as units of the Federal Land Bank System which was given authority to generate funds for loan to farmers by the sale of bonds.

1932—Reconstruction Finance Act. Created the Reconstruction Finance Corporation which was designed to, among other things, provide liquidity to commercial banks.

1932—Federal Home Loan Bank Act. Established the Federal Home Loan Bank Board and 12 regional banks to provide central credit facilities for home finance institutions which were members of the FHLB.

1933—Home Owners' Loan Act. This act produced two results: 1) created the Home Owners' Loan Corporation with authority to purchase defaulted home mortgages and to refinance as many as prudently feasible; 2) provided the basic lending authority for federally chartered savings and loan associations.

1934—National Housing Act. Authorized the creation of the Federal Housing Administration and the Federal Savings and Loan Insurance Corporation.

1938—National Mortgage Association of Washington. This governmental agency, soon renamed Federal National Mortgage Association, was authorized to provide secondary mortgage market support for FHA mortgages.

1944—Servicemen's Readjustment Act. Established within the Veterans Administration a mortgage guarantee program for qualified veterans.

1949—Housing Act. Stated that the national housing goal was to provide, ". . . a decent home and suitable living environment for every American family . . ." Consolidated past lending programs of the Farmers Home Administration.

1961—Consolidated Farmers Home Administration Act. Extended authority for the agency to make mortgage loans to non farmers in rural areas.

1965—Housing and Urban Development Act. Consolidated many federal housing agencies into a new Department of Housing and Urban Development with expanded authority.

1966—Interest Rate Adjustment Act. Authorized the setting of maximum savings rates and the creation of a differential between commercial bank and thrift institutions savings rates.

1968—Fair Housing Act. Prohibited discrimination in real estate sales and mortgage lending based on race, color, national origin and religion.

1968—Interstate Land Sales Full Disclosure Act. Required complete and full disclosure of all facts regarding interstate sale of real estate.

1968—Consumer Credit Protection Act. Contained Title I, better known as Truth-in-Lending, which authorized the Federal Reserve Board to formulate regulations (Reg Z) requiring advanced disclosure of the amount and type of finance charge and a calculation of the annual percentage rate. Title VI, better known as the Fair Credit Reporting Act, established disclosure requirements regarding the nature of credit information used in determining whether to grant a loan.

1968—Housing and Urban Development Act. This act privatized the existing Federal National Mortgage Association and authorized it to continue secondary mortgage market support. The act also created a new governmental agency, Government National Mortgage Association, and authorized it to continue the FNMA special assistance function and issue mortgage-backed securities.

1969—National Environmental Policy Act. Required the preparation of an Environmental Impact Statement for the Council on Environmental Quality in order to determine the environmental impact of a real estate development.

1970—Emergency Home Finance Act. Created a new secondary mortgage market participant, Federal Home Loan Mortgage Corporation, which had as its stated objective providing secondary mortgage support for conventional mortgages originated by thrift institutions. The act also gave FNMA authority to purchase conventional mortgages in addition to FHA/VA.

1974—Flood Disaster Protection Act. Effective in 1975, mortgage loans could not be made in a flood hazard area unless flood insurance had been purchased.

1974—Real Estate Settlement Procedures Act (as amended in 1976). This act as amended requires mortgage lenders to provide mortgage borrowers with an advance disclosure of loan settlement costs and charges.

Further, this act prohibited kickbacks to any person for referring business. The 1976 amendment requires lenders to provide applicants with a Good Faith Estimate of Settlement Costs and a HUD booklet. A Uniform Settlement Statement (HUD-1) must be furnished to the borrower before or at the settlement.

1974—Equal Credit Opportunity Act (as amended in 1976). This act as amended prohibits discrimination in lending on the basis of sex, marital status, age, race, religion or the fact that a borrower receives public assistance. In addition, if an application is rejected, the borrower must be notified within 30 days of the reason for rejection.

1974—Emergency Home Purchase Act. Permitted the Secretary of HUD to declare an emergency in the housing market and allow GNMA to purchase home mortgages at a below-market interest rate.

1975—Home Mortgage Disclosure Act. This act requires disclosure, in order to prevent redlining, of geographic distribution of loans in standard metropolitan statistical areas.

1976—RESPA amendments (see 1974).

1976—ECOA amendments (see 1974).

1978—Fair Lending Practices Regulations. These FHLB regulations require members to develop written underwriting standards, keep a loan registry, not deny loans because of age of dwelling or condition of neighborhood, and to direct advertising to all segments of the community.

1978—Community Reinvestment Act. This act requires FSLIC insured institutions to adopt a community reinvestment statement which delineates the community in which they will invest; maintain a public comment file, and post a CRA notice.

1979—Housing and Community Development Amendments. This legislation exempted FHA insured mortgages from state and local usury ceilings. (Other concurrent legislation exempted VA and conventional mortgages.)

1980—Depository Institutions Deregulation and Monitory Control Act. Congress extended the savings interest rate control and thrift institution ¼ of 1% differential for six years. The act also extended the federal override of state usury ceilings on certain mortgages: other loans, simplified truth-in-lending standards and eased or removed lending restrictions, including geographical limitations, loan-to-value ratios and treatment of one-family loans exceeding specified dollar amounts.

The purpose of this chapter is to: (1) review the laws and regulations affecting mortgage lending; and (2) analyze the impact of these laws and regulations on mortgage lending. Although it can be argued that much of the recent regulatory action has been generated by state and local governments (in particular, many poorly and hastily conceived zoning regulations and building codes), this chapter will be limited only to those laws and regulations of the federal government. (For an interesting discussion of local regulations, see Center for Urban Policy Research, Rutgers University, *Government Regulations and Housing Costs.* 1977).

GOVERNMENT INTERVENTION

The Great Depression provided the economic and political environment for a change from the existing *laissez-faire* attitude of government toward business in general to a more interventionist or direction-providing attitude. The need for this change was obvious since only the federal government had both the political and fiscal resources necessary to help American economy recover from the staggering impact of the Great Depression. The basic concern of government at this point in history was survival. Financial institutions were in chaos, hundreds of thousands of homes were in foreclosure, and 25 percent of the work force was unemployed. In order to prevent total collapse of the economy with the resulting danger to political institutions, the federal government instituted within a few short years a series of legislative actions which would change mortgage lending forever.

The first step was taken in the last year of the Hoover Administration with the creation of the *Reconstruction Finance Corporation* (RFC) in January 1932. The RFC was intended to provide stability to the economy by providing funds to financial institutions, primarily commercial banks, in order to help with the liquidity crisis.

Shortly after the creation of the RFC, new legislation creating the *Federal Home Loan Bank System* (FHLB) was enacted, but only after heated debate within the mortgage lending community. Many believed this type of governmental activity was unjustified and detrimental to capitalism. The FHLB established 12 regional banks which could provide funds as needed to member savings and loan associations and similar institutions engaged in home financing. The FHLB generated these funds by selling bonds and notes on the open market and making the funds available at nominal markup.

In the summer of 1933, the *Home Owners' Loan Corporation* (HOLC) was established to help solve the home mortgage default problems. Before the creation of the HOLC, more than 40 percent of the nation's home mortgage debt of $20 billion was in default. To alleviate this problem, the HOLC provided: (1) the exchange of HOLC government-backed bonds to mortgagees for home mortgages in default; and (2) some cash loans to mortgagors for payment of real estate taxes.

The importance of this governmental agency cannot be overstated. It provided the opportunity for mortgagees to receive something of value (HOLC bonds) for a debt instrument that was diminishing in value almost daily. By providing a system of refinancing, the defaulted mortgages did not have to be foreclosed during a time of decreasing real estate values, thus preventing a further decline in property values.

An often overlooked part of the HOLC program gave aid to homeowners to help pay local real estate taxes. Without the real estate tax revenue paid by these homeowners, many municipalities could have been bankrupt.

The mortgages HOLC obtained usually were refinanced on an installment plan for a 15-year term. This was the first extensive use of a self-amortizing, long-term mortgage. During its three-year lending period, HOLC refinanced more than one million nonfarm homes. This action by the government not only helped to restabilize the economy, but also prevented the foreclosure of thousands of homes.

National Housing Act of 1934

As far as mortgage lending is concerned, the *National Housing Act of 1934* was the most important piece of federal legislation ever enacted. This act created the *Federal Housing Administration* (FHA) and authorized the creation of the *Federal Savings and Loan Insurance Corporation* (FSLIC). In addition to providing insurance on deposits in member institutions, the FSLIC, an FHLB controlled corporation, is responsible for issuing regulations controlling the operations of insured associations. These regulations govern both the savings and lending side of the savings and loan business, and the FSLIC periodically inspects associations to determine compliances. Most FSLIC regulations on the lending side have followed the general principles and trends of mortgage lending as practiced by other lenders. When they have differed, it has usually been on the conservative side.

The Federal Deposit Insurance Corporation (FDIC) created by the *Banking Act of 1933* has basically the same function in relation to commercial banks as the FSLIC has to savings associations. Some mutual savings banks have deposits insured by the FDIC and are therefore regulated and examined by the FDIC.

Federal Housing Administration (FHA)

The National Housing Act of 1934 created the Federal Housing Administration (FHA) and gave it three primary objectives:

1. To encourage the improvement of the nation's housing standards and conditions.
2. To provide an adequate home financing system.
3. To exert a stabilizing influence on the mortgage and residential real estate markets.

The mortgage insurance programs of FHA furthered the concept of installment (or amortized) loans begun by the thrift institutions (and expanded by HOLC). This type of loan is the most common today.

The FHA was not popular with the financial communities when it first appeared. The concept of government-guaranteed mortgages was suspect because many companies and individuals had suffered financially as a result of the mortgage guaranty companies of the 1930s. (See Chapter 8, Mortgage Insurance—Government and Private). Others felt that this intrusion by the government into the housing market eventually would be detrimental to private capitalism.

The FHA-insured mortgage provided the elements of dependability, transferability and minimal risk vital to the development of a national mortgage market. Prior to the creation of FHA, only local mortgage markets existed. Most of the loans were made either by individuals who wanted to keep their loans local or by thrift institutions which were limited to specific lending areas and originated loans only for their own portfolios.

By using FHA standards for homes and borrowers, the correspondent system between mortgage companies and insurance companies (which was already in existence to a limited extent) helped establish a national mortgage market by allowing for movement of funds from capital-rich areas to capital-poor areas of the nation. Today, the mortgage banking industry undoubtedly owes its success and growth to the basic decision by life insurance companies to engage in national lending, with FHA providing the insurance. About 80 percent of all mortgage companies now in existence were formed after the creation of FHA. This fact alone is evidence of the effect FHA has had on the mortgage industry.

Thrift institutions did not use FHA-insured mortages to any great extent because they were primarily local organizations which promoted local home ownership. The legal limitations on their lending activity also had an effect, as did the belief by some thrift institution leaders that the government should not become involved in insuring home mortgages.

Commercial banks, also important as a residential lender, did participate in FHA-insured mortgages, but not as extensively as mortgage companies which have originated more than 75 percent of such mortgages. Until recently, other residential lenders (excluding mortgage companies) have originated most conventional mortgages, usually on a local basis.

Until the creation of FHA, mortgage lenders serviced few if any loans. However, with the practice of monthly loan amortization being reinforced by FHA and the requirement of escrowing for taxes and insurances, the need for lenders to service loans became evident. Servicing now is considered an integral part of mortgage lending and one of the means by which mortgage lenders persevere despite fluctuating financial conditions. (See Chapter 12, Closing and Administering the Mortgage Loan.)

In 1938, Congress created as a governmental agency the *Federal National Mortgage Association* (FNMA) to provide a secondary mortgage market for FHA-insured loans. FNMA became more active after World War II and helped provide the necessary facilities for a truly national market. FNMA later was reorganized as a private corporation and is now the largest holder of single-family mortgages, including FHA-insured, VA-guaranteed and conventional mortgages. (For a complete discussion of FNMA, see Chapter 7, Secondary Mortgage Markets and Institutions.)

Veterans Administration (VA)

Partially as a reward for winning the war, and partially as a recognition of the fact that most returning veterans were young and undereducated and had accumulated little financial resources during the war, Congress enacted into law the *Servicemen's Readjustment Act of 1944*. As amended in 1945, and later years, this act gave returning veterans an opportunity to obtain loans for vocational and academic training, businesses and, most importantly for family men, purchase of farms and homes. The necessary credit was available at the end of the war because individuals and financial institutions had invested most of their savings in safe but low-yielding investments. Veterans were able to borrow these funds since the Veterans Administration would guarantee the repayment of a qualified loan made to a veteran. The original guarantee on a home loan was $2,000 or 50 percent of the loan whichever was less. The guarantee has increased through the years:

1945	$ 4,000
1950	$ 7,500 or 60 percent
1968	$12,500
1974	$17,500
1978	$25,000
1980	$27,500

One of the reasons for these periodic increases was to continue the normal situation whereby a veteran need make no downpayment. As an example, if a lender made a $100,000 mortgage loan to a veteran, the risk of loss to the lender was only 72 percent since $27,500 was guaranteed. Therefore no downpayment would be required, although this could change if the loan exceeded $100,000.

The success of this program over the years has allowed for over 11.5 million veterans and their families to purchase a home that many would not have been able to purchase otherwise. In addition, many veterans have taken advantage of the opportunity to acquire an education.

It should be emphasized that the VA guarantee is at no cost to the veteran since any claims are paid by the federal government directly. This contrasts with the FHA insurance programs and private mortgage insurance which have a mutual insurance fund supported by premiums paid by mortgage borrowers. Similar to FHA programs though, the maximum interest rate that can be charged on a VA-guaranteed mortgage is set administratively which, therefore, often requires discount points to be charged a seller in order to increase a lender's yield to the market. This fact often puts a restraint on VA-guaranteed mortgages since the discount points charged a seller can reach a point where a seller would not agree to a VA mortgage and the discount. An example is early 1980, when the VA interest rate reached the unprecedented high of 12 *but* the market rate was close to 14 percent.

Mortgage companies have originated nearly 78 percent of all VA-guaranteed mortgage loans and, as is their practice, sold these loans either directly to investors or into the secondary market. Until recently, many of these loans originated by mortgage companies would have been sold to mutual savings banks, savings and loan associations or FNMA, but today practically all of these loans are put into GNMA mortgage-backed securities. Savings and loan associations originate approximately 11 percent of VA mortgage loans while commercial banks originate another 8 percent.

One of the prime benefits of this program is that it started at a time when single-family home construction needed a stimulus (in addition to FHA) to break out of the low volume construction mode it had been in since the early 1930s. VA guarantees and FHA insurance, combined with the liquid position of financial institutions after the war, provided the opportunity for a decade of greatly increased housing production.

Housing Act of 1949

The Housing Act of 1949 is one of the most important pieces of social legislation in the past 30 years because of the national commitment made to provide ". . . a decent home and suitable living environment for every American family. . . ." Much of the legislative action in the housing and mortgage lending field since then has been an attempt to fulfill that commendable but probably unrealistic goal.

The 1950s and early 1960s were a period of national optimism, economic growth and, as far as mortgage lending is concerned, a relatively quiet period in the legislative arena. This period of tranquility soon dissipated in the face of an onslaught of such national crises as political assassinations, civil rights demonstrations, urban blight and Vietnam.

HUD

The lack of adequate housing, a situation often associated with poverty, was partially addressed in 1965 by the consolidation of many federal housing agencies into a new cabinet-level department, Department of Housing and Urban Development (HUD). HUD was to be the focal point of much of the new legislation in the years to come as it assumed a dominant position in real estate and mortgage lending.

A few years after HUD was created, the avalanche of legislation and regulation that was to so change mortgage lending began when the *Housing and Urban Development Act of 1968* was enacted. This was the first major legislation in the mortgage lending field in over a decade. The act committed the government to a goal of 26 million new housing starts in the next decade. At the time, many argued that this goal was not practical on either fiscal or political grounds. However, the act introduced a new concept in government programs for residential real estate by adopting the principle of subsidizing interest rates. The two major subsidy programs of the 1968 act were: 1) Section 235, which encourages home ownership for low- and moderate-income families by providing special mortgage insurance and by subsidizing the mortgage interest rate in excess of one percent; and 2) Section 236, which was basically the same as 235 but was geared to multi-family rental units.

These government subsidy programs, combined with general national growth, stimulated housing production in 1972 to more than three million units. This was the highest ever. With this large housing increase, problems developed almost immediately. In 1971, news reports of possible scandals in subsidized housing began to appear; thus, the concept was in grave danger. The scandals were followed by congressional investigations which spotlighted the unforeseen high program costs. In January of 1973, President Nixon ordered a freeze on all subsidy programs. This was partially lifted later, but only after a thorough review of government programs by a special task force created by the Department of Housing and Urban Development (HUD). This task force reviewed the history of government involvement in real estate and analyzed the impact of the various subsidy programs on housing. One result of the task force review was a change in the basic government philosophy regarding shelter for the poor. The task force concluded that the goal of providing home ownership for everyone was neither practical nor desirable when weighed against the cost. The report stated:

> "Although home ownership has been encouraged by a variety of Federal laws, no major programs offering home ownership to the poor in the 20th century were enacted until the 1960s. Since that time, the problems that have arisen from the operation of these programs—principally the Section 235 and Section 221(d)(2) programs—are so serious that they raise questions about the validity of the concept itself."[1]

The government's concept changed from subsidizing home ownership to subsidizing rent. *The Housing and Community Development Act of 1974* formalized this change with the "Section 8" program. This program allows low- and moderate-income families to choose the rental unit in the community in which they want to live with the government subsidizing the amount of "fair market rent" that is in excess of 25 percent of the family's monthly income. This program provides assistance to families who could not afford the minimal housing expenses stipulated in prior programs and to families whose incomes were just over the maximum income limit qualifying them for assistance in home purchasing.

Consumer Protection

The Consumer Protection Act of 1968 was the first in a series of legislative acts which redefined the concept of consumer protection regarding mortgage lending, and therefore, changed forever the manner in which mortgage lending is practiced. Much of this early effort helped to provide the consumer with more information about mortgage lending, but later legislative action may have produced more information than can be handled by the consumer and at the same time, imposed incredible amounts of paperwork on the mortgage lender.

The major section of this omnibus bill was Title I, better known as *Truth-in-Lending*. Title I authorized the Federal Reserve Board to draft regulations implementing this law—these regulations became known to mortgage lenders as *Regulation Z*. The regulations require a lender to provide a borrower with complete written information about the terms of a loan and a disclosure of the annual percentage rate (APR).

This disclosure of terms includes the amount of the payment, when due, and the number of such payments. The particulars of the repayment clause, finance charge and the sum of all monthly payments are also required to be disclosed. The finance charge is defined as the total of all borrowing costs imposed by a lender and payable by a borrower. These include interest, points or discount, initial service charge, time-price differential, insurance premiums required by a lender and any underwriting fee.

The APR disclosure includes interest charged and total prepaid items. Tables exist for translating the amount paid to an understandable percentage figure.

The 1980 Truth-in-Lending Simplification Act revised Regulation Z. The act requires that the TIL disclosure be provided to a borrower three days after application. Consequently, lenders have to compute the disclosed figures twice in order to determine if a second disclosure to the customer is necessary.

The Consumer Protection Act of 1968 also contained Title VI which is better known as the *Fair Credit Reporting Act*. This act did not have major impact on mortgage lending with the possible exception of limiting the use of investigative credit reports.

The *Fair Housing Act of 1968*, a civil rights law, was designed to prohibit racial discrimination in sales and financing of real estate, but procedurally its impact was minor. The other laws which were enacted before 1974 that affected mortgage lending were primarily to add new government mortgage support agencies and extend the authority of older existing ones. For a more complete discussion of these, see Chapter 7, Secondary Mortgage Markets and Institutions.

RESPA and ECOA

The 1970s is often described as the decade of the consumer. In many areas of society, consumer protection was a cresting wave, but nowhere was it as

LOAN COST DISCLOSURE STATEMENT
as required by Federal Reserve Regulation "Z"
Real Property Transaction Secured By First Lien on a Dwelling

Loan No.　　　　　　　　　　　　　　Date

1. The **AMOUNT OF THE LOAN** in this transaction is $

2. The **FINANCE CHARGE** on this transaction will begin to accrue on

3. The **ANNUAL PERCENTAGE RATE** on this transaction is　　　　　%. The Interest component of the Finance Charge will be computed at the annual contractual rate of　　　　　% on the outstanding balance of the loan from time to time.

4. The **PREPAID FINANCE CHARGE** includes:
   Loan Origination Fee . . . . $
   Assumption Fee . . . . $
   Interest From Date of Settlement
   　Until Amortized Interest Begins. . . $
   Initial Mortgage/F.H.A. Insurance
   　Premium . . . . $
   　　　　　　　　　　　　　　　　$
   　　　　　　　　　　　　　　　　$

4a. Total **PREPAID FINANCE CHARGE** $

5. The **AMOUNT FINANCED** in this transaction (Subtract 4a from Amount of Loan) . . . . $

6. Itemized Charges Excludable from **FINANCE CHARGE:**

	6a. Paid By Cash	6b. Paid From Loan Proceeds
Title Examination/Insurance . . . . $		$
Appraisal Fee . . . . $		$
Credit Report Fee . . . . $		$
Survey . . . . $		$
Initital Hazard Insurance Premium $		$
Insurance Reserve/Escrow . . . . . $		$
Tax Reserve/Escrow . . . . $		$
Recording Fees . . . . $		$
		$

Total Itemized Charges **Paid From Loan Proceeds (6b)** $ and included in the **Amount Financed**

7. **NET PROCEEDS** (Subtract Total 6b from Line 5) . . $

8. The **FINANCE CHARGE** on this transaction totals $　　　　　This amount includes:
   Total Prepaid Finance Charge (from 4a) . . . . $
   Total Interest to be Earned over life of Loan . . . . $
   Private or F.H.A. Mortgage Insurance collected after the outset of the transaction . . . . $
   　　　　　　　　　　　　　　　　　　　　　　　　　　　　　　　　　　　　　　　$

   TOTAL OF PAYMENTS on this transaction (**Amount Financed (5) plus total FINANCE CHARGE (8)** will be) . . . $

9. Payments of principal and Finance Charge exclusive of mortgage insurance premiums on this transaction shall number　　　　　with the first payment due on the　　　　　day of　　　　　and all subsequent payments due on the　　　　　day of every month thereafter. Such payments shall be in the amount of $

   In addition, the first　　　　　payments will include additional amounts for mortgage insurance premiums. These additional amounts will range from $　　　　　in the first payment due　　　　　to $ in the payment due　　　　　, which is the last payment on which mortgage insurance premiums are due. Thereafter, all monthly payments, if any, will be $

10. This institution's security interest in this transaction is a　　　　　on property located at　　　　　also specifically described in the documents furnished for this loan. The documents executed in connection with this transaction stand as security for future advances, the terms for which are described in the documents. Such documents also cover the following after-acquired property, if any.

11. Late payment formula:

12. Prepayment formula:

13. Miscellaneous disclosures:

14. **PROPERTY INSURANCE:** Hazard insurance, if written in connection with this loan, may be obtained by borrower through any person of his choice, provided, however, the creditor reserves the right to refuse, for reasonable cause, to accept an insurer offered by the borrower. If borrower desires hazard insurance to be obtained from or through the creditor, the cost will be:
    $　　　　　for the　　　　　year term of the initial policy.

15. **OTHER INSURANCE:** Credit life, accident, health or loss of income insurance is not required to obtain this loan. No charge is made for such insurance and no such insurance may be provided unless the borrower signs the appropriate statement below.
    　　　　　is available at a cost of $　　　　　for the　　　　　year term of the initial policy.
    I desire　　　　　insurance coverage.
    　　　　　　　　　　　Signature　　　　　　　　　　　　　　　　　Date

    I hereby acknowledge receipt of the disclosures made in this notice.

    Lender　　　　　　　　　　　Borrower　　　　　　　　　　　Date

    Authorized Signature　　　Date　　　Borrower　　　　　　　　Date

43011-6 (6/78)
TIL DISCLOSURE

SAF SYSTEMS & FORMS
American Savings & Accounting Supply, Inc.

WORK SHEET — DETACH AND COMPLETE BEFORE-TYPING

Figure 13–1. *Loan cost disclosure statement.*

strong or as pervasive as in mortgage lending. 1974 witnessed much of this movement coming to fruition in Congress with three important legislative acts—*Flood Disaster Protection Act, Real Estate Settlement Procedures Act* (RESPA), and *Equal Credit Opportunity Act* (ECOA).

The Flood Disaster Protection Act requires all lenders to ascertain before loan closing whether real estate securing a mortgage is located within a designated flood hazard area. If so located, this fact must be disclosed to a borrower before closing. A borrower then must obtain flood insurance from the National Flood Insurance Administration, and the flood insurance policy should remain in the loan file.

RESPA, originally enacted in 1974 and then extensively amended in 1976, requires mortgage lenders to provide mortgage borrowers with advance disclosures regarding loan settlement costs and charges, as well as information regarding the settlement process itself—the latter to be found in a booklet prepared by HUD. Another part of RESPA prohibited any person from receiving kickbacks for referring settlement business. Limits were also set on the amount of real estate tax and insurance escrows required by a lender. The 1976 amendments require mortgage lenders to supply both a "good faith estimate of settlement costs" and the HUD booklet three days after the loan application is received. The amendments also require the use of a document prepared by HUD, the complex Uniform Settlement Statement (HUD-1), at closing (see Figure 12–3).

ECOA, originally enacted in 1974 and then extensively amended in 1976, further extended the original Consumer Protection Act of 1968. The law as it applies today, prohibits discrimination based on age, sex, race, marital status, receipt of public assistance, color, religion and national origin. The additional paperwork required of mortgage lenders because of this law include:

1. Revising loan application forms to conform to ECOA terminology.
2. Providing a written ECOA notice at time of application.
3. Notifying applicant of action taken within 30 days (if application rejected, explain why).
4. Reporting both names in credit information if both spouses are contractually liable for the loan.
5. Retention of application and action taken thereon for 25 months.
6. And finally, other miscellaneous monitoring and recordkeeping requirements.

Home Mortgage Disclosure Act

Congress in 1975 attempted to redress the "redlining" issue with this act which requires mortgage lenders to make disclosures regarding the geographic distribution of loans within the Standard Metropolitan Statistical Area (SMSA). These disclosure statements must be available for any interested group to review; and, at least once each year, the mortgage lender must notify their depositors of this information. These disclosures must be retained for five years.

Date_____, 19_____

IMPORTANT INFORMATION ABOUT THE ADJUSTABLE MORTGAGE LOAN
PLEASE READ CAREFULLY

You have received an application form for an adjustable mortgage loan ("AML"). The AML may differ from other mortgages with which you are familiar.

General Description of Adjustable Mortgage Loan

The adjustable mortgage loan is a flexible instrument. Its interest rate may be adjusted by the lender from time to time. Such adjustments will result in increases or decreases in your payment amount, in the outstanding principal loan balance, in the loan term, or in all three (see discussion below relating to these types of adjustments). Federal regulations place no limit on the amount by which the interest-rate may be adjusted either at any one time or over the life of the loan, or on the frequency with which it may be adjusted. Adjustments to the interest rate must reflect the movement of a single, specified index. This does not mean that the particular loan agreement you sign must, by law, permit unlimited interest rate changes. It merely means that, if you desire to have certain rate-adjustment limitations placed in your loan agreement, that is a matter you should negotiate with the lender. You may also want to make inquiries concerning loan terms offered by other lenders on AMLs to compare the terms and conditions.

Another flexible feature of the AML is that the regular payment amount may be increased or decreased by the lender from time to time to reflect changes in the interest rate. Again, Federal regulations place no limitations on the amount by which the lender may adjust payments at any one time, or on the frequency of payment adjustments. If you wish to have particular provisions in your loan agreement regarding adjustments to the payment amount, you should negotiate such terms with the lender.

A third flexible feature of the AML is that the outstanding principal loan balance (the total amount you owe) may be increased or decreased from time to time when, because of adjustments to the interest rate, the payment amount is either too small to cover interest due on the loan, or larger than is necessary to pay off the loan over the remaining term of the loan.

The final flexible feature of the AML is that the loan term may be lengthened or shortened from time to time, corresponding to an increase or decrease in the interest rate. When the term is extended in connection with a rate increase, the payment amount does not have to be increased to the same extent as if the term had not been lengthened. In no case may the total term of the loan exceed 40 years.

The combination of these four basic features allows an association to offer a variety of mortgage loans. For example, one type of loan could permit rate adjustments with corresponding changes in the payment amount. Alternatively, a loan could permit rate adjustments to occur more frequently than payment adjustments, limit the amount by which the payment could be adjusted, and/or provide for corresponding adjustments to the principal loan balance.

Index

Adjustments to the interest rate of an AML must correspond directly to the movement of an index, subject to such rate-adjustment limitations as may be contained in the loan contract. If the index has moved down, the lender must reduce the interest rate by at least the decrease in the index. If the index has moved up, the lender has the right to increase the interest rate by that amount. Although taking such an increase is optional by the lender, you should be aware that the lender has this right and may become contractually obligated to exercise it.

DESCRIPTION OF THE INDEX TO BE USED_____

INITIAL INDEX VALUE (IF KNOWN)_____DATE OF INITIAL INDEX VALUE_____, 19_____

SOURCE(S) WHERE THE INDEX MAY BE READILY OBTAINED _____

HIGH AND LOW POINTS ON THE INDEX THE PREVIOUS CALENDAR YEAR: High_____Low_____

KEY TERMS OF THIS LENDER'S ADJUSTABLE MORTGAGE LOAN

Following is a summary of the basic terms on the type of AML to be offered to you. This summary is intended for reference purposes only. Important information relating specifically to your loan will be contained in the loan agreement.

Only the boxes checked below reflect the key terms of your AML:

☐ *Loan Term _____years.*

☐ *Frequency of Interest Rate Changes _____months*

☐ *Frequency of Payment Changes _____months*

☐ *Maximum Interest Rate Increase at One Time _____%*

☐ *Maximum Interest Rate Increase Over the Life of the Loan _____%*

☐ *Maximum Interest Rate Decrease Over the Life of the Loan _____%*

☐ *Maximum Interest Rate Decrease at One Time _____%*

☐ *Maximum Payment Increase at One Time _____%*

☐ *Minimum Interest Rate Change Increment _____%*

☐ *Rounding of Interest Rate Changes to nearest _____%*

☐ *Possible Adjustment to Principal Loan Balance*

HOW YOUR ADJUSTABLE MORTGAGE LOAN WOULD WORK

The initial interest rate offered by this lender will be established and disclosed to you _____ based on the market conditions at the time.

A narrative description of all the "Key Terms" of this Lender's AML program is contained on the reverse side. Note that only those "Key Terms" that are checked apply to your AML.

The box(es) checked below will reflect the basic overall operation of your AML. **Please see the reverse for a detailed explanation of the "Key Terms" of your AML.**

☐ Your loan term may either be shortened, or be extended, up to total loan term of 40 years, to (partially) offset a payment change increase.

☐ Your monthly payment will remain fixed for _____ months. Rate changes that occur during this fixed period may increase or decrease the principal loan balance. Payment changes will be made to amortize your AML over the remaining term at the end of each fixed period.

☐ All rate changes will result in a corresponding payment change, subject to the terms stated above for rate change increases.

☐ Your payment change will have a "cap" or limit of _____ % per rate change increase. Rate change increases might exceed the payment change "cap" causing increases in the principal loan amount through "negative amortization."

☐ _____
_____
_____
_____

Notice of Payment Adjustments

_____(LENDER) will send you notice of an adjustment to the payment amount at least 30 but not more than 45 days before it becomes effective. The notice will contain the following information:

1. The fact that the payment on the loan with the association, secured by a mortgage or deed of trust on property located at the appropriate address, is scheduled to be adjusted on a particular date;

2. The outstanding balance of the loan on the adjustment date, assuming timely payment of the remaining payments due by that date;

3. The interest rate on the loan as of the adjustment date, the index value on which that rate is based, the period of time for which that interest rate will be in effect, the next following payment adjustment date, and the rate adjustment dates, if any, between the upcoming payment adjustment date and the next following payment adjustment date;

4. The payment amount as of the payment adjustment date;

5. The date(s), if any, on which the rate was adjusted since the last payment adjustment, the rates on each such rate adjustment date, and the index values corresponding to each such date;

6. The dates, if any, on which the outstanding principal loan balance was adjusted since the last payment adjustment, and the net change in the outstanding principal loan balance since the last payment adjustment;

7. The fact that the borrower may pay off the entire loan or a part of it without penalty at any time; and

8. The title and telephone number of an association employee who can answer questions about the notice.

Prepayment Penalty

You may prepay an AML in whole or in part **without penalty at any time** during the term of the loan.

Fees

You will be charged fees by _____(LENDER) and other persons in connection with the origination of your AML. The association will give you an estimate of these fees after receiving your loan application. However, you will not be charged any costs or fees in connection with any regularly-scheduled adjustment to the interest rate, the payment, the outstanding principal loan balance, or the loan term initiated by the lender.

I/We acknowledge receipt of the above AML disclosure and a separate example of the operation of the type of AML to be offered to us.

_____   _____
Signature   Signature

Borrower

43072-8 (3/82*)
AML Application Disclosure

SAF Systems and Forms
1982 American Savings & Accounting Supply, Inc.

Figure 13-2. *AML disclosure statement.*

EQUAL HOUSING
LENDER

**WE DO BUSINESS IN ACCORDANCE WITH THE FEDERAL
FAIR HOUSING LAW AND THE EQUAL CREDIT OPPORTUNITY ACT
IT IS ILLEGAL TO:**

■ DISCOURAGE a loan inquiry or refuse to accept a written loan application;

■ DISCRIMINATE in fixing the amount, interest rate, duration, application procedures, or other terms or conditions of a loan; or

■ DENY a loan for the purpose of purchasing, constructing, improving, repairing or maintaining a dwelling

**ON THE BASIS OF
RACE, COLOR, NATIONAL ORIGIN, RELIGION, SEX,
MARITAL STATUS OR AGE;
OR BECAUSE
A PERSON RECEIVES INCOME FROM A PUBLIC ASSISTANCE PROGRAM,
OR HAS IN GOOD FAITH EXERCISED ANY RIGHT UNDER THE
CONSUMER CREDIT PROTECTION ACT.**

IF YOU BELIEVE YOU HAVE BEEN DISCRIMINATED AGAINST, YOU MAY:

SPEAK with the management of this institution;

COMPLAIN TO The Office of Community Investment, Federal Home Loan Bank Board, Washington, D.C. 20552, or the Assistant Secretary for Fair Housing and Equal Opportunity, Department of Housing and Urban Development, Washington, D.C. 20010; or

CONSIDER filing a civil suit under Federal laws.

Figure 13–3. *Equal housing lender emblem.*

Closely related to the above act is the *Community Reinvestment Act* (CRA), effective in 1979. The purpose of this act was to require regulated financial institutions to meet their communities' need for credit for low- and moderate-income neighborhoods "consistent with safe and sound operation" of the institution. In order to accomplish this, institutions must define their community and then publish a CRA statement which lists the types of credit available to the community, and finally maintain a public file for inspection of written comments in regard to the institutions' CRA statement.

Fair Lending Practices Regulations

In 1978, the Federal Home Loan Board imposed on FSLIC-insured savings associations a new set of regulations which were developed as a settlement to a lawsuit brought against the board by a coalition of civil rights groups. (The Federal Reserve Board was also a party to that suit, but refused the settlement, and the suit was later dropped). These regulations do not apply to all mortgage lenders, only FSLIC-insured institutions. Among other items, these regulations require:

1. A written nondiscrimination underwriting statement which is available to the public.
2. A loan application register with 23 possible entries (see Figure 13–4).
3. A disclosure notice that declares the association must determine race and sex for monitoring purposes even if not supplied.
4. Affirmative marketing of mortgage services.
5. Institutions to not deny a loan based on age or location of a dwelling.
6. Institutions to base loan decision on a realistic evaluation of all pertinent factors without giving undue weight to any one factor.

THE NET EFFECT

Obvious questions that should arise after reviewing the wealth of new laws and regulations governing the current practice of mortgage lending are: What is the net effect? Has it allowed for more families to finance home purchases? Has it made the practice of mortgage lending more professional or proficient? Has it allowed for more minority or disadvantaged classes to purchase homes? Has the nation as a whole benefitted?

It is the author's opinion that these recent laws and regulations (i.e., enacted in the '70s and into the '80s) have had a negative effect. The main reason for this negative reaction is based on the staggering increase in the cost of housing, the high cost of home financing and the shortage of funds with which to extend mortgage credit. During the decade of the '70s, the cost for the average priced existing home increased at a rate twice as fast as the increase in median family income.

LOAN APPLICATION REGISTER
MORTGAGE LOANS
(Codes (•) and Footnotes are listed below)

ADDRESS OF DECISION CENTER

PAGE

LOAN IDENTIFICATION
- APPLICATION NUMBER
- LOAN PURPOSE •
- DATE OF APPLICATION: MO / DAY / YEAR
- LOAN NUMBER
- DISPOSITION •
- DATE: MO / DAY / YEAR

LOAN DISPOSITION

PROPERTY LOCATION
- SMSA
- CENSUS TRACT
- ZIP CODE

AREA DATA •
- LOW INC
- MOD INC

APPLICANT(S) INFORMATION
- RACE • CA / A
- SEX • CA / A
- MARITAL STATUS • CA / A
- AGE A / CA
- PROPERTY TYPE •

PROPERTY DATA
- PURCHASE PRICE
- APPRAISED VALUE
- YEAR BUILT

LOAN TERMS
- LOAN AMOUNT
- LOAN TO VALUE RATIO
- CONTRACT INTEREST RATE
- MATURITY TERM (Months)
- TYPE OF FINANCING •

4703Y-0 (REV 3/80**)
FHLBB Loan Register - Mortgage
FHLBB Form 1154-O

SAF Systems and Forms
American Savings & Accounting Supply, Inc.

* CODES

LOAN PURPOSE
1 = Purchase/Owner-Occupied
2 = Purchase/Investment
3 = Construction/Permanent
4 = Construction
5 = Refinance
9 = Other

DISPOSITION
1 = Approved as Requested
2 = Approved with Changes - Applicant Accepts
3 = Approved with Changes - Applicant Refuses
4 = Denied - Decision based on Applicant's Creditworthiness
5 = Denied - Decision based on Collateral
6 = Denied - Decision based on Other Considerations
7 = Withdrawn by Applicant

AREA DATA
Y = Yes
N = No

APPLICANT(S) INFORMATION
RACE
1 = American Indian or Alaskan Native
2 = Asian or Pacific Islander
3 = Black
4 = Hispanic
5 = White

SEX
M = Male
F = Female

MARITAL STATUS
M = Married
U = Unmarried
S = Separated

PROPERTY TYPE
1 = Single-Family Dwelling
2 = 2-4 Family Dwelling
3 = Combination Home and Business

TYPE OF FINANCING
1 = Conventional without Private Mortgage Insurance
2 = Conventional with Private Mortgage Insurance
3 = FHA
4 = VA
5 = Other

FOOTNOTES

1/ DATE
• FOR LOANS GRANTED (Codes 1 and 2)
Give Date of Loan Settlement
• FOR LOANS REJECTED OR WITHDRAWN (Codes 3, 4, 5, 6, and 7)
Give Date of Disposition

2/ YEAR BUILT
Give Year Built or Approximate Year Built

Figure 13–4. *Loan application register.*

PRICE OF HOMES PURCHASED NATIONWIDE

Price	1981		1979	1977
Less than $30,000	6.9%		10.1%	18.6%
$30,000–$49,999	16.9%		27.9%	43.8%
$50,000–$69,999	24.4%		28.6%	22.7%
$70,000–$89,999	19.2%		17.1%	9.4%
$90,000–$99,999	6.0%			
$100,000–$119,999	8.2%	32.6%	16.3%	5.5%
$120,000–$139,999	6.2%			
$140,000 or more	12.2%			
Median	$72,000		$58,000	$44,000

Source: U.S. League of Savings Associations.

Figure 13–5.

While many of the recent laws and regulations have a positive objective, such as preserving the environment, making homes safer, reducing sprawl, helping settlement procedures, preventing discriminatory lending, etc., all too frequently, they have had the effect of stifling the housing development market and increasing the cost of housing. The average price for an existing single-family residential unit has increased from $25,700 in 1970 to in excess of $72,000 in 1981.

If the cost of housing was increasing at a rate that was keeping pace with inflation, the problem, although great, would not be insurmountable. But the annual average percentage increase for housing costs in the 1970s was 15 percent. It is estimated that in 1970, fifty percent of the American families could afford the average priced existing house. At the end of 1979, less than 20 percent of the American families could afford the average priced existing house.

The regulations imposed on the mortgage lending community over the past ten years have had the effect of mortgage lenders suffering increased origination, underwriting, servicing and appraising expenses. The increase in mortgage lending expense has not and cannot be expected to be absorbed by mortgage lenders. These costs ultimately must be passed on to the consumer. The increased expense to the mortgage lender, and therefore, to the consumer, in both the price of housing and financing expenses has one result: fewer families are able to afford the average priced home.

SUGGESTED READINGS

Burchell, Robert W. and Listoken, David. *Future Land Use*, New Brunswick, New Jersey, The Center for Urban Policy Research, 1975.

Dennis, Warren L. "How Do You Know You're Not Discriminating?" *Federal Home Loan Bank Board Journal* (May 1977), pp. 15–24.

Frieden, Bernard J. *The Environmental Protection Hustle*, MIT Press, 1979.

King, A. Thomas. "The Loan Application Register: A Tool for Examiners," *Federal Home Loan Bank Board Journal* (August 1980), pp. 8–13.

Seidel, Stephen R. *Housing Costs and Government Regulations: Confronting the Regulatory Maze*, New Brunswick, New Jersey, The Center for Urban Policy Research, 1978.

Weidenboum, Murry L. "Government Regulations Blamed for Much of Housing Cost Insurance," *The Mortgage Banker*, (March, 1978), pp. 21–22.

Winningham, Scott and Hagan, Donald G. "Regulation Q: An Historical Perspective," *Economic Review* (April 1980), pp. 3–17.

NOTES

1.   Center for Urban Policy Research, Rutgers University, Government Regulations and Housing Costs, A study conducted for the Smith-Richardson Foundation; June, 1977.

2.   Housing in the Seventies, National Housing Policy Review, Department of Housing and Urban Development, Washington, D.C. 1974, p. 136.

Chapter 14

Fundamentals of Real Estate Law

INTRODUCTION

This chapter provides reference material for other chapters of the book, as well as a fundamental review of the basic principles of American real estate law.

Possibly no other segment of the U.S. social-economic system is more involved with law than real estate. Whether as a homeowner, a developer or a financier, those involved with real estate must understand the legal framework upon which real estate is defined and the interests therein protected relating both to the business and the commodity. Obviously, mortgage lenders who rely on legally-defined and enforced rights must be aware of their own and possibly other conflicting rights to the real property securing the obligation. This can occur only if the legal principles involved are understood.

Law and real estate have been inseparable since the early days of the development of Anglo-American jurisprudence. This close relationship continues because of custom and the perception that real estate is normally its owner's most precious possession. However, this also has hindered the changes in real estate concepts needed in an evolving society.

A fundamental review of how this relationship between law and real estate developed and a discussion of the interests a person can have in real estate appear in the following sections. Nonlegal terminology is used where the meaning or concept is not altered or affected in any way.

In light of broad differences in state law, this review covers only the general principles of real estate law with no discussion of the unique features of any one state's law. In those situations where there is a basic conflict in the general principles, the majority position is reviewed. Nevertheless, the laws of individual jurisdictions should be carefully determined. This is best accomplished by consulting a competent local attorney.

ENGLISH COMMON LAW

The real estate laws of the 50 jurisdictions, including the District of Columbia but excluding Louisiana, which is based primarily on French civil law, are based almost entirely on the English common law as it existed at the time of the American Revolutionary War. As individual state laws were changed by statute or court decisions, the chief problem of American real estate law was 50 different bodies of law written in an archaic language often difficult to understand, with a conceptual basis different from that which exists in modern America. A short review of this development is vital since our current real estate laws evolved from the English common law.

Before the Norman invasion of England in 1066, there was no well-developed system of land ownership in England. Land was owned by the family unit rather than the individual, and when the head of the household died, the new head of the household would represent the ownership of the family in a particular piece of land. In 1066, when William the Conqueror invaded England, he imposed a European concept of land ownership upon the English called the feudal system of land tenure, an economic, military and political system of government which held that the King exclusively owned all land. The most valuable and important commodity in such a society was land. Land represented wealth, and all wealth came from the land. Money hardly existed and barter was the means of exchange. Since the King owned all land, he had complete control over the country and the economy.

A king, of course, needed arms for protection of the realm. For this he depended on the loyalty, fidelity, and allegiance of the lords. In return for their allegiance and military service, the King allowed the lords to use the land, although no ownership was being conveyed. The lords, in turn, allowed lesser lords to use a portion of this land in return for a share of the profits and for swearing allegiance to them. Finally, these lesser lords allowed serfs, who were nothing more than slaves indentured to the land, to use the land in return for a promise of military service. In this pyramid of military allegiance, the serfs owed military service to the lesser lords, who in turn owed service to the lords, who swore allegiance to the King.

The right to own land didn't exist for many years, but one of the incidents of ownership, the inability to pass the use of land to heirs, produced a confrontation with King John in 1215. The result was the Magna Carta, which provided greater rights for the lords, including the right to pass the use of the land on to their sons. Land was passed on to sons only as a result of the doctrine of primogeniture, which dictated that the oldest male child had the right to inherit the land. This was desirable at the time, since it prevented estates from being broken up into smaller tracts and allowed for the development of a landed gentry, which eventually developed the English society. Out of this society evolved the common law and, eventually, English real estate law. Although modified over the years, the feudal system survived until 1660 when it was abolished by law.

As contrasted with the feudal system, the *allodial* system recognizes that an owner of real estate has title irrespective of the sovereign and thus owes no duty, such as rent or the rendering of military service, to the sovereign. This system developed throughout the world with the exception of Western Europe and certain other areas where the feudal system remained.

The feudal system was an early part of the American land-ownership system in a few locations such as New York and Maryland. With those exceptions, the allodial system was paramount in America based on either conquest, discovery or purchase.

PRINCIPLES OF REAL ESTATE LAW

The first step in understanding the principles of real estate law is to define terms. *Real property* is land and everything permanently attached to it. Under the common law, and as a general rule today, this included ownership from the center of the earth, the surface, and up to the heavens. All other property is *personal property*. *Real estate* is used to denote both real property and the business of real estate, including financing.

Property can change from one classification to another fairly rapidly. For example, a tree standing in a forest is real property. When it is felled, it becomes personal property and, finally, after being made into lumber and becoming part of a house, it is real property again. The term *fixture* is used to describe a piece of personal property that has been attached in such a manner that it is now considered real property. This distinction is important, since title to real property is normally transferred by a deed, while personal property is transferred by a bill of sale.

Estate

Today, when people talk about their ownership of land, they are legally talking about the type of estate they have in real estate. This is as true in America as it was in England 500 years ago. An estate is defined as *an interest in real property which is measured by its potential duration.* There are two recognized classifications of estate in real property; *freehold,* and *leasehold,* sometimes referred to as non-freehold. The classification *freehold estate* is the highest form of interest possible in real property, as it involves all the rights in real property including use, passing the property to one's heirs, or selecting who is going to take it in a transfer. It is an estate of infinite duration, in that the chain of title could theoretically last forever. An example of a freehold estate would be a *fee simple absolute.*

On the other hand, the classification *leasehold estate* is an inferior interest in real property, because the owner of a leasehold interest only has the right of possession for a period of time. The owner of this interest does not have *seisin,* which is defined as the ability to pass title to one's heirs or assigns. An example of a leasehold estate would be a tenant's interest in leased property.

Fee Simple Absolute

There has never been nor will there ever be complete ownership of land. Examples of the restraints or limitations on ownership of land include, among others, eminent domain, adverse possession, and easements.

The greatest interest a person can have in real property is known as a *fee simple absolute.* Any owner of real property, whether it be a large corporation or John Doe, has a fee simple absolute if all possible rights to that piece of real property are possessed.

In order to explain a fee simple absolute, legal pedagogues use the *bundle of rights* concept. For example, assume that all rights, such as the right to sell, mortgage and build on, among others, to a piece of real property are represented by "sticks," contained in this bundle of rights. If all of the "sticks" are present and the owner has all possible rights to the real property, then the bundle of rights is complete and is called a *fee simple absolute.* If a "stick" is missing, such as the right to use the property the way one wants, then the interest is less than a fee simple absolute.

Defeasible or Conditional Fee

A freehold estate, which is similar to a fee simple absolute but minus a "stick" (or a right) from the bundle of rights, is the *defeasible fee simple.* This is a freehold estate that could but will not necessarily last forever. An example of a defeasible fee simple occurs when conditions are placed on how the property may be used.

Grantors of land may put any restrictions they desire on how the land is to be used after it has been conveyed. There are, of course, a few exceptions, such as those that are racially oriented. Grantors can always give less than the full interests they own in conveying land, but never more. They can give possession for any desired period of time, or for any specific use—only as a church, for example. If so conveyed, a defeasible fee simple is created that could last forever, but it could also be terminated.

An example of a defeasible fee simple that would automatically end if a certain event occurs is when A grants land to B church on condition that the premises are used only for church purposes. The church has a defeasible fee simple that could last forever but will automatically end if the property ceases to be used for church purposes. When that happens, the title automatically reverts to A or A's heirs. This interest is classified as a fee simple since it could last forever if the property is always used for church purposes.

A distinction is made legally between two types of defeasible fee simple. They are a fee simple subject to a condition subsequent, and a fee simple determinable. The typical person involved in real estate does not need to know the distinction, but counsel for that person should. An example of a fee simple subject to a condition subsequent would occur when A conveys property to B as long as liquor is never sold on the premises. In this situation, the grantee B (the person to whom the land has been conveyed) has a fee simple, but it is subject to a condition subsequent in that if liquor is ever sold on the premises the land will revert to the grantor (the one making the conveyances). The grantor must make an affirmative action for the property to revert, that is, re-enter the property and sue to terminate the estate.

The fee simple determinable has been described. Most courts lump these together as being basically the same. If forced to distinguish, courts attempt to find a fee on a condition subsequent in order that the grantor must re-enter to terminate rather than have the estate terminate automatically.

Fee Tail

This type of estate came into being from a desire in feudal England to keep land in whole parcels within the family. A fee tail is an estate of potentially infinite duration, but is inheritable only by the grantee's lineal descendants, such as children or grandchildren. For a fee tail to be created under the common law it was necessary to state in the conveyance that the land was being transferred to A and "the heirs of his body." This differed from the wording of any other common law transfer, which required only "and his heirs" to be used.

There were various types of the fee tail. The *fee tail general* meant the property was inheritable by any issue of the grantee. A *fee tail special* meant the land was inheritable only by the issue of the grantee and a specifically named spouse. (*A conveyance to A and the heirs of his body, by his wife Mary,* would be an example.) A fee tail general could specify whether the issue need be male or female, and there also was the possibility of a fee tail special, male or female. Although the fee tail is still allowed in some New England states, the practical effect of it has been abolished in all states today.

Life Estates

A *life estate* is a freehold estate like the fee simple absolute and others already mentioned, but it is not inheritable. Life estates can be either conventional (created by the grantor) or legal (created by operation of law). The creation of a life estate is a tool often used in estate planning and is fairly common interest in real estate. By the creation of a life estate the life tenant (the one granted the right) has the use of real estate for a period of time measured by a human life. The human life used to measure the duration of the life estate may be that of another human life, but is most commonly measured by the life of the life tenant. An example is: A conveys a life estate to B for life, and as long as B is alive, B has the right to use the real estate, with certain exceptions, as if he owned it. The only incident of ownership that B lacks is the power to pass a fee simple absolute. The right to sell or mortgage the interest is not expressly given but a person could acquire only that which B had, which was the use of the land for a period measured by a life.

When A created this life estate, only a part of the complete interest was transferred. In other words someone else was allowed to use the land for a period of time. However, at the expiration of that period of time, the remaining rights to the real estate are with the grantor. A may have retained it to pass the real property to someone else. In the example given, where A conveyed land to B for B's life, the land will revert to A (the grantor) or the heirs upon the death of B (the life tenant) since no other conveyance was made.

When A created the life estate in B, the remainder could have been transferred in this way: A to B for life, and then to C. In this situation, C is the *vested remainderman,* because the grantor has transferred the remaining interest to C. The rights of C are vested irrespective of whether C survives the life tenant or not. If a vested remainderman does die before a life tenant, then the vested remainderman's heirs would inherit the fee interest.

On the other hand, a life estate could be created this way: A to B for B's life, and then to C if C is alive, in which case C must survive B to acquire any rights to the land. If C dies before B, the land reverts to the original owner. If it is impossible to determine at the time of the creation of the life estate who definitely will take the fee simple after the death of the life tenant, the remainderman is referred to as a *contingent remainderman.*

Another common example of this situation would be: A to B for life, and then to B's children. B may not have any children; therefore, their interest is contingent upon being born. To complicate it even further, the conveyance could read: A to B for B's life, and then to B's surviving children. The children, if any, must survive B before they can acquire any interest.

In summary, a conventional life estate is an interest which an individual has in real estate providing most of the incidences of ownership, with the exception of the ability to pass a fee simple absolute. The person who takes possession after the life tenant dies could be either the grantor, if the grantor did not convey the remainder, or it could be a third person who would be classified as either a contingent or a vested remainderman, depending on whether the identify can be determined precisely at the time of the creation of the life estate.

In contrast with the conventional life estate, created intentionally by the grantor, a *legal life estate* is created by operation of the law. An example of a legal life estate is the *right of dower.* Dower was originally conceived to prevent a widow from being penniless during a period of English history when life insurance, welfare and social security were unknown. Dower is a common-law right of a widow still present in many jurisdictions. The equivalent right of the husband is *curtesy,* which has either been abolished or merged with dower in nearly all states.

Basically, the right of dower gives a wife, at her husband's death, a life estate in one-third of the real estate owned by her husband during marriage.

Generally, the widow has a choice of which real estate will be subject to her dower right and this right is applicable to all real estate owned by the husband during the marriage, even if he had transferred it before death. In those states where this right exists, a wife's potential dower interest is extinguished if she executes a deed with her husband transferring the land to another.

Currently, in some states, the right of dower has been abolished as unnecessary. This is probably because the need for a right such as dower has been eliminated in most states by the creation of a statutory right of each spouse to a minimum one-third share of the decedent's estate, and because of life insurance, social security and other benefits.

Leasehold Estates (non-freehold estates)

As mentioned earlier, this estate gives the owner the right to possession of real estate for a period of time. The actual duration may or may not be ascertainable at the beginning, but it does not carry with it the ability to pass title to the real estate. The owner of the land (the fee) has given up possession for a period of time, but retains the legal title to the real estate, and the owner (or heirs or assigns) will eventually retake possession. The legal term to describe the missing element in a leasehold estate is seisin.

Although the use of leases can be traced to the beginning of written history, the leasehold estate in England was originally used to circumvent the prohibition against lending money for interest since any interest was usury under early Church law. The person borrowing money would allow the lender to use some or all of the land for a period of time in lieu of interest. Therefore, under the common law, a leasehold was considered personal property, but now is considered an estate in real estate. A lease, which creates the leasehold estate, is a peculiar instrument in that it is both a conveyance giving the tenant possession for a period of time, and a contract establishing rights and duties for the parties. The essential elements for a lease are:

- Name of landlord and tenant
- Agreement to lease
- Description of leased property
- Duration of lease
- Rental agreement
- Rights and duties of the parties
- Signature

A lease for a year or less may be verbal or in writing, but one for more than a year must be in writing. For the safety of both the landlord and tenant, all leases should be in writing. Most states have a 99-year limitation on a lease, although the vast majority of leases are for less than 10 years. The degree of complexity in leases increases from the relatively simple residential lease to the very complex shopping center lease. The type of tenancy acquired form a lease depends on whether or not the term is renewable and whether notice to terminate must be given by either party. (See Chapter 10, The Lease and Leasehold Financing, for more details.)

Additional Interests in Real Estate

In addition to the freehold and leasehold estates in real estate, there are certain other limited interests or rights to real estate. These include easements, profits and covenants. The effect of these interests is to create a limited right to the real estate of another, although the fact that a piece of real property is subject to an easement, for instance, does not prevent it from being owned in fee simple absolute.

Easements. An easement is a non-possessory interest in the real estate of another, giving the holder the right to a limited use of real estate. An example is the right to drive across the real estate of another to reach a highway. An easement is either in gross (a personal right) or appurtenant (belonging to whoever owns the benefitted real estate). Although most easements are expressed in writing, they can be simply implied. The right of a gas company to install a gas line on a back property line is an example of an expressed easement appurtenant.

Profit. A profit resembles an easement because the holder has an interest in the real estate of another. However, a profit creates the right to enter the property of another and take a portion of the property, such as the soil, or the product of the property such as trees or oil.

Covenant. Like the previous interests discussed, this interest is in the real estate of another. The difference between a covenant or a promise to do or not to do something and other interests is that it restricts or limits how the owner can use the real estate. An example of a covenant is the requirement a farmer may put on the part of a farm being sold that the grantee use the real estate only for residential purposes. This interest is of benefit to the grantor because it allows control of the use of the real estate. Therefore, it is an interest in the real estate of another. This interest can be either in gross or appurtenant, although the term often used with covenants is *running with the land.* This interest should not be confused with a defeasible fee simple since title cannot be lost if a covenant is breached—only damages or an injunction can be sought.

JOINT OR CONCURRENT OWNERSHIP

Joint Tenancy

Ownership in land can be and usually is held by more than one person. The most common type of joint or concurrent ownership is the joint tenancy, which can exist between any two or more persons. Although joint tenants share a single title to the real estate, each owns an equal share of the whole. Joint tenancies are quite common, but a few states have abolished or limited them for reasons that will be discussed later. Most states will allow the creation of a joint tenancy by simply referring to A and B as joint tenants. But other jurisdictions require reference to A and B as joint tenants with the right of survivorship. This interest can be created only by affirmative action of the grantor, not by operation of law. The right of survivorship is the key concept of a joint tenancy. Upon the death of one of the joint tenants, all the deceased's interests in the real property terminate and the ownership in the land is retained by the surviving joint tenant or tenants. In other words, a joint tenancy is not an inheritable estate. Therefore, it does not pass through the estate of the decedent and does not pass to the heirs. Instead, it passes to or is possessed automatically by the surviving joint tenants. For this reason, some states have abolished joint tenancy, and most courts disfavor joint tenancy because it automatically prevents property from flowing through the estate of an individual to the heirs. Therefore, if one wishes to create a joint tenancy, it is mandatory to follow the strict statutory requirements of the respective state. To avoid the possibility that a court could misunderstand a grantor's intention, a joint tenancy should be created by using this phrase: *to A and B, as joint tenants with right of survivorship and not as tenants in common.*

During the time a joint tenancy is in existence, the portion of the whole belonging to any one of the joint tenants usually may be attached to satisfy that individual's legal debts. But the portion belonging to the other joint tenant(s) may not. Some states have laws that modify this approach if the joint tenants are man and wife and the property in question is their home.

Although any joint tenant may sell or mortgage interest (with some exceptions for married joint tenants), the effect is a termination of the joint tenancy by either a voluntary or involuntary transfer. It is also terminated by the death of one of two joint tenants, but not by the death of one of more than two. The survivors in that case still have a joint tenancy among themselves.

Under the common law, if both parties did not acquire ownership to real estate at the same time, a joint tenancy could not exist. Consequently, a husband owning property before marriage could not create a joint tenancy with his wife. One method devised to circumvent this requirement was the usage of a "straw man". For instance, the husband would convey title to his real estate to a friend or relative (the so-called "straw man") who would then transfer the title back to the husband and wife as joint tenants and the unity of time requirement would be satisfied.

Tenancy by the Entirety

A form of concurrent ownership much like the joint tenancy is the *tenancy by the entirety,* which is allowed in about 20 states. The reason for its existence is because of a vestige from the common law of some technical requirement for a joint tenancy, such as the unity of time, or the state had abolished joint tenancy. The primary difference between this form of ownership and the joint tenancy is a tenancy by the entirety can exist only between a legally-married husband and wife, while a joint tenancy can exist between any two or more persons.

Another important feature of a tenancy by the entirety is that the interest of one of the parties cannot be attached for the legal debts of that person. Only if the debts are of both parties can an attachment be made. For this reason, both a husband and wife in some states will be asked to sign the mortgage note if the form of ownership to the real estate is to be as tenants by the entirety, even if only one has income. Many states allowing tenancy by the entirety presume that a conveyance to a husband and wife, silent as to the type of ownership, will be a tenancy by the entirety.

The surviving tenant becomes the sole owner like the surviving joint tenant, but this survivorship right stems from the concept that the husband and wife were one, so ownership was already with the survivor. Divorce or annulment will terminate this tenancy.

Tenants in Common

Tenancy in common is a concurrent estate with no right of survivorship. Therefore, when a person dies, the interest held in the real property passes through the estate. This interest can exist between any two or more individuals and, in effect, jointly gives them the rights and duties of a sole owner. Each of the co-tenants is considered an owner of an undivided interest (not necessarily equal) in the whole property, and each has separate legal title, unlike joint tenants who share a single title. Courts of law look with favor on a tenancy in common, because a co-tenant's share of ownership passes upon death to the heirs and is not forfeited. As contrasted with a joint tenancy or a tenancy by the entirety, a tenancy in common can arise by operation of law, e.g., when a person dies intestate (without a will), heirs automatically inherit as tenants in common.

Any tenant in common can sell his interest, mortgage it and have it attached for debts without destroying the joint interest. A grantee of a tenancy in common acquires only the percentage of the whole owned by the grantor. A tenancy in common is terminated by agreement between the parties or upon a petition to a court.

Community Property

Another form of concurrent ownership is community property, which is the law primarily in those states located in the western part of the United States.[1] Basically, the concept is that half of all property, personal and real, created during marriage belongs to each spouse. The underlying theory of this concept is that both have contributed to the creation of the family's wealth, even though only one was gainfully employed. There are three exceptions to this rule:

1. Property acquired from separate funds, such as a trust account
2. Property acquired individually before the marriage
3. Property inherited from another's estate.

With these exceptions, if the necessity of terminating the marriage occurs each should receive a one-half share. Since each has equal interests, both must sign a mortgage note and security agreement.

Tenancy in Partnership

The last form of concurrent ownership is tenancy in partnership. Under the common law, a partnership could not own real estate in its partnership name. Therefore, one of the partners had to own the real estate in his or her own name. This presented the possibility of fraud. The Uniform Partnership Act, as adopted by many states, provides that a partnership can own real property in its firm name. Upon the death of a partner in a partnership, the surviving partners are vested with the share of the decedent or a percentage ownership of all property owned by the partnership. One partner's share of ownership may not necessarily be equal to that of another. It is quite common for partnerships to provide for a means of compensation for a deceased partner's estate, usually by insurance or a buy-sell agreement.

TRANSFER OF LAND

All title to real estate in America can be traced to one of three origins; conquest, discovery, or purchase. Today, title to real property can be transferred either voluntarily or involuntarily.

Voluntary Transfers

Most transfers of land are voluntary in that a grantor usually intends to transfer title to land to a grantee by the use of a deed or possibly a will. A deed is a legal instrument that purports to transfer a grantor's interest. If a grantor had no actual interest in a particular piece of real estate, an executed deed would transfer nothing. In addition, a properly executed deed from a grantor who did have title but lacked legal capacity (the grantor was legally insane, for example) would also transfer nothing. The validity of the title of the grantor can be determined by *abstracting* or checking the chain of title for defects.

All states have a law known as a statute of frauds requiring written transfers of real estate. Today, technical words are not needed in a deed, since any words that clearly show the grantor's intention to transfer are sufficient. There are eight essential elements of a modern deed:

1. Grantor's name
2. Grantee's name
3. Description of real estate to be conveyed
4. Consideration (does not have to be actual amount paid)
5. Words of conveyance
6. Signature of grantor
7. Delivery and acceptances
8. Proper execution

Three basic types of deed are used, each having a specific purpose and function to perform. The least complicated is a *quit claim deed* which is used to clear title to real estate. A person signing this deed makes no title guarantee. Instead, a grantor is simply transferring whatever interest owned, if any. This deed can be used to clear a cloud on the title caused by a widow having a potential right of dower. She would be requested to execute the deed, possibly for a fee, whereby she transferred whatever interest she had (in this case dower), thus clearing the title.

A *general warranty deed* is the most common deed used to transfer interest in real estate. With this deed a grantor guarantees to a grantee that the title transferred is good against the whole world. This guarantee extends past the grantor to those in the chain of title. If a grantor refuses to use this deed, it may be an indication that the title is defective.

The *special warranty deed* is a relatively rare deed used in situations where a grantor wants to limit the guarantee. This instrument would be used by an executor of an estate to convey real estate to those specified in a will. By this deed the grantor only guarantees that nothing was done to interfere with the title to the real estate while under the grantor's control and makes no guarantee about a decedent's claim to the real estate.

Real estate that passes according to a will is also a voluntary conveyance, since it passes as the testator or the one making the will intended.

Involuntary Transfers

An involuntary conveyance occurs when a legal owner of real estate loses title contrary to the owner's intention. An example of this would be *eminent domain.* Any sovereign in the United States (federal, state, city or county) and some quasi-public entities (such as the telephone company or gas line company) can exercise the right of eminent domain. This right is inherent in a sovereign and is not granted by a constitution, although it is limited by it. The key elements are that it must be exercised for a valid public purpose or use, and that it requires compensation to be paid the legal owner.[2]

Another example of involuntary transfer of title is *adverse possession*. The public policy behind the doctrine of adverse possession is the encouragement of the usage of land, in addition to settling old claims to real property. Normally, a person possessing the real property of another holds that real estate for the legal owner's benefit. But if certain requirements are satisfied, the one occupying the real property could acquire legal title.

To claim title to real property by adverse possession, the one occupying the real property must prove:

- Actual possession
- Hostile intent
- Notorious and open possession
- Exclusive and continuous possession
- Possession for a statutory period (which ranges from five to twenty years)

Some states also require that the party claiming title by adverse possession base the claim on some written instrument—even if the instrument is not valid. Other states require the claimant to pay real estate taxes for the statutory period.

Other examples of the possibility of involuntary transfer would include *foreclosure and subsequent sale* if an owner of real estate does not pay the mortgage, real estate tax or other encumbrances.

When a person dies intestate the title to real property along with the personal property passes, not according to the dictates of the owner, but according to the statutes of that particular state. If the individual had no discernible heirs, the property would escheat (pass) to the state.

Recording

Any time an interest in real estate is being created, transferred or encumbered, that transaction should be recorded. As in England centuries ago, the reason for recording is to prevent fraud. For example, situations existed where the owner of land would sell, possibly inadvertently, the same real estate to two or more innocent purchasers. Therefore, it was necessary to develop a system by which fraudulent transactions could be prevented. This was accomplished by devising a system of recording transactions affecting real estate. In order to protect a buyer's interest, recording statutes require purchasers of real estate to record the instrument by which they acquired the interest. If recorded, any subsequent purchaser will have either actual knowledge of the prior interest (because he checked the record), or constructive notice (because if he did check he would have discovered the interest).

If the party (the prior purchaser, for instance) who could have prevented a subsequent fraud by recording does not record, then that party will suffer the loss. An individual who wants to purchase real property has an obligation to check the record, usually in a county court house, to determine if there have been any transactions involving that particular real estate. Recording gives constructive notice to the whole world that a party has acquired an interest in a particular real property. Therefore, any subsequent purchaser could not acquire the same interest. If no transaction appears, an innocent purchaser acquiring an interest will be protected against the whole world, even against a prior purchaser.

In summary, a prior purchaser is protected if a record is made, whether a subsequent purchaser checks the record or not. The same is true if there is actual notice. If A sold land to B, and B failed to record, and C, knowing of that transaction, buys the same land and records, B will be protected since C had actual notice of the transaction between A and B. If C did not have actual notice and recorded before B, C would be protected in any dispute between B and C.

All states have a "race statute" which dictates that the first of two innocent parties to record will be protected.

SUGGESTED READINGS

Hebard, Edna L., and Meisel, Gerald S. *Principles of Real Estate Law*. Cambridge, Massachusetts: Schenkman Publishing Co., 1967.

Kratovil, Robert. *Modern Mortgage Law and Practice*. Englewood Cliffs, New Jersey: Prentice-Hall, Inc., 1972.

_____. *Modern Real Estate Documentation*. Englewood Cliffs, New Jersey: Prentice-Hall, Inc., 1975.

_____. *Real Estate Law*. Englewood Cliffs, New Jersey: Prentice-Hall Inc., 1974.

Lusk, Harold F. *The Law of the Real Estate Business*. Homewood, Illinois: Richard D. Irwin, Inc., 1975.

NOTES

1. Arizona, California, Idaho, Louisiana, Nevada, New Mexico, Oklahoma, Texas, and Washington.

2. This should not be confused with the exercise of police power, such as zoning, which does not require compensation.

Chapter 15

Residential Mortgage Loan Case Studies

INTRODUCTION

Both the practitioner and student of residential mortgage lending should be aware of and fully understand the essential elements and documents in a mortgage loan submission. This chapter discusses those documents required for each of the three types of residential mortgage loan:

1. Conventional residential loan with private mortgage insurance
2. Federal Housing Administration insured loan (FHA)
3. Veterans Administration guaranteed loan (VA)

Preceding chapters explained that the type of mortgage loan made depends on the qualifications of the borrower as well as the classification of the mortgage lender. For example, a mortgage company typically originates either VA or FHA mortgage loans, while a savings and loan almost exclusively originates conventional loans, and a commercial bank typically originates all three types.

All of these cases are actual requests for mortgage loans which were made to the mortgagees whose names appear on the documents. These mortgage lenders provided invaluable assistance in preparing the cases for this chapter. The identities of the borrowers have been disguised and a few facts changed for clarity.

The reader is cautioned that the forms used are those currently required but which could change at any time. Some states may have particular requirements which are not included in these cases.

CASE STUDY: CONVENTIONAL RESIDENTIAL LOAN WITH PRIVATE MORTGAGE INSURANCE

This first case study is a conventional loan made by the A.B.C. Lending Institution to Jeffrey Brenner and Susan Brenner. Since this is a 90 percent loan to value mortgage, application is made to General Electric Mortgage Insurance Corporation for private mortgage insurance.

This case is a typical conventional mortgage loan and the underwriting, verification and processing produced no surprises; therefore, this loan could easily be sold into the secondary mortgage market, in this case to FHLMC.

- Purchase agreement
- Residential loan application
- Request for verification of employment (3)
- Request for verification of deposit (2)
- Credit report
- FHLMC Form 70 Residential Appraisal Report
- Private mortgage insurance application

Jeffrey and Susan Brenner

Good	Bad
Both professionals	Housing ratio 29%
Borrower good tenure	Overall ratio 38%
Fixed rate—30 years	Co-borrower only 1 year on job
Condo pending sale could pay off debts	May need to pay child care
Could rent condo if it does not sell	Down payment will wipe out savings
Co-borrower probably could work more hours	Condo pending sale—not sold; overall ratio will be 53% if not sold
Present mortgage payment good	Some slow payments on credit report
Good security, good subdivision and good comp	

Copyright April 1978: Cincinnati Board of REALTORS, Inc.

CONTRACT TO PURCHASE
for use only by Members of the
CINCINNATI BOARD OF REALTORS, INC.
Approved by Board Legal Counsel
(This is a legally binding contract. If not understood seek
legal advice. For real estate advice consult your REALTOR.)

REALTOR®

1 McNeal, Inc. _____, Ohio. __April 23__ , 19 82
   NAME OF SELLING REALTOR/(BROKER)

2 PROPERTY DESCRIPTION: The undersigned Purchaser offers to purchase __7882 Village Drive, Cincinnati__ _____
   _____ Ohio ("REAL ESTATE") from the undersigned Owner through __McNeal Inc.__ _____ ("REALTOR").
   (Listing REALTOR/(Broker)

3 PRICE AND TERMS: Purchaser hereby agrees to pay $ __70,000.00__ ("Purchase Price") for the REAL ESTATE, payable as follows:
   EARNEST MONEY: $ __2,000.00__ as earnest money ("Earnest Money") to apply toward the Purchase Price to be held by the listing REALTOR in a
   trust account pending closing. If the offer is not accepted, if Owner defaults in the performance of this contract, or if Purchaser terminates this contract as hereafter provided, the Earnest Money shall be promptly returned to Purchaser. If Purchaser defaults in the performance of this contract, then the Earnest Money
   shall be paid one-half to Owner and one-half, but not in excess of the commission, to REALTOR, not as liquidated damages, but to apply to damages which Owner
   and REALTOR may suffer on account of the default of Purchase.
   BALANCE: The balance of the Purchase Price shall be paid by cash, certified, building and loan or cashier's check on date of closing.
   FINANCING CONTINGENCY: __This offer is contigent upon buyer obtaining a first mortgage__
   __loan for at least $62,000 at 16.25% fixed rated for a term of 30 years.__

4 OBTAINING FINANCING: Purchaser agrees to apply for and to make a diligent effort to obtain said financing. The commitment for said financing shall be
   obtained on or before __May 30__ , 19 __82__ , or this contract shall become null and void unless the parties agree to an extension of such time period.

5 OTHER CONTINGENCIES: __none__

6 INCLUDED IN THE SALE: The REAL ESTATE shall include the land, together with all improvements thereon, all appurtenant rights, privileges, easements,
   fixtures and all of the following items if they are now located on the REAL ESTATE and used in connection therewith: electrical; plumbing; heating and air conditioning equipment, including window units; bathroom fixtures; shades, venetian blinds; awnings; curtain/drapery/traverse rods; window/door screens, storm win-
   dows/doors; shrubbery/landscaping; affixed mirrors/floor covering; wall-to-wall/stair carpeting; television aerials/rotor operating boxes; water softeners; garage
   door openers/operating devices; built-in ranges/ovens/refrigerators/dishwashers/garbage disposers/trash compactors/humidifiers; and all affixed/built-in furniture/
   fixtures; and utility/storage buildings or sheds; except: __no exceptions__ .
   Owner certifies that he owns all of the above items included in the sale and that they will be free and clear of any debt, lien or encumbrances at Closing except
   __no exceptions__ ; and shall be delivered to Purchaser on Possession.

7 PERSONAL PROPERTY: The following personal property shall be included in the sale: __none__

8 OWNER'S CERTIFICATION: Owner certifies to Purchaser that, to the best of Owner's knowledge (a) there is no termite damage to the Real Estate; (b) the
   fireplaces, chimneys, electrical, plumbing, heating, air conditioning equipment and systems, and other items included herein will be operational on Possession,
   except __no exceptions__ ; (c) there are no pending orders or ordinances or resolutions that have been enacted or adopted authorizing work
   or improvements for which the REAL ESTATE may be assessed, except __no exceptions__ ; (d) the REAL ESTATE is zoned __residential__
   and is ( ) is not (x) located in an Environmental Quality District; and (e) no City, County or State orders have been served upon him requiring work to be done or
   improvements to have not been performed, except: __no exceptions__

9 CONVEYANCE AND CLOSING: Owner shall be responsible for transfer taxes, deeds preparation; and shall convey marketable title to the REAL ESTATE by
   deed of general warranty in fee simple absolute, with release of dower, on or before __June 15__ , 19 __82__ , or at such sooner time as mutually agree-
   able to the parties hereto ("Closing"), free, clear and unencumbered as of Closing, except restrictions and easements of record which do not adversely affect the
   use of the REAL ESTATE, except __no exceptions__ and except the following assessments (certified or otherwise): __none__
   . Owner shall have the right to remove any and all encumbrances or liens at the Closing out of the Purchase Price.

10 PRORATIONS: There shall be prorated between Owner and Purchaser as of Closing all (a) real estate taxes and installments of assessments as shown on the
   latest available tax duplicate; (b) interest on encumbrances assumed by Purchaser and (c) rents and operating expenses; with Purchaser assuming liability for such
   items following Closing. Security and/or damage deposits held by Owner shall be transferred to Purchaser at Closing without proration.

11 CONDITION OF IMPROVEMENTS: Owner agrees that on Possession, the REAL ESTATE shall be in the same condition as it is on the date of this offer, except for ordinary wear and tear and casualty damage from perils insurable under a standard fire policy with extended coverage. If the REAL ESTATE be damaged
   or destroyed by fire or other casualty and if, prior to Closing, the REAL ESTATE shall not be repaired or restored by, and at the cost of Owner, to a condition as
   good as it was prior to the damage or destruction, then Purchaser, at his option, may terminate this contract by written notice to Owner, and the Earnest Money
   deposit shall be returned to Purchaser without delay.

12 POSSESSION: Possession shall be given subject to tenants' rights on or before __15 days after closing__ Possession ("Possession") shall be deemed
   given as of said date or such earlier date as of which Purchaser receives actual notice from Owner of Owner's vacating the REAL ESTATE. Until such date, Owner
   shall have the right of possession free of rent, but shall pay for all utilities used.

13 AUTHORIZATION TO MLS: Owner and Purchaser authorize REALTOR to disclose this sales information to the Multiple Listing Service of Greater Cincinnati, Inc., and to any other multiple listing service to which REALTOR is a member and further authorize M.L.S. to report this sales information to other M.L.S.
   participants, affiliates and to those governmental agencies authorized to receive M.L.S. information.

14 SOLE CONTRACT: The parties agree that this contract constitutes their entire agreement and that no oral or implied agreement exists. Any amendments to this
   contract shall be made in writing, signed by all parties and copies shall be attached to all copies of the original contract. This contract shall be binding upon the
   parties, their heirs, administrators, executors, successors and assigns.

15 PURCHASER'S EXAMINATION: PURCHASER IS RELYING SOLELY UPON HIS OWN EXAMINATION OF THE REAL ESTATE, THE OWNER'S CER-
   TIFICATIONS HEREIN, AND INSPECTIONS HEREIN REQUIRED, IF ANY, FOR ITS PHYSICAL CONDITION AND CHARACTER, AND NOT UPON ANY
   REPRESENTATIONS BY THE REAL ESTATE AGENTS INVOLVED, EXCEPT FOR THOSE MADE BY SAID AGENTS DIRECTLY TO THE PURCHASER
   IN WRITING.

16 EXPIRATION AND APPROVAL: This offer is void if not accepted in writing on or before __12:00__ o'clock (A.M.) (P.M.) (Noon) (Midnight) CINCINNATI
   TIME __April 28__ , 19 82 . The Purchaser has read, fully understands and approves the foregoing offer and acknowledges receipt of a signed copy.

WITNESS: _Bria Coyle_   PURCHASER _Jeffl Brenner_   PURCHASER _Susan A. Brenner_

ADDRESS OF PURCHASER __973 Captain Court, Cincinnati, OH 45239__

RECEIPT BY REALTOR/Broker: __Cincinnati__ , Ohio. __April 23__ , 19 __82__ I hereby acknowledge receipt of $ __2,000.00__
in accordance with the terms herein provided.

__McNeal Inc.__ _____ M.L.S. # __1150__ By: _____ M.L.S. # __110110__
(REALTOR/Broker)   (Salesperson)

ACTION BY OWNER: The undersigned Owner has read and fully understands the foregoing offer and hereby: (X) accepts said offer and agrees to convey
the REAL ESTATE according to the above terms and conditions, ( ) rejects said offer, or ( ) counteroffers according to the above modifications
initialed by Owner, which counteroffer shall become null and void if not accepted in writing on or before _____ o'clock (A.M.) (P.M.) (Noon) (Midnight)
CINCINNATI TIME _____ , 19 — . In the event of acceptance, Owner further agrees to pay the listing REALTOR/(Broker) a commission of
__8__ % for services rendered in this transaction.

WITNESS: _Bria Coyle_   OWNER _Tom Crockett_   OWNER _____

General Electric Mortgage Insurance Corporation

RESIDENTIAL LOAN APPLICATION

MORTGAGE APPLIED FOR	☒ Conventional ☐ FHA ☐ VA ☐	Amount $62,000	Interest Rate 16¼%	No. of Months 360	Monthly Payment Principal & Interest $846.26	Escrow/Impounds (to be collected monthly) ☒ Taxes ☒ Hazard Ins. ☒ Mtg. Ins. ☐

Prepayment Option
Standard FNMA/FHLMC Option

SUBJECT PROPERTY

Property Street Address 7882 Village Drive	City Cincinnati	County Hamilton	State Ohio	Zip 45242	No. Units 1

Legal Description (Attach description if necessary) Lot #145 Township of Sycamore	Year Built 1977

Purpose of Loan: ☒ Purchase ☐ Construction-Permanent ☐ Construction ☐ Refinance ☐ Other (Explain)

Complete this line if Construction-Permanent or Construction Loan ☛	Lot Value Data	Original Cost	Present Value (a)	Cost of Imps. (b)	Total (a + b)	ENTER TOTAL AS PURCHASE PRICE IN DETAILS OF PURCHASE.
	Year Acquired $	$	$	$	$	

Complete this line if a Refinance Loan	Purpose of Refinance	Describe Improvements [ ] made [ ] to be made
Year Acquired / Original Cost / Amt. Existing Liens $ / $		Cost: $

Title Will Be Held In What Name(s) Jeffrey B. and Susan A. Brenner	Manner In Which Title Will Be Held Tenancy by the Entirety

Source of Down Payment and Settlement Charges
Savings, Equity in Present Home

This application is designed to be completed by the borrower(s) with the lender's assistance. The Co-Borrower Section and all other Co-Borrower questions must be completed and the appropriate box(es) checked if ☒ another person will be jointly obligated with the Borrower on the loan, or ☐ the Borrower is relying on income from alimony, child support or separate maintenance or on the income or assets of another person as a basis for repayment of the loan, or ☐ the Borrower is married and resides, or resided, in a community property state.

BORROWER	CO-BORROWER

Name Jeffrey B. Brenner	Age 42	School Yrs 16	Name Susan A. Brenner	Age 41	School Yrs 15

Present Address No. Years 8 ☒ Own ☐ Rent	Present Address No. Years 8 ☒ Own ☐ Rent
Street 973 Captain Court	Street 973 Captain Court
City/State/Zip Cincinnati, OH 45239	City/State/Zip Cincinnati, OH 45239
Former address if less than 2 years at present address	Former address if less than 2 years at present address
Street	Street
City/State/Zip	City/State/Zip
Years at former address ☐ Own ☐ Rent	Years at former address ☐ Own ☐ Rent

Marital Status ☒ Married ☐ Separated ☐ Unmarried (incl. single, divorced, widowed)	DEPENDENTS OTHER THAN LISTED BY CO BORROWER NO. 2 AGES 7 - 5	Marital Status ☒ Married ☐ Separated ☐ Unmarried (incl. single, divorced, widowed)	DEPENDENTS OTHER THAN LISTED BY BORROWER NO. 2 AGES 7 - 5

Name and Address of Employer Robots Unlimited 729 Vine Street Cincinnati, OH 45241	Years employed in this line of work or profession? 10 years Years on this job 10 ☐ Self Employed*	Name and Address of Employer Bellin Hospital 10233 Montgomery Road Cincinnati, OH 45242	Years employed in this line of work or profession? 6 years Years on this job 1 ☐ Self Employed*

Position/Title Industrial Robot Spec.	Type of Business Machinery	Position/Title Registered Nurse	Type of Business Hospital

Social Security Number*** 123-45-6789	Home Phone 439-4704	Business Phone 984-7623	Social Security Number*** 987-65-4321	Home Phone 439-4704	Business Phone 891-0935

GROSS MONTHLY INCOME				MONTHLY HOUSING EXPENSE**			DETAILS OF PURCHASE	
Item	Borrower	Co-Borrower	Total		PRESENT	PROPOSED	Do Not Complete If Refinance	
Base Empl. Income	$ 2417	$ 850	$ 3267	Rent $			a. Purchase Price	$ 70,000
Overtime				First Mortgage (P&I)	356.75	$846.26	b. Total Closing Costs (Est.)	2,100
Bonuses				Other Financing (P&I)			c. Prepaid Escrows (Est.)	165
Commissions				Hazard Insurance	12.00	16.00	d. Total (a + b + c)	$ 72,265
Dividends/Interest				Real Estate Taxes	50.00	75.00	e. Amount This Mortgage	(62,000)
Net Rental Income				Mortgage Insurance	7.80	12.40	f. Other Financing	(0)
Other† (Before completing, see notice under Describe Other Income below.)				Homeowner Assn. Dues	75.00	0	g. Other Equity	(0)
				Other:	0	0	h. Amount of Cash Deposit	(2,000)
				Total Monthly Pmt.	$ 501.55	$949.66	i. Closing Costs Paid by Seller	(0)
				Utilities	110.00	210.00	j. Cash Reqd. For Closing (Est.)	$ 8,265
Total	$ 2417	$ 850	$ 3267	Total	$ 611.55	$1159.66		

DESCRIBE OTHER INCOME

B—Borrower   C—Co-Borrower

NOTICE:† Alimony, child support, or separate maintenance income need not be revealed if the Borrower or Co-Borrower does not choose to have it considered as a basis for repaying this loan.

	Monthly Amount
None	$

IF EMPLOYED IN CURRENT POSITION FOR LESS THAN TWO YEARS COMPLETE THE FOLLOWING

B/C	Previous Employer/School	City/State	Type of Business	Position/Title	Dates From/To	Monthly Income
C	Cincinnati Memorial	Cincinnati, OH	Hospital	Registered Nurse	1972-1975	$ 1,000

THESE QUESTIONS APPLY TO BOTH BORROWER AND CO BORROWER

If a "yes" answer is given to a question in this column, explain on an attached sheet.	Borrower Yes or No	Co-Borrower Yes or No	If applicable, explain Other Financing or Other Equity (provide addendum if more space is needed).
Have you any outstanding judgments? In the last 7 years, have you been declared bankrupt?	No	No	
Have you had property foreclosed upon or given title or deed in lieu thereof?	No	No	
Are you a co-maker or endorser on a note?	No	No	
Are you a party in a law suit?	No	No	
Are you obligated to pay alimony, child support, or separate maintenance?	No	No	
Is any part of the down payment borrowed?	No	No	

*FHLMC/FNMA require business credit report, signed Federal Income Tax returns for last two years, and, if available, audited Profit and Loss Statements plus balance sheet for same period.
**All Present Monthly Housing Expenses of Borrower and Co-Borrower should be listed on a combined basis.
***Neither FHLMC nor FNMA requires this information.

FHLMC 65 (Rev. 1/82)   FNMA 1003 (Rev. 1/82)

This Statement and any applicable supporting schedules may be completed jointly by both married and unmarried co-borrowers if their assets and liabilities are sufficiently joined so that the Statement can be meaningfully and fairly presented on a combined basis; otherwise separate Statements and Schedules are required (FHLMC 65A/FNMA 1003A). If the co-borrower section was completed about a spouse, this statement and supporting schedules must be completed about that spouse also. ☐ Completed Jointly ☐ Not Completed Jointly

ASSETS		LIABILITIES AND PLEDGED ASSETS			

Indicate by (*) those liabilities or pledged assets which will be satisfied upon sale of real estate owned or upon refinancing of subject property

Description	Cash or Market Value	Creditors' Name, Address and Account Number	Acct. Name If Not Borrower's	Mo. Pmt. and Mos. left to pay	Unpaid Balance
Cash Deposit Toward Purchase Held By $ McNeal, Incorporated	2,000	Installment Debts (include "revolving" charge accts)		$ Pmt./Mos. /	$
Checking and Savings Accounts First National 4578-3	1,500	Shillitos 727-385-392-1 2533-5210-0166-7334		25/8	185
ABC Lending Institution 179854	7,000	Master Card 5504-300-216-629		25/20	500
Stocks and Bonds (No./Description)		Visa 403-41488		25/11	275
		Sears		20/12	240
				/	
Life Insurance Net Cash Value Face Amount ($ 50,000)	1,000	Other Debts Including Stock Pledges		/	
SUBTOTAL LIQUID ASSETS $	11,500				
Real Estate Owned	49,500	Real Estate Loans		/	
Vested Interest in Retirement Fund	2,500	ABC Lending Institution			37,000
Net Worth of Business Owned					
Automobiles 1982 Buick Regal	10,000	Automobile Loans First National Bank			
1979 Chevrolet	3,500	796403		230 36	8280
Furniture and Personal Property	10,000	Alimony, Child Support and Separate Maintenance Payments Owed To			
Other Assets (Itemize)				/	
		TOTAL MONTHLY PAYMENTS		$ 325	
TOTAL ASSETS A $87,000		NET WORTH (A minus B) $ 40,520		TOTAL LIABILITIES B	$46,480

SCHEDULE OF REAL ESTATE OWNED (If Additional Properties Owned Attach Separate Schedule)

Address of Property (Indicate S if Sold, PS if Pending Sale or R if Rental being held for income)		Type of Property	Present Market Value	Amount of Mortgages & Liens	Gross Rental Income	Mortgage Payments	Taxes, Ins. Maintenance and Misc.	Net Rental Income
973 Captain Court	PS	Condo	$ 49,500	$ 37,000	$	$356.75	$ 144.80	$ 0
TOTALS →			$	$	$	$	$	$

LIST PREVIOUS CREDIT REFERENCES

B-Borrower C-Co-Borrower	Creditor's Name and Address	Account Number	Purpose	Highest Balance	Date Paid
B-C	Wickes Furniture	729-4128	Furniture	$ 350	1-81

List any additional names under which credit has previously been received _____

AGREEMENT: The undersigned applies for the loan indicated in this application to be secured by a first mortgage or deed of trust on the property described herein, and represents that the property will not be used for any illegal or restricted purpose, and that all statements made in this application are true and are made for the purpose of obtaining the loan. Verification may be obtained from any source named in this application. The original or a copy of this application will be retained by the lender, even if the loan is not granted. The undersigned ☒ intend or ☐ do not intend to occupy the property as their primary residence.

I/we fully understand that it is a federal crime punishable by fine or imprisonment, or both, to knowingly make any false statements concerning any of the above facts as applicable under the provisions of Title 18, United States Code, Section 1014.

Borrower's Signature _____ Date 5/1/82 Co-Borrower's Signature _____ Date 5/1/82

INFORMATION FOR GOVERNMENT MONITORING PURPOSES

Instructions: Lenders must insert in this space, or on an attached addendum, a provision for furnishing the monitoring information required or requested under present Federal and/or present state law or regulation. For most lenders, the inserts provided in FHLMC Form 65-B/FNMA Form 1003-B can be used.

FOR LENDER'S USE ONLY

(FNMA REQUIREMENT ONLY) This application was taken by ☒ face to face interview ☐ by mail ☐ by telephone

Joanne Plain (Interviewer)   ABC Lending Institution Name of Employer of Interviewer

FHLMC 65 (Rev. 1/82)   REVERSE   FNMA 1003 (Rev. 1/82)

General Electric Mortgage Insurance CORPORATION

REQUEST FOR
VERIFICATION OF EMPLOYMENT

HOME OFFICE ADDRESS:
11353 Reed Hartman Highway
P.O. Box 41910
Cincinnati, Ohio 45241

(513) 984-8064
Toll Free (800) 543-4549
In Ohio/Toll Free (800) 582-7128

INSTRUCTIONS: LENDER- Complete items 1 thru 7. Have applicant complete item 8. Forward directly to employer named in item 1.

EMPLOYER-Please complete either Part II or Part III as applicable. Sign and return directly to lender named in item 2.

PART I · REQUEST

1. TO *(Name and address of employer)*	2. FROM *(Name and address of lender)*
Robots Unlimited 729 Vine Street Cincinnati, Ohio 45239	ABC Lending Institution 987 East Ohio Avenue Cincinnati, Ohio 45241

3. SIGNATURE OF LENDER	4. TITLE	5. DATE	6. LENDER'S NUMBER *(optional)*
Joanne Plain	Loan Officer	5/2/82	

I have applied for a mortgage loan and stated that I am now or was formerly employed by you. My signature below authorizes verification of this information.

7. NAME AND ADDRESS OF APPLICANT *(Include employee or badge number)* Jeffrey B. Brenner 973 Captain Court, Cincinnati, Ohio	8. SIGNATURE OF APPLICANT *Jeffrey B Brenner*

PART II · VERIFICATION OF PRESENT EMPLOYMENT

EMPLOYMENT DATA

9. APPLICANT'S DATE OF EMPLOYMENT		
6/1/72		

10. PRESENT POSITION
Industrial Robot Specialist

11. PROBABILITY OF CONTINUED EMPLOYMENT
Excellent

13. IF OVERTIME OR BONUS IS APPLICABLE, IS ITS CONTINUANCE LIKELY?

OVERTIME	☐ YES	☒ NO
BONUS	☐ YES	☒ NO

PAY DATA

12A. CURRENT BASE PAY (Enter Amount and Check Period)
☒ ANNUAL ☐ HOURLY ☐ MONTHLY ☐ OTHER *(Specify)* ☐ WEEKLY $ 29,000

12B. EARNINGS

TYPE	YEAR TO DATE	PAST YEAR
BASE PAY	$9,667	$26,500
OVERTIME	$ 0	$ 0
COMMISSIONS	$ 0	$ 0
BONUS	$ 0	$ 0

12C. FOR MILITARY PERSONNEL ONLY
PAY GRADE

TYPE	MONTHLY AMOUNT
BASE PAY	$
RATIONS	$
FLIGHT OR HAZARD	$
CLOTHING	$
QUARTERS	$
PRO PAY	$
OVER SEAS OR COMBAT	$

14. REMARKS *(if paid hourly, please indicate average hours worked each week during current and past year)*

PART III · VERIFICATION OF PREVIOUS EMPLOYMENT

15. DATES OF EMPLOYMENT	16. SALARY/WAGE AT TERMINATION PER (Year) (Month) (Week)
	BASE _____ OVERTIME _____ COMMISSIONS _____ BONUS _____

17. REASON FOR LEAVING	18. POSITION HELD

19. SIGNATURE OF EMPLOYER	20. TITLE	21. DATE
Imogene C Dunbar	Personnel Administrator	5/3/82

The confidentiality of the information you have furnished will be preserved except where disclosure of this information is required by applicable law. The form is to be transmitted directly to the lender and is not to be transmitted through the applicant or any other party.

PREVIOUS EDITION WILL BE USED UNTIL STOCK IS EXHAUSTED

FNMA Form 1005
Rev. June 78

General Electric Mortgage Insurance CORPORATION

REQUEST FOR
VERIFICATION OF EMPLOYMENT

HOME OFFICE ADDRESS:
11353 Reed Hartman Highway
P.O. Box 41910
Cincinnati, Ohio 45241

(513) 984-8064
Toll Free (800) 543-4549
In Ohio/Toll Free (800) 582-7128

INSTRUCTIONS: LENDER- Complete items 1 thru 7. Have applicant complete item 8. Forward directly to employer named in item 1.

EMPLOYER-Please complete either Part II or Part III as applicable. Sign and return directly to lender named in item 2.

PART I - REQUEST

1. TO *(Name and address of employer)* Bellin Hospital 10233 Montgomery Road Cincinnati, Ohio 45242	2. FROM*(Name and address of lender)* ABC Lending Institution 987 East Ohio Avenue Cincinnati, Ohio 45241

3. SIGNATURE OF LENDER *Joanne Plain*	4. TITLE Loan Officer	5. DATE 5/2/82	6. LENDER'S NUMBER *(optional)*

I have applied for a mortgage loan and stated that I am now or was formerly employed by you. My signature below authorizes verification of this information.

7. NAME AND ADDRESS OF APPLICANT *(Include employee or badge number)* Susan A. Brenner 973 Captain Court, Cincinnati, Ohio	8. SIGNATURE OF APPLICANT *Susan A. Brenner*

PART II - VERIFICATION OF PRESENT EMPLOYMENT

EMPLOYMENT DATA	**PAY DATA**

9. APPLICANT'S DATE OF EMPLOYMENT 5/15/81	12A. CURRENT BASE PAY (Enter Amount and Check Period) ☐ ANNUAL ☒ HOURLY ☐ MONTHLY ☐ OTHER ☐ WEEKLY *(Specify)* $ 7.85	12C. FOR MILITARY PERSONNEL ONLY

12C. continued	PAY GRADE	

10. PRESENT POSITION Registered Nurse	12B. EARNINGS			TYPE	MONTHLY AMOUNT
11. PROBABILITY OF CONTINUED EMPLOYMENT excellent	TYPE	YEAR TO DATE	PAST YEAR	BASE PAY	$
13. IF OVERTIME OR BONUS IS APPLICABLE, IS ITS CONTINUANCE LIKELY?	BASE PAY	$ 3140	$ 5887	RATIONS	$
	OVERTIME	$ 0	$ 0	FLIGHT OR HAZARD	$
	COMMISSIONS	$ 0	$ 0	CLOTHING	$
				QUARTERS	$
OVERTIME ☐ YES ☒ NO	BONUS	$ 0	$ 0	PRO PAY	$
BONUS ☐ YES ☒ NO				OVER SEAS OR COMBAT	$

14. REMARKS *(if paid hourly, please indicate average hours worked each week during current and past year)*

Susan Brenner works an average of 25 hours per week

PART III - VERIFICATION OF PREVIOUS EMPLOYMENT

15. DATES OF EMPLOYMENT	16. SALARY/WAGE AT TERMINATION PER (Year) (Month) (Week) BASE _____ OVERTIME _____ COMMISSIONS _____ BONUS _____

17. REASON FOR LEAVING	18. POSITION HELD

19. SIGNATURE OF EMPLOYER *Karen Kuntz*	20. TITLE Nursing Administrator	21. DATE 5/4/82

The confidentiality of the information you have furnished will be preserved except where disclosure of this information is required by applicable law. The form is to be transmitted directly to the lender and is not to be transmitted through the applicant or any other party.

PREVIOUS EDITION WILL BE USED UNTIL STOCK IS EXHAUSTED

FNMA Form 1005
Rev. June 78

General Electric
Mortgage Insurance
CORPORATION

REQUEST FOR
VERIFICATION OF EMPLOYMENT

HOME OFFICE ADDRESS:
11353 Reed Hartman Highway
P.O. Box 41910
Cincinnati, Ohio 45241

(513) 984-8064
Toll Free (800) 543-4549
In Ohio/Toll Free (800) 582-7128

INSTRUCTIONS: LENDER- Complete items 1 thru 7. Have applicant complete item 8. Forward directly to employer named in item 1.
EMPLOYER-Please complete either Part II or Part III as applicable. Sign and return directly to lender named in item 2.

PART I - REQUEST

1. TO *(Name and address of employer)*	2. FROM *(Name and address of lender)*
Cincinnati Memorial Hospital 747 Oak Street Cincinnati, Ohio 45241	ABC Lending Institution 987 East Ohio Avenue Cincinnati, Ohio 45241

3. SIGNATURE OF LENDER	4. TITLE	5. DATE	6. LENDER'S NUMBER *(optional)*
Joanne Flair	Loan Officer	5/2/82	

I have applied for a mortgage loan and stated that I am now or was formerly employed by you. My signature below authorizes verification of this information.

7. NAME AND ADDRESS OF APPLICANT *(Include employee or badge number)*	8. SIGNATURE OF APPLICANT
Susan A. Brenner 973 Captain Court, Cincinnati, OH	*Susan A. Brenner*

PART II - VERIFICATION OF PRESENT EMPLOYMENT

EMPLOYMENT DATA	PAY DATA		

9. APPLICANT'S DATE OF EMPLOYMENT	12A. CURRENT BASE PAY (Enter Amount and Check Period) ☐ ANNUAL ☐ HOURLY ☐ MONTHLY ☐ OTHER ☐ WEEKLY *(Specify)* $_____	12C. FOR MILITARY PERSONNEL ONLY PAY GRADE

10. PRESENT POSITION		TYPE	MONTHLY AMOUNT
	12B. EARNINGS	BASE PAY	$

11. PROBABILITY OF CONTINUED EMPLOYMENT	TYPE	YEAR TO DATE	PAST YEAR	RATIONS	$
13. IF OVERTIME OR BONUS IS APPLICABLE, IS ITS CONTINUANCE LIKELY?	BASE PAY	$	$	FLIGHT OR HAZARD	$
	OVERTIME	$	$	CLOTHING	$
	COMMISSIONS	$	$	QUARTERS	$
OVERTIME ☐ YES ☐ NO				PRO PAY	$
BONUS ☐ YES ☐ NO	BONUS	$	$	OVER SEAS OR COMBAT	$

14. REMARKS *(if paid hourly, please indicate average hours worked each week during current and past year)*

PART III - VERIFICATION OF PREVIOUS EMPLOYMENT

15. DATES OF EMPLOYMENT	16. SALARY/WAGE AT TERMINATION PER (Year) (Month)(Week)
1972 – 1975	BASE $12,000 OVERTIME 0 COMMISSIONS 0 BONUS 0

17. REASON FOR LEAVING	18. POSITION HELD
Raise a family	Registered Nurse

19. SIGNATURE OF EMPLOYER	20. TITLE	21. DATE
Donna Durkan	Nursing Supervisor	5/4/82

The confidentiality of the information you have furnished will be preserved except where disclosure of this information is required by applicable law. The form is to be transmitted directly to the lender and is not to be transmitted through the applicant or any other party.

PREVIOUS EDITION WILL BE USED UNTIL STOCK IS EXHAUSTED

FNMA Form 1005
Rev. June 78

REQUEST FOR
VERIFICATION OF DEPOSIT

General Electric Mortgage Insurance Corporation

HOME OFFICE ADDRESS:
11353 Reed Hartman Highway
P.O. Box 41910
Cincinnati, Ohio 45241

(513) 984-8064
Toll Free (800) 543-4549
In Ohio/Toll Free (800) 582-7128

INSTRUCTIONS: LENDER - Complete Items 1 thru 8. Have applicant(s) complete Item 9. Forward directly to depository named in Item 1.
DEPOSITORY - Please complete Items 10 thru 15 and return DIRECTLY to lender named in Item 2.

PART I - REQUEST

1. TO *(Name and address of depository)*	2. FROM *(Name and address of lender)*
ABC Lending Institution 987 East Ohio Street Cincinnati, Ohio 45241	ABC Lending Institution 987 East Ohio Street Cincinnati, Ohio 45241

3. SIGNATURE OF LENDER	4. TITLE	5. DATE	6. LENDER'S NUMBER *(Optional)*
Joanne Plain	Loan officer	5/2/82	

7. INFORMATION TO BE VERIFIED

TYPE OF ACCOUNT	ACCOUNT IN NAME OF	ACCOUNT NUMBER	BALANCE
Savings	Jeffrey and Susan Brenner	179854	$ 7,000
			$
			$
			$

TO DEPOSITORY: *I have applied for a mortgage loan and stated in my financial statement that the balance on deposit with you is as shown above. You are authorized to verify this information and to supply the lender identified above with the information requested in Items 10 thru 12. Your response is solely a matter of courtesy for which no responsibility is attached to your institution or any of your officers.*

8. NAME AND ADDRESS OF APPLICANT(s)	9. SIGNATURE OF APPLICANT(s)
Jeffrey and Susan Brenner 973 Captain Court Cincinnati, Ohio 45239	*Jeffrey B. Brenner* *Susan A. Brenner*

TO BE COMPLETED BY DEPOSITORY

PART II - VERIFICATION OF DEPOSITORY

10. DEPOSIT ACCOUNTS OF APPLICANT(s)

TYPE OF ACCOUNT	ACCOUNT NUMBER	CURRENT BALANCE	AVERAGE BALANCE FOR PREVIOUS TWO MONTHS	DATE OPENED
Savings	179854	$ 7,000	$ 9,000	7/23/76
		$	$	
		$	$	
		$	$	

11. LOANS OUTSTANDING TO APPLICANT(s)

LOAN NUMBER	DATE OF LOAN	ORIGINAL AMOUNT	CURRENT BALANCE	INSTALLMENTS *(Monthly/Quarterly)*	SECURED BY	NUMBER OF LATE PAYMENTS
7954640	1974	$ 39,000	$ 37,050	$356.75 per Month	home	0
		$	$	$ per		
		$	$	$ per		

12. ADDITIONAL INFORMATION WHICH MAY BE OF ASSISTANCE IN DETERMINATION OF CREDIT WORTHINESS:
(Please include information on loans paid-in-full as in Item 11 above)

13. SIGNATURE OF DEPOSITORY	14. TITLE	15. DATE
Karen Carucci	Vice President	5/3/82

The confidentiality of the information you have furnished will be preserved except where disclosure of this information is required by applicable law. The form is to be transmitted directly to the lender and is not to be transmitted through the applicant or any other party.

PREVIOUS EDITION WILL BE USED UNTIL STOCK IS EXHAUSTED

FNMA Form 1006
Rev. June 78

General Electric Mortgage Insurance CORPORATION

HOME OFFICE ADDRESS:
11353 Reed Hartman Highway
P.O. Box 41910
Cincinnati, Ohio 45241

(513) 984-8064
Toll Free (800) 543-4549
In Ohio/Toll Free (800) 582-7128

REQUEST FOR
VERIFICATION OF DEPOSIT

INSTRUCTIONS: LENDER - *Complete Items 1 thru 8. Have applicant(s) complete item 9. Forward directly to depository named in Item 1.*

DEPOSITORY - *Please complete Items 10 thru 15 and return DIRECTLY to lender named in Item 2.*

PART I - REQUEST

1. TO (Name and address of depository)	2. FROM (Name and address of lender)
First National Bank 111 Adam Street Cincinnati, Ohio 45239	ABC Lending Institution 987 East Ohio Avenue Cincinnati, Ohio 45241

3. SIGNATURE OF LENDER	4. TITLE	5. DATE	6. LENDER'S NUMBER (Optional)
Joanne Plain	Loan Officer	5/2/82	

7. INFORMATION TO BE VERIFIED

TYPE OF ACCOUNT	ACCOUNT IN NAME OF	ACCOUNT NUMBER	BALANCE
Checking	Jeffrey and Susan Brenner	4578-3	$ 1,500
			$
			$
			$

TO DEPOSITORY: *I have applied for a mortgage loan and stated in my financial statement that the balance on deposit with you is as shown above. You are authorized to verify this information and to supply the lender identified above with the information requested in Items 10 thru 12. Your response is solely a matter of courtesy for which no responsibility is attached to your institution or any of your officers.*

8. NAME AND ADDRESS OF APPLICANT(s)	9. SIGNATURE OF APPLICANT(s)
Jeffrey and Susan Brenner 973 Captain Court Cincinnati, Ohio 45239	*Jeffrey B Brenner* *Susan A. Brenner*

TO BE COMPLETED BY DEPOSITORY

PART II - VERIFICATION OF DEPOSITORY

10. DEPOSIT ACCOUNTS OF APPLICANT(s)

TYPE OF ACCOUNT	ACCOUNT NUMBER	CURRENT BALANCE	AVERAGE BALANCE FOR PREVIOUS TWO MONTHS	DATE OPENED
Checking	4578-3	$ 1,500	$1,100	5/1/72
		$	$	
		$	$	
		$	$	

11. LOANS OUTSTANDING TO APPLICANT(s)

LOAN NUMBER	DATE OF LOAN	ORIGINAL AMOUNT	CURRENT BALANCE	INSTALLMENTS (Monthly/Quarterly)	SECURED BY	NUMBER OF LATE PAYMENTS
796403	4/15/82	$ 8,280	$ 8,280	$ 230 per month	auto	new acct.
		$	$	$ per		
		$	$	$ per		

12. ADDITIONAL INFORMATION WHICH MAY BE OF ASSISTANCE IN DETERMINATION OF CREDIT WORTHINESS:
(Please include information on loans paid-in-full as in Item 11 above)

13. SIGNATURE OF DEPOSITORY	14. TITLE	15. DATE
Ed Hensley	Vice President	5/15/82

The confidentiality of the information you have furnished will be preserved except where disclosure of this information is required by applicable law. The form is to be transmitted directly to the lender and is not to be transmitted through the applicant or any other party.

PREVIOUS EDITION WILL BE USED UNTIL STOCK IS EXHAUSTED

FNMA Form 1006
Rev. June 78

NAME AND ADDRESS OF CREDIT BUREAU MAKING REPORT:

TYPE OF REPORT:

SAMPLE

COMPUTER FORM 2000
MEMBER ASSOCIATED CREDIT BUREAUS, INC.

CONFIDENTIAL crediscope® REPORT

ABC Lending Institution
987 East Ohio Avenue
Cincinnati, Ohio 45241

BUREAU NUMBER	DATE RECEIVED
90-51183	5/3/82
MEMBER NUMBER	**DATE MAILED**
3-763	5/4/82
COMPUTER ID NUMBER	DATE TRADE CLEARED
28027756	5/3/82

IN FILE SINCE
1974

REPORT ON	SOCIAL SECURITY NUMBER	SPOUSE'S NAME
Brenner, Jeffrey B.	123-45-6789	Susan A.

ADDRESS:		SINCE	SPOUSE'S SOCIAL SEC. NO.
973 Captain Court, Cincinnati, Ohio 45239		1974	987-65-4321

COMPLETE TO HERE FOR TRADE REPORT AND SKIP TO CREDIT HISTORY

PRESENT EMPLOYER:	POSITION HELD:	SINCE	DATE EMP. VER.	EST. MONTHLY INCOME
Robots Unlimited	Robot Specialist	1972	5/3/82	$ 2417

COMPLETE TO HERE FOR EMPLOYMENT AND TRADE REPORT AND SKIP TO CREDIT HISTORY

DATE OF BIRTH	NUMBER OF DEPENDENTS INCLUDING SELF:		OTHER: (EXPLAIN)
2/8/40	4	[X] OWNS OR IS BUYING HOME [ ] RENTS HOME	

FORMER ADDRESS:	FROM:	TO:

FORMER EMPLOYER:	POSITION HELD:	FROM:	TO:	EST. MONTHLY INCOME: $

SPOUSE'S EMPLOYER:	POSITION HELD:	SINCE:	DATE EMP. VER.	EST. MONTHLY INCOME:
Bellin Hospital	Registered Nurse	1981	5/3/82	$ 7.85

CREDIT HISTORY (COMPLETE THIS SECTION FOR ALL REPORTS)

WHOSE	KIND OF BUSINESS AND ID CODE	DATE REPORTED AND METHOD OF REPORTING	DATE OPENED	DATE OF LAST PAYMENT	HIGHEST CREDIT	BALANCE OWING	PAST DUE AMOUNT	PAST DUE PMTS	MONTH REV'D	30-59	60-89	90+	TYPE ACCT, TERMS, MANNER PMT	REMARK CODE
2	D (Department) 727-385-392-1	5/82 A	4/80	4/82	300	185	0	0	24	1	0	0	R-25	
2	N (Credit Card) 2533-5210-0166-7334	5/82 A	6/78	4/82	1000	500	0	0	48	0	0	0	R-20	
2	N (Credit Card) 5504-300-216-629	5/82 A	1/81	4/82	390	275	0	0	15	0	0	0	R-25	
2	D (Department) 403-41488	5/82 A	4/78	4/82	600	240	0	0	48	2	0	0	R-20	
2	H (Home Furnishings) 729-4128	5/82 A	7/80	1/81	350	0	0	0	15	0	0	0	I-60	

Present mortgage at ABC Lending Institution will not rate.
Check of legal items clear - no suits, liens or judgments.

SAMPLE NOT TO BE USED FOR CREDIT EXTENSION PURPOSES

General Electric Mortgage Insurance

RESIDENTIAL APPRAISAL REPORT   File No.

To be completed by Lender

Borrower **Jeffrey Brenner**   Census Tract **02134**   Map Reference **21-B**
Property Address **7882 Village Drive**
City **Cincinnati**   County **Hamilton**   State **Ohio**   Zip Code **45242**
Legal Description **Lot #145, Township of Sycamore**
Sale Price $ **70,000**   Date of Sale **5/82**   Loan Term **30** yrs   Property Rights Appraised ☒Fee ☐Leasehold ☐DeMinimis PUD
Actual Real Estate Taxes $**900** (yr) Loan charges to be paid by seller $ **0**   Other sales concessions **None**
Lender/Client **ABC Lending Institution**   Address **987 E. Ohio Ave., Cincinnati, Ohio**
Occupant **Thomas Crockett** Appraiser **Bill Smith**   Instructions to Appraiser **Key left at McNeal Realty**

NEIGHBORHOOD

						Good	Avg.	Fair	Poor
Location	☐Urban	☒Suburban	☐Rural		Employment Stability	☐	☒	☐	☐
Built Up	☒Over 75%	☐25% to 75%	☐Under 25%		Convenience to Employment	☒	☐	☐	☐
Growth Rate ☒Fully Dev.	☐Rapid	☒Steady	☐Slow		Convenience to Shopping	☒	☐	☐	☐
Property Values	☐Increasing	☒Stable	☐Declining		Convenience to Schools	☒	☐	☐	☐
Demand/Supply	☐Shortage	☒In Balance	☐Over Supply		Adequacy of Public Transportation	☐	☐	☐	☒
Marketing Time	☐Under 3 Mos.	☒4–6 Mos.	☐Over 6 Mos.		Recreational Facilities	☐	☒	☐	☐

Present Land Use **85** % 1 Family **10** % 2–4 Family ___% Apts. ___% Condo ___% Commercial
___% Industrial **5** % Vacant ___%
Change in Present Land Use ☒Not Likely ☐Likely (*) ☐Taking Place (*)
(*) From ___ To ___
Predominant Occupancy ☒Owner ☐Tenant ___% Vacant
Single Family Price Range $**60,000** to $**125,000** Predominant Value $**72,000**
Single Family Age **1** yrs to **10** yrs Predominant Age **5** yrs

	Good	Avg.	Fair	Poor
Adequacy of Utilities	☐	☒	☐	☐
Property Compatibility	☒	☐	☐	☐
Protection from Detrimental Conditions	☒	☐	☐	☐
Police and Fire Protection	☐	☒	☐	☐
General Appearance of Properties	☒	☐	☐	☐
Appeal to Market	☒	☐	☐	☐

Note: FHLMC/FNMA do not consider race or the racial composition of the neighborhood to be reliable appraisal factors.
Comments including those factors, favorable or unfavorable, affecting marketability (e.g. public parks, schools, view, noise) **No detrimental factors in neighborhood other than public transportation is not available in this subdivision.**

SITE

Dimensions **50 X 125** = **6250** Sq. Ft. or Acres ☐Corner Lot
Zoning classification **R4 Single and Multi family**   Present improvements ☒do ☐do not conform to zoning regulations
Highest and best use: ☒Present use ☐Other (specify) ___

	Public	Other (Describe)	OFF SITE IMPROVEMENTS	
Elec.	☒		Street Access: ☒Public ☐Private	Topo **Level**
Gas	☒		Surface **cement**	Size **Average**
Water	☒		Maintenance: ☒Public ☐Private	Shape **Rectangular**
San.Sewer	☒		☒Storm Sewer ☒Curb/Gutter	View **Average**
	☐Underground Elect. & Tel	☒Sidewalk ☒Street Lights	Drainage **Good**

Is the property located in a HUD Identified Special Flood Hazard Area? ☒No ☐Yes
Comments (favorable or unfavorable including any apparent adverse easements, encroachments or other adverse conditions) **None noted**

IMPROVEMENTS

☒Existing ☐Proposed ☐Under Constr.   No. Units **1**   Type (det, duplex, semi/det, etc.) **Detached**   Design (rambler, split level, etc.) **Rambler**   Exterior Walls **Brick**
Yrs. Age: Actual **5** Effective **3** to **4**   No. Stories **1**
Roof Material **Shingle**   Gutters & Downspouts ☐None **Galvanized**   Window (Type): **Wood** ☐Storm Sash ☐Screens ☒Combination   Insulation ☐None ☐Floor ☐Ceiling ☒Roof ☒Walls

☐Manufactured Housing
Foundation Walls **Concrete**

BSMT
75% Basement ☒Floor Drain   Finished Ceiling
☐Outside Entrance ☒Sump Pump   Finished Walls
☒Concrete Floor ___% Finished   Finished Floor
☐Slab on Grade ☐Crawl Space   Evidence of: ☐Dampness ☐Termites ☐Settlement

Comments **Good, dry basement which could be made into a recreational room — no finished floor ceiling or wall at this time.**

ROOM LIST

Room List	Foyer	Living	Dining	Kitchen	Den	Family Rm	Rec. Rm	Bedrooms	No. Baths	Laundry	Other
Basement										X	
1st Level	X	X	X	X				3	1½		
2nd Level											

Finished area above grade contains a total of **6** rooms **3** bedrooms **1½** baths. Gross Living Area **1525** sq. ft. Bsmt Area **1145** sq. ft.

INTERIOR FINISH & EQUIPMENT

Kitchen Equipment: ☒Refrigerator ☒Range/Oven ☒Disposal ☒Dishwasher ☒Fan/Hood ☐Compactor ☐Washer ☐Dryer
HEAT: Type **F/A** Fuel **Gas** Cond. **Good** AIR COND ☒Central ☐Other ☒Adequate ☐Inadequate

Floors	☒Hardwood ☒Carpet Over ☐
Walls	☒Drywall ☐Plaster ☐
Trim/Finish	☐Good ☒Average ☐Fair ☐Poor
Bath Floor	☒Ceramic ☐
Bath Wainscot	☒Ceramic ☐

Special Features (including energy efficient items) **Insulation**

PROPERTY RATING

	Good	Avg.	Fair	Poor
Quality of Construction (Materials & Finish)	☐	☒	☐	☐
Condition of Improvements	☐	☒	☐	☐
Room sizes and layout	☐	☒	☐	☐
Closets and Storage	☐	☒	☐	☐
Insulation–adequacy	☐	☒	☐	☐
Plumbing–adequacy and condition	☐	☒	☐	☐
Electrical–adequacy and condition	☐	☒	☐	☐
Kitchen Cabinets–adequacy and condition	☒	☐	☐	☐
Compatibility to Neighborhood	☒	☐	☐	☐
Overall Livability	☐	☒	☐	☐
Appeal and Marketability	☒	☐	☐	☐

ATTIC: ☒Yes ☐No ☐Stairway ☒Drop-stair ☐Scuttle ☐Floored
Finished (Describe) ☐Heated
CAR STORAGE: ☒Garage ☐Built-in ☒Attached ☐Detached ☐Car Port
No. Cars **2** ☒Adequate ☐Inadequate Condition

Yrs Est Remaining Economic Life **30** to **40** . Explain if less than Loan Term

FIREPLACES, PATIOS, POOL, FENCES, etc. (describe) **10' x 12' patio off living room**

COMMENTS (including functional or physical inadequacies, repairs needed, modernization, etc.) **None noted – property in good repair.**

FHLMC Form 70 Rev. 7/79   ATTACH DESCRIPTIVE PHOTOGRAPHS OF SUBJECT PROPERTY AND STREET SCENE   FNMA Form 1004 Rev. 7/79

VALUATION SECTION

Purpose of Appraisal is to estimate Market Value as defined in Certification & Statement of Limiting Conditions (FHLMC Form 439/FNMA Form 1004B). If submitted for FNMA, the appraiser must attach (1) sketch or map showing location of subject, street names, distance from nearest intersection, and any detrimental conditions and (2) exterior building sketch of improvements showing dimensions.

COST APPROACH

Measurements		No. Stories		Sq. Ft.
25 x 61	x	1	=	1525
25 x 20	x	Garage	=	500
10 x 12	x	patio	=	120
x	x		=	
x	x		=	
x	x		=	

Total Gross Living Area (List in Market Data Analysis below) __1525__

Comment on functional and economic obsolescence:

None

ESTIMATED REPRODUCTION COST – NEW – OF IMPROVEMENTS:

Dwelling 1525 Sq. Ft. @ $ 45.00	=	$68,625
Sq. Ft. @ $	=	
Extras	=	
Special Energy Efficient Items	=	
Porches, Patios, etc. 120 sq ft @ 12	=	1,440
Garage/Car Port 500 Sq. Ft. @ $15	=	7,500
Site Improvements (driveway, landscaping, etc.)	=	
Total Estimated Cost New	=	$77,565

Less | Physical | Functional | Economic
Depreciation $13,950 | $ 0 | $ 0 | = $ (13,950)
Depreciated value of improvements . . . . . . = $63,615
ESTIMATED LAND VALUE . . . . = $12,000
(If leasehold, show only leasehold value)

INDICATED VALUE BY COST APPROACH . . $75,615

MARKET DATA ANALYSIS

The undersigned has recited three recent sales of properties most similar and proximate to subject and has considered these in the market analysis. The description includes a dollar adjustment, reflecting market reaction to those items of significant variation between the subject and comparable properties. If a significant item in the comparable property is superior to, or more favorable than, the subject property, a minus (-) adjustment is made, thus reducing the indicated value of subject; if a significant item in the comparable is inferior to, or less favorable than, the subject property, a plus (+) adjustment is made, thus increasing the indicated value of the subject.

ITEM	Subject Property	COMPARABLE NO. 1	+(-)$ Adjustment	COMPARABLE NO. 2	+(-)$ Adjustment	COMPARABLE NO. 3	+(-)$ Adjustment
Address	7882 Village Drive	7945 Montgomery Rd		8103 Carlton Drive		8472 Carlton Drive	
Proximity to Subj.		2 blocks		3 blocks		6 blocks	
Sales Price	$70,000	$75,000		$66,000		$72,000	
Price/Living area	$45.90	$47.62		$ 44.00		$47.21	
Data Source	Contract						
Date of Sale and	DESCRIPTION	DESCRIPTION		DESCRIPTION		DESCRIPTION	
Time Adjustment	Same time	2/82		11/81		1/82	
Location	Average	Average		Average		Average	
Site/View	Average	Average		Average		Average	
Design and Appeal	Ranch	Ranch		Ranch		Ranch	
Quality of Const.	Average	Average		Average		Average	
Age	5 years	6 years		5 years		5 years	
Condition	Average	Average		Average		Average	
Living Area Room Count and Total	Total 6 B-rms 3 Baths 1.5	Total 7 B-rms 3 Baths 1.5	- 2381	Total 6 B-rms 3 Baths 1.5	+ 1000	Total 6 B-rms 3 Baths 1.5	
Gross Living Area	1525 Sq.Ft.	1575 Sq.Ft.		1500 Sq.Ft.		1525 Sq.Ft.	
Basement & Bsmt. Finished Rooms	Full	Full		Full		Full	
Functional Utility	Average	Average		Average		Average	
Air Conditioning	Central	Central		Central		Central	
Garage/Car Port	2 car	2 car		1 car	+ 3000	2 car	
Porches, Patio, Pools, etc.	Patio slab	Patio slab		None	+ 1440	Patio slab	
Special Energy Efficient Items	Insulation	Insulation		Insulation		Insulation	
Other (e.g. fireplaces, kitchen equip., remodeling)	Equipped kitchen	Equipped kitchen		Equipped kitchen		Fireplace	- 1200
Sales or Financing Concessions	None	None		None		None	
Net Adj. (Total)		☐ Plus; ☒ Minus $ 2381		☒ Plus; ☐ Minus $ 5440		☐ Plus; ☒ Minus $ 1200	
Indicated Value of Subject		$ 72,619		$71,440		$ 70,800	

Comments on Market Data Sales are recent and in subject area.

INDICATED VALUE BY MARKET DATA APPROACH . . . . $ 71,300

INDICATED VALUE BY INCOME APPROACH (If applicable) Economic Market Rent $ /Mo. x Gross Rent Multiplier = $

This appraisal is made ☒ "as is" ☐ subject to the repairs, alterations, or conditions listed below ☐ completion per plans and specifications.

Comments and Conditions of Appraisal:

Final Reconciliation: Heaviest emphasis based upon Market approach
Since all comparisons are approximately same age
Income approach not applicable

Construction Warranty ☐ Yes ☒ No Name of Warranty Program None Warranty Coverage Expires N/A

This appraisal is based upon the above requirements, the certification, contingent and limiting conditions, and Market Value definition that are stated in
☐ FHLMC Form 439 (Rev. 10/78)/FNMA Form 1004B (Rev. 10/78) filed with client May 3 19 82 ☒ attached.

I ESTIMATE THE MARKET VALUE, AS DEFINED, OF SUBJECT PROPERTY AS OF May 3 19 82 to be $ 71,000

Appraiser(s) _Bill Smith_

Review Appraiser (If applicable)
☒ Did ☐ Did Not Physically Inspect Property

HOME OFFICE ADDRESS:
11353 Reed Hartman Highway
P.O. Box 41910
Cincinnati, Ohio 45241

(513) 984-8064
Toll Free (800) 543-4549
In Ohio/Toll Free (800) 582-7128

APPLICATION FOR MORTGAGE LOAN INSURANCE

Lender Name __ABC Lending Institution__ **Master Policy No.** _36000056_

Lender Address _987 East Ohio Avenue_

Cincinnati, Ohio 45241

Borrower Name and Property Address ___Jeffrey and Susan Brenner___

Premium Plan No. [4116]   _7882 Village Drive_

Cincinnati, OH 45242 **Mortgage Amount** $62,000

Borrower Name and Property Address _____

Premium Plan No. [   ]   _____

_____ **Mortgage Amount** _____

Borrower Name and Property Address _____

Premium Plan No. [   ]   _____

_____ **Mortgage Amount** _____

Borrower Name and Property Address _____

Premium Plan No. [   ]   _____

_____ **Mortgage Amount** _____

Borrower Name and Property Address _____

Premium Plan No. [   ]   _____

_____ **Mortgage Amount** _____

Documents Required for Each Loan

1. Copy of lender's loan application
2. Copy sales contract
3. Current credit report
4. Employment verification
5. Deposit verification
6. Tax returns if self employed
7. Past payment record in refinanced
8. Current appraisal report and photo
9. Purchase affidavit may be submitted when loan closes

For Telephone Reply Enter Phone Number _770-0900_ **Contact** _Janice Hyde_

Date: _5/10/82_ **By:** _Joanne Plain_
Lender's Authorized Signature

GEMIC Form 20 (6/..)

May 8, 1982

Ms. Joanne Plain
ABC Lending Institution
987 East Ohio Avenue
Cincinnati, Ohio   45241

Dear Ms. Plain:

This letter is in response to your request of an explanation
for the slow payments reflected on my credit report for the
Shillitos and Sears accounts.

My job calls for some traveling and this fact and mail delays
are the only reasons I can come up with for the adverse ratings.

I hope this letter answers your questions regarding my credit.

Sincerely,

Jeffrey Brewer

CASE STUDY: FEDERAL HOUSING ADMINISTRATION
INSURED MORTGAGE LOAN

This residential mortgage loan case study (based on actual facts) involves John Buyer and Betty Buyer, both of whom desire to purchase a $64,000 home in Phoenix, Arizona.

The loan applied for is a mortgage loan insured by FHA under its basic program, Section 203(b). Before FHA will insure any mortgage loan, it must approve both the borrower and the structure. This approval process begins with the *application for appraisal* which is submitted to FHA by the mortgage lender.

After the FHA receives an estimate of value, it issues a *conditional commitment* which contains requirements relative to the real estate that must be satisfied before insurance will be approved. The processing of the loan itself follows normal procedures in that the borrower's credit, employment and financial liquidity must be verified. This information and all other pertinent facts are submitted to FHA for approval in a formal *application for mortgage insurance.*

The closing process is much the same as described in Chapter 12, Closing and Administering the Mortgage Loan.

After closing, applicable documents are submitted to FHA which issues a *mortgage insurance certificate.* This loan is to be sold and is warehoused for an interim period with a commercial bank. On the designated date, the mortgage, note and associated documents are shipped to the buyer and FHA is finally informed of the transaction.

The following documents are required and would appear in the loan file for this mortgage loan which is insured by FHA, warehoused at a commercial bank, and finally sold to FNMA.

- Purchase contract and receipt for deposit
- Initial loan application
- Application for property appraisal and commitment
- HUD Conditional Commitment for insurance
- Certificate of Commitment
- Home energy checklist
- Highest permissible rate affidavit
- Request for verification of employment (2)
- Request for verification of deposit
- Credit report
- Mortgage insurance certificate
- FHA Escrow Instructions
- FHA's Debt Ratio Calculation

- Hazard Insurance/Flood Insurance
- Regulation Z Truth-in-Lending disclosure statement
- Pest inspection report and clearance (*not* included here)
- Title insurance policy (*not* included here)
- Deed of Trust Note
- Deed of Trust
- Settlement Statement (HUD-1) (2 pages)
- Good Faith Estimate

REAL ESTATE DEPOSIT RECEIPT AND PURCHASE CONTRACT

Phoenix........., Arizona.........., January 18,.........., 19 82....

RECEIVED FROM..John J. Buyer & Betty J. Buyer, Husband and wife, JTWRS

the sum of...Five Hundred Dollars and no/100------------............DOLLARS ($ .500.00.........)

as an earnest money deposit to be applied toward the purchase price of the following described property, situated in the County of ....

Maricopa........., State of......Arizona.........., to wit:...Lot 0, NAVAJO ESTATES, AKA, 0000 E. Indian
Way , Phoenix, Arizona

The full purchase price of said premises being:....Sixty-four Thousand dollars and no/100------------
DOLLARS ($ __64,000.00__).

The full purchase price, including the above amount paid as deposit, shall be paid as follows:

$ ....500.00...... by above deposit...at Escrow Co. Inc. upon acceptance of this contract by

$ ....all parties

$ ......9,500.00...... at close of escrow

$ ....54,000.00...... FHA 203b loan obtained by buyers from FIRST FEDERAL SAVINGS & LOAN ASSOC.

Interest on deferred payments at the rate of ....percent per annum, from ....

payable ....

IT IS HEREBY AGREED: First, that in the event said purchaser shall fail to pay the balance of said purchase price, or complete said purchase as herein provided, the seller may demand specific performance of this Contract, or may retain the amount paid herein as liquidated and agreed damages, as he may elect.

Second: The purchaser and seller agree that if the title to the above property be defective, ninety days from this time will be given the seller, or his agent, to perfect same. If said title can not be perfected within said time limit the earnest money receipted for herein shall, upon the demand of the purchaser, be returned to the purchaser and this contract cancelled;

Third: That the evidence of title is to be a Title Insurance Policy issued by the....Escrow Co. Inc.
insuring the purchaser in the full amount of the purchase price shown herein, and to be issued and paid for by the seller; said title insurance policy to
show title to said premises to be subject to the usual exceptions contained in the regular form of title insurance in use by the ....
and subject to building and other restrictive convenants of record pertaining to the use of said premises and encumbrances, taxes and assessments or
other matters affecting said property as follows: ....
....
....

I CERTIFY THIS ... OF THE
AND CORRE...
ORIGINAL

Fourth: It is understood and agreed that the Buyer is of legal age and that said property has been inspected by the Buyer or the Buyer's duly authorized agent; that the same is, and has been, purchased by the Buyer as the result of said inspection and not upon any representation made by the Seller, or any Selling agent, or other agent of the Seller, and the Buyer hereby expressly waives any and all claims for damages because of any representation made by any person whomsoever other than as contained in this agreement, and the Seller or his agent shall not be responsible or liable for any inducement, promise, respresentation, agreement, condition or stipulation not specifically set forth herein.

Fifth: That the taxes, insurance, rents, etc., affecting said premises shall be prorated in the following manner:

Taxes:..prorated at close of escrow..........; Irrigation Assessments:..........;
Insurance:..buyers to obtain..........; Interest:..........;
Paving:..........; Possession:..at close of escrow..........;
Rents:..n/a..........

Sixth: This contract shall become binding only when executed by the purchaser and by the seller, and shall be in force and effect from the date of such execution;

Seventh: Time is declared to be the essence of this contract;

Eighth: This earnest money to be deposited with the...Escrow Co. Inc.......... and all other funds to be
paid by the parties hereto are to be paid in escrow to the....Escrow Co. Inc..........and the parties hereto
agree to pay, in equal portions, the fee for escrow services in connection with this transaction, and the purchaser agrees to pay the costs of recording any instruments which directly convey title to the purchaser, or which evidence the rights of the purchaser in these premises, or which evidence any deferred balance due upon this purchase;

Ninth: The parties hereto agree also (within 10 days from the date of acceptance hereof by Seller) to execute escrow instructions
Escrow Co., Inc..........upon its ordinary form for the guidance of said Company
in the handling of this transaction; providing the terms of said escrow instructions do not conflict with the terms and conditions hereof;

Tenth: The seller agrees to deliver or cause to be delivered to the....Escrow Co. Inc.......... all
instruments which are required to carry out this contract and to cause said Title Company to issue the insurance policy herein provided for; and the conveyance of these premises by the Seller to the purchaser shall be by warranty deed, subject to the conditions of this agreement.

Eleventh: This deposit is accepted subject to prior sale and subject to approval of owner.

..........*Randolph Smith*..........
(Broker)

By ....

I agree to purchase the above described property on the terms and conditions herein stated, provided acceptance of this agreement by the seller,
or his authorized agent, is made on or before 19

Bennet Gainer..........
(Witness)

John J. Buyer (Purchaser) *Betty J. Buyer*
John J. Buyer   (Purchaser) Betty J. Buyer

000 N. Hill Street (Address) Phoenix, Arizona 85003

229

January 18, ..., 19 82

I agree to sell the premises described upon the reverse side hereof, upon the terms and conditions set forth upon the reverse side hereof, and agree to pay the broker (agent) mentioned in said contract and receipt, as commission the sum of . Three. Thousand. two. Hundred. Dollars .and .no/100 .....(5%) .... DOLLARS ($ 3,200.00);

or one-half of the amount receipted for in said contract and receipt in case same is forfeited by purchaser, provided the said one-half shall not exceed the full amount of the commission.

....
(Witness)

William Seller   Emma Seller
(Seller)

(Please secure signatures of both husband and wife)

0000 E. Indian Way, Phoenix, Arizona 85032
....
(Address)

FHA AMENDMENT TO PURCHASE CONTRACT

Date 1/20/82   Case No. 021-000000-203b

It is expressly agreed that, notwithstanding any other provisions of this contract, the purchaser shall not be obligated to complete the purchase of the property described herein or to incur any penalty by forfeiture of earnest money deposits or otherwise, unless the seller has delivered to the purchaser a written statement issued by the Federal Housing Commissioner setting forth the appraised value of the property for mortgage insurance purposes of not less than $ 64,000.00   which statement the seller hereby agrees to deliver to the purchaser promptly after such appraised value statement is made available to the seller. The purchaser shall, however, have the privilege and option of proceeding with the consummation of this contract without regard to the amount of the appraised valuation made by the Federal Housing Commissioner. The appraised valuation is arrived at to determine the maximum mortgage the Department of Housing and Urban Development will insure. HUD does not warrant the value or the condition of the property. The purchaser should satisfy himself/herself that the price and condition of the property are acceptable.

Buyer _____John J. Buyer_____   Seller _____William Seller_____

Buyer _____Betty J. Buyer_____   Seller _____Emma Seller_____

Required on FHA loans when Purchase Contract is dated prior to the Appraisal.

VETERANS OPTION CLAUSE TO SALES CONTRACT

Date _____   Case No. _____

It is expressly agreed that, notwithstanding any other provisions of this contract, the purchaser shall not incur any penalty by forfeiture of earnest money or otherwise be obligated to complete the purchase of the property described herein, if the contract purchase price or cost exceeds the reasonable value of the property established by the Veterans Administration. The purchaser shall, however, have the privilege and option of proceeding with the consummation of this contract without regard to the amount of reasonable value established by the Veterans Administration.

Buyer _____   Seller _____

Buyer _____   Seller _____

Required on VA loans when Veteran is buying over appraised value.

ESCROW INSTRUCTIONS ONLY BINDING AGREEMENT

Date _____   Escrow No. _____

The undersigned parties, being the Buyer and Seller respectively under the above numbered escrow, hereby certify that the executed Escrow Instructions at_____
_____ form the only binding agreement between said parties as no formal agreements have been prepared or executed such as purchase contract.

Buyer _____   Seller _____

Buyer _____   Seller _____

Required when Escrow Instructions are the only agreement between Buyer and Seller.

RENTAL AGREEMENT

Date _____   Address _____

We are now residing in the above described property. We do/do not have a rental agreement. The rent is/is not being applied to down payment. We are paying $_____ per month.

Buyer _____   Seller _____

Buyer _____   Seller _____

Required on all FHA loans when Borrower is living in house at time of Application.

ML-272 (7-78)

FIRST FEDERAL SAVINGS

3003 NORTH CENTRAL AVENUE / PHOENIX, ARIZONA
P.O. BOX 2263 / PHOENIX, ARIZONA 85002

Date: January 25, 1982

Smith Realty
0000 Address Street
Phoenix, Arizona 85000

RE: Buyer __John J. & Betty J. Buyer__
Property Address __0000 E. Indian Way__
__Phoenix, Arizona 85032__

Dear Dan Smith

Thank you for referring the above referenced buyers to First Federal Savings for an FHA insured or VA guaranteed mortgage loan. Based on the information contained in the buyer's application, First Federal is interested in providing the permanent financing and is processing the application at the following terms.

Loan Amount:	54,000.00	Seller's Discount:	5%
Term in Years:	30	Origination Fee:	1%
Current FHA or VA Rate:	15.50	Expiration of Commitment:	3/26/82

The above loan terms are subject to the following conditions:

1.   Both the property and the borrowers must meet the credit and underwriting requirements of First Federal Savings and/or FHA and VA.

2.   The discount stated above is committed for a period of 60 days from the application date and subject to loan closing within that period of time and the rate remaining the same as stated above. After 60 days have expired, and if First Federal elects to extend the commitment for an additional 30 days, it may do so at the discount quoted above or at our new higher discount should it be higher at that particular time.

3.   In the event of a change in the government interest rate between now and the time of closing, this discount commitment shall remain the same should the FHA/VA rate increase, and shall be null and void should the FHA/VA interest rate decrease and a new commitment issued based upon the new FHA/VA rate in effect.

4.   This loan will be closed at the highest permissible rate allowable by law at the time of closing, but in no event lower than the prevailing rate in existence at the time of the application.

We sincerely hope that this letter is an aid to you in selling this property, and we are glad to have been a service to you. If we can be of any further assistance in regard to this or any other property, please contact us.

Sincerely,

ML-313 (1-79)

Form Approved
OMB No. 2900-0045

VA REQUEST FOR DETERMINATION OF REASONABLE VALUE (Real Estate) HUD APPLICATION FOR PROPERTY APPRAISAL AND COMMITMENT	HUD Section of Act 203	1. CASE NUMBER 021-000000

PROPERTY ADDRESS *(Include ZIP Code and county)*	3. LEGAL DESCRIPTION	4. TITLE LIMITATIONS AND RESTRICTIVE COVENANTS
0000 E. Indian Way Phoenix, Arizona 85032 Maricopa County, Arizona	Lot 0, NAVAJO ESTATES Maricopa County, Arizona Parcel #000-00-000	none

1 ☐ CONDOMINIUM   2 ☐ PLANNED UNIT DEVELOPMENT

5. NAME AND ADDRESS OF FIRM OR PERSON MAKING REQUEST/APPLICATION *(Include ZIP Code)*

FIRST FEDERAL SAVINGS & LOAN ASSOC.
3003 N. Central Ave.
Phoenix, Arizona 85012

Att: Teri

6. LOT DIMENSIONS: N. 117.02 S. 62.35 E. 100 W. 57.07

1 ☐ IRREGULAR: SQ/FT   2 ☐ ACRES:

7. UTILITIES (√)	ELEC.	GAS	WATER	SAN. SEWER
1. PUBLIC	X	X	X	X
2. COMMUNITY				
3. INDIVIDUAL				

BEQUIP	1. ☐	RANGE/OVEN	4. ☐	CLOTHES WASHER	7. ☐	VENT FAN
	2. ☐	REFRIG.	5. ☐	DRYER	8. X	W/W CARPET
	3. X	DISH WASHER	6. X	GARBAGE DISP.	9. ☐	

9. BUILDING STATUS	10. BUILDING TYPE	11. FACTORY FABRICATED?	12. NUMBER OF UNITS	13A. STREET ACCESS	13B. STREET MAINT.
1. ☐ PROPOSED 3. ☐ UNDER CONSTR. 2. ☐ SUBSTANTIAL REHABILITATION 4. X EXISTING	1. X DETACHED 3. ☐ ROW 2. ☐ SEMI-DETACHED 4. ☐ APT. UNIT	1. ☐ YES 2. X NO	1	1. ☐ PRIVATE 2. X PUBLIC	1. ☐ PRIVATE 2. X PUBLIC

14A. CONSTRUCTION WARRANTY INCLUDED?	14B. NAME OF WARRANTY PROGRAM	14C. EXPIRATION DATE *(Month, day, year)*	15. CONSTR. COMPLETED *(Mo., yr.)*
1. ☐ YES 2. ☐ NO *(If "Yes" complete Items 14B and C also.)*			

16. NAME OF OWNER William & Emma Seller	17. PROPERTY: X OCCUPIED BY OWNER ☐ NEVER OCCUPIED ☐ VACANT ☐ OCCUPIED BY TENANT *(Complete Item 18 also)*	18. RENT *(If applic.)* $ /MONTH

19. NAME OF OCCUPANT William & Emma Seller	20. TELEPHONE NO. 602-000-0000	21. NAME OF BROKER Dan Smith Smith Realty	22. TELEPHONE NO. 248-0000	23. DATE AND TIME AVAILABLE FOR INSPECTION call for appt. ☐ AM ☐ PM

24. KEYS AT *(Address)* Brokers office	25. ORIGINATOR'S IDENT. NO. 02014-001-4	26. SPONSOR'S IDENT. NO.	27. INSTITUTION'S CASE NO.

28. PURCHASER'S NAME AND ADDRESS *(Complete mailing address. Include ZIP code.)*

John J. & Betty J. Buyer
000 N. Hill Street
Phoenix, Arizona 85003

EQUAL OPPORTUNITY IN HOUSING

NOTE – Federal laws and regulations prohibit discrimination because of race, color, religion, sex, or national origin in the sale or rental of residential property. Numerous State statutes and local ordinances also prohibit such discrimination. In addition, section 805 of the Civil Rights Act of 1968 prohibits discriminatory practices in connection with the financing of housing.

If HUD/VA finds there is noncompliance with any antidiscrimination laws or regulations, it may discontinue business with the violator.

29. NEW OR PROPOSED CONSTRUCTION – *Complete Items 29A through 29G for new or proposed construction cases only.*

A. COMPLIANCE INSPECTIONS WILL BE OR WERE MADE BY: ☐ FHA ☐ VA ☐ NONE MADE	B. PLANS *(check one)* ☐ FIRST SUBMISSION ☐ REPEAT CASE *(If checked complete Item 29C.)*	C. PLANS SUBMITTED PREVIOUSLY UNDER CASE NO.:
D. NAME AND ADDRESS OF BUILDER	E. TELEPHONE NO.	F. NAME AND ADDRESS OF WARRANTOR	G. TELEPHONE NO.

30. COMMENTS ON SPECIAL ASSESSMENTS OR HOMEOWNERS ASSOCIATION CHARGES none	31. ANNUAL REAL ESTATE TAXES $ 360.00	33. LEASEHOLD CASES *(Complete if applicable)*
	32. MINERAL RIGHTS RESERVED? ☐ YES *(Explain)* X NO	LEASE IS: ☐ 99 YEARS ☐ RENEWABLE ☐ HUD/VA APPROVED	EXPIRES *(Date)* ANNUAL GROUND RENT $

34. SALE PRICE OF PROPERTY $ 64,000.00	35. REFINANCING – AMOUNT OF PROPOSED LOAN $	36. PROPOSED SALE CONTRACT ATTACHED X YES ☐ NO	37. CONTRACT NUMBER PREVIOUSLY APPROVED BY VA THAT WILL BE USED

CERTIFICATIONS FOR SUBMISSIONS TO HUD

In submitting this application for a conditional commitment for mortgage insurance, it is agreed and understood by the parties involved in the transaction, that if, at the time of application for a Firm Commitment, the identity of the seller has changed, the application for a Firm Commitment will be rejected and the application for a Conditional Commitment will be reprocessed upon request by the mortgagee.

It is further agreed and understood that in submitting the request for a Firm Commitment for mortgage insurance, the seller, the purchaser and the broker involved in the transaction shall each certify that the terms of the contract for purchase are true to his or her best knowledge and belief, and that any other agreement entered into by any of these parties in connection with this transaction is attached to the sales agreement.

BUILDER/SELLER'S AGREEMENT: **All Houses:** The undersigned agrees to deliver to the purchaser HUD's statement of appraised value. **Proposed Construction:** The undersigned agrees, upon sale or conveyance of title within one year from date of initial occupancy, to deliver to the purchaser Form HUD-92544, warranting that the house is constructed in substantial conformity with the plans and specifications on which HUD based its value and to furnish HUD a conformed copy with the purchaser's receipt thereon that the original warranty was delivered to him/her. **All Houses:** In consideration of the issuance of the commitment requested by this application, I (we) hereby agree that any deposit or down payment made in connection with the purchase of the property described above, whether received by the undersigned, or an agent of the undersigned, shall upon receipt be deposited in escrow or in trust or in a special account which is not subject to the claims of my creditors and where it will be maintained until it has been disbursed for the benefit of the purchaser or otherwise disposed of in accordance with the terms of the contract of sale.

Signature of: X Mortgage ☐ Builder ☐ Seller ☐ Other X_____	Date 2/5/82 19___

MORTGAGEE'S CERTIFICATE: The undersigned mortgagee certifies that to the best of his/her knowledge, all statements made in this application and the supporting documents are true, correct and complete.

Signature and Title of Mortgage Officer: X *Paul Smith* Loan Processor	Date 2/5/82 19___

CERTIFICATIONS FOR SUBMISSIONS TO VA

1. On receipt of "Certificate of Reasonable Value" or advice from the Veterans Administration that a "Certificate of Reasonable Value" will not be issued, we agree to forward to the appraiser the approved fee which we are holding for this purpose.

2. CERTIFICATION REQUIRED ON CONSTRUCTION UNDER FHA SUPERVISION *(Strike out inappropriate phrases in parentheses)*
I hereby certify that plans and specifications and related exhibits, including acceptable FHA Change Orders, if any, supplied to VA in this case, are identical to those (submitted to) (to be submitted to) (approved by) FHA, and that FHA inspections (have been) (will be) made pursuant to FHA approval for mortgage insurance on the basis of proposed construction under Sec.

38. SIGNATURE OF PERSON AUTHORIZING THIS REQUEST	39. TITLE	40. DATE

41. DATE OF ASSIGNMENT 2/5/82	42. NAME OF APPRAISER Bill Appraiser

WARNING: Section 1010 of Title 18, U.S.C. provides: "Whoever for the purpose of . . . influencing such Administration . . . makes, passes, utters or publishes any statement knowing the same to be false . . . shall be fined not more than $5,000 or imprisoned not more than two years or both."

VA FORM 26-1805, AUG 1980 HUD FORM 92800-1	SUPERSEDES VA FORM 26-1805, AUG 1977, AND HUD 92800, JUL 1979, WHICH WILL NOT BE USED.	VA/HUD FILE COPY 1

Form Approved
OMB No. 2900-0144

VA Application for Home Loan Guaranty ☐	USDA-FmHA Application for FmHA Guaranteed Loan ☐	HUD/FHA Application for Commitment for Insurance under the National Housing Act ☒	1. AGENCY CASE NUMBER ▲ 021-000000	2A. LENDER'S CASE NUMBER	2B. SECTION OF THE ACT (HUD Only) 203 (b)

3. NAME AND PRESENT ADDRESS OF BORROWER (Include ZIP Code)
BUYER, John J. & Betty J.
000 N. Hill Street
Phoenix, Arizona 85003

5A. BORROWER: If you do not wish to complete Items 5B or 5C, please initial in the space to the right. | INITIALS

5B. RACE/NATIONAL ORIGIN
▲1 ☒ WHITE, NOT HISPANIC 4 ☐ ASIAN OR PACIFIC ISLANDER
2 ☐ BLACK, NOT HISPANIC 5 ☐ HISPANIC
3 ☐ AMERICAN INDIAN OR ALASKAN NATIVE

5C. SEX
▲1 ☒ MALE 2 ☐ FEMALE

4A. NAME AND ADDRESS OF LENDER (Include ZIP Code)
FIRST FEDERAL SAVINGS & LOAN ASSOCIATION
3003 N. Central Ave.
Phoenix, Arizona 85012
602-248-4274

6A. SPOUSE OR OTHER BORROWER: If you do not wish to complete Items 6B or 6C, please initial in space to the right. | INITIALS

6B. RACE/NATIONAL ORIGIN
▲1 ☒ WHITE, NOT HISPANIC 4 ☐ ASIAN OR PACIFIC ISLANDER
2 ☐ BLACK, NOT HISPANIC 5 ☐ HISPANIC
3 ☐ AMERICAN INDIAN OR ALASKAN NATIVE

6C. SEX
▲1 ☐ MALE 2 ☒ FEMALE

4B. ORIGINATORS'S I.D. (HUD Only) 02014-001-4	4C. SPONSOR'S I.D. (HUD Only)

7. PROPERTY ADDRESS INCLUDING NAME OF SUBDIVISION, LOT AND BLOCK NO., AND ZIP CODE	8A. LOAN AMOUNT	8B. INT. RATE	8C. PROPOSED MATURITY
0000 E. Indian Way Lot 0, NAVAJO ESTATES Phoenix, Arizona 85032 Maricopa County, Arizona	$ 54,000.00	15.50 %	30 YRS. 0 MOS.

DISCOUNT: (Only if borrower to pay) ➡ | 8D. PERCENT % | 8E. AMOUNT $

VA ONLY: Veteran and lender hereby apply to the Administrator of Veterans Affairs for Guaranty of the loan described here under Section 1810, Chapter 37, Title 38, United States Code to the full extent permitted by the veteran's entitlement and severally agree that the Regulations promulgated pursuant to Chapter 37, and in effect on the date of the loan shall govern the rights, duties, and liabilities of the parties.
HUD/FHA ONLY: Mortgagee's application for mortgagor approval and commitment for mortgage insurance under the National Housing Act.

SECTION I - PURPOSE, AMOUNT, TERMS OF AND SECURITY FOR PROPOSED LOAN

9A. PURPOSE OF LOAN – TO:		9B. HUD ONLY – BORROWER WILL BE	10. VA ONLY – TITLE WILL BE VESTED IN:
▲1 ☒ PURCHASE EXISTING HOUSE PREVIOUSLY OCCUPIED 4 ☐ PURCHASE NEW CONDO. UNIT 7 ☐ CONSTRUCT A HOME - PROCEEDS TO BE PAID OUT DURING CONSTRUCTION		▲1 ☒ OCCUPANT 5 ☐ ESCROW COMMITMENT	☐ VETERAN ☐ VETERAN AND SPOUSE
2 ☐ FINANCE IMPROVEMENTS TO EXISTING PROPERTY 5 ☐ PURCHASE EXISTING CONDO. UNIT 8 ☐ HUD ONLY – FINANCE COOP-PURCHASE		2 ☐ LANDLORD 3 ☐ BUILDER 4 ☐ OPERATIVE BUILDER	☐ OTHER (Specify)
3 ☐ REFINANCE 6 ☐ PURCHASE EXISTING HOME NOT PREVIOUSLY OCCUPIED			

11. LIEN: ☒ FIRST MORTGAGE ☐ OTHER (Specify)	12. ESTATE WILL BE: ☒ FEE SIMPLE ☐ LEASEHOLD (Show expiration date)	13. IS THERE A MANDATORY HOMEOWNERS ASSOC.? ☐ YES ☒ NO (If "Yes," complete Item 14F.)

14. ESTIMATED TAXES, INSURANCE AND ASSESSMENTS

		15. ESTIMATED MONTHLY PAYMENT	
A. ANNUAL TAXES	$ 336.00	A. PRINCIPAL AND INTEREST	$ 704.44
B. AMOUNT OF HAZARD INSURANCE ON SECURITY	54,000.00	B. TAXES AND INSURANCE DEPOSITS 15/28	43.00
C. ANNUAL HAZARD INSURANCE PREMIUM	180.00	C. OTHER MIP	22.49
D. ANNUAL SPECIAL ASSESSMENT PAYMENT			
E. UNPAID SPECIAL ASSESSMENT BALANCE			
F. ANNUAL MAINTENANCE ASSESSMENT		TOTAL $	769.53

SECTION II - PERSONAL AND FINANCIAL STATUS OF APPLICANT

16. PLEASE CHECK APPROPRIATE BOX(ES). IF ONE OR MORE ARE CHECKED, ITEMS 18B, 21, 22 AND 23 MUST INCLUDE INFORMATION CONCERNING BORROWER'S SPOUSE (or former spouse if box "D" is checked). IF NO BOXES ARE CHECKED, NO INFORMATION CONCERNING THE SPOUSE NEED BE FURNISHED IN ITEMS 18B, 21, 22 AND 23.

A. ☒ THE SPOUSE WILL BE JOINTLY OBLIGATED WITH THE BORROWER ON THE LOAN.
B. ☐ THE BORROWER IS RELYING ON THE SPOUSE'S INCOME AS A BASIS FOR REPAYMENT OF THE LOAN.
C. ☒ THE BORROWER IS MARRIED AND THE PROPERTY TO SECURE THE LOAN IS LOCATED IN A COMMUNITY PROPERTY STATE.
D. ☐ THE BORROWER IS RELYING ON ALIMONY, CHILD SUPPORT, OR SEPARATE MAINTENANCE PAYMENTS FROM A SPOUSE OR FORMER SPOUSE AS A BASIS FOR REPAYMENT OF THE LOAN.

17A. MARITAL STATUS OF BORROWER	17B. MARITAL STATUS OF COBORROWER OTHER THAN SPOUSE	17C. MONTHLY CHILD SUPPORT OBLIGATION	17D. MONTHLY ALIMONY OBLIGATION	18A. AGE OF BORROWER	18B. AGE OF SPOUSE OR COBORROWER	18C. AGE(S) OF DEPENDENT(S)
1 ☒ MARRIED 3 ☐ UNMARRIED 2 ☐ SEPARATED	1 ☐ MARRIED 3 ☐ UNMARRIED 2 ☐ SEPARATED	$ n/a	$ n/a	28	25	n/a

19. NAME AND ADDRESS OF NEAREST LIVING RELATIVE (Include telephone number, if available).	20A. CURRENT MONTHLY HOUSING EXPENSE	20B. UTILITIES INCLUDED?
John Jones Phoenix, Arizona 85000 000 E. 6th St. Phone #602-000-0000	$ 295.00	☐ YES ☒ NO

21. ASSETS

		22. LIABILITIES (Itemize all debts)		
		NAME OF CREDITOR	MO. PAYMENT	BALANCE
A. CASH (Including deposit on purchase)	$ 11,515.22	FIB (auto)	$ 131.00	$ 2,231.00
B. SAVINGS BONDS - OTHER SECURITIES		McMahans	38.00	1,018.00
C. REAL ESTATE OWNED		Visa	21.00	500.00
D. AUTO (2) 76 Ford PU/78 Ply	8,000.00	Transamerican Fin *(pd in 7ms)	(34.00)	238.00
E. FURNITURE AND HOUSEHOLD GOODS	16,000.00			
F. OTHER (Use separate sheet, if necessary)		JOB-RELATED EXPENSE (Specify)		
G. TOTAL	$ 28,015.22	TOTAL $	190.00	$ 3,987.00

23. INCOME AND OCCUPATIONAL STATUS

ITEM	BORROWER	SPOUSE OR COBORROWER
A. OCCUPATION	Field Representive	Ass't Buyer Shoe Dept.
B. NAME OF EMPLOYER	Acme Ins. Co.	Penney's Dept. St
C. NUMBER OF YEARS EMPLOYED	4	3
D. GROSS PAY	▲ MONTHLY $ 2083.00 HOURLY $ n/a	▲ MONTHLY $ 1,052.1 HOURLY 6.07
E. OTHER INCOME (Disclosure of child support, alimony and separate maintenance income is optional.)	▲ MONTHLY n/a $	▲ MONTHLY n/a $

24. ESTIMATED TOTAL COST

ITEM	AMOUNT
A. PURCHASE EXISTING HOME	$ 64,000.00
B. ALTERATIONS, IMPROVEMENTS, REPAIRS	
C. CONSTRUCTION	
D. LAND (If acquired separately)	
E. PURCHASE OF CONDOMINIUM UNIT	
F. REFINANCE	
G. PREPAID ITEMS	400.00
H. ESTIMATED CLOSING COSTS	1,050.00
I. DISCOUNT (Only if borrower permitted to pay)	
J. TOTAL COSTS (Add Items 24A through 24I)	65,450.00
K. LESS CASH FROM BORROWER	11,450.00
L. LESS OTHER CREDITS	
M. AMOUNT OF LOAN	$ 54,000.00

NOTE — If land acquired by separate transaction, complete Items 25A and 25B.

25A. DATE ACQUIRED	25B. UNPAID BALANCE $

VA FORM 26-1802a, JAN 1982
HUD FORM 92900.1

SUPERSEDES VA FORM 26-1802a, APR 1979, WHICH WILL NOT BE USED.
HUD FORM 92900, JUL 1980, MAY BE USED FOR HUD PURPOSES.

VA/HUD COPY 1

SECTION III - LENDER'S CERTIFICATION *(Must be signed by lender)*

The undersigned lender makes the following certifications to induce the Veterans Administration to issue a certificate of commitment to guarantee the subject loan under Title 38, U.S. Code, or to induce the Department of Housing and Urban Development - Federal Housing Commissioner to issue a firm commitment for mortgage insurance under the National Housing Act.

26A. The information furnished in Section I is true, accurate and complete.
26B. The information contained in Section II was obtained directly from the borrower by a full-time employee of the undersigned lender or its duly authorized agent and is true to the best of the lender's knowledge and belief.
26C. The credit report submitted on the subject borrower *(and spouse, if any)* was ordered by the undersigned lender or its duly authorized agent directly from the credit bureau which prepared the report and was received directly from said credit bureau.
26D. The verification of employment and verification of deposits were requested and received by the lender or its duly authorized agent without passing through the hands of any third persons and are true to the best of the lender's knowledge and belief.
26E. This application was signed by the borrower after Sections I, II and V were completed.
26F. This proposed loan to the named borrower meets the income and credit requirements of the governing law in the judgment of the undersigned.
26G through 26I - TO BE COMPLETED OR APPLICABLE FOR VA LOANS ONLY.
26G. The names and functions of any duly authorized agents who developed on behalf of the lender any of the information or supporting credit data submitted are as follows:

	NAME	ADDRESS	FUNCTION *(e.g., obtained information in Sec. II; ordered credit report, verification of employment, verif. of deposits, etc.)*
(1)			
(2)			
(3)			

☒ *(Check box if all information and supporting credit data were obtained directly by the lender.)*
26H. The undersigned lender understands and agrees that it is responsible for the acts of agents identified in item 26G as to the functions with which they are identified.
26I. The proposed loan conforms otherwise with the applicable provisions of Title 38, U.S. Code, and of the regulations concerning guaranty or insurance of loans to veterans.

27. Date	28. Name of Lender	29. Telephone Number *(Include Area Code)*	30. Signature and Title of Officer of Lender
	FIRST FEDERAL SAVINGS & LOAN ASSOC.	602-248-4274	*Paul Smith* Loan Processor

SECTION IV - NOTICE TO BORROWERS

PRIVACY ACT INFORMATION - The information requested in this form is authorized by 38 U.S.C. 1810 *(if VA)* and 12 U.S.C. 1701 et seq., *(if HUD/FHA)* and will be used in determining whether you qualify as a mortgagor. Any disclosure of information outside VA or HUD/FHA will only be made as permitted by law. Disclosure of this information is voluntary but no loan may be approved unless a completed application is received.
NOTICE TO BORROWERS - This is notice to you as required by the Right to Financial Privacy Act of 1978 that the VA or HUD/FHA has a right of access to financial records held by financial institutions in connection with the consideration or administration of assistance to you. Financial records involving your transaction will be available to VA and HUD/FHA without further notice or authorization but will not be disclosed or released to another Government Agency or Department without your consent except as required or permitted by law.

SECTION V - BORROWERS CERTIFICATION *(Must be signed by Borrower(s))*

31A. COMPLETE FOR HUD/FHA INSURED MORTGAGE ONLY.
(1) Do you own or have you sold, within the past 12 months, other real estate?
☐ Yes ☒ No   Is it to be sold? ☐ Yes ☐ No   HUD/FHA Mortgage? ☐ Yes ☐ No   Sales Price $_____ Original Mortgage Amount $_____

Address: _____ Lender: _____

(2) Have you ever been obligated on a home loan, home improvement loan or a mobile home loan which resulted in foreclosure, transfer of title in lieu of foreclosure or judgment? ☐ Yes ☒ No. If "Yes" give details including date, property address, name and address of lender, FHA or VA Case Number, if any, and reasons for the action.

(3) If dwelling to be covered by this mortgage is to be rented, is it a part of, adjacent or contiguous to any project, subdivision, or group rental properties involving eight or more dwelling units in which you have any financial interest? ☐ Yes ☒ No ☐ Not to be rented. If "Yes" give details. Do you own four or more dwelling units with mortgages insured under any title of the National Housing Act? ☐ Yes ☒ No. If "Yes" submit form HUD-92561.

31B. APPLICABLE FOR BOTH VA AND HUD. As a home loan borrower, you will be legally obligated to make the mortgage payments called for by your mortgage loan contract. The fact that you disposed of your property after the loan has been made WILL NOT RELIEVE YOU OF LIABILITY FOR MAKING THESE PAYMENTS. PAYMENT OF THE LOAN IN FULL IS ORDINARILY THE WAY LIABILITY ON A MORTGAGE NOTE IS ENDED. Some home buyers have the mistaken impression that if they sell their homes when they move to another locality, or dispose of it for any other reasons, they are no longer liable for the mortgage payments and that liability for these payments is solely that of the new owners. Even though the new owners may agree in writing to assume liability for your mortgage payments, this assumption agreement will not relieve you from liability to the holder of the note which you signed when you obtained the loan to buy the property. Also, unless you are able to sell the property to a buyer who is acceptable to the VA or to HUD/FHA and who will assume the payment of your obligation to the lender, you will not be relieved from liability to repay any claim which the VA or HUD/FHA may be required to pay your lender on account of default in your loan payments. The amount of any such claim payment will be a debt owed by you to the Federal Government. This debt will be the object of established collection procedures.

I, THE UNDERSIGNED BORROWER(S) CERTIFY THAT:
(1) I have read and understand the foregoing concerning my liability on the loan.
(2) VA Only *(check applicable box)* ☐ Purchase or Construction Loan. I now actually occupy the above-described property as my home or intend to move into and occupy said property as my home within a reasonable period of time. ☐ Home Improvement or Refinancing Loan. I own and personally occupy as my home the property described in Item 7 of the Application.
(3) Check applicable box *(not applicable for Home Improvement or Refinancing Loan)*, I have been informed that $64,000.00 is ☐ the reasonable value of the property as determined by the VA, ☒ the statement of appraised value as determined by HUD/FHA. IF THE CONTRACT PRICE OR COST EXCEEDS THE VA REASONABLE VALUE OR HUD/FHA STATEMENT OF APPRAISED VALUE, COMPLETE EITHER ITEM (a) or (b), WHICHEVER IS APPLICABLE.
(a) ☐ I was aware of this valuation when I signed my contract and I have paid or will pay in cash from my own resources at or prior to loan closing a sum equal to the difference between the contract purchase price or cost and the VA or HUD/FHA established value. I do not and will not have outstanding after loan closing any unpaid contractual obligation on account of such cash payment;
(b) ☒ I was not aware of this valuation when I signed my contract but have elected to complete the transaction at the contract purchase price or cost. I have paid or will pay in cash from my own resources at or prior to loan closing a sum equal to the difference between contract purchase price or cost and the VA or HUD/FHA established value. I do not and will not have outstanding after loan closing any unpaid contractual obligation on account of such cash payment.
(4) Neither I, nor anyone authorized to act for me, will refuse to sell or rent, after the making of a bona fide offer, or refuse to negotiate for the sale or rental of, or otherwise make unavailable or deny the dwelling or property covered by this loan to any person because of race, color, religion, sex or national origin. I recognize that any restrictive covenant on this property relating to race, color, religion, sex or national origin is illegal and void and civil action for preventive relief may be brought by the Attorney General of the United States in any appropriate U.S. District Court against any person responsible for the violation of the applicable law.
(5) The Borrower certifies that all information in this application is given for the purpose of obtaining a loan to be insured under the National Housing Act, or guaranteed by the Veterans Administration and the information in Section II is true and complete to the best of his/her knowledge and belief. Verification may be obtained from any source named herein.
HUD ONLY {(6) For properties constructed prior to 1950 - I have received the brochure "Watchout for Lead Paint Poisoning" ☐ ☒ NA
(7) ☒ I have read and understand the contents of the Home Energy Checklist attached to HUD-92800-4.

READ CERTIFICATIONS CAREFULLY - DO NOT SIGN UNLESS APPLICATION IS FULLY COMPLETED.	32. DATE	33. SIGNATURE OF BORROWER(S) *(Before signing, review accuracy of application and certifications.)*
		John J. Buyer & Betty J. Buyer

Federal statutes provide severe penalties for any fraud, intentional misrepresentation, or criminal connivance or conspiracy purposed to influence the issuance of any guaranty or insurance by the VA or USDA-FmHA Administrator or the HUD/FHA Commissioner.

Form Approved
OMB No. 2900-0045

☐ VA CERTIFICATE OF REASONABLE VALUE ☒ HUD CONDITIONAL COMMITMENT		HUD Section of Act **203**	1. CASE NUMBER **021-000000**

2. PROPERTY ADDRESS *(Include ZIP Code and county)*	3. LEGAL DESCRIPTION	4. TITLE LIMITATIONS AND RESTRICTIVE COVENANTS
0000 E. Indian Way Phoenix, Arizona 85032 Maricopa County, Arizona	Lot 0, NAVAJO ESTATES Maricopa County, Arizona Parcel #000-00-000	**none**

1. ☐ CONDOMINIUM   *2.* ☐ PLANNED UNIT DEVELOPMENT

5. NAME AND ADDRESS OF FIRM OR PERSON MAKING REQUEST/APPLICATION *(Include ZIP Code)*	6. LOT DIMENSIONS: N. 117.02 S. 62.35 E. 100 W. 57.07

FIRST FEDERAL SAVINGS & LOAN ASSOC.
3003 N. Central Ave.
Phoenix, Arizona 85012

Att: Teri

1. ☐ IRREGULAR: SQ/FT   *2.* ☐ ACRES:

7. UTILITIES (✓)	ELEC.	GAS	WATER	SAN. SEWER
1. PUBLIC	X	X	X	X
2. COMMUNITY				
3. INDIVIDUAL				

8. EQUIP.	*1.* RANGE/OVEN	*4.* CLOTHES WASHER	*7.* VENT FAN
	2. X REFRIG.	*5.* DRYER	*8.* X W/W CARPET
	3. X DISH. WASHER	*6.* X GARBAGE DISP.	*9.*

9. BUILDING STATUS	10. BUILDING TYPE	11. FACTORY FABRICATED?	12. NUMBER OF UNITS	13A. STREET ACCESS	13B. STREET MAINT.
1. ☐ PROPOSED *3.* ☐ UNDER CONSTR. *2.* ☐ SUBSTANTIAL REHABILITATION *4.* ☒ EXISTING	*1.* ☒ DETACHED *3.* ☐ ROW *2.* ☐ SEMI-DETACHED *4.* ☐ APT UNIT	*1.* ☐ YES *2.* ☒ NO	1	*1.* ☐ PRIVATE *2.* ☒ PUBLIC	*1.* ☐ PRIVATE *2.* ☒ PUBLIC

14. ESTIMATED REASONABLE VALUE OF PROPERTY	15. REMAINING ECONOMIC LIFE OF PROPERTY IS ESTIMATED TO BE NOT LESS THAN:	16. EXPIRATION DATE
$ 64,000.00	50 YEARS	8/8/82

17. HUD COMMITMENT TERMS	
A. MAXIMUM MORTGAGE AMOUNT	$ 62,250.00
B. NO. OF MONTHS	360
C. NOTICE OF REJECTION	
D. "AS IS" VALUE	$

18. ☐ This Certificate of Reasonable Value is valid only if VA Form 26-1843p showing VA General Conditions and the applicable Specific Conditions is attached.

19. ADMINISTRATOR OF VETERANS AFFAIRS, BY *(Signature of authorized agent)*, OR HUD AUTHORIZED AGENT	20. DATE ISSUED	21. VA OR HUD OFFICE
HUD Authorized Agent	2/8/82	PHX

E. MONTHLY EXPENSE ESTIMATE	
FIRE INSURANCE	$ 15.00
TAXES	$ 21.00

22. PURCHASER'S NAME AND ADDRESS *(Complete mailing address. Include ZIP Code.)*	

John J. & Betty J. Buyer
000 N. Hill Street
Phoenix, Arizona 85003

CONDO. COMMUNITY EXPENSE	$
MAINTENANCE AND REPAIRS	$ 21.00
HEAT AND UTILITIES	$ 125.00
F. ESTIMATED CLOSING COST	$ 1,050.00
G. ☒ EXISTING ☐ PROPOSED	*(See General Condition 3 on attachment.)*
H. IMPROVED LIVING AREA	1292.00 SQ/FT

I. ☒ This Conditional Commitment is valid only if HUD Form 92800-5a showing HUD General Conditions and the applicable Specific Conditions is attached.

VA FORM 26-1843, AUG 1980   HUD FORM 92800-5

REQUESTER'S COPY 2

U.S. DEPARTMENT OF HOUSING AND URBAN DEVELOPMENT HOUSING - FEDERAL HOUSING COMMISSIONER **ADDENDUM TO CONDITIONAL COMMITMENT**	FHA CASE NUMBER 021-000000-203

This form is required by law. It is a "Statement of Appraised Value" that borrowers who will be using HUD-insured financing must receive prior to the purchase of the property. If the sales contract has been signed before the borrower receives such a statement, the contract must contain, or must be amended to include, the following language:

"It is expressly agreed that, notwithstanding any other provisions of the contract, the purchaser shall not be obligated to complete the purchase of the property described herein or to incur any penalty by forfeiture of earnest money deposits or otherwise unless the seller has delivered to the purchaser a written statement issued by the Federal Housing Commissioner setting forth the appraised value of the property (excluding closing costs) of not less than $ _____ which statement the seller hereby agrees to deliver to the purchaser promptly after such appraised value statement is made available to the seller. The purchaser shall, however, have the privilege and option of proceeding with the consummation of the contract without regard to the amount of the appraised valuation made by the Federal Housing Commissioner. The appraised valuation is arrived at to determine the maximum mortgage the Department of Housing and Urban Development will insure. HUD does not warrant the value nor the condition of the property. The purchaser should satisfy himself/herself that the price and condition of the property are acceptable."

ESTIMATED REASONABLE VALUE OF PROPERTY - - Is the same thing as the appraised value. These terms can be defined as the amount that HUD considers the property to be worth. The HUD "Estimated Reasonable Value of Property" does not fix a sales price, except when the mortgage is to be insured under Section 235(i), which is a homeownership assistance program. By providing this estimate, HUD is not approving the purchase of the property nor is HUD indicating the amount of an insured mortgage that will be approved.

REPLACEMENT COST - - Is used instead of value in the Section 213 and Section 220 programs. This is an estimate by HUD of the current cost to reproduce the property including land, labor, site survey, materials and marketing expenses. The "Estimated Reasonable Value of Property" shall be considered to mean replacement cost under those two programs.

MAXIMUM MORTGAGE AMOUNT - - Is the maximum mortgage which HUD can insure and it is based on the sum of the "Estimated Reasonable Value of Property" plus the "Estimated Closing Costs." *IF THE PURCHASE PRICE OF THE PROPERTY IS MORE THAN THE "ESTIMATED REASONABLE VALUE OF THE PROPERTY," AND YOU PAY CLOSING COSTS, YOU ARE PAYING MORE FOR THE PROPERTY THAN HUD CONSIDERS IT TO BE WORTH.*

ESTIMATED CLOSING COSTS - - Is the amount HUD considers to be customarily paid by the buyer in order to complete the mortgage loan transaction. However, these costs may be paid by the buyer or the seller. They normally include items such as fees for preparing the mortgage documents, title insurance, loan origination fees and transfer and recording taxes.

PREPAID ITEMS - - Are charges that normally will also be paid at closing and are recurring in nature. They include such items as funds for real estate taxes and hazard insurance. *BECAUSE THE AMOUNT OF THESE ITEMS WILL VARY DEPENDING UPON THE CLOSING DATE, HUD DOES NOT PROVIDE AN ESTIMATE WITH THIS STATEMENT.*

ATTENTION HOMEBUYERS

EXISTING HOUSES - - *IF YOU ARE BUYING A HOUSE WHICH HAS BEEN LIVED IN BEFORE, BE SURE THE HOUSE IS IN THE CONDITION YOU WANT BEFORE SIGNING A PURCHASE CONTRACT. HUD MAKES AN APPRAISAL ONLY TO ESTIMATE THE VALUE OF THE PROPERTY. THIS APPRAISAL DOES NOT GUARANTEE THAT THE HOUSE IS FREE OF DEFECTS. HUD CANNOT GIVE YOU MONEY FOR REPAIRS SO YOU MUST PROTECT YOURSELF BEFORE YOU BUY. YOU SHOULD INSPECT THE PROPERTY CAREFULLY. IF YOU NEED HELP, A PRIVATE INSPECTION SERVICE CAN BE HIRED IN MANY LOCALITIES. LOOK IN THE TELEPHONE BOOK FOR SUCH SERVICES.*

ADVICE TO HOMEBUYERS

ESCROW ACCOUNT - - This is a special account that your lender will keep on your behalf to save the necessary funds to pay certain future bills. Your mortgage payment will include, in addition to an amount for interest and principal, amounts to cover such items as property taxes, hazard insurance, and the mortgage insurance premium. These charges are collected in advance so that your lender will have enough money in the account to apply the charge when it comes due. Generally, 1/12 of the next estimated charges will be the amount collected with each of your monthly mortgage payments. Bear in mind that in most communities taxes and other operating costs are increasing. The estimates should give some idea of what you can expect the costs to be at the beginning. In some areas the HUD estimate of taxes may also include charges such as sewer charges, garbage collection fee, water rates, etc.

MORTGAGE INSURANCE PREMIUM - - The amount charged for insuring your mortgage. The charge is ½ of 1 percent of your average loan balance not taking into account additional payments or late payments you might make. Each month as part of your mortgage payment you will pay 1/12 of the amount of the mortgage insurance premium which will be due each year, For example, if your average loan balance is $10,000, your mortgage insurance premium for that year will be $50 which you will pay in monthly payments of $4.16. As your loan balance grows smaller, the charge for insurance will also go down.

ESTIMATED MONTHLY EXPENSES - - Costs which are associated with homeownership which HUD believes the home-owners will have to pay when living in the property. Two examples of "Estimated Monthly Expenses" are fire insurance and taxes, which are paid to your lender each month as part of your mortgage payment. These are put into your escrow account.

OTHER COSTS OF HOMEOWNERSHIP - - Utilities are usually paid monthly to whomever provides the service. Also, you should save a certain amount each month to cover repair and maintenance costs which will come up while you own your home.

LATE PAYMENTS - - If you do not pay your mortgage payment within 15 days from the 1st day of the month, you can be charged a penalty. This may be 4 cents for each dollar of your payment.

NEW CONSTRUCTION - - When HUD approves plans and specifications before construction, the builder is required to warrant that the house conforms to approved plans. This warranty is for 1 year following the date on which title is transferred to the original buyer or the date on which the house was first lived in whichever happens first. If during the warranty period you notice defects for which you believe the builder is responsible, ask him in writing to fix them. If he does not fix them, write the HUD Field Office. Mention the FHA case number shown above. If inspection shows the builder to be at fault, HUD will try to persuade him to fix the defect. If he does not, you may be able to obtain legal relief under the builder's warranty. Where a structural defect is involved HUD can provide money for corrections under certain conditions. You cannot expect the builder to fix damage caused by ordinary wear and tear or by poor maintenance. Keeping the house in good condition is your responsibility.

☐ *THIS HOUSE WAS CONSTRUCTED BEFORE 1950. THERE IS A POSSIBILITY THAT IT MAY CONTAIN LEAD PAINT THAT WAS IN USE BEFORE THAT TIME. THE LENDING INSTITUTION IS REQUIRED TO GIVE YOU A COPY OF THE BROCHURE ENTITLED "WATCH OUT FOR LEAD PAINT POISONING.*

OMB No. 2502-0111

U.S. DEPARTMENT OF HOUSING AND URBAN DEVELOPMENT HOUSING - FEDERAL HOUSING COMMISSIONER **ADDENDUM TO CONDITIONAL COMMITMENT**	FHA CASE NUMBER 021–000000–203

INFORMATION

The estimates of fire insurance, taxes, maintenance repairs, heat utilities and closing costs are furnished for mortgagee's and mortgagor's information. They must be used to prepare Form HUD-92900, Application for Credit Approval, when a firm commitment is desired.

GENERAL COMMITMENT CONDITIONS

1. MAXIMUM MORTGAGE AMOUNT AND TERMS -
(a) **OCCUPANT MORTGAGORS:** - the mortgage amount and term set forth on HUD-92800-5 are the maximum approved for this property assuming a satisfactory owner-occupant mortgagor. The maximum amount and term may be changed depending upon HUD's rating of the borrower, his income and credit.

(b) **NONOCCUPANT MORTGAGORS:**- If the mortgagor does not occupy the house, the law limits the maximum mortgage amount to not exceed 85% of the maximum amount available to an eligible mortgagor who will occupy the house (85% of value if Sec. 203(i) or 221). In the case of nonoccupant mortgagors, the firm commitment when issued will reduce the mortgage amount and terms below that stated in the heading.

(c) **COMMITMENT CHANGES:** - The Commissioner may, upon request of the approved mortgagee, change the mortgage amount and term set forth on HUD-92800-5. If the application is accompanied by a VA CRV, changes will be made only if VA issues an amendment.

2. FIRM COMMITMENT: - A firm commitment to insure a mortgage will be issued upon receipt of an Application for Credit Approval. Form HUD-92900, executed by an approved mortgagee and a borrower satisfactory to the Commissioner.

3. COMMITMENT TERM: - This commitment shall expire **SIX MONTHS** from the issue date in the case of an EXISTING HOUSE or **ONE YEAR** from its date in the case of PROPOSED CONSTRUCTION. *(FHA classifies all cases as either "EXISTING" or "PROPOSED" for the purpose of determining when a commitment expires. Accordingly, a house, even though still under construction, may be classified as an existing house if it was not approved by FHA or VA prior to the beginning of construction.)*

4. CANCELLATION: - This commitment may be cancelled after 60 days from the date of issuance if construction has not started, unless the mortgagee has disbursed loan proceeds.

5. PROPERTY STANDARDS: All construction, repairs, or alterations proposed in the application or on the drawings and specifications returned herewith, shall equal or exceed the HUD Minimum Property Standards.

SPECIFIC COMMITMENT CONDITIONS *(Applicable when checked)*

1. ☐ HEALTH AUTHORITY APPROVAL: - Execution of Form FHA-2573 by the Health Authority indicating approval of the water supply and/or sewage disposal installation is required. *(Approval by letter or Health Authority Form may be used.)*

2. ☒ TERMITE CONTROL: - (a) EXISTING HOUSE - Furnish certificate from a recognized termite control operator that the house and other structures within the legal boundaries of the property shows no evidence of active termite infestation. (b) PROPOSED CONSTRUCTION - Furnish one copy of Termite Soil Treatment Guarantee Form FHA-2052.

3. ☐ PREFABRICATOR'S CERTIFICATE: - Provide Prefabrication Certificate required by related Engineering Bulletin.

4. ☐ CARPET UNDERFLOORING: - Notice of subflooring or finish flooring installed under carpet shall be posted at a conspicuous location within the dwelling.

5. ☐ SUBDIVISION REQUIREMENTS: - Comply with Requirements No. _____ from Report dated _____ for _____ _____ Subdivision.

6. ☐ BUILDER'S WARRANTY: - The builder shall execute Form HUD-92544, Builder's Warranty.

7. ☐ PROPERTY INSPECTIONS: - A notice of construction status shall be given by Form FHA-2289X, letter or telephone at the time indicated below. Unless instructed otherwise, the builder may proceed with construction uninterrupted after the two day notification required in a.(1).
a. Proposed Construction Cases:
(1) ☐ Notification shall be given for all Proposed Construction Cases at least two work days before "beginning of construction" and as may be instructed below.
(2) ☐ When the building is enclosed, structural framing completely exposed and roughing in of plumbing, heating and electrical work installed and visible.
(3) ☐ When construction completed and property ready for occupancy.

b. ☐ REPAIRS: Notify FHA upon completion of required repairs.
c. ☐ CERTIFICATE OF COMPLETION: A certificate stating that the mortgagee has examined the proposed or required repairs and that they have been satisfactorily completed will be accepted.

8. ☐ VA INSPECTIONS: - Furnish a copy of a clear VA final report.

9. ☐ ASSURANCE OF COMPLETION: - If the required repairs cannot be completed prior to submission of closing papers, a Form HUD-92300 escrow in the amount of $ _____ *(or such additional amount as the lender desires)* may be established as the means to assure completion.

10. ☐ SECTION 223
This Commitment is issued under Section _____ Pursuant to Section 223e.

11. ☐ SECTION 221(d)(2)
The Maximum Insurable mortgage for a mortgagor other than a displaced family presenting a Certificate of Eligibility, FHA Form 3476, is $ _____ .

12. ☐ CODE ENFORCEMENT
Submit a statement from Public Authority that the subject property meets Code Requirements. If the mortgage encumbering the property is to be insured under Section 221(d)(2) a code compliance inspection is required.

13. ☐ The property is located in a flood hazard area as identified on the latest FIA Flood Hazard Boundary Map in effect for the community. The property must be covered by flood insurance in accordance with HUD Regulations published at 24 CFR 203.16A.

14. ☐ See special conditions No. _____ _____ below or on attached sheet.

CERTIFICATE OF COMMITMENT (FOR HUD INSURED MORTGAGE)	1. AGENCY CASE NUMBER 021-000000	2A. LENDER'S CASE NUMBER	2B. SECTION OF THE ACT (HUD Only) 203 (b)

3. NAME AND PRESENT ADDRESS OF BORROWER *(Include ZIP Code)*
BUYER, John J. & Betty J.
000 N. Hill Street
Phoenix, Arizona 85003

X   X

4A. NAME AND ADDRESS OF LENDER *(Include ZIP Code)*
FIRST FEDERAL SAVINGS & LOAN ASSOC.
3003 N. Central Ave.
Phoenix, Arizona 85012
602-248-4274

X

X

4B. ORIGINATOR'S I.D. 02014-001-4	4C. SPONSOR'S I.D.

5. PROPERTY ADDRESS INCLUDING NAME OF SUBDIVISION, LOT AND BLOCK NO., AND ZIP CODE	6A. LOAN AMOUNT	6B. INT. RATE	6C. PROPOSED MATURITY
0000 E. Indian Way Lot 0, NAVAJO ESTATES Phoenix, Arizona 85032 Maricopa County, Arizona	$ 54,000.00	15.50 %	30 YRS. 0 MOS.
	DISCOUNT: *(Only if borrower to pay)*	6D. PERCENT %	6E. AMOUNT $

☒ ACCEPTED: A note and mortgage described above or as modified below will be insured under the National Housing Act provided one of the mortgagors will be an owner-occupant and all conditions appearing in any outstanding commitment issued under the above case number and those set forth below are fulfilled.
                                                                    IMPROVED FLOOR AREA =   square feet.

☐ MODIFIED AND ACCEPTED AS FOLLOWS	Mortgage Amount $	Interest Rate %	No. of Months	Monthly Payment $	ESTIMATE OF VALUE AND CLOSING COSTS

ADDITIONAL CONDITIONS

VALUE OF PROPERTY $_____

☐ 2544 · Builders warranty required. ☐ Owner-occupancy NOT required. *(Delete (b) · Mtgrs. Cert.)*
☐ The property is to be insured under Section 221(d)(2); a code compliance inspection is required.

Closing Costs $_____

This is to certify, in compliance with the Right to Financial Privacy Act of 1978, that, in connection with any subsequent request for access to financial records for the purpose of considering or administering assistance to this applicant, the Department of Housing and Urban Development is in compliance with the applicable provisions of said Act.

DATE OF THIS COMMITMENT:

THIS COMMITMENT EXPIRES:

_____, 19 _____

_____, 19 ____
(Expiration Date)

FHA AGENT WILL SIGN
(Authorized Agent for the Federal Housing Commissioner)

PHOENIX
(Field Office)

INSTRUCTIONS TO MORTGAGEE · Forward to the HUD Field Office; (1) this commitment signed by the mortgagee and mortgagor; (2) a copy of the note or other credit instrument; (3) a copy of the mortgage or other security instrument; (4) a copy of the settlement statement, *(Form HUD-1)* signed by the mortgagee which itemizes all charges and fees collected by the mortgagee from the mortgagor and seller; and (5) HUD/FHA Mortgage Insurance Certificate completed with case number, Section of the National Housing Act, mortgage amount, property address, mortgagors' names and mortgagee's name and address. Attach Form HUD-92900 Supplement.

HUD 92900.4, JAN 1982   LENDER COPY 4

MORTGAGOR'S CERTIFICATE - The undersigned certifies that:

(a) I will not have outstanding any other unpaid obligations contracted in connection with the mortgage transaction or the purchase of the said property except obligations which are secured by property or collateral owned by me independently of the said mortgaged property, or obligations approved by the Commissioner.

(b) One of the undersigned is the occupant of the subject property. *(NOTE: Delete item (b) if owner occupancy not required by commitment.)*

(c) All charges and fees collected from me as shown in the settlement statement have been paid from my own funds, and no other charges have been or will be paid by me in respect to this transaction.

(d) Check applicable box:

☐ Amendatory clause not required in this transaction.

☐ The FHA Statement of Appraised Value or VA Certificate of Reasonable Value was given to me prior to my signing the purchase contract for the property.

☒ The FHA Statement of Appraised Value or VA Certificate of Reasonable Value was not received by me prior to my signing the contract to purchase, but the contract to purchase contained the following language: "It is expressly agreed that, notwithstanding any other provisions of this contract the purchaser shall not be obligated to complete the purchase of the property described herein or to incur any penalty by forfeiture of earnest money deposits or otherwise unless the seller has delivered to the purchaser a written statement issued by the Federal Housing Commissioner setting forth the appraised value of the property *(excluding closing costs)* of not less than $ _____ which statement the seller hereby agrees to deliver to the purchaser promptly after such appraised value statement is made available to the seller. The purchaser shall, however, have the privilege and option of proceeding with the consummation of the contract without regard to the amount of the appraised valuation made by the Federal Housing Commissioner. The appraised valuation is arrived at to determine the maximum mortgage the Department of Housing and Urban Development will insure. HUD does not warrant the value or the condition of the property. The purchaser should satisfy himself that the price and condition of the property are acceptable.

(IF THE AMENDMENT PROCEDURE WAS NECESSARY, THE DOLLAR AMOUNT USED IN THE AMENDATORY CLAUSE IS INSERTED IN THE ABOVE BLANK.)

(e) Neither I, nor anyone authorized to act for me, will refuse to sell or rent, after the making of a bona fide offer, or refuse to negotiate for the sale or rental of, or otherwise make unavailable or deny the dwelling or property covered by this loan to any person because of race, color, religion, sex, marital status or national origin. I recognize that any restrictive covenant on this property relating to race, color, religion, sex, marital status or national origin is illegal and void and any such covenant is hereby specifically disclaimed. I understand that civil action for preventative relief may be brought by the Attorney General of the United States in any appropriate U.S. District Court against any person responsible for a violation of this certification. NOTE: The interest rate shown is the FHA-VA maximum rate in effect on the date of this commitment and may increase prior to closing unless buyer and lender agree otherwise.

Signature(s): X _John J. Buyer_   X _Betty J. Buyer_   Date: _____ , 19 ____

John J. Buyer   Betty J. Buyer

MORTGAGEE'S CERTIFICATE - The undersigned certifies that to the best of its knowledge: Date: _____ , 19 ____

(a) The statements made in its application for insurance and in the Mortgagor's Certificate are true and correct to our best knowledge.

(b) The conditions listed above or appearing in any outstanding commitment issued under the above case number have been fulfilled.

(c) Complete disbursement of the loan has been made to the Mortgagor, or to his creditors for his account and with his consent.

(d) The security instrument has been recorded and is a good and valid first lien on the property described.

(e) No charge has been made to or paid by the Mortgagor except as permitted under HUD Regulations.

(f) The copies of the credit and security instruments which are submitted herewith are true and exact copies as executed and filed for record.

(g) It has not paid any kickbacks, fees or consideration of any type, directly or indirectly, on or after May 1, 1972, to any party in connection with this transaction except as permitted under Section 203.7(a)(6) of the HUD Regulations and administrative instructions issued pursuant thereto.

NOTE: If commitment is executed by an agent in name of the mortgagee, the agent must enter the mortgagee's code number and type code number in blocks below.

Code   Type

Mortgagee *(Please use FHA imprint stamp, or other approved device.)*

Signature and title of officer

COPY 5 - MORTGAGOR/MORTGAGEE CERTIFICATE – MᴏᴿTGAGEE COPY

	HOME ENERGY CHECKLIST	CASE NUMBER
VA Veterans Administration	(Attachment to VA Form 26-1843 and HUD Form 92800-5)	021-999999-203

NOTE: The amount of value shown in Item 14 of VA Form 26-1843/HUD Form 92800-5 may be increased by up to one of the following if such increase is expended for weatherization and/or energy conservation improvements to the property: (a) $2000, without a separate value determination; (b) $3500, if supported by a value determination by a designated appraiser; or, (c) more than $3500, subject to appraisal by VA or HUD, as applicable, and subsequent endorsement of the VA Certificate of Reasonable Value or HUD Conditional Commitment.

The specific areas of the property listed below are those that have been identified as potential sites where home energy can be lost. Examine those areas listed and check each that, if corrected or improved could result in energy and monetary savings for the homeowner.

AREA(S) FOR POTENTIAL ENERGY SAVINGS *(Check each applicable box)*

☐ 1. THERMOSTATS — Consideration should be given to clock thermostats.

☒ 2. WATER HEATERS — Consideration should be given to an insulation wrap.

☐ 3. HEATING/COOLING SYSTEM — Insulate ducts and pipes in unheated spaces.

☐ 4. ATTIC INSULATION — See map below for location of the property and recommended minimum insulation.
CAUTION: Do not forget to consider ventilation.

☐ 5. FLOORS AND FOUNDATION WALLS — Adequate insulation is needed:

    ☐☐ A. UNDER FLOORS   ☐☐ C. CRAWL SPACE
          B. AROUND BASEMENT   D. FOUNDATION WALLS

☒ 6. WINDOWS AND DOORS — Storm windows are recommended in areas D, E and F for all fuels and for electric heat in areas B and C (see map below). Consideration should be given to installation of

    ☒ A. WEATHER-STRIPPING/CAULKING TO PREVENT AIR   ☐ C. _____ STORM DOORS
         ESCAPES FROM OPENINGS *(Including pipes/ducts)*
    ☐ B. _____ STORM WINDOWS   ☐ D. DOUBLE OR TRIPLE GLAZED PRIME WINDOWS
                                      WITH WEATHER-STRIPPING

RECOMMENDED CEILING INSULATION BY ENERGY TYPE AND DEGREE-DAY ZONE

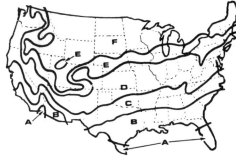

	INSULATION CONVERSION TABLE	
R VALUE	**EQUIVALENTS**	
	BATT OR BLANKET	LOOSE-FILL
19	5½ – 6½ inches	6½ – 8½ inches
22	6½ inches	7 – 9½ inches
30	9 inches	10 – 11 inches
38	12 inches	13 – 17 inches

The minimum amounts of ceiling insulation that the Department of Energy considers desirable for existing homes are listed below.

The amounts range from R-38 to R-19, according to heating degree-days and type of energy – gas, oil, or electricity – used for heating. Electricity is divided into two categories, resistance heat and the heat pump. The DOE minimums, as shown on the map, are:

     Zone A   ((0-1000 degree-days) (Includes Hawaii and Puerto Rico)) – All energy types, R-19.
     Zone B   (1001-2500 degree-days) – Gas, oil and electric heat pump, R-19. Electric resistance heat, R-22.
     Zone C   (2501-3500 degree-days) – Gas, oil and electric heat pump, R-22. Electric resistance heat, R-30.
     Zone D   (3501-6000 degree-days) – All energy types, R-30.
     Zone E   (6001-7000 degree-days) – Gas and oil, R-30. All electric heat, R-38.
     Zone F   ((7001 or more degree-days) (Includes Alaska)) – All energy types, R-38.

Duct and pipe insulation, and water heater insulation are recommended in all climate zones. Floor insulation is recommended for electric resistance heating in all zones with more than 2500 degree-days and for other energy sources and heat pumps in zones above 3500 degree-days; either R-19 or R-11 is recommended.

HIGHEST PERMISSIBLE RATE AFFIDAVIT

TO: First Federal Savings & Loan Association

RE: Borrowers: ___John J. & Betty J. Buyers___

        Address: ___0000 E. Indian Way   Phoenix, Arizona   85032___

        Legal Description: ___Lot 0, NAVAJO ESTATES___

Gentlemen:

I (we) desire to buy a home on the property described above. To enable me (us) to complete the transaction on the purchase of this home, it is necessary for me (us) to obtain a loan either guaranteed by the Veterans Administration or insured by the Department of Housing and Urban Development.

I (we) understand that interest rates on FHA and VA loans are set by the government and are subject to change from time to time without notice. Because of this, although the present maximum permissible interest rate on government loans is ___15.50___ percentage per annum, I (we) understand that this maximum rate may change by the time I (we) am (are) ready to close the loan. If this should happen, I (we) realize that it would effect First Federal's willingness to make requested loan based upon the changed market conditions and the discount points quoted to the seller in connection with the present maximum interest rate.

Therefore, as an inducement to First Federal Savings to accept my application and process my loan request for an FHA or VA loan, I (we) agree to close the loan at the highest permissible interest rate allowed by law at the time of loan closing, but in no event less than the present maximum interest rate as stated above.

_____
Name John J. Buyer

_____
Name Betty J. Buyer

_____
Date 1/25

Form Approved
OMB No. 63R-1062

VETERANS ADMINISTRATION,
U.S.D.A. FARMERS HOME ADMINISTRATION, AND
U.S.DEPARTMENT OF HOUSING AND URBAN DEVELOPMENT
HOUSING - FEDERAL HOUSING COMMISSIONER

REQUEST FOR VERIFICATION OF EMPLOYMENT

PRIVACY ACT NOTICE: This information is to be used by the agency collecting it in determining whether you qualify as a prospective mortgagor under its program. It will not be disclosed outside the agency without your consent except to your employer(s) for verification of employment and as required and permitted by law. You do not have to give us this information, but if you do not your application for approval as a prospective mortgagor may be delayed or rejected. The information requested in this form is authorized by Title 38, U.S.C., Chapter 37 (If VA); by 12 U.S.C.,Section 1701 et.seq. (If HUD/FHA) and Title 42 U.S.C., 1471 et.seq., or U.S.C., 1921 et.seq. (If U.S.D.A. FmHA).

| INSTRUCTIONS | *LENDER: Complete Items 1 through 7. Have the applicant complete item 8. Forward the completed form directly to the employer named in Item 1.* | *EMPLOYER: Complete either Parts II and IV or Parts III and IV. Return form directly to Lender named in Item 2 of Part I.* |

PART I - REQUEST

1. TO: *(Name and Address of Employer)*
   Acme Insurance Co.
   000 N. 1st Street
   Phoenix, ARizona 85003

2. FROM: *(Name and Address of Lender)*
   FIRST FEDERAL SAVINGS & LOAN ASSOC.
   3003 N. Central Ave.
   Phoenix, Arizona 85012

3. *I certify that this verification has been sent directly to the employer and has not passed through the hands of the applicant or any other interested party.*

   _____
   (Signature of Lender)

4. TITLE OF LENDER

5. DATE 1/21/82

6. FHA,VA, or FmHA NUMBER

I have applied for a mortgage loan and stated that I am/was employed by you. My signature in the block below authorizes verification of my employment information.

7. NAME AND ADDRESS OF APPLICANT
   JOHN J. BUYER
   000 N. HIll Street
   Phoenix, Arizona 85003

8. EMPLOYEE'S IDENTIFICATION

   John J Buyer
   SIGNATURE OF APPLICANT

PART II - VERIFICATION OF PRESENT EMPLOYMENT

| EMPLOYMENT DATA | PAY DATA |

9. APPLICANT'S DATE OF EMPLOYMENT
   11/30/77

12A. BASE PAY IS $ 2,083.00
☐ ANNUAL ☐ HOURLY
☒ MONTHLY ☐ WEEKLY
☐ OTHER *(Specify)*

FOR MILITARY PERSONNEL ONLY

Type	Monthly Amount
BASE PAY	$
RATIONS	$
FLIGHT OR HAZARD	$
CLOTHING	$
QUARTERS	$
PRO PAY	$
OVERSEAS OR COMBAT	$

10. PRESENT POSITION
    Field Representative

11. PROBABILITY OF CONTINUED EMPLOYMENT
    Excellent

12B. EARNINGS

Type	Year to Date	Past Year
BASE PAY	$ 2083.00	$ 24,996.00
OVERTIME	$	$
COMMISSIONS	$	$
BONUS	$	$

13. IF OVERTIME OR BONUS IS APPLICABLE, IS ITS CONTINUANCE LIKELY?

   OVERTIME ☐ Yes ☐ No
   BONUS ☐ Yes ☐ No

14. REMARKS *(If paid hourly, please indicate average hours worked each week during current and past year)*

PART III - VERIFICATION OF PREVIOUS EMPLOYMENT

15. DATES OF EMPLOYMENT

16. SALARY/WAGE AT TERMINATION PER (YEAR) (MONTH) (WEEK)

   $_____ BASE $_____ OVERTIME $_____ COMMISSIONS $_____ BONUS

17. REASONS FOR LEAVING

18. POSITION HELD

PART IV - CERTIFICATION

"Federal statutes provide severe penalties for any fraud, intentional misrepresentation, or criminal connivance or conspiracy purposed to influence the issuance of any guaranty or insurance by the VA Administrator, the HUD/FHA Commissioner, or the USDA Farmers Home Administrator."

19. SIGNATURE
    John James

20. TITLE OF EMPLOYER
    Personnel

21. DATE
    1/27/82

Previous Editions are Obsolete

HUD-92004-g VA-26-8497; FmHA-410-5 (12-79)

RETURN DIRECTLY TO SENDER

ML-778 (5-80)   ***This form must be signed by an officer of the company or the employee's immediate supervisor.

Form Approved
OMB No. 63R-1062

PRIVACY ACT NOTICE: This information is to be used by the agency collecting it in determining whether you qualify as a prosepctive mortgagor under its program. It will not be disclosed outside the agency without your consent except to your employer(s) for verification of employment and as required and permitted by law. You do not have to give us this information, but if you do not your application for approval as a prospective mortgagor may be delayed or rejected. The information requested in this form is authorized by Title 38, U.S.C., Chapter 37 (If VA); by 12 U.S.C.,Section 1701 et.seq. (If HUD/FHA) and Title 42 U.S.C., 1471 et.seq., or U.S.C., 1921 et.seq. (If U.S.D.A. FmHA).	VETERANS ADMINISTRATION, U.S.D.A. FARMERS HOME ADMINISTRATION, AND U.S.DEPARTMENT OF HOUSING AND URBAN DEVELOPMENT HOUSING - FEDERAL HOUSING COMMISSIONER **REQUEST FOR VERIFICATION OF EMPLOYMENT**
INSTRUCTIONS *LENDER: Complete Items 1 through 7. Have the applicant complete item 8. Forward the completed form directly to the employer named in Item 1.*	*EMPLOYER: Complete either Parts II and IV or Parts III and IV. Return form directly to Lender named in Item 2 of Part I.*

PART I - REQUEST

1. TO: *(Name and Address of Employer)* PENNEY'S DEPT. STORE 000 Main Street Phoenix, Arizona 85000	2. FROM: *(Name and Address of Lender)* FIRST FEDERAL SAVINGS & LOAN ASSOC. 3003 N. Central Ave. Phoenix, Arizona 85012		
3. I certify that this verification has been sent directly to the employer and has not passed through the hands of the applicant or any other interested party. _____ *(Signature of Lender)*	4. TITLE OF LENDER	5. DATE 1/21/82	
	6. FHA,VA, or FmHA NUMBER		
7. NAME AND ADDRESS OF APPLICANT BUYER, Betty J. 000 N. Hill Street Phoenix, Arizona 85003	*I have applied for a mortgage loan and stated that I am/was employed by you. My signature in the block below authorizes verification of my employment information.* 8. EMPLOYEE'S IDENTIFICATION *Betty J. Buyer* SIGNATURE OF APPLICANT		

PART II - VERIFICATION OF PRESENT EMPLOYMENT

EMPLOYMENT DATA	PAY DATA		

9. APPLICANT'S DATE OF EMPLOYMENT 6/1/78	12A. BASE PAY IS $ 6.07 ☐ ANNUAL ☒ HOURLY ☐ MONTHLY ☐ WEEKLY ☐ OTHER *(Specify)*	FOR MILITARY PERSONNEL ONLY	
10. PRESENT POSITION Ass't Shoe Buyer		Type	Monthly Amount
		BASE PAY	$
11. PROBABILITY OF CONTINUED EMPLOYMENT Excellent	12B. EARNINGS	RATIONS	$
	Type / Year to Date / Past Year	FLIGHT OR HAZARD	$
	BASE PAY $ 1052.13 $12,625.56	CLOTHING	$
13. IF OVERTIME OR BONUS IS APPLICABLE, IS ITS CONTINUANCE LIKELY? OVERTIME ☐ Yes ☐ No BONUS ☐ Yes ☐ No	OVERTIME $ $	QUARTERS	$
	COMMISSIONS $ $	PRO PAY	$
	BONUS $ $	OVERSEAS OR COMBAT	$
14. REMARKS *(If paid hourly, please indicate average hours worked each week during current and past year)* 40 hour week			

PART III - VERIFICATION OF PREVIOUS EMPLOYMENT

15. DATES OF EMPLOYMENT	16.SALARY/WAGE AT TERMINATION PER (YEAR) (MONTH) (WEEK)		
	$ _____ BASE	$ _____ OVERTIME	$ _____ COMMISSIONS	$ _____ BONUS
17. REASONS FOR LEAVING	18. POSITION HELD		

PART IV - CERTIFICATION

"Federal statutes provide severe penalties for any fraud, intentional misrepresentation, or criminal connivance or conspiracy purposed to influence the issuance of any guaranty or insurance by the VA Administrator, the HUD/FHA Commissioner, or the USDA Farmers Home Administrator."

19. SIGNATURE Ruth Jones	20. TITLE OF EMPLOYER Personnel	21. DATE 1/28/82

Previous Editions are Obsolete

RETURN DIRECTLY TO SENDER

HUD-92004-g VA-26-8497; FmHA-410-5 (12-79)

ML-778 (5-80)   ***This form must be signed by an officer of the company or the employee's immediate supervisor.

FHA FORM NO. 2004-F (Rev. 12/75) VA FORM NO. 26-8497a (Rev. 12/75)	VETERANS ADMINISTRATION AND U.S. DEPARTMENT OF HOUSING AND URBAN DEVELOPMENT FEDERAL HOUSING ADMINISTRATION	OMB NO. 63-R0266 Approval Expires 4/76

REQUEST FOR VERIFICATION OF DEPOSIT

INSTRUCTIONS: LENDER - Complete Items 1 through 7. Have applicant complete Items 8 and 9. Forward directly to bank or other depository named in Item 1.

BANK or DEPOSITORY - Please complete Items 10 through 13. Return directly to Lender named in Item 2.

Right to Financial Privacy Act of 1978 authorizes financial institutions to release financial information to the Veteran's Administration or the Federal Housing Administration in connection with a customer's request for an FHA Insured or VA Guaranteed loan. FHA, VA and this institution are in compliance with the applicable provisions of the law.

PART I - REQUEST

1. TO: (Name and Address of Bank or other Depository)

FIRST FEDERAL SAVINGS & LOAN ASSOC.
3003 N. Central Ave.
Phoenix, Arizona 85012

2. FROM: (Name and Address of Lender)

FIRST FEDERAL SAVINGS & LOAN ASSOC.
3003 N. Central Ave.
Phoenix, Arizona 85012

3. I certify that this verification has been sent directly to the bank or other depository and has not passed through the hands of the applicant or any other interested party.

Signature of Lender:

4. Title: Loan Processor

5. Date: 1/21/82

6. FHA or VA Number:

7. STATEMENT OF APPLICANT:

7A. Name and Address of Applicant:

BUYER, John J. & Betty J.
000 N. Hill Street
Phoenix, Arizona 85003

7B. TYPE OF ACCOUNT	BALANCE	ACCOUNT NUMBER
CHECKING	$ 12.00	0000-0000
SAVINGS	$ 10,000.00	111111
CERTIFICATE OF DEPOSIT	$	

8. I have applied for a mortgage loan and stated that I maintain account(s) with the bank or other depository named in Item 1. My signature below authorizes that bank or other depository to furnish the lender named in Item 2 the information set forth in Part II. Your response is solely a matter of courtesy for which no responsibility is attached to your institution or any of your officers.

John J. Buyer
Signature of Applicant

7C. TYPE OF LOAN	BALANCE	ACCOUNT NUMBER
SECURED	$	
UNSECURED	$	

9. Date:

PART II - VERIFICATION

10A. Does Applicant have any outstanding loans?
☐ Yes ☐ No (If Yes, enter total in Item 10B.)

10B. TYPE OF LOAN	MONTHLY PAYMENT	PRESENT BALANCE
SECURED	$	$
UNSECURED	$	$

10C. Payment Experience:
☐ Favorable
☐ Unfavorable (If Unfavorable, explain in Remarks.)

CURRENT STATUS OF ACCOUNTS			
	CHECKING	SAVINGS	CERT. of DEPOSIT
11A. Is account less than two months old? (If Yes, give date account was opened in Item 12B)	☒ Yes ☐ No	☒ Yes ☐ No	☐ Yes ☐ No
11B. Date the account was opened.	2/25/80	3/20/81	
11C. Present Balance	$ 13.01	$11,002.21	$
11D. Is account other than individual, e.g., Joint or Trust? (If Yes, explain in Remarks.)	☐ Yes ☐ No	☐ Yes ☐ No	☐ Yes ☐ No
11E. Is account satisfactory?	☐ Yes ☐ No		☐ Yes ☐ No

12. REMARKS:

Please return both copies of this verification to lender.

The above information is provided in response to your request.

13A. Signature of Official of Bank or other Depository:	13B. Title:	13C. Date:
Joe Banker	Operations Teller	1/29/82

THIS INFORMATION IS FOR THE SOLE PURPOSE OF ASSISTING THE APPLICANT IN OBTAINING A MORTGAGE LOAN.
RETURN DIRECTLY TO LENDER

c43—16—83508-1 GPO

ML-779 (5-79)

standard factual data report — CREDCO

FILE NO:	PREPARED FOR:			ATTENTION:		ACCOUNT NO.
	FIRST FEDERAL SAVINGS AND LOAN			TERI		

DATE COMPLETED	DATE RECEIVED	FHA NO.			CHARGES	
1-25-82	1-21-82	02014-001-4	BASE 27.00	NON LOCAL	MISC 12.00 SPOUSAL	

SUBJECT(S):

BUYER, JOHN J. (BETTY)
000 N. HILL STREET (1 YEAR)
PHOENIX, ARIZONA

This STANDARD FACTUAL DATA REPORT meets all underwriting requirements set by: US Department of H.U.D. (FHA): US Veteran's Administration (VA): Federal National Mortgage Association (FNMA): and Federal Home Loan Mortgage Corporation (FHLMC).

YES	Do name & address agree with those on application?
28	Approximate age of subject
MARRIED −0−	Marital Status — number of dependents
3-7-81	Length of time married
ACME INSURANCE COMPANY	Employer
FIELD REPRESENTATIVE	Position held
4 YEARS	Approximate length of present employment
NO	Has employment status changed in the past two years?
$2083	Monthly Income
NONE	Approximate income, if any, from other sources
PENNEY'S	Employer
ASSISTANT BUYER	Position held
3 YEARS	Approximate length of present employment
NO	Has employment status changed in the past two years?
$1052	Monthly Income
NONE	Approximate income, if any, from other sources

REMARKS: 1. Amplify business history (This report shall contain information as to the subject's previous employment status, if there has been a change in employment status within the past two years.)
2. The reporting bureau certifies (a) ☒ public records have been checked for suits, judgements, foreclosures, garnishments, bankruptcies, and other legal actions involving the subject with the results indicated below, or (b) ☐ equivalent information has been obtained through use of a qualified public records report; ing service with the results indicated below. (Give details.) (The records of real estate transfers which do not involve foreclosure may be excluded.)
3. The reporting bureau certifies that the subject's credit record in the payment of bills and other obligations has been checked; (a) ☒ through the credit accounts extended by the designated credit grantors under the Classes and Trades identified in the contract for the community in which the subject resides, with the results indicated below, or (b) ☒ through accumulated credit records at such credit grantors of the community in which the subject resides, with the results indicated below.
4. (No reference shall be made in this report to race, creed, color, or national origin.)

TRADE LINES	DATE OPENED	HIGHEST CREDIT	TERMS	BALANCE	PAYING HABITS
VISA/0000000000000	1980	500L	REV	500	SATIS
TRANSAMERICA FINANCE/000000000	7-80	816	34	238	SATIS
MCMAHANS/000000000	1-81	LOW 4	38	1018	SATIS
THE FOLLOWING REPRESENT SPOUSAL CREDIT:					
FIRST INTERSTATE BANK/0000000000	6-79	6300	131	2231	SATIS
ARIZONA CENTRAL C.U./00000	6-78	1500L	REV	−0−	SATIS

INQUIRIES IN THE LAST 90 DAYS: NONE

PREVIOUS RESIDENCE: 000 N. CENTER − 8 MONTHS

HUSBAND'S PREVIOUS RESIDENCE: 0000 INDIAN BLEND − 1 YEAR

WIFE'S PREVIOUS RESIDENCE: 0000 SNOW − 8 YEARS

PUBLIC RECORDS: NONE

LOCAL REPOSITORY CHECKED

JS

222 W. OSBORN • P.O. BOX 16101 • PHOENIX, AZ 85011 • TELEPHONE (602) 248-7952

U.S. DEPARTMENT OF HOUSING AND URBAN DEVELOPMENT
HOUSING — FEDERAL HOUSING COMMISSIONER

Mortgage Insurance Certificate

Section
203B

FHA Case No.

021-000000-203

Mortgagor's Name *(Last Name First)*

BUYER, JOHN J

Property Address

0000 E Indian Way

City, State and ZIP Code

Phoenix, AZ   85032

02014-001-4
FIRST FEDERAL SAVINGS
3003 N Central Ave
Phoenix, AZ   85012

MORTGAGEE'S NAME AND ADDRESS

Mortgage Amount

$54,000.00

This Certificate, when endorsed in the block below, is evidence of insurance of the mortgage loan described herein under the indicated Section of the National Housing Act *(12 USC 1701 et seq.)* and Regulations of the Department of Housing and Urban Development Published at 24 CFR 200.1 et.seq.

Endorsed for insurance by an Authorized Agent of the Federal Housing Commissioner.

William Wilson

(Signature)

1/25

(Date)

(REMOVE CERTIFICATE BEFORE SIGNING)

Previous Edition is Obsolete

HUD-59100.1 (1-81)

247

F **First Federal**

FHA
ESCROW INSTRUCTIONS

To: TITLE INSURANCE CO
Escrow Officer   SALLY ESCROW
JOHN J BUYER AND BETTY J BUYER
000 N Hill St   Phoenix,AZ

Escrow No: 27,000,000   at   MAIN   Office
                         19 82   regarding escrow
              June 24   herein called Borrower whose address is
Phone 248-0000   First Federal Savings,

herein called Lender, whose address is: 3003 N Central Ave   Phoenix,AZ   85012
hereby employs the above title company to act as Escrow Agent in connection with a real estate loan made by Lender to Borrower
in the sum of: $54,000.00

Loan Closer: Address: 3003 N Central Ave   Phone: 248-0000

ESCROW INSTRUCTIONS: ALL DOCUMENTS MUST BE PROPERLY EXECUTED (AND NOTARIZED WHERE REQUIRED)
The signed original of each is to be returned to the Lender and one copy each may be distributed to the Borrower when applicable.
DO NOT MAKE ANY CHANGES, ALTERATIONS OR ADDITIONS TO OUR DOCUMENTS. Cash down payment plus closing costs
must be deposited in this escrow. Borrower(s) to sign all documents as typed **ALL DOCUMENTS MUST BE RETURNED TO US FOR**
APPROVAL PRIOR TO THE DEED OF TRUST BEING RECORDED AND FUNDS DISBURSED.

___**X**___ Disclosure Statement to be executed and **DATED PRIOR** to any of the following:
_____ Notice of Right of Rescission. Comply with C on reverse.
___**X**___ Note.
___**X**___ Loan Settlement Statement.
___**X**___ Copy of executed Deed of Trust is required for review prior to recording.
___**X**___ Prepare Disclosure Settlement Statement (HUD Form 1). Original to Borrower, and executed copy to Lender with completed
         Affidavit of Delivery (attached). Comply with A on reverse.
___**X**___ Original Insurance Policy for not less than $ 54,000.00   [xx] HAZARD   [ ] FLOOD
         Fire Insurance must be acceptable to Lender with a Best Guide Rating of **A CLASS X**   . Comply with E on reverse.
___**X**___ Order Tax Service from Transamerica Real Estate Tax Service. [X] C [ ] B Type Service for   **30**   years. PAY FEE.
_____ Proof of sale of present home (copy of Closing Statement).
___**X**___ FHA Form 2900-4 (Firm Commitment), dated by Borrower. (Return both copies.)
___**X**___ Provide CLEAR Termite Inspection Report. Must be original signed by examiner, license holder & Borrower.
_____ Provide 5-year Termite Soil Treatment Guarantee, FHA Form 2052. Must be orignal signed by company official.
_____ Certification of Proof of Flood Insurance from insurance agent.
_____ Warranty of Completion executed by Borrower and Contractor.
_____ Provide Clear ASP-9 Report.
_____ Provide Code Compliance Inspection.
_____ Provide CLEAR Inspection Report. [ ] Carpet Cushioning [ ] Landscaping Certification to be signed by Contractor.
_____ One and the Same Letter.
___**X**___ Address Information;

TITLE COMPANY INSTRUCTIONS:
___**X**___ COMMITMENT ON POINTS WILL EXPIRE   **July 1, 1982**   IF NOT FUNDED BY THIS DATE,
         CALL CLOSER.
Collect fees and expenses from Borrower. NOTE: Borrower is permitted to pay 1% Origination Fee. Seller must pay Discount Fee, Tax
    Service Fee, Escrow Fee, Termite Inspection Fee, Document Preparation Fee, and Warehouse Fee, if applicable.
YOU ARE INSTRUCTED TO COLLECT ANY AND ALL PAYMENTS WHICH BECOME DUE PRIOR TO CLOSE OF ESCROW.
Deliver copy of FHA appraisal to Borrower.
Title must be vested at time of closing in the name(s) of the Trustor(s) cited in our Deed of Trust, and the recording of the Deed of
    Trust is conditioned upon First Federal Savings receiving ALTA Title Insurance Policy for $54,000.00   , the amount of
    our loan, INSURING OUR DEED OF TRUST AS A VALID FIRST LIEN subject only to the following as set forth in the
    Preliminary Title Report approved by First Federal Savings:
         City and County Taxes - PAY   **all 1981**   taxes and all prior
         Pay improvement liens in full.
Upon recording the Deed of Trust, issue an ALTA Title Policy in DUPLICATE with a schedule of subordinate items and endorsements
3R and 5 without deletion. SHOW LENDER LOAN NUMBER ON THE TITLE POLICY WHEN ISSUED. Any assessments, liens, and
charges on Schedule B to state: ALL ASSESSMENTS DUE AND PAYABLE ARE PAID.

SEE REVERSE SIDE FOR ADDITIONAL INSTRUCTIONS

ML-667b FHA (5-81)   TITLE CO. - White   FILE COPY - Canary

FHA'S DEBT RATIO CALCULATION

BORROWER BUYER, JOHN J. & BETTY J.   **LOAN AMOUNT** $ 54,000.00

A. Mortgagor's Base Pay	2,083.00	B. P & I	704.44	
Co-Mortgagor Base Pay	1,052.13	MIP	22.49	
Other Income	n/a	1 Mo. Ins.	15.00	
Total Earnings	3,135.13	1 Mo. taxes	28.00	
Minus Federal Tax	486.00	Maintenance	21.00	
ADJUSTED MO. INCOME	2,649.13	(A) Utilities	125.00	
		TOTAL HOUSING EXPENSE	915.93	(B)
C. Payments over 6 mo.		D. State Income Tax (10% of Federal Tax)	48.60	
Payment	Balance	Total Mo. Obligations from "C"	190.00	
		Social Security (.0670* × Gross Earnings)	210.05	
		Retirement (If city or state employee)		
		Total Fixed pymt	448.65	(D)
(C)		E. Total Housing Expense (B)	915.93	
TOTAL MONTHLY	TOTAL BALANCE	Total Fixed + Pymt (D)	448.65	
To find the percentage—divide the greater figure into the lesser figure		Total Fixed Obligation	1,364.58	

$$\frac{\text{TOTAL HOUSING EXPENSE (B)}}{\text{ADJUSTED MONTHLY INCOME (A)}} = \frac{915.93}{2,649.13} = 35 \ \% \quad \text{(No more than 35\%)}$$

$$\frac{\text{TOTAL FIXED OBLIGATIONS (E)}}{\text{ADJUSTED MONTHLY INCOME (A)}} = \frac{1,364.58}{2,649.13} = 52 \ \% \quad \text{(No more than 50\%)}$$

Section A will be the same as Section II on 2900 application.
Section B will be the same as Section 13,

FHA'S GUIDELINES ARE 35% and 50% AT THE TOP OF THE RANGE.
*If self employed the social security factor would be .0935%.

Ⓕ / FIRST FEDERAL SAVINGS

HAZARD INSURANCE - FLOOD INSURANCE

Name ·BUYER, John J. & Betty J.   Loan Officer _____

Property Address   0000 E. Indian Way   Branch   Home office

Legal Description Lot 0, NAVAJO ESTATES   Phone   602-248-4146

In accordance with regulations, First Federal Savings requires a hazard insurance policy for fire and extended coverage in the minimum amount of our loan as a condition for granting your loan request. The first year's premium must be prepaid in advance and may be paid directly to your agent or collected at the close of escrow. Thereafter, 1/12th the annual premium will be collected in your regular monthly payment (See Part A).

In addition to hazard insurance, flood insurance may be required if your property lies in a HUD designated flood hazard area (See Part B).

A.   HAZARD INSURANCE

We will require the following information as soon as possible:

Company Allstate Insurance Co.   Agent Bill Smith   Phone 602-000-0000

Coverage Amount 55,000.00   Premium 167.00   Effective Date   close of escrow
Please contact your insurance agent for this information and notify the loan officer above. The policy should be sent to the following title company, with a copy of a paid receipt if the premium has been paid, prior to your scheduled close of escrow.

    Escrow Co., Inc.   Attn: Sheila Officer
    Title Company & Address   Escrow Officer
The hazard insurance policy should contain the following mortgagee clause:
"First Federal Savings, and or their assigns, as their interests may appear, P.O. Box 2235, Phoenix, AZ 85002."

B.   NOTICE TO BORROWER OF SPECIAL FLOOD HAZARD

[X]   FLOOD INSURANCE IS OPTIONAL - First Federal Savings hereby notifies you that the above described property does not lie in a designated Flood Hazard area as determined by the Secretary of Housing and Urban Development.

[ ]   FLOOD INSURANCE IS REQUIRED - Notice is given to _____ that the improved real estate or mobile home described in the attached instrument is or will be located in an area designated by the Secretary of the Department of Housing and Urban Development as a special flood hazard area. This area is delineated on _____ 's Flood Insurance Rate Map (FIRM) or, if the FIRM is unavailable, on the Flood Hazard Boundary Rate Map (FHBM). This area has a 1% chance of being flooded within any given year. The risk of exceeding the 1% chance increases with time periods longer than one year. For example, during the life of a 30 year mortgage, a structure located in a special flood hazard area has a 26% chance of being flooded.

We will require the following information as soon as possible:

Company _____   Agent _____   Phone _____

Coverage Amount _____   Premium _____ Effective Date _____
Please contact your insurance agent for this information and notify the loan officer above. The policy should be sent to the title company and escrow officer in Part A above with a copy of a paid receipt if the premium has been paid, prior to your scheduled close of escrow.

The flood insurance policy should contain the following mortgagee clause:
"First Federal Savings, and or their assigns, as their interests may appear, P.O. Box 2235, Phoenix, AZ 85002."

NOTICE TO BORROWER ABOUT FEDERAL FLOOD DISASTER ASSISTANCE

Lender Check One:

[X]   NOTICE IN PARTICIPATING COMMUNITIES - The improved real estate or mobile home securing your loan is or will be located in a community which is now participating in the National Flood Insurance Program. In the event your property is damaged by flooding in a Federally declared disaster, Federal disaster relief may be available. However, such relief will be unavailable if your community is not participating in the National Flood Insurance Program at the time such assistance would be approved (assuming your community has been identified as flood-prone for at least one year). This assistance, usually in the form of a loan with a favorable interest rate, may be available for damages incurred in excess of your flood insurance.

[ ]   NOTICE IN NONPARTICIPATING COMMUNITIES - The improved real estate or mobile home securing your loan is or will be located in a community which is not participating in the National Flood Insurance Program. This means that you are not eligible for Federal flood insurance. In the event your property is damaged by flooding in a Federally declared disaster, Federal disaster relief will be unavailable (assuming your community has been identified as flood-prone for at least one year). Federal flood disaster relief will be available only if your community is participating in the National Flood Insurance Program at the time such assistance would be approved.

Determination of Flood Hazard Area: Receipt of the Foregoing Notice Acknowledged by the
FIRST FEDERAL SAVINGS   Undersigned.

By _Paul Smith_   _John J. Buyer_
                                        John J. Buyer
Its: _Loan Officer/Agent_   _Betty J. Buyer_
                                        Betty J. Buyer
Date _1/20/82_   Date _____

ML-234 (3-78)   WHITE: Association Copy   CANARY: Customer Copy   PINK: Insurance Agent Copy

FIRST FEDERAL SAVINGS

DEED OF TRUST
REAL ESTATE LOAN
DISCLOSURE STATEMENT

LOAN NO. 012999999
NAME(S) of BORROWER   JOHN J BUYER BETTY J BUYER

MAILING ADDRESS: 0000 E Indian Way   Phoenix, AZ 85032

1. First Federal Savings, whose home office address is 3003 N. Central Ave., Phoenix, Az. 85012, hereinafter called "Lender," will lend to the "Borrower" the sum of $54,000.00   hereinafter referred to as the "Loan Amount."

2. The following PREPAID FINANCE CHARGE must be paid by or on behalf of Borrower at the loan closing:

3. The following itemized charges are either included in the amount financed or must be paid separately by Borrower. They are not a part of the finance charge:

ORIGINATION FEE	$ 540.00	(C) ANNUAL HAZ INS PREM	$ 180.00*
PREPAID INTEREST	$ 116.25 *	(C) RECORDING FEE	$ 8.00*
TAX SERVICE FEE	$ 22.50	(C) ESCROW FEE	$ 164.00*
DISCOUNT FEE	$2,700.00	(C) TITLE INSURANCE PREM	$ 158.00*
DOCUMENT PREP FEE	$ 35.00	(C) APPRAISAL FEE	$ 35.00
		(C) COUNTY TAX IMPOUND	$ 85.00
		(F) CREDIT REPORT FEE	$ 140.35
		(F) HAZARD INS IMPOUND	$ 30.00
		(F) MORTGAGE INSURANCE IMP	$ 22.49

Total PREPAID FINANCE CHARGE $3,413.75 *

4. Property insurance (fire and extended coverage) ☐ and, if box is marked, flood insurance is/are required and may be purchased through any person of Borrower's choice who is acceptable to Lender.

5. Amount financed: Loan Amount (Item 1) minus total PREPAID FINANCE CHARGE (Item 2) $ 50,586.25*

6. The total **FINANCE CHARGE** consists of:

PREPAID FINANCE CHARGES (Item 2)	$ 3,413.75*
interest at 15.500 % per annum included in monthly payments.	$199,598.40
MORTGAGE INSURANCE PREMIUMS INCLUDED IN MONTHLY PAYMENTS	$ 6,376.64
TOTAL FINANCE CHARGE	$209,388.79*

7. The **ANNUAL PERCENTAGE RATE** of the FINANCE CHARGE is   17.00%.

8. Borrower will pay the loan amount plus interest in 360 monthly payments, payable on the 1st day of each month beginning August 1, 1982, in the amount of $704.44. Additional amounts for Mortgage Insurance Premiums will be required in all payments. These additional amounts will range from $22.49* in the first payment due August 1, 1982 to $1.30* in the payment due July 1, 2012, which is the last payment due. The total of all monthly payments is $259,975.04*.

9. **FINANCE CHARGES** will begin to accrue on the date lender disburses the loan proceeds, estimated to be   June 26, 1982*

10. LATE CHARGE - 4.000% of the monthly installment if the payment is not received within 15 days after the installment is due.

11. Security interest. Lender's security interest in this transaction is a first deed of trust on property located at
0000 E Indian Way   Phoenix, AZ 85032
more particularly described in the copy of the first deed of trust attached hereto. Said security interest covers all after-acquired property now or hereafter on, in or attached to the aforesaid property and any future advances, the terms of which are described in the deed of trust. Regardless of any other existing agreement between Borrower and Lender, this loan will not be secured except as indicated above. Lender hereby specifically waives its right of offset as security for this loan.

12. PREPAYMENT PENALTY - NONE

The document preparation fee charged above is for the preparation of loan documents other than those required by the Consumer Credit Protection Act.

I acknowledge receipt of a completed copy of this statement on   , 19   , prior to the execution of the note and/or first deed of trust.

John J. Buyer
John J Buyer

Betty J. Buyer
Betty J Buyer

*ASTERISK, IF USED, DENOTES ESTIMATE.

ML-312 (6-80)   WHITE: Original   CANARY: Customer(s)

LOAN NUMBER		FHA CASE NUMBER
012999999	**NOTE**	021-000000-203

(To be used with Deed of Trust or Mortgage)

$ 54,000.00   PHOENIX   , Arizona

JUNE 24,   , ¹⁹82

FOR VALUE RECEIVED, I, or We, promise to pay to **FIRST FEDERAL SAVINGS,**
A FEDERALLY CHARTERED ASSOCIATION
or order, the principal sum of **FIFTY FOUR THOUSAND AND NO/100**

Dollars ($ **54,000.00**   ),

with interest from date at the rate of **FIFTEEN AND ONE-HALF**   per
centum (**15.500**   %) per annum on the unpaid balance until paid. Said principal and interest shall be
payable at the office of

    FIRST FEDERAL SAVINGS   **3003 N Central Ave**

in **Phoenix, AZ 85012**
or at such other place as the holder hereof may designate in writing, in monthly installments of

    SEVEN HUNDRED FOUR AND 44/100

Dollars ($ **704.44**   ), commencing on the first day of **August, 1982**   , and on the
first day of each month thereafter until the principal and interest are fully paid, except that the final payment
of principal and interest, if not sooner paid, shall be due and payable on the first day of

    If default be made in the payment of any installment under this note, and if default is not made good
.prior to the due date of the next such installment, the entire principal sum and accrued interest shall at once
become due and payable without notice at the option of the holder of this note. Failure to exercise this option
shall not constitute a waiver of the right to exercise the same in the event of any subsequent default.

    I, or We, agree to pay all costs incurred in the collection thereof, including a reasonable attorney's fee.
Principal and interest payable in lawful money of the United States.

    No extension of time for the payment of this note or any installment hereof made by agreement with any
person now or hereafter liable for the payment of this note shall operate to release, discharge, modify, change
or affect the original liability under this note, either in whole or in part, of any of the undersigned not a party
to such agreement.

    I, or We, and each of us, whether principal, surety, guarantor or endorser, agree to be jointly and severally
bound, and I, or We, severally waive any homestead or exemption right against said debt and waive demand,
protest and notice of demand, protest and nonpayment.

_____   _____
John J Buyer   Betty J Buyer

_____   _____

ML-369 (2-79)   **WHITE: Original**   **CANARY: Customer**   **GREEN: FHA**   **PINK: File Copy**

STATE OF ARIZONA

	This form is used in connection with deeds of trust insured under the one- to four-family provisions of the National Housing Act.

DEED OF TRUST

With Assignment of Rents

THIS DEED OF TRUST, made this ___24th___ day of _____ JUNE _____, 19 82,

BETWEEN _____ JOHN J BUYER AND BETTY J BUYER, HUSBAND AND WIFE _____

_____ , as TRUSTOR,

whose mailing address is ___ 0000 E Indian Way _____ PHOENIX, AZ _____ 85032
(Street and number)   (City)   (State)

FIRST SERVICE CORPORATION, AN ARIZONA CORPORATION _____

3003 N Central Ave   Phoenix, Arizona   85012 _____ , as TRUSTEE, and

FIRST FEDERAL SAVINGS, A FEDERALLY CHARTERED ASSOCIATION _____

3003 N Central Ave   Phoenix, Arizona   85012 _____ , as BENEFICIARY.

WITNESSETH: That Trustor irrevocably GRANTS, TRANSFERS, and ASSIGNS to TRUSTEE IN TRUST, WITH POWER OF SALE,

the property in _____ MARICOPA _____ County, Arizona, described as:

LOT 0, NAVAJO ESTATES, ACCORDING TO BOOK 00 OF MAPS, PAGE 00, RECORDS OF
MARICOPA COUNTY, ARIZONA

PROPERTY ADDRESS: 0000 E Indian Way   Phoenix, AZ 85032

TOGETHER WITH the rents, issues, and profits thereof, SUBJECT, HOWEVER, to the right, power, and authority hereinafter given to and conferred upon Beneficiary to collection and apply such rents, issues, and profits;

FOR THE PURPOSE OF SECURING Performance of each agreement of Trustor herein contained and payment of the sum of

FIFTY FOUR THOUSAND AND NO/100 ---

$ 54,000.00 with interest thereon according to the terms of a promissory note of even date herewith, payable to Beneficiary or order and made by Trustor.

1. Privilege is reserved to pay the debt secured hereby in whole or in an amount equal to one or more principal payments next due on the note, on the first day of any month prior to maturity, provided written notice of intention so to do is given at least thirty days prior to prepayment

2. Trustor agrees to pay to Beneficiary in addition to the monthly payments of principal and interest payable under the terms of said note, on the first day of each month until said note is fully paid, the following sums:

a. An amount sufficient to provide the holder hereof with funds to pay the next mortgage insurance premium if this instrument and the note secured hereby are insured, or a monthly charge (in lieu of a mortgage insurance premium) if they are held by the Secretary, Department of Housing and Urban Development, as follows:

(I) If and so long as said note of even date and this instrument are insured or are reinsured under the provisions of the National Housing Act, an amount sufficient to accumulate in the hands of the holder one (1) month prior to its due date the annual mortgage insurance premium, in order to provide such holder with funds to pay such premium to the Secretary, Department of Housing and Urban Development pursuant to the National Housing Act, as amended, and applicable Regulations thereunder; or

(II) If and so long as said note of even date and this instrument are held by the Secretary, Department of Housing and Urban Development, a monthly charge (in lieu of a mortgage insurance premium) which shall be in an amount equal to one-twelfth (1/12) of one-half (1/2) per centum of the average outstanding balance due on the note computed without taking into account delinquencies or prepayments;

b. An installment of the ground rents, if any, and of the taxes and special assessments levied or to be levied against the premises covered by this Deed of Trust; and an installment of the premium or premiums that will become due and payable to renew the insurance on the premises covered hereby against loss by fire or such other hazard as may be required by Beneficiary in amounts and in a company or companies satisfactory to Beneficiary; trustor agreeing to deliver promptly to Beneficiary all bills and notices therefor. Such installments shall be equal respectively to one-twelfth (1/12) of the annual ground rent, if any, plus the estimated premium or premiums for such insurance, and taxes and assessments next due (as estimated by Beneficiary) less all installments already paid therefor, divided by the number of months that are to elapse before one month prior to the date when such premium or premiums and taxes and assessments will become delinquent. Beneficiary shall hold such payments in trust to pay such ground rents, premium or premiums and taxes and special assessments before the same become delinquent; and

c. All payments mentioned in the two preceding subsections of this paragraph and all payments to be made under the note secured hereby shall be added together and the aggregate amount thereof shall be paid each month in a single payment to be applied by Beneficiary to the following items in the order set forth:

(I) premium charges under the contract of insurance with the Secretary, Department of Housing and Urban Development, or monthly charge (in lieu of mortgage insurance premium), as the case may be;
(II) grounds rents, taxes, special assessments, fire and other hazard insurance premiums;
(III) interest on the note secured hereby; and
(IV) amortization of the principal of said note.

Any deficiency in the amount of any such aggregate monthly payment shall, unless made good prior to the due date of the next such payment, constitute an event of default under this Deed of Trust.

Replaces Form FHA-2101 DT, which is Obsolete
Previous Edition may be used until Supply is Exhausted

HUD-92101-DT (11-78)

3. If the total of the payments made under (*b*) of paragraph 2 preceding shall exceed the amount of payments actually made by Beneficiary for ground rents, taxes or assessments, or insurance premiums, as the case may be, such excess, if the loan is current, at the option of the Trustor, shall be credited on subsequent payments to be made by the Trustor, or refunded to the Trustor. If, however, the monthly payments made under (*b*) of paragraph 2 preceding shall not be sufficient to pay ground rents, taxes and assessments, and insurance premiums, as the case may be, when the same shall become due and payable, then Trustor shall pay to Beneficiary any amount necessary to make up the deficiency on or before the date when payment of such ground rents, taxes, assessments, or insurance premiums shall be due. If at any time Trustor shall tender to Beneficiary, in accordance with provisions hereof, full payment of the entire indebtedness secured hereby, Beneficiary shall, in computing the amount of indebtedness, credit to the account of Trustor all payments made under the provisions of (*a*) of paragraph 2, which the Beneficiary has not become obligated to pay to the Secretary, Department of Housing and Urban Development, and any balance remaining in the funds accumulated under the provisions of (*b*) of paragraph 2 hereof. If there shall be a default under any of the provisions of the Deed of Trust and thereafter a sale of the premises in accordance with the provisions hereof, or if the Beneficiary acquires the property otherwise after default, Beneficiary shall apply, at the time of the commencement of such proceedings, or the time the property is otherwise acquired, the balance then remaining in the funds accumulated under (*b*) of paragraph 2 preceding, as a credit against the amount of principal then remaining unpaid under said note and shall properly adjust any payments which shall have been made under (*a*) of paragraph 2.

4. In the event that any payment or portion thereof is not paid within fifteen (15) days from the date the same is due, Trustor agrees to pay a "late charge" of four cents (4¢) for each dollar so overdue, if charged by Beneficiary.

To Protect the Security of This Deed of Trust, Trustor Agrees:

5. To protect and preserve said property and to maintain it in good condition and repair.

6. Not to remove or demolish any building or improvement thereon.

7. To complete or restore promptly and in good and workmanlike manner any building or improvement which may be constructed, damaged, or destroyed thereon, and pay when due all costs incurred therefor, and, if the loan secured hereby or any part thereof is being obtained for the purpose of financing construction of improvements on said property, Trustor further agrees:

    a. to commence construction promptly and in any event within 30 days from the date of the commitment of the Department of Housing and Urban Development, and complete same in accordance with plans and specifications satisfactory to beneficiary.

    b. to allow Beneficiary to inspect said property at all times during construction.

    c. to replace any work or materials unsatisfactory to Beneficiary, within fifteen (15) calendar days after written notice from Beneficiary of such fact, which notice may be given to the Trustor by registered mail, sent to his last known address, or by personal service of the same,

    d. That work shall not cease on the construction of such improvements for any reason whatsoever for a period of fifteen (15) calendar days.

The Trustee, upon presentation to it of an affidavit signed by Beneficiary, setting forth facts showing a default by Trustor under this numbered paragraph, is authorized to accept as true and conclusive all facts and statements therein, and to act thereon hereunder.

8. Not to commit or permit waste of said property.

9. To comply with all laws, ordinances, regulations, covenants, conditions, and restrictions affecting said property.

10. To cultivate, irrigate, fertilize, fumigate, prune, and do all other acts which from the character and use of said property may be reasonable proper or necessary, the specific enumerations herein not excluding the general.

11. To provide and maintain insurance against loss by fire and other hazards, casualties, and contingencies including war damage as may be required from time to time by the Beneficiary in such amounts and for such periods as may be required by the Beneficiary, with loss payable solely to Beneficiary and to deliver all policies to Beneficiary, which delivery shall constitute an assignment to Beneficiary of all return premiums.

12. To appear in and defend any action or proceeding purporting to affect the security hereof or the rights or powers of Beneficiary or Trustee; and should Beneficiary or Trustee elect to also appear in or defend any such action or proceeding, to pay all cost and expenses, including cost of evidence of title and attorney's fees in a reasonable sum incurred by Beneficiary or Trustee.

13. To pay at least 10 days before delinquency all assessments upon water company stock, and all rents, assessments and charges for water, appurtenant to or used in connection with said property; to pay, when due, all encumbrances, charges and liens with interest, on said property or any part thereof, which at any time appear to be prior or superior hereto; to pay all costs, fees, and expenses of this Trust.

14. Should Trustor fail to make any payment or to do any act as herein provided, then Beneficiary or Trustee, but without obligation so to do and without notice to or demand upon Trustor and without releasing Trustor from any obligation hereof, may: Make or do the same in such manner and to such extent as either may deem necessary to protect the security hereof, Beneficiary to Trustee being authorized to enter upon the property for such purposes; commence, appear in and defend any action or proceeding purporting to affect the security hereof or the rights or powers of Beneficiary or Trustee; pay, purchase, contest, or compromise any encumbrance, charge or lien which in the judgement of either appears to be prior or superior hereto; and in exercising any such powers, incur any liability, expend whatever amounts in its absolute discretion it may deem necessary therefor, including cost of evidence of title, employ counsel, and pay his reasonable fees.

15. To pay within 30 days after demand all sums expended hereunder by Beneficiary or Trustee, with interest from date of expenditure at the rate provided on the principal debt, and the repayment thereof shall be secured hereby.

16. Trustor agrees to do all acts and make all payments required of Trustor and of the owner of the property to make said note and this Deed eligible for insurance by Beneficiary under the provisions of the National Housing Act and amendments thereto, and agrees not to do, or cause or suffer to be done, any act which will void such insurance during the existence of this Deed.

IT IS MUTUALLY AGREED THAT:

17. Should the property or any part thereof be taken or damaged by reason of any public improvement or condemnation proceeding, or damaged by fire, or earthquake or in any other manner, Beneficiary shall be entitled to all compensation, awards, and other payments or relief therefor, and shall be entitled at its option to commence, appear in and prosecute in its own name, any action or proceedings, or to make any compromise or settlement, in connection with such taking or damage. All such compensation, awards, damages, rights of action and proceeds, including the proceeds of any policies of fire and other insurance affecting said property, are hereby assigned to Beneficiary, who may after deducting therefrom all its expenses, including attorney's fees, release any moneys so received by it or apply the same on any indebtedness secured hereby. Trustor agrees to execute such further assignments of any compensation, award, damage, and rights of action and proceeds as Beneficiary or Trustee may require.

18. By accepting payment of any sum secured hereby after its due date, Beneficiary does not waive its right either to require prompt payment when due of all other sums so secured or to declare default for failure so to pay.

19. This Deed of Trust shall remain in full force and effect during any postponement or extension of the time of payment of the indebtedness or any part thereof secured hereby.

20. At any time and from time to time upon written request of Beneficiary, payment of its fees and presentation of this Deed and the note for endorsement (in case of full reconveyance, for cancelation and retention), without affecting the liability of any person for the payment of the indebtedness, Trustee may (*a*) consent to the making of any map or plat of said property; (*b*) join in granting any easement or creating any restriction thereon; (*c*) join in any subordination or other agreement affecting this Deed or the lien or charge thereof; (*d*) reconvey, without warranty, all or any part of the property. The grantee in any reconveyance may be described as the "person or persons legally entitled thereto," and the recitals therein of any matters or facts shall be conclusive proof of the truthfulness thereof. Trustee's fees for any of the services mentioned in this paragraph shall be $ MAXIMUM

21. Trustor hereby absolutely assigns to Beneficiary during the continuance of these trusts, all rents, issues, royalties, and profits of the property affected by this Deed and of any personal property located thereon. Until Trustor shall default in the payment of any indebtedness secured hereby or in the performance of any agreement hereunder, Trustor shall have the right to collect all such rents, issues, royalties, and profits earned prior to default as they become due and payable save and excepting rents, issues, royalties, and profits arising or accruing by reason of any oil, gas, or mineral lease of said property. If Trustor shall default as aforesaid Trustor's right to collect any of such moneys shall cease and Beneficiary shall have the right, without taking possession of the property affected hereby, to collect all rents, royalties, issues, and profits. Failure or discontinuance of Beneficiary at any time, or from time to time to collect any such moneys shall not in any manner affect the subsequent enforcement by Beneficiary of the right, power, and authority to collect the same. Nothing contained herein, nor the exercise of the right by Beneficiary to collect, shall be, or be construed to be, an affirmation by Beneficiary of any tenancy, lease or option, nor an assumption of liability under, nor a subordination of the lien or charge of this Deed to any tenancy, lease, or option.

22. Upon any default by Trustor hereunder, Beneficiary may at any time without notice, either in person, by agent, or by a receiver to be appointed by a court, and without regard to the adequacy of any security for the indebtedness hereby secured, enter upon and take possession of said property or any part thereof, in its own name sue for or otherwise collect said rents, issues, and profits, including those past due and unpaid, and apply the same, less costs and expenses of operation and collection, including reasonable attorney's fees, upon any indebtedness secured hereby, and in such order as Beneficiary may determine.

23. The entering upon and taking possession of said property, the collection of such rents, issues, and profits, or the proceeds of fire and other insurance policies, or compensation or awards for any taking or damage of the property, and the application or release thereof as aforesaid, shall not cure or waive any default or notice of default hereunder or invalidate any act done pursuant to such notice.

24. Upon default by Trustor in payment of any indebtedness secured hereby or in performance of any agreement hereunder, or should this Deed and said note not be eligible for insurance under the National Housing Act within 90 days from the date hereof (written statement of any officer of the Department of Housing and Urban Development or authorized agent of the Secretary, Department of Housing and Urban Development dated subsequent to 90 days time from the date of this Deed, declining to insure said note and this Deed, being deemed conclusive proof of such ineligibility), or should the commitment of the Department of Housing and Urban Development to insure this loan cease to be in full force and effect for any reason whatsoever, Beneficiary may declare all sums secured hereby immediately due and payable.

25. After the lapse of such time as may then be required by law following the recordation of notice of sale, and said notice of sale having been given as then required by law, Trustee, without demand on Trustor, shall sell said property at the time and place fixed by it in said notice of sale, either as a whole or in separate parcels, and in such order as it may determine (but subject to any statutory right of Trustor to direct the order in which such property, if consisting of several known lots or parcels, shall be sold), at public auction to the highest bidder for cash in lawful money of the United States, payable at time of sale. Trustee may postpone sale of all or any portion of said property by public announcement at the time and place of sale, and from time to time thereafter may postpone the sale by public announcement at the time fixed by the preceding postponement. Trustee shall deliver to the purchaser its Deed conveying the property so sold, but without any covenant or warranty, express or implied. The recitals in the Deed of any matters or facts shall be conclusive proof of the truthfulness thereof. Any person, including Trustor, Trustee, or Beneficiary, may purchase at the sale. Trustee shall apply the proceeds of sale to payment of (1) the expenses of such sale, including, but not limited to, reasonable Trustee's and Attorney's fees; (2) cost of any evidence of title procured in connection with such sale and revenue stamps on Trustee's Deed; (3) all sums expended under the terms thereof, not then repaid, with accrued interest at the rate provided on the principal debt; (4) all other sums then secured hereby; and (5) remainder, if any, to the person or persons legally entitled thereto.

26. Upon the occurrence of any default hereunder, Beneficiary shall have the option to foreclose this Trust Deed in the manner provided by law for the foreclosure of mortgages on real property.

No power or remedy herein conferred is exclusive of, or shall prejudice any other power or remedy of Trustee or Beneficiary.

The exercise of any power or remedy on one or more occasions shall not exclude the future exercise thereof from time to time upon the conditions prescribed herein or by operation of law.

27. If a final decree in favor of plaintiff is entered in a suit brought to foreclose this Trust Deed, it may include the amount of all costs and expenses incident to such proceedings, including reasonable attorney's fees actually incurred.

28. Beneficiary may from time to time, for any reason or cause, substitute a successor or successors to any Trustee named herein or acting hereunder to execute this Trust. Upon such appointment, and without any conveyance to any successor Trustee, the latter shall be vested with all title, powers, and duties conferred upon any Trustee herein named or acting hereunder. Each such appointment and substitution shall be made by written notice through registered or certified mail, postage prepaid, to Trustor, Trustee, and the successor Trustee and by recording notice of such in the office of the County Recorder of the county in which the trust property is situated. Such notice of substitution of trustee shall be executed and acknowledged by Beneficiary and shall contain reference to this Trust Deed and its place of record and describe the trust property and when so recorded shall be conclusive proof of proper appointment of the successor Trustee.

29. The waiver by Trustee or Beneficiary of any default of Trustor under this Trust Deed shall not be or be deemed to be a waiver of any other or similar defaults subsequently occurring.

30. This Deed shall inure to and bind the heirs, legatees, devisees, administrator, executors, successors, and assigns of the parties hereto. All obligations of Trustor hereunder are joint and several. The term "Beneficiary" shall mean the owner and holder, including pledgees, of the note secured hereby, whether or not named as Beneficiary herein.

31. Trustee accepts this Trust when this Deed, duly executed and acknowledged, is made a public record as provided by law. Trustee is not obligated to notify any party hereto of pending sale under any other Deed of Trust or of any action or proceeding in which Trustor, Beneficiary, or Trustee shall be a party, unless brought by Trustee.

32. Whenever used in this Deed of Trust, the singular number shall include the plural, the plural the singular, and the use of any gender shall include all genders.

33. This Deed shall be construed according to the laws of the State of Arizona.

34. The Undersigned Trustor requests that a copy of any notice of default and of any notice of sale hereunder be mailed to him at the address hereinbefore set forth.

WHEN RECORDED MAIL TO
FIRST FEDERAL SAVINGS
3003 N Central Ave
Phoenix, AZ 85012
Closer ID#000

Signature of Trustor

John J Buyer

Betty J Buyer

(Copyist will copy) Index as Trust Deed and Assignment of Rents

STATE OF ARIZONA
COUNTY OF **MARICOPA** } ss:

On this _____ day of _____, 19 ____, before me, _____, A Notary Public in and for said County, personally appeared

_____ **John J Buyer and Betty J Buyer** _____

known to me to be the person whose name**s** **are** subscribed to the within instrument, and acknowledged that **they** executed the same.

WITNESS my hand and official seal.
[NOTARIAL SEAL]

Notary Public in and for said County and State.

REQUEST FOR FULL RECONVEYANCE

Do not record. To be used only when note has been paid

TO: TRUSTEE.

The undersigned is the legal owner and holder of the note and all other indebtedness secured by the within Deed of Trust. Said note, together with all other indebtedness secured by said Deed of Trust, has been fully paid and satisfied; and you are hereby requested and directed, on payment to you of any sums owing to you under the terms of said Deed of Trust, to cancel said note above mentioned, and all other evidences of indebtedness secured by said Deed of Trust delivered to you herewith, together with the said Deed of Trust, and to reconvey, without warranty, to the parties designated by the terms of said Deed of Trust, all the estate now held by you thereunder.

Dated_____, 19_____

Mail reconveyance to_____

HUD-92101-DT (11-78)

P.C.S. FORM 1

A.

U.S. DEPARTMENT OF HOUSING AND URBAN DEVELOPMENT

SETTLEMENT STATEMENT

Form Approved
OMB No. 63 - R1501

B. TYPE OF LOAN:		
1. ☒ FHA	2. ☐ FMHA	3. ☐ CONV. UNINS.
4. ☐ VA	5. ☐ CONV. INS.	

6. FILE NUMBER	7. LOAN NUMBER
27-000,000	012999999

8. MORTGAGE INS. CASE NO.
021-000000-203

C. NOTE: This form is furnished to give you a statement of actual settlement costs. Amounts paid to and by the settlement agent are shown. Items marked "(p.o.c.)" were paid outside the closing; they are shown here for informational purposes and are not included in the totals.

D. BORROWER NAME AND ADDRESS
JOHN J BUYER   BETTY J BUYER
0000 E Indian Way   Phoenix, AZ 85032

E. SELLER NAME AND ADDRESS
JOHN J SELLER   BETTY J SELLER

F. LENDER NAME AND ADDRESS
FIRST FEDERAL SAVINGS
3003 N Central Ave   Phoenix, AZ 85012

G. PROPERTY LOCATION
0000 E Indian Way   Phoenix, AZ 85032

H. SETTLEMENT AGENT PLACE OF SETTLEMENT
TITLE INSURANCE COMPANY
0000 Central St   Phoenix, AZ 85003

I. DATE OF SETTLEMENT	DATE OF LOAN COMMITMENT
June 26, 1982	

J. SUMMARY OF BORROWER'S TRANSACTION		K. SUMMARY OF SELLER'S TRANSACTION	
100. GROSS AMOUNT DUE FROM BORROWER		400. GROSS AMOUNT DUE TO SELLER	
101. Contract sales price	$64,000.00	401. Contract sales price	$64,000.00
102. Personal property		402. Personal property	
103. Settlement charges to borrower (line 1400)	1,367.59	403.	
104.		404.	
105.		405.	
Adjustments for items paid by seller in advance		Adjustments for items paid by seller in advance	
106. City/town taxes to		406. City/town taxes to	
107. County taxes to		407. County taxes to	
108. Assessments to		408. Assessments to	
109. to		409. to	
110.		410.	
111.		411.	
112.		412.	
120. GROSS AMOUNT DUE FROM BORROWER	65,367.59	420. GROSS AMOUNT DUE TO SELLER	64,000.00
200. AMOUNTS PAID BY OR IN BEHALF OF BORROWER		500. REDUCTIONS IN AMOUNTS DUE TO SELLER	
201. Deposits or earnest money	500.00	501. Excess deposits (see instructions)	
202. Principal amount of new loan(s)	54,000.00	502. Settlement charges to seller (line 1400)	6,374.00
203. Existing loan(s) taken subject to		503. Existing loan(s) taken subject to	
204. Cash from Borrower at	10,704.34	504. Payoff of first mortgage loan	
205. settlement		505. Payoff of second mortgage loan	
206.		506.	
207.		507.	
208.		508.	
209.		509.	
Credit to borrower for items unpaid by seller		Credit to borrower for items unpaid by seller	
210. City/town taxes to		510. City/town taxes to	
211. County taxes 1/1 to 6/26	163.25	511. County taxes 1/1 to 6/26	163.25
212. Assessments to		512. Assessments to	
213.		513.	
214.		514.	
215.		515.	
216.		516.	
217.		517.	
218.		518.	
219.		519.	
220. TOTAL PAID BY/FOR BORROWER	65,367.59	520. TOTAL REDUCTION AMOUNT DUE SELLER	6,537.25
300. CASH AT SETTLEMENT FROM/TO BORROWER		600. CASH AT SETTLEMENT TO/FROM SELLER	
301. Gross amount due from borrower (line 120)	65,367.59	601. Gross amount due to seller (line 420)	64,000.00
302. Less amounts paid by/for borrower (line 220) (	65,367.59)	602. Less reductions in amount due seller (line 520) (	6,537.25)
303. CASH (☐ FROM) (☐TO) BORROWER	- 0 -	603. CASH (x TO) (FROM) SELLER	57,462.75

U.S. DEPARTMENT OF HOUSING AND URBAN DEVELOPMENT   **SETTLEMENT STATEMENT**

PAGE 1 OF 3

P.C.S. FORM 2

SETTLEMENT STATEMENT

L. SETTLEMENT CHARGES		PAID FROM BORROWER'S FUNDS AT SETTLEMENT	PAID FROM SELLER'S FUNDS AT SETTLEMENT
700. Sales/Broker's commission based on price $ 64,000.00 @ 5. %			
Division of Commission (line 700) as follows:			
701. $ 3,200.00 to Real Estate Company			
702. $ to			
703. Commission paid at settlement			3,200.00
704.			
800. ITEMS PAYABLE IN CONNECTION WITH LOAN			
801. Loan origination fee 1 %		540.00	
802. Loan discount 5 %			2,700.00
803. Appraisal fee to POC $85.00			
804. Credit report to CREDCO		35.00	
805. Lender's inspection fee			
806. Mortgage insurance application fee to			
807. Assumption fee/Refinancing fee			
808. TRANSAMERICA TAX SERVICE		22.50	
809. DOCUMENT PREP FEE		35.00	
810.			
811.			
900. ITEMS REQUIRED BY LENDER TO BE PAID IN ADVANCE			
901. Interest from 06/26/82 to 07/1/82 @ 23.25 /day		116.25	
902. Mortgage insurance premium for mo. to			
903. Hazard insurance premium for 1 yrs. to FIRE INSURANCE COMPANY		180.00	
904. yrs. to			
905.			
1000. RESERVES DEPOSITS WITH LENDER			
1001. Hazard insurance 2 /mo. @ 15.00 /mo.		30.00	
1002. Mortgage insurance 1 /mo. @ 22.49 /mo.		22.49	
1003. City property taxes /mo. @ /mo.			
1004. County property taxes 5 /mo. @ 28.07 mo.		140.35	
1005. Annual assessments /mo. @ /mo.			
1006. Flood insurance /mo. @ mo.			
1007. Sanitary tax /mo. @ /mo.			
1008. /mo. @ mo.			
1100. TITLE CHARGES			
1101. Settlement or closing fee to			
1102. Abstract or title search to			
1103. Title examination to			
1104. Title insurance binder to			
1105. Document preparation to			
1106. Notary fees to			
1107. Attorney's fees to			
(includes above items numbers:			
1108. Title insurance to TITLE INSURANCE COMPANY		158.00	355.00
(includes above items numbers:			
1109. Lender's coverage $ 54,000.00			
1110. Owner's coverage $ 64,000.00			
1111. ESCROW FEE TO TITLE INSURANCE COMPANY		82.00	82.00
1112.			
1113.			
1200. GOVERNMENT RECORDING AND TRANSFER CHARGES			
1201. Recording fees: Deed $ 3.00 Mortgage $ 3.00 Releases $		6.00	
1202. City County tax stamps: Deed $ Mortgage $			
1203. State tax/stamps: Deed $ Mortgage $			
1204. Affidavit $2.00			2.00
1205.			
1300. ADDITIONAL SETTLEMENT CHARGES			
1301. Survey to			
1302. Pest inspection to TERMITE COMPANY			35.00
1303.			
1304.			
1305.			
1400. TOTAL SETTLEMENT CHARGES (enter on lines 103, Section J and 502, Section K)		1,367.59	6,374.00

LOAN SETTLEMENT STATEMENT
AUTOMATED

Date: June 24, 1982   Loan Number: 012999999

Mortgagor: JOHN J BUYER   BETTY J BUYER

Mailing Address: 0000 E Indian Way   Property Address: 0000 E Indian Way
Phoenix, AZ 85032   Phoenix, AZ 85032

Legal: LOT 0, NAVAJO ESTATES

Rate: 15.500   Term: 360 Mos.   Ratio: 84   First Payment Due: August 01, 1982

P and I: 704.44   Impounds: 65.56   Total Pmt: 770.00   By: Loan Closer

DESCRIPTION			
Amount of Loan: FHA	13104005200	54,000.00	
Interest to 07/01/82 @ $23.25	31103005200		*
Escrow:	24200005200		192.84
Taxes: (5 mos. @ 28.07)$140.35			
Insurance: (2 mos. @ 15.00)$ 30.00			
PMI or MIP: (1 mos. @ 22.49)$ 22.49			
Flood Ins. (mos. @)$			
(mos. @)$			
Appraisal Fee :			
Deferred Acquisition Credits: Const. Other X	26250025402		540.00
DISCOUNT FEE	26250025402		2,700.00
CREDIT REPORT FEE	31506005952		35.00
DOCUMENT PREPARATION FEE	31518005205		35.00
Refinance Old Loan No. Date:			
Inv. Class % Owned			
Loan Payoff Transaction			
Principal Balance			
Interest To			
Prepayment Fee			
Escrow Balance			
NET PROCEEDS Check No. Date:	13200005952		*
Loan Settlement Prepayments:			
Due Balance on Loan in Process:			
Due Balance on Loan in Process:			
	TOTALS	54,000.00	54,000.00

ML-317 (8-81)   *TO BE COMPLETED ON FINAL

We welcome you as a member of our Association and look forward with pleasure to serving you.

Satisfaction in any business relationship is dependent to a great degree upon the complete understanding of all details by all parties to the transaction. Therefore, in order that you will fully understand your privileges and obligations as a borrower, we ask that you read all documents relating to this loan before signing your name.

Thank you.

FIRST FEDERAL SAVINGS

1. PAYMENT COUPONS: I will include with each loan payment a loan payment coupon, a set of which will be supplied by the association. In lieu of a monthly record of my account, a statement of my account will be sent to me at the end of each year.

2. LATE CHARGE: I understand that to avoid a late charge, payment must be received by the Association before the close of business on the due date.

3. TAXES AND ASSESSMENTS: If my loan payments do not include an impound for taxes, the first one-half of my annual tax must be paid on or before the first of November, and the second one-half on or before the first of May of the following year. On assessments for street paving, sewers, etc., interest installments must be paid prior to June 1st, and interest and principal installments must be paid prior to December 1st of each year. I understand it is my obligation to pay these taxes or assessments even though we have not received a tax or assessment notice and that failure on our part to pay these taxes or assessments when due, constitutes a default under the terms of the mortgage or deed of trust, making it subject to foreclosure.

4. INSURANCE: It is my obligation to provide the Association with fire and extended coverage insurance from the date of closing this loan until the loan is paid in full. The insurance policy must be in a face amount equal to the unpaid balance of the loan with the policy form, term and insurance company all being acceptable to the Association. It is further understood that the Association will not accept a reciprocal insurer. The original of the policy must be delvered to the Association at the closing of the loan and all renewal policies must be delivered to the Association at least 30 days prior to the expiration date of the policy held by the Association. The Association will accept substitution of policies during the term of a policy held by the Association will not accept a reciprocal insurer. The original of the policy must be delivered to the Association at the closing by the Association; however, the Association wll never advance its own funds to renew such a policy. To facilitate fulfilling the insurance requirements of the mortgage or deed of trust, I hereby authorize the Association to secure and/or renew during the term of the loan the required insurance coverage, and the association is hereby authorized to disclose expiration or other policy information to any agent or person directly or indirectly, for the purpose of permitting said person or agent to solicit the required insurance or any renewal thereof. Should I deliver to the association an insurance policy insuring more than the mortgage or deed of trust security and for risks other than fire and extended coverage, the Association is authorized to pay the full amount of the premium out of reserve funds impounded with the Association to pay for renewal premiums on insurance. However, should the *premium on such additional risk insurance or should this coverage be allowed to expire or be cancelled, I agree that the Association may then order the minimum required insurance adequate to protect the mortgage and allow the additional coverage to lapse.

5. PAYMENT OF POINTS AND FEES: I hereby agree to pay all service charges, points, fees, interest or other charges, however indicated as set forth on the reverse side of this document and in the Note, and Truth-in-Lending disclosure statement and any riders to these documents.

I HAVE READ AND UNDERSTAND THE ABOVE AND ALL OTHER DOCUMENTS WHICH I HAVE SIGNED IN RELATION TO THIS LOAN AND MY SIGNATURE INDICATES MY APPROVAL AND ACCEPTANCE OF THESE DOCUMENTS.

I acknowledge receipt of a copy of this statement and the closing escrow statement. I authorized the disbursement of the funds as stated on the reverse side hereon.

Date: _____

_____
John J. Buyer

*impounded fund not be sufficient to pay the full premium on such

_____
Betty J. Buyer

F / **FIRST FEDERAL SAVINGS**

BUYER _____ John J. & Betty J. Buyer _____

ADDRESS ___ 0000 E, Indian Way _____ Phoenix, Arizona _____

TYPE OF LOAN ___ FHA _____ LOAN AMT. 54,000.00 ___ INT RT 15.50 _____

GOOD FAITH ESTIMATE

In accordance with the Real Estate Settlement Procedures Act (RESPA) of 1974, outlined below are your estimated costs in connection with the above referenced transaction.

	Buyer	Seller
DOWN PAYMENT	$ 10,000.00	
CLOSING COSTS:		
Broker's Commission		$
FHA-VA Loan Discount or Points _5%_		$ 2,700.00
Origination Fee or Service Charge _1%_	$ 540.00	$
Initial Private Mortgage Insurance Premium	$ n/a	$
Appraisal Fee	$ 85.00	$
Inspection Fee	$	$
Escrow or Settlement Fee	$ 82.00	$ 82.00
Owner's Title Policy		$ 355.00
Title Insurance — Lenders Coverage (ALTA)	$ 158.00	$
Recording Fees	$ 8.00	$
Credit Report Charges	$ 35.00	$
Tax Service Contract	$ 22.50	$
Document Preparation Fee	$ 35.00	$
Termite Inspection	$	$ 35.00
_____	$	$
Total Closing Costs	$ 965.50	$ 3,172.00
IMPOUNDS OR PREPAID ITEMS:		
First Year's Fire Insurance Policy plus _2_ months	$ 210.00	$
Taxes _2 months_	$ 56.00	$
MIP or PMI _1 months_	$ 22.49	$
Initial or Prepaid Interest From C.O.E. _2/25/82_ to _2/28/82_ @ 22.93	$ 68.79	$
_____	$	$
Total Impounds	$ 357.28	$
TOTAL MOVE-IN COSTS (Down Payment + Closing Costs + Impounds)	$ 11,322.78	$
ESTIMATED MONTHLY PAYMENT:		
Principal and Interest		$ 704.44
MIP or PMI		$ 22.49
Taxes		$ 28.00
Insurance		$ 15.00
_____		$
Total		$ 769.53

This form does not necessarily cover all items you may be required to pay in cash at settlement. It does, however, estimate the amount you will likely pay to the best of our knowledge as of the date of application.

The above estimate should not be construed as either a commitment by First Federal Savings to make a loan or a commitment of terms should your loan application be approved.

If you have further questions regarding this form, please contact the branch office where your application was taken.

I (We) have received a copy of the Good Faith Estimate and HUD Booklet and Financial Privacy Notice.

FIRST FEDERAL SAVINGS

By _Paul Smith_

Title _Loan Officer/Agent_ Date _1/20/82_

ML-300 (5-79)

Signature _John J. Buyer_ Date _____
John J. Buyer

Signature _Betty J. Buyer_ Date _____
Betty J. Buyer

ASSOCIATION COPY - WHITE
CUSTOMER COPY - YELLOW

CASE STUDY: VETERANS ADMINISTRATION—
GUARANTEED MORTGAGE LOAN

The following case study (based on actual facts) involves Bryan James Robinson and Marie Williams Robinson who have decided to use Bryan's veterans entitlement to purchase a home for $60,000 in Metairie, Louisiana. The Robinson's decide to make mortgage application at Carruth Mortgage Corporation, a large mortgage company in New Orleans.

A mortgage loan application by the borrowers on the mortgagee's own application form begins the case. This form has been specially designed for Carruth's computer system and complies with all current regulations and is therefore acceptable, although most mortgage lenders use the FNMA-FHLMC form.

After the application is made, a loan processor or underwriter must determine the veteran's eligibility for a VA guaranteed loan. Many veterans already have a *Certificate of Eligibility* on hand. However, if they do not, one can be ordered for the veteran by submitting Form 26-1880, *Request for Determination of Eligibility and Available Loan Guaranty Entitlement*. This form is completed from information taken from the veteran's DD214, *Report of Transfer or Discharge*. If the veteran is eligible, a *Certificate of Eligibility* will be sent to the mortgagee by the Veterans Administration within a short period of time. In order to save time, a loan processor, prior to taking the application, should instruct the veteran to bring the DD214 or the *Certificate of Eligibility*, a valid purchase agreement, and all asset and liability account numbers.

Assuming all is in order to qualify, the processor would follow the Credit Questionnaire to obtain the necessary data to begin the preliminary stages of underwriting. A *Good Faith Estimate of Closing Costs* is given to the borrowers to comply with RESPA, along with the RESPA booklet.

The next step is to order an appraisal by submitting the *Request for Determination of Reasonable Value*. The form is sent to the VA which in turn has a VA approved appraiser visit the property. The resulting estimate of value is placed on a *Certificate of Reasonable Value (CRV)* and returned to the mortgagee. It is important to note that the CRV establishes the conditions under which the loan should be closed to assure the VA guaranty. A credit report and verifications of employment and deposit are required for a VA approval and guaranty.

Every loan application taken faces the possibility of an interest rate change and all prospective mortgagors are asked to sign a certification protecting all parties against such possibilities, i.e., *No Commitment to Lend*.

Upon receipt of all verifications, credit reports, and other documents, an *Application for Home Loan Guaranty* is prepared by the mortgagee and signed by the veteran. A cover letter is sent to the VA indicating the documentation being sent for VA review.

After the VA underwrites and approves the loan submission, it returns a *Certificate of Commitment* to the mortgagee. The mortgage lender then notifies the mortgagor of the loan approval and sends closing instructions to the closing notary/attorney. All documents needed by the attorney for the closing are indicated and are prepared by Carruth when a closing date has been set.

When the loan is ready to close, the closing attorney must furnish the mortgage lender with all items necessary to satisfy the conditions of the lender set forth by the Veterans Administration and the mortgage lender. Evidence of *Flood Insurance* is required by the VA along with a *Termite Certificate*, as indicated on the CRV. A *Title Binder* and *Survey* are required prior to the closing attorney setting the Act of Sale to assure clear title. Along with these documents, the closing attorney must submit a *Request for Authority to Close* and *A Statement of Sellers and Buyers Costs*. These costs and the rate derived from the calculation of annual percentage rate required by the Federal Consumer Protection Act allows the mortgage lender to prepare the *Disclosure Statement*. The disclosure statement and proper legal documents along with the *Authority to Close Letter* are sent back to the attorney with the funds for the sale.

At the sale, the borrower is required to sign the Disclosure Statement, Note, Mortgage, HUD-1 Form, and other various documents. In the state of Louisiana, a Credit Sale of Property is the accepted mortgage form. It conveys the land and dwelling simultaneously and provides for a more expeditious foreclosure proceeding, if necessary. In other states a mortgage or deed of trust would serve the same purpose.

After all documents are returned to the mortgage lender, they are checked for compliance and the loan is assigned to an investor commitment. This particular mortgage was placed in a GNMA Mortgage Backed Security Pool. The original note, mortgage, and *Assignment of Note and Mortgage* are forwarded to a custodian to initiate the pool proceedings.

Within this same time frame, the loan file is transferred to the loan administration area via computer communication lines for future maintenance of the account. Once the loan is "set-up," a first payment letter is sent to the mortgagors, congratulating them on their purchase.

The following documents are required for a mortgage loan guaranteed by the Veterans Administration and placed in a mortgage pool guaranteed by GNMA:

- Credit Questionnaire and Loan Data Input Worksheet
- Agreement to purchase or sell
- Good faith estimate of borrower's closing costs and monthly payment estimate
- Compliance disclosures

- Request for determination of eligibility and available loan guaranty entitlement
- Certificate of eligibility
- VA request for determination of reasonable value
- VA certificate of reasonable value
- Photographs
- Request for verification of employment (2)
- Request for verification of deposit (2)
- Credit report
- Character and credit statement
- Mortgagees cover letter for submission to VA
- Processing check sheet
- Status of housing availability
- Loan analysis
- VA application for home loan guaranty
- Certificate of commitment
- Mortgagees notification of approval letter
- Mortgagees closing instructions
- Loan discount guaranty agreement
- Commitment for title insurance
- Survey
- Hazard insurance policy (not included in this case)
- Flood insurance
- Termite certificate
- Request for authority to close and statement of seller's and buyer's costs
- Calculation of annual percentage rate
- Truth-in-lending disclosure statement
- Authorization to close letter
- Note
- Credit sale of property
- HUD-1, settlement statement
- Supplement to disclosure/settlement statement
- Assignment of note and mortgage

ROBINSON, B.J.
APPLICANT

ROBINSON, M.W.
APPLICANT

100400
WORKSHEET NO. (1

CREDIT QUESTIONAIRE AND LOAN DATA IMPUT WORKSHEET

NO. 2 GENERAL	2—INVESTOR NO. 010	3—DATE WAREHOUSED	4—LOAN STATUS CODE 1	5—FHA, VA, PMI CASE NO. LH 123456	6—APPLICATION DATE 052482
7—ORIGINATOR NO. 1000	8— ☒ S — SPOT ☐ B — BLDR		9—BUILDER CODE OTHR	10—LOAN TYPE CODE 20	11—LOAN GRADE CODE 01
12—PURCHASE PRICE $ 60,000.00	13—LOAN AMT. $ 60,000.00	14—INTEREST RATE 15.50%	15—LOAN in mos. 360	16 Will Advise? Y N	17 DISCOUNT % 1.5	18—DISC. EXP DATE 063082
19—CASH DEPOSIT HELD BY N/A	20—CASH DEPOSIT AMOUNT $ -0-	21—FIRST MORTGAGE ☒ YES ☐ NO		22—CREDIT REPORT $ 30.00	23—APPRAISAL FEE $ 80.00
24—UNDERWRITER FEE $	25—ORIGINATION FEE $	26—OTHER FEE (EXPLAIN) $	27—OTHER FEE AMOUNT $	27—SETTLEMENT COST-SELLER $	29—DISCOUNT PD. BY SELLER $ 900.00	30—PMI PD. BY SELLER
31—INTERVIEWER NAME Carla Rody		32—SELLER NAME — 1 John Hunter		33—SELLER NAME — 2	
34—SELLER ADDRESS 1804 Homer Street		35—SELLER CITY, STATE, ZIP Metairie, Louisiana 70005			
36—Mortgagor Will be: A	37—Source of cash code 1	38—AUTHORIZATION NAME Patricia Misiek		39—AUTHORIZATION TITLE Loan Officer	
40—LISTING AGENT Linda Keanan		41—SELLING AGENT Mike Crane		42—Buydown.plan.code A-B-C-D-E-F-G	
43 Title.held manner 1					
44—PROCESSOR NAME Carla Rody		45—PROCESSOR TITLE Loan Processor		46-47-48-49 COMPLETE FOR AUDIT PURPOSE	

NO. 8 — PRESENT HOUSING EXPENSE	2—RENT $ 450.00	3—P & I $	4—OTHER P & I $	5—HAZD. INS. $	6—R.E. TAXES $
7—MORTGAGE INSURANCE $	8—ASSOC. DUES $	9—FLOOD INS. $	10—UTILITIES $ 150.00	11—MAINT. $	

NO. 8 — PROPOSED HOUSING EXPENSE	12—OTHER P & I $	13—R. E. TAXES $ 12.00	14—ASSOC. DUES $	15—FLOOD INS. $ 7.00
16—UTILITIES $ 90.00	17—MAINTENANCE $ 35.00	18—TOT. OPER. EXP. $	19—GROSS MO. RENTAL 2-4 $	

NO. 9 PROPERTY INFORMATION	2—STREET 1804 Homer Street		3—CITY Metairie	4—COUNTY Jefferson
5—STATE .Abbr. La.	6—ZIP 70005	7—SUBDIVISION Bonnabel Heights		8—CENSUS TRACT 17.12
9—YEAR BUILT 1980	10—LOT NO. 12	11—SQ. NO. 16	12—NO. OF UNITS 1	13—PROPERTY CODE E	14—property type.code 11	15—LOT DIMENSIONS 60 X 130
16—PROPERTY PROJECT TYPE 1 – PUD 3 – D-PUD 2 – CONDO 4 – S/D	17—PROPERTY RIGHTS CODE F – FEE L – LEASEHOLD P – PUD	18—TOTAL APPRAISED VALUE $ 60,000.00	19—APPRAISED land value $ 17,000.00	20—Appraiser name DeMarcay

NO. 18 ESTIMATE OF CLOSING COST	2—% ORIG. FEE 1.00 %	3—ORIG. FEE $ 600.00	4—DISCOUNT % 1.50 %	5—DISCOUNT $	6—APPRAISAL FEE $ 80.00
7—CREDIT REPORT $ 30.00	8—LEND INP. FEE $	9—UNDERWRITING Fee $	10—EST. CLOSING DT. 063082	11—DAILY INT ☒ B ☐ S	12—PMI 12 MOS. ☒ B ☐ S
13—MIP/pmi 2 MOS. ☒ B ☐ S	14—TITLE EXAM $ 150.00	15—DOC. PREP. $	16—NOTARY FEES $ 90.00	17—ATTORNEY Fee $	18—TITLE INS. $ 284.00
19—LENDER'S COVERAGE $ 212.00	20—OWNER'S COVERAGE $ 72.00	21—RECORDING FEES $ 35.00	22—SURVEY $ 125.00	23—PHOTOGRAPHS $ 10.00	24—AMORTIZA-TION SCHED. $ 3.00
P-1 (R4/82)	25—Warehousing fee $	26—Commitment fee or Yield Conf. Fee $		27. Delivery fee or Buydown Ratio/Fee,buyer $	

WORKSHEET NO:

NO. 3 BORROWER – 1	2–FIRST NAME	3–MIDDLE NAME (MAIDEN)	4–LAST NAME
	Bryan	James	Robinson

5–AGE	6 –SCHOOL YRS.	7–PRES. ADD. YRS.	8–PRES. ADDRESS
40	16	2	☐ OWN ☒ RENT

9–PRESENT STREET	10–PRESENT CITY	11 –PRESENT STATE & ZIP
5 Opelousas Street	New Orleans	Louisiana 70114

12–PREVIOUS STREET	13–PREVIOUS CITY	14–PREVIOUS STATE & ZIP

15–PREV. ADD. YRS.	16–PREV. ADD.	17–MARITAL STATUS	18–NO. DEP.	19- 24-AGES OF DEPENDENTS
	☐ OWN ☐ RENT	☒MAR ☐ SEP ☐ UNMARRIED	2	16,14

25–SOCIAL SECURITY NO.	26–HOME PHONE	27–BUSINESS PHONE
222-45-7183	241-7100	241-3000

28–BUYER 1 – JOMT/BNKRPT?	29–BUYER 1 – FRCLS/LIENS?	30–BUYER 1 – COMAKER?
☐ YES ☒NO	☐ YES ☒NO	☐ YES ☒NO

31–BUYER 1 – LAWSUIT?	32–BUYER 1 – ALIMONY?	33–BUYER 1 – DWNPMT BOR.?
☐ YES ☒NO	☐ YES ☒NO	☐ YES ☒NO

NO. 4 CO-BORROWER–1	2–FIRST NAME	3–MIDDLE NAME (MAIDEN)	4–LAST NAME
	Maria	Williams	Robinson

5–AGE	6 –SCHOOL YRS.	7–PRES. ADD. YRS.	8–PRES. ADDRESS
35	16	2	☐ OWN ☒ RENT

9 –PRESENT STREET	10–PRESENT CITY	11 –PRESENT STATE & ZIP
5 Opelousas Street	New Orleans	Louisiana 70114

12–PREVIOUS STREET	13–PREVIOUS CITY	14–PREVIOUS STATE & ZIP

15–PREV. ADD. YRS.	16–PREV. ADD.	17–MARITAL STATUS	18–NO. DEP.	19- 24-AGES OF DEPENDENTS
	☐ OWN ☐ RENT	☒MAR ☐ SEP ☐ UNMARRIED		

25–SOCIAL SECURITY NO.	26–HOME PHONE	27–BUSINESS PHONE
127-34-1906	241-7000	586-4312

28–BUYER 2 – JOMT/BNKRPT?	29–BUYER 2 – FRCLS/LIENS?	30–BUYER 2 – COMAKER?
☐ YES ☒NO	☐ YES ☒ NO	☐ YES ☒ NO

31–BUYER 2 – LAWSUIT?	32–BUYER 2 – ALIMONY?	33–BUYER 2 – DWNPMT BOR.?
☐ YES ☒NO	☐ YES ☒ NO	☐ YES ☒ NO

NO. 5 BORROWER – 1 EMPLOYMENT	2–EMPLOYER NAME	3–EMPLOYER STREET ADDRESS
	U. S. Navy	4400 Dauphine Street

4–EMPLOYER CITY	5–STATE AND ZIP	6–YRS/PROFESS.	7–YRS/JOB	8–SELF EMP.
New Orleans	Louisiana 70119	14	14	☐ YES ☒NO

9–POSITION	10–TYPE OF BUSINESS
Chief Petty Officer	Government/Military

11–BASE INCOME $	12–OVERTIME $	13–BONUSES $	14–COMMISSIONS $
$ 2200.00	$	$	$

15–DIV/INT $	16–FED $	17–STATE $	18–S/S $	19–OTHER DED.
$	$ 648.90	$ 55.00	$ 197.00	$

NO. 6 CO-BORROWER–2 EMPLOYMENT	2–EMPLOYER NAME	3–EMPLOYER STREET ADDRESS
	D. H. Holmes	500 Canal Boulevard

4–EMPLOYER CITY	5–STATE AND ZIP	6–YRS/PROFESS	7–YRS/JOB	8–SELF EMP.
New Orleans	Louisiana 70153	6	2	☐ YES ☒NO

9–BUYER 2 – POSITION	10–BUYER 2 TYPE OF BUSINESS	11–BASE INCOME	12–OVERTIME	13–BONUSES	14–COMMISSIONS
Hosiery Mgr.	Retail	$ 1200.00	$	$	$ 100.00

15–DIV/INT	16–FED $	17–STATE $	18–S/S $	19–OTHER DED.
$	$	$ 18.00	$ 80.00	$

20–LIST ADDITIONAL NAMES	21–BUYER 3 – GROSS MO. INCOME	22–BUYER 4 GROSS MO. INCOME
	$	$

NOTICE: † Alimony, child support, or separate maintenance income need not be revealed if the Borrower or Co-Borrower does not choose to have it considered as a basis for repaying this loan.

NO. 7 OTHER INCOME 1	2—OTHER INCOME ☒ B ☐ C	3—DESCRIPTION Quarters/Rations		4—INCOME $ $ 600.00
NO. 7 cont'd OTHER INCOME 2	5—OTHER INCOME ☐ B ☐ C	6—DESCRIPTION		7—INCOME $ $
NO 7 cont'd OTHER INCOME 3	8—OTHER INCOME ☐ B ☐ C	9—DESCRIPTION		10—INCOME $ $
NO. 7 cont.d PREVIOUS EMPLOYMENT – 1	11—PREV. EMPLOY. ☐ B ☐ C	12—PREV. EMPLOYER – 1		
13—PREV. EMPLOYER STREET		14—PREV. EMPLOY. CITY, ST., ZIP	15—TYPE OF BUSINESS	
16—PREV. POSITION	17—PREV. DATE FROM	18—PREV. DATE TO	19—PREV. MONTHLY $ $	
NO. 7 cont'd PREVIOUS EMPLOYMENT – 2	20—PREV. EMPLOY ☐ B ☐ C	21—PREVIOUS EMPLOYER – 2		
22—PREV. EMPLOYER STREET		23—PREV. EMPLOY. CITY, ST., ZIP	24—TYPE OF BUSINESS	
25—PREV. POSITION	26—PREV. DATE FROM	27—PREV. DATE TO	28—PREV. MONTHLY $ $	
NO. 7 cont'd PREVIOUS EMPLOYMENT – 3	29—PREV. EMPLOY. ☐ B ☐ C	30—PREVIOUS EMPLOYER – 3		
31—PREV. EMPLOYER STREET		32—PREV. EMPLOY. CITY, ST., ZIP	33—TYPE OF BUSINESS	
34—PREV. POSITION	35—PREV. DATE FROM	36—PREV. DATE TO	37—PREV. MONTHLY $ $	
NO. 7 cont'd PREVIOUS EMPLOYMENT – 4	38—PREV. EMPLOY. ☐ B ☐ C	39—PREVIOUS EMPLOYER – 4		
40—PREV. EMPLOYER STREET		41—PREV. EMPLOY. CITY, ST., ZIP	42—TYPE OF BUSINESS	
43—PREV. POSITION	44—PREV. DATE FROM	45—PREV. DATE TO	46—PREV. MONTHLY $ $	

NO. 10 ASSETS BANK ONE	2—BANK 1 NAME Bank of New Orleans		3—BANK 1 ADDRESS 502 Kabel Drive		4—CITY, STATE, ZIP New Orleans, La. 70153	
5—ACCOUNT 1 NO. 25-7592	6—TYPE CB CC SB SC	7—AMOUNT $ 1000.00	8—ACCOUNT 2 NO. 25-75930		9—TYPE CB CC SB SC	10—AMOUNT $ 8000.00
11—ACCOUNT 3 NO.	12—TYPE CB CC SB SC	13—AMOUNT $	14—ACCOUNT 4 NO.		15—TYPE CB CC SB SC	16—AMOUNT $
NO. 10 ASSETS BANK TWO	17—BANK 2 NAME First Homestead		18—BANK 2 ADDRESS 105 WB Expressway		19—CITY, STATE, ZIP Algiers, La. 70114	
20—ACCOUNT 1 NO. CD 250	21—TYPE CB CC SB SC	22—AMOUNT $ 10,000.00	23—ACCOUNT 2 NO.		24—TYPE CB CC SB SC	25—AMOUNT $
26—ACCOUNT 3 NO.	27—TYPE CB CC SB SC	28—AMOUNT $	29—ACCOUNT 4 NO.		30—TYPE CB CC SB SC	31—AMOUNT $
NO. 10 ASSETS BANK THREE	32—BANK 3 NAME		33—BANK 3 ADDRESS		34—CITY, STATE, ZIP	
35—ACCOUNT 1 NO.	36—TYPE CB CC SB SC	37—AMOUNT $	38—ACCOUNT 2 NO.		39—TYPE CB CC SB SC	40—AMOUNT $
41—ACCOUNT 3 NO.	42—TYPE CB CC SB SC	43—AMOUNT $	44—ACCOUNT 4 NO.		45—TYPE CB CC SB SC	46—AMOUNT $

NO. 10
ASSETS — cont'd.

WORKSHEET NO.

47—STOCKS/BONDS NO/DESC	48—AMOUNT	49—STOCKS/BONDS NO/DESC	50—AMOUNT	51—STOCKS/BONDS NO/DESC	52—AMOUNT
U.S.Sav.Bnds $ 100 @ $25	2500.00	$	$		$

53—LIFE INS. FACE VALUE	54—LIFE INS. NET CASH $	55—VESTED INT. RET. FND.	56—NETWORTH OF BUSINESS
$	$	$	$

57—AUTO 1 - YR. MAKE	58—AUTO 1 - VALUE	59—AUTO 2 - YR. MAKE	60—AUTO 2 - VALUE
1980 Buick	$ 6000.00	1978 Chevrolet	$ 3000.00

61—FURNITURE/PERSONAL	62—OTHER ASSET 1 - DESC.	63—OTHER ASSET - 1	64—OTHER ASSET 2 - DESC
$ 30,000.00	Boat, Motor, Trailer	$ 5000.00	

65—OTHER ASSET - 2	66—OTHER ASSET 3 - DESC.	67—OTHER ASSET - 3	68—GIFT $
$		$	$

NO. 11
INSTALLMENT
OTHER DEBT — 1

2—NAME DEBT	3—ADDRESS	4—CITY, STATE, ZIP
VISA/Bank of New Orleans	502 Kabel Drive	New Orleans, La.

5—ACCT. NO.	6—ACCT. NAME	7—PAYMENT $	8—BALANCE
4312-51196001	B - C	30 days	$300.00

NO. 11
INSTALLMENT
OTHER DEBT — 2

9—NAME DEBT	10—ADDRESS	11—CITY, STATE, ZIP
D. H. Holmes	500 Canal Blvd.	New Orleans, La.

12—ACCT. NO.	13—ACCT. NAME	14—PAYMENT $	15—BALANCE
127-34	B - C	$15.00	$200.00

NO. 11
INSTALLMENT
OTHER DEBT — 3

16—NAME DEBT	17—ADDRESS	18—CITY, STATE, ZIP

19—ACCT. NO.	20—ACCT. NAME	21—PAYMENT $	22—BALANCE
	B - C		

NO. 11
INSTALLMENT
OTHER DEBT — 4

23—NAME DEBT	24—ADDRESS	25—CITY, STATE, ZIP

26—ACCT. NO.	27—ACCT. NAME	28—PAYMENT $	29—BALANCE
	B - C		

NO. 11
INSTALLMENT
OTHER DEBT — 5

30—NAME DEBT	31—ADDRESS	32—CITY, STATE, ZIP

33—ACCT. NO.	34—ACCT. NAME	35—PAYMENT $	36—BALANCE
	B - C		

NO. 11
INSTALLMENT
OTHER DEBT — 6

37—NAME DEBT	38—ADDRESS	39—CITY, STATE, ZIP

40—ACCT. NO.	41—ACCT. NAME	42—PAYMENT $	43—BALANCE
	B - C		

44—OTHER DEBT DESC.	45—OTHER DEBT ACCT. NAME	46—PAYMENT	47—BALANCE

48—CHILD SUPPORT	49—ALIMONY PMT	50—ALIMONY MOS
$	$	

REMARKS:

WORKSHEET NO. - 1

NO. 12 REAL ESTATE LOAN – 1	2–NAME		3–STREET ADDRESS	
4–CITY, STATE, ZIP		5–LOAN NO.	6– ☐ B ☐ C ☐ O	

NO. 12 REAL ESTATE LOAN – 2	7–NAME		8–STREET ADDRESS	
9–CITY, STATE, ZIP		10–LOAN NO.	11– ☐ B ☐ C ☐ O	

NO. 12 REAL ESTATE LOAN – 3	12–NAME		13–STREET ADDRESS	
14–CITY, STATE, ZIP		15–LOAN NO.	16– ☐ B ☐ C ☐ O	

NO. 12 AUTO – 1 LOAN	17–DESCRIPTION Navy Federal Credit Union	18–ACCOUNT NO. 222-45-7183
19–ACCOUNT NAME B – C – O	20–PAYMENT AMT. $ 125.00	21–BALANCE $2300.00

NO. 12 AUTO – 2 LOAN	22–DESCRIPTION	23–ACCOUNT NO.
24–ACCOUNT NAME B – C – O	25–PAYMENT AMT. $	26–BALANCE

NO. 12 SCHEDULE – 1 REAL ESTATE	27–ADDRESS			28–STATUS O–P–R–S	29–TYPE
30–VALUE $	31–MORTGAGE AMOUNT $	32–GROSS RENT $		33–PAYMENT $	34–TIM. $

NO. 12 SCHEDULE – 2 REAL ESTATE	35–ADDRESS			36–STATUS O–P–R–S	37–TYPE
38–VALUE $	39–MORTGAGE AMOUNT $	40–GROSS RENT $		41–PAYMENT $	42–TIM. $

NO. 12 SCHEDULE – 3 REAL ESTATE	43–ADDRESS				44–STATUS O–P–R–S
45–TYPE	46–VALUE $	47–MORTGAGE AMT. $	48–GROSS RENT $	49–PAYMENT $	50–TIM. $

I have been advised that flood insurance is, or may be in the future, available in this area in which I am purchasing property, and it has been recommended that I obtain this type of coverage when available from the insurance agent of my choice.

THIS IS TO ACKNOWLEDGE that I am aware of my right to select the insurance company or agent of my choice, provided they meet the requirements of Carruth Mortgage Corporation to write the hazard insurance on the home on which I am applying for financing through Carruth Mortgage Corporation.

I am aware that I have the right to select the carrier of my private mortgage insurance (if applicable) and the carrier of the required Mortgage Title Insurance, subject to the approval of Carruth Mortgage Corporation. However, I hereby designate Carruth Mortgage Corporation as my agent to select such companies.

I have applied to you for a loan and you have made a commitment which you have advised me is purely tentative and is subject to approval by the Federal Housing Administration or The Veterans Administration and/or your investor. I understand the present interest rate on this type of loan is_____% per annum. In the event the interest rate is increased prior to passing of the Act of Sale, I realize that my loan would be closed at the increased interest rate. In the event I elect not to close because of the foregoing: the only adverse consequence I would realize as far as Carruth Mortgage Corporation is concerned would be the loss of the amount paid to you for the application and appraisal fee, if any.

If this application is approved by Carruth Mortgage Corporation, I agree to pay to Carruth Mortgage Corporation_____% of the amount of the loan applied for as a lender's fee for services rendered.

THIS STATEMENT (including that on the foregoing pages) is made by the undersigned for the purpose of obtaining the benefits of a mortgage loan which may be insured under the provisions of the National Housing Act and/or the Servicemen's Readjustment Act of 1944 as amended and/or Conventional Financing, and the undersigned hereby represents that to the best of the undersigned's knowledge and belief, the statements and information contained herein are, in all respects, true and correct and complete. The Federal Housing Administration Commissioner and/or the Administrator of Veterans Affairs and Carruth Mortgage Corporation or their representative, may verify the items contained herein by communicating with any of the persons or institutions named in this statement. The statements will otherwise be treated as confidential. The undersigned further understands that the information furnished herewith will be transcribed to the Veterans Administration, or the Federal Housing Administration and/or Carruth Mortgage Corporation investor forms as applicable in order to complete the processing of the application. The undersigned has read the statements contained over the affixed signature on such forms and hereby authorizes Carruth Mortgage Corporation to complete the forms with the information furnished herewith.

Applicant: *Bryan J. Robinson*

Co-Applicant: *Marie W. Robinson*

Date: 5/25/82

Date: 5/25/82

Date of Application *May 25, 1982*

Application Interview Taken By *Carla Rody*

No. 13 - CONVENTIONAL DATA

WORKSHEET NO. - 1

2—APPRAISER NUMBER		3—PMI FIRST YEAR %	4—LOAN PURPOSE CODE
5—FNMA APPROVAL TYPE	6—FNMA SUBMISSION TYPE	7—FNMA RECOMMENDATION	

8—YR. CONST. LOT ACQUIRED	9—CONST. LOT COST $	10—CONST. LOT VALUE $	11—CONST. LOT IMPROVE. $
12—REFIN. YEAR ACQUIRED	13—REFIN — ORIG. COST $	14—REFIN — LIEN $	15—REFIN. PURPOSE $
16—REFIN — IMPROVE? $	17—REFIN — IMPROVE. $	18—OTHER FIN. $	19—OTHER EQTY. $	20—PMI Code

21 GPARM PLAN CODE A–B–C–D–E–F–G	22 GPARM ORIG. INDEX	23 YIELD CONFIRMATION DATE
24 —UNDERWRITER NAME	25 —UNDERWRITER NUMBER	26—UNDERWRITER TITLE

No. 14 - VA/FHA DATA

WORKSHEET NO. - 1

2—VA LOAN — PURPOSE CODE A	3—FHA LOAN — PURPOSE CODE

4—ELECTRIC TYPE C – COMM N – N/A I – INDV P – PUB	5—GAS TYPE C – COMM N – N/A I – INDV P – PUB	6—WATER TYPE C – COMM I – INDV P – PUB	7—SEWER TYPE C – COMM P – PUB I – INDV S – SEP	8—RANGE ☐ YES ☐ NO
9—REFRIGERATOR ☐ YES ☒ NO	10—DISHWASHER ☐ YES ☒ NO	11—AUTOWASHER ☐ YES ☒ NO	12—DRYER ☐ YES ☒ NO	13—CARPETING ☒ YES ☐ NO
14—OTHERS ☒ YES ☐ NO	Disposal, Ceiling Fan		15— D—DET S—SEMI R—ROW C—CONDO	
16—STREET ACCESS PRIVATE ☐ YES ☒ NO	17—STREET MAINT PRIVATE ☐ YES ☒ NO	18—DATE COMPLETED 1980	19—PROPERTY OCCUPIED N—NEVER OCCUPIED O—OWNER OCCUPIED T—TENANT V— VACANT	
20—OCCUPANT'S NAME John Hunter			21—OCCUPANT'S PHONE NO. 821-1526	
22—INSPECTION TIME Anytime	23—KEYS AT (NAME)		24—KEYS AT (PHONE)	
25—COMPLIANCE INSP. B—FHA-VA V—VA F—FHA H—HOW N—None Made	26—PLAN — SUBMISSION F—FIRST R—REPEAT	27—MASTER CRV NO.	28—BUILDER NAME	
29—WARRANTOR NAME		30—WARRANTOR ADDRESS	31—WARRANTOR PHONE NO	
32—MINERAL RIGHTS ☐ YES ☒ NO	33—LEASE TERM 9 = 99 YRS. O = OTHER F = FHA R = RENEW	34—GROUND RENT YR. $	35—REFINANCE — IMPROVEMENTS $	
		36—FHA CLOSING COST $		
37 —WHICH BUYER VETERAN (CODE) 1—BUYER 1 2—BUYER 2 N—NEITHER		38 JOB RELATED EXP. $	39 —LIFE INS. PREM. $	
40 —REL. NAME Mr . Tom Hunter	41 —REL. STREET ADDRESS 502 Helois Street		42 REL. CITY, STATE, ZIP Metairie, Louisiana 70005	

APPLICANT'S SIGNATURE *Bryan J. Robinson*	CO-APPLICANT'S SIGNATURE *Maine W. Robinson*	DATE 5/25/82
INTERVIEWER *Carla Roth*		DATE 5/25/82

Agreement
To Purchase
Or Sell

Agreement
To Purchase
Or Sell

_____ Agent   New Orleans, La._____ May 24, ____ 19 82
                    Sell

1. ____ I ____ offer and agree to purchase 1804 Homer Street, Metairie, Louisiana
2. house, lot and all improvements theron. All electric, plumbing, air-condi-
3. tioning & heating & builtins to be in working order. Termite inspection at
4. purchasers expense. On grounds measuring about_____ 60 X 130 _____or as per title, and subject to title restrictions if any,
5. for the sum of Sixty thousand dollars ********($ 60,000.00 _____) Dollars, on the terms of
6. _____ No _____ Cash balance secured by a VA loan. Subject to
7. a satisfactory roof inspection at purchasers expense. Seller to furnish a
8. clear termite certificate.
9. This sale is conditioned upon the ability of the purchaser to borrow upon this property as security the sum of $60,000.
10. by a mortgage loan or loans at a rate of interest not to exceed 15.5% per annum, interest and principal payable in equal
11. _____ Monthly _____; installments, over a period of_____ 30 _____years.
    (monthly)   (quarterly)   (semi-annual)   (annual)
12. Should the loan stipulated above be unobtainable by the purchaser, seller or agent within _60_ days from date of accept-
13. ance hereof, this contract shall then become null and void, and the agent is hereby authorized to return the purchaser's deposit
14. in full.
15. Property sold subject to the following lease or leases:
16. Tenant_____ Rental_____ Expiration_____ Options_____
17.
18. Occupancy_ At Act of Sale
19. Paving charges bearing against the property, if any, to be paid by_ Seller
20. Real Estate Taxes and rentals (if any) to be prorated to date of Act of Sale.
21. All proper and necessary certificates and revenue stamps to be paid by seller.
22. Cost of survey by_ Purchaser _____.
23. _____
24. _____
25. _____
26. Act of Sale to be passed before_ Purchaser's _____Notary, on or prior to_ July 24, ____ 1982
27. at expense of purchaser.
28. If this offer is accepted, purchaser must deposit with seller's agent immediately in cash n/a % of purchase price
29. amounting to $ -0-
30. This deposit is to be non-interest bearing and may be placed in any bank in the City of New Orleans, without
31. responsibility on the part of the agent in case of failure or suspension of such bank.
32. The seller shall deliver to purchaser a merchantable title.
33. In the event the purchaser fails to comply with this agreement within the time specified, the seller shall have the
34. right to declare the deposit, ipso facto, forfeited, without formality beyond tender of title to purchaser; or the seller may de-
35. mand specific performance.
36. In the event the seller does not comply with this agreement within the time specified, the purchaser shall have the
37. right either to demand the return of his deposit in full plus an equal amount to be paid as penalty by the seller; or the
38. purchaser may demand specific performance, at his option.
39. In the event the deposit is forfeited, the commission shall be paid out of this deposit, reserving to the seller the right
40. to proceed against the purchaser for the recovery of the amount of the commission.
41. If this offer is accepted, seller agrees to pay the agent's commission of____ 6% ____which commission is earned by
42. agent when this agreement is signed by both parties and when the mortgage loan, if any, has been secured.
43. Seller agrees to pay no more than 1.5% discount.
44. Either party hereto who fails to comply with the terms of this offer, if accepted, is obligated and agrees to pay the
45. agent's commission and all fees and costs incurred in enforcing collection and damages.
46. This offer remains binding and irrevocable through May 25, 1982
47. Submitted to _Linda Kearns_   . (Signed) _Marie W. Robinson_
              (Listing Agent)   (Owner)   _Bryan James Robinson_

48. By _____   New Orleans, La._____ May 24 ____ 19 82
        Selling Agent

        I/We accept the above in all its terms and conditions.
        (Signed) _John Hunter_

Mortgage Corporation
MEMBER OF THE MELLON NATIONAL MORTGAGE GROUP

GOOD FAITH ESTIMATE OF BORROWER'S CLOSING COSTS
AND
MONTHLY PAYMENT ESTIMATE

P 432/48 (R 11/81)

Borrower(s) MARIE WILLIAMS ROBINSON BRYAN JAMES ROBINSON	Property Address 1805 HOMER STREET, METAIRIE, LA. 70005		Loan Amount $ 60,000.00
Loan Type: ☐ FHA ☒ VA ☐ CONV	Rate 15.500	Term 30 Yrs. A.P.R. 15.875 (e)	Date: 5-25-82

ESTIMATED CLOSING COSTS		MONTHLY PAYMENT	
801. Origination Fee 1.00 %	$ 600.00	Principal & Interest	$ 782.72
802. Loan Discount 1.50 %	$	Hazard Insurance Escrow	29.75
803. Appraisal Fee	$ 80.00		
804. Credit Report	$ 30.00	Flood Insurance Escrow	7.00
805. Lender's Inspect.	$	Taxes Escrow	12.00
806. Underwriting Review Fee	$		
902. Private Mortgage Insurance Premium-1st yr.	$	Mortgage Insurance ☐ FHA ☐ PMI	
808. Amortization Schedule	$ 3.00	Total Payment	$ 831.47
901. 30 Days Interest at 25.479 Per Day	$ 764.37	ITEMS REQUIRED	
1002. Mortgage Insurance Premium _____ mos.	$	☐ Bank Account Numbers and Addresses	
807. Photographs	$ 10.00		
1103. Title Examination	$ 150.00	☐ Charge Account Numbers and Addresses	
1104. Title Insurance Binder	$	☐ W-2 Forms for Last 3 Years ☐ 1040 Forms for Last 3 Years	
1105. Document Preparation	$		
1106. Notary Fee	$ 90.00	☐ Profit and Loss Statements ☐ Balance Sheet	
1107. Attorney's Fees	$	☐ Closing Statement of Sale of Home (Prior or Present)	
1108. Title Insurance:	$ 284.00	☒ Certificate of Eligibility ☐ DD 214	
1109. Lender's Coverage $ 212.00		☒ DD 1747 ☐ DD 802	
1110. Owner's Coverage $ 72.00			
1201. Recording Fees	$ 35.00	☐ Resume	
1301. Survey	$ 125.00	☐ Gift Letter	
1302. Pest Inspection	$		
810.			
		SELLER TO PAY PER SALES CONTRACT	

ESTIMATE—CLOSING COSTS	$ 2,171.37	APPLICATION FEE & RECEIPT	
Plus: 1001. 14 Mos. Hazard Insurance (Est)	416.50	Application Fee: (Credit Report)	$ 30.00
904. 1006. 14 Mos. Flood Insurance (Est)	98.00	Appraisal Fee: ☒ VA ☐ FHA ☐ CONV	80.00
1003. 1004. 2 Mos. Tax (Est)	24.00	Underwriter's Fee:	
Down Payment		Origination Fee:	
ESTIMATE—TOTAL CASH REQUIREMENT	$ 2,709.87	TOTAL FEES COLLECTED	$ 110.00

I/We, the undersigned, have received full notification regarding the facts of ECOA, Flood & Title Insurance and have received copies of this estimate and RESPA booklet, on the above date.

This amount cannot be guaranteed, and this figure could change by time of closing. This form does not cover all items you will be required to pay in cash at settlement, you may be requested to pay other additional amounts, and you may wish to inquire as to the nature of the amounts.

Receipt of Copy of Estimated Closing Costs is Hereby Acknowledged.

Bryan James Robinson
BRYAN JAMES ROBINSON Borrower

Marie W. Robinson
MARIE WILLIAMS ROBINSON

Paid By:

☒ CASH ☐ CHECK

Received:

By _____ Carla Rody *Carla Rody*
CARRUTH MORTGAGE CORPORATION

CARRUTH
Mortgage Corporation
MEMBER OF THE MELLON NATIONAL MORTGAGE GROUP

As a result of applying to CARRUTH MORTGAGE CORPORATION for a mortgage, receipt is hereby acknowledged of the following (appropriate notices as checked:)

Equal Credit Opportunity Act (ECOA) Notice and Additional Disclosure:

The Board of Governors of the Federal Reserve System have issued Regulation B implementing the Equal Credit Opportunity Act, and require that the public be alerted to the existence of the general rule prohibiting discrimination on a prohibited basis. Below is the (1) Notice and (2) Additional Disclosures required by Regulation B:

(1) EQUAL CREDIT OPPORTUNITY ACT NOTICE
   The Federal Equal Credit Opportunity Act prohibits creditors from discriminating against credit applicants on the basis of race, color, religion, national origin, sex, marital status, age (provided that the applicant has the capacity to enter into a binding contract); because all or part of the applicant's income derives from any public assistance program; or because the applicant has in good faith exercised any right under the Consumer Credit Protection Act. The Federal agency that administers compliance with this law concerning this creditor is the Federal Trade Commission, Equal Credit Opportunity, Washington, D. C. 20580.

(2) ADDITIONAL DISCLOSURE
   Alimony, child support, or separate maintenance income need not be revealed if applicant does not wish to have it considered as a basis for repaying a loan.

NOTICE TO APPLICANTS: Right of Privacy Act of 1978

☐ FHA

This is notice to you as required by the Right of Financial Privacy Act of 1978 that the Department of Housing and Urban Development has a right of access to financial records held by a financial institution in connection with the consideration or administration of assistance to you. Financial records involving your transaction will be available to the Department of Housing and Urban Development without further notice or authorization but will not be disclosed or released to another Government agency or Department without your consent except as required or permitted by law.

☒ VA

This is notice to you as required by the Right to Financial Privacy Act of 1978 that the Veterans Administration Loan Guaranty Service or Division has a right of access to financial records held by a financial institution in connection with the consideration or administration of assistance to you. Financial records involving your transaction will be available to the Veterans Administration Loan Guaranty Service or Division without further notice or authorization but will not be disclosed or released to another Government agency or department without your consent except as required or permitted by law.

NO COMMITMENT TO LEND

I have applied to you for a loan and you have made a commitment which you have advised me is purely tentative and is subject to approval by the Federal Housing Administration or Veterans Administration and/or your investor.

I understand the present interest rate on this type of loan is ___15.5___ % per annum. In the event the interest rate is increased prior to passing of the Act of Sale, I realize that my loan will be closed at the increased interest rate. In the event that I elect not to close because of the foregoing, the only adverse consequence I would realize as far as Carruth Mortgage Corporation is concerned would be the loss of the amount paid to you for the appraisal, credit report, and any other out-of-pocket expenses.

INFORMATION FOR GOVERNMENT MONITORING PURPOSES

If this loan is for purchase or construction of a home, the following information is requested by the Federal Government to monitor this lender's compliance with Equal Credit Opportunity and Fair Housing Laws. The law provides that a lender may neither discriminate on the basis of this information nor on whether or not it is furnished. Furnishing this information is optional. If you do not wish to furnish the following information, please initial below.

BORROWER: I do not wish to furnish this information (initials) _____

RACE/ NATIONAL ORIGIN: ☐ American Indian, Alaskan Native ☐ Asian, Pacific Islander ☐ Black ☐ Hispanic ☒ White ☐ Other (specify) _____

SEX: ☒ Male ☐ Female

CO-BORROWER: I do not wish to furnish this information (initials) _____

RACE/ NATIONAL ORIGIN: ☐ American Indian, Alaskan Native ☐ Asian, Pacific Islander ☐ Black ☐ Hispanic ☒ White ☐ Other (specify) _____

SEX: ☒ Female ☐ Male

I/We hereby acknowledge receipt of a copy of the above notices.

Applicant	Date	Co-Applicant	Date
Bryan J. Robinson	5/25/82	*Marie W. Robinson*	5/25/82

CMC651 11/79

Form Approved
OMB No. 76-R0371

Veterans Administration		TO	VETERANS ADMINISTRATION ATTN. LOAN GUARANTY DIVISION 701 Loyola Avenue New Orleans, Louisiana
REQUEST FOR DETERMINATION OF ELIGIBILITY AND AVAILABLE LOAN GUARANTY ENTITLEMENT			

NOTE. Please read instructions on reverse before completing this form. If additional space is required attach separate sheet.

1. FIRST - MIDDLE - LAST NAME OF VETERAN	2A. ADDRESS OF VETERAN (No., Street or rural route, City or P.O., State and ZIP Code)
BRYAN JAMES ROBINSON	5 Opelousas Street
2B. VETERAN'S DAYTIME TELEPHONE NO. (Include Area Code)	3. DATE OF BIRTH	New Orleans, Louisiana 70123
504-241-7100	12-1-42	

4. MILITARY SERVICE DATA *(SEE INSTRUCTIONS ON REVERSE - ITEM 4)*

PERIOD OF ACTIVE SERVICE		NAME (Show your name exactly as it appears on your separation papers (DD214) or Statement of Service)	SERVICE NUMBER (Enter Social Security No. if appropriate)	BRANCH OF SERVICE
DATE FROM	DATE TO			
A. 01/68	present	ROBINSON, BRYAN JAMES	222-45-7183	NAVY
B.				
C.				
D.				

5A. WERE YOU DISCHARGED, RETIRED OR SEPARATED FROM SERVICE BECAUSE OF DISABILITY OR DO YOU NOW HAVE ANY SERVICE-CONNECTED DISABILITIES? ☐ YES ☒ NO *(If "Yes," Complete Item 5D)*	5B. VA FILE NUMBER C-	6. IS A CERTIFICATE OF ELIGIBILITY FOR LOAN GUARANTY PURPOSES ENCLOSED? ☐ YES ☒ NO *(If "No," Complete Items 7A and 7B)*
7A. HAVE YOU PREVIOUSLY APPLIED FOR A CERTIFICATE OF ELIGIBILITY FOR VA LOAN PURPOSES? ☐ YES ☒ NO *(If "Yes," give location of VA office(s))*	7B. HAVE YOU PREVIOUSLY RECEIVED SUCH A CERTIFICATE? ☐ YES ☒ NO *(If "Yes," give location of VA office(s))*	7C. THE CERTIFICATE OF ELIGIBILITY PREVIOUSLY ISSUED TO ME HAS BEEN LOST OR STOLEN, IF RECOVERED IT WILL BE RETURNED TO THE VA *(Check if applicable)* ☐

ALL APPLICANTS MUST COMPLETE ITEMS 19 THROUGH 21

8. HAVE YOU PREVIOUSLY ACQUIRED PROPERTY WITH THE ASSISTANCE OF A GI LOAN? ☐ YES ☐ NO *(If "Yes," complete Items 9 through 18. Please attach a separate sheet if more than one loan is involved)*	9. ADDRESS OF REGIONAL OFFICE WHERE LOAN WAS OBTAINED (City and State)
10. STATE TYPE OF LOAN (Home, Mobile home, Condominium, Direct, Farm, Business, etc.)	11. ADDRESS OF PROPERTY PREVIOUSLY PURCHASED WITH GUARANTY ENTITLEMENT	12. DATE YOU PURCHASED THE PROPERTY
13. DO YOU NOW OWN THE REAL PROPERTY DESCRIBED IN ITEM 11? ☐ YES ☐ NO *(If "Yes," do not complete Items 14 through 18)*	14. DATE THE DEED, IF ANY, WAS DELIVERED TO PURCHASER	15. IS THERE ANY UNDERSTANDING OR AGREEMENT WRITTEN OR ORAL, BETWEEN YOU AND THE PURCHASERS THAT THEY WILL RECONVEY THE PROPERTY TO YOU? ☐ YES ☐ NO

NOTE. It will speed processing if you can complete Items 16, 17, and 18.

16. NAME AND ADDRESS OF LENDER TO WHOM LOAN PAYMENTS WERE MADE	17. LENDER'S LOAN OR ACCOUNT NUMBER
	18. VA LOAN NO. (LH)

I certify that the statements herein are true to the best of my knowledge and belief.

19. SIGNATURE OF VETERAN	20. DATE SIGNED
Bryan James Robinson	5/25/82

FEDERAL STATUTES PROVIDE SEVERE PENALTIES FOR FRAUD, INTENTIONAL MISREPRESENTATION, CRIMINAL CONNIVANCE OR CONSPIRACY PURPOSED TO INFLUENCE THE ISSUANCE OF ANY GUARANTY OR INSURANCE BY THE ADMINISTRATOR.

THIS SECTION FOR VA USE ONLY

DATE CERTIFICATE ISSUED AND DISCHARGE OR SEPARATION PAPERS GIVEN TO VETERAN OR MAILED TO ADDRESS SHOWN BELOW	TYPE OF DISCHARGE OR SEPARATION PAPERS RETURNED	SIGNATURE AND TITLE OF APPROPRIATE OFFICIAL (If applicable)	STATION NUMBER

VA FORM 26-1880, APR 1980   DO NOT DETACH

IMPORTANT - You must complete Item 21 since the Certificate of Eligibility along with all discharge and separation papers will be mailed to the address shown in Item 21 below. If they are to be sent to you, your current mailing address should be indicated, or if they are to be sent elsewhere, the name and address of such person or firm should be shown in Item 21.

The amount of loan guaranty entitlement available for use is endorsed on the reverse of the enclosed Certificate of Eligibility. This certificate must be returned to the VA at the time a loan application or loan report is submitted.

NOTE - PLEASE DELIVER THE ENCLOSED PAMPHLETS AND DISCHARGE OR SEPARATION PAPERS TO THE VETERAN PROMPTLY

VA FORM 26-1880
APR 1980   SUPERSEDES VA FORM 26-1880, JAN 1977,
WHICH WILL NOT BE USED.

DO NOT DETACH

---

21. PLEASE BE SURE THAT NAME AND ADDRESS ARE ENTERED IN THE SPACE INDICATED TO INSURE PROMPT DELIVERY OF DOCUMENTS ▶

CARRUTH MORTGAGE CORPORATION
P. O. Box 53334
NEW ORLEANS, LA. 70153

Veterans Administration

Certificate of Eligibility CANCELLED

7656225

FOR LOAN GUARANTY BENEFITS

NAME OF VETERAN (First, Middle, Last)	SERVICE SERIAL NUMBER/SOCIAL SECURITY NUMBER
BRYAN JAMES ROBINSON	222-45-7183

ENTITLEMENT CODE	BRANCH OF SERVICE	DATE OF BIRTH
4	NAVY	December 1, 1942

IS ELIGIBLE FOR THE BENEFITS OF CHAPTER 37, TITLE 38, U.S. CODE, AND HAS THE AMOUNT OF ENTITLEMENT SHOWN AS AVAILABLE ON THE REVERSE, SUBJECT TO THE STATEMENT BELOW, IF CHECKED.

☐   Valid unless discharged or released subsequent to date of this certificate. A certification of continuous active duty as of date of note required.

ADMINISTRATOR OF VETERANS AFFAIRS

Bruce C. Loree

Veterans Administration (Authorized Agent)
Regional Office
701 Loyola Avenue
New Orleans, Louisiana 70113
(Issuing Office)

CANCELLED

June 3, 1982
(Date Issued)

Form Approved
OMB No. 2900-0045

VA REQUEST FOR DETERMINATION OF REASONABLE VALUE (Real Estate) HUD APPLICATION FOR PROPERTY APPRAISAL AND COMMITMENT	HUD Section of Act	1. CASE NUMBER LH123-456

2. PROPERTY ADDRESS *(Include ZIP Code and county)*
1804 Homer Street
Metairie, Louisiana 70005

3. LEGAL DESCRIPTION
Lot 12 Square 16
Bonnabel Heights S/D
Jefferson Parish

4. TITLE LIMITATIONS AND RESTRICTIVE COVENANTS
None Known

1. ☐ CONDOMINIUM   2. ☐ PLANNED UNIT DEVELOPMENT

5. NAME AND ADDRESS OF FIRM OR PERSON MAKING REQUEST/APPLICATION *(Include ZIP Code)*

CARRUTH MORTGAGE CORPORATION
P. O. Box 53334
NEW ORLEANS, LOUISIANA 70153

Carla- 885-4811   Census Tract 17.12

6. LOT DIMENSIONS:
60' x 130'
1. ☐ IRREGULAR: SQ/FT   2. ☐ ACRES:

7. UTILITIES (✓)   ELEC.   GAS   WATER   SAN. SEWER
1. PUBLIC   x   x   x   x
2. COMMUNITY
3. INDIVIDUAL

8. E Q U I P.	1. ☒ RANGE/OVEN	4. ☐ CLOTHES WASHER	7. ☒ VENT FAN	
	2. ☐ REFRIG.	5. ☐ DRYER	8. ☒ W/W CARPET	
	3. ☒ DISH WASHER	6. ☒ GARBAGE DISP.	9. ☒ ceiling fan	

9. BUILDING STATUS
1. ☐ PROPOSED   3. ☐ UNDER CONSTR.
2. ☐ SUBSTANTIAL REHABILITATION   4. ☒ EXISTING

10. BUILDING TYPE
1. ☒ DETACHED   3. ☐ ROW
2. ☐ SEMI-DETACHED   4. ☐ APT. UNIT

11. FACTORY FABRICATED?
1. ☐ YES   2. ☒ NO

12. NUMBER OF UNITS

13A. STREET ACCESS
1. ☐ PRIVATE
2. ☒ PUBLIC

13B. STREET MAINT.
1. ☐ PRIVATE
2. ☒ PUBLIC

14A. CONSTRUCTION WARRANTY INCLUDED?
1. ☐ YES   2. ☒ NO *(If "Yes" complete items 14B and C also.)*

14B. NAME OF WARRANTY PROGRAM

14C. EXPIRATION DATE *(Month, day, year)*

15. CONSTR. COMPLETED *(Mo., yr.)*
1980

16. NAME OF OWNER
John Hunter

17. PROPERTY:
☒ OCCUPIED BY OWNER   ☐ NEVER OCCUPIED   ☐ VACANT   ☐ OCCUPIED BY TENANT *(Complete Item 18 also)*

18. RENT *(If applic.)*
$ -0- /MONTH

19. NAME OF OCCUPANT
John Hunter

20. TELEPHONE NO.
821-1526

21. NAME OF BROKER
Linda Keanan

22. TELEPHONE NO.
888-2192

23. DATE AND TIME AVAILABLE FOR INSPECTION
Anytime   ☒ AM   ☐ PM

24. KEYS AT *(Address)*
Call for access 821-1526

25. ORIGINATOR'S IDENT. NO.

26. SPONSOR'S IDENT. NO.

27. INSTITUTION'S CASE NO.
100400

28. PURCHASER'S NAME AND ADDRESS *(Complete mailing address. Include ZIP code.)*

Bryan James Robinson
5 Opelousas Street
New Orleans, Louisiana 70114

EQUAL OPPORTUNITY IN HOUSING

NOTE – Federal laws and regulations prohibit discrimination because of race, color, religion, sex, or national origin in the sale or rental of residential property. Numerous State statutes and local ordinances also prohibit such discrimination. In addition, section 805 of the Civil Rights Act of 1968 prohibits discriminatory practices in connection with the financing of housing.

If HUD/VA finds there is noncompliance with any antidiscrimination laws or regulations, it may discontinue business with the violator.

29. NEW OR PROPOSED CONSTRUCTION – *Complete Items 29A through 29G for new or proposed construction cases only.*

A. COMPLIANCE INSPECTIONS WILL BE OR WERE MADE BY:
☐ FHA   ☒ VA   ☐ NONE MADE

B. PLANS *(check one)*
☐ FIRST SUBMISSION   ☐ REPEAT CASE *(If checked complete Item 29C.)*

C. PLANS SUBMITTED PREVIOUSLY UNDER CASE NO.:

D. NAME AND ADDRESS OF BUILDER
none

E. TELEPHONE NO.

F. NAME AND ADDRESS OF WARRANTOR

G. TELEPHONE NO.

30. COMMENTS ON SPECIAL ASSESSMENTS OR HOMEOWNERS ASSOCIATION CHARGES
none

31. ANNUAL REAL ESTATE TAXES
$ 144.00

32. MINERAL RIGHTS RESERVED?
☐ YES *(Explain)*   ☒ NO

33. LEASEHOLD CASES *(Complete if applicable)*
LEASE IS: ☐ 99 YEARS   ☐ RENEWABLE   ☐ HUD/VA APPROVED
EXPIRES *(Date)*
ANNUAL GROUND RENT $

34. SALE PRICE OF PROPERTY
$ 60,000.00

35. REFINANCING – AMOUNT OF PROPOSED LOAN
$

36. PROPOSED SALE CONTRACT ATTACHED
☒ YES   ☐ NO

37. CONTRACT NUMBER PREVIOUSLY APPROVED BY VA THAT WILL BE USED

CERTIFICATIONS FOR SUBMISSIONS TO HUD

In submitting this application for a conditional commitment for mortgage insurance, it is agreed and understood by the parties involved in the transaction, that if, at the time of application for a Firm Commitment, the identity of the seller has changed, the application for a Firm Commitment will be rejected and the application for a Conditional Commitment will be reprocessed upon request by the mortgagee.

It is further agreed and understood that in submitting the request for a Firm Commitment for mortgage insurance, the seller, the purchaser and the broker involved in the transaction shall each certify that the terms of the contract for purchase are true to his or her best knowledge and belief, and that any other agreement entered into by any of these parties in connection with this transaction is attached to the sales agreement.

BUILDER/SELLER'S AGREEMENT: All Houses: The undersigned agrees to deliver to the purchaser HUD's statement of appraised value. **Proposed Construction:** The undersigned agrees, upon sale or conveyance of title within one year from date of initial occupancy, to deliver to the purchaser Form HUD-92544, warranting that the house is constructed in substantial conformity with the plans and specifications on which HUD based its value and to furnish HUD a conformed copy with the purchaser's receipt thereon that the original warranty was delivered to him/her. **All Houses:** In consideration of the issuance of the commitment requested by this application, I (we) hereby agree that any deposit or down payment made in connection with the purchase of the property described above, whether received by the undersigned, or an agent of the undersigned, shall upon receipt be deposited in escrow or in trust or in a special account which is not subject to the claims of my creditors and where it will be maintained until it has been disbursed for the benefit of the purchaser or otherwise disposed of in accordance with the terms of the contract of sale.

Signature of: ☒ Mortgagee   ☐ Builder   ☐ Seller   ☐ Other *(signed)* Patricia Misiek   Date 5/25 19 82

MORTGAGEE'S CERTIFICATE: The undersigned mortgagee certifies to the best of his/her knowledge, all statements made in this application and the supporting documents are true, correct and complete.

Signature and Title of Mortgage Officer: x *Patricia Misiek* Patricia Misiek, Loan Officer   Date 5-25 19 82

CERTIFICATIONS FOR SUBMISSIONS TO VA

1. On receipt of "Certificate of Reasonable Value" or advice from the Veterans Administration that a "Certificate of Reasonable Value" will not be issued, we agree to forward to the appraiser the approved fee which we are holding for this purpose.
2. CERTIFICATION REQUIRED ON CONSTRUCTION UNDER FHA SUPERVISION *(Strike out inappropriate phrases in parentheses)*

I hereby certify that plans and specifications and related exhibits, including acceptable FHA Change Orders, if any, supplied to VA in this case, are identical to those (submitted to) (to be submitted to) (approved by) FHA, and that FHA inspections (have been) (will be) made pursuant to FHA approval for mortgage insurance on the basis of proposed construction under Sec.

38. SIGNATURE OF PERSON AUTHORIZING THE REQUEST
Patricia Misiek *Patricia Misiek*

39. TITLE
Loan Officer

40. DATE
5-25-82

41. DATE OF ASSIGNMENT
May 25, 1982

42. NAME OF APPRAISER
Larry DeMarcay, Jr.

WARNING Section 1010 of Title 18, U.S.C. provides: "Whoever for the purpose of . . . influencing such Administration . . . makes, passes, utters or publishes any statement knowing the same to be false . . . shall be fined not more than $5,000 or imprisoned not more than two years or both."

VA FORM 26-1805, AUG 1980
HUD FORM 92800-1

SUPERSEDES VA FORM 26-1805, AUG 1977, AND
HUD 92800, JUL 1979, WHICH WILL NOT BE USED.

VA/HUD FILE COPY 1

Form Approved
OMB No. 2900-0045

VA CERTIFICATE OF REASONABLE VALUE [X] / HUD CONDITIONAL COMMITMENT [ ]	HUD Section of Act	1. CASE NUMBER LH123456

2. PROPERTY ADDRESS (Include ZIP Code and county)	3. LEGAL DESCRIPTION	4. TITLE LIMITATIONS AND RESTRICTIVE COVENANTS
1804 Homer Street Metairie, Louisiana 70005	Lot 12 Square 16 Bonnabel Heights S/D Jefferson Parish	None Known 1. [ ] CONDOMINIUM 2. [ ] PLANNED UNIT DEVELOPMENT

5. NAME AND ADDRESS OF FIRM OR PERSON MAKING REQUEST/APPLICATION (Include ZIP Code)

CARRUTH MORTGAGE CORPORATION
P. O. Box 53334
New Olreans, Louisiana 70153

Tel. 885-4811   Census Tract 17.12

6. LOT DIMENSIONS:

60 X 130

1. [ ] IRREGULAR: SQ/FT   2. [ ] ACRES:

7. UTILITIES (✓)	ELEC.	GAS	WATER	SAN. SEWER
1. PUBLIC	X	X	X	X
2. COMMUNITY				
3. INDIVIDUAL				

8. EQUIP.								
1. [X] RANGE/OVEN		4. [ ] CLOTHES WASHER		7. [X] VENT FAN				
2. [ ] REFRIG.		5. [ ] DRYER		8. [X] W/W CARPET				
3. [ ] DISH-WASHER		6. [X] GARBAGE DISP.		9. [X] Ceiling fan				

9. BUILDING STATUS	10. BUILDING TYPE	11. FACTORY FABRICATED?	12. NUMBER OF UNITS	13A. STREET ACCESS	13B. STREET MAINT.
1. [ ] PROPOSED 3. [ ] UNDER CONSTR. 2. [ ] SUBSTANTIAL REHABILITATION 4. [X] EXISTING	1. [X] DETACHED 3. [ ] ROW 2. [ ] SEMI-DETACHED 4. [ ] APT. UNIT	1. [ ] YES 2. [X] NO	1	1. [ ] PRIVATE 2. [X] PUBLIC	1. [ ] PRIVATE 2. [X] PUBLIC

14. ESTIMATED REASONABLE VALUE OF PROPERTY	15. REMAINING ECONOMIC LIFE OF PROPERTY IS ESTIMATED TO BE NOT LESS THAN:	16. EXPIRATION DATE
$ 60,000.00	30 YEARS	12/2/82

17. HUD COMMITMENT TERMS

A. MAXIMUM MORTGAGE AMOUNT	$
B. NO. OF MONTHS	
C. NOTICE OF REJECTION	
D. "AS IS" VALUE	$

18. [ ] This Certificate of Reasonable Value is valid only if VA Form 26-1843p showing VA General Conditions and the applicable Specific Conditions is attached.

19. ADMINISTRATOR OF VETERANS AFFAIRS, BY (Signature of authorized agent), OR HUD AUTHORIZED AGENT	20. DATE ISSUED	21. VA OR HUD OFFICE
Bruce C. Lowe Bruce C. Lowe	6/2/82	NOLA

E. MONTHLY EXPENSE ESTIMATE

FIRE INSURANCE	$
TAXES	$

22. PURCHASER'S NAME AND ADDRESS (Complete mailing address. Include ZIP Code.)

Bryan James Robinson
5 Opelousas Street
New Orleans, Louisiana 70114

CONDO. COMMUNITY EXPENSE	$
MAINTENANCE AND REPAIRS	$
HEAT AND UTILITIES	$
F. ESTIMATED CLOSING COST	$
G. [ ] EXISTING [ ] PROPOSED	(See General Condition 3 on attachment.)
H. IMPROVED LIVING AREA	SQ/FT

I. [ ] This Conditional Commitment is valid only if HUD Form 92800-5a showing HUD General Conditions and the applicable Specific Conditions is attached.

VA FORM 26-1843, AUG 1980   HUD FORM 92800-5

REQUESTER'S COPY 2

VA Veterans Administration	**GENERAL AND SPECIFIC CONDITIONS FOR VA CERTIFICATE OF REASONABLE VALUE (VA Form 26-1843)**	1. CASE NUMBER
		LH 123456

GENERAL CONDITIONS

(NOTE: THE VETERANS ADMINISTRATION DOES NOT ASSUME ANY RESPONSIBILITY FOR THE CONDITION OF THE PROPERTY. THE CORRECTION OF ANY DEFECTS NOW EXISTING OR THAT MAY DEVELOP WILL BE THE RESPONSIBILITY OF THE PURCHASER.)

1. This certificate will remain effective as to any written contract of sale entered into by an eligible veteran within the validity period indicated.

2. This dwelling conforms with the Minimum Property Requirements prescribed by the Administrator of Veterans Affairs.

3. The aggregate of any loan secured by this property plus the amount of any assessment consequent on any special improvements as to which a lien or right to a lien shall exist against the property, except as provided in Item 12 below, may not exceed the reasonable value in Item 14 on VA Form 26-1843.

4. Proposed construction shall be completed in accordance with the plans and specifications identified below, relating to both on-site and off-site improvements upon which this valuation is based and shall otherwise conform fully to the VA Minimum Property Requirements. Satisfactory completion must be evidenced by either

    A. VA Final Compliance Inspection Report (VA Form 26-1839), or

    B. VA Acceptance of FHA Compliance Inspection Reports or other evidence of completion under FHA supervision applicable to proposed construction.

5. By contracting to sell property, as proposed construction or existing construction not previously occupied, to a veteran purchaser who is to be assisted in the purchase by a loan made, guaranteed, or insured by VA, the builder or other seller agrees to place any down payment received by the seller or agent of the seller in a special trust account as required by section 1806 of Title 38, U.S. Code.

6. The VA guaranty is subject to and conditioned upon the lending institution's compliance, at the time of the making, increasing, extending or renewing of the proposed loan, with section 102 of P.L. 93-234, "Flood Disaster Protection Act of 1973."

SPECIFIC CONDITIONS *(Applicable when checked or completed)*

2. THE REASONABLE VALUE ESTABLISHED HEREIN FOR THE RELATED PROPERTY IS

[X] BASED UPON OBSERVATION OF THE PROPERTY IN ITS "AS IS" CONDITION

[ ] PREDICATED UPON COMPLETION OF PROPOSED CONSTRUCTION *(If checked complete Item 3.)*

[ ] PREDICATED UPON COMPLETION OF REPAIRS LISTED IN ITEM 5

3. PROPOSED CONSTRUCTION TO BE COMPLETED *(Identify plans, specifications and exhibits)*

4. INSPECTIONS REQUIRED

[ ] FHA COMPLIANCE INSPECTIONS FOR PROPOSED CONSTRUCTION

[ ] VA COMPLIANCE INSPECTIONS   [ ] LENDER TO CERTIFY

6. NAME OF COMPLIANCE INSPECTOR

5. REPAIRS TO BE COMPLETED

7. HEALTH AUTHORITY APPROVAL–Execution of VA Form 26-6395 by the Health Authority indicating approval of the water supply and/or sewage disposal installation is required. (Approval by letter or Health Authority Form may be used.)

8. This document is subject to the provisions of Executive Orders 11246 and 11375, and the Rules and Regulations of the Secretary of Labor in effect this date, and VA Regulations 4390 through 4393, and also the provisions of the certification executed by the builder, sponsor or developer named herein which is on file in this office.

9. TERMITE CERTIFICATE–The seller shall furnish the veteran-purchaser at no cost to settlement a written statement (or certification) from a recognized exterminator that based on careful visual inspection of accessible areas and on sounding of accessible structural members, there is no evidence of termite or other wood-destroying insect infestation in [X] the subject property, and, if such infestation previously existed, it has been corrected and any damage due to such infestation has also been corrected or alternatively been fully disclosed.

10. WARRANTY

[ ] *(If checked, complete Item 11)*

11. NAME OF WARRANTOR

12. EXCEPTIONS TO GENERAL CONDITION NO. 3 ABOVE

[ ] ENERGY CONSERVATION IMPROVEMENTS *(See VA Form 26-1843n attached.)*

[ ] OTHER *(Cite and explain in Item 13 below.)*

13. OTHER REQUIREMENTS

"Since this property is located in a special flood hazard area, Flood insurance will be required in accordance with VA regulation 4326."

VA FORM 26-1843p
AUG 1980

Competent
Mortgage
Counseling

CARRUTH Mortgage Corporation

MEMBER OF THE MELLON NATIONAL MORTGAGE GROUP

3601 I-10 SERVICE ROAD   METAIRIE, LOUISIANA   PHONE 885-4811

MAILING ADDRESS
P. O. BOX 53334
NEW ORLEANS, LA. 70153

SUBJECT PROPERTY

STREET SCENE

1804 HOMER STREET
METAIRIE, LOUISIANA 70005

CMC 531

Form Approved
OMB No. 2502-0059

PRIVACY ACT NOTICE: This information is to be used by the agency collecting it in determining whether you qualify as a prospective mortgagor or borrower under its program. It will not be disclosed outside the agency without your consent except to your employer(s) for verification of employment and as required and permitted by law. You do not have to give us this information, but if you do not your application for approval as a prospective mortgagor or borrower may be delayed or rejected. The information requested in this form is authorized by Title 38, U.S.C., Chapter 37 *(if VA)*; by 12 U.S.C., Section 1701 et seq. *(if HUD/FHA)*; by 42 U.S.C., Section 1452b *(if HUD/CPD)*; and Title 42, U.S.C., 1471 et seq., or 7 U.S.C., 1921 et seq. *(if U.S.D.A., FmHA)*.	VETERANS ADMINISTRATION, U.S.D.A., FARMERS HOME ADMINISTRATION, AND U.S. DEPARTMENT OF HOUSING AND URBAN DEVELOPMENT - (Community Planning and Development, and Housing - Federal Housing Commissioner) **REQUEST FOR VERIFICATION OF EMPLOYMENT**

INSTRUCTIONS

LENDER OR LOCAL PROCESSING AGENCY (LPA): Complete Items 1 through 7. Have the applicant complete Item 8. Forward the completed form directly to the employer named in Item 1. EMPLOYER: Complete either Parts II and IV or Parts III and IV. Return form directly to the Lender or Local Processing Agency named in Item 2 of Part I.

PART I - REQUEST

1. TO: *(Name and Address of Employer)* U.S. NAVY 4400 DAUPHINE STREET NEW ORLEANS, LA., 70119	2. FROM: *(Name and Address of Lender or Local Processing Agency)* CARRUTH MORTGAGE CORPORATION P. O. BOX 53334 NEW ORLEANS, LOUISIANA 70153		
3. I certify that this verification has been sent directly to the employer and has not passed through the hands of the applicant or any other interested party. *Carla Rody* *(Signature of Lender, Official of LPA, or FmHA Loan Packager)*	4. TITLE OF LENDER, OFFICIAL OF LPA, OR FmHA LOAN PACKAGER CARLA RODY LOAN PROCESSOR	5. DATE JUNE 2, 1982	
		6. HUD/FHA/CPD, VA, OR FmHA NO. LH-123456	
7. NAME AND ADDRESS OF APPLICANT BRYAN JAMES ROBINSON 5 OPELOUSAS STREET NEW ORLEANS, LA., 70114	I have applied for a mortgage loan or a rehabilitation loan and stated that I am/was employed by you. My signature in the block below authorizes verification of my employment information. 8. EMPLOYEE'S IDENTIFICATION 222-45-7183 SIGNATURE OF APPLICANT *Bryan James Robinson*		

PART II - VERIFICATION OF PRESENT EMPLOYMENT

EMPLOYMENT DATA	PAY DATA		
9. APPLICANT'S DATE OF EMPLOYMENT Jan. 1968	12A. BASE PAY *(Current)* $_____ ☐ Annual $_____ ☐ Hourly $_____ ☐ Monthly $_____ ☐ Weekly $_____ ☐ Other *(Specify)*	FOR MILITARY PERSONNEL ONLY	
		Type	Monthly Amount
10. PRESENT POSITION Chief Petty Officer		BASE PAY	$ 2200.
		RATIONS	$ 200.
11. PROBABILITY OF CONTINUED EMPLOYMENT Career Officer, Very Good	12B. EARNINGS	FLIGHT OR HAZARD	$ -0-
	Type / Year to Date / Past Year		
	BASE PAY $ $	CLOTHING	$ 20.
13. IF OVERTIME OR BONUS IS APPLICABLE, IS ITS CONTINUANCE LIKELY?	OVERTIME $ $	QUARTERS	$ 400.
OVERTIME ☐ Yes ☒ No	COMMISSIONS $ $	PRO PAY	$ -0-
BONUS ☐ Yes ☒ No	BONUS $ $	OVERSEAS OR COMBAT	$ -0-

14. REMARKS *(If paid hourly, please indicate average hours worked each week during current and past year)*

NONE

PART III - VERIFICATION OF PREVIOUS EMPLOYMENT

15. DATES OF EMPLOYMENT	16. SALARY/WAGE AT TERMINATION PER ☐ YEAR ☐ MONTH ☐ WEEK			
	BASE PAY	OVERTIME	COMMISSIONS	BONUS
	$	$	$	$
17. REASONS FOR LEAVING	18. POSITION HELD			

PART IV - CERTIFICATION

Federal statutes provide severe penalties for any fraud, intentional misrepresentation, or criminal connivance or conspiracy purposed to influence the issuance of any guaranty or insurance by the VA Administrator, the U.S.D.A., FmHA Administrator, the HUD/FHA Commissioner, or the HUD/CPD Assistant Secretary.

19. SIGNATURE *Tim Hartley* Tim Hartley	20. TITLE OF EMPLOYER Base Personnel Officer	21. DATE 5/27/82

Previous Editions May be Used until Supply is Exhausted

HUD-6233/92004-g; VA 26-8497; FmHA-410-5 (12-80)

RETURN DIRECTLY TO LENDER OR LOCAL PROCESSING AGENCY

Form Approved
OMB No. 2502-0059

| PRIVACY ACT NOTICE: This information is to be used by the agency collecting it in determining whether you qualify as a prospective mortgagor or borrower under its program. It will not be disclosed outside the agency without your consent except to your employer(s) for verification of employment and as required and permitted by law. You do not have to give us this information, but if you do not your application for approval as a prospective mortgagor or borrower may be delayed or rejected. The information requested in this form is authorized by Title 38, U.S.C., Chapter 37 *(if VA)*; by 12 U.S.C., Section 1701 et seq. *(if HUD/FHA)*; by 42 U.S.C., Section 1452b *(if HUD/CPD)*; and Title 42, U.S.C., 1471 et seq., or 7 U.S.C., 1921 et seq. *(if U.S.D.A., FmHA)*. | VETERANS ADMINISTRATION, U.S.D.A., FARMERS HOME ADMINISTRATION, AND U.S. DEPARTMENT OF HOUSING AND URBAN DEVELOPMENT - (Community Planning and Development, and Housing - Federal Housing Commissioner)

REQUEST FOR VERIFICATION OF EMPLOYMENT |

INSTRUCTIONS

LENDER OR LOCAL PROCESSING AGENCY (LPA): Complete Items 1 through 7. Have the applicant complete Item 8. Forward the completed form directly to the employer named in Item 1. EMPLOYER: Complete either Parts II and IV or Parts III and IV. Return form directly to the Lender or Local Processing Agency named in Item 2 of Part I.

PART I - REQUEST

1. TO: *(Name and Address of Employer)* D. H. HOLMES, LTD. 500 CANAL BLVD. NEW ORLEANS, LA., 70153	2. FROM: *(Name and Address of Lender or Local Processing Agency)* CARRUTH MORTGAGE CORPORATION P. O. BOX 53334 NEW ORLEANS, LOUISIANA 70153	
3. I certify that this verification has been sent directly to the employer and has not passed through the hands of the applicant or any other interested party. *Carla Rody* *(Signature of Lender, Official of LPA, or FmHA Loan Packager)*	4. TITLE OF LENDER, OFFICIAL OF LPA, OR FmHA LOAN PACKAGER CARLA RODY LOAN PROCESSOR	5. DATE JUNE 2, 1982 6. HUD/FHA/CPD, VA, OR FmHA NO. LH 123456
7. NAME AND ADDRESS OF APPLICANT MARIE WILLIAMS ROBINSON 5 OPELOUSAS STREET NEW ORLEANS, LA., 70114	I have applied for a mortgage loan or a rehabilitation loan and stated that I am/was employed by you. My signature in the block below authorizes verification of my employment information. 8. EMPLOYEE'S IDENTIFICATION 127-34-1906 SIGNATURE OF APPLICANT *Marie W. Robinson*	

PART II - VERIFICATION OF PRESENT EMPLOYMENT

EMPLOYMENT DATA	PAY DATA		
9. APPLICANT'S DATE OF EMPLOYMENT May 1980	12A. BASE PAY *(Current)* $_____ ☐ Annual $_____ ☐ Hourly $ 1200. ☐ Monthly $_____ ☐ Weekly $ 100. ☐ Other *(Specify)* avg. comm.	FOR MILITARY PERSONNEL ONLY	
10. PRESENT POSITION Hosiery Manager		Type	Monthly Amount
		BASE PAY	$
		RATIONS	$
11. PROBABILITY OF CONTINUED EMPLOYMENT Very Good	12B. EARNINGS	FLIGHT OR HAZARD	$

	Type	Year to Date	Past Year		
	BASE PAY	$ 6000.	$ 14,400.	CLOTHING	$
13. IF OVERTIME OR BONUS IS APPLICABLE, IS ITS CONTINUANCE LIKELY?	OVERTIME	$	$	QUARTERS	$
OVERTIME ☐ Yes ☒ No	COMMISSIONS	$ 500.	$ 1,200.	PRO PAY	$
BONUS ☐ Yes ☒ No	BONUS	$	$	OVERSEAS OR COMBAT	$

14. REMARKS *(If paid hourly, please indicate average hours worked each week during current and past year)*

NONE

PART III - VERIFICATION OF PREVIOUS EMPLOYMENT

15. DATES OF EMPLOYMENT	16. SALARY/WAGE AT TERMINATION PER ☐ YEAR ☐ MONTH ☐ WEEK			
	BASE PAY	OVERTIME	COMMISSIONS	BONUS
	$	$	$	$
17. REASONS FOR LEAVING	18. POSITION HELD			

PART IV - CERTIFICATION

Federal statutes provide severe penalties for any fraud, intentional misrepresentation, or criminal connivance or conspiracy purposed to influence the issuance of any guaranty or insurance by the VA Administrator, the U.S.D.A., FmHA Administrator, the HUD/FHA Commissioner, or the HUD/CPD Assistant Secretary.

19. SIGNATURE *Mary Jones* Mary Jones	20. TITLE OF EMPLOYER Personnel Director	21. DATE May 27, 1982

Previous Editions May be Used until Supply is Exhausted

HUD-6233/92004-g; VA 26-8497; FmHA-410-5 (12-80)

RETURN DIRECTLY TO LENDER OR LOCAL PROCESSING AGENCY

Form Approved
OMB No. 63R-1062

VETERANS ADMINISTRATION AND U.S. DEPARTMENT OF HOUSING AND URBAN DEVELOPMENT
HUD COMMUNITY PLANNING AND DEVELOPMENT
HUD HOUSING - FEDERAL HOUSING COMMISSIONER
REQUEST FOR VERIFICATION OF DEPOSIT

PRIVACY ACT NOTICE STATEMENT - This information is to be used by the agency collecting it in determining whether you qualify as a prospective mortgagor for mortgage insurance or guaranty or as a borrower for a rehabilitation loan under the agency's program. It will not be disclosed outside the agency without your consent except to financial institutions for verification of your deposits and as required and permitted by law. You do not have to give us this information, but, if you do not, your application for approval as a prospective mortgagor for mortgage insurance or guaranty or as a borrower for a rehabilitation loan may be delayed or rejected. This information request is authorized by Title 38, U.S.C., Chapter 37 *(if VA);* by 12 U.S.C., Section 1701 et seq., *(if HUD/FHA);* and by 42 U.S.C., Section 1452b *(if HUD/CPD).*

INSTRUCTIONS

LENDER OR LOCAL PROCESSING AGENCY: Complete Items 1 through 8. Have applicant(s) complete Item 9. Forward directly to the Depository named in Item 1. DEPOSITORY: Please complete Items 10 through 15 and return DIRECTLY to Lender or Local Processing Agency named in Item 2.

PART I - REQUEST

1. TO *(Name and Address of Depository)*	2. FROM *(Name and Address of Lender or Local Processing Agency)*
FIRST HOMESTEAD 105 WB EXPRESSWAY ALGIERS, LA. 70114	CARRUTH MORTGAGE CORPORATION P. O. BOX 53334 NEW ORLEANS, LOUISIANA 70153

I certify that this verification has been sent directly to the bank or depository and has not passed through the hands of the applicant or any other party.

3. Signature of Lender or Official of Local Processing Agency *Carla Rody*	4. Title CARLA RODY LOAN PROCESSOR	5. Date 05/24/82	6. Lender's Number *(Optional)* 100400

7. INFORMATION TO BE VERIFIED:

Type of Account and/or Loan	Account/Loan in Name of	Account/Loan Number	Balance
SAVINGS	BRYAN JAMES ROBINSON	CD250	$ 10,000.00
			$
			$
			$

TO DEPOSITORY: I have applied for mortgage insurance or guaranty or for a rehabilitation loan and stated that the balance on deposit and/or outstanding loans with you are as shown above. You are authorized to verify this information and to supply the lender or the local processing agency identified above with the information requested in Items 10 through 12. Your response is solely a matter of courtesy for which no responsibility is attached to your institution or any of your officers.

8. NAME AND ADDRESS OF APPLICANT(S)	9. SIGNATURE OF APPLICANT(S)
BRYAN JAMES ROBINSON MARIE WILLIAMS ROBINSON 5 OPELOUSAS STREET NEW ORLEANS, LA., 70114	*Bryan James Robinson* *Marie W. Robinson*

TO BE COMPLETED BY DEPOSITORY
PART II - VERIFICATION OF DEPOSITORY
10. DEPOSIT ACCOUNTS OF APPLICANT(S)

Type of Account	Account Number	Current Balance	Average Balance for Previous Two Months	Date Opened
savings/CD	250	$ 10,000.	$ 10,000.	4/80
		$	$	
		$	$	
		$	$	

11. LOANS OUTSTANDING TO APPLICANT(S)

Loan Number	Date of Loan	Original Amount	Current Balance	Installments *(Monthly/Quarterly)*	Secured by	Number of Late Payments within Last 12 Months
		$	$	$ per		
NONE		$	$	$ per		
		$	$	$ per		

12. ADDITIONAL INFORMATION WHICH MAY BE OF ASSISTANCE IN DETERMINATION OF CREDIT WORTHINESS: *Please include information on loans paid-in-full as in Item 11 above)*

13. Signature of Depository Official *Joyce Hinckley* Joyce Hinckley	14. Title Asst. Vice President	15. Date 5/27/82

The confidentiality of the information you have furnished will be preserved except where disclosure of this information is required by applicable law. The completed form is to be transmitted directly to the lender or local processing agency and is not to be transmitted through the applicant or any other party.

Replaces Form FHA-2004-F, which is Obsolete

VA 26-8497a/HUD-92004-F-6234 (7-80)

Form Approved
OMB No. 63R-1062

VETERANS ADMINISTRATION AND U.S. DEPARTMENT OF HOUSING AND URBAN DEVELOPMENT
HUD COMMUNITY PLANNING AND DEVELOPMENT
HUD HOUSING - FEDERAL HOUSING COMMISSIONER
REQUEST FOR VERIFICATION OF DEPOSIT

PRIVACY ACT NOTICE STATEMENT - This information is to be used by the agency collecting it in determining whether you qualify as a prospective mortgagor for mortgage insurance or guaranty or as a borrower for a rehabilitation loan under the agency's program. It will not be disclosed outside the agency without your consent except to financial institutions for verification of your deposits and as required and permitted by law. You do not have to give us this information, but, if you do not, your application for approval as a prospective mortgagor for mortgage insurance or guaranty or as a borrower for a rehabilitation loan may be delayed or rejected. This information request is authorized by Title 38, U.S.C., Chapter 37 (if VA); by 12 U.S.C., Section 1701 et seq., (if HUD/FHA); and by 42 U.S.C., Section 1452b (if HUD/CPD).

INSTRUCTIONS

LENDER OR LOCAL PROCESSING AGENCY: Complete Items 1 through 8. Have applicant(s) complete Item 9. Forward directly to the Depository named in Item 1. DEPOSITORY: Please complete Items 10 through 15 and return DIRECTLY to Lender or Local Processing Agency named in Item 2.

PART I - REQUEST

1. TO (Name and Address of Depository)	2. FROM (Name and Address of Lender or Local Processing Agency)
BANK OF NEW ORLEANS 502 KABEL DRIVE NEW ORLEANS, LA. 70114	CARRUTH MORTGAGE CORPORATION P. O. BOX 53334 NEW ORLEANS, LOUISIANA 70153

I certify that this verification has been sent directly to the bank or depository and has not passed through the hands of the applicant or any other party.

3. Signature of Lender or Official of Local Processing Agency *Carla Rody*	4. Title CARLA RODY LOAN PROCESSOR	5. Date 05/24/82	6. Lender's Number (Optional) 100400

7. INFORMATION TO BE VERIFIED:

Type of Account and/or Loan	Account/Loan in Name of	Account/Loan Number	Balance
CHECKING	MARIE WILLIAMS ROBINSON	25-7592	$ 1,000.00
SAVINGS	BRYAN JAMES ROBINSON	25-75930	$ 8,000.00
			$

TO DEPOSITORY: I have applied for mortgage insurance or guaranty or for a rehabilitation loan and stated that the balance on deposit and/or outstanding loans with you are as shown above. You are authorized to verify this information and to supply the lender or the local processing agency identified above with the information requested in Items 10 through 12. Your response is solely a matter of courtesy for which no responsibility is attached to your institution or any of your officers.

8. NAME AND ADDRESS OF APPLICANT(S)	9. SIGNATURE OF APPLICANT(S)
BRYAN JAMES ROBINSON MARIE WILLIAMS ROBINSON 5 OPELOUSAS STREET NEW ORLEANS, LA., 70114	*Bryan James Robinson* *Marie W. Robinson*

TO BE COMPLETED BY DEPOSITORY
PART II - VERIFICATION OF DEPOSITORY
10. DEPOSIT ACCOUNTS OF APPLICANT(S)

Type of Account	Account Number	Current Balance	Average Balance for Previous Two Months	Date Opened
Checking	257592	$ 1000.00	$ 1200.00	8/79
Savings	2575930	$ 8000.00	$ 8000.00	8/79
		$	$	
		$	$	

11. LOANS OUTSTANDING TO APPLICANT(S)

Loan Number	Date of Loan	Original Amount	Current Balance	Installments (Monthly/Quarterly)	Secured by	Number of Late Payments within Last 12 Months
		$	$	$ per		
NONE		$	$	$ per		
		$	$	$ per		

12. ADDITIONAL INFORMATION WHICH MAY BE OF ASSISTANCE IN DETERMINATION OF CREDIT WORTHINESS: Please include information on loans paid-in-full as in Item 11 above)

13. Signature of Depository Official *Janice Moody*	14. Title Credit Officer	15. Date 5/27/82

The confidentiality of the information you have furnished will be preserved except where disclosure of this information is required by applicable law. The completed form is to be transmitted directly to the lender or local processing agency and is not to be transmitted through the applicant or any other party.

Replaces Form FHA-2004-F, which is Obsolete

VA 26-8497a/HUD-92004-F-6234 (7-80)

REPORTING BUREAU

CREDIT BUREAU SERVICES—NEW ORLEANS
110 VETERANS BLVD., ANNEX BLDG., 200A
METAIRIE, LA 70005
01

INQUIRER

01--4412

CARRUTH MORTGAGE
3000 GEN DE GAULLE DR 201
NEW ORLEANS, LA 70114

CONFIDENTIAL CREDIMATIC REPORT TYPE

FACT DATA		JOINT INQUIRY
CROSS REF	01=ID-0000000	
BUREAU NUMBER	DATE RECEIVED	DATE ISSUED
90--20700	5/25/82	5/25/82
DATE TRADE CLEARED	DATE EMP VER (MO/YR)	INCOME VERIFIED
SEE BELOW	5/82	YES ☐ NO ☒

THIS INFORMATION, THE COMPLETE ACCURACY OF WHICH IS NOT GUARANTEED, HAS BEEN OBTAINED FROM RELIABLE SOURCES AND IS FURNISHED PURSUANT TO THE TERMS OF APPLICABLE LAW. THE RECIPIENT AGREES TO INDEMNIFY REPORTING BUREAU FOR ANY DAMAGE ARISING FROM MISUSE OF THIS INFORMATION.

FILE SINCE (MO/YR)	COMPUTER I.D. NO	SOCIAL SECURITY NO
10/79	01-0000001	222-45-7183
		SPOUSE'S NAME

SUBJECT

ROBINSON, BRYAN JAMES
CURRENT ADDRESS

SPOUSE'S NAME: MARIE

5 OPELOUSAS ST, NEW ORLEANS, LA 70114   S5/80

COMPLETE TO HERE FOR TRADE REPORT AND SKIP TO CREDIT HISTORY

| PRESENT EMPLOYER: | POSITION HELD | SINCE (MO/YR) | MONTHLY INCOME |
| US NAVY | CHIEF PETTY OFF | 00/68 | $ — |

COMPLETE TO HERE FOR EMPLOYMENT AND TRADE REPORT AND SKIP TO CREDIT HISTORY

| DATE OF BIRTH: (MO/YR) | NUMBER OF DEPENDENTS INCLUDING SELF | | |
| 00/42 | 4 | OWNS OR BUYING HOME ☐ | RENTS HOME ☒ |

FORMER ADDRESS: FROM: (MO/YR)   TO: (MO/YR)

NONE REPORTED
FORMER EMPLOYER:

| | POSITION HELD: | FROM (MO/YR) | TO (MO/YR) | MONTHLY INCOME: |
| NONE REPORTED | | | | $ |

SPOUSE'S EMPLOYER:

| | POSITION HELD: | SINCE: (MO/YR) | MONTHLY INCOME: |
| --- | | | $ |

CREDIT HISTORY

ECOA DESIG	FIRM NAME / KIND OF BUSINESS AND ID CODE	DATE REPORTED AND METHOD	DATE ACCOUNT OPENED	DATE OF LAST CUSTOMER TRANSACTION	HIGHEST CREDIT	BALANCE OWING	PAST DUE AMOUNT	NO PMT	MOS REV	MONTHLY PAYMENTS LATE PRIOR TO DATE REPORTED 1 2 3 4 5 6 7 8 9 10 11 12 13 14 15 16 17 18 19 20 21 22 23 24	TYPE TERMS CURRENT STATUS (MOP)	ATTN

REPORTING BUREAU CERTIFIES COMPLIANCE WITH CONTRACTUAL REQUIREMENTS GOVERNING CHECK OF PUBLIC RECORDS AS WELL AS CREDIT INFORMATION INVOLVING SUBJECT

4	BK N O VISA BB-01----6082 #431251196001	5/82M	4/79	5/82	600	300	00	—	12	00/00/00	R
4	D H HOLMES DC-01---6025 #12734	4/82A	5/80	3/82	500	200	00	0	12	000000000000	R$15
4	BK N O BB-01----6976 #257592	5/82M	5/80	CHECKING							
4	BK N O BB-01----6576 #2575930	5/82M	4/79	SAVINGS							

REF— 1ST HOMESTEAD SAVINGS   REFUSES INFORMATION
REF— NAVY FEDERAL CR UN   RECORDS NOT LOCAL

MISCELLANEOUS INFORMATION--5/82 ,
NO PUBLIC RECORDS FOUND AS OF 5/25/82

END OF REPORT
CREDIMATIC SYSTEM
FORM 2000   PLEASE SEE REVERSE SIDE FOR EXPLANATORY CODES

REPORTING BUREAU

CREDIT BUREAU SERVICES—NEW ORLEANS
110 VETERANS BLVD., ANNEX BLDG., 200A
METAIRIE, LA 70005
    01

INQUIRER

                              01--4412

CARRUTH MORTGAGE
3000 GEN DE GAULLE DR 201
NEW ORLEANS, LA 70114

CONFIDENTIAL CREDIMATIC REPORT TYPE

FACT DATA   JOINT INQUIRY
CROSS REF   01-ID-0000001

BUREAU NUMBER	DATE RECEIVED	DATE ISSUED
90--20700	5/25/82	5/25/82

DATE TRADE CLEARED	DATE EMP VER (MO YR)	INCOME VERIFIED
SEE BELOW	5/82	YES NO X

THIS INFORMATION, THE COMPLETE ACCURACY OF WHICH IS NOT GUARANTEED, HAS BEEN OBTAINED FROM RELIABLE SOURCES AND IS FURNISHED PURSUANT TO THE TERMS OF APPLICABLE LAW. THE RECIPIENT AGREES TO INDEMNIFY REPORTING BUREAU FOR ANY DAMAGE ARISING FROM MISUSE OF THIS INFORMATION

FILE SINCE (MO. YR.)	COMPUTER I.D. NO	SOCIAL SECURITY NO.
9/80	01-0000000	127-34-1906

SUBJECT

ROBINSON, MARIE WILLIAMS
CURRENT ADDRESS

5 OPELOUSAS ST, NEW ORLEANS, LA 70114

SPOUSE'S NAME
BRYAN
S5/80

COMPLETE TO HERE FOR TRADE REPORT AND SKIP TO CREDIT HISTORY

PRESENT EMPLOYER:	POSITION HELD:	SINCE: (MO.-YR.)	MONTHLY INCOME:
D H HOLMES	HOSIERY MGR	5/80	$ -

COMPLETE TO HERE FOR EMPLOYMENT AND TRADE REPORT AND SKIP TO CREDIT HISTORY

DATE OF BIRTH (MO.-YR.)	NUMBER OF DEPENDENTS INCLUDING SELF ——→		OWNS OR BUYING HOME	X RENTS HOME
00/47				

FORMER ADDRESS:		FROM (MO.-YR.)	TO: (MO.-YR.)
NONE REPORTED			

FORMER EMPLOYER:	POSITION HELD:	FROM (MO.-YR.)	TO (MO.-YR.)	MONTHLY INCOME:
NONE REPORTED				$

SPOUSE'S EMPLOYER:	POSITION HELD:	SINCE: (MO.-YR.)	MONTHLY INCOME:
---			$

CREDIT HISTORY

ECOA DESIG	FIRM NAME KIND OF BUSINESS AND ID CODE	DATE REPORTED AND METHOD	DATE ACCOUNT OPENED	DATE LAST CUSTOMER TRANSACTION	CURRENT STATUS					HISTORICAL STATUS		TYPE TERMS CURRENT STATUS (MOP)	ATTN
					HIGHEST CREDIT	BALANCE OWING	PAST DUE AMOUNT	NO PMT	MOS REV	PAST DUE 30 / 60 / 90+ OR MONTHLY PAYMENTS LATE PRIOR TO DATE REPORTED 1 2 3 4 5 6 7 8 9 10 11 12 13 14 15 16 17 18 19 20 21 22 23 24			

REPORTING BUREAU CERTIFIES COMPLIANCE WITH CONTRACTUAL REQUIREMENTS GOVERNING CHECK OF PUBLIC RECORDS AS WELL AS CREDIT INFORMATION INVOLVING SUBJECT

4 BK N O VISA	5/82M	4/79	5/82	600	300	00	-	12	00/00/00	R
BB-01----6082	#431251196001									
4 D H HOLMES	4/82A	5/80	3/82	500	200	00	0	12	000000000000	R$15
DC-01----6025	#12734									
4 BK N O	5/82M	5/80		CHECKING						
BB-01----6576	#257592									
4 BK N O	5/82M	4/79		SAVINGS						
BB-01----6576	#2575930									

MISCELLANEOUS INFORMATION--5/82 ,
NO PUBLIC RECORDS FOUND AS OF 5/25/82

END OF REPORT
CREDIMATIC SYSTEM
FORM 2000

PLEASE SEE REVERSE SIDE FOR EXPLANATORY CODES

Mortgage Corporation
MEMBER OF THE MELLON NATIONAL MORTGAGE GROUP

MAY 25, 1982

NAVY FEDERAL CR. UNION
Washington, D. C. 20391

RE:

BRYAN JAMES ROBINSON
5 OPELOUSAS STREET
NEW ORLEANS, LA., 70114
222-45-7183

We are processing an application for a first mortgage loan on subject with whom it is believed you have had credit experience. Therefore, a statement of your experience including any other information that will enable us to make an intelligent decision is respectfully requested. Such information will be held in strictest confidence.

You may use the form below or any other method of acknowledgement most convenient to you.

Your prompt consideration of this request will be sincerely appreciated and, for your convenience, a business reply envelope is enclosed.

Yours very truly,

Carla Rody

CARLA RODY
LOAN PROCESSOR

Processing Department

Enc.

PLEASE RELEASE THE ABOVE REQUESTED INFORMATION TO CARRUTH MORTGAGE CORPORATION. THANK YOU.

Bryan J. Robinson

Marie W. Robinson

CHARACTER AND CREDIT STATEMENT

HOW LONG HAVE YOU KNOWN SUBJECT?	HOW LONG HAVE YOU GIVEN CREDIT ACCOMMODATIONS?		KIND OF CREDIT ACCOMMODATIONS?
	10 years		Auto loan
HIGHEST CREDIT ALLOWED?	**AMOUNT OWING $**	**MONTHLY PAYMENT**	**PAID ACCORDING TO TERMS?**
$6000.00	$2300.00	$ 125.00	☒ YES ☐ NO IF NO, EXPLAIN BELOW.

REAL ESTATE MORTGAGE EXPERIENCE

MORTGAGE DATE	ORIGINAL AMOUNT	MATURITY DATE	PRESENT BALANCE
	$ NONE		
TERMS OF PAYMENT			

IS INTEREST IN DEFAULT	AMOUNT	PERIOD	HAVE YOU ADVANCED UNPAID TAXES	AMOUNT
☐ YES ☐ NO			☐ YES ☐ NO	
HAS ACCOUNT BEEN SATISFACTORY?				

TYPE OF FINANCING			REMARKS
☐ FHA	☐ VA	☐ CONV	

Marlyne Doyle
SIGNATURE

CMC 62 MG R 10/79

3601 I-10 Service Rd., Metairie, La.
Mailing Address: P.O. Box 53334, New Orleans, La. 70153
Phone: 885-4811

Mortgage Corporation
MEMBER OF THE MELLON NATIONAL MORTGAGE GROUP

June 3, 1982

Loan Guaranty Division
Veterans Administration
701 Loyola Avenue
New Orleans, Louisiana 70113

ATTENTION: (xxx) EXAMINATION SECTION
( ) APPRAISAL SECTION

RE: BRYAN JAMES ROBINSON

MARIE WILLIAMS ROBINSON

PROPERTY: 1804 Homer Street

Metairie,

Louisiana, 70005

V. A. Case No. LH 123456

CMC Loan No. 100400

Gentlemen:

Enclosed is/are the following with regard to the above captioned matter:

Certificate of Eligibility, Application for Home Loan Guaranty (1802a),
Certificate of Reasonable Value (1843, 1843p), Credit Report, VOE's,
VOD's, Ecoa, No Commitment to Lend, Government Monitoring Information,
Purchase Agreement, 1747
(xx) PLEASE ISSUE YOUR:

( ) Certificate of Eligibility   ( ) Certificate of Reasonable Value
( ) Final Compliance Inspection   (xxx Certificate of Commitment
( ) Loan Guaranty Certificate   ( ) _____

OR

( ) PLEASE TAKE THE FOLLOWING ACTION ON THE ABOVE CAPTIONED MATTER:

Your prompt attention in this matter is greatly appreciated.

Sincerely,

Patricia Misiek

CARRUTH MORTGAGE CORPORATION
PATRICIA MISIEK

Enclosures
P-6
Rev. 6/81

(V. A. Request for forms/information/action)

3601 I-10 Service Rd., Metairie, La.
Mailing Address: P. O. Box 53334, New Orleans, La. 70153
Phone 885-4811

SET UP DATE 5/25/82
RESET _____
RESET _____

CARRUTH MORTGAGE CORPORATION

PROCESSING CHECK SHEET

APPLICANT: Bryan James Robinson   CO-APPLICANT Marie Williams Robinso

PROPERTY ADDRESS: 1804 Homer Street   TYPE: VA

_____ Metairie, La. 70005   TERM: 30 years

DATE OF APPLICATION: May 25, 1982   S.P.: $60,000.00

SOURCE: Homes Realty-Linda Keanan   LOAN: $60,000.00

X	REQUIRED ITEMS		DATE REQUESTED	DATE RECEIVED	REMARKS
	APPRAISAL & APPLIC. FEES			5/25/82	
	PURCHASE AGREEMENT			5/25/82	
	PLANS & SPECS. (PROPOSED)				
	TITLES (EXISTING)			5/25/82	
	CREDIT REPORT Pauline		5/25/82	5/27/82	OK
	EMPLOYMENT	APPLICANT	5/25/82	5/27/82	OK
	VERIFICATIONS	CO-APPLICANT	5/25/82	5/27/82	OK
	PREVIOUS	APPLICANT			
	EMPLOYMENT	CO-APPLICANT			
	VERIFICATIONS				
	UNION VERIFICATION				
		1. BNO	5/25/82	5/27/82	OK
	DEPOSIT	2. 1st Homestd	5/25/82	5/27/82	OK
	VERIFICATIONS	3.			
		4.			
	APPRAISAL - TYPE VA		5/25/82	6/3/82	OK
	FHA APPRAISAL ACKNOWLEDGEMENT LETTER SENT TO APPLICANT				
	APPRAISAL SENT TO LISTING AND SELLING AGENT (Where permitted)				
	DIVORCE DECREES/DEATH CERT.				
	W-2 FORMS				
	FIN. & P & L STATEMENTS				
	PROP. INSP. & PHOTOGRAPHS		6/3/82	6/4/82	
	INS. PREFERENCE LETTER				
	CUSTOMER MEMO		5/25/82	5/25/82	
	CERTIFICATE OF ELIGIBILITY		5/25/82	6/2/82	
	DD-802 (FHA IN SERVICE)				
	DD-214				
	DD-1747		5/25/82	5/26/82	
	STATEMENT OF SERVICE				
		1. Navy Fed C.U.	5/25/82	6/1/82	OK
	MORTGAGE	2.			
	RATING	3.			
	LETTERS	4.			
	LOAN APPROVAL		6/3/82	6/8/82	

P-89 (Rev 1/82)

TO: *(Name of Applicant)*		**DATE** *(Month, Day Year)*
ROBINSON, Bryan James		5/24/82

ADDRESS *(Street, City, State and Zip Code)*	**FROM:**	Family Housing Office
5 Opelousas Street, New Orleans, La. 70114		*(Name of Installation)*

1. YOUR APPLICATION FOR MILITARY FAMILY HOUSING WILL BE EFFECTIVE AS OF:

5/24/82

(Month, Day, Year and Hour)

2. YOU ARE ADVISED THAT:

a. ☐ Family housing will be made available immediately upon your arrival. Comments: _____

b. ☐ You can expect family housing to be available within approximately 30 days of your arrival and for the interim period you should make temporary housing arrangements.

c. ☐ You can expect family housing to be available within approximately 90 days of your arrival and for the interim period you should make temporary housing arrangements.

d. ☐ You can expect family housing to be available within the first 12 months of your arrival and therefore you should make temporary or semipermanent housing arrangements in the interim.

e. ☒ It is unlikely that family housing will be available for at least a year, and perhaps not at all during your tour; therefore you should make permanent private housing arrangements.

f. ☐ Because of your particular circumstances you are authorized to make permanent private housing arrangements. You will not be mandatorily assigned to military family housing.

g. ☐ It is anticipated that occupancy of family housing will be on a voluntary basis. At this time it appears that there will be sufficient voluntary occupants to assure full utilization of family housing units. However, it may be necessary to make a mandatory assignment should the situation warrant.

h. ☐ It is anticipated that occupancy of family housing will be on a mandatory basis.

3. HOUSING AVAILABILITY IN THE COMMUNITY IS:

☐ Good ☐ Fair ☒ Limited ☐ Reasonable ☐ Expensive

4. YOU MUST CONTACT THE FAMILY HOUSING OFFICE *(HOUSING REFERRAL)* **UPON ARRIVAL BEFORE YOU MAKE ANY ARRANGEMENTS FOR HOUSING, AND TO BE INFORMED OF ANY CHANGES TO THE ABOVE.**

DD FORM 1747   0102-LF-023-1000
1 OCT 70

STATUS OF HOUSING AVAILABILITY

GENERAL INSTRUCTIONS

This form is to be issued to each applicant for Military Family Housing immediately upon receipt by the Family Housing Office of the DD Form 1746, "Application for and Assignment to Military Family Housing."

Item 1 - Effective date of application. Enter the effective date of change in installation of assignment or such date as the application was received in the family housing office as applicable. This must be the same as Section B, Item 13b.. on DD Form 1746.

Item 2 - Check items a. through h., as appropriate. If item a., b., c., or d. is checked, item g. or h. must also be checked.

Item 3 - Community Housing. Check as appropriate to advise applicant in a general way of the local community housing situation.

SIGNATURE *(Family Housing Office)*

Kay Arnold

LOAN ANALYSIS

LOAN NUMBER: 100400

SECTION A—LOAN DATA

1. NAME OF BORROWER	2. AMOUNT OF LOAN	3. CASH DOWN PAYMENT ON PURCHASE PRICE
Bryan James Robinson and Marie Williams Robinson	$ 60,000.00	$ 0.00

SECTION B—BORROWER'S PERSONAL AND FINANCIAL STATUS

4. APPLICANT'S AGE	5 OCCUPATION OF APPLICANT	6 NUMBER OF YEARS AT PRESENT EMPLOYMENT	7 LIQUID ASSETS (Cash, savings, bonds, etc.)	8. CURRENT MONTHLY RENTAL OR OTHER HOUSING EXPENSE
40	Chief Petty Officer	14	$ 22,610.00	$ 450.00

9. IS SPOUSE EMPLOYED?	10 SPOUSE'S AGE	11 OCCUPATION OF SPOUSE	12 NUMBER OF YEARS AT PRESENT EMPLOYMENT	13. AGE OF OTHER DEPENDENTS
☐ YES ☒ NO	35	Hosiery Manager	6	16, 14

NOTE: ROUND ALL DOLLAR AMOUNTS BELOW TO NEAREST WHOLE DOLLAR.

SECTION C – ESTIMATED MONTHLY SHELTER EXPENSES (This Property)

	ITEMS	AMOUNT
14.	TERM OF LOAN: 30 YEARS	
15.	MORTGAGE PAYMENT (Principal and Interest) 15.50	$ 782.72
16.	REALTY TAXES	12.00
17.	HAZARD INSURANCE	29.75
18.	SPECIAL ASSESSMENTS	0.00
19.	MAINTENANCE	35.00
20.	UTILITIES (Including heat)	90.00
21.	OTHER (HOA, Condo fees, etc.) Flood Ins.	7.00
22.	TOTAL	$ 956.47

SECTION D – DEBTS AND OBLIGATIONS
(Itemize and indicate by (√) which debts considered in Section E, Line 41)

	ITEMS	(√)	MO. PAYMENT	UNPAID BAL.
23.	VISA/BNO		$ 30 days	$ 300.00
24.	D.H. Holmes, Ltd.	*	15.00	200.00
25.	Navy Fed. Credit Union	*	125.00	2300.00
26.				
27.				
28.				
29.				
30.	JOB RELATED EXPENSE		None	
31.	TOTAL		$ 140.00	$ 2800.00

SECTION E – MONTHLY INCOME AND DEDUCTIONS

	ITEMS		SPOUSE	BORROWER	TOTAL
32.	GROSS SALARY OR EARNINGS FROM EMPLOYMENT		$ 1200.00	$ 2200.00	$ 3400.00
33.	DEDUCTIONS	FEDERAL INCOME TAX	250.00	648.90	
34.		STATE INCOME TAX	18.00	55.00	
35.		RETIREMENT OR SOCIAL SECURITY	80.00	197.00	
36.		OTHER (Specify)			
37.		TOTAL DEDUCTIONS	$ 348.00	$ 900.90	$ 1248.90
38.	NET TAKE-HOME PAY		852.00	1299.10	2151.10
39.	PENSION, COMPENSATION OR OTHER NET INCOME (Specify) Rations/Barracks		0.00	700.00	700.00
40.	TOTAL (Sum of lines 38 and 39)		$ 952.00	$ 1899.10	$ 2851.10
41.	LESS THOSE OBLIGATIONS LISTED IN SECTION D WHICH SHOULD BE DEDUCTED FROM INCOME				140.00
42.	TOTAL NET EFFECTIVE INCOME				$ 2711.10
43.	LESS ESTIMATED MONTHLY SHELTER EXPENSE (Line 22)				956.47
44.	BALANCE AVAILABLE FOR FAMILY SUPPORT				$ 1754.63

45. PAST CREDIT RECORD	46. DOES LOAN MEET VA CREDIT STANDARDS? (Give reasons for decision under "Remarks," if necessary, e.g., borderline case)
☒ SATISFACTORY ☐ UNSATISFACTORY	☒ YES ☐ NO

47. REMARKS (Use reverse, if necessary)

Ratio: 35.28

SECTION F – DISPOSITION OF APPLICATION

☐ Recommend that the application be approved since it meets all requirements of Chapter 37, Title 38, U.S. Code and applicable VA Regulations and directives.

☐ Recommend that the application be disapproved for the reasons stated under "Remarks" above.

48. DATE	49. SIGNATURE OF EXAMINER	
50. FINAL ACTION ☐ APPROVE APPLICATION ☐ REJECT APPLICATION	51. DATE	52. SIGNATURE AND TITLE OF APPROVING OFFICIAL

VA FORM 26-6393 MAY 1979

EXISTING STOCKS OF VA FORM 26-6393, OCT 1976, WILL BE USED.

* U.S.GPO:1979-0-311-545/1033

Form Approved
OMB No. 2900-0144

VA Application for Home Loan Guaranty [X]	USDA-FmHA Application for FmHA Guaranteed Loan	HUD/FHA Application for Commitment for Insurance under the National Housing Act	1. AGENCY CASE NUMBER ▲ LH123-456	2A. LENDER'S CASE NUMBER 100400	2B. SECTION OF THE ACT (HUD Only)

3. NAME AND PRESENT ADDRESS OF BORROWER (Include ZIP Code)
Bryan James Robinson
5 Opelousas Street
New Orleans, Louisiana 70114

5A. BORROWER: If you do not wish to complete Items 5B or 5C, please initial in the space to the right. | INITIALS

5B. RACE/NATIONAL ORIGIN ▲1 [X] WHITE, NOT HISPANIC 4 [ ] ASIAN OR PACIFIC ISLANDER 2 [ ] BLACK, NOT HISPANIC 5 [ ] HISPANIC 3 [ ] AMERICAN INDIAN OR ALASKAN NATIVE

5C. SEX ▲1 [X] MALE 2 [ ] FEMALE

4A. NAME AND ADDRESS OF LENDER (Include ZIP Code)
CARRUTH MORTGAGE CORPORATION
P. O. Box 53334
New Orleans, Louisiana 70153

Tel.504-885-4811   Census Tract 17.12

6A. SPOUSE OR OTHER BORROWER: If you do not wish to complete Items 6B or 6C, please initial in space to the right. | INITIALS

6B. RACE/NATIONAL ORIGIN ▲1 [X] WHITE, NOT HISPANIC 4 [ ] ASIAN OR PACIFIC ISLANDER 2 [ ] BLACK, NOT HISPANIC 5 [ ] HISPANIC 3 [ ] AMERICAN INDIAN OR ALASKAN NATIVE

6C. SEX ▲1 [ ] MALE 2 [X] FEMALE

4B. ORIGINATORS' I.D. (HUD Only) | **4C. SPONSOR'S I.D.** (HUD Only)

7. PROPERTY ADDRESS INCLUDING NAME OF SUBDIVISION, LOT AND BLOCK NO., AND ZIP CODE
1804 Homer Street
Lot 12 Square 16, Bonnabel Heights S/D
Jefferson Parish, Metairie, Louisiana 70005

8A. LOAN AMOUNT $60,000.00 **8B. INT. RATE** 15.5% **8C. PROPOSED MATURITY** 30 YRS. 0 MOS.
DISCOUNT: (Only if borrower to pay) **8D. PERCENT** % **8E. AMOUNT** $

VA ONLY: Veteran and lender hereby apply to the Administrator of Veterans Affairs for Guaranty of the loan described here under Section 1810, Chapter 37, Title 38, United States Code to the full extent permitted by the veteran's entitlement and severally agree that the Regulations promulgated pursuant to Chapter 37, then in effect on the date of the loan shall govern the rights, duties, and liabilities of the parties.
HUD/FHA ONLY: Mortgagee's application for mortgagor approval and commitment for mortgage insurance under the National Housing Act.

SECTION I - PURPOSE, AMOUNT, TERMS OF AND SECURITY FOR PROPOSED LOAN

9A. PURPOSE OF LOAN – TO:
▲1 [X] PURCHASE EXISTING HOUSE PREVIOUSLY OCCUPIED
2 [ ] FINANCE IMPROVEMENTS TO EXISTING PROPERTY
3 [ ] REFINANCE
4 [ ] PURCHASE NEW CONDO. UNIT
5 [ ] PURCHASE EXISTING CONDO. UNIT
6 [ ] PURCHASE EXISTING HOME NOT PREVIOUSLY OCCUPIED
7 [ ] CONSTRUCT A HOME - PROCEEDS TO BE PAID OUT DURING CONSTRUCTION
8 [ ] HUD ONLY – FINANCE COOP-PURCHASE

9B. HUD ONLY – BORROWER WILL BE
▲1 [ ] OCCUPANT 5 [ ] ESCROW COMMITMENT
2 [ ] LANDLORD
3 [ ] BUILDER
4 [ ] OPERATIVE BUILDER

10. VA ONLY – TITLE WILL BE VESTED IN:
[ ] VETERAN [X] VETERAN & SPOUSE [ ] OTHER (Specify)

11. LIEN: [X] FIRST MORTGAGE [ ] OTHER (Specify)
12. ESTATE WILL BE: [X] FEE SIMPLE [ ] LEASEHOLD (Show expiration date)
13. IS THERE A MANDATORY HOMEOWNERS ASSOC.? [ ] YES [X] NO (If "Yes," complete Item 14F.)

14. ESTIMATED TAXES, INSURANCE AND ASSESSMENTS

		15. ESTIMATED MONTHLY PAYMENT	
A. ANNUAL TAXES	$ 144.00	A. PRINCIPAL AND INTEREST	$ 782.72
B. AMOUNT OF HAZARD INSURANCE ON SECURITY	51,000.00	B. TAXES AND INSURANCE DEPOSITS	12.00
C. ANNUAL HAZARD INSURANCE PREMIUM	357.00	C. OTHER Flood & Taxes	29.75
D. ANNUAL SPECIAL ASSESSMENT PAYMENT			
E. UNPAID SPECIAL ASSESSMENT BALANCE			
F. ANNUAL MAINTENANCE ASSESSMENT		TOTAL $ 831.47	

SECTION II - PERSONAL AND FINANCIAL STATUS OF APPLICANT

16. PLEASE CHECK APPROPRIATE BOXES. IF ONE OR MORE ARE CHECKED, ITEMS 18B, 21, 22 AND 23 MUST INCLUDE INFORMATION CONCERNING BORROWER'S SPOUSE (or former spouse if box "D" is checked). IF NO BOXES ARE CHECKED, NO INFORMATION CONCERNING THE SPOUSE NEED BE FURNISHED IN ITEMS 18B, 21, 22 AND 23.

A [X] THE SPOUSE WILL BE JOINTLY OBLIGATED WITH THE BORROWER ON THE LOAN
B [X] THE BORROWER IS RELYING ON THE SPOUSE'S INCOME AS A BASIS FOR REPAYMENT OF THE LOAN.
C [X] THE BORROWER IS MARRIED AND THE PROPERTY TO SECURE THE LOAN IS LOCATED IN A COMMUNITY PROPERTY STATE.
D [ ] THE BORROWER IS RELYING ON ALIMONY, CHILD SUPPORT, OR SEPARATE MAINTENANCE PAYMENTS FROM A SPOUSE OR FORMER SPOUSE AS A BASIS FOR REPAYMENT OF THE LOAN.

17A. MARITAL STATUS OF BORROWER ▲ 1 [X] MARRIED 3 [ ] UNMARRIED 2 [ ] SEPARATED
17B. MARITAL STATUS OF COBORROWER OTHER THAN SPOUSE ▲ 1 [ ] MARRIED 3 [ ] UNMARRIED 2 [ ] SEPARATED
17C. MONTHLY CHILD SUPPORT OBLIGATION $ none
17D. MONTHLY ALIMONY OBLIGATION $ none
18A. AGE OF BORROWER 40
18B. AGE OF SPOUSE OR COBORROWER 35
18C. AGE(S) OF DEPENDENT(S) 16, 14

19. NAME AND ADDRESS OF NEAREST LIVING RELATIVE (Include telephone number, if available).
Mr. Tom Hunter   Phone 885-2376
502 Helois Street, Metairie, Louisiana 70005

20A. CURRENT MONTHLY HOUSING EXPENSE $ 600.00
20B. UTILITIES INCLUDED? [X] YES [ ] NO

21. ASSETS / 22. LIABILITIES (Itemize all debts)

21. ASSETS		22. LIABILITIES NAME OF CREDITOR	MO. PAYMENT	BALANCE
A. CASH (Including deposit on purchase)	$20,110.00			
B. SAVINGS BONDS - OTHER SECURITIES	2,500.00	Visa/BNO	$ 300.00	$ 300.00
C. REAL ESTATE OWNED		D.H.Holmes	15.00	200.00
D. AUTO	9,000.00	Navy Federal Credit Union	125.00	2,300.00
E. FURNITURE AND HOUSEHOLD GOODS	30,000.00			
F. OTHER (Use separate sheet, if necessary) Boat,Motor,Trailer	5,000.00	JOB-RELATED EXPENSE (Specify)		
G. TOTAL	$ 66,610.00	TOTAL	$ 440.00	$ 2,800.00

23. INCOME AND OCCUPATIONAL STATUS / 24. ESTIMATED TOTAL COST

ITEM	BORROWER	SPOUSE OR COBORROWER	ITEM	AMOUNT
A. OCCUPATION	Chief Petty Off	Hosiery Manager	A. PURCHASE EXISTING HOME	$ 60,000.00
B. NAME OF EMPLOYER	U. S. Navy	D.H. Holmes	B. ALTERATIONS, IMPROVEMENTS, REPAIRS	
			C. CONSTRUCTION	
C. NUMBER OF YEARS EMPLOYED	14	2	D. LAND (If acquired separately)	
			E. PURCHASE OF CONDOMINIUM UNIT	
			F. REFINANCE	
D. GROSS PAY	▲ MONTHLY $2,200 HOURLY $	▲ MONTHLY $1,200 HOURLY $	G. PREPAID ITEMS	538.50
E. OTHER INCOME (Disclosure of child support, alimony and separate maintenance income is optional)	▲ MONTHLY Barracks/Rations $600.00	▲ MONTHLY $	H. ESTIMATED CLOSING COSTS	2,171.37
			I. DISCOUNT (Only if borrower permitted to pay)	
			J. TOTAL COSTS (Add Items 24A through 24I)	62,709.87
NOTE — If land acquired by separate transaction, complete Items 25A and 25B.			K. LESS CASH FROM BORROWER	1,809.87
25A. DATE ACQUIRED	25B. UNPAID BALANCE $		L. LESS OTHER CREDITS By Seller	900.00
			M. AMOUNT OF LOAN	$ 60,000.00

VA FORM 26-1802a, JAN 1982
HUD FORM 92900.1
SUPERSEDES VA FORM 26-1802a, APR 1979, WHICH WILL NOT BE USED.
HUD FORM 92900, JUL 1980, MAY BE USED FOR HUD PURPOSES.
VA/HUD COPY 1

SECTION III - LENDER'S CERTIFICATION *(Must be signed by lender)*

The undersigned lender makes the following certifications to induce the Veterans Administration to issue a certificate of commitment to guarantee the subject loan under Title 38, U.S. Code, or to induce the Department of Housing and Urban Development - Federal Housing Commissioner to issue a firm commitment for mortgage insurance under the National Housing Act.

26A. The information furnished in Section I is true, accurate and complete.

26B. The information contained in Section II was obtained directly from the borrower by a full-time employee of the undersigned lender or its duly authorized agent and is true to the best of the lender's knowledge and belief.

26C. The credit report submitted on the subject borrower *(and spouse, if any)* was ordered by the undersigned lender or its duly authorized agent directly from the credit bureau which prepared the report and was received directly from said credit bureau.

26D. The verification of employment and verification of deposits were requested and received by the lender or its duly authorized agent without passing through the hands of any third persons and are true to the best of the lender's knowledge and belief.

26E. This application was signed by the borrower after Sections I, II and V were completed.

26F. This proposed loan to the named borrower meets the income and credit requirements of the governing law in the judgment of the undersigned.

26G through 26I - TO BE COMPLETED OR APPLICABLE FOR VA LOANS ONLY.

26G. The names and functions of any duly authorized agents who developed on behalf of the lender any of the information or supporting credit data submitted are as follows:

	NAME	ADDRESS	FUNCTION	*(e.g., obtained information in Sec. II; ordered credit report, verification of employment, verif. of deposits, etc.)*
(1)				
(2)				
(3)				

☒ *(Check box if all information and supporting credit data were obtained directly by the lender.)*

26H. The undersigned lender understands and agrees that it is responsible for the acts of agents identified in item 26G as to the functions with which they are identified.

26I. The proposed loan conforms otherwise with the applicable provisions of Title 38, U.S. Code, and of the regulations concerning guaranty or insurance of loans to veterans.

27. Date	28. Name of Lender	29. Telephone Number *(Include Area Code)*	30. Signature and Title of Officer of Lender
6/3/82	CARRUTH MORTGAGE CORP.	504-885-4811	*Patricia Misiek* Patricia Misiek, Loan Officer

SECTION IV - NOTICE TO BORROWERS

PRIVACY ACT INFORMATION - The information requested in this form is authorized by 38 U.S.C. 1810 *(if VA)* and 12 U.S.C. 1701 et seq., *(if HUD/FHA)* and will be used in determining whether you qualify as a mortgagor. Any disclosure of information outside VA or HUD/FHA will only be made as permitted by law. Disclosure of this information is voluntary but no loan may be approved unless a completed application is received.

NOTICE TO BORROWERS - This is notice to you as required by the Right to Financial Privacy Act of 1978 that the VA or HUD/FHA has a right of access to financial records held by financial institutions in connection with the consideration or administration of assistance to you. Financial records involving your transaction will be available to VA and HUD/FHA without further notice or authorization but will not be disclosed or released to another Government Agency or Department without your consent except as required or permitted by law.

SECTION V - BORROWERS CERTIFICATION *(Must be signed by Borrower(s))*

31A. COMPLETE FOR HUD/FHA INSURED MORTGAGE ONLY.

(1) Do you own or have you sold, within the past 12 months, other real estate? ☐ Yes ☐ No Is it to be sold? ☐ Yes ☐ No HUD/FHA Mortgage? ☐ Yes ☐ No

Sales Price $_____

Original Mortgage Amount $_____

Address: _____ Lender: _____

(2) Have you ever been obligated on a home loan, home improvement loan or a mobile home loan which resulted in foreclosure, transfer of title in lieu of foreclosure or judgment? ☐ Yes ☐ No. If "Yes" give details including date, property address, name and address of lender, FHA or VA Case Number, if any, and reasons for the action.

(3). If dwelling to be covered by this mortgage is to be rented, is it a part of, adjacent or contiguous to any project, subdivision, or group rental properties involving eight or more dwelling units in which you have any financial interest? ☐ Yes ☐ No ☐ Not to be rented. If "Yes" give details. Do you own four or more dwelling units with mortgages insured under any title of the National Housing Act? ☐ Yes ☐ No. If "Yes" submit form HUD-92561.

31B. APPLICABLE FOR BOTH VA AND HUD. As a home loan borrower, you will be legally obligated to make the mortgage payments called for by your mortgage loan contract. The fact that you disposed of your property after the loan has been made WILL NOT RELIEVE YOU OF LIABILITY FOR MAKING THESE PAYMENTS. PAYMENT OF THE LOAN IN FULL IS ORDINARILY THE WAY LIABILITY ON A MORTGAGE NOTE IS ENDED. Some home buyers have the mistaken impression that if they sell their homes when they move to another locality, or dispose of it for any other reasons, they are no longer liable for the mortgage payments and that liability for these payments is solely that of the new owners. Even though the new owners may agree in writing to assume liability for your mortgage payments, this assumption agreement will not relieve you from liability to the holder of the note which you signed when you obtained the loan to buy the property. Also, unless you are able to sell the property to a buyer who is acceptable to the VA or to HUD/FHA and who will assume the payment of your obligation to the lender, you will not be relieved from liability to repay any claim which the VA or HUD/FHA may be required to pay your lender on account of default in your loan payments. The amount of any such claim payment will be a debt owed by you to the Federal Government. This debt will be the object of established collection procedures.

I, THE UNDERSIGNED BORROWER(S) CERTIFY THAT:

(1) I have read and understand the foregoing concerning my liability on the loan.

(2) VA Only *(check applicable box)* ☐ Purchase or Construction Loan. I now actually occupy the above-described property as my home or intend to move into and occupy said property as my home within a reasonable period of time. ☐ Home Improvement or Refinancing Loan. I own and personally occupy as my home the property described in Item 7 of the Application.

(3) Check applicable box *(not applicable for Home Improvement or Refinancing Loan)*, I have been informed that $ 60,000.00 is the reasonable value of the property as determined by the VA, ☐ the statement of appraised value as determined by HUD/FHA. IF THE CONTRACT PRICE OR COST EXCEEDS THE VA REASONABLE VALUE OR HUD/FHA STATEMENT OF APPRAISED VALUE, COMPLETE EITHER ITEM (a) or (b), WHICHEVER IS APPLICABLE.

(a) ☐ I was aware of this valuation when I signed my contract and I have paid or will pay in cash from my own resources at or prior to loan closing a sum equal to the difference between the contract purchase price or cost and the VA or HUD/FHA established value. I do not and will not have outstanding after loan closing any unpaid contractual obligation on account of such cash payment;

(b) ☐ I was not aware of this valuation when I signed my contract but have elected to complete the transaction at the contract purchase price or cost. I have paid or will pay in cash from my own resources at or prior to loan closing a sum equal to the difference between contract purchase price or cost and the VA or HUD/FHA established value. I do not and will not have outstanding after loan closing any unpaid contractual obligation on account of such cash payment.

(4) Neither I, nor anyone authorized to act for me, will refuse to sell or rent, after the making of a bona fide offer, or refuse to negotiate for the sale or rental of, or otherwise make unavailable or deny the dwelling or property covered by this loan to any person because of race, color, religion, sex or national origin. I recognize that any restrictive covenant on this property relating to race, color, religion, sex or national origin is illegal and void and civil action for preventive relief may be brought by the Attorney General of the United States in any appropriate U.S. District Court against any person responsible for the violation of the applicable law.

(5) The Borrower certifies that all information in this application is given for the purpose of obtaining a loan to be insured under the National Housing Act, or guaranteed by the Veterans Administration and the information in Section II is true and complete to the best of his/her knowledge and belief. Verification may be obtained from any source named herein.

HUD ONLY { (6) For properties constructed prior to 1950 - I have received the brochure "Watchout for Lead Paint Poisoning" ☐ ☐ NA

(7) ☐ I have read and understand the contents of the Home Energy Checklist attached to HUD-92800-4.

READ CERTIFICATIONS CAREFULLY - DO NOT SIGN UNLESS APPLICATION IS FULLY COMPLETED.	32. DATE 6/3/82	33. SIGNATURE OF BORROWER(S) *(Before signing, review accuracy of application and certifications.)* Bryan James Robinson

Federal statutes provide severe penalties for any fraud, intentional misrepresentation, or criminal connivance or conspiracy purposed to influence the issuance of any guaranty or insurance by the VA or USDA-FmHA Administrator or the HUD/FHA Commissioner.

CERTIFICATE OF COMMITMENT (FOR VA LOAN GUARANTY)	1. AGENCY CASE NUMBER LH123456	2A. LENDER'S CASE NUMBER 100400	2B. SECTION OF THE ACT *(HUD Only)*

3. NAME AND PRESENT ADDRESS OF BORROWER *(Include ZIP Code)*
Bryan James Robinson
5 Opelousas Street
New Orleans, Louisiana 70114

4. NAME AND ADDRESS OF LENDER *(Include ZIP Code)*

CARRUTH MORTGAGE CORPORATION
P. O. Box 53334
New Orleans, Louisiana 70153

Tel. 504-885-4811   Census Tract 17.12

5. PROPERTY ADDRESS INCLUDING NAME OF SUBDIVISION, LOT AND BLOCK NO., AND ZIP CODE	6A. LOAN AMOUNT	6B. INT. RATE	6C. PROPOSED MATURITY
1804 Homer Street Lot 12 Square 16, Bonnabel Heights S/D Jefferson Parish, Metairie, Louisiana 70005	$ 60,000.00 DISCOUNT: *(Only if borrower to pay)* ➤	15.5 % 6D. PERCENT %	30 YRS. 0 MOS. 6E. AMOUNT $

FOR VA USE ONLY *(To be completed by VA and returned to lender.)*

PERCENT OF GUARANTY
43.0 % ☐ CERTIFICATION OF ACTIVE DUTY STATUS AS OF DATE OF NOTE REQUIRED
(Applicable if checked)

TERMS OF COMMITMENT

The documents submitted in connection with the loan described above on this certificate have been examined and the loan has been determined to be eligible under Chapter 37, Title 38, U.S.C., and the regulations effective thereunder.

Upon receipt of a duly executed "Certificate of Loan Disbursement"* showing full compliance with the applicable regulations, the Administrator will issue: A Loan Guaranty Certificate as indicated above on this Certificate; subject to any adjustment necessary under Section 36:4303(g) of the Regulations upon ascertainment of the exact principal amount of the loan, or upon submission of the loan disbursement report under Section 36:4305 thereof.

In the case of a joint loan as defined in Section 36:4307 of the Regulations the portion of such loan eligible for guaranty shall be as provided therein.

This Certificate of Commitment will expire and will be invalid 6 months from the date hereof, unless the loan described herein is closed prior to such expiration date.

*If the loan described above on this Certificate is made by the lending institution named herein this certificate need not be returned to the VA. Otherwise this certificate or a copy of the agreement assigning this certificate must accompany the Certificate of Loan Disbursement.

ADMINISTRATOR OF VETERANS AFFAIRS, BY *(Authorized Agent)* Bruce C. Lowe	ISSUING OFFICE nola	DATE 6/8/82

VA FORM
JAN 1982 **26-1866a**   VA COPY 3

(CARRUTH)

Mortgage Corporation
MEMBER OF THE MELLON NATIONAL MORTGAGE GROUP

Bryan James Robinson &	**DATE** June 8, 1982 **LOAN TYPE:**
Marie Williams Robinson	XX VA ☐ FHA
5 Opelousas Street	**LOAN NO.** 100400 ☐ CONVENTIONAL
New Orleans, La. 70114	**PROPERTY DESCRIPTION**
	1804 Homer Street
	Metairie, Louisiana 70005

DEAR Customers:

We are pleased to inform you that your application for a loan on the above cited property has been approved as a result of a satisfactory review of the financial and credit information you furnished to us at the time of your application. This review and approval was done by:

The Veterans Administration

The mortgage loan will be made to you subject to the conditions as cited below and for the amount, term, and rate of interest as shown below. Upon the below checked conditions being met and a date of the Act of Sale being set, you will be notified of the time and place of the Act of Sale.

Sincerely,
CARRUTH MORTGAGE CORP.

By _Patricia Misiek_

Patricia Misiek, Loan Officer

LOAN AMOUNT	TERM (YEARS)	RATE OF INTEREST	ANNUAL PERCENTAGE RATE
$60,000.00	30	15.50	15.875

CONDITIONS OF APPROVAL

1. (X) THAT WE HAVE A VALID AND SUBSISTING LIEN AGAINST THE PROPERTY;
2. (X) THAT ALL REQUIREMENTS OF OUR LEGAL COUNSEL BE MET;
3. ( ) THAT THE DOWN PAYMENT REPRESENT A TRUE EQUITY AND NO OTHER FINANCING IN CONNECTION WITH THIS TRANSACTION, EITHER DIRECTLY OR INDIRECTLY IS PERMITTED. IF ANY VIOLATION OF THIS REQUIREMENT IS FOUND, THIS PERMANENT LOAN TRANSACTION SHALL BECOME NULL AND VOID.
4. (X) Subject to _1.5_ % discount points to be paid by the _Seller_; and good thru _6/30/82_;
5. ( ) Private Mortgage Insurance (PMI) Certificate;
6. (X) Termite Certificate;
7. (X) Flood Insurance;
8. ( ) Certificate of Completion;
9. ( ) Photographs;
10. ( ) Proof of sale of home netting at least $_____
11. ( ) Gift letter in the amount of $_____;
12. ( ) Pay off of debts designated on 1003;
13. ( ) Location map;
14. ( ) Floor plans;
15. ( ) Borrower(s) must sign and date original and copy of 1003;
16. ( ) Completion of repairs as shown on appraisal;
17. ( ) Board of Health approval of well and/or septic tank;
18. ( ) Satisfactory explanation from borrower(s) regarding late payments shown on credit report;
19. ( ) Code Compliance;
20. ( ) Borrower(s) to initial correction(s) on original and copy of 1003;
21. ( ) Letter of recommendation from applicant/co-applicant employer;
22. (X) Return to Carruth a signed copy of this Commitment Letter (SIGNED BELOW BY PURCHASER).

FLOOD INSURANCE NOTIFICATION

As you were previously advised, Flood Insurance under the National Flood Insurance Program is required for the life of your loan by Carruth. If you have not made arrangements with your insurance agent to have your flood insurance policy presented to the closing attorney at the time of the Act of Sale, please do so immediately.

PURCHASER'S SIGNATURE	PURCHASER'S SIGNATURE
Bryan J. Robinson	_Marie W. Robinson_

P13 (R 8/81)

CARRUTH MORTGAGE CORPORATION
P. O. BOX 53334
NEW ORLEANS, LOUISIANA 70153
Phone (504) 885-4811

CLOSING DATA SHEET
CMC CASE # __100400__

June 8, 1982
DATE

TO: Shirley Kirkes   TITLE COMPANY: Lawyer's Title of La.

MORTGAGOR(S): Bryan James Robinson and Marie Williams Robinson
    MARITAL STATUS: Attorney to Obtain
REALTOR: Linda Keanan - Homes Realty   CONTRACTOR: N/A
    Mike Crane - Crane Realty
SELLER-OWNER: John Hunter   SURVEY FROM: Attorney to Obtain

MORTGAGEE: CARRUTH MORTGAGE CORPORATION, AN ARKANSAS CORPORATION

LEGAL DESCRIPTION: LOT__12__ SQ.__16__ SUBDIVISION__Bonnabel Heights__

STREET ADDRESS__1804 Homer Street__ CITY__Metairie__ STATE__Louisiana__
CHANGES IN TERMS OF SALE & LOAN RECITED BELOW ARE NOT TO BE MADE (SEE REVERSE ITEM #2)

SALE PRICE: $__60,000.00__ CONTRACT PRICE: $_____ SALE PRICE OF LOT: $_____

LOAN AMOUNT: $__60,000.00__ RATE__15.5__% TERM__30__YRS. MO. PRIN. & INT. $__782.72__
Purchaser to pay closing costs and prepaids   ATTORNEY TO VERIFY
Seller to pay discount
HAZARD INSURANCE AGENT/AGENCY: Will Advise   COVERAGE: $__51,000.00__
    FIRST MORTGAGEE CLAUSE
    (XX) CARRUTH MORTGAGE CORPORATION, P. O. BOX 53334, NEW ORLEANS, LA. 70153

FLOOD INSURANCE AGENT/AGENCY: Will Advise   COVERAGE: $__51,000.00__
    FIRST MORTGAGEE CLAUSE
    (XX) CARRUTH MORTGAGE CORPORATION, P. O. BOX 53334, NEW ORLEANS, LA. 70153

NOTE PREPARED ON:
    (X) VA FORM 26-6316a ( ) FHA FORM 9123 ( ) FNMA/FHLMC UNIFORM INSTRUMENT

MORTGAGE PREPARED ON:
    (XX) VA FORM 26-6316b ( ) FHA FORM 2123m V-L ( ) FNMA/FHLMC UNIFORM INST.

PREPAYMENT CLAUSE IN THE CONVENTIONAL NOTE SHOULD BE COMPLETED AS FOLLOWS:
    __NONE__ DURING EACH OF THE FIRST THREE LOAN YEARS
    __NONE__ DURING EACH OF THE FOURTH AND FIFTH LOAN YEARS
THE ENTIRE PREPAYMENT PARAGRAPH OF THE NOTE SHOULD BE INCORPORATED IN THE CONVENTIONAL MORTGAGE FORM.

THE FUNDS FOR ITEMS MARKED BELOW WILL BE COLLECTED AT CLOSING AND FORWARDED TO CARRUTH MORTGAGE CORORATION.

(x)	PHOTOGRAPHS	By Seller	$ 10.00
(x)	AMORTIZATION SCHEDULE	By Seller	$ 3.00
(x)	CREDIT REPORT FEE		$ 30.00
(x)	APPRAISAL FEE		$ 80.00
(x)	ORIGINATION FEE		$ 600.00
( )	2 MO. FHA/PMI MTG. INS. ____ @ ____ PER MO.		$
(x)	2 MO. FLOOD INS. ESCROW ____ @ ____ PER MO.		$
(x)	HAZARD INSURANCE PREMIUM PAYABLE TO ISSUING INSURANCE AGENCY		$
(x)	DISCOUNT PAID BY __Seller__ 1.5 % OF LOAN (ATTORNEY TO VERIFY COMPUTATIONS)		$ 900.00
(x)	ACCRUED INTEREST IF APPLICABLE — ATTORNEY TO COMPUTE (SEE ITEM #3 ON REVERSE SIDE)		$
(x)	ESCROW FUNDS FOR TAXES FOR CURRENT YEAR FROM SELLER & PURCHASER, IF NOT BEING PAID BY ATTORNEY.		
( )	____ OF 1%, FIRST YEARS PRIVATE MORTGAGE INSURANCE PREMIUM		$
( )	PRIVATE MORTGAGE INSURANCE REVIEW FEE		$
( )	FNMA UNDERWRITING FEE		$
( )	PROPERTY INSPECTION FEE		$

ALLOW CREDIT TO: __Purchaser__ FOR FUNDS IN THE AMOUNT OF $110.00 PAID TO CARRUTH MORTGAGE CORPORATION. Credit Report-$30.00, Appraisal-$80.00

ALL CONDITIONS OF VA CRV AND VA CERTIFICATE OF COMMITMENT AND/OR FHA CONDITIONAL COMMITMENT WITH ATTACHMENT(S) AND FHA FIRM COMMITMENT MUST BE SATISFIED PRIOR TO CLOSING THIS LOAN.

ENCLOSURES:
(X) PURCHASE CONTRACT
(X) VA CERTIFICATE OF REASONABLE VALUE
(X) VA CERTIFICATE OF COMMITMENT
(X) VA FORM 1876 FOR SIGNATURE OF VETERAN
( ) DIVORCE DECREES
( ) WARRANTY OF COMPLETION OF CONSTRUCTION (MUST BE COMPLETED)
(X) HUD-1 FORM AND ADDENDUM
(X) LOAN CLOSING SETTLEMENT SHEET CMC FORM 118 (MUST BE COMPLETED)
( ) FHA FIRM COMMITMENT FOR MORTGAGOR'S SIGNATURE (2)
(X) CMC 218

( ) ATTACHMENT "A" FIRM COMMITMENT WITH CONDITIONS
( ) FHA CONDITIONAL COMMITMENT
( ) ATTACHMENT "A", "B" OF CONDITIONAL COMMITMENT
(X) TERMITE STATEMENT CMC FORM 33 FOR SIGNATURES
( ) CONVENTIONAL NOTE & MORTGAGES
( ) BUILDER & PURCHASER AFFIDAVIT
(X) CMC 157 ( ) FNMA 1009
(X) CMC 176/178 ( ) CMC 1009A
( ) PREVIOUS TITLE EVIDENCE

FINAL/REPAIR INSPECTION REQUIRED: ( ) YES (X) NO: TERMITE CERTIF. REQUIRED: (X) YES ( ) NO

ADDITIONAL INSTRUCTIONS & REMARKS: Flood insurance policy to be submitted with closing papers. Equipment in value to be included in mortgage.

294

CARRUTH
Mortgage Corporation
MEMBER OF THE MELLON NATIONAL MORTGAGE GROUP

Branch <u>Metairie</u>

Loan Rep. <u>Carla Rody</u>

LOAN DISCOUNT GUARANTY AGREEMENT

Name of Applicant <u>Bryan James Robinson and Marie Williams Robinson</u>

Property Description <u>1804 Homer Street, Metairie, Louisiana 70005</u>

Application Date <u>5/25/82</u> Type <u>VA</u> Rate <u>15.50%</u> Loan Amount <u>$60,000.00</u>

Name of Seller <u>John Hunter</u>

Name of Seller's Agent <u>Mike Crane- Crane Realty</u>

Carruth Mortgage Corp. hereby agrees to close the above captioned mortgage loan at a discount of <u>1.5</u> % of the loan amount. In addition to the discount a 1% origination fee will be collected at the time of closing.

It is understood and agreed that this loan will be closed at the highest permissible interest rate of the FHA and/or VA, or conventional, but in no event less than <u>15.50</u> %. Should the interest rate be reduced from the present <u>15.50</u> %, or this applicant fails to qualify for the loan request, this agreement shall become null and void.

This agreement is conditioned upon approval by the appropriate governmental or other agency and/or Carruth Mortgage Corp. of the loan application and upon compliance with the terms of their commitment. This agreement is also conditioned upon this loan being eligible for purchase by FNMA and/or GNMA.

This commitment will expire on <u>June 30</u> , 19 <u>82</u> .

ACCEPTED BY:

_____
Loan Representative

_____
Branch Manager

_____
Agent/Seller/Applicant

<u>May 25, 1982</u>
Date Accepted

COMMITMENT:
1 Office Location	4 Transaction Code	7 Endorsement Code	10 State Code	13 Source of Business
2 Date Income Reported	5 Liability	8 Endorsement Charge	11 County Code	14 Commission Retention
3 Case Number	6 Charge	9 Total Revenue	12 Property type	

1	3	4 0	5 0	6 0	7	9	10	12	14
2		M	M	M	8 M		11	13	

Lawyers Title Insurance Corporation
A STOCK COMPANY
Home Office—Richmond, Virginia
COMMITMENT FOR TITLE INSURANCE
SCHEDULE A

1. Effective Date   June 10, 1982, at 8:00 a.m.   Case No. __12345__ SPECIMEN

Bryan James Robinson, and wife
Marie Williams Robinson

2. Policy or policies to be issued:

(a)

☐ ALTA Owner's Policy—Form B-1970 (Rev. 10-17-70)   Amount $_____

☐ ALTA Residential Title Insurance Policy—1979   None

Proposed insured:

(b) ALTA Loan Policy, 1970 (Rev. 10-17-70)   Amount $__60,000.00__

Proposed insured:

     Carruth Mortgage Corporation, and/or
     Administrator of Veterans' Affairs,
     his successors and assigns as their interest may appear
     c/o Mrs. Shirley H. Kirkes

(c)   3100 Division Street   Amount $_____

Proposed insured: Metairie, Louisiana 70002

     None

3. Title to the   fee simple   estate or interest in the land
described or referred to in this Commitment is at the effective date hereof vested in:

         JOHN HUNTER

4. The land referred to in this Commitment is described as follows:

     1804 HOMER STREET
     METAIRIE, LOUISIANA, 70005
     LOT 12
     SQUARE 16
     BONNABEL HEIGHTS SUBDIVISION
     PARISH OF JEFFERSON
     STATE OF LOUISIANA

Countersigned at __New Orleans, Louisiana__

LAWYERS TITLE OF LOUISIANA, INC.

BY __SPECIMEN__

     Authorized Officer or Agent

Form No. 91-88 (SCH. A)
035-1-088-0001/2   **ORIGINAL**

Commitment No. __AB 987456__

Schedule A—Page 1   SPECIMEN

This commitment is invalid unless
the Insuring Provisions and Schedules A and B are attached.

Lawyers Title Insurance Corporation

A STOCK COMPANY

Home Office—Richmond, Virginia

SPECIMEN

SCHEDULE B—Section 1

Requirements

The following are the requirements to be complied with:

Item (a) Payment to or for the account of the grantors or mortgagors of the full consideration for the estate or interest to be insured.

Item (b) Proper instrument(s) creating the estate or interest to be insured must be executed and duly filed for record, to-wit:

Item (c) Furnishing two copies of current satisfactory survey showing improvements, certified to Lawyers Title Insurance Corporation. Adverse matters disclosed will be shown as policy exceptions.

Item (d) Submission of completed Inchoate Lien Affidavit, disclosing all facts relative to mechanics' laborers' and material-men's liens. The company reserves the right to make additional requirements.

Item (e) Submission of marital status and/or corporate charter information of the parties, and appropriate corporate resolutions. The company reserves the right to make additional requirements.

Item (f) ANNEXATION to the instrument creating the estate or interest to be insured, of the following:

1. Tax research certificates showing payment of all taxes due and payable.
2. Orleans Parish property: a. Clear paving certificate from the Recorder of Mortgages, and
                          b. Clear P.O.L.I.C. from the City of New Orleans.
    Jefferson Parish property: Clear Paving and Sewerage lien certificate from an approved source.
3. Clear Mortgage and Conveyance Certificates, dated or timed subsequent to the filing for record of the insured instrument,

(searched in ⎱ Present owners
name(s) of ⎰ Additional required certificate names.
            MORTGAGORS—TO ACQUIRE (except for vendor's liens).
4. The approved survey,
5. Corporate resolutions, powers of attorney and other pertinent documents.

Item (g) Cancellation of record of adverse inscriptions shown on certificates required under Item (f)-3., above, and the following:

This commitment is invalid unless the Insuring Provisions and Schedules A and B are attached.

Form No. 91-88
035-1-088-1703

SPECIMEN

Lawyers Title Insurance Corporation
A STOCK COMPANY
Home Office — Richmond, Virginia

SCHEDULE B—Section 2

Exceptions

The policy or policies to be issued will contain exceptions to the following unless the same are disposed of to the satisfaction of the Company:

1. Defects, liens, encumbrances, adverse claims or other matters, if any, created, first appearing in the public records or attaching subsequent to the effective date hereof but prior to the date the proposed insured acquires for value of record the estate or interest or mortgage thereon covered by this Commitment.

NOTE: If policy is to be issued in support of a mortgage loan, attention is directed to the fact that the Company can assume no liability under its policy, the closing instructions, or Insured Closing Service for compliance with the requirements of any consumer credit protection or truth in lending law in connection with said mortgage loan.

This commitment is invalid unless the Insuring Provisions and Schedules A and B are attached.

Schedule B-Section 2-Page 1-Commitment No. _____SPECIMEN_____

Form No. 91-88 (B-2)
035-1-088-0004/1

ORIGINAL

Lawyers Title Insurance Corporation

Home Office — Richmond, Virginia

COMMITMENT FOR TITLE INSURANCE

LAWYERS TITLE INSURANCE CORPORATION, a Virginia corporation, herein called the Company, for valuable consideration, hereby commits to issue its policy or policies of title insurance, as identified in Schedule A, in favor of the proposed Insured named in Schedule A, as owner or mortgagee of the estate or interest covered hereby in the land described or referred to in Schedule A, upon payment of the premiums and charges therefor; all subject to the provisions of Schedules A and B and to the Conditions and Stipulations hereof.

This Commitment shall be effective only when the identity of the proposed Insured and the amount of the policy or policies committed for have been inserted in Schedule A hereof by the Company, either at the time of the issuance of this Commitment or by subsequent endorsement.

This Commitment is preliminary to the issuance of such policy or policies of title insurance and all liability and obligations hereunder shall cease and terminate six (6) months after the effective date hereof or when the policy or policies committed for shall issue, whichever first occurs, provided that the failure to issue such policy or policies is not the fault of the Company. This Commitment shall not be valid or binding until countersigned by an authorized officer or agent.

IN WITNESS WHEREOF, the Company has caused this Commitment to be signed and sealed, to become valid when countersigned by an authorized officer or agent of the Company, all in accordance with its By-Laws. This Commitment is effective as of the date shown in Schedule A as "Effective Date."

CONDITIONS AND STIPULATIONS

1. The term "mortgage," when used herein, shall include deed of trust, trust deed, or other security instrument.

2. If the proposed Insured has or acquires actual knowledge of any defect, lien, encumbrance, adverse claim or other matter affecting the estate or interest or mortgage thereon covered by this Commitment other than those shown in Schedule B hereof, and shall fail to disclose such knowledge to the Company in writing, the Company shall be relieved from liability for any loss or damage resulting from any act of reliance hereon to the extent the Company is prejudiced by failure to so disclose such knowledge. If the proposed Insured shall disclose such knowledge to the Company, or if the Company otherwise acquires actual knowledge of any such defect, lien, encumbrance, adverse claim or other matter, the Company at its option may amend Schedule B of this Commitment accordingly, but such amendment shall not relieve the Company from liability previously incurred pursuant to paragraph 3 of these Conditions and Stipulations.

3. Liability of the Company under this Commitment shall be only to the named proposed Insured and such parties included under the definition of Insured in the form of policy or policies committed for and only for actual loss incurred in reliance hereon in undertaking in good faith (a) to comply with the requirements hereof, or (b) to eliminate exceptions shown in Schedule B, or (c) to acquire or create the estate or interest or mortgage thereon covered by this Commitment. In no event shall such liability exceed the amount stated in Schedule A for the policy or policies committed for and such liability is subject to the insuring provisions and the Conditions and Stipulations and the Exclusions from Coverage of the form of policy or policies committed for in favor of the proposed Insured which are hereby incorporated by reference and are made a part of this Commitment except as expressly modified herein.

4. Any action or actions or rights of action that the proposed Insured may have or may bring against the Company arising out of the status of the title to the estate or interest or the status of the mortgage thereon covered by this Commitment must be based on and are subject to the provisions of this Commitment.

Lawyers Title Insurance Corporation

Robert C. Dawson

President

Attest:

Roy Brushead

Secretary.

NOTE: ACCORDING TO H.Ü.D. F.I.A. FLOOD HAZARD BOUNDARY MAP 220204
THIS PROPERTY IS:
_____ NOT IN A FLOOD PRONE AREA
__X__ IS LOCATED IN FLOOD ZONE ___C___

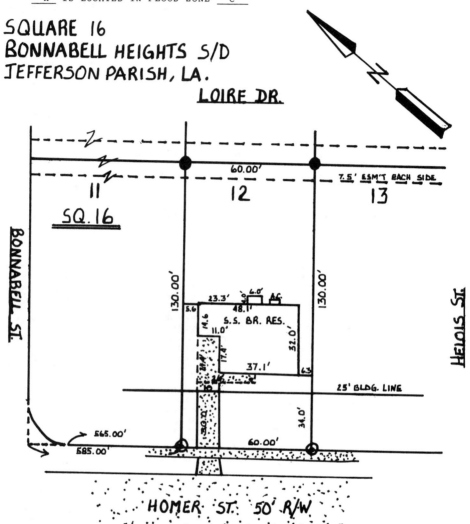

SQUARE 16
BONNABELL HEIGHTS S/D
JEFFERSON PARISH, LA.

SET IRON

FOUND IRON

FENCE POST

SCALE : 1" = 30'

FLOOD INSURANCE
APPLICATION
EMERGENCY AND REGULAR PROGRAMS
IMPORTANT — SEE REVERSE SIDE — IMPORTANT

OMB - 026-R-00025

National Flood Insurance Program
federal emergency management agency

NOTE: THE NUMBERED SECTIONS 1-14 CORRESPOND TO INSTRUCTIONS IN THE FLOOD INSURANCE MANUAL

① CURRENT POLICY NUMBER
NEW ☒ RENEWAL ☐ FL IF NEW, LEAVE BLANK

② ONE YEAR POLICY ☒ THREE YEAR POLICY ③
DIRECT BILL INSTRUCTIONS
BILL INSURED ☐1 BILL FIRST MORTGAGEE ☒2 BILL SECOND MORTGAGE ☐3 BILL LOSS PAYEE ☐4 BILL OTHER ☐5

POLICY TERM IS FROM 6/10/82 TO 6/10/83
MO/DA/YR   MO/DA/YR
1201 A.M. LOCAL TIME AT THE INSURED PROPERTY LOCATION.
IS IT INTENDED THAT THIS POLICY BE EFFECTIVE AT THE TIME THAT THE DESCRIBED BUILDING IS ACQUIRED? YES ☒ NO ☐N

③ ADDRESS OF LICENSED PROPERTY OR CASUALTY INSURANCE AGENT OR BROKER
CARRUTH INSURANCE AGENCY INC.,
P. O. Box 8861
Metairie, Louisiana 70011-8861
AGENTS TAX ID ☒ OR SSN ☐ 72-0856901

④ NAME AND MAILING ADDRESS OF INSURED
ROBINSON, Bryan James and wife
Marie Williams Robinson
1804 Homer Street
Metairie, Louisiana 70005
TELEPHONE (AREA) NUMBER

⑤ IS COVERAGE REQUIRED FOR DISASTER ASSISTANCE?
YES ☐Y NO ☒
SBA ☐1 FEMA ☐2 FHA ☐3 HEW ☐4
IF YES, CHECK (✓) GOVERNMENT AGENCY AND ENTER CASE FILE NUMBER OR INSURED'S SOCIAL SECURITY NUMBER
IF OTHER, PLEASE SPECIFY

⑥ NAME AND ADDRESS OF FIRST MORTGAGEE
LOAN # 12345
CARRUTH MORTGAGE CORPORATION
their successors and/or assigns ATIMA
P. O. Box 53334
New Orleans, Louisiana 70153

⑦ IF SECOND MORTGAGEE, LOSS PAYEE OR OTHER, IS TO BE BILLED THE FOLLOWING MUST BE COMPLETED, INCLUDING THE NAME AND ADDRESS:
2ND MORTGAGEE ☐1 LOSS PAYEE ☐2 DISASTER AGENCY ☐3
OTHER, PLEASE SPECIFY ☐4

Dummy Policy

⑧ IS INSURED PROPERTY LOCATION SAME AS INSURED MAILING ADDRESS? YES ☒ NO ☐N IF NO, ENTER PROPERTY ADDRESS. IF RURAL, DESCRIBE PROPERTY LOCATION.

⑨ NAME OF COUNTY/PARISH? JEFFERSON   LOCATED IN AN UNINCORPORATED AREA OF THE COUNTY? YES ☒ NO ☐N
COMMUNITY NUMBER AND SUFFIX FOR LOCATION OF PROPERTY INSURED   225199B
COMMUNITY PROGRAM TYPE IS REGULAR ☒ EMERGENCY ☐E IS BUILDING IN SPECIAL FLOOD HAZARD AREA? YES ☐Y NO ☒
FLOOD INSURANCE RATE MAP ZONE   C   INFORMATION MAP INFO ☐1 COMMUNITY ☐2 FLOOD ☒ OTHER ☐4
SOURCE   FACILITY   OFFICIAL   MAP

⑩ CHECK (✓) ONE APPLICABLE BLOCK IN EACH A, B, C, D, E, F, G, AND H BELOW AND COMPLETE I THEN J IF APPLICABLE

(A) BUILDING OCCUPANCY	(B) BUILDING TYPE (INCLUDING BASEMENT IF ANY)	(C) BASEMENT IS	(E) IS PROPERTY A CONDOMINIUM?	(G) IS THIS BUILDING IN THE COURSE OF CONSTRUCTION? (BUILDERS RISK)
RESIDENTIAL		NONE ☒ FINISHED ☐1		
SINGLE FAMILY ☒	ONE FLOOR ☒	UNFINISHED ☐2	YES ☐Y NO ☒	YES ☐Y NO ☒
2-4 FAMILY ☐2	TWO FLOORS ☐2			
OTHER RESIDENTIAL ☐3	THREE OR MORE FLOORS ☐3	(D) INSURED QUALIFIES AS A SMALL BUSINESS RISK?	(F) IS BUILDING OWNED BY STATE GOVERNMENT?	(H) IS BUILDING INSURED'S PRINCIPAL RESIDENCE?
	SPLIT LEVEL ☐4			
NON-RESIDENTIAL ☐4 (INCLUDING HOTEL/MOTEL)	MOBILE HOME ON FOUNDATION ☐5	YES ☐Y NO ☒	YES ☐Y NO ☒	YES ☐Y NO ☒

(I) ESTIMATED REPLACEMENT COST OF INSURED BUILDING? 51,000.
(J) IF NOT SINGLE FAMILY DWELLING, NUMBER OF OCCUPANCIES _____
DESCRIBE USES OF BUILDING _____

⑪ IS BUILDING MULTIPLE OCCUPANCY? YES ☐Y NO ☒
IF YES, INSURED OCCUPIES (CHECK ONE BLOCK BELOW)
BASEMENT ONLY ☐1   FIRST FLOOR ONLY ☐3
BASEMENT AND ABOVE ☐2   FIRST FLOOR AND ABOVE ONLY ☐4
SECOND FLOOR AND ABOVE ONLY ☐5

IS PERSONAL PROPERTY HOUSEHOLD CONTENTS?
YES ☐Y NO ☐N
IF NO, PLEASE DESCRIBE BELOW

⑫ IS BUILDING POST FIRM CONSTRUCTION OR SUBSTANTIAL IMPROVEMENT? YES ☐Y NO ☒ (SEE REVERSE SIDE FOR DEFINITION.)
IF YES, BUILDING PERMIT DATE OR DATE CONSTRUCTION STARTED _____ MO/DA/YR
IF POST FIRM CONSTRUCTION IN ZONES A1-A30, AH, V1-V30, OR IF PRE FIRM CONSTRUCTION IS ELEVATION RATED, COMPLETE ELEVATION DATA BELOW.
LOWEST FLOOR ELEVATION _____ (−) BASE FLOOD ELEVATION _____ (=) DIFFERENCE TO NEAREST FOOT _____ (+ OR −)
IS BUILDING FLOOD-PROOFED? YES ☐Y NO ☒
ATTACH ELEVATION OR FLOOD-PROOFING CERTIFICATION (SEE FLOOD INSURANCE MANUAL FOR SUGGESTED CERTIFICATE FORM.)
IF PREVIOUSLY SUBMITTED, INDICATE POLICY NUMBER TO WHICH CERTIFICATION WAS ATTACHED. FL

⑬ COVERAGE REQUESTED – CHECK ONE BLOCK BELOW AND COMPLETE REMAINDER OF SECTION 13
BUILDING AND CONTENTS ☒   BUILDING ONLY ☐2   CONTENTS ONLY ☐3

COVERAGE	BASIC LIMITS			ADDITIONAL LIMITS (REGULAR PROGRAM ONLY)			BASIC AND ADDITIONAL	TOTAL PREMIUM
	AMOUNT OF INSURANCE	RATE	ANNUAL PREMIUM	AMOUNT OF INSURANCE	RATE	ANNUAL PREMIUM	TOTAL AMOUNT OF INSURANCE REQUESTED	
BUILDING	35,000	.20	70 00	16,000	.06	10 00	51,000	80 00
CONTENTS	10,000	.35	35 00	10,000	.11	11 00	20,000	46 00

BLANKET COVERAGE NOT PERMITTED
ONE YEAR POLICY ☒
THREE YEAR POLICY ☐3
(FOR COMPUTATION OF A THREE YEAR POLICY MULTIPLY THE ANNUAL SUBTOTAL BY THREE, AND THEN ADD THE EXPENSE CONSTANT)

ANNUAL SUBTOTAL	126 00
THREE YEAR SUBTOTAL (ANNUAL X THREE)	
EXPENSE CONSTANT +	20 00
TOTAL PREPAID PREMIUM	146 00

⑭ THE ABOVE STATEMENTS ARE CORRECT TO THE BEST OF MY KNOWLEDGE. I UNDERSTAND THAT ANY FALSE STATEMENTS MAY _____
Jackie Reynolds
SIGNATURE OF INSURANCE AGENT/BROKER

5/28/82
MO/DA/YR
DATE OF APPLICATION

PLEASE ATTACH TO NFIP COPY OF APPLICATION THE CHECK OR MONEY ORDER FOR THE TOTAL PREPAID PREMIUM MADE PAYABLE TO THE NATIONAL FLOOD INSURANCE AGENT.
SPECIAL NOTE TO INSURANCE AGENT:
Attach check to original and send to NFIP. Keep second part for your records and give third part to insured, and fourth part to mortgagee.

FEMA 81-16 (2-80)

N F I P C O P Y

Form Approved
OMB No. 63-R1395

VETERANS ADMINISTRATION, U.S. DEPARTMENT OF HOUSING AND URBAN DEVELOPMENT **WOOD DESTROYING INSECT INFORMATION EXISTING CONSTRUCTION**	1A. VA CASE NUMBER LH 123456	2. DATE
	1B. HUD/FHA CASE NUMBER	6/8/82

PRIVACY ACT INFORMATION - The information requested on this form will be used in evaluating the property for a VA or HUD insured loan. Although you are not required by law to provide this information, failure to provide it can result in rejection of the property as security for your loan. The information collected will not be disclosed outside VA or HUD except as permitted by law. VA and HUD are authorized to request this information by statute (38 U.S.C., 1804(a) and 12 U.S.C., 1701 et seq.).

READ THESE INSTRUCTIONS CAREFULLY BEFORE COMPLETING THIS FORM

1. The VA case number or HUD/FHA case number shall be inserted in Item 1 by the lender or the pest control company.
2. When treatment is indicated in Item 8C, the insects treated will be named, the data on application method and chemicals used shall be entered in Item 10. Proper control measures may include issuance of warranty. Warranty information should also be entered below. Proper control measures are those which follow good acceptable industry practices.
3. If visual evidence is found, the insects causing such evidence will be listed in Item 8A and damage resulting from such infestation will be noted in Item 8D.
4. Areas that were inaccessible or obstructed (item 7) may include, but are not limited to, wall covering, fixed ceilings, floor coverings, furniture or stored articles. The Pest Control Operator (PCO) should list, in item 7, those obstructions or areas which inhibit the inspection.
5. Item 8A may be checked when the PCO is not authorized to perform control measures by the owner/seller or control measures cannot be performed due to conditions beyond your control, e.g., obstructions, weather, etc.
6. Visible evidence of conditions conducive to infestation from subterranean termites shall be reported on reverse of the form (earth-wood contact, faulty grades, insufficient ventilation. etc.).

3A. NAME OF INSPECTION COMPANY BEST PEST CONTROL, INC.	5A. NAME OF PROPERTY OWNER/SELLER J. HUNTER
3B. ADDRESS OF INSPECTION COMPANY (Include ZIP Code) 332 VETERANS HIGHWAY METAIRIE, LOUISIANA 70002	5B. ADDRESS OF PROPERTY 1804 HOMER STREET METAIRIE, LOUISIANA 7000S
3C. TELEPHONE NUMBER (Include Area Code) 504-889-7321	4. PEST CONTROL OPERATOR LICENSE NUMBER B-12	5C. STRUCTURE(S) INSPECTED 1

FINDINGS

6. WERE ANY AREAS OF THE PROPERTY OBSTRUCTED OR INACCESSIBLE? ☐ Yes ☒ No (If "Yes" complete Item 7.)	7. OBSTRUCTIONS OR INACCESSIBLE AREAS (specify) (Read Item 11B before completing.)

8. BASED ON CAREFUL VISUAL INSPECTION OF THE READILY ACCESSIBLE AREAS OF THE PROPERTY (See Item 11A below completing):

☐ A. Visible evidence of wood destroying insects was observed. No control measures were performed. Insects observed: _____

☒ B. No visible evidence of infestation from wood destroying insects was observed.

☐ C. Visible evidence of infestation was noted; proper control measures were performed.

☐ D. Visible damage due to _____ has been observed in the following areas: _____

☐ E. Visible evidence of previously treated infestation, which is now inactive, was observed. (Explain in Item 10.)

9. DAMAGE OBSERVED ABOVE, IF ANY: (Check One) ☐ A. Will be/has been corrected by this company. ☐ B. Will be corrected by another company (see attached contract). ☐ C. Will not be corrected by this company. Recommend that damage be evaluated by qualified building expert and that needed repairs be made.	10. ADDITIONAL COMMENTS (If necessary, continue on reverse.) NONE

11. STATEMENT OF PEST CONTROL OPERATOR

A. The inspection covered the readily accessible areas of the property, including attics and crawl spaces which permit entry. Special attention was given to those accessible areas which experience has shown to be particularly susceptible to attack by wood destroying insects. Probing and/or sounding of those areas and other visible accessible wood members showing evidence of infestation was performed.

B. The inspection did not include areas which were obstructed or inaccessible at the time of inspection. (See instruction number 4 above.)

C. This is not a structural damage report. Neither is this a warranty as to absence of wood destroying insects.

D. Neither I nor the company for which I am acting have had, presently have, or contemplate having any interest in the property. I do further state that neither I nor the company for which I am acting is associated in any way with any party to this transaction.

12A. SIGNATURE OF AUTHORIZED COMPANY REPRESENTATIVE *Albert Best, Sr.* ALBERT BEST, SR.	12B. TITLE PRESIDENT	13. DATE 6/8/82

STATEMENT OF PURCHASER

I have received the original or a legible copy of this form

14. SIGNATURE OF PURCHASER *Bryan James Robinson*	15. DATE 6-10-82

VA FORM 26-8850
HUD-92053 (4-80)

REQUEST FOR AUTHORITY TO CLOSE AND STATEMENT
OF SELLERS' AND BUYERS' COSTS

The information furnished by you on the attached form will be
used by Carruth Mortgage Corporation in preparation of the
"DISCLOSURE OF COST OF LOAN" as required by the Federal Consumers
Protection Act (Truth in Lending). This form should be prepared
as soon as you are able to determine the date of closing and
actual costs.

The figures listed must be accurate and represent all costs to
buyer and seller incident to this transaction.

Receipt of this form in our office will be considered as your
formal request for the authority to close this loan. We will
furnish to you, within two (2) working days from receipt in our
office, written authority to close this loan in accordance with
our General Loan Closing Instructions along with a completed
"DISCLOSURE OF COST OF LOAN" statement to be signed by the
borrower(s) PRIOR TO THE CLOSING.

You are NOT to close this loan under any circumstances without
our prior written authority.

Borrower(s) _Marie Williams Robinson and Bryan James Robinson_

Address of Property ___1804 Homer Street_____

_____ Metairie, Louisiana 70005_____

FHA/VA Case No. _____LH 123456_____

CMC Loan # _____100400_____

Sales Price $_____60,000.00_____

Payment (P&I)$_____782.72_____

Loan Amount $_____60,000.00_____

Date of Closing _____June 10, 1982_____

Date of First Payment August 1, 1982_____

Date of Final Payment June 1, 2012_____

Hazard Insurance Type Homeowners_____

Amt. Coverage $_____60,000.00_____

City Where Closing Will Take Place ____Metairie_____

C-5 (9/81)

Date __6-9-82__   Attorney_____
                              (signature)

This Statement represents actual costs incurred
by buyer and seller pertinent to this transaction.
This loan will not be closed by me if these figures
do not agree with the actual charges at the time
of the loan closing.

_6-8-82_
Date

Attorney Signature

C-5 pg 2 12/81

J. SUMMARY OF BORROWER'S TRANSACTION		K. SUMMARY OF SELLER'S TRANSACTION	
100. GROSS AMOUNT DUE FROM BORROWER:		400. GROSS AMOUNT DUE TO SELLER:	
101. Contract sales price	60,000.	401. Contract sales price	60,000.
102. Personal property		402. Personal property	
103. Settlement charges to borrower (line 1400)	2598.90	403.	
104.		404.	
105.		405.	
Adjustments for items paid by seller in advance	Year amt.	Adjustments for items paid by seller in advance	Year Amt.
106. City/town taxes to		406. City/town taxes to	
107. County taxes to		407. County taxes to	
108. Assessments to		408. Assessments to	
109.		409.	
110.		410.	
111.		411.	
112.		412.	
120. GROSS AMOUNT DUE FROM BORROWER	62,598.90	420. GROSS AMOUNT DUE TO SELLER	60,000.
200. AMOUNTS PAID BY OR IN BEHALF OF BORROWER:		500. REDUCTIONS IN AMOUNT DUE TO SELLER:	
201. Deposit or earnest money		501. Excess deposit (see instructions)	
202. Principal amount of new loan(s)	60,000.	502. Settlement charges to seller (line 1400)	2778.00
203. Existing loan(s) taken subject to		503. Existing loan(s) taken subject to	
204. CREDIT REPORT	30,00	504. Payoff of first mortgage loan	
205. APPRAISAL FEE	80,00	505. Payoff of second mortgage loan	
206. UNDERWRITER FEE		506.	
207. ORIGINATION FEE		507.	
208. OTHER COLLECTED AMOUNT		508.	
209.		509.	
Adjustments for items unpaid by seller	Year Amt.	Adjustments for items unpaid by seller	Year Amt.
210. City/town taxes to		510. City/town taxes to	
211. County taxes to		511. County taxes to	
212. Assessments to		512. Assessments to	
213.		513. PRO RATION TAXES	60,00
214.		514.	
215.		515.	
216.		516.	
217.		517.	
218.		518.	
219.		519.	
220. TOTAL PAID BY/FOR BORROWER	60,110.	520. TOTAL REDUCTION AMOUNT DUE SELLER	2838.00
300. CASH AT SETTLEMENT FROM/TO BORROWER		600. CASH AT SETTLEMENT TO/FROM SELLER	
301. Gross amount due from borrower (line 120)	62,598.90	601. Gross amount due to seller (line 420)	60,000.
302. Less amounts paid by/for borrower (line 220)	(60,110.)	602. Less reductions in amount due seller (line 520)	(2838.00
303. CASH (☒ FROM) (☐ TO) BORROWER	2488.90	603. CASH (☒ TO) (☐ FROM) SELLER	57,162.

L	SETTLEMENT CHARGES	PAID FROM BORROWER'S FUNDS AT SETTLEMENT	PAID FROM SELLER'S FUNDS AT SETTLEMENT
700.	TOTAL SALES/BROKER'S COMMISSION based on price $ 60,000. @ 3.0 % = 1800.		
	Division of Commission (line 700) as follows:		
701.	$ 900. to Linda Keanan		
702.	$ 900. to Mike Crane		
703.	Commission paid at Settlement		1800.00
704.			
800.	ITEMS PAYABLE IN CONNECTION WITH LOAN		
801.	Loan Origination Fee 1.0 %	600.00	
802.	Loan Discount 1.5 %		900.00
803.	Appraisal Fee to DE MARCAY	80.00	
804.	Credit Report to	29.00	
805.	Lender's Inspection Fee (CONV.)		
806.	~~Mortgage Insurance Application Fee~~ UNDERWRITER FEE		
807.	~~Assumption Fee~~ PHOTOGRAPHS		10.00
808.	AMORTIZATION SCHEDULE		3.00
809.	PROPERTY INSPECTION FEE (VA-FHA ONLY)		
810.	WAREHOUSING FEE		
811.			
900.	ITEMS REQUIRED BY LENDER TO BE PAID IN ADVANCE		
901.	Interest from 6/10/82 to 7/1/82 @ $ 25.479 /day	535.06	
902.	Mortgage Insurance Premium for months to		
903.	Hazard Insurance Premium for 1 years to EZQ HAZARD INS., INC.	357.00	
904.	FLOOD INSURANCE PREMIUM years to CARRUTH INS.	146.00	
905.			
1000.	RESERVES DEPOSITED WITH LENDER		
1001.	Hazard insurance 2 months @ $ 29.75 per month	59.50	
1002.	Mortgage insurance months @ $ per month		
1003.	City property taxes 7 months @ $ 12.00 per month	84.00	
1004.	County property taxes months @ $ per month		
1005.	Annual assessments months @ $ per month		
1006.	FLOOD INSURANCE 2 months @ $ 12.17 per month	24.34	
1007.	ASSOCIATION DUES months @ $ per month		
1008.	months @ $ per month		
1100.	TITLE CHARGES		
1101.	Settlement or closing fee to		
1102.	Abstract or title search to		
1103.	Title examination to LAWYER'S TITLE OF LA., INC.	150.00	
1104.	Title insurance binder to		
1105.	Document preparation to		
1106.	Notary fees to LAWYER'S TITLE OF LA., INC.	90.00	
1107.	Attorney's fees to		
	(includes above items numbers;)		
1108.	Title insurance to LAWYER'S TITLE OF LA., INC.	284.00	
	(includes above items numbers;)		
1109.	Lender's coverage $ 212.00		
1110.	Owner's coverage $ 72.00		
1111.			
1112.			
1113.			
1200.	GOVERNMENT RECORDING AND TRANSFER CHARGES		
1201.	Recording fees: Deed $; Mortgage $; Releases $	35.00	30.00
1202.	City/county tax/stamps: Deed $; Mortgage $		
1203.	State tax/stamps: Deed $; Mortgage $		
1204.	CERTIFICATES		
1205.			
1300.	ADDITIONAL SETTLEMENT CHARGES		
1301.	Survey to MIDLER, INC.	125.00	
1302.	Pest inspection to BEST PEST CONTROL		35.00
1303.			
1304.	DELIVERY FEE/ BUYDOWN FUNDS		
1305.	COMMITMENT FEE/ YIELD CONFIRMATION FEE		
1400.	TOTAL SETTLEMENT CHARGES *(enter on lines 103, Section J and 502, Section K)*	2,598.90	2,778.00

CALCULATION OF ANNUAL PERCENTAGE RATE
FOR
REGULAR FHA/VA/CONVENTIONAL LOANS
REQUIRED BY THE FEDERAL CONSUMER CREDIT PROTECTION ACT

NAME(S): BRYAN JAMES ROBINSON AND MARIE WILLIAMS ROBINSON

PROPERTY ADDRESS: 1804 HOMER STREET, METAIRIE, LOUISIANA 70005

FHA/VA CASE NO. LH 123456   CMC LOAN NO.: 100400

A. FIRST PAYMENT DUE AUGUST 1, 1982   B. LOAN AMOUNT $ 60,000.00
FINAL PAYMENT DUE JULY 1, 2012
TOTAL NUMBER OF   PREPAID F.C.   -   1,148.06
PAYMENTS   360   AMOUNT
                                                FINANCED $ 58,851.94

Prepaids   C. MONTHLY P&I $ 782.72
Origination $_____   TOTAL NUMBER
Discount (if applicable) $_____   OF PAYMENTS X   360
Mtg. Ins. __12__ mos. $_____   TOTAL P&I $ 281,779.20
Photos $_____   LOAN AMOUNT $ 60,000.00
Amortization $_____   INTEREST FOR
Underwriting $_____   LIFE OF LOAN $ 221,779.20
30 days of interest $_____
Other   (L.A. × 1st mo. PMI $_____
__2__ mos. premium from chart × 2) = $_____   FOR FHA LOANS ONLY
TOTAL $_____   INTEREST FOR
                                                LIFE OF LOAN $_____
                                                FHA FACTOR   X_____
CONVENTIONAL LOANS ONLY   MTG. INSURANCE
LOAN AMOUNT $ 60,000.00   FOR LIFE OF LOAN $_____
PMI LIFE OF LOAN
FACTOR (from chart) X PRECOMPUTED
MORTGAGE INSURANCE
FOR 29 YEARS $ 0.00
                                             FHA/PMI INSURANCE
                                             FOR LIFE OF LOAN $ 0.00
                                             INTEREST FOR
                                             LIFE OF LOAN   + 221,779.20
                                             CONTINUING
                                             FINANCE CHARGE $ 221,779.20

                                             D. CONTINUING FINANCE
                                                CHARGE $ 221,779.20
                                                PREPAID
                                                FINANCE CHGS.   + 1,148.06
                                                TOTAL
                                                FINANCE CHGS. $ 222,927.26
                                                              X   100
                                                TOTAL $ 22,292,726.00
                                                AMOUNT
                                                  FINANCED   ÷ 58,851.94
                                                FINANCE CHG.
                                                per $100.00
                                                of Amt. Financed $ 378.79
                                                ANNUAL PERCENTAGE
                                                RATE   15.875 %

PREPARED BY CARLA RODY   DATE: JUNE 2, 1982

CHECKED BY: *Carla Rody*   DATE: _____

P-177-A (REGULAR FHA/VA/CONVENTIONAL ONLY)
(REV. 1/82)

THIS FORM IS TO BE USED BY ALL BRANCHES

(For All Transactions Except ARMS And VRMS)

CARRUTH MORTGAGE CORPORATION

TRUTH-IN-LENDING DISCLOSURE STATEMENT

NAME(S): BRYAN JAMES ROBINSON AND MARIE WILLIAMS ROBINSON

PROPERTY ADDRESS: 1804 HOMER STREET, METAIRIE, LOUISIANA 70005

CMC LOAN NO.: 100400   FHA/VA CASE NO.: LH 123456

ANNUAL PERCENTAGE RATE The cost of your credit as a yearly rate.	FINANCE CHARGE The dollar amount the credit will cost you.	Amount Financed The amount of credit provided to you or on your behalf.	Total Of Payments The amount you will have paid after you have made all payments as scheduled.	Total Sales Price The total cost of your, purchase on credit, including your downpayment of: $ 0.00
15.875 %	$ 222,927.26	$ 58,851.94	$ 281,779.20	$ 60,000.00

YOUR PAYMENT SCHEDULE WILL BE:

NUMBER OF PAYMENTS	AMOUNT OF PAYMENTS	WHEN PAYMENTS ARE DUE
360	782.72	MONTHLY, BEGINNING AUGUST 1, 1982

INSURANCE

You may obtain property insurance from anyone you want that is acceptable to Carruth Mortgage Corporation. If you get the insurance from Carruth Mortgage Corporation, you will pay

$ N/A per N/A for Hazard/Homeowner's and

$ N/A per N/A for Flood Insurance.

SECURITY INTEREST:

You are giving a security interest in real property known as

1804 HOMER STREET, METAIRIE, LOUISIANA 70005

FILING FEES: $ 35.00

LATE CHARGE: IF A PAYMENT IS LATE, YOU WILL BE CHARGED 4.00 % OF:

XXX the principal and interest portion of the payment;

_____ the total payment including mortgage insurance, if any, and escrow.

PREPAYMENT: IF YOU PAY OFF EARLY, YOU

☐ MAY ☒ WILL NOT Have to pay a penalty.

☐ MAY ☐ WILL NOT Be entitled to a refund of part of the finance charge.

ASSUMPTION POLICY: SOMEONE BUYING YOUR HOUSE

☒ MAY, Subject To Conditions

☐ WILL NOT,

Be allowed to assume the remainder of the mortgage on its original terms.

See your contract documents for information about nonpayment, default, any required repayment in full before the scheduled date, and prepayment refunds and penalties.

Borrower(s) acknowledge that they have received a completed copy of this disclosure statement before a contractual relationship was created between the borrower(s) and the lender.

Bryan James Robinson   _June 10, 1982_

Borrower   Date

Marie W. Robinson   _June 10, 1982_

Borrower   Date

NOTARY PUBLIC

e = means an estimate

CM-176A (Rev. 1/82)

CARRUTH
Mortgage Corporation

MEMBER OF THE MELLON NATIONAL MORTGAGE GROUP

Shirley Kirkas
Lawyer's Title of La., Inc.
3100 Division Street
Metairie, Louisiana 70002

                                    RE: Authorization to Close

                                    BRYAN JAMES ROBINSON
                                    1804 Homer Street
                                    Metairie, Louisiana 70005

Dear Shirley Kirkas:

Enclosed is Disclosure of Cost of Loan (CMC Form 176) which
we have prepared for the above captioned transaction in
accordance with information furnished by you on CMC Form C-5.
The enclosed form is to be completed, properly executed, and
distributed in accordance with our General Loan Closing
Instructions, as supplemented and amended, and in accordance
with instructions below.

AFTER the enclosed Disclosure of Cost of Loan Form has been
properly executed, you are authorized to close this loan on
_____June 10_____, 19 _82_ .

                            Yours very truly,

                            CARRUTH MORTGAGE CORPORATION

                            Donna J. Pillard
                            Vice President

INSTRUCTIONS

1. Verify that there has been no change in the figures
given to us on CMC Form C-5, and the figures indicated on
the attached agree with figures as shown on all statements
in connection with this loan transaction.

2. Borrower(s) are to sign Form 176 where indicated, and
the form is to be properly dated, witnessed and notarized.

3. Distrubution is to be made in accordance with General
Loan Closing Instructions.

3601 I-10 Service Rd., Metairie, La.
Mailing Address: P.O. Box 53334, New Orleans, La. 70153
Phone: 885-4811

VA Form 26-6316a (Home Loan)
Rev. Apr. 1974. Use Optional. Section 1810, Title 38, U.S.C. Acceptable to Federal National Mortgage
Association.

LOUISIANA

NOTE

$ 60,000.00   METAIRIE   , Louisiana.

                                        JUNE 10   , 19 82

FOR VALUE RECEIVED, without grace, the undersigned, in solido, promise(s) to pay to the order of

the principal sum of SIXTY THOUSAND AND NO/100   **Dollars**
($ 60,000.00   ), with interest from date at the rate of FIFTEEN AND ONE HALF per centum (15.500%)
per annum on the unpaid balance until paid. The said principal and interest shall be payable at the office of
CARRUTH MORTGAGE CORPORATION, P. O. BOX 53334
in NEW ORLEANS, LA , 70153   , or at such other place as the holder hereof may
designate in writing delivered or mailed to the debtor, in monthly installments of
SEVEN HUNDRED EIGHTY-TWO AND 72/100 Dollars ($ 782.72   ), commencing on the first day of
AUGUST   , 19 82 , and continuing on the first day of each month thereafter until this note is fully
paid, except that, if not sooner paid, the final payment of principal and interest shall be due and payable on the
first day of JULY   , 2012.

Privilege is reserved to prepay at any time, without premium or fee, the entire indebtedness or any part thereof
not less than the amount of one installment, or $100, whichever is less. Prepayment in full shall be cred-
ited on the date received. Partial prepayment, other than on an installment due date, need not be credited
until the next following installment due date or thirty days after such prepayment, whichever is earlier.

If any deficiency in the payment of any installment under this note is not made good prior to the due date of
the next such installment, the entire principal sum and accrued interest shall at once become due and payable
without notice at the option of the holder of this note. Failure to exercise this option shall not constitute a waiver
of the right to exercise the same in the event of any subsequent default. In the event of default in payment
of this note, and if the same is collected by an attorney at law, I, we, or either of us, in solido, further agree
to pay all costs of collection, including a reasonable attorney's fee actually incurred or paid by the holder of
this note.

This note is secured by Mortgage or Notarial Act of even date on certain property described therein and
represents money actually used for the acquisition of said property or the improvements thereon.

The undersigned hereby waive presentment, protest, and notice.

"NE VARIETUR" in conformity with an act   *Bryan James Robinson*
of mortgage passed this day before me, Notary.   BRYAN JAMES ROBINSON
                                           Marie Williams Robinson
                                    MARIE WILLIAMS ROBINSON

METAIRIE   .La., JUNE 10   , 19 82

SHIRLEY KIRKES   *Notary Public.*
      JEFFERSON   Parish, La.

THIS IS TO CERTIFY that this is the note described in and secured by mortgage of even date herewith and in
the same principal amount as herein stated and secured by real estate situated in
                             JEFFERSON   Parish, State of Louisiana.
Dated JUNE 10   , 19 82 .

                                    SHIRLEY KIRKES   *Notary Public.*

VA Form 26-4316b (Home Loan)
Revised December 1976. Use Op-
tional. Section 1810, Title 38 U.S.C.
Acceptable to Federal National
Mortgage Association.

CREDIT SALE OF PROPERTY

BY

JOHN HUNTER

TO

BRYAN JAMES ROBINSON AND
MARIE WILLIAMS ROBINSON

JUNE 10   , 19 82

STATE OF LOUISIANA
PARISH OF JEFFERSON

BE IT KNOWN, That on this TENTH   day of
JUNE   , in the year nineteen hundred and
EIGHTY-TWO

Before me, the undersigned authority, a notary public
in and for said PARISH and STATE duly commissioned
and qualified, and in the presence of witnesses hereinafter named and undersigned,

PERSONALLY CAME AND APPEARED:

JOHN HUNTER BEING OF FULL AGE OF MAJORITY AND RESIDENT OF THE PARISH OF
JEFFERSON, STATE OF LOUISIANA, WHO DECLARED UNDER OATH TO ME, NOTARY,
THAT HE IS SINGLE AND NEVER BEEN MARRIED.

[VENDOR], who declared that he does, by these presents, sell, convey, and deliver, with full guaranty of
title, and with complete transfer and subrogation of all rights and actions of warranty against all former pro-
prietors of the property herein conveyed, together with all rights of prescription, whether acquisitive or libera-
tive, to which said vendor may be entitled unto
MARIE WILLIAMS WIFE OF/AND BRYAN JAMES ROBINSON, BOTH PERSONS OF THE FULL
AGE OF MAJORITY AND RESIDENTS OF THE PARISH OF JEFFERSON, STATE OF
LOUISIANA, WHO DECLARED UNDER THE OATH TO ME, NOTARY, THAT THEIR MARITAL
STATUS IS AS FOLLOWS: BOTH HAVE BEEN MARRIED ONCE AND THEN TO EACH OTHER.

MAILING ADDRESS: 1804 HOMER STREET, METAIRIE, LOUISIANA 70005

[PURCHASER], here present, accepting and purchasing for said purchaser, his heirs and assigns, who
acknowledges due delivery and possession thereof, the following described property, to-wit:
A CERTAIN PORTION OF GROUND, TOGETHER WITH ALL THE BUILDINGS AND THEIR
IMPROVEMENTS, AND ALL OF THE RIGHTS, WAYS, PRIVILEGES, SERVITUDES, AND
APPURTENANCES AND ADVANTAGES THEREUNTO BELONGING OR IN ANYWISE APPERTAINING
SITUATED IN THE PARISH OF JEFFERSON, STATE OF LOUISIANA, BONNABEL SUBDIVISION
ALL IN ACCORDANCE WITH A PLAN OF SUBDIVISION BY MIDLER, INC., C.C., DATED
OCTOBER 26, 1964, REVISED NOVEMBER 19, 1964, APPROVED BY THE JEFFERSON
PARISH COUNCIL UNDER ORDINANCE NUMBER 6877 ON NOVEMBER 19, 1964, REGISTERED
IN C.O.B. 603, FOLIO 861 ON DECEMBER 7, 1964, WHICH PORTION OF GROUND IS
DESIGNATED AS FOLLOWS:
     LOT 12 IN SQUARE 16, WHICH IS SQUARE BOUNDED BY HELOIS STREET, LOIRE
DRIVE, AND BONNABEL STREET. LOT 12 MEASURES 60 FEET FRONT ON HOMER STREET,
SAME WIDTH IN THE REAR, BY A DEPTH ON THE SIDE LINE OF LOTS 11 AND 13 OF
130 FEET. ALL IN ACCORDANCE WITH ANNEXED SURVEY BY MIDLER, INC., C.C.,
DATED JUNE 8, 1982.

To HAVE AND TO HOLD the above-described property and its appurtenances to the said purchaser, his heirs and assigns, forever.

This sale is made and accepted for and in consideration of the sum of
SIXTY THOUSAND AND NO/100   Dollars ($ 60,000.00   ) XXXXXXX

payable as follows

($ -0-   )

DOLLARS, cash in hand paid, the receipt of which is hereby acknowledged, and the balance represented in one note of said purchaser in the amount of SIXTY THOUSAND AND NO/100   ($ 60,000.00)
DOLLARS, which is dated with this act, made payable to the order of bearer, with interest from date at the rate of FIFTEEN AND ONE HALF per centum (15.500%) per annum on the unpaid balance until paid, the principal and interest thereon being payable at the office of CARRUTH MORTGAGE CORPORATION, P. O. BOX 53334
NEW ORLEANS in LOUISIANA , or at such other place as the holder thereof might designate in writing delivered or mailed to the purchaser, in monthly installments of
SEVEN HUNDRED EIGHTY-TWO AND 72/100   ($ 782.72)
DOLLARS, commencing on the first day of AUGUST   , 19 82 , and continuing on the first day of each month thereafter until the principal and interest are fully paid, except that, if not sooner paid, the final payment of principal and interest shall be due and payable on the first day of JULY   , 2012
Said promissory note, after having been paraphed "Ne Varietur" by me, notary, to identify it herewith, was delivered unto the said vendor, who, after acknowledging receipt therefor, for value received, the receipt and sufficiency of which value was acknowledged, transferred, assigned, and delivered said note, without recourse as to said vendor, together with all of his rights and actions as vendor herein, including those relating to the vendor's lien and privilege, to CARRUTH MORTGAGE CORPORATION
[CREDITOR], through its undersigned agent, who acknowledges receipt thereof.

In order to secure the payment of said promissory note, in capital and interest, according to its tenor and the provisions herein contained, and to secure the faithful performance of all of the obligations contained herein, and the reimbursement and payment of attorneys' fees, taxes, paving assessments, premiums of insurance, costs, fines, late charges, and all advances and expenses as herein authorized, the said purchaser does, by these presents, specially mortgage, affect, and hypothecate the above-described property, unto and in favor of the said creditor, the purchaser hereby confessing judgment in favor of the creditor, and any future holder or holders of said note, for the full amount of the said promissory note or obligation, together with all interest, taxes, paving assessments, premiums of insurance, fines, penalties, attorneys' fees, and all costs, late charges, advances, and expenses, as authorized herein.

Said creditor retains its vendor's lien and privilege as security for all of the purchaser's obligations hereinunder, and the said purchaser hereby binds and obligates himself not to sell, alienate, or encumber the said property to the prejudice of these presents.

XXXXXXXXXXXXXXXXXXXXXXXXXXXXXXXXXXXXXXXXXXXXXXXXXXXXXXXXXXXXXXXXXXXXXXXXXXXXXXXXX
XXXXXXXXXXXXXXXXXXXXXXXXXXXXXXXXXXXXXXXXXXXXXXXXXXXXXXXXXXXXXXXXXXXXXXXXXXXXXXXXX
XXXXXXXXXXXXXXXXXXXXXXXXXXXXXXXXXXXXXXXXXXXXXXXXXXXXXXXXXXXXXXXXXXXXXXXXXXXXXXXXX
XXXXXXXXXXXXXXXXXXXXXXXXXXXXXXXXXXXXXXXXXXXXXXXXXXXXXXXXXXXXXXXXXXXXXXXXXXXXXXXXX
XXXXXXXXXXXXXXXXXXXXXXXXXXXXXXXXXXXXXXXXXXXXXXXXXXXXXXXXXXXXXXXXXXXXXXXXXXXXXXXXX

The purchaser further covenants and agrees:

1. That he will pay the indebtedness as hereinbefore provided. Privilege is reserved to prepay at any time, without premium or fee, the entire indebtedness or any part thereof not less than the amount of one installment, or one hundred dollars ($100.00), whichever is less. Prepayment in full shall be credited on the date received. Partial prepayment, other than on an installment due date, need not be credited until the next following installment due date or thirty days after such prepayment, whichever is earlier.

2. He will pay to said creditor, as trustee (under the terms of this trust as hereinafter stated) together with and in addition to the monthly payments hereinbefore specified, on the first day of each month until the note is fully paid:

    (a) A sum equal to the ground rents, if any, next due, plus the premium that will next become due and payable on policies of fire and other hazard insurance covering the mortgaged property, plus taxes and assessments next due on the mortgaged property (all as estimated by creditor, and of which the purchaser is notified) less all sums already paid therefor divided by the number of months to elapse before one month prior to the date when such ground rents, premiums, taxes, and assessments will become delinquent, such sums to be held by creditor in trust to pay said ground rents, premiums, taxes, and special assessments.

    (b) The aggregate of the amounts payable pursuant to subparagraph (a) and those payable on the note secured hereby, shall be paid in a single payment each month, to be applied to the following items in the order stated:

        (I) ground rents, taxes, special assessments, fire and other hazard insurance premiums;

        (II) interest on the indebtedness secured hereby; and

        (III) amortization of the principal of said indebtedness.

Any deficiency in the amount of such aggregate monthly payment shall constitute an event of default under this act.

XXXXXXXXXXXXXXXXXXXXXXXXXXXXXXXXXXXXXXXXXXXXXXXXXXXXXXXXXXXXXXXXXXXXXXXXXXXXXXXXX
XXXXXXXXXXXXXXXXXXXXXXXXXXXXXXXXXXXXXXXXXXXXXXXXXXXXXXXXXXXXXXXXXXXXXXXXXXXXXXXXX.

3. If the total of the payments made by the purchaser under (a) of paragraph 2 preceding shall exceed the amount of payments actually made by creditor as trustee for ground rents, taxes or assessments or insurance premiums, as the case may be, such excess shall be credited on subsequent payments due or to become due by the purchaser for such items or, at the creditor's option, as trustee shall be refunded to the purchaser. If, however, such monthly payments shall not be sufficient to pay such items when the same shall become due and payable, then the purchaser shall pay to creditor as trustee any amount necessary to make up the deficiency. Such payments shall be made within thirty (30) days after written notice stating the amount of the deficiency, which notice may be given by mail. If at any time the purchaser shall tender to the creditor in accordance with the provisions of this act full payment of the purchaser's entire indebtedness the creditor as trustee shall, in computing the amount of such indebtedness, credit to the account of the purchaser the credit balance accumulated under the provisions of (a) of paragraph 2 hereof. If there shall be a default under any of the provisions of this act resulting in a public sale of the premises covered hereby, or if creditor acquires the property otherwise after default, creditor as trustee shall apply, at the time of the commencement of such proceedings, or at the time the property is otherwise acquired, the amount then remaining to credit of purchaser under (a) of paragraph 2 preceding, as a credit on the interest accrued and unpaid and the balance to the principal then remaining unpaid on said note.

(NOTE.—If lender is *not* a Building and Loan or Homestead Association delete paragraphs (X) and (Y) above.)

4. He will promptly pay all taxes, assessments, water rates, and other governmental or municipal charges, fines, or impositions, and ground rents, except when payment for all such items has theretofore been made under (a) of paragraph 2 hereof, and he will promptly deliver the official receipts therefor to creditor. If the purchaser fails to make such payment creditor may make them, and any sums so advanced shall bear interest at the same rate as and become a part of the principal debt from the date of payment, and shall be secured by the pledge and mortgage herein granted and by the vendor's lien herein retained.

5. Sums advanced by creditor for the payment of any taxes, special assessments, premiums on insurance, or any other charges, expense or costs herein authorized to be made shall bear interest at the same rate as and become a part of the principal debt from the date of payment, and the reimbursement thereof shall be ratably secured by the pledge and mortgage herein granted and the vendor's lien herein retained.

6. Upon the request of creditor, the purchaser shall execute and deliver a supplemental note or notes for the sum or sums advanced by creditor for any alteration, modernization or improvement made at the purchaser's request; or for maintenance or repair of said premises or taxes, assessments against the same or hazard insurance premiums and for any other purpose elsewhere authorized hereunder. Said note or notes shall be secured hereby on a parity with as fully as if the advance evidenced thereby were included in the note first described above. Said supplemental note or notes shall bear interest at the same rate as the principal debt and shall be payable in approximately equal monthly payments of such period as may be agreed upon by the creditor and debtor. Failing to agree on the maturity, the whole of the sum or sums so advanced shall be due and payable thirty (30) days after demand by the creditor. In no event should the aggregate of the sums so advanced, together with interest, exceed fifty (50%) percent of the original principal amount of the note secured hereby, nor shall the ultimate maturity of the said secured note first described above be extended. The mortgaging and confession of judgment clauses herein shall be deemed to include all such advances in the event the same are not specifically included therein. The holder of the note shall have no obligation to make any such advances.

7. He will continuously maintain hazard insurance, of such type or types and amounts as creditor may from time to time require, on the improvements now or hereafter on said premises, and except when payment for all such premiums has theretofore been made under (a) of paragraph 2 hereof, he will pay promptly when due any premiums therefor. All insurance shall be carried in companies approved by the creditor and the policies and renewals thereof shall have attached thereto standard mortgagee or loss payable clauses in favor of and in form acceptable to creditor. He will transfer and deliver the policy or policies of such insurance or insurances, and their renewals, to creditor; in default of which the creditor is hereby authorized, at its option, to avail itself of the rights hereafter set forth, or to cause such insurance to be made and effected at the cost, charge, and expense of said purchaser.

8. If the property covered hereby, or any part thereof, shall be damaged or destroyed by fire or other hazard against which insurance is held, the amounts due by any insurance company shall, to the extent of the indebtedness then remaining unpaid, be paid to creditor, and, when so paid, may, at its option, be applied to the debt or be used for the repairing or rebuilding of the said property.

9. The lien of this instrument shall remain in full force and effect during any postponement or extension of the time of payment of the indebtedness or any part thereof secured hereby.

10. If any of the monthly payments provided for in paragraph (2) (b) preceding shall not be paid when due, he will, at creditor's option, pay to creditor a "late charge" not exceeding four per centum (4%) of any installment which is paid more than fifteen (15) days after the due date thereof, to cover the extra expense involved in handling delinquent payments, but such "late charge" shall not be payable out of the proceeds of any sale made to satisfy the indebtedness secured hereby, unless such proceeds are sufficient to discharge the entire indebtedness and all proper costs and expenses secured thereby.

11. He will not commit or permit waste; and shall maintain the property in as good condition as at present, reasonable wear and tear excepted. Upon any failure so to maintain, creditor, at its option, may cause reasonable maintenance work to be performed at the cost of the purchaser. Any amounts paid therefor shall bear interest at the same rate as, and become a part of, the principal debt from the date of payment, and the reimbursement thereof shall be secured by the pledge and mortgage herein granted and the vendor's lien herein retained.

12. The balance due by the purchaser, at any time, on his note shall be the face of said note, together with the interest herein stipulated, plus any amount which may have been advanced by or be due to the creditor for taxes, insurance premiums, paving assessments, late charges, or for any other charge or expense elsewhere authorized herein, minus proper credits.

13. In the event of default in any of the terms, conditions, or covenants under this act, creditor shall have the right and is hereby authorized, at its option, to collect and receipt for all rents and revenues from the property, and to apply the same to the purchaser's indebtedness.

14. If purchaser violates any of the conditions of this act, or fails promptly to perform any obligation hereunder, or fails to make any installment or installments on the above described promissory note in accordance with its terms, or upon the cancellation of any insurance covering the property, for whatever reason, if the purchaser fails immediately to replace said insurance in a company, or companies satisfactory to creditor, the creditor may, at its option, without demand, and without putting in default, purchaser having by these presents waived the demand and delay provided for by Article 2639 of the Code of Civil Procedure of Louisiana, declare the entire balance immediately due, exigible and payable together with interest, costs, attorney's fees, advances, and all proper expenses and charges.

15. In the event of any default or the violation of any of the conditions of this act, or the happening of any one or more of the events hereinabove mentioned, the creditor shall have the right, without the necessity of demand or of putting in default, to cause the property herein described, together with all the improvements thereon, to be seized and sold under executory or other process issued by any competent court, or it may proceed to the enforcement of its rights in any other manner provided by law, and the property may be sold with or without appraisement, at the option of the creditor, to the highest bidder for cash, the present purchaser herein waiving hereby the benefit of all laws relative to the appraisement of property seized and sold under executory or other process.

16. If legal proceedings are instituted for the recovery of any amount due hereunder, or if any past due claim hereunder is placed in the hands of an attorney for collection, the purchaser agrees to pay the reasonable fees of the attorney at law employed for that purpose.

17. The failure of creditor to exercise any of its privileges or options at any time shall not constitute a waiver of its right to exercise the same in the event of any subsequent default.

18. Nothing in this act contained shall be so construed as to limit any right or remedy otherwise granted or available to the creditor.

The covenants herein contained shall bind, and the benefits and advantages shall inure to, the respective heirs, executors, administrators, successors, and assigns of the parties hereto. Whenever used, the singular number shall include the plural, the plural the singular, the use of any gender shall be applicable to all genders, and the term "creditor" shall include any payee of the indebtedness hereby secured or any transferee thereof, whether by operation of law or otherwise.

The production of Mortgage, Conveyance, and United States District, and Circuit Court Certificates is hereby waived by the parties hereto, who relieve and release me, Notary, from all responsibility and liability in the premises for such nonproduction.

This conveyance is subject to any paving or other special assessment lien for public improvements, charged against the herein conveyed property. All State and city taxes up to and including taxes due and exigible in 1981, are paid as per TAX RESEARCH

All taxes for year 19   are assumed by the present purchaser.

THE MORTGAGOR COVENANTS AND AGREES THAT SO LONG AS THIS MORTGAGE AND THE NOTE SECURED HEREBY ARE INSURED UNDER THE PROVISIONS OF THE SERVICEMEN'S READJUSTMENT ACT, HE WILL NOT EXECUTE OR FILE FOR RECORD ANY INSTRUMENT WHICH IMPOSES A RESTRICTION UPON THE SALE OR OCCUPANCY OF THE MORTGAGED PROPERTY ON THE BASIS OF RACE, COLOR OR CREED. UPON ANY VIOLATION OF THIS UNDERTAKING, THE MORTGAGEE MAY, AT ITS OPTION, DECLARE THE UNPAID BALANCE OF THE DEBT SECURED HEREBY IMMEDIATELY DUE AND PAYABLE.

SHOULD THE VETERANS ADMINISTRATION FAIL OR REFUSE TO ISSUE ITS GUARANTY, IN THE FULL AMOUNT COMMITTED UPON BY THE VETERANS ADMINISTRATION, UNDER THE PROVISIONS OF THE SERVICEMEN'S READJUSTMENT ACT OF 1944, AS AMENDED, WITHIN 60 DAYS FROM THE DATE THIS LOAN WOULD NORMALLY BECOME ELIGIBLE FOR SUCH GUARANTY, THE HOLDER MAY DECLARE THE INDEBTEDNESS HEREBY SECURED AT ONCE DUE AND PAYABLE AND MAY FORECLOSE IMMEDIATELY OR MAY EXERCISE ANY OTHER RIGHTS HEREUNDER OR TAKE ANY OTHER PROPER ACTION AS BY LAW PROVIDED.

THE SAID MORTGAGOR FURTHER DECLARES THAT IN FAVOR OF THE MORTGAGEE HEREIN, AND ALL FUTURE HOLDERS OF THE NOTE SECURED HEREBY AND AS REGARDS THE PROPERTY HEREBY MORTGAGED, MORTGAGOR WAIVES ANY AND ALL HOMESTEAD EXEMPTIONS TO WHICH MORTGAGOR IS OR MAY BE ENTITLED UNDER THE CONSTITUTION AND LAWS OF THE STATE OF LOUISIANA.

THUS DONE AND PASSED in my office in the Parish and State aforesaid on the day, month and year first above written and in the presence of the undersigned competent witnesses of lawful age, who have signed their names with the said appearers, and me, Notary, after reading thereof.

WITNESSES:

_____ *John Hunter*
JOHN HUNTER   *Vendor*

_____
                                                              Vendor

Patricia R. Mader.

James Arnold

Bryan James Robinson
BRYAN JAMES ROBINSON   *Purchaser*

Marie Williams Robinson
MARIE WILLIAMS ROBINSON   *Purchaser*

By _____
        Agent   *Creditor*
        CARRUTH MORTGAGE CORPORATION

_____
                                                        Notary Public
SHIRLEY KIRKES

STATE OF LOUISIANA

Credit Sale of Property

TO

HUD-1 REV. 5/76

FORM APPROVED
OMB NO. 63-R-1501

A.			B.		TYPE OF LOAN	

U. S. DEPARTMENT OF HOUSING AND URBAN DEVELOPMENT

SETTLEMENT STATEMENT

TYPE OF LOAN
1. ☐ FHA   2. ☐ FmHA   3. ☐ CONV. UNINS.
4. ☒ VA   5. ☐ CONV. INS.

6. FILE NUMBER: 7. LOAN NUMBER: 100400

8. MORTGAGE INSURANCE CASE NUMBER: LH 123456

C. *NOTE: This form is furnished to give you a statement of actual settlement costs. Amounts paid to and by the settlement agent are shown. Items marked "(p.o.c.)" were paid outside the closing; they are shown here for informational purposes and are not included in the totals.*

D. NAME OF BORROWER:	E. NAME OF SELLER:	F. NAME OF LENDER:
BRYAN JAMES ROBINSON MARIE WILLIAMS ROBINSON 5 OPELOUSAS STREET NEW ORLEANS, LA., 70114	JOHN HUNTER 1804 HOMER STREET METAIRIE, LOUISIANA 70005	CARRUTH MORTGAGE CORPORATION P. O. BOX 53334 NEW ORLEANS, LA 70153

G. PROPERTY LOCATION:	H. SETTLEMENT AGENT:	I. SETTLEMENT DATE:
1804 HOMER STREET METAIRIE, LOUISIANA 70005	LAWYER'S TITLE OF LA., INC. SHIRLEY KIRKES PLACE OF SETTLEMENT: 3100 DIVISION STREET METAIRIE, LOUISIANA 70002	JUNE 10, 1982

J. SUMMARY OF BORROWER'S TRANSACTION		K. SUMMARY OF SELLER'S TRANSACTION	
100. GROSS AMOUNT DUE FROM BORROWER:		400. GROSS AMOUNT DUE TO SELLER:	
101. Contract sales price	60,000.00	401. Contract sales price	60,000.00
102. Personal property		402. Personal property	
103. Settlement charges to borrower *(line 1400)*	2,598.90	403.	
104.		404.	
105.		405.	
Adjustments for items paid by seller in advance		*Adjustments for items paid by seller in advance*	
106. City/town taxes to		406. City/town taxes to	
107. County taxes to		407. County taxes to	
108. Assessments to		408. Assessments to	
109.		409.	
110.		410.	
111.		411.	
112.		412.	
120. GROSS AMOUNT DUE FROM BORROWER	62,598.90	420. GROSS AMOUNT DUE TO SELLER	60,000.00
200. AMOUNTS PAID BY OR IN BEHALF OF BORROWER:		500. REDUCTIONS IN AMOUNT DUE TO SELLER:	
201. Deposit or earnest money		501. Excess deposit *(see instructions)*	
202. Principal amount of new loan(s)	60,000.00	502. Settlement charges to seller *(line 1400)*	2,778.00
203. Existing loan(s) taken subject to		503. Existing loan(s) taken subject to	
204. CREDIT REPORT	30.00	504. Payoff of first mortgage loan	
205. APPRAISAL FEE	80.00	505. Payoff of second mortgage loan	
206.		506.	
207.		507.	
208.		508.	
209.		509.	
Adjustments for items unpaid by seller		*Adjustments for items unpaid by seller*	
210. City/town taxes to		510. City/town taxes to	
211. County taxes to		511. County taxes to	
212. Assessments to		512. Assessments to	
213.		513. TAX PRO-RATION	60.00
214.		514.	
215.		515.	
216.		516.	
217.		517.	
218.		518.	
219.		519.	
220. TOTAL PAID BY/FOR BORROWER	60,110.00	520. TOTAL REDUCTION AMOUNT DUE SELLER	2,838.00
300. CASH AT SETTLEMENT FROM/TO BORROWER		600. CASH AT SETTLEMENT TO/FROM SELLER	
301. Gross amount due from borrower *(line 120)*	62,598.90	601. Gross amount due to seller *(line 420)*	60,000.00
302. Less amounts paid by/for borrower *(line 220)*	60,110.00)	602. Less reductions in amount due seller *(line 520)*	(2,838.00)
303. CASH ☒ FROM (☐ TO) BORROWER	2,488.90	603. CASH ☒ TO) (☐ FROM) SELLER	57,162.00

Bryan James Robinson
Marie Williams Robinson

John Hunter

Page 2

L.	SETTLEMENT CHARGES		PAID FROM BORROWER'S FUNDS AT SETTLEMENT	PAID FROM SELLER'S FUNDS AT SETTLEMENT
700.	TOTAL SALES/BROKER'S COMMISSION based on price $ 60,000.00 @3.000% 1,800.00			
	Division of Commission (line 700) as follows:			
701. $	900.00 to LINDA KEANAN			
702. $	900.00 to MIKE CRANE			
703.	Commission paid at Settlement			
704.				1,800.00
800.	ITEMS PAYABLE IN CONNECTION WITH LOAN			
801.	Loan Origination Fee 1.000%		600.00	
802.	Loan Discount 1.50 %			900.00
803.	Appraisal Fee to DE MARCAY		80.00	
804.	Credit Report to		29.00	
805.	Lender's Inspection Fee			
806.	Mortgage Insurance Application Fee to			
807.	Assumption fee PHOTOGRAPHS			10.00
808.	AMORTIZATION SCHEDULE			3.00
809.				
810.				
811.				
900.	ITEMS REQUIRED BY LENDER TO BE PAID IN ADVANCE			
901.	Interest from 06/10/82 to 07/01/82 @$ 25.479 /day		535.06	
902.	Mortgage Insurance Premium for months to			
903.	Hazard Insurance Premium for 1 years to EZQ HAZARD INSURANCE CO.		357.00	
904.	FLOOD INS. PREMIUM FOR 1 years to CARRUTH INS.		146.00	
905.				
1000.	RESERVES DEPOSITED WITH LENDER			
1001.	Hazard insurance 2 months @ $ 29.75 per month		59.50	
1002.	Mortgage insurance months @ $ per month			
1003.	City property taxes 7 months @ $ 12.00 per month		84.00	
1004.	County property taxes months @ $ per month			
1005.	Annual assessments months @ $ per month			
1006.	FLOOD INSURANCE 2 months @ $ 12.17 per month		24.34	
1007.	months @ $ per month			
1008.	months @ $ per month			
1100.	TITLE CHARGES			
1101.	Settlement or closing fee to			
1102.	Abstract or title search to			
1103.	Title examination to LAWYER'S TITLE OF LA., INC.		150.00	
1104.	Title insurance binder to			
1105.	Document preparation to			
1106.	Notary fees to LAWYER'S TITLE OF LA., INC.		90.00	
1107.	Attorney's fees to			
	(includes above items numbers;)			
1108.	Title insurance to LAWYER'S TITLE OF LA., INC.		284.00	
	(includes above items numbers;)			
1109.	Lender's coverage $ 212.00			
1110.	Owner's coverage $ 72.00			
1111.				
1112.				
1113.				
1200.	GOVERNMENT RECORDING AND TRANSFER CHARGES			
1201.	Recording fees: Deed $; Mortgage $; Releases $		35.00	
1202.	City/county tax/stamps: Deed $; Mortgage $			
1203.	State tax/stamps: Deed $; Mortgage $			
1204.	CERTIFICATES			30.00
1205.				
1300.	ADDITIONAL SETTLEMENT CHARGES			
1301.	Survey to MIDLER, INC.		125.00	
1302.	Pest inspection to BEST PEST CONTROL			35.00
1303.				
1304.				
1305.				
1400.	TOTAL SETTLEMENT CHARGES (enter on lines 103, Section J and 502, Section K)		2,598.90	2,778.00

HUD-1 REV. 5/76

Bryan Jane Robinson   John Hunter

Marie Williams Johnson

CARRUTH MORTGAGE CORPORATION

Supplement to Disclosure/Settlement Statement
(HUD-1 Form)

FHA/VA CASE NUMBER

LH 123456

Loan Number 100400
Borrower .... MARIE WILLIAMS ROBINSON AND . BRYAN JAMES ROBINSON
Property Address ...... 1804 HOMER STREET, METAIRIE, LOUISIANA 70005
Amount of Loan ....$ 60,000.00
Date of Disbursement .... JUNE 10, 1982
Date of First Payment .... AUGUST 1, 1982

Monthly Payment Amount:
Principal and Interest ....$ 782.72
Tax Reserve 12.00
Insurance Reserve ..... +FLOOD INS. 41.92
FHA Mortgage Insurance Reserve ....
TOTAL PAYMENT ....$ 836.64

This is to certify that we have examined and received a copy of the Disclosure/Settlement Statement, HUD-1 form, on the above captioned transaction and that no other fees, deposits or commissions other than those stated therein have been paid by the seller and/or borrower either directly or indirectly and that the disbursements listed thereon have been made with our approval.

Seller JOHN HUNTER   Borrower BRYAN JAMES ROBINSON

Seller   Borrower MARIE WILLIAMS ROBINSON

JUNE 10, 1982   JUNE 10, 1982
Date   Date

The Disclosure/Settlement Statement, HUD-1 form, on the above captioned transaction is a complete, true and correct account of the funds received and disbursed by me in the closing of this loan.

Attorney/Notary SHIRLEY KIRKES

JUNE 10, 1982
Date

To the best of our knowledge, all above certifications have been complied with according to all HUD regulations.

CARRUTH MORTGAGE CORPORATION

Mortgagee PATRICIA MISIEK

JUNE 10, 1982
Date

C-424
Rev. 11/81

STATE OF LOUISIANA
PARISH OF JEFFERSON

<u>ASSIGNMENT OF NOTE AND MORTGAGE</u>

     BE IT KNOWN, That on this ____ day of _____, 1982, before me,
a Notary Public duly commissioned and qualified, in and for the Parish
and State aforesaid, and therein residing, personally came and appeared
<u>J. O. Hecker, Jr.</u>, who declared unto me, Notary, that he is PRESIDENT
of CARRUTH MORTGAGE CORPORATION and who, acting in said capacity and
duly authorized hereunto, declared that, for value received, the said
CARRUTH MORTGAGE CORPORATION does hereby assign, transfer, sell and
deliver to

GOVERNMENT NATIONAL MORTGAGE ASSOCIATION

without recourse, one certain mortgage note made and subscribed by____
<u>Bryan James Robinson and Marie Williams Robinson</u>, Dated <u>June 10, 1982</u>
in the original principle sum of <u>$60,000.00</u>, payable to the order of
<u>Ourselves</u>   Paraphed Ne Varietur by <u>Shirley Kirkes</u>, Notary Public
and the said CARRUTH MORTGAGE CORPORATION does hereby assign, transfer
and deliver to GOVERNMENT NATIONAL MORTGAGE ASSOCIATION

     Real estate located in the Parish of <u>Jefferson</u>   , State of
Louisiana, and being:
     Lot 12 of Square 16, Bonnabel Heights Subdivision,
     Parish of Jefferson, State of Louisiana.

the mortgage, passed before <u>Shirley Kirkes</u> , Notary Public, by which
the aforesaid note is secured, recorded in <u>Jefferson</u> Parish, Louisiana,
on the <u>15th</u> day of <u>June</u>, 1982, in MOB <u>848 Folio 387</u>, and the said
CARRUTH MORTGAGE CORPORATION does hereby warrant that the principle
remaining unpaid on the aforesaid note as of this date is the sum of
$_____, that CARRUTH MORTGAGE CORPORATION has full power
and authority to assign, transfer and deliver same; that it has executed no prior assignment thereof; that it has executed no release,
discharge satisfaction or cancellation of said note or mortgage and
that it has not released any portion of the security or released the
liability of the maker or makers thereof.

     To fully accomplish, effectuate and evidence said assignment and
transfer, the CARRUTH MORTGAGE CORPORATION, through its proper officer,
endorsed the hereinabove described note, without recourse, to the order
of

GOVERNMENT NATIONAL MORTGAGE ASSOCIATION

whereupon I, Notary, did paraph said note for identification herewith.

     THUS DONE AND PASSED IN <u>DUPLICATE</u> ORIGINALS IN MY OFFICE IN THE
CITY OF <u>METAIRIE</u>, STATE OF LOUISIANA, on the day and in the month and
year first hereinabove written in the presence of the undersigned
competent witnesses who have affixed their signatures hereunto with
said appearer and me, Notary, after due reading of the whole.

WITNESSES:

_____

_____

                     CARRUTH MORTGAGE CORPORATION

                     By: _____
                         Julian O. Hecker, Jr.
                         President

                          NOTARY PUBLIC
                 My commission expires at death

Glossary of Real Estate and Mortgage Lending Terms

AAA tenant. A tenant with the highest credit rating.

Abandonment of property. A property status indicating the property has been abandoned, is not being maintained, and is not offered for sale or rent.

Abstract of title. A written history of the title transaction or condition bearing on the title to a designated real estate. An abstract of title covers the period from the original source of title to the present and summarizes all subsequent instruments of public record by setting forth their material parts.

Acceleration clause. A common provision of a mortgage, trust deed and note providing that the entire principal shall become immediately due and payable in the event of default.

Accrued interest. The interest earned for the period of time that has elapsed since interest was last paid.

Acknowledgment. A formal declaration, attached to or a part of an instrument, made before a duly authorized officer (usually a notary public) by the person who has executed the instrument, who declares the execution to be a free act and deed.

Acre. A measure of land, 43,560 square feet.

Action to quiet title. A court action to remove any interest or claim to the title to real property. To remove a cloud on the title.

Administrator. A person appointed by a probate court to administer the estate of a person who died intestate (without a will).

Ad valorem. "According to the value," used in connection with taxation.

Advance. In real estate, a partial disbursement of funds under a note. Most often used in connection with construction lending.

Advance commitment (conditional). A written promise to make an investment at some time in the future if specified conditions are met.

Adverse possession. The right by which someone occupying a piece of land might acquire title against the real owner, if the occupant's possession has been actual, continuous, hostile, visible, and distinct for a statutory period of time.

Affidavit. A sworn statement in writing before a proper official, usually a notary (see acknowledgement).

After-acquired property. Property acquired after the execution of a security agreement and which will serve as additional security for the underlying debt.

Agent. One who legally represents another, called a principal, from whom authority has been derived.

Agreement for sale. A written document in which the purchaser agrees to buy certain real estate (or personal property) and the seller agrees to sell under stated terms and conditions. Also called sales contract, binder, or earnest money contract.

Air rights. The ownership of the right to use, control or occupy the air space over designated real estate.

Alienation. To transfer real property from one person to another.

ALTA. American Land Title Association. A national association of title insurance companies, abstractors, and attorneys, specializing in real property law. The association speaks for the title insurance and abstracting industry and establishes standard procedures and title policy forms.

Amenity. An aspect of a property that enhances its value. Examples are offstreet reserved parking within a condominium community, the nearness of good public transportation, tennis courts, or a swimming pool.

Amortization. Gradual debt reduction. Normally, the reduction is made according to a predetermined schedule of installment payments.

Amortization schedule. A table showing the amounts of principal and interest due at regular intervals and the unpaid balance of the loan after each payment is made.

Annual percentage rate (APR). A rate which represents the relationship of the total finance charge (interest, loan fees, points) to the amount of the loan.

Application. A form used to apply for a mortgage loan and to record pertinent information concerning a prospective mortgagor and the proposed security.

Appraisal. A report by a qualified person setting forth an opinion or estimate of value. Also, the process by which this estimate is obtained.

Appraised value. An opinion of value reached by an appraiser based upon knowledge, experience, and a study of pertinent data.

Appraiser. A person qualified by education, training, and experience to estimate the value of real and personal property.

Appreciation. An increase in value, the opposite of depreciation.

Appurtenance. Anything attached to the land and thus part of the property, such as a barn, garage, or an easement.

Assessed valuation. The value that a taxing authority places upon real or personal property for the purpose of taxation.

Assessment. The process of placing a value on property for the strict purpose of taxation. May also refer to a levy against property for a special purpose, such as a sewer assessment.

Assignee. The person to whom property or a right is assigned or transferred.

Assignment of mortgage. A document that evidences a transfer of ownership of a mortgage from one party to another.

Assignment of rents. An agreement between a property owner and mortgagee specifically fixing the rights and obligations of each regarding rent transferred to a mortgagee if a mortgagor defaults.

Assignor. A person who transfers or assigns a right or property.

Assumption. A written agreement by one party to pay an obligation originally incurred by another.

Assumption fee. The fee paid to a lender (usually by the purchaser of real property) resulting from the assumption of an existing mortgage.

Assumption of mortgage. Assumption by a purchaser of the primary liability for payment of an existing mortgage or deed of trust. The seller remains secondarily liable unless specifically released by the lender.

Attachment. A seizure of defendant's property by court order as security for any judgment plaintiff may recover in a legal action.

Balance sheet. A financial statement showing assets, liabilities and the net worth as of a specific date.

Balloon mortgage. A mortgage with periodic installments of principal and interest that do not fully amortize the loan. The balance of the mortgage is due in a lump sum at the end of the term.

Balloon payment. The unpaid principal amount of a mortgage or other long-term loan due at a certain date in the future. Usually the amount that must be paid in a lump sum at the end of the term.

Band of investment. A method of deriving capitalization rates by weighting the return on and of various interests in real estate.

Bankrupt. A person, firm or corporation, who, through a court proceeding, is relieved from the payment of all debts after the surrender of all assets to a court appointed trustee.

Base rent. The minimum fixed guaranteed rent in a commercial property lease.

Basis point. 1/100 of 1 percent. Used to describe the amount of change in yield in many debt instruments, including mortgages.

Basket provision. A provision contained in the regulatory acts governing the investments of insurance companies, savings and loan associations, and mutual savings banks. It allows for a certain small percentage of total assets to be placed in investments not otherwise permitted by the regulatory acts.

Beneficiary.   The person designated to receive the income from a trust, estate or trust deed.

Bequeath.   A transfer of personal property by will.

Bill of sale.   A document in writing that transfers title to personal property.

Binder, insurance.   A written evidence of temporary hazard or title coverage that only runs for a limited time and must be replaced by a permanent policy.

Blanket mortgage.   A lien on more than one parcel or unit of land frequently incurred by subdividers or developers who have purchased a single tract of land for the purpose of dividing it into smaller parcels for sale or development.

Bona fide.   In good faith, without fraud.

Borrower.   One who receives funds with the expressed or implied intention of repaying the loan in full.

Breach.   Violation of a legal obligation.

Break-even point.   In residential or commercial property, the figure at which occupancy income is equal to all required expenses and debt service.

Broker.   The person who, for a commission or a fee, brings parties together and assists in negotiating contracts between them.

Building code.   Local regulations that control design, construction, and materials used in construction. Building codes are based on safety and health standards.

Bundle of rights.   The rights or interests a person has in property. It is the exclusive right of an individual to own, possess, use, enjoy and dispose of real property.

Buy-sell agreement.   An agreement entered into by an interim and a permanent lender for the sale and assignment of the mortgage to the permanent lender when a building has been completed. Often the mortgagor is a party to this agreement on the theory that the mortgagor should have a contractual right to insist that the permanent lender buy the mortgage.

Call provision.   A clause in the mortgage or deed of trust giving the mortgagee or beneficiary the right to accelerate payment of the mortgage debt in full on a certain date or on the happening of specified conditions.

Capital.   Money used to create income, either as investment in a business or income property. The money or property comprising the wealth owned or used by a person or business enterprise. The accumulated wealth of a person or business. The net worth of a business represented by the amount by which its assets exceed liabilities.

Capitalization.   The process of converting into present value a series of anticipated future installments of net income by discounting them into a present worth using a specific desired rate of earnings.

Capitalization rate.   The rate which is believed to represent the proper relationship between real property and the net income it produces.

Cash flow.   The income from an investment after gross income is subtracted from all operating expenses, loan payments, and the allowance for the income tax attributed to the income.

Cash-on-cash return. The rate of return on an investment measured by the cash returned to the investor based on the investor's cash investment without regard to income tax savings or the use of borrowed funds.

Certificate of occupancy. Written authorization given by a local municipality that allows a newly completed, or substantially completed structure to be inhabited.

Certificate of reasonable value (CRV). A document issued by the VA establishing maximum value and loan amount for a VA guaranteed mortgage.

Certificate of title. A statement furnished by an abstract or title company or an attorney to a client stating that the title to real estate is legally vested in the present owner.

Chain of title. The history of all the documents transferring title to a parcel of real property, starting with the earliest existing document and ending with the most recent.

Chattel. Personal property.

Closing. The conclusion or consummation of a transaction. In real estate, closing includes the delivery of a deed, financial adjustments, the signing of notes, and the disbursement of funds necessary to the sale or loan transaction.

Closing costs. Expenses incidental to a sale of real estate, such as loan fees, title fees, appraisal fees, and others.

Closing statement. A financial disclosure accounting for all funds received and expected at the closing, including the escrow deposits for taxes, hazard insurance, and mortgage insurance for the escrow account.

Cloud on title. Any conditions revealed by a title search that adversely affect the title to real estate. Usually they cannot be removed except by a quitclaim deed, release, or court action.

CMB. Certified Mortgage Banker. A professional designation of the mortgage banking industry.

Coinsurance. A sharing of insurance risk between insurer and insured depending on the relation of the amount of the policy and a specified percentage of the actual value of the property insured at the time of loss.

Collateral. Any property pledged as security for a debt.

Collection. Procedure followed to bring the mortgage account current and to file the necessary notices to proceed with foreclosure when necessary.

Commercial loan. A mortgage loan on property that produces income.

Commercial paper. Short-term unsecured promissory notes of large firms sold to meet short-term capital needs.

Commission. An agent's fee for negotiating a real estate or loan transaction.

Commitment. An agreement, often in writing, between a lender and a borrower to loan money at a future date subject to compliance with stated conditions.

Commitment fee. Any fee paid by a borrower to a lender for the lender's promise to lend money at a specified date in the future. The lender may or may not expect to fund the commitment.

Community property. In some western and southwestern states, a form of ownership under which property acquired during a marriage is presumed to be owned jointly unless acquired as separate property of either spouse.

Common law. An unwritten body of law based on general custom in England and used to an extent in the United States.

Comparables. An abbreviation for comparable properties used for comparative purposes in the appraisal process; facilities of reasonably the same size and location with similar amenities; properties which have been recently sold, which have characteristics similar to property under consideration, thereby indicating the approximate fair market value of the subject property.

Compensating balance. A demand deposit usually required by a commercial bank as a condition for extending a line of credit or a bank loan.

Compound interest. Interest paid on original principal and on the accrued and unpaid interest which has accumulated.

Condemnation. The court proceedings for taking private property under the right of eminent domain for public use with just compensation to the owner.

Condominium. A form of ownership of real property. The purchaser receives title to a particular unit and a proportionate interest in certain common areas. A condominium generally defines each unit as a separately-owned space to the interior surfaces of the perimeter walls, floor and ceilings.

Constant. The percentage of the original loan paid in equal annual payments that provide for interest and principal reduction over the life of the loan.

Construction contract. An agreement between a general contractor and an owner-developer stating the specific duties the general contractor will perform according to blueprints and specifications at a stipulated price and terms of payment.

Construction loan. A short-term, interim loan for financing the cost of construction. The lender makes payments to the builder at periodic intervals as the work progresses.

Construction loan agreement. A written agreement between a lender and a builder or borrower in which the specific terms and conditions of a construction loan, including the schedule of payments, are spelled out.

Construction loan draw. The partial disbursement of the construction loan, based on the schedule of payments in the loan agreement. Also called takedown.

Contract. An oral or written agreement to do or not to do a certain thing.

Conventional loan. A mortgage loan neither insured by FHA nor guaranteed by VA.

Cooperative. A form of multiple ownership of real estate in which a corporation or business trust entity holds title to a property and grants the occupancy rights to particular apartments or units to shareholders by means of proprietary leases or similar arrangements.

Corporation. An artificial person created by law with certain rights, privileges and duties of natural persons.

Correspondent. A mortgage banker who services mortgage loans as a representative or agent for the owner of the mortgage or investor. Also applies to the mortgage banker's role as originator of mortgage loans for an investor.

Cost approach. An appraisal technique used to establish value by estimating the cost to reproduce the improvement, allowing for depreciation, then adding in the fair market value of the land.

Coupon rate. The annual interest rate on a debt instrument. In mortgage lending, the term is used to describe the contract interest rate on the face of the note or bond.

Covenant. A legally enforceable promise or restriction in a mortgage. For example, the borrower may covenant to keep the property in good repair and adequately insured against fire and other casualties. The breach of a covenant in a mortgage usually creates a default as defined by the mortgage or deed of trust and can be the basis for foreclosure.

Credit deal. A mortgage made based primarily on the credit of a borrower or tenant with a net lease.

Credit report. A report to a prospective lender on the credit standing of a prospective borrower, or tenant used to help determine credit worthiness.

Curtesy. The common law interest a husband had in the real estate owned by the wife at the time of her death.

Debenture. An unsecured debt instrument backed only by the general credit standing and earning capacity of the issuer.

Debt coverage ratio. The ratio of effective annual net income to annual debt service.

Debt service. The periodic payment of principal and interest earned on mortgage loans.

Deed. A written legal document which purports to transfer ownership of land from one party to another.

Deed in lieu. A deed given by a mortgagor to a mortgagee to satisfy a debt and avoid foreclosure.

Deed of reconveyance. The transfer of legal title from the trustee to the trustor (the borrower) after the trust deed debt is paid in full.

Deed of trust. In some states it is the document used in place of a mortgage; a type of security instrument conveying title in trust to a third party covering a particular piece of property; used to secure the payment of a note; a conveyance of the title land to a trustee as collateral security for the payment of a debt with the condition that the trustee shall reconvey the title upon the payment of the debt, and with power of the trustee to sell the land and pay the debt in the event of a default on the part of the debtor.

Deed Restriction. A limitation placed in a deed limiting or restricting the use of real property.

Default. A breach or nonperformance of the terms of a note or the covenants of a mortgage or deed of trust.

Default point. See break-even point.

Defeasance clause. The clause in a mortgage that gives the mortgagor the right to redeem property upon the payment to the mortgagee of the obligation due.

Deficiency judgment. A court order to pay the balance owed on a loan if the proceeds from the sale of the security are insufficient to pay off the loan.

Delinquent. The status of a mortgage with a payment past due.

Delivery. The legal, final and absolute transfer of a deed from seller to buyer in such a manner that it cannot be recalled by the seller; a necessary requisite to the transfer of title; in mortgage banking, the physical delivery of loan documents to an investor or agent in conformance with the commitment.

Demand note. A note that is due whenever the holder demands payment.

Deposit. A sum of money given to bind a sale of real estate, or a sum of money given to assure payment or an advance of funds in the processing of a loan. Also known as earnest money.

Depository Institutions Deregulation Committee (DIDC). A committee established by the U. S. Congress in 1980 to oversee the orderly phasing out of interest rate ceilings in depository institutions.

Depreciation. A loss of value in real property brought about by age, physical deterioration or functional or economic obsolescence. Broadly, a loss in value from any cause. The opposite of appreciation.

Depreciation allowance. The accounting charge made to allow for the fact that the asset may become economically obsolete before its physical deterioration. The purpose is to write off the original cost by distributing it over the estimated useful life of the asset. It appears in both the profit and loss statement and the balance sheet.

Developer. A person or entity who prepares raw land for building sites, and sometimes builds on the sites.

Development loan. A loan made for the purpose of preparing raw land for the construction of buildings. Development may include grading and installation of utilities and roadways (see construction loan).

Disbursements. The payment of monies on a previously-agreed-to basis. Used to describe construction loan draws.

Discount. In loan originations, a discount refers to an amount withheld from loan proceeds by a lender. In secondary market sales, a discount is the amount by which the sale price of a note is less than its face value. In both instances, the purpose of a discount is to adjust the yield upward, either in lieu of interest or in addition to interest. The rate or amount of discount depends on money market conditions, the credit of the borrower, and the rate and terms of the note.

Discount point. See point.

Disintermediation. The flow of funds out of savings institutions into short-term investments in which interest rates are higher. This shift normally results in a net decrease in the amount of funds available for long-term real estate financing. Also the market condition that exists when this shift occurs.

Dower. The rights of a widow in the property of her husband at his death.

Due-on-sale clause. See alienation clause.

Earnest money. See deposit.

Easement. Right or interest in the land of another entitling the holder to a specific limited use, privilege, or benefit such as laying a sewer, putting up electric power lines, or crossing the property.

ECOA. Equal Credit Opportunity Act. ECOA is a federal law that requires lenders and other creditors to make credit equally available without discrimination based on race, color, religion, national origin, age, sex, marital status, or receipt of income from public assistance programs. Also known as Regulation "B".

Economic rent. The rent that a property would bring if offered in the open market at the fair rental value. Not necessarily the contract rent.

Economic value. The valuation of real property based on its earning capabilities.

Effective gross income (personal). Normal annual income including overtime that is regular or guaranteed. It may be from more than one source. Salary is generally the principal source, but other income may qualify if it is significant and stable.

Effective gross income (property). Stabilized income that a property is expected to generate after a vacancy allowance.

Effective rate. The actual rate of return to the investor. It may vary from the contract rate for a variety of reasons. Also called yield (see yield).

Eminent domain. The right of a government to take private property for public use upon payment of its fair value. It is the basis for condemnation proceedings (see condemnation).

Encroachment. An improvement that intrudes illegally upon another's property.

Encumbrance. Anything that affects or limits the fee simple title to property, such as mortgages, leases, easements, or restrictions.

Equity. In real estate, equity is the difference between fair market value and current indebtedness, usually referring to the owner's interest.

Equity of redemption. The common law right to redeem property during the foreclosure period. In some states the mortgagor has a statutory right to redeem property after a foreclosure sale.

Equity participation. Partial ownership of income property, given by the owner to the lender, as part of the consideration for making the loan.

Escalator clause. A clause providing for the upward or downward adjustment of rent payments to cover specified contingencies, such as the provision in a lease to provide for increases in property tax and operating expenses.

Escheat. The reversion of property to the state if the owner dies intestate and without heirs.

Escrow. A transaction in which a third party, acting as the agent for the buyer and the seller, carries out instructions of both and assumes the responsibilities of handling all the paperwork and disbursement of funds.

Escrow analysis. The periodic examination of escrow accounts to determine if current monthly deposits will provide sufficient funds to pay taxes, insurance and other bills when due.

Escrow payment. That portion of a mortgagor's monthly payments held by the lender to pay for taxes, hazard insurance, mortgage insurance, lease payments, and other items as they become due. Known as impounds or reserves in some states.

Estate. The ownership interest of an individual in real property. The sum total of all the real and personal property owned by an individual at time of death.

Estoppel letter. A statement that in itself prevents its issuer from later asserting different facts.

Eviction. The lawful expulsion of an occupant from real property.

Exclusive listing. A written contract giving a licensed real estate agent the exclusive right to sell a property for a specified time, but reserving the owner's right to sell the property alone without the payment of a commission.

Exclusive right to sell. The same as exclusive listing, but the owner agrees to pay a full commission to the broker even though the owner may sell the property.

Executor. A person named in a will to administer an estate. The court will appoint an administrator if no executor is named. Executrix is the feminine form.

Fair market value. The price at which property is transferred between a willing buyer and a willing seller, each of whom has a reasonable knowledge of all pertinent facts and neither of whom is under any compulsion to buy or sell.

Fannie Mae. See Federal National Mortgage Association.

Farmers Home Administration (FmHA). An agency within the Department of Agriculture which operates principally under the Consolidated Farm and Rural Development Act of 1921 and Title V of the Housing Act of 1949. This agency provides financing to farmers and other qualified borrowers who are unable to obtain loans elsewhere. Funds are borrowed from the U.S. Treasury.

Federal Home Loan Mortgage Corporation (FHLMC). A private corporation authorized by Congress to provide secondary mortgage market support for conventional mortgages. It also sells participation sale certificates secured by pools of conventional mortgage loans, their principal and interest guaranteed by the federal government through the FHLBB. Popularly known as Freddie Mac.

Federal Housing Administration (FHA). A division of HUD. Its main activity is the insuring of residential mortgage loans made by private lenders. It sets standards for construction and underwriting. FHA does not lend money, plan, or construct housing.

Federal National Mortgage Association (FNMA). A privately-owned corporation created by Congress to support the secondary mortgage market. It purchases and sells residential mortgages insured by FHA or guaranteed by VA, as well as conventional home mortgages. Popularly known as Fannie Mae.

Fee simple. The greatest possible interest a person can have in real estate.

Fiduciary. A person in a position of trust and confidence for another.

Financial intermediary. A financial institution which acts as a middleman between savers and borrowers by selling its own obligations or serving as a depository and, in turn, lending the accumulated funds to borrowers.

Financing package. The total of all financial interest in a project. It may include mortgages, partnerships, joint venture capital interests, stock ownership, or any financial arrangement used to carry a project to completion.

Financing statement. Under the Uniform Commercial Code, this is a prescribed form filed by a lender with the registrar of deeds, or secretary of state to perfect a security interest. It gives the name and address of the debtor and the secured party (lender), along with a description of the personal property securing the loan. It may show the amount of indebtedness.

Finder's fee. A fee or commission paid to a broker for obtaining a mortgage loan for a client or for referring a mortgage loan to a broker. It may also refer to a commission paid to a broker for locating a property.

Firm commitment. A lender's agreement to make a loan to a specific borrower on a specific property. An FHA or PMI agreement with a designated borrower to insure a loan on a specific property.

First mortgage. A real estate loan that creates a primary lien against real property.

Fixture. Personal property that becomes real property when attached in a permanent manner to real estate.

Floor loan. A portion or portions of a mortgage loan commitment that is less than the full amount of the commitment. It may be funded upon conditions less stringent than those required for funding the full amount. For example, the floor loan, equal to perhaps 80 percent of the full amount, may be funded upon completion of construction without occupancy requirements, but substantial occupancy of the building may be required for funding the full amount of the loan.

FNMA. See Federal National Mortgage Association.

Forbearance. The act of refraining from taking legal action despite the fact that a mortgage is in arrears. It is usually granted only when a mortgagor makes a satisfactory arrangement by which the arrears will be paid at a future date.

Foreclosure. An authorized procedure taken by a mortgagee or lender under the terms of a mortgage or deed of trust for the purpose of having the property applied to the payment of a defaulted debt.

Forward delivery. The delivery of mortgages or mortgage-backed securities to satisfy cash or future market transactions of an earlier date.

Front-end money. Funds required to start a development and generally advanced by the developer or equity owner as a capital contribution to the project.

Freehold estate. An estate in real estate that could last forever.

Gap financing. An interim loan given to finance the difference between the floor and the maximum permanent loan as committed (see floor loan).

Garnishment. A proceeding that applies specified monies, wages, or property to a debt or creditor by proper statutory process against a debtor.

Government National Mortgage Association (GNMA). On Sept. 1, 1968, Congress enacted legislation to partition FNMA into two continuing corporate entities within HUD. GNMA has assumed responsibility for the special assistance loan program and the management and liquidation function of the older FNMA. Also, GNMA administers the mortgage-backed securities program which channels new sources of funds into residential financing through the sale of privately-issued securities carrying a GNMA guaranty. Popularly known as Ginnie Mae.

GNMA futures market. A regulated central market in which standardized contracts for the future delivery of GNMA securities are traded.

GNMA mortgage-backed securities. Securities, guaranteed by GNMA, that are issued by mortgage bankers, commercial banks, savings and loan associations, savings banks and other institutions. The GNMA security holder is protected by the "full faith and credit of the U.S." GNMA securities are backed by FHA, VA or FmHA mortgages.

Grantee. The person to whom an interest in real property is conveyed.

Grantor. The person conveying an interest in real property.

Gross rent multiplier. A figure used to compare rental properties to determine value. It gives the relationship between the gross rental income and the sales price. Synonyms are gross multiplier, and gross income multiplier.

Ground rent. The earnings of improved property allocated to the ground itself after allowance is made for earnings of the improvement. Also, payment for the use of land in accordance with the terms of a ground lease.

Guaranteed loan. A loan guaranteed by VA, FmHA or any other interested party.

Hazard insurance. A contract whereby an insurer, for a premium, undertakes to compensate the insured for loss on a specific property due to certain hazards.

Hedging. In mortgage lending, the purchases or sale of mortgage futures contracts to offset cash market transactions to be made at a later date.

Highest and best use. The available present use or series of future uses that will produce the highest present property value and develop a site to its full economic potential.

Holdback. That portion of a loan commitment not funded until some additional requirement such as rental or completion is attained (See floor loan). In construction or interim lending it is a percentage of the contractor's draw held back to provide additional protection for the interim lender, often in an amount equal to the contractor's profit given over when the interim loan is closed.

Home Owners Loan Corporation (HOLC). An agency formed in 1933 to help stabilize the economy. The HOLC issued government guaranteed bonds to lenders for delinquent mortgages and then refinanced homeowner indebtedness.

Homeowners policy. A multiple peril policy commonly called "package policy". It is available to owners of private dwellings and covers the dwelling and contents in the case of fire or wind damage, theft, liability for property damage, and personal liability.

Homestead estate. In some states, the home and property occupied by an owner are protected by law up to a certain amount from attachment and sale for the claims of creditors.

HUD. The Department of Housing and Urban Development established by the Housing and Urban Development Act of 1965 to supersede the Housing and Home Finance Agency. It is responsible for the implementation and administration of government housing and urban development programs. The broad range of programs includes community planning and development, housing production and mortgage credit (FHA), equal opportunity in housing, research and technology.

Hypothecate. To give a thing as security without the necessity of giving up possession of it.

Impound. See escrow payment.

Income and expense statement. The actual or estimated schedule of income and expense items reflecting net gain or loss during a specified period.

Income approach to value. The appraisal technique used to estimate real property value by capitalizing net income (see capitalization).

Income property. Real estate developed or improved to produce income.

Industrial park. A controlled development designed for specific types of businesses. These developments provide required appurtenances including public utilities, streets, railroads sidings, auto parking, and water and sewage facilities.

Installment. The regular periodic payment that a borrower agrees to make to the mortgagee.

Institutional lender. A financial institution that invests in mortgages carried in its own portfolio. Mutual savings banks, life insurance companies, commercial banks, pension and trust funds, and savings and loan associations are examples.

Insurance. A contract for indemnification against loss.

Insured loan. A loan insured by FHA or a private mortgage insurance company.

Interest. Consideration in the form of money paid for the use of money, usually expressed as an annual percentage. Also, a right, share, or title in property.

Interim financing. Financing during the time from project commencement to closing of a permanent loan, usually in the form of a construction loan or development loan.

Intestate. To die leaving no valid will.

Investor. The holder of a mortgage or the permanent lender for whom a mortgage lender services the loan. Any person or institution investing in mortgages.

Involuntary lien. A lien imposed against property without consent of an owner. Examples include taxes, special assessments, federal income tax liens, mechanics liens, and materials liens.

Joint tenancy. An equal undivided ownership of property by two or more persons, whose survivors take the interest upon the death of any one of them.

Joint venture. An association between two or more parties to own or develop real estate. It may take a variety of legal forms including partnership, tenancy in common, or a corporation. It is formed for a specific purpose and duration.

Judgment. That which has been adjudicated, allowed, or decreed by a court.

Judgment lien. A lien upon the property of a debtor resulting from the decree of a court.

Judicial foreclosure. A type of foreclosure proceeding used in some states that is handled as a civil lawsuit and conducted entirely under auspices of a court.

Junior mortgage. A lien subsequent to the claims of the holder of a prior (senior) mortgage.

Kicker. A term describing any benefit to a lender above ordinary interest payments. It may be an equity in a property or a participation in the income stream.

Land contract. A contract ordinarily used in connection with the sale of property in cases where the seller does not wish to convey title until all or a certain part of the purchase price is paid by the buyer. The financing vehicle is often used when property is sold on a small downpayment.

Landlord. Owner or lessor of real property.

Late charge. An additional charge a borrower is required to pay as penalty for failure to pay a regular installment when due.

Lease. A written document containing the conditions under which the possession and use of real or personal property are given by the owner to another for a stated period and for a stated consideration.

Leaseback. See sale-leaseback.

Leasehold. An interest in real property held by virtue of a lease.

Leasehold mortgage. A loan to a lessee secured by a leasehold interest in a property.

Legal description. A property description recognized by law which is sufficient to locate and identify the property without oral testimony.

Legal lists. A term describing investments that life insurance companies, mutual savings banks, or other regulated investors may make under a state charter or court order.

Lessee (tenant). That person(s) holding rights of possession and use of property under terms of a lease.

Lessor (landlord). The one leasing property to a lessee.

Leverage. The use of borrowed money to increase the return on a cash investment. For leverage to be profitable, the rate of return on the investment must be higher than the cost of the money borrowed (interest plus amortization).

Lien. A legal hold or claim of one person on the property of another as security for a debt or charge. The right given by law to satisfy debt.

Limited partnership. A partnership that consists of one or more general partners who are fully liable and one or more limited partners who are liable only for the amount of their investment.

Line of credit. An agreement by a commercial bank or other financial institution to extend credit up to a certain amount for a certain time to a specific borrower.

Lis pendens. A notice recorded in the official records of a county to indicate that there is a pending suit affecting the lands within that jurisdiction.

Loan. A sum of money loaned at interest to be repaid.

Loan submission. A package of pertinent papers and documents regarding specific property or properties. It is delivered to a prospective lender for review and consideration for the purpose of making a mortgage loan.

Loan-to-value ratio. The relationship between the amount of the mortgage loan and the appraised value of the security expressed as a percentage of the appraised value.

MAI (Member, Appraisal Institute). The highest professional designation awarded by the American Institute of Real Estate Appraisers.

Marketable title. A title that may not be completely clear but has only minor objections that a well-informed and prudent buyer of real estate would accept.

Market approach to value. In appraising, the market value estimate is predicated upon actual prices paid in market transactions. It is a process of correlation and analysis of similar recently sold properties. The reliability of this technique is dependent upon the degree of comparability of each property with the subject property, the time of sale, the verification of the sale dates, the absence of unusual conditions affecting the sale, and the terms of the sale.

Market rent. The price a tenant pays a landlord for the use and occupancy of real property based upon current prices for comparable property.

Market value. The highest price that a buyer, willing but not compelled to buy, would pay, and the lowest a seller, willing but not compelled to sell, would accept.

Maturity. The terminating or due date of a note, time, draft, acceptance, bill of exchange, or bond. The date a time instrument or indebtedness becomes due and payable.

Metes and bounds. A description in a deed of the land location in which the boundaries are defined by directions and distances.

Moratorium. A period during which a borrower is granted the right to delay fulfillment of an obligation.

Mortgage. A conveyance of an interest in real property given as security for the payment of a debt.

Mortgage-backed securities. Bond-type investment securities representing an undivided interest in a pool of mortgages or trust deeds. Income from the underlying mortgage is used to pay off the securities (see GNMA mortgage-backed securities).

Mortgage banker. A firm or individual active in the field of mortgage banking. Mortgage bankers, as local representatives of regional or national institutional lenders, act as correspondents between lenders and borrowers.

Mortgage banking. The packaging of mortgage loans secured by real property to be sold to a permanent investor with servicing retained for the life of the loan for a fee. The origination, sale, and servicing of mortgage loans by a firm or individual. The investor-correspondent system is the foundation of the mortgage banking industry.

Mortgage broker. A firm or individual bringing the borrower and lender together and receiving a commission. A mortgage broker does not retain servicing.

Mortgage company. A private corporation (sometimes called a mortgage banker) whose principal activity is the origination and servicing of mortgage loans which are sold to other financial institutions.

Mortgage discount. The difference between the principal amount of a mortgage and the amount for which it actually sells. Sometimes called points, loan brokerage fee, or new loan fee. The discount is computed on the amount of the loan, not the sales prices.

Mortgagee. A person or firm to whom property is conveyed as security for a loan made by such person or firm (a creditor).

Mortgagee in possession. A mortgagee who, by virtue of a default under the terms of a mortgage, has obtained possession but not ownership of the property.

Mortgage insurance. The function of mortgage insurance (whether government or private) is to insure a mortgage lender against loss caused by a mortgagor's default. This insurance may cover a percentage of or virtually all of the mortgage loan depending on the type of mortgage insurance.

Mortgage life insurance. A type of term life insurance often bought by mortgagors. The amount of coverage decreases as the mortgage balance declines. In the event that the borrower dies while the policy is in force, the debt is automatically satisfied by insurance proceeds.

Mortgage insurance premium (MIP). The consideration paid by a mortgagor for mortgage insurance either to FHA or a private mortgage insurance (PMI) company. On an FHA loan, the payment is one-half of one percent annually on the declining · balance of the mortgage.

Mortgage note. A written promise to pay a sum of money at a stated interest rate during a specified term. It is secured by a mortgage.

Mortgage portfolio. The aggregate of mortgage loans held by an investor, or serviced by a mortgage lender.

Mortgagor. One who borrows money giving a mortgage or deed of trust on real property as security (a debtor).

Mutual mortgage insurance fund. One of four FHA insurance funds into which all mortgage insurance premiums and other specified revenue of the FHA are paid and from which losses are met.

Mutual savings bank. A state chartered financial institution, located primarily in the Northeast, that is a heavy purchaser of mortgage loans.

Negative cash flow. Cash expenditures of an income producing property in excess of the cash receipts.

Net income. The difference between effective gross income and the expenses including taxes and insurance. The term is qualified as net income before depreciation and debt service.

Net lease. A lease calling for the lessee to pay all fixed and variable expenses associated with the property. Also known as a pure net lease, as opposed to a gross lease. The terms net-net and net-net-net are ill-defined and should be avoided.

Net worth. The value of all assets, including cash, less total liabilities. It is often used as an underwriting guideline to indicate an individual's credit worthiness and financial strength.

Net yield. That part of gross yield that remains after the deductions of all costs, such as servicing, and any reserves for losses.

Nondisturbance agreement. An agreement that permits a tenant under a lease to remain in possession despite any foreclosure.

Notice of default. A notice recorded after the occurrence of a default under a deed of trust or mortgage or a notice required by an interested third party insuring or guaranteeing a loan (FHA, VA, or PMI).

Novation. The substitution of a new contract or obligation between the same or different parties. The substitution, by mutual agreement, of one debtor for another or one creditor for another whereby the existing debt is extinguished.

Obsolescence. The loss of value of a property occasioned by going out of style, by becoming less suitable for use, or by other economic influences.

Open-end mortgage. A mortgage with a provision that the outstanding loan amount may be increased upon mutual agreement of the lender and the borrower.

Option. A contract agreement granting a right to purchase, sell, or otherwise contract for the use of a property at a stated price during a stated period of time.

Origination fee. A fee or charge for the work involved in the evaluation, preparation, and submission of a proposed mortgage loan.

Originator. A person who solicits builders, brokers, and others to obtain applications for mortgage loans. Origination is the process by which the mortgage lender brings into being a mortgage secured by real property.

Package mortgage. A mortgage or deed of trust that includes items which are technically chattels, such as appliances, carpeting, and drapery.

Par. The principal amount of a mortgage with no premium or discount.

Participation loan. A mortgage made by one lender, known as the lead lender, in which one or more other lenders, known as participants, own a part interest, or a mortgage originated by two or more lenders.

Percentage lease. A lease in which a percentage of the tenant's gross business receipts constitutes the rent. Although a straight percentage lease is occasionally encountered, most percentage leases contain a provision for a minimum rent amount.

Personal property. Any property that is not real property.

PITI (principal, interest, taxes, and insurance). The principal and interest payment on most loans is fixed for the term of the loan; the tax and insurance portion may be adjusted to reflect changes in taxes or insurance costs.

Plans and specifications. Architectural and engineering drawings and specifications for construction of a building or project including a description of materials to be used and the manner in which they are to be applied.

Point. An amount equal to one percent of the principal amount of an investment or note. Loan discount points are a one-time charge assessed at closing by the lender to increase the yield on the mortgage loan to a competitive position with other types of investments.

Police power. That right by which the state or other governmental authority may take, condemn, destroy, impair the value of, limit the use of, or otherwise invade property rights. It must be affirmatively shown that the property was taken to protect the public health, public morals, public safety, or the general welfare.

Preclosing. A transaction preceding the formal closing, often used to distinguish between transactions affecting title to real property where there are events that appear to be the formal closing.

Premium. The amount, often stated as a percentage, paid in addition to the face value of a note or bond. Also, the charge for insurance coverage.

Prepayment fee. A consideration paid to the mortgagee for the prepayment privilege. Also known as prepayment penalty or reinvestment fee.

Prepayment privilege. The right given a borrower to pay all or part of a debt prior to its maturity. The mortgagee cannot be compelled to accept any payment other than those originally agreed to.

Principal. The amount of debt.

Principal balance. The outstanding balance of a mortgage, exclusive of interest and any other charges.

Priority. As applied to claims against property, priority is the status of being prior or having precedence over other claims. Priority is usually established by filing or recordation in point of time, but may be established by statute or agreement.

Private mortgage insurance (PMI). Insurance written by a private company protecting the mortgage lender against loss occasioned by a mortgage default.

Proforma statement. A financial or accounting statement projecting income and performance of real estate within a period of time (usually one year) based on estimates and assumption.

Purchase money mortgage. A mortgage given by the purchaser of real property to the seller as part of the consideration in the sales transaction.

Quitclaim deed. A deed that transfers (with no warranty) only such interest, title or right a grantor may have at the time the conveyance is executed.

Real estate investment trust (REIT). A financial institution which can own and hold mortgages on real estate and pass earnings from these assets on free of tax to the corporation but taxable to shareholders.

Real estate owned (REO). A term frequently used by lending institutions as applied to ownership of real property acquired for investment or as a result of foreclosure.

Real property. Land and appurtenances, including anything of a permanent nature such as structures, trees, minerals, and the interest, benefits and inherent rights thereof.

Realtor. A real estate broker or an associate holding active membership in a local real estate board affiliated with the National Association of Realtors.

Recapture. An owner's recovery of money invested in real estate, usually referring to a depreciation allowance.

Recision. The cancellation or annulment of a transaction or contract by the operation of law or by mutual consent.

Reconveyance. The transfer of the title of land from one person to the immediate preceding owner. It is used when the performance of debt is satisfied under the terms of a deed of trust.

Recorder. The public official in a political subdivision who keeps records of transactions affecting real property in the area. Sometimes known as a registrar of deeds or county clerk.

Recording. The noting in the registrar's office of the details of a properly executed legal document, such as a deed, mortgage, a satisfaction of mortgage, or an extension of mortgage, thereby making it a part of the public record.

Redemption, right of. The right allowed by law in some states whereby a mortgagor may buy back property by paying the amount owed on a foreclosed mortgage, including interest and fees.

Refinancing. The repayment of a debt from the proceeds of a new loan using the same property as security.

Release of lien. An instrument discharging secured property from a lien.

Remainder. That part of an estate that remains after the termination of a prior estate.

Rent. Consideration paid for use or occupancy of property, buildings, or dwelling units.

Reproduction cost. The money required to reproduce a building under current market conditions less an allowance for depreciation.

RESPA. Real Estate Settlement Procedures Act.

Restrictive covenant. A clause in a deed limiting use of the property conveyed for a certain period of time.

Return on equity. The ratio of cash flow after debt service to the difference between the value of property and the total financing (see cash-on-cash return).

Reverse leverage. A situation that arises when financing is too costly. It results when total yield on cash investment is less than the financing constant on borrowed funds (see negative cash flow).

Reversion. A right to future possession retained by an owner at the time of a transfer of an owner's interest in real property.

Reversionary clause. A clause providing that any violations of restrictions will cause title to the property to revert to the party who imposed the restriction.

Right of survivorship. In joint tenancy, the right of survivors to acquire the interest of a deceased joint tenant.

Right-of-way. A privilege operating as an easement upon land, whereby a land owner, by grant or agreement, gives another the right to pass over land (see easement).

Sale-leaseback. A technique in which a seller deeds property to a buyer for a consideration and the buyer simultaneously leases the property back to the seller, usually on a long-term basis.

Sandwich lease. A lease in which the "sandwiched party" is a lessee, paying rent on a leasehold interest to one party, and also is a lessor, collecting rents from another party or parties.

Satisfaction of mortgage. The recordable instrument given by the lender to evidence payment in full of the mortgage debt. Sometimes known as a release deed.

Savings and loan association. A mutual or stock association chartered and regulated by either the federal government or a state. S&Ls accept time deposits and lend funds primarily on residential real estate.

Secondary financing. Financing real estate with a loan, or loans, subordinate to a first mortgage or first trust deed.

Secondary mortgage market. An unorganized market where existing mortgages are bought and sold. It contrasts with the primary mortgage market where mortgages are originated.

Secured party. The party holding a security interest or lien; may be referred to as the mortgagee, the conditional seller, or the pledgee.

Security. The collateral given, deposited, or pledged to secure the fulfillment of an obligation or the payment of a debt.

Security instrument. The mortgage or trust deed evidencing the pledge of real estate security as distinguished from the note or other credit instrument.

Security interest. According to the U.C.C., Uniform Commercial Code, security interest is a term designating the interest of the creditor in the property of the debtor in all types of credit transactions. It thus replaces such terms as chattel mortgage, pledge, trust receipt, chattel trust, equipment trust, conditional sale, and inventory lien (see financing statement).

Seller-servicer. FNMA term for an approved corporation that sells and services mortgages for FNMA.

Servicing. The duties of the mortgage lender as a loan correspondent as specified in the servicing agreement for which a fee is received. The collection for an investor of payments, interest, principal, and trust items such as hazard insurance and taxes, on a note by the borrower in accordance with the terms of the note. Servicing also consists of operational procedures covering accounting, bookkeeping, insurance, tax records, loan payment follow-up, delinquency loan follow-up, and loan analysis.

Soft costs. Architectural, engineering, and legal fees as distinguished from land and construction costs.

Special warranty deed. A deed containing a covenant whereby the grantor agrees to protect the grantee against any claims arising during the grantor's period of ownership.

Specific performance. A remedy in a court of equity compelling the defendant to carry out the terms of an agreement or contract.

SREA. The designation of an appraiser who is a member of the Society of Real Estate Appraisers. The designations are: senior residential appraiser (SRA), senior real property appraiser (SRPA), and senior real estate analyst (SREA).

Standby commitment. A commitment to purchase a loan or loans with specified terms, both parties understanding that delivery is not likely, unless circumstances warrant. The commitment is issued for a fee with willingness to fund in the event that a permanent loan is not obtained. Such commitments are typically used to enable the borrower to obtain construction financing at a lower cost on the assumption that permanent financing of the project will be available on more favorable terms when the improvements are completed and the project is generating income.

Standby fee. The fee charged by an investor for a standby commitment. The fee is earned upon issuance and acceptance of the commitment.

Statute of frauds. A state law requiring that certain contracts be in writing. In real estate, a contract for the sale of land must be in writing to be enforceable.

Statute of limitations. A law that limits the length of time in which a lawsuit must be commenced or the right to sue is lost. It varies from state to state.

Step-down-lease. A lease calling for one initial rent to be followed by a decrease in rent over stated periods.

Step-up-lease. A lease calling for one initial rent followd by an increase in rent over stated periods.

Subject to mortgage. When a purchaser buys subject to a mortgage but does not endorse the same or assume to pay mortgage, a purchaser cannot be held for any deficiency if the mortgage is foreclosed and the property sold for an amount not sufficient to cover the note (see assumption of mortgage).

Sublease. A lease executed by a lessee to a third person for a term no longer than the remaining portion of the original lease.

Subordinate. To make subject to, or junior to.

Subordination. The act of a party acknowledging, by written recorded instrument, that a debt due is inferior to the interest of another in the same property. Subordination may apply not only to mortgages, but to leases, real estate rights, and any other types of debt instruments.

Subrogation. The substitution of one person for another in reference to a debt, claim, or right.

Takeout commitment. A promise to make a loan at a future specified time. It is commonly used to designate a higher cost, shorter term, back-up commitment as a support for construction financing until a suitable permanent loan can be secured.

Tandem plan. A mortgage assistance program in which GNMA agrees to purchase qualified, below-market interest rate mortgages at prices favorable to sellers. The mortgages purchased by GNMA are accumulated and periodically sold at auction as either GNMA securities or whole mortgages. As the subsidy cost of the program, GNMA absorbs the difference between the price it paid for the loan and the market price paid by the investor. If the seller or assignee assumes GNMA's obligation to purchase, then GNMA will pay the seller a differential of the excess of the specified purchase price over a published interim selling price (ISP). The term is also used to describe any of the many forms of special assistance programs sponsored by GNMA to affect mortgage finance activity and costs.

Tax deed. A deed on property purchased at public sale for nonpayment of taxes.

Tax lien. A claim against property for the amount of its due and unpaid taxes.

Tenancy. A holding of real estate under any kind of right of title. Used alone, tenancy implies a holding under a lease.

Tenancy at will. A holding of real estate that can be terminated at the will of either the lessor or the lessee, usually with notice.

Tenance by entirety. The joint ownership of property by a husband and wife where both are viewed as one person under common law that provides for the right of survivorship.

Tenancy in common. In law, the type of tenancy or estate created when real or personal property is granted, devised or bequeathed to two or more persons, in the absence of expressed words creating a joint tenancy. There is no right of survivorship (see joint tenancy).

Tenant. One who is not the owner but occupies real property under consent of the owner and in subordination to the owner's title. The tenant is entitled to exclusive possession, use and enjoyment of the property, usually for a rent specified in the lease.

Term. The period of time between the commencement date and termination date of a note, mortgage, legal document, or other contract.

Testate. The estate or condition of leaving a will at death.

Title. The evidence of the right to or ownership in property. In the case of real estate, the documentary evidence of ownership is the title deed which specifies in whom the legal state is vested and the history of ownership and transfers. Title may be acquired through purchase, inheritance, devise, gift, or through foreclosure of a mortgage.

Title insurance policy. A contract by which the insurer, usually a title insurance company, agrees to pay the insured a specific amount for any loss caused by defects of title to real estate, wherein the insured has an interest as purchaser, mortgagee, or otherwise.

Triple A tenant. See AAA tenant.

Trust deed. The instrument given by a borrower (trustor) to a trustee vesting title to a property in the trustee as security for the borrower's fulfillment of an obligation (see deed of trust).

Trustee. A fiduciary who holds or controls property for the benefit of another.

Underwriting.   The analysis and matching of risk to an appropriate rate and term.

Unencumbered property.   A property the title to which is free and clear.

Uniform Commerical Code (UCC).   A comprehensive law regulating commercial transactions. It has been adopted, with modification, by all states.

Usury.   Charging more for the use of money than allowed by law.

Vacancy factor.   A percentage rate expressing the loss from gross rental income due to vacancy and collection losses.

VA certificate of reasonable value.   The VA issues a certificate of reasonable value at a specific figure, agreeing to guarantee a mortgage loan to an eligible qualified veteran buyer upon completion and sale of the house. The veteran must be aware of the VA's appraised value of the property.

Valuation.   See appraisal.

Variable rate mortgage.   A mortgage agreement that allows for adjustment of the interest rate in keeping with a fluctuating market and terms agreed upon in the note.

Vendee.   The party to whom personal or real property is sold.

Veterans Administration (VA).   The Servicemen's Readjustment Act of 1944 authorized this agency to administer a variety of benefit programs designed to facilitate the adjustment of returning veterans to civilian life. The VA home loan guaranty program is designed to encourage lenders to offer long-term, low down payment mortgages to eligible veterans by guaranteeing the lender against loss.

Warehousing.   The borrowing of funds by a mortgage banker on a short-term basis at a commercial bank using permanent mortgage loans as collateral. This form of interim financing is used until the mortgages are sold to a permanent investor.

Warranty deed.   A deed in which the grantor or seller warrants or guarantees that good title is being conveyed, as opposed to a quit-claim deed that contains no representation or warranty as to the quality of title being conveyed.

Waste.   Damage to real estate by neglect or other cause.

Will.   A written document providing for the distribution of property at death.

Wrap-around.   A mortgage which secures a debt that includes the balance due on an existing senior mortgage and an additional amount advanced by the wrap-around mortgagee. The wrap-around mortgagee thereafter makes the amortizing payments on the senior mortgage. An example is when a landowner has a mortgage securing a debt with an outstanding balance of $3,000,000. A lender now advances the same mortgagor another $1,500,000 and undertakes to make the remaining payments due on the $3,000,000 debt and takes a $4,500,000 wrap-around junior mortgage on the real estate to secure the total indebtedness.

Yield.   In real estate, the term refers to the effective annual amount of income which is being accrued on an investment. Expressed as a percentage of the price originally paid.

Yield to maturity.   A percent returned each year to the lender on actual funds borrowed considering that the loan will be paid in full at the end of maturity.

Zoning.   The act of city or county authorities specifying the type of use to which property may be put in specific areas (see restriction).

Index